The University of Law

14 Store Street
London
WC1E 7DE

Financial Services Law Guide
Fourth Edition

D1330487

The University of Law

incorporating The College of Law

Financial Services Law Guide

Fourth Edition

General Editor

Professor Andrew Haynes
School of Law,
University of Wolverhampton

Visiting Professor of Law
University of Macau
People's Republic of China

Bloomsbury Professional

Bloomsbury Professional, Maxwelton House, 41–43 Boltro Road, Haywards Heath, West Sussex, RH16 1BJ

© Bloomsbury Professional 2014

Bloomsbury Professional is an imprint of Bloomsbury Publishing Plc

British Library Cataloguing-in-Publication Data.

A catalogue record for this book is available from the British Library.

ISBN 978 1 84766 978 0

Typeset by Phoenix, Chatham, Kent
Printed and bound in Great Britain by CPI Group (UK) Ltd, Croydon, CR0 4YY

Preface

Since the previous edition of this book there have been extensive and substantial changes to the financial services regulatory regime. There are new regulators, new statutes, new rules and a new approach to regulation. The book has therefore had to be largely rewritten. In the light of the new regulations a chapter has been added on Approved Persons but the chapter on European issues has been removed due to the range and detail of the new issues which are emerging on that front. Once their form has become clear and the various Regulations and Directives are in place a future edition of the book will deal with them.

The range of authors remains, as with the previous editions, a mixture of academics and practitioners to achieve the best all-round view of the laws and regulations and their application. The book continues to be aimed at legal practitioners, accountants, academics and those holding senior positions in banks and financial services firms.

The law is as stated on 1 June 2014.

Professor Andrew Haynes

School of Law
University of Wolverhampton

General editor and contributors

GENERAL EDITOR AND CONTRIBUTOR

Professor Andrew Haynes

Professor Andrew Haynes BA (Hons) Law, PhD, Cert Ed, FRSA, FSALS has written, edited and contributed to a wide range of books, encyclopaedias and articles on financial services law and regulation, financial crime and international capital markets law including writing *The Law Relating to International Banking*, also published by Bloomsbury Professional. He has also spoken at a wide range of international conferences as well as delivering training sessions for judges, banking regulators, banks, financial services firms and solicitors throughout the world.

The University of Wolverhampton Law School offers a range of PhDs, specialist postgraduate programmes in financial services law as well as undergraduate programmes in law in Wolverhampton, Hong Kong, Russia, Mauritius and Sri Lanka.

Email: andrew@andrewhaynes.co.uk

CONTRIBUTORS

Peter Bibby

Peter Bibby is a partner in the White Collar Defence & Government Investigations group in the London office of Brown Rudnick LLP.

Peter is a specialist financial regulatory lawyer with over 20 years of contentious regulatory enforcement experience. He was Head of Enforcement at the FSA and was responsible for writing the statements of Principle and Code of Practice for Approved Persons. Whilst in private practice Peter has been recognised by both *Chambers UK* and the *Legal 500* as one of the leading individuals in the area with an excellent breadth of knowledge. Peter's practice focuses on advising in relation to matters concerning the Financial Services and Markets Act 2000 and the rules of the Financial Conduct Authority and the Prudential Regulation Authority.

He advises on all aspects of the regime, with a particular emphasis on enforcement, from the initial identification of a potential problem, through the different stages of the investigation process, to the representation of clients in front of the regulators' decision making committees and the external Tribunal.

Clients include fund managers, banks, insurance companies and other financial institutions together with individuals who are subject to financial regulation. He has also advised regulators in the UK and overseas in relation to the exercise of their powers in contentious regulatory matters and has been appointed as a skilled person under s 166 of the Financial Services and Markets Act 2000.

Email: pbibby@brownrudnick.com

Tel: 0207 851 6017

Brown Rudnick LLP
8 Clifford Street
London
W1S 2LQ

Ian Kelly

Ian Kelly is a Manager in PwC's Regulatory Centre of Excellence. He specialises in prudential regulation. He advises banks and investment firms on compliance with all aspects of the prudential framework including capital, liquidity, leverage, risk management and regulatory reporting. He is a regular contributor to PwC's external publications.

Prior to this Ian was a policymaker and firm supervisor at the FSA. He worked on reforms to the original Capital Requirements Directive before later moving on to supervise firms directly. Ian has spoken at conferences on financial regulation and is a regular contributor to financial publications. He holds a Masters in Commercial Law from the University of Edinburgh.

Richard Parlour

Richard Parlour is an experienced international financial markets lawyer. He started in the derivatives team at Clifford Chance and worked as general counsel at LIFFE, as well as in Brussels with the European institutions. He then worked closely with Accenture setting up new financial institutions and restructuring others across Europe. Richard now runs Financial Markets Law International (www.fmli.co.uk), a new kind of law firm focusing on international financial markets, and making compliance profitable. FMLI's network covers 140 countries worldwide. Richard advises on compliance transformation for financial markets and their participants, including regulation, restructuring, new product and service development, deterrence of financial crime, enhanced due diligence, and accelerated learning. He won and ran the largest EBRD project (restructuring the capital markets of a CEE country) the first time all recommendations were adopted by a Parliament. He was also involved in the UK's leading example of compliance transformation, and was awarded UK Strategic Regulatory Advisor of the Year 2013. He has been part of the UK's money laundering experts group and was the UK expert on an EU anti-corruption project, winning AML Law Firm of the

Year 2014. He has published widely on financial markets issues and is a regular conference speaker.

Christopher Robinson

Christopher Robinson is a London-based partner in the Financial Institutions Disputes Group at Freshfields Bruckhaus Deringer LLP. He advises on a wide range of litigation and regulatory proceedings in the banking and financial services sector. His recent regulatory experience includes leading a cross-jurisdictional internal investigation arising from regulatory enquiries for a leading investment bank and advising a leading European retail bank on regulatory and criminal liability issues arising from allegations of bribery. He is a member of the firm's global investigations practice and frequently works on cross-border investigations with a financial services or financial crime focus.

Christopher holds first class degrees in law from Durham University (LL.B) and Christ's College Cambridge (LL.M).

Email: christopher.robinson@freshfields.com

Direct T: +44 20 7785 5781

F: +44 20 7832 7001

Freshfields Bruckhaus Deringer LLP
65 Fleet Street
London
EC4Y 1HS

Rebeka Smith

Rebeka Smith is a Senior Manager in PwC's Financial Services Risk and Regulation practice. She has extensive experience working with banks and investment firms, particularly in relation to the FCA and PRA's regulatory capital regimes, capital markets transactions, recovery planning and governance and risk management. Most recently Rebeka has been focused on the Capital Requirements Regulation and Directive (CRDIV) introduced across the European Union.

Rebeka holds a Bachelor of Arts/Bachelor of Laws (BA/LLB) from the Australian National University and a Diploma in Investment Compliance from the Chartered Institute for Securities and Investment.

Robert Surridge

Robert is Chief Counsel in the Legal Department of Friends Life and concentrates on providing legal and regulatory support on product related matters. Recent work has included such issues as the Retail Distribution Review, Pensions changes arising out of the Budget, Unfair Contract Terms reviews and the transitioning of policies between administration systems. He is one of the authors of *Houseman's Law of Life Assurance* (also published by Bloomsbury Professional) and has contributed to other publications. He also helps maintain some of the Fact Files for the Chartered Insurance Institute.

Email: Robert.Surridge@friendslife.co.uk

Owen Watkins

Owen Watkins MA, DPhil is a barrister in the corporate department at Lewis Silkin. He has been involved in financial services regulation for more than 20 years, first at the UK regulator (the Financial Services Authority and before that the Securities and Investments Board), more recently in private practice. His work primarily involves advising firms and individuals on the scope and application of relevant financial services legislation (in particular the Financial Services and Markets Act 2000) and of regulatory rules.

Lewis Silkin LLP is focused on providing effective and commercial solutions to clients' needs from offices in London, Oxford and Cardiff. In addition to expertise in the legal fields of real estate, corporate, employment, litigation and dispute resolution, the firm focuses in particular on the creative industries, media, people, urban regeneration and mixed use development.

Email: owen.watkins@lewissilkin.com

Lewis Silkin - www.lewissilkin.com

Contents

Contents

Contents

Table of Statutes

Table of Statutory Instruments

Table of EU Legislation

Table of Sourcebooks and Materials

Table of Cases

Chapter 1

Financial services regulation

Andrew Haynes

INTRODUCTION

1.1   The main purpose of the regulatory structure which the Financial Services and Markets Act 2000 ('FSMA') as amended by the Financial Services Acts of 2010 ('FSA 2010') and 2012 ('FSA 2012') brought
about was to create a system of joint regulation in which the Prudential Regulation Authority ('PRA') and the Financial Conduct Authority
('FCA') regulate almost the entire financial services industry. The PRA's
remit is to deal with the prudential regulation of firms and the FCA
deals with the other issues, primarily relating to consumer protection
and the conduct of business. The PRA also functions as the lead regulator of banks, building societies, credit unions and insurance companies.
The FCA deals with the prudential regulation of smaller organisations
and brokers.

1 See FSMA 2000, Pt XIX, ss 314–324 and also the FSA Lloyd's Sourcebook.

1.2   Thus between them, the PRA and the FCA regulate banks, building societies, credit unions and insurance companies, whilst the FCA is
essentially responsible for friendly societies, stockbrokers, derivatives,
dealers, fund managers, financial advisers, and insurance intermediaries.
It also retains an overriding power in relation to insurance underwriting
at Lloyd's of London, subject to PRA prudential supervision. The FCA has
to keep in touch with the regulation of Lloyd's by the Council of Lloyd's
and, should it deem it necessary, has the power to take over Lloyd's financial regulation in association with the PRA.

1.3   The prudential aspects of regulation are split between the PRA,
which handles micro prudential regulation and the Bank of England's
Financial Policy Committee ('FPC') which handles the macro prudential
issues. The FPC in turn works closely with the Financial Policy Committee
and the Special Resolutions Unit at the Bank. Thus the overall regulatory
structure looks as follows:

Bank of England
Financial Policy Committee
(macro prudential regulation)
↓

FCA————————————————**PRA**
(all regulation other than that   (micro prudential regulation of
covered by PRA)   banks, building societies, credit
                                     unions and insurance companies)

1

The Financial Conduct Authority

1.4   The FCA has three main objectives which are set out in the FSA 2012, s 1B(3). They are:

−   consumer protection;

−   integrity (which in this context is taken to mean that the system should be sound, not be used in connection with organised crime or market abuse, maintain the orderly operation of the financial markets and be transparent regarding price operation); and

−   competition.

Although this appears to leave the FCA with an enormous degree of power, it is scrutinised by both Parliamentary Committees and the Treasury, as is the PRA. The end result is therefor that they are subject to political control.

1.5   The FCA's primary function is to carry out the functions mentioned above (see **1.2** and **1.3**) under the FSMA 2000 and the FSAs of 2010 and 2012. It is also required to regulate the categories of financial business and to deal with the official listing of securities. The FSMA 2000 confirmed the FCA as the competent authority for Official Listing of securities, which entails, inter alia, specifying the requirements to be complied with by issuers of listed securities. The FCA is responsible for maintaining the official list and applications for listing have to be made to them. The Treasury maintain the capacity under FSMA 2000, s 95 to keep the FCA's performance under review. A detailed analysis of the listing rules is however beyond the scope of this chapter.

1.6   The aim of the regulations is to keep a balance between the interests of those in industry who wish to raise capital and those of the public at large who may wish to subscribe. In this context the purpose of the listing rules is to provide a regulatory framework for the issuing of new (primary) securities and the selling of existing (secondary) ones. Securities will only be admitted to listing if the applicant is suitable and it is appropriate for the securities concerned to be publicly held and traded. They must be brought to the market in a way that is appropriate to their nature and number and that will facilitate an open and efficient market for trading in those securities. Issuers must make full and timely disclosures about themselves and the listed securities both at the time of issue and afterwards. The continuing obligations imposed on issuers are designed to promote investor confidence in standards of disclosure, in the conduct of listed companies' affairs and in the market as a whole. Holders of equity securities must be given adequate opportunity to consider in advance and vote upon major changes in the company's management and constitution.

1.7   Thus the FCA's functions beyond the immediate matters of investment business regulation and supervision are:

−   overseeing the conduct regulation of Lloyd's of London (although the PRA deals with the prudential supervision of Lloyd's managing agents);

−   combating market abuse;

- recognising and supervising investment exchanges and clearing houses;

- regulating competition scrutiny;

- overseeing the compensation scheme; and

- overseeing the ombudsman scheme.

1.7A That this will lead to change is clear. In the words of Martin Wheatley, Chief Executive of the FCA[1]:

'The important point here is that this is a new epoch in financial regulation. Thematic reviews, market studies, and the increased use of judgement, these are regulatory features that are here to stay.

Like Icarus, financial services flew too close to the sun in the boom years. They pivoted too far towards commercial interests and too far away from consumer interests. Poor regulation provided an impetus for that fall and market failure.

But it is in all our interests to correct the balance now. Good regulation is not a zero-sum game. It's not like a game of tennis or football, where for one side to win the other has to lose. We each have a vested interest in making markets work well for all participants'.

1 Speech 9 July 2013.

The Prudential Regulation Authority

1.8 The PRA was established pursuant to FSA 2012, s 2B to promote the safety and soundness of PRA authorised firms. It was a response to the banking crisis that started in 2008 amidst a general belief that the previous regulatory structure was not fully fit for purpose. The aim was to create a structure which would make sure that business is carried on so that it avoids adversely affecting the stability of the UK financial system. It should also seek to minimise the adverse effect that the failure of a PRA authorised person could have on the stability of the UK financial system. Within the context of this, key figures, called 'controlled functions' are regulated as well as the institutions themselves. The 'controlled functions' relating to PRA authorised persons being the governing functions of chief executives, directors, including non-executives, partners, key functions at friendly societies and actuarial functions and small friendly society functions.

1.9 In essence the PRA exists to promote the safety and soundness of banks, building societies, credit unions, insurers and major investment firms and also to protect the position of insurance policy holders. In so doing its regulatory approach has three characteristics:

- judgement-based regulation to determine whether financial firms are safe, whether insurers provide appropriate protection for policyholders and whether firms meet the Threshold Conditions;

- forward-looking to assess firms against risks that may arise in the future and, where necessary, to intervene at an early stage; and

–   focused on those issues that pose the greatest risk to the stability of the UK financial system and policyholders.

To achieve this, the PRA is not proposing a zero risk approach as this would require heavy handed and intrusive regulation and a huge diminution in the risks firms could adopt.

1.10   The PRA also has a close relationship with the Bank's Financial Policy Committee and the Special Resolution Unit. The former is charged with the objective of identifying, monitoring and taking action to reduce or remove any systemic risks to the UK's financial system. The latter seeks resolution for issues involving distressed banks. It also has an important function in refining the UK's approach to bank resolution through formulating and implementing policy.

Bank of England's Monetary Policy Committee

1.11   The MPC's responsibilities go well beyond its macro prudential regulation and its liaison with the PRA. It publishes an inflation report each quarter which includes its forecasts for growth and inflation. Monetary stability is its core function and this means maintaining stable prices and the value of the currency. It thus has an influence on interest rates and was responsible for managing the policy of quantitative easing. It is through its involvement in the conduct of monetary policy that it also has an involvement in macro prudential regulation relating to the more significant financial services firms.

AUTHORISATION

1.12   It is necessary to be authorised[1] to carry on business in relation to specified investments in any of the areas already discussed unless the party concerned is exempt. 'Exemption' covers a narrow range of people including, inter alia, appointed representatives, but it is not going to be relevant for most of those wishing to carry on business in relation to specified investments. Failure to obtain authorisation prior to carrying on business in relation to specified investments is a criminal offence[2]. In addition, should contracts be entered into without a PRA/FCA licence, that contract will be enforceable against the person so acting, but can only be enforced by them at the discretion of a judge[3]. This is essentially a consumer protection measure and it is likely that enforcement by a person acting illegally would only be permitted where this is necessary to enable the criminal to repay his clients. There are also civil rights available to private clients who have a direct right of action where they suffer loss as a result of either a breach of the PRA/FCA rules by a regulated person who is a private client[4] or as a result of such a person breaching a PRA/FCA enforcement order[5].

1 FSMA 2000, s 19.
2 FSMA 2000, s 23.
3 FSMA 2000, s 26–29.
4 FSMA 2000, s 150.
5 FSMA 2000, s 71.

1.13   All 'authorised persons' must apply for and be accepted for registration by the FCA and where the firm is a bank, insurance company, deposit taker, insurer, Lloyd's managing agent or a credit union, the PRA. The institutions are generally described in the handbooks as 'firms', whilst individuals who also need to be registered are known as 'approved persons'. Together, these two requirements enable the individuals and their firms to carry on the specified activities in relation to investments.

The FCA and PRA websites provide guidance as to what is required. Applicants are expected to:

–   determine the exact scope of the permission that they should apply for, subject to any applicable limitations and requirements;

–   make sure which category of authorisation is needed to cover the specified activities. This is because the license when issued will only cover those specific areas of operation that have been approved. The license does not operate in a more general sense;

–   find out which FCA rules apply to the specified activities that they propose to carry on and make sure that the applicant is in a position to satisfy them;

–   prepare a business plan covering the activities, risks, resources and a budget that will satisfy the financial resources or capital adequacy requirement as is appropriate;

–   ascertain which people are covered by the approved person's scheme and make any necessary applications as there must be a license for each relevant individual as well as for the firm. This is considered further below;

–   obtain such reports by auditors or reporting accountants as are required by the rules. These reports may also be asked for by the PRA/FCA. If matters are not straightforward it is a good idea to involve the auditors or accountants at an early stage in planning the application; and

–   where appropriate, ascertain whether it is necessary to apply to the Society of Lloyd's for admission as an underwriting agent.

APPROVED PERSONS

1.14   All significant individuals involved in a business that requires authorisation must be 'approved' by the PRA/FCA as appropriate. They must be convinced that the person concerned is fit and proper and possesses appropriate abilities, relevant qualifications and/or experience and a suitable degree of honesty and integrity. The people covered by this requirement are found in two areas of financial services firms performing 'controlled functions'. The first group are those who are in such senior positions that the regulator(s) need to be satisfied that they are suitable. Examples are: the chief executive, directors, partners (if relevant), senior managers, compliance officers, money laundering reporting officers and finance officers. The second group are those who carry on controlled functions in a context that affects customers directly, such as advising clients or arranging contracts, and those who manage them.

1.15 In the case of banks, deposit taking institutions, friendly societies, insurance companies, actuaries and Lloyd's key personnel the PRA have to approve the persons concerned. In other cases the FCA is responsible for approval and their definitions of the relevant controlled functions are the same as the PRA's except that certain additional ones arise. These are: appointment and oversight functions (non-MiFiD only), compliance oversight, CASS oversight, money laundering reporting, systems and control functions, senior management, customer functions and finally LIBOR benchmark and LIBOR administration functions.

1.16 To put this in context the controlled functions fall into seven categories of job function.

CONTROLLED FUNCTIONS

Governing body functions

1.17 These consist of the following significant influence functions:

– Executive directors of a company. * PRA/FCA CF 1

– Non-executive directors of a company. * PRA/FCA CF2

– Chief executive officers. In the case of a UK branch of a non-EEA insurer the role includes the principal UK executive. It also covers joint chief executives operating under the immediate control of the board where there is more than one. * PRA/FCA CF 3

– Partners or limited partners, as is appropriate, are regarded as carrying on controlled functions where the firm is primarily involved in regulated investment business. Limited partners whose role is purely that of an investor are excluded from the need to be regulated. If a partnership's primary business does not relate to specified investments but a separate part of the business does, then, provided the partnership has decided that only a distinct partner or set of partners deal with that aspect of the business, only they need be approved. * PRA/FCA CF4

– Directors of unincorporated associations. * PRA/FCA CF 5

– Those directing or regulating the specified activities of a small friendly society. * PRA/FCA CF 6

– Apportionment and oversight functions for non MiFiD firms. PRA/FCA CF 8

– Compliance oversight functions. PRA/FCA CF 10

– CASS oversight operation function. PRA/FCA CF 10A

– Money laundering reporting function. PRA/FCA CF 11

– Actuarial function * PRA/FCA CF 12

– With profits actuary function * PRA/FCA CF 12A

– Lloyd's actuary function * PRA/FCA CF 12B

– Systems and controls functions. PRA/FCA CF 28

– Significant management functions. PRA/FCA 29

* Indicates a PRA Designated Controlled Function that applies to Dual Regulated Firms. The PRA leads the assessment of applications for approval but also requires the FCA's consent before approval of an individual to perform any PRA designated Significant Influence Function.

Significant management functions in relation to business and control

1.18　The significant management functions set out below are added to cover those situations where the firm concerned has senior managers whose function is equivalent to that of a member of the firm's governing body. They do not apply if the activity is a specified activity as this would automatically then be an approved persons' role. They fall into five categories of senior management:

(1)　Those operating in relation to investment services, such as the head of equities. This will often be a controlled function in any event.

(2)　Those operating in relation to other areas of the firm's business than specified investment activity, eg head of personal lending or corporate lending, head of credit card issues etc.

(3)　Those responsible for carrying out insurance underwriting other than in relation to contractually based investments, eg head of aviation underwriting.

(4)　Those responsible for making decisions concerning the firm's own finances, eg chief corporate treasurer.

(5)　Those responsible for back office functions.

1.19　The LIBOR function is categorised as a 'controlled function' at CF40 (benchmark submission function) and CF 50 (benchmark administration function). This was brought in as a specific requirement following the LIBOR scandal and the limited control which seemed to be applied to the setting of LIBOR under the previous arrangements.

Temporary and emergency functions

1.20　Should the function of undertaking such a role continue for more than eight weeks in a twelve month period then the person primarily responsible will need to be an approved person.

Dealing with customer functions

1.21　There are seven main functions within this category:

(1)　life and pensions advisers;

(2)　life and pensions advisers when acting under supervision;

(3)　pension transfer advisers. Such people can also give ancillary advice in relation to packaged products;

(4)　investment advisers, including those advising in relation to packaged products, but not life and pensions advice;

(5)　investment advisers acting under supervision;

(6) corporate finance advisers; and

(7) advisers to underwriting members of Lloyd's in relation to becoming a syndicate member.

Dealing with customers' property

1.22 This covers two main types of activity under PRA/FCA CF 30 relating to dealing with customers' property, namely:

(1) The customer trading functions, ie those individuals who deal or arrange deals on behalf of customers. It does not extend to execution only business and feeding orders into automatic execution systems.

(2) Discretionary fund management.

APPLYING FOR APPROVAL

1.23 When a firm is making an application to the PRA/FCA for permission for an employee or other individual they must submit an application including the following:

– A business plan covering any proposed regulated and unregulated activities. The latter may impact on the financial stability of the firm. It must also show the management and organisation structure together with any proposed outsourcing. There are additional requirements for those wishing to carry on insurance business.

– The budget and financial projections analysed to show that the applicant will satisfy the financial resources or capital adequacy requirements.

– The proposed compliance procedures and systems.

– A statement listing the people controlling the business and anyone connected with them.

1.24 Despite the above it is important to bear in mind that the regulated firm remains primarily responsible for compliance with the regulations. There is however a Code of Practice affecting approved persons that set out the conduct to be expected of them. Its main purpose is to make sure that the people concerned realise the legal obligations being imposed on them in the area of risk-based compliance.

1.25 In addition to the firms being subject to general Principles in addition to the rules, the approved persons are also subject to a series of ongoing requirements in the form of general principles. Principles 5-7 only apply to those in positions of significant influence whereas the first four apply to all approved persons.

APPOINTED REPRESENTATIVES

1.26 An 'appointed representative' is defined[1] as being someone who is:

'(a) a party to a contract with an unauthorised person (his principal) which-

    (i) permits or requires him to carry on business of a prescribed description, and

    (ii) complies with such requirements as may be prescribed, and

(b) is someone for whose activities in carrying on the whole or part of that business his principal has accepted responsibility in writing'.

1 FSMA 2000, s 39(1)(a), (b).

1.27 Anyone satisfying this description is exempt from the general prohibition in relation to any regulated activity when they are acting within the remit of the area of business for which their principal has accepted responsibility. Thus the principal will be responsible for the appointed representative's acts and the principal will therefore need to be an authorised person. There is some protection for the principal though:

'nothing … is to cause the knowledge or intentions of an appointed representative to be attributed to his principal for the purpose of determining whether the principal has committed an offence, unless in all the circumstances it is reasonable for them to be attributed to him[1]'

Applications to carry on regulated activities can be made by individuals as well as corporate entities, partnerships and unincorporated associations[2].

1 FSMA 2000, s 39(6).
2 FSMA 2000, s 40.

FCA/PRA PRINCIPLES FOR BUSINESS

1.28 The Principles for Business are the initial part of the rules and in many respects the most important as they can be used a basis for disciplinary proceedings by the regulators even without evidence of a breach of one of the rules themselves. That said, in practice the vast majority of disciplinary proceedings are evidenced by a breach of the rules. The Principles themselves overarch the various detailed regulations and although a breach of the Principles will not in itself give rise to potential civil action by clients, this is in contrast to the PRA/FCA rules which can give rise to civil liability where the action is at the suit of a private person (see above at **1.12**)[1]. The Principles are widely worded and thus can represent an opportunity for the PRA/FCA to bring proceedings where the regulations do not themselves precisely deal with the issue that has arisen. In practice however the vast majority of disciplinary actions for breach of a Principle are likely to involve clear breaches of the other rules. It should be added that it is expected that the PRA Principles may be amended in the future and then differ from those of the FCA.

1 FSMA 2000, s 150(1).

The Eleven PRA/FCA Principles

1.29

(1) Integrity

A firm must conduct its business with integrity.

(2) Skill, care and diligence

A firm must conduct its business with due skill, care and diligence.

(3) Management and control

A firm must take reasonable care to organise and control its affairs responsibly and effectively, with adequate risk management systems.

(4) Financial prudence

A firm must maintain adequate financial resources.

(5) Market conduct

A firm must observe proper standards of market conduct.

(6) Customers' interests

A firm must pay due regard to the interests of its customers, and treat them fairly.

(7) Communications with customers

A firm must pay due regard to the information needs of its customers, and communicate information to them in a way which is clear, fair and not misleading.

(8) Conflicts of interest

A firm must manage conflicts of interest fairly, both between itself and its customers and between one customer and another.

(9) Customers' relationships of trust

A firm must take reasonable care to ensure the suitability of its advice and discretionary decisions for any customer who is entitled to rely upon its judgment.

(10) Customers' assets

A firm must arrange adequate protection for customers' assets when it is responsible for them.

(11) Relations with regulators

A firm must deal with its regulator in an open and co-operative way, and must tell the PRA/FCA promptly anything relating to the firm of which the PRA/FCA would reasonably expect notice.

PART 6 STATEMENTS OF PRINCIPLE FOR APPROVED PERSONS

1.30 The Principles themselves are:

(1) An Approved Person must act with integrity in carrying out his controlled function.

(2) An Approved Person must act with due skill, care and diligence in carrying out his controlled function.

(3) An Approved Person must observe proper standards of market conduct in carrying out his controlled function.

(4) An Approved Person must deal with the PRA/FCA and with other regulators in an open and co-operative way and must disclose appropriately any information of which the PRA/FCA would reasonably expect notice.

(5) An Approved Person performing a significant influence function must take reasonable steps to ensure that the business of the firm for which he is responsible in his controlled function is organised so that it can be controlled effectively.

(6) An Approved Person performing a significant influence function must exercise due skill, care and diligence in managing the business of the firm for which he is responsible in his controlled function.

(7) An Approved Person performing a significant influence function must take reasonable steps to ensure that the business of the firm for which he is responsible in his controlled function complies with the regulatory requirements imposed on that business'.

FCA RULES

1.31   The FCA has the power to issue rules, both generally[1] and has statutory authority to issue them in certain specific areas[2] such as price stabilisation, financial promotion and the control of information. The full FCA handbook includes a glossary and standards on high level issues, prudential matters, business, regulation, and redress together with specialist sourcebooks, listing and prospectus rules, and handbook and regulatory guides.

1 FSMA 2000, s 138.
2 FSMA 2000, ss 144–147.

1.32   The rules themselves are preceded by general principles (see above) which the PRA and FCA require authorised persons to obey and are followed by guidance notes, which are not technically part of the rules but which assist in explaining how the rules are expected to operate. The PRA and FSA have made clear that should the guidance notes be followed a firm or approved person will be safe from disciplinary proceedings should the guidance transpire to be inaccurate.

1.33   A firm must notify new clients at the outset of their client classification, which will be either as a retail client, professional or eligible counterparty and any limitations on the level of protection that they will receive[1]. The client may request re-categorisation to obtain a greater degree of protection should they wish[2]. In essence the default setting is that a client is a retail client unless they are otherwise so classified[3]. Turning to professional clients, anyone who satisfies the regulatory requirements is a professional client per se. Such firms are:

•   entities required to be authorised or regulated to operate in the financial markets. The following list includes all authorised entities carrying out the characteristic activities of the entities mentioned, whether authorised by an EEA State or a third country and whether or not authorised by reference to a directive:

- ○ a credit institution;
- ○ an investment firm;
- ○ any other authorised or regulated financial institution;
- ○ an insurance company;
- ○ a collective investment scheme or the management company of such a scheme;
- ○ a pension fund or the management company of a pension fund;
- ○ a commodity or commodity derivatives dealer;
- ○ a local;
- ○ any other institutional investor;

- in relation to MiFID or equivalent third country business a large undertaking meeting two of the following size requirements on a company basis:

  - ○ balance sheet total of EUR 20,000,000;
  - ○ net turnover of EUR 40,000,000;
  - ○ own funds of EUR 2,000,000;

- in relation to business that is not MiFID or equivalent third country business a large undertaking meeting any of the following conditions:

  - ○ a body corporate (including a limited liability partnership) which has (or any of whose holding companies or subsidiaries has) (or has had at any time during the previous two years) called up share capital or net assets of at least £5 million (or its equivalent in any other currency at the relevant time);
  - ○ an undertaking that meets (or any of whose holding companies or subsidiaries meets) two of the following tests:

- a balance sheet total of EUR 12,500,000;
- (ii) a net turnover of EUR 25,000,000;
- (iii) an average number of employees during the year of 250;

  - ○ a partnership or unincorporated association which has (or has had at any time during the previous two years) net assets of at least £5 million (or its equivalent in any other currency at the relevant time) and calculated in the case of a limited partnership without deducting loans owing to any of the partners;
  - ○ a trustee of a trust (other than an occupational pension scheme, SSAS, personal pension scheme or stakeholder pension scheme) which has (or has had at any time during the previous two years) assets of at least £10 million (or

its equivalent in any other currency at the relevant time) calculated by aggregating the value of the cash and designated investments forming part of the trust's assets, but before deducting its liabilities;

- ○ a trustee of an occupational pension scheme or SSAS, or a trustee or operator of a personal pension scheme or stakeholder pension scheme where the scheme has (or has had at any time during the previous two years):

at least 50 members; and

(ii) assets under management of at least £10 million (or its equivalent in any other currency at the relevant time);

- ○ a local authority or public authority.

- a national or regional government, a public body that manages public debt, a central bank, an international or supranational institution (such as the World Bank, the IMF, the ECP, the EIB) or another similar international organisation;

- another institutional investor whose main activity is to invest in financial instruments (in relation to the firm's MiFID or equivalent third country business) or designated investments (in relation to the firm's other business). This includes entities dedicated to the securitisation of assets or other financing transactions.

1 COBS 3.3.1.
2 COBS 3.7.1 R.
3 COBS 3.4.1.

1.34 A client may elect to be a professional client[1], either generally or for a particular service or transaction, but the firm accepting them as such must undertake an adequate assessment of their expertise and knowledge to determine whether such a classification is appropriate given their understanding of the relevant risks. In the case of MiFID or equivalent third country businesses the client must have carried out transactions of a significant size on the relevant market at least ten times per quarter in the previous year and the size of their investment portfolio must exceed €500,000. That client must also have worked in the financial services sector for at least a year in a professional position. Should the client fail to continue to satisfy these requirements the firm should re-categorise them as appropriate, and if this results in them becoming a retail client they must be so notified in writing[2].

1 COBS 3.5.3.
2 COBS 3.5.9.

1.35 The client must be warned in writing of the loss of protections that will happen and the investors' compensation rights that will be lost and the client must confirm in writing, in a document other than the main contract that they are aware of the fact[1]. Even then they cannot be presumed to possess all the market knowledge and experience of a per se professional client[2].

1 COBS 3.5.5.
2 COBS 3.5.7.

1.36 The same distinction between a per se client and an elective one arises with eligible counterparties[1]. Any of the following area per se eligible counterparty[2]:

- an investment firm;

- a credit institution;

- an insurance company;

- a collective investment scheme authorised under the UCITS Directive or its management company;

- a pension fund or its management company;

- another financial institution authorised or regulated under EU legislation or the national law of an EEA State;

- an undertaking exempted from the application of MiFID under either Article 2(1)(k) (certain own account dealers in commodities or commodity derivatives) or Article 2(1)(l) (locals) of that directive;

- a national government or its corresponding office, including a public body that deals with the public debt;

- a central bank;

- a supranational organisation.

1 COBS 3.6.1.
2 COBS 3.6.2.

1.37 In addition a client can be treated as an elective eligible counterparty if:

- the client is an undertaking and

  o is a per se professional client (except for a client that is only a per se professional client because it is an institutional investor under COBS 3.5.2 R (5)) and, in relation to business other than MiFID or equivalent third country business:

  o is a body corporate (including a limited liability partnership) which has (or any of whose holding companies or subsidiaries has) called up share capital of at least £10 million (or its equivalent in any other currency at the relevant time); or

  o meets the criteria in the rule on meeting two quantitative tests (COBS 3.5.2 R (3)(b)); or

  o requests such categorisation and is an elective professional client, but only in respect of the services or transactions for which it could be treated as a professional client; and

- the firm has, in relation to MiFID or equivalent third country business, obtained express confirmation from the prospective counterparty that it agrees to be treated as an eligible counterparty.

1.38 A firm may reclassify a client to give them more protection, i.e., eligible counterparty to professional, or professional to retail[1]. The client should then be so notified[2]. The protection to be provided on this basis can

be done generally, on a trade by trade basis, in respect of a particular rule
or transaction or a product[3].

1 COBS 3.7.3.
2 FCA Principle 7 and COBS 3.7.6.
3 COBS 3.7.7.

PRA RULES

1.39   The PRA deals with the regulation of banks, building societies,
credit unions and insurance companies. A detailed analysis of the prudential rules if beyond the scope of this book, although **Chapter 9** provides
an overview.

INVESTMENT BUSINESS IN THE UK

Specified Investments

1.40   The Financial Services and Markets Act 2000 (Regulated Activities) Order 2001 as amended[1] provides full definitions of specified investments and activities.

1 SI 2002/1518, SI 2003/1475, SI 2003/1476, SI 2004/1610, SI 2004/2737, SI 2005/1518,
   SI 2005/2114, SI 2006/196, SI 2006/2383, SI 2006/3384, SI 2009/1342, SI 2012/1906,
   SI 2013/556, SI 2013/655, Alternative Investment Fund Managers Regulations, SI 2013/
   1773, SI 2013/1881, SI 2013/3128, SI 2014/334 and SI 2014/366.

1.41   As far as the Order is concerned, the investments that are specified are as follows.

(1) **Deposits**[1]. the investment itself is effectively left undefined but there
     is a definition of 'accepting deposits' at **1.48** below.

(2) **Issuing electronic money**[2].

(3) **Contracts of insurance**[3]. These are defined in Schedule 1, to the Instru-
     ment. The definition covers the following categories of insurance
     policy: accident, sickness, land, vehicles, railway rolling stock, aircraft,
     ships, goods in transit, fire and natural forces, damage to property,
     motor vehicle liability, aircraft liability, liability of ships, general lia-
     bility, credit, suretyship, miscellaneous financial loss, legal expenses,
     travel assistance, life and annuity, marriage and birth, linked long term,
     permanent health, tontines, capital redemption contracts, pension fund
     management, collective insurance contracts and social insurance.

(4) **Shares**[4]. This is widely defined as 'shares or stock in the share capital
     of:

     (a) any body corporate (wherever incorporated), and

     (b) any unincorporated body constituted under the law of a coun-
          try or territory outside the United Kingdom'.

1 SI 2001/544, art 74, as amended.
2 Inserted by SI 2002/682, art 4.
3 SI 2001/544, art 75.
4 SI 2001/544, art 76.

1.42   It also includes deferred shares within the meaning of s 119 of the
Building Societies Act 1986 and any transferable shares in a body incorpo-

rated under the UK law relating to industrial and provident societies or credit unions, or under equivalent laws in other EEA states.

Shares were defined by Farwell J as being 'the interest of a shareholder in the company measured by a sum of money, for the purpose of liability in the first place, and of interest in the second, but also consisting of a series of mutual covenants entered into by all the shareholders *inter se*'. The definition appears to extend to stock.

The Instrument's definition excludes shares in open ended investment companies, building societies, industrial and provident societies, credit unions or an equivalent entity in another EEA jurisdiction.

1.43

(5)   **Instruments creating or acknowledging indebtedness**[1]. The definition of debentures is a wide one and in addition to normal debentures, loan stock and bonds it includes certificates of deposit and any other instrument creating or acknowledging indebtedness.

It is generally accepted that 'debenture' has never been properly defined. The most widely accepted definition is that of Chitty J, who described a debenture as being 'a document which either creates a debt or acknowledges it'. This is the wording adopted by the Statutory Instrument, and as a result of it being so wide certain other financial instruments are specifically excluded, namely:

- an instrument acknowledging indebtedness for money borrowed to provide the cost of goods or services;

- cheques, bills of exchange, bank drafts and letters of credit, but not a bill of exchange accepted by a banker;

- bank notes and bank statements, a lease or other disposition of property or a heritable security; and

- contracts of insurance.

1 SI 2001/544, art 77.

1.44

(6)   **Alternative finance investment bonds**[1]. These are arrangements which provide for the holder to pay a sum to the issuer. The arrangements relating to such a bond must identify a class of assets which the bond holder will acquire to generate an income or gain which are known as 'the bond assets'. It must be arranged for a fixed term. There must be a redemption payment and additional payment up to the amount necessary to provide a reasonable commercial return on a loan of that amount.

If a bond falls under the definitions in (5) above and (7) below then that definition applies.

1 At SI 2001/544, art 77A.

1.45

(7) **Government and public securities**[1]. This covers loan stock, bonds and other instruments issued by central, regional and local government in the EEA. Excluded are those instruments excluded under 'debentures' above and instruments issued by the National Savings Bank and under the National Loans Act 1968 and s 11(3) of the National Debt Act 1972.

1 SI 2001/544, art 7.

1.46

(8) **Warrants**[1]. The definition applies regardless of whether the instrument relates to something that is or is not already in existence. They have been defined as 'transferable option certificates issued by companies and trusts which entitle the holder to buy a specific number of shares in that company at a specific price ... at a specific time in the future'. As is made clear in the definition this state of affairs applies regardless of whether the shares are already in existence.

1 SI 2001/544, art 7.

1.47

(9) **Certificates Representing Securities**[1]. Certificates providing contractual rights in respect of shares, instruments creating or acknowledging indebtedness, government and public securities and warrants where the interest is held by someone other than the person on whom the rights are conferred and where the transfer can be carried out without the consent of that person. This paragraph effectively debars the creation of investments which amount to an indirect interest so as to facilitate carrying on business in such investments outside the jurisdiction of the FCA/PRA regime.

Excluded are instruments conferring rights in respect of two or more investments issued by different persons, or in respect of two or more types of government or public security issued by the same person. The first of these exclusions covers legal and equitable mortgages because such an arrangement involves a transfer of property interest from the party granting the mortgage to that receiving it.

1 SI 2001/544, art 80.

1.48

(10) **Units in collective investment schemes**[1]. Such schemes are defined in s 235 of the Act as:

> '(1) any arrangements with respect to property of any description, including money, the purpose or effect of which is to enable persons taking part ... (whether by becoming owners of the property or any part of it or otherwise) to participate in or receive profits or income arising from the acquisition, holding, management or disposal of the property or sums paid out of such profits or income.

17

(2) The arrangements must be such that the persons who are to participate ... do not have day-to-day control over the management of the property, whether they have the right to be consulted or give directions.

(3) The arrangements must also have either or both of the following characteristics:

(a) the contributions of the participants and the profits or income out of which payments are to be made to them are pooled;

(b) the property is managed as a whole by or on behalf of the operator of the scheme'.

If the property is held on trust for the participants the fund will be known as a unit trust. An open ended investment company on the other hand is a collective investment scheme where the property concerned belongs beneficially to and is managed by or on behalf of a body corporate. The aim of such a scheme must be to spread investment risk and give the members the benefit. The investment must however appear to a reasonable investor to be one from which he can realise the investment within a reasonable period and be satisfied that the value of that investment would be calculated by reference to the value of property into which the scheme has invested.

1 SI 2001/544, art 81.

1.49

(11) **Rights under stakeholder or personal pension schemes**[1]. These are defined by s 1 of the Welfare Reform and Pensions Act 1999 which in essence states that such a scheme is one which is registered with Pensions Regulator and meets a series of conditions which are set out in s 1(2)–(9) and any others that may be added by statutory instrument.

1 SI 2001/544, art 81.

1.50

(12) **Greenhouse gas emissions allowances**[1] These are covered when auctioned as financial instruments or as two day spot contracts within Art 3.3 of the Emission Allowances Auctioning Regulation.

1 SI 2001/544, art 82A.

1.51

(13) **Options**[1]. The definition covers options to buy or sell:

- a security or contractually based investment;

- UK or foreign currency; or

- palladium, platinum, gold or silver.

There are two main categories: put options, which involve the party paying a deposit acquiring the right to sell one of the above commodities whilst the counterparty takes on the obligation to buy, and call options which operate in reverse. The party paying a deposit acquires a right to perform whilst the counterparty is obligated to. In each instance the party who has the right to perform can also decide to walk away from the contract and the only cost to them will be the loss of the deposit. Their counterparty has no such right.

1 SI 2001/544, art 83.

1.52

(14) **Futures**[1]. This covers rights under a contract to sell a commodity or property where the price is agreed now but delivery is in the future where such an agreement is made for an investment rather than a commercial purpose. A contract will be regarded as being for investment purposes if it is traded on a recognised investment exchange or where it is not but is expressed to be traded as such. A contract will be regarded as being for commercial purposes if delivery is to be made within seven days or where one of the parties is a producer of the commodity or property or uses it in their business, or where delivery is intended.

1 SI 2001/544, art 84.

1.53

(15) **Contracts for differences**[1]. This covers agreements the aim of which is to secure a profit or avoid a loss by either or both of the parties by reference to fluctuations in the value of property or an index or other factor. There are two types of contract which would potentially appear to be caught by this wording: swaps and forward rate agreements.

Swap contracts exist in a number of forms, but essentially they all consist of a contractual arrangement whereby two counterparties will agree to notionally swap similar or dissimilar assets or debts. The original modern type – currency swaps – evolved as a method of circumventing exchange control restrictions prior to their suspension in 1979. Rather than use traditional methods, such as parallel and back-to-back loans, the parties would enter into a spot exchange transaction to sell one currency and use a forward exchange contract to reverse the original contract. As loans were not being made as such it did not constitute borrowing and the transaction could be left off the balance sheet. Any necessary payments between the parties were then made on a net basis, commonly every six months. The next major development was the emergence of the interest rate swap, where one party who had a greater quantity of fixed rate debt that they wished to retain arranged with a counterparty who had a surplus of floating rate debt, to 'swap' the respective debts. The arrangement did not consist of a transference of the legal title to the debts but the periodic payment of net amounts needed to place the parties in the financial position they would have been had the legal transfer of the debt taken place. Recent years have seen the emergence of a wide range of swap contracts of which the most important are credit swaps where one party exchanges an income stream against another's asset holdings and credit default swaps which are effectively insurance against non-payment of a debt by a third party. This can facilitate a transfer of risk that better suits the respective parties' financial needs.

Excluded by the Instrument are contracts under which delivery is going to take place to one of the parties, and contracts in relation to money deposits where interest or another return will be paid by reference to fluctuations in an index or other factor. Also excluded are contracts in relation to deposits at the National Savings Bank or money raised under the National Loans Act 1968 or under s 11(3) of the National Debt Act 1972.

1 SI 2001/544, art 85.

1.54

(16) **Lloyd's syndicate capacity and syndicate membership**[1]. Lloyd's is an insurance underwriting market. Those who underwrite risks are the underwriters who work in syndicates to spread the risk between them. They do not carry all this risk themselves but spread it to 'names' in return for passing them a share of the premium. These names fall into two categories. The traditional names who are wealthy individuals who risk all their assets in return for a premium income and the corporate names who, subject to limited liability receive a premium income on behalf of their shareholders. By 2014 wealthy individuals only amounted to 14% of the Names. Today this function is normally carried out by limited liability companies and partnerships. Syndicate capacity and membership are specified investments.

Largely as a consequence of the problems that beset Lloyd's in the 1990's The Council of Lloyd's that traditionally ran the market is now subject to oversight by the FCA. S 314 FSMA requires the FCA to keep itself informed about the Council's running of Lloyd's and the manner in which regulated activities are being carried out with a view to exercising their own powers if necessary.

1 SI 2001/544, art 86.

1.55

(17) **Funeral plan contracts**[1]. This issue is discussed below at **1.86**.

1 SI 2001/544, art 87.

1.56

(18) **Regulated mortgage contracts**[1]. This is arguably the most important addition to the range of investments covered by the financial services regulatory regime. It is for most people the largest or second largest financial investment they make. Although the banks and other main lending institutions had adopted a code of practice with regard to mortgage lending, the involvement of the FCA now means that tighter control can be taken of advice given to those taking out one of the various types of mortgage contract now available. The definition has kept being extended in line with the new types of private mortgage product entering the market. These are defined as **regulated home reversion plans**[2], **regulated home purchase plans**[3] and **regulated sale and rent back agreements**[4].

1 SI 2001/544, art 88.
2 SI 2001/544, art 88A.

3 SI 2001/544, art 88B.
4 SI 2001/544, art 88C.

1.57

(19) Credit agreements[1] **and** consumer hire **agreements.**[2]

1 SI 2001/544, art 88D.
2 SI 2001/544, art 88E.

1.58

(20) **Rights or interests in investments**[1]. Essentially this covers any right or interest in the above. This is effectively a safety net provision to catch instruments that would otherwise have been covered by one of the above but are technically outside it, for example because the beneficiary of the investment has a legal or equitable charge or mortgage over the property or a beneficial interest in a trust rather than a direct involvement with the investment. Excluded are interests under trusts of an occupational pension scheme and certain interests in contracts of insurance or under certain trusts.

1 SI 2001/544, art 89.

SPECIFIED ACTIVITIES

1.59   The Financial Services and Markets Act 2000 (Regulated Activities) Order 2001, SI 2001/544, as amended also defines the activities that are regulated in the new regime where they relate to specified investments. These activities are:

1.60

(1) **Accepting deposits**[1]. This covers the receipt of deposits (other than those immediately exchanged for electronic money[2]) that will be repaid, either with or without interest, and either on demand or at another time agreed by the parties. It does not cover payments referable to the provision of property other than currency, or services or giving security. There are a range of exclusions, namely sums paid by[3]:

- central banks in Europe;
- an authorised person who has permission to accept deposits;
- EEA authorised firms;
- The National Savings Bank;
- A municipal bank;
- Keesler Federal Credit Union;
- A certified school bank;
- Local authorities;
- A body which is enacted to issue a precept to local authorities in England and Wales or by requisition in Scotland;

- The European Community, the European Atomic Energy Community or the European Coal and Steel Community;
- The European Investment Bank;
- The International Bank for Reconstruction and Development;
- The International Finance Corporation;
- The International Monetary Fund;
- The African Development Bank;
- The Asian Development Bank;
- The Caribbean Development Bank;
- The inter-American Development Bank;
- The European Bank for Reconstruction and Development;
- The Council of Europe Resettlement Fund

Also sums paid by any other party in the course of wholly or significantly carrying on the business of money lending; sums paid by one company to another where they are both members of the same group or when the same individual is a majority shareholder in both of them; or the making of a payment by a person who is a close relative of the person receiving it or who is a close relative of a director or manager of that person or a partner in it. Likewise, a sum received by a solicitor[4], or anyone dealing in investments[5], acting as agent in relation to investments, arranging deals in investments, managing investments, or establishing, operating or winding up a collective investment scheme or stakeholder pension scheme. Also excluded are sums received in consideration of the issue of debt securities[6], in exchange for electronic money[7], for information society services, by mangers of UCITS and AIFs[8] and funds received for payment services[9].

1 SI 2001/544, art 5.
2 Inserted by SI 2002/682, art 3(2).
3 SI 2001/544, art 6.
4 SI 2001/544, art 7.
5 SI 2001/544, art 8.
6 SI 2001/544, art 9.
7 SI 2001/544, art 9A.
8 SI 2001/544, art 9AA.
9 SI 2001/544, art 9AB.

1.61

(2) **Issuing electronic money**[1]. This definition covers credit institutions, credit unions and municipal banks any anyone else granted permission under reg 74 or 76(1) Electronic Money regulations 2011. It excludes those categorised as 'small issuers' the definition of which is set out at SI 2001/544, art 9C(1)–(10).

1 SI 2001/544, art 9B.

1.62

(3) **Insurance**[1]. This covers both effecting and carrying out a contract of insurance. Excluded from this are where such contracts are effected

or carried out by an EEA firm falling within Sch 3, para 5(d) of the 2000 Act (community co-insurers) and motor vehicle breakdown insurance. Contracts of insurance are defined in Sch 1 to the Instrument in two main categories: general and long-term insurance. These are explained at **1.29(3)** above

1 SI 2001/544, art 10.

1.63

(4) **Dealing in investments as principal**[1]. This covers buying, selling, subscribing for or underwriting securities or contractually based investments[2] (other than funeral plan contracts and rights to, or interests in, investments). Excluded are[3] situations where the person concerned holds themselves out as willing to deal at prices determined by him generally and continuously or hold themselves out as engaging in the business of buying or underwriting investments of the type concerned. Also excluded are those who hold over 20% of the shares in a company and who seek to buy the shares of other shareholders or sell those shares to them, or someone acting on behalf of such a person. Finally, there is a general exception for those whose head office is outside the UK and whose ordinary business consists of dealing as principal or agent, arranging, managing, safeguarding and administering investments and advising on investments. Likewise those who are establishing, running or winding up a collective investment scheme or stakeholder pension scheme, and, where relevant, those agreeing to carry on any of these.

This category does not extend to those who:

- accept instruments creating or acknowledging indebtedness[4];

- are companies issuing or dealing in its own shares or share warrants[5];

- enter into contractually based transactions with or through an authorised or exempt person[6];

- are contracting as principal in relation to futures, options, contracts for differences and rights or interests in investments where the counterparties are not individuals and the principal is contracting with a view to limiting an identifiable business risk other than one arising as a result of regulated activities (or matters that would be regulated activities but for the exclusions in Part III of the Instrument)[7].

- trustees[8];

- contracts for the sale of goods and supply of services;

- groups and joint enterprises;

- sale of a body corporate; and

- overseas persons.

1 SI 2001/544, art 14.
2 SI 2001/544, art 16.
3 SI 2001/544, art 15.
4 SI 2001/544, art 17.

5 SI 2001/544, art 18.
6 SI 2001/544, art 16.
7 SI 2001/544, art 19.
8 SI 2001/544, art 20 which applies to the rest of this list.

1.64

(4) **Dealing in investments as agent**[1]. This covers buying, selling, subscribing for or underwriting securities or contractually based investments (other than funeral plan contracts and rights or interests in specified investments) as agent.

The exclusions are:

- dealing through authorised persons where the transaction is entered into or the advice given to the client by an authorised person or where it is clear that the client is not seeking and has not sought advice from the agent regarding the transaction. This exclusion does not apply if the agent receives payment from anyone other than the client, for which he does not account to the client[2];

- transactions relating to futures, options, contracts for differences or rights or interests in either of those, between parties who are not individuals where the sole or main purpose is that of limiting the extent to which the business may be affecting by an identifiable risk other than one arising as a result of carrying on a regulated activity[3].

- activities carried on in the course of a profession or non-investment business;[4]

- activities carried on in connection with the sale of goods or supply of services;

- groups and joint enterprises;

- activities carried on in connection with the sale of a body corporate;

- activities carried on in connection with employee share schemes;

- overseas persons;

- information society services;

- activities carried on by a provider of relevant goods and services.

- managers of UCITS and AIFs; and

- large risks contracts where the risk is situated outside the EEA.

1 SI 2001/544, art 21.
2 SI 2001/544, art 22.
3 SI 2001/544, art 23.
4 SI 2001/544, art 24 which applies to the rest of this list.

1.65

(5) **Bidding in emissions auctions**[1]. The reception, transmission or submission of a bid at an auction of this type of investment is an

investment activity if it is carried out on a recognised auction platform or any other platform appointed under the emission allowance auctioning regulation. Excluded are[2] activities carried out by aircraft operators or business groupings bidding on their own account and public bodies and state owned entities.

1 SI 2001/544, art 24A.
2 SI 2001/544, art 24B.

1.66

(6)   **Arranging deals in investments**[1]. This covers the making of arrangements for another person to buy, sell, subscribe for or underwrite investments which are either a security, a contractually based investment, an interest in investments or syndicate capacity or membership of Lloyd's. It also extends to making such arrangements with a view to someone participating. It does not extend to merely introducing someone to another party unless it is done for a fee or on a recurrent basis. The wording is clear in that it makes it overt that the act of arranging must be a causative element in the transaction following.

The exclusions are:

- arranging regulated mortgage contracts[2];

- arranging regulated home reversion plans;[3]

- arranging regulated home purchase plans;[4]

- operating a multilateral trading facility;[5]

- arranging regulated sale and rent back agreements;[6]

- arrangements which would not bring about the transaction[7];

- merely providing the means of communication[8];

- where the person entering into the contract does so as principal or as agent for another[9] and where the arranger is a party[10];

- arranging deals through authorised persons where the client is acting on the advice of an authorised person, or where it is clear that the client is not seeking advice from the person acting[11];

- arrangements made in the course of administration by an authorised person[12];

- arranging transactions in connection with lending on the security of insurance policies[13];

- arranging the acceptance of debentures in connection with loans[14];

- providing finance to enable a person to buy, sell, subscribe for or underwrite investments[15];

- introducing persons to either an authorised person, an exempt person acting in the course of a regulated activity for which he is exempt, or someone who is lawfully dealing, dealing as agent, arranging, managing, safeguarding and administering investments, sending dematerialised securities, establishing, operating or winding up a collective investment scheme or stakeholder pensions scheme or advising. The introduction must be made with a view to the provision of independent advice or the independent exercise of a discretion[16];

- introducing to authorised persons[17];

- arrangements for the issue of shares, share warrants, debentures or debenture warrants by the company issuing them;

- international securities self-regulating organisations who have been approved as such by the Treasury[18];

- arrangements for the issue of shares[19];

- trade repositories[20];

- trustees[21];

- activities carried on in the course of a profession or non-investment business;

- activities carried on in connection with the sale of goods or supply of services;

- groups and joint enterprises;

- sale of a body corporate;

- employee share schemes;

- overseas persons;

- information society services;

- managers of UCITS and AIFs;

- activities carried out by a provider of relevant goods and services;

- provision of information about contracts of insurance on an incidental basis;

- managers of UCITS and AIFs; and

- large risk contracts where the risks are situated outside the EEA.

1 SI 2001/544, art 25.
2 SI 2001/544, art 25A.
3 SI 2001/544, art 25B.
4 SI 2001/544, art 25C.
5 SI 2001/544, art 25D.
6 SI 2001/544, art 25E.
7 SI 2001/544, art 26.
8 SI 2001/544, art 27.
9 SI 2001/544, art 28.
10 SI 2001/544, art 28A.
11 SI 2001/544, art 29.
12 SI 2001/544, art 29A.
13 SI 2001/544, art 30.
14 SI 2001/544, art 31.
15 SI 2001/544, art 32.
16 SI 2001/544, art 33.
17 SI 2001/544, art 33A.
18 SI 2001/544, art 35.

19 SI 2001/544, art 34.
20 SI 2001/544, art 35A.
21 SI 2001/544, art 36 for the remainder of the list.

1.67

(7) **Credit broking**[1]. This covers introducing an individual or recipient of credit who wish to enter into a credit agreement to a lender. It also applies to so doing with someone wishing to enter a consumer hire agreement. Excluded from this definition is the process of introducing by individuals in the course of canvassing off trade premises[2], activities for which no fee is paid[3], transactions to which the broker is a party[4], activities in certain agreements relating to land[5], activities carried on by members of the legal profession and information society services[7].

1 SI 2001/544, art 36A.
2 SI 2001/544, art 36B.
3 SI 2001/544, art 36C.
4 SI 2001/544, art 36D.
5 SI 2001/544, art 36E.
6 SI 2001/544, art 36F.
7 SI 2001/544, art 36G.

1.68

(8) **Operating an electronic system in relation to lending**[1]. This covers operating an electronic system where that system is capable of determining what amount the lender will provide to the borrower.

1 SI 2001/544, art 36H.

1.69

(9) **Managing investments**[1]. This is a specified activity if the assets concerned consist of or include an investment which is a security or a contractually based investment. It is limited to discretionary management. If there is no discretion it would normally then be covered by 'arranging deals in investment' at (6) above.

The exclusions are:

- where the assets are being managed under a power of attorney and all day to day decisions are taken by an authorised person acting within the scope of their authorisation or an exempt or overseas person[2];

- trustees[3];

- activities carried on in connection with the sale of goods or supply of services;

- groups and joint enterprises;

- information society services;

- managers of UCITS and AIFs; and

- the provision of information about contracts of insurance on an incidental basis.

1 SI 2001/544, art 37.

2 SI 2001/544, art 38.
3 SI 2001/544, art 39 covers the rest of the list.

1.70

(10) **Assisting in the administration and performance of a contract of insurance** is a specified activity.[1] This excludes claims management on behalf of an insurer[2], acting as trustee[3], professional of non-investment business activity, information society services, activities carried on by a provider of relevant goods and services, the provision of information about contracts of insurance on an incidental basis, mangers of UCITS and AIFs and large risk insurance where the risk is situated outside the EEA.

1 SI 2001/544, art 39A.
2 SI 2001/544, art 39B.
3 SI 2001/544, art 39C covers the remainder of the list.

1.71

(11) **Debt adjusting**[1]. This covers the activities of negotiating with a lender on the borrower's behalf with a view to discharging a debt, taking over the obligation to discharge it in return for a payment by the borrower or similar activities to discharge the debt. The equivalent situation also covers consumer hire agreements. There is an exception to this and also to (12) and (13) below covering activities where the person has a connection with the agreement[2]. There is a separate exception both here and to (12) (13) and (14) below where the activities concerned are carried out by certain energy suppliers[3] and to relevant agreements in land[4], by members of the legal profession[5] and by information society services[6].

1 SI 2001/544, art 39D.
2 SI 2001/544, art 39H.
3 SI 2001/544, art 39I.
4 SI 2001/544, art 39J.
5 SI 2001/544, art 39K.
6 SI 2001/544, art 39L.

1.72

(12) **Debt counselling**[1]. This covers giving advice to a borrower about the liquidation of a debt under a credit agreement and to a hirer about the liquidation of a debt due under a consumer hire agreement.

1 SI 2001/544, art 39E.

1.73

(13) **Debt collecting**[1]. This covers procuring the payment of a debt due under a credit agreement or a consumer hire agreement.

1 SI 2001/544, art 39F.

1.74

(14) **Debt administration**[1]. This covers performing duties under a credit agreement on behalf of the lender or enforcing rights on their behalf. It also covers consumer hire agreements.

1 SI 2001/544, art 39G.

1.75

(15) **Safeguarding and administering assets**[1]. This covers safeguarding assets which are securities or contractually based investments belonging to another and administering them. It applies regardless of whether the securities are held in a certified form.

The exclusions are:

- where responsibility has been accepted by a qualified third party[2];
- making introductions to a qualified custodian[3];
- depositaries of UCITS and AIFs[4];
- providing information as to the units or value of assets held, converting currency or receiving documents relating to an investment solely for the purpose of onward transmission to, from, or at the direction of the person to whom it belongs[5];
- trustees[6];
- activities carried on in connection with professional or non-investment business;
- activities carried on in connection with the sale of goods or supply of services;
- groups and joint enterprises;
- employee share schemes;
- information society services;
- managers of UCITS and AIFs; and
- the provision of information about contracts of insurance on an incidental basis.

1 SI 2001/544, art 40.
2 SI 2001/544, art 41.
3 SI 2001/544, art 42.
4 SI 2001/544, art 42A.
5 SI 2001/544, art 43.
6 SI 2001/544, art 44 covers the rest of this list.

1.76

(16) **Sending dematerialised instructions.**[1]

The exclusions here are:

- acting on behalf of a participating issuer[2];
- acting on behalf of settlement banks[3];
- instructions in connection with takeover offers[4];
- instructions in the course of providing a network[5];
- trustees[6];
- groups and joint enterprises;
- information society services; and
- managers of UCITS and AIFs.

1 SI 2001/544, art 45.
2 SI 2001/544, art 46.
3 SI 2001/544, art 47.
4 Art 48.
5 SI 2001/544, art 49.
6 SI 2001/544, art 50 covers the rest of the list.

1.77

(17) **Managing a UCITS**[1]. This is achieved by the person arranging a collective portfolio within the definition of Annex 2 UCITS Directive.

1 SI 2001/544, art 51ZA.

1.78

(18) Acting as trustee or depositary of UCITS[1] **or AIF**[2].

1 SI 2001/544, art 51ZB.
2 SI 2001/544, art 51ZD.

1.79

(19) **Establishing, operating or winding up a collective investment scheme in relation to a UCITS or an AIF**[1]. The definition of 'collective investments schemes' is considered at **1.48** above.

1 SI 2001/544, art 51ZE.

1.80

(20) **Information society services and mangers of UCITS and AIFs**[1].

1 SI 2001/544, art 51A.

1.81

(21) **Establishing, operating or winding up a stakeholder or personal pension scheme**[1]. This excludes information society services and mangers of ICITS and AIFs[2].

1 SI 2001/544, art 52.
2 SI 2001/544, art 52A.

1.82

(22) **Providing basic advice on stakeholder products**[1]. This covers asking a retail customer questions to enable them to assess whether a stakeholder product is suitable for them and relying on the information that customer has provided in carrying out the assessment and then describing a product or making a recommendation.

1 SI 2001/544, art 52B.

1.83

(23) **Advising on investments**[1]. This covers giving advice to an investor or prospective investor on the merits of buying, selling, subscribing for or underwriting an investment which is a security or a contractually based investment or exercising any right conferred by such an investment. It applies whether the advice is given to someone in their own capacity or as agent or another. However, generic advice

is not covered, so for example it is possible to advise on the relative merits of direct and indirect investments or of investments of a particular nature.

The exclusions are:

- advice given in newspapers, journals or broadcast transmissions where that media is neither essentially giving advice or leading or enabling people to buy, sell, subscribe for or underwrite securities or contractually based investments[2];

- trustees[3];

- activities carried on in connection with professional or on-investment business;

- activities carried on in connection with the sale of goods or supply of services;

- groups and joint enterprises;

- sale of a body corporate;

- overseas persons;

- information society services;

- activities carried on by a provider of relevant goods or services;

- managers of UCITS and AIFs; and

- large risk contracts where the risk is situated outside the EEA.

1 SI 2001/544, art 53.
2 SI 2001/544, art 54.
3 SI 2001/544, art 55 covers the rest of this list.

1.84

(24) **Advising on regulated mortgage contracts[1], regulated home reversion plans[2], regulated home purchase plans[3] and regulated sale and rent back agreements[4].** The same exclusions listed at **1.82** apply here and in addition there are exclusions for:

- trustees[5];

- professional or non-investment businesses;

- information society services; and

- mangers of UCITS and AIFs.

1 SI 2001/544, art 53A.
2 SI 2001/544, art 53B.
3 SI 2001/544, art 53C.
4 SI 2001/544, art 53D.
5 SI 2001/544, art 55(2) covers this list.

1.85

(25) **Lloyd's[1].** This covers advising a person to become or to cease to be a member of a Lloyd's syndicate; managing the underwriting capacity of a Lloyd's syndicate as a managing agent or arranging deals in contracts of insurance written at Lloyd's. The background to this is

discussed at (**1.54**) above. The Society of Lloyd's itself is an authorised person and has permission to carry on the following regulated activities

- arranging deals in insurance written at Lloyd's (basic market activity);

- arranging deals in participation in Lloyd's syndicates (secondary market activity); and

- activities carried on in connection with basic and primary market activities.

However, the FCA retains the legal capacity to involve itself by applying core provisions of the FSMA to a member of Lloyd's or the Society of Lloyd's generally if it thinks so fit bearing in mind the interests of policyholders and potential policyholders. The FCA can do this either by giving a direction to the Council of Lloyd's or to the Society acting through the Council.

Former underwriting members can carry out each contract of insurance that they have underwritten at Lloyd's whether or not they are authorised. However, the FCA can impose on them such requirements as the FCA thinks fit to protect policyholders against the risk that the underwriter may not be able to meet their liabilities.

1 Arts 56, 57 and 58.

1.86

(26) **Funeral plan contracts**[1]. This covers contracts under which one person makes payments to another in return for the provision of a funeral on the first person's death provided it is not expected to occur within the first month.

The exclusion is that of plans covered by insurance or trust arrangements[2], information society services and mangers of UCITS and AIFs[3].

1 SI 2001/544, art 59.
2 SI 2001/544, art 60.
3 SI 2001/544, art 60A.

1.87

(27) **Regulated credit agreements**[1]. This covers a lender or another person exercising or having the right to exercise the lender's rights and duties under a regulated credit agreement. SI 2001/544, arts 60C to 60K provide a list of exemptions.

1 SI 2001/544, art 60B.

1.88

(28) **Regulated consumer hire agreements**[1]. This covers an owner or another person exercising or having the right to exercise the owner's rights and duties under a regulated consumer hire agreement. There are exclusions in Arts 60O to Q.

1 SI 2001/544, art 60N.

1.89

(29) **Regulated mortgage contracts**. This covers entering into or administering a regulated mortgage contract. Such an arrangement arises where a lender provides the credit to an individual or trustee in return for an obligation to repay which is secured by a first legal mortgage on land in the U.K., at least 40% of which is to be used as a dwelling by the borrower (or if it is the beneficiary of a trust the beneficiary), or a related person. In this context administering means notifying the borrower of changes in interest rates on payments due and taking any necessary steps to collect or recover payments from the borrower. Merely exercising the right to take action does not amount to administering.

Exclusions cover arranging administration by an authorised person[1] or pursuant to an agreement with one[2], trustees[3], overseas persons, information society services and mangers of UCITS and AIFs.

1 SI 2001/544, art 62.
2 SI 2001/544, art 63.
3 SI 2001/544, art 63A covers the rest of the list.

1.90

(30) **Entering into and administering regulated home reversion plans[1], regulated home purchase plans[2] and regulated sale and rent back agreements[3]**. This extends the regulation of traditional mortgages to the newer arrangements which have entered the market place and fulfil a very similar economic function. The risks to the public remain largely the same with the new products and so equivalent regulatory protection is provided to consumers.

1 SI 2001/544, art 63B.
2 SI 2001/544, art 63F.
3 SI 2001/544, art 63J.

1.91

(31) **Agreeing to carry on activities[1]**. An agreement to carry on any other specified activity other than accepting deposits, effecting and carrying out contracts of insurance, or establishing, operating or winding up a collective investment scheme or stakeholder pension scheme. There are a range of exceptions in Arts 64 and 65.

1 SI 2001/544, art 64.

COMPENSATION SCHEME

1.92   The Act requires the FCA to operate a compensation scheme. The purpose of this is to provide a fall-back position for those who have a claim against an authorised firm which cannot be satisfied financially by a claim against the firm or their insurers. The compensation scheme applies even if the firm is acting outside or in breach of its authorisation, but not if it is unauthorised. The claim may be for money that has been paid over to an authorised person, money due to be paid to them by an authorised person or an amount owing as a result of a legal claim or an ombudsman's ruling.

1.93   As the function of the compensation scheme is to provide cover for those who need it, claims may only be made by a restricted group of people, which excludes larger businesses. As is normally the way with compensation schemes there is a limit on the size of pay outs for any individual claim. The funds that finance the scheme cover three areas of the financial services markets: investment services, deposit protection and insurance. The authorised firms are required to pay a levy according to which of these areas the business concerned operates in.

1.94   The scheme manager can require the authorised person against whom a claim is being made to provide information and documents within a given period where this is believed by the manager to be necessary to fairly determine the claim. The manager can also inspect documents held by an administrative receiver, administrator or liquidator, or trustee in bankruptcy of an insolvent person or in Scotland a permanent trustee of an insolvent person where this is necessary for the manager to discharge his function. This will normally occur where the authorised person against whom a claim has been made is in insolvency. If either type of request is not met it is possible to request a court order to that effect.

FINANCIAL SERVICES OMBUDSMAN

1.95   An ombudsman scheme has been created to assist those who have a complaint against an authorised person or appointed representative and which has not been satisfactorily resolved by complaining to them. Those who are authorised under the Act must agree as part of that process to honour rulings by the ombudsman once the complainant has accepted it. Such a ruling may involve a compensatory award up to a maximum figure, or a direction that specified steps be taken. However, the ombudsman could recommend that an additional sum be paid above the maximum, but the extra amount would be legally unenforceable. That said the regulators have considerable powers of persuasion in such cases. The Ombudsman has the power to require any of the parties involved in a complaint to provide specified information or documents. Finally, the complainant can if they wish pursue a complaint in the courts even after a ruling of the ombudsman.

RELEVANT DOMESTIC BODIES OTHER THAN THE FINANCIAL SERVICES AUTHORITY

The Bank of England

1.96   The Bank's main role is that of central bank to the United Kingdom whose functions are:

(a)   setting interest rates for sterling;

(b)   advising the government on economic and monetary policy and implementing agreed monetary policy decisions, mainly through the bank's operations in the markets;

(c)   promoting an efficient and competitive framework for financial activity in the UK, particularly through its involvement in payments and settlements systems;

(d)   responsibility for note issue;

(e)   acting as banker to the commercial banks and to the government.

(f)   acting at its discretion to provide assistance to the money market when it is short of funds, both directly and through the discount houses;

(g)   advising on and managing the government's short and long term borrowings, for which it acts as registrar; and

(h)   managing on behalf of the Treasury the nation's gold and foreign currency reserves.

In addition of course it is engaged in regulatory activities to the extent mentioned at **1.3** to **1.11** above.

1.97   The Bank's involvement in payment and settlement systems includes membership of UK Payments Administration Ltd, active participation in the development of new real-time payment procedures as well as the provision of the Central Gilts Office and Moneymarkets Office services which provide on-line settlement facilities for gilts and money market instruments. These are now owned by Euroclear.

Lloyd's

1.98   Lloyd's is a society, incorporated by statute[1], which provides the facilities for the Lloyd's market to carry on business. In so doing it is overseen by the FCA for regulatory purposes, though member's agents and Lloyd's advisers are regulated directly. The members are syndicates managed by an underwriting agent. The members of the syndicates who are provided with financial backing by names who are fully liable for their share of the accepted risk in the case of individuals and to the extent of their share capital in the case of limited company names. The insurance business itself falls into four main categories: marine, aviation, non-marine and motor.

1 Lloyd's Act 1982.

1.99   The members do not deal directly with the public. Those requiring insurance will approach a Lloyd's broker. They place business both with Lloyd's syndicates and insurance companies. If it is placed at Lloyd's, the broker will first approach a lead underwriter and then follow up by approaching other underwriters to take a share.

1.100   Lloyd's is now a part of the FCA regulatory regime. Lloyd's syndicate capacity and syndicate membership are specified investments and advising a person to become or cease to be a member of a Lloyd's syndicate; managing the underwriting capacity of a Lloyd's syndicate as a managing agent or arranging deals in contracts of insurance written at Lloyd's, are specified activities. The Council of Lloyd's retains the capacity to make rules regulating the market and has responsibility for the functioning of it.

1.101   In addition, the FSMA requires the FCA to keep itself informed about the way in which Lloyd's Council supervises and regulates Lloyd's market and the way in which regulated activities are being carried out there. The FCA's concern will be twofold: protecting policy holders and protecting the names who are using their capital to underwrite the policies. The Society of Lloyd's has been made an authorised person and consequently has authority to carry out its basic market activity, namely arranging deals in contracts of insurance on the Lloyd's market. The relationship between the parties can be varied where the FCA believes that the Society is failing to satisfy its threshold conditions, has failed to carry on a regulated activity for at least one year, or where the FCA believe it is necessary in the interests of consumers. The FCA can also apply the FSMA to a member of Lloyd's or its Society by applying a general prohibition or a core provision to the carrying on of an insurance market activity or give a direction to the Council or Society of Lloyd's.

1.102   The element of duality in the regulation of Lloyd's between the FCA and the Society of Lloyd's necessitates having arrangements in place to make sure that those being regulated do not find themselves in a position of double jeopardy where complaints were concerned. Thus, an eight point agreement was reached to determine the relationship between the FCA and Lloyd's in this respect.

(*i*)   All Lloyd's participants should not be subject to more than one investigation or set of disciplinary proceedings for the same alleged wrongdoing unless it is appropriate for both the FCA and Lloyd's to exercise their different powers against the firm or the investigation or discipline relates to different aspects of the misconduct.

(*ii*)   Disciplinary action should not usually be taken by both bodies concurrently although there may occasionally be instances where consecutive action is appropriate for example in relation to de-authorisation proceedings conducted by FCA following Lloyd's disciplinary proceedings.

(*iii*) The body whose powers are most appropriate to discipline a firm for, or otherwise deal with, the appropriate wrongdoing should in most cases be responsible for leading the investigation.

(*iv*)   The relative effectiveness of the FCA's or Lloyd's powers to obtain the required information and evidence should, however, be taken into account in all cases.

(*v*)   If the FCA is investigating a concern about a Lloyd's participant it may require Lloyd's Regulatory Proceedings Department to assist by providing technical advice, information and documents or by carrying out its own enquiries and reporting its findings to the FCA.

(*vi*)   If appropriate, the FCA may formally appoint a member of Lloyd's Regulatory Proceedings Department together with a member of the FCA's staff or another competent person to investigate concerns about a Lloyd's participant.

(*vii*) The FCA will always have power to carry out investigations itself and to take such disciplinary action as it considers appropriate.

(*viii*) Cases of joint interest will be reviewed regularly as they develop to determine whether the lead responsibility should be transferred from Lloyd's to the FCA or vice versa.

1.103   Complaints by members against each other and against managing agents are dealt with by Lloyd's Complaints Department. If that does not resolve matters it can be taken to Lloyd's Arbitration scheme. If the complaint relates to the corporation of Lloyd' itself, it will be taken to Lloyd's Members Corporation.

1.104   Compensation arrangements are dealt with separately from the FCA Compensation Scheme. In the event of a claim being made against a Lloyd's underwriting syndicate and not being met it would be paid from the following sources in the following order:

(a)   premium trust funds;

(b)   balances due from brokers;

(c)   names' deposits and reserves;

(d)   names' other assets (subject to limited liability in the case of limited liability corporate names);

(e)   names' stop loss insurance;

(f)   Lloyd's central fund;

(g)   The Society of Lloyd's assets.

The London Stock Exchange

1.105   Since the FSMA made the FCA the official listing authority, the Exchange's primary role is now in relation to trading equities already in existence. The Board is the governing body of the Exchange and has power to manage the property and affairs of the Stock Exchange. Most importantly it governs strategic policy direction. It also has the power to determine the use of the Exchange's facilities and to manage property belonging to the Exchange, including its acquisition, disposal and letting, borrowing money and the investment of surplus funds. Applicants for membership must have obtained appropriate authorisation to carry on investment business from the FCA, unless they are exempt or in some way excluded from the requirement. Special requirements apply to EU and certain other overseas businesses. Branch membership of the Exchange is permitted and is available to any office that is not the main office of the relevant business, where either the company operating the branch, or another company in its group, is a member of another appropriate investment exchange.

1.106   Settlement of transactions in gilt edged securities is effected either on the basis of payment against documents of title and transfers or through the Central Gilts Office (CGO Service). This operates on a cash against delivery basis and incorporates a system of assured payments, by which each member procures that a settlement bank acting on its behalf undertakes to pay at the end of each business day, the amounts due in respect of securities transferred to that member through the CGO Service on that day.

1.107   As the main derivatives exchanges do not clear their own contracts the clearing houses act in this regard. Clearing is necessary to facilitate the legal change of ownership and it brings in the facility of netting. In the case of exchange traded options multi-lateral netting can greatly reduce the financial risk to the participants to the trades. The exchanges concerned are the CME Group, ICE Clear Europe, Euro CCP and LCH Clearnet Group. In addition the upsurge in over-the-counter ('OTC') derivatives (ie, those contracted between parties privately rather than on an exchange) has led to a need for a similar facility for these contracts. The LCH Clearnet Group therefore provides clearing for repos, and a range of interbank, interest rate swaps and credit default swaps. It serves a wide range of major European exchanges and platforms, equity markets, exchange traded derivatives markets, energy markets, the interbank interest rate swaps market and the majority of Euro denominated, sterling bond and repo markets.

1.108   The clearing function itself is not limited to facilitating the smooth completion of contracts. Facilities are provided to assist in the performance of completion and to manage problems caused by default. The latter is handled by requiring each party to contract with the exchange. The contract is then sold by the seller to the exchange, who in turn sells it to the buyer. The clearing house then guarantees the contract by taking financial cover and sometimes other security from these parties. The proportion of the cover taken is measured in relation to the risk on the contract. The clearing house's capital reserves can also be called on if necessary.

NYSE Euronext Liffe

1.109   NYSE Euronext LIFFE provides exchange facilities to deal in a very wide range of financial futures contracts and options on futures. The precise range of contracts being traded keeps developing and if precise information on this is required it can be obtained from the website. Suffice to say that they cover a range of futures and options in equities and financial products. LIFFE also trades agricultural commodity products, both as futures and options and short term interest rates.

ICE Futures

1.110   This exchange focuses on energy-related contracts. The contracts traded as futures and options are: Brent Crude, WTI Crude, ASCI, ASCI Differential, Gas Oil, UK Natural Gas, TYF Natural Gas, UK Power, Emissions and Coal. There is also OTC trading, ie off exchange, in Natural Gas, Electricity, Oil, Natural Gas Liquid, Iron Ore and Credit Derivatives. Some financial contract trading takes place, namely Russell futures, US $ indexes, currencies and credit derivatives. The exchange clears through ICE Clear Europe. The contracts on offer regularly change in the light of market demand.

The London Metal Exchange

1.111   The Exchange provides facilities for producers and consumers through futures and options contracts for defined grades of eight metals, ie aluminium (both alloy and prime grade), copper, lead, NSAAC, nickel, silver, tin, zinc, cobalt, molybdenum and steel billet. It also trades certain plastics contracts, such as polypropylene and polythylene. It administers its own functions and formulates the regulations governing trading. It also investigates complaints, settles disputes and provides conciliation and arbitration facilities for disputes in respect of transactions relating to the Exchange. It clears through LCH Clearnet.

SWX Europe

1.112   Formerly known as virt-x, it was taken over by the Swiss SWX Exchange and changes its name 2008. It is a UK equities stock exchange operating by electronic order. Its clients are the wholesale traders of funds such as market makers, brokers and fund managers.

EEA authorities

1.113   Businesses established in another European Economic Area member state and who have their head office there, who are recognised by that state as one of their nationals and who do not carry on investment business from a permanent place of business in the U.K. are treated as authorised to the extent that the investment laws of that state afford protection to investors equivalent to that afforded in this country. Whether such a state of affairs exists will normally be determined by the Chancellor issuing a certificate to that effect. Passport rights are governed by Sch 3 of the Act and in this context 'EEA firm' means any of the following:

- an investment firm authorised by its home state regulator;

- a credit institution which is authorised by its home state regulator;

- a financial institution which is a subsidiary;

- an undertaking pursuing the activity of direct insurance which is authorised by its home state regulator.

RELEVANT INTERNATIONAL BODIES

Introduction

1.114   Recent years have seen the increasing internationalisation of banking, insurance and other financial services businesses. Coupled with this has been a breaking down of the barriers that traditionally existed between the various parts of the financial services industry. This is against a background of an ever increasing proportion of the world's wealth being reflected in capital flows, some related to international trade but the majority by way of investment. As a consequence, the regulation of financial services has become a task requiring a far wider range of activities than used to be the case. This is a primary reason for the creation of the FCA in its previous form as the Financial Services Authority in the UK. In addition, it is necessary in an increasingly inter-linked world for there to be an agreed set of international standards by which financial institutions should be regulated. This does not require total commonality, but a large degree of equivalence is certainly highly desirable to facilitate economic stability and sustained economic growth. A failure to create high quality economic regulation can also both facilitate a financial crisis and aggravate it when it arises. In addition, the extent to which world capital markets have become integrated has limited the ability of national regulators to monitor firms effectively without a considerable degree of international co-operation.

1.115   The proposals considered below which help develop a set of international financial regulations articulate five key features. It represents a reform of the nexus of international financial regulation; a bringing together of a group of limited codes and standards; international collaboration between a disparate set of linked codes and standards; international collaboration between a disparate set of states, markets, financial regulators and financial institutions. It engages both international and domestic compliance assessments and there is a clear acceptance that there is a direct relationship between adopting such regulation and codes, and maintaining financial stability.

1.116   The motivation is also clear. In the words of a G7 Communiqué:

'Close international co-operation in the regulation and supervision of financial institutions and markets is essential to the continued safeguarding of the financial system and to prevent erosion of necessary prudential standards'.

Organisations

1.117   A number of bodies stand out as being key players in this process. In alphabetical order they are:

The Basel Committee on Banking Supervision

1.118   This provides a meeting place for the central banks of the G10 countries and facilitates co-operation on the regulation of banking. Member countries are represented on the Committee by their central bank and also by the authority with formal responsibility for the prudential supervision of banking if this is a separate body. Its secretariat is provided by the Bank for International Settlements in Basel. Over recent years it has developed into a standard setting body on all aspects of banking supervision, although its rules carry no legal force. Its purpose is to design minimum standards for the prudential regulation of banks, especially those active in the international markets. Those states who are represented on the Committee are expected to adopt the standards once they have been agreed. However, the extremely complexity of some of the standards, especially in the latest set of Basel III rules are such that it will take a number of years to implement them, even when political will is present. The Committee also produces guidelines and sound practice papers.

Committee on Payment and Settlement Systems

1.119   Also created by the G10 central banks this, as its name suggests, provides a meeting place for those central banks on matters arising in relation to payment and settlement systems. Their concern is not limited to domestic considerations but extends to cross border operations and netting. Much of their work concerns supervisory standards and recommendations of best practice. It sates its aim as 'strengthening the financial market infrastructure through promoting sound and efficient payment and settlement systems'. Like the Basel Committee it operates under the auspices of the Bank for International Settlements

Financial Action Task Force

1.120   Created by the G7, its role is to ascertain the threat to financial institutions from money laundering and to recommend steps that can be taken to counter this. There are now a large number of member states and a key function of the Task Force is to monitor the extent to which these countries are taking appropriate steps to deal with the problem. Its role is to set standards and promote effective implementation of legal regulatory and operational measures for combating money laundering and terrorist financing. It has over the years produced a number of recommendations in the form of a series of principles which states are expected to adopt. Originally the organisation was set up for a fixed period of four years which has been repeatedly extended. There is a danger that it becomes an engine for producing ongoing developments and changes in the principles to justify its existence rather than because they are really needed.

Financial Stability Board

1.121   Following a meeting of the Finance Ministers and Central Bank Governors of the G7 countries, Hans Tietmeyer the then President of the Bundesbank was commissioned to draft a report considering what new structures might be appropriate to improve co-operation between the existing national and international regulatory bodies. The aim was to facilitate increased stability in the regulation of world finance and financial services. As a consequence of the report he produced the Financial Stability Forum was created, which changed its name to the Financial Stability Board in 2009. It now includes members of the G20 although it has 25 nations as members and six major international bank related organisations.

International Accounting Standards Board

1.122   The aim of this institution is to bring about the convergence of accounting standards. This is of importance, partly in increasing the financial safety by having high common standards, and also in reducing the risk of financial failure or loss to investors due to accounts not representing a true and fair view in the generally understood meaning of the words. Its progress in this area is well advanced.

International Association of Insurance Supervisors

1.123   Its purpose is to develop a set of generally accepted standards in this area to increase the effectiveness and global consistency of insurance regulation and to help develop and maintain fair, safe and stable insurance markets. It is a voluntary member organisation of insurance supervisors and regulators. Over 140 states have become members and over 130 observers attend representing international institutions, professional associations and reinsurance companies. As well as setting and implementing principles and standards it also acts as a forum for members and observers to share their experience.

International Federation of Accountants

1.124   Originally created in 1977, it is made up of the national accountancy bodies that represent those accountants who are involved in the public sector, large organisations and commerce and industry. Its primary aim is to increase the quality of the accounting regulations and increase their international equivalence. It develops high quality international standards in auditing and assurance, public sector accounting, ethics and education for professional accountants and supports their adoption and use. It also facilitates collaboration among its members, co-operates with other international bodies and serves as an international spokesman for the accountancy profession.

International Monetary Fund

1.125   This is the body that sets international standards in relation to overseeing the world's monetary system. It has created a range of standards in relation to monetary and fiscal policy and has assisted in creating methods of assessment for the standards used for the supervision of banking and insurance. It works to foster global economic growth and economic stability. It provides members in financial difficulty with both advice and finance. Connected with this it promotes monetary co-operation, exchange rate stability, helps promote balanced growth in international trade and assists in the reduction of poverty. Although a specialised agency of the United Nations it has its own charter, governing structure and finances.

International Organization of Securities Commissions

1.126   As its name implies, this is an organisation made up of the securities and derivatives regulators of the member countries. Its main purpose is to create high standards to govern the regulation of the securities markets to exchange information, provide effective surveillance of international securities markets and to protect the integrity of markets. Its approach has changed radically since a series of financial failures, such as Enron, Worldcom, Parmalat and Vivendi made it realise that it needed to adopt a more decisive role. It has a permanent headquarters in Madrid.

Organisation for Economic Cooperation and Development

1.127   The aim of this body is to promote world economic growth and to this end it promotes the development of financial markets regulation to a high common standard. Much of its significance arises from the statistics that it provides. It plays a prominent role in fostering good governance in both public service and corporate activity. It also assists governments in ensuring the responsiveness of key economic areas with sectoral monitoring.

The World Bank

1.128   The World Bank is a key source of financial and technical assistance for developing countries. It is a combination of two institutions, the International Bank for Reconstruction and Development and the International Development Association. It aims to reduce poverty in the world by facilitating private investment in the regions concerned through low interest loans, interest free credit and grants. It is not technically a bank but a provider of finance and technical assistance to the developing world. Its aims include promoting the development of education, health, public administration, infrastructure, financial and private sector development, agriculture and environmental and natural resources management.

Financial Stability Forum – Key standards

1.129   In its role as a facilitator of increased international co-operation the Financial Stability Forum has issued a set of twelve standards which it believes are a pre-requisite to creating a system of stable, well regulated financial systems. These are as follows:

Code of Good Practices on Transparency in Monetary and Financial Policies

1.130   The essence of this is that it highlights the approaches that creates the appropriate level of transparency to enable the public to assess what is happening and thus facilitate accountability. The Code specifically highlights four key areas:

- roles, responsibility and objectives should be clearly stated;

- policy decisions should have clearly defined processes determining how they are reached and reported;

- policies and information pertinent to them should be publicly available; and

- accountable systems should exist to guarantee integrity.

Code of Good Practices on Fiscal Transparency

1.131   The role of transparency is critical in that it makes the regulatory authorities more accountable. To facilitate this the code provides four principles:

- that the roles and responsibilities of those involved should be clear;

- there should be access to the information by the public;

- that key financial steps such as budgets, accounts and financial reports should be publicly available; and

- integrity should be underpinned by independent means.

43

Data Dissemination

1.132   There are two key agreements in this area. The first is the Special Data Dissemination Standard issued by the IMF. This was produced to resolve the problem of instability induced, if only in part, by insufficient information being available in the market place. Those countries who subscribe (and the significant economies already do) agree to satisfy this function in four key regards and to do so in standard form:

- that data, particularly regarding reserves and foreign currency holdings should be made publicly available, promptly and at appropriate periods;

- that the public should be informed of the dates on which such data will be available;

- clear laws determining both the above and proposed changes in the same, coupled with government access to data and comment being released by the relevant government officials; and

- the making available to the public of information to articulate how the data should be formulated and of any other material against which it can be assessed.

1.133   The second is that General Data Dissemination System, also issued by the IMF. This is more severe in its demands than the Special Data Dissemination Standard and the developed economies are expected to apply it. It requires that detailed, high quality information relating to financial, economic and social issues be made publicly available on a timely basis. It adopts the same four stage structure as the Special Data Dissemination Standard.

Principles and Guidelines for effective Insolvency and Creditor Rights Systems

1.134   The existence of a clear, fair set of rights for creditors is a key ingredient for a stable economy. It also assists commercial lenders in determining the degree of risk they are taking on. This has been primarily driven by the World Bank, the United Nations Commission of International Trade Law, the IMF and INSOL.

Principles of Corporate Governance

1.135   This is a system of corporate regulation which applies to a company when it determines its objectives, when it seeks to achieve them and in assessing its performance. It is crucial to have such regulation to create a high quality corporate environment to attract international capital. Key issues to be found within corporate governance regulations are:

- shareholder rights;

- stakeholder rights (this is a contentious area in terms of its future development);

- disclosure of information; and

- Board responsibility.

International Accounting Standards

1.136   A succession of international accounting standards have been issued to determine the extent of the detail, range, relevance and reliability of the information to be included in the accounts. To represent a true and fair view accounts must be regulated by clear and detailed regulation. There are specific types of accounts, those relating to banks, securities houses and insurance companies for example, which give rise to specific issues when determining what should be included.

International Standards on Auditing

1.137   If there are to be accepted standards of accountancy then it follows that there must also be internationally accepted standards of auditing to maintain it. The standards on auditing that have been issued cover:

- audit responsibilities;
- audit planning;
- internal controls;
- evidence;
- practice statements relating to international auditing;
- external auditing; and
- audit characteristics and considerations.

Core Principles for Systemically Important Payment Systems

1.138   To function in a stable way financial markets require stable, effective settlement systems. The aim of the Core Principles is to facilitate this by requiring a degree of safety and efficiency in these systems. The Principles themselves require that domestic and international payment systems satisfy criteria relating to design and operation. Guidance is also provided on interpreting the Principles.

The Forty Recommendations of the Financial Action Task Force on Money Laundering

1.139   These were intended to provide a set of recommendations which, if followed, would optimise the response of banking and financial bodies that were being used to launder illegal money. They cover areas such as:

- criminal justice systems;
- law enforcement;
- the banking and financial systems;
- banking and financial regulation; and
- international co-operation.

Money Laundering is discussed in detail in **Chapter 5**.

1.140   All members states are subject to periodic mutual analysis to determine whether they are satisfying the recommendations. They must also carry out an annual self-assessment exercise to the same end.

Core Principles for Effective Banking Supervision

1.141   To assist in stabilising the world's banking system the Basel Committee on Banking Supervision have published a set of twenty five core principles and additional criteria for banking supervision. These cover issues such as:

- the preconditions for effective banking supervision;
- licensing requirements;
- ongoing banking supervision;
- powers of supervisors; and
- cross-border banking.

Objectives and Principles of Securities Regulation

1.142   IOSCO have published a set of objectives and principles to help bring about a system of sound regulation of the securities markets. The key objectives are:

- protecting investors;
- making sure the markets function in a manner that is fair, efficient and transparent; and
- reducing the risk of systemic failure.

There are also thirty principles relating to securities regulation.

Insurance Core Principles

1.143   As their name implies these were produced to facilitate that the regulatory supervision of the insurance industry is taking place at a suitably proficient and effective manner. The Principles themselves cover key areas such as:

- the role of supervisors;
- licensing insurance companies;
- corporate governance of insurance companies;
- prudential controls;
- market conduct;
- monitoring by the regulator; and
- sanctions for failure to satisfy the regulations.

Monitoring regulatory observance

1.144   Clearly it is insufficient to create a series of desirable standards without some system for ascertaining whether they are being subscribed to in practice. States themselves will sometimes carry out research into the state of affairs within their own jurisdiction. In addition the IMF and the World Bank both produce reports on the extent to which the standards and codes discussed above are being met. The IMF has produced them in relation to the distribution of data and fiscal transparency. The World Bank has done so in relation to accounting, auditing, corporate governance, insolvency and creditors' rights. How well standards in the financial sector are carried out and what the priorities need to be to rectify any shortcomings are dealt with under the auspices of the joint IMF and World Bank 'Financial Sector Assessment Programme'.

Facilitating regulatory observance

1.145   The Financial Stability Forum has suggested that member states could take a number of key steps to facilitate awareness and observance of regulatory standards.

- an ongoing campaign should be run to raise the level of awareness in their financial centres as to the requirements of the standards;

- that the bodies creating the standards in the first place should themselves facilitate and encourage this process of education;

- that the bodies creating the standards and the national regulators should help explain how satisfying the requirements of the standards will help avoid certain types of risk. In this context explaining how past market problems have led to the standards will assist;

- external assessments of the application of standards should be undertaken by the bodies setting the standards;

- peer discussions should be encouraged to facilitate the implementation of standards; and

- technical advice and training should be provided by the more developed states to the others.

1.146   There are a number of reasons why this is thought necessary. The importance of the standards is primarily in that they facilitate a sound financial system. To this end it is important that not only the authorities but also relevant private bodies should put them into effect.

Key issues other than regulatory observance

1.147   Turning to the regulated financial institutions themselves, there are factors other than the quality of regulation that will determine whether institutions will proceed with a financial arrangement. A suitable legal system and framework are vital. Key elements are efficiency, transparency and a predictable outcome in the sense that it should be determined by clearly stated laws rather than other factors. In some states it can prove difficult to successfully pursue certain parties through their courts due to corruption. Political risk and economic fundamentals also need to be within acceptable levels. If not there will be no point pursuing a financial arrangement further. Parties do not always fully understand how the regulations relate to the risks they were created to try and manage.

1.148 Some firms are by their very nature less concerned with regulatory issues. The international investment portfolios managed by those such as hedge funds, pension funds and insurance companies are more concerned with market analysis that relates to capitalisation.

Rating agencies are a key source of information and their role in providing assessments will involve an analysis of supervisory and regulatory issues as well as financial and market issues.

Consequences of regulatory failure

1.149 There are instances of countries having lax regulatory controls and surviving for some time with no serious problems. However, the absence of a system of decent controls both increases the risk of a crisis arising and of it becoming systemic, leading to a larger scale problem when it does. The Asian financial crisis of 1998 has been generally regarded as having been partly caused by lax regulation. In addition the crisis was able to develop to a greater extent before it became apparent that it was occurring than should have been the case because of poor corporate governance and a lack of transparency. This was exacerbated by the high proportion of businesses in the area that were owned and managed by the same people, which coupled with traditional business practices resulted in weak corporate governance. Then as the crisis accelerated those outside the countries concerned were unable to draw a distinction between those institutions in the states concerned that were a real risk and those that were not. This resulted in a flight of matured short term debt and a refusal by those outside the jurisdictions to hold debt and equity securities denominated in those states' currencies due to fear of devaluation.

1.150 The key steps that were deemed necessary to reduce the risk of such a crisis in the future were:

- increasing transparency;

- enhancing the free flow of capital;

- strengthening states' financial systems;

- leaving the responsibility and risk associated with lending with the private institutions responsible; and

- increasing the involvement of international financial institutions.

It has been suggested that the larger credit rating agencies have an important role to play in this context.

CO-OPERATION BETWEEN REGULATORS

Introduction

1.151 At a national level co-operation is much less of a problem. Home state regulators have long since had agreements in place to deal with the issues of co-operation. In the United Kingdom the wideness and extent of the FCA and PRA's powers reduce the scale of the problem. It can carry out most of the regulatory steps itself. In instances where it cannot do so there are provisions in place to facilitate them. The real issues arise in the context of international and pan European regulation.

Memoranda of Understanding

1.152   The main way in which international co-operation has been put in place is through memoranda of understanding. Originally these tended to be bi-lateral, but more recently a multi-lateral approach seems to have gained ground. A considerable amount of work has gone into key issues such as the exchange of information between regulators to arrive at the best design for such memoranda. These agreements do not impose legally binding obligations on the signatories. Nor can they override domestic laws and regulations. What they can do however is give rise to a much freer flow of information between regulators than would otherwise be the case. This facilitates the national regulators building a more accurate picture of the financial scene of which they are regulating one part. It is important to bear in mind that an MoU is not always a pre-requisite to co-operation being provided. For example, the US Exchange Act specifically allows the SEC to utilise its powers to assist foreign regulators if there is not an MoU in place. They are also mandated to try and develop reciprocal arrangements with states that are not in a position to sign them. Nonetheless they represent the most effective and comprehensive way of proceeding.

1.153   The Principles that the IOSCO Report suggested as giving rise to an optimal Memorandum of Understanding are:

That Memoranda should provide for assistance to an investigation from an overseas state requesting information even if the behaviour under investigation would not be a breach of the laws or regulations of the country from which it is requested. If that is not possible because of the laws of a state signing a memorandum then they should request a change in their domestic law to permit it. This Principle overrides what has been a long standing principle of extradition type laws, namely that someone can only be extradited if the offence concerned is one in both the requesting state and the requested. This has to be overridden in the context of financial regulation as otherwise it would be impossible to police international financial organisations effectively. A decision could be made in a part of a financial organisation in one country to do something that was a breach of financial regulation in another. If the regulator in the state where the offence occurred were to find out there would often be little they could do to proceed against the parties responsible without a Memorandum drafted on the basis of this principle. They could otherwise only take steps against the branch or subsidiary in their own jurisdiction which may be insufficient.

1.154   This has been a particular issue for the United States. US law does not require that when a non US regulator seeks assistance the events concerned must also be an offence in the US. This is important as US securities laws generally tend to be wider than the securities laws of other countries. However, reciprocity arises in another way in that the Exchange Act requires the SEC to consider whether the overseas regulator would reciprocate were the SEC to request assistance from them. If not then assistance should be refused.

1.155 That a memorandum should provide that information received by a regulator should be treated 'with the highest possible level of confidentiality'. This is stated to mean that the information should be treated with the same degree of confidentiality as domestically acquired information. The memorandum should also give the authority that is asked for information the opportunity to say what degree of confidentiality should be attached to the information provided.

1.156 The memorandum should also set out the procedures to be followed in requesting information and in responding to such requests. This is a fundamental issue to be agreed, and in most cases one that should not be too difficult for the parties to agree on.

1.157 The memorandum should state that when an investigation is going on in one state as a result of a request from a regulator in a second state it should not impact on the rights that a person has in the first state. This is necessary because otherwise the memorandum will find itself inoperable in the first state. In many nations the rights concerned will be constitutional ones, and so the matter is not negotiable.

1.158 The memoranda should contain an agreement that the signatories will consult with each other during the period of operation of the memorandum. The need for this could become apparent when there is a difference of view as to whether assistance should be provided in a particular case. It is also hoped that the facility for consultation will give rise to a relaxed relationship between the regulators concerned. Highlighted by IOSCO are three situations where consultation is likely to be particularly important; namely where unforeseen circumstances arise, where there is an overlap of jurisdiction and where one country's laws or regulations change.

1.159 As a matter of political and legal reality it is accepted that there must be a public policy exclusion. This permits a regulator to refuse to provide assistance to a request where to do so would violate the public policy of its state. The IOSCO Report defines public policy in this context as being 'issues affecting sovereignty, national security or other essential interests'. This may prove a narrower definition than that which some state's judges may give it.

1.160 The memoranda should provide that the signatories should take all reasonable steps to fully utilise their powers when faced with a request for information. This should include obtaining documents, where appropriate testimony from witnesses, giving access to any relevant non-public files they may have and carrying out inspections of the regulated entity concerned in the investigation. This is a particularly important principle given that there have been instances of regulators refusing to provide information that it can obtain from the regulated firm on a voluntary basis because of an unwillingness to enforce requests for information against the firm. In some cases this has occurred for legal reasons.

1.161   There should be an agreement allowing an authority requesting assistance to take part directly in its execution. This can be useful in cases where the investigating authority is the one with most of the background information on the issue concerned. In addition it may be the case when the investigation proceeds further that the requesting authority starts to find information that it would not have been able to request in the first place because it could not have known of its existence.

1.162   Finally, the memorandum should allow the regulator being requested to provide assistance to share the costs with the regulator requesting it. This would be important in cases where an investigation were likely to prove expensive, especially where the regulator being requested to provide assistance has limited resources. It could also prove relevant if, over a period of time, one regulator finds itself requesting more information from another than is requested in return. It is useful to have a mechanism for dealing with this.

Chapter 2

Authorisation

Richard Parlour

FINANCIAL MARKETS LAW INTERNATIONAL (WWW.FMLI.CO.UK)

2.1   This chapter covers the authorisation of those wanting to carry on financial markets business in the UK. The introduction to this chapter covers the background, history and key concepts of authorisation. It then focuses on the latest regulatory regime architecture and grandfathering into the new system from the old. The chapter then considers the scope of authorisation, the types of investment and investment activity covered, as well as the exemptions which may apply. It sets out the decision tree which those wanting to carry on financial markets business in the UK will need to go through when deciding whether they need to apply for authorisation to carry on the activities which they wish to carry on. The following section then addresses applying for authorisation, the threshold conditions applicable, and the regime applying to approved persons (ie individuals as opposed to firms). The chapter then examines the authorisation process itself, covering practicalities and fees. It then goes on to cover the decision making process and the appeals process. Once authorised, firms have certain obligations of authorisation, and the chapter introduces the concepts of high level standards and business standards. There follows some discussion of the relationship of the regulator with the regulated. A number of special cases are dealt with, including credit unions, the oil market regime, payment institutions, electronic money institutions and crowdfunding. There is an introduction to the increasingly important European dimension, and the final section concludes with a brief look at the future.

This chapter is designed to give a relatively detailed overview and introduction to the subject of authorisation. Naturally, it is not intended to amount to professional advice as to the application to any particular business of the various primary legislation, delegated legislation, regulatory rules and industry guidance.

Introduction

Background

2.2   The UK is the world's leading financial jurisdiction. The history of the UK as a financial jurisdiction is a long and complex one. The growth of the British Empire required financial support and brought the UK into contact with many different parts of the world. This internationalisation has continued apace despite the decline of empire and the UK has always been willing to step in and assist with the financial needs of others following local difficulties. Examples range from the growth of foreign exchange markets following the collapse of the Bretton Woods agreement, to the 'Swedish invasion' of the late 1980s, to more recent growth in Sharia based finance. The UK has grown up in a different way to other financial centres. The general approach in the UK has been to establish specialist financial institutions, which has increased competition and diversity, as well as having encouraged innovation. The continental European approach, on the other hand, has been to keep all services under the same roof. This is reflected in concepts such as the German 'Allfinanz' and French 'bancassurance', where there are only banks to approach for finance.

2.3   The UK has traditionally been very open to market entrants, and authorisation has been a fairly straightforward process, though becoming more and more complex. There are many other commercial advantages to establishment in the UK, which have made it the most popular destination in Europe to start up a new financial institution. There are now around 600 authorised banks in the UK, and 24,000 financial institutions. The financial services sector amounts to 10% of UK GDP and employs 1 million people. There are more than 1,200 foreign owned authorised financial institutions including over 250 branches and subsidiaries of foreign banks, more than any other country. Half of European investment banking is conducted in the UK.

The UK is the world's largest foreign exchange market. 80% of European hedge fund assets are managed in the UK. The UK is the world's largest market for OTC interest rate derivatives and the world's second largest market for exchange traded derivatives. It has the largest market in nonferrous metals and energy derivatives. It is the largest centre for global gold trading and Europe's largest centre for commodities trading.

2.4   The London Stock Exchange is one of the leading centres for foreign listed companies and foreign equity trading. It has around 7% of the world's IPOs, is Europe's largest centre for funding of SMEs, and is also a leading centre of international bond trading. UK investment managers have GBP 3.2 trillion under management. The UK is one of the leading centres of private wealth management. The UK banking sector originates more cross border bank lending than any other centre. London is the largest international insurance centre. It is also the world's centre of reinsurance. The UK is the leading western centre for Islamic finance. The UK is also one of the leading centres worldwide for dispute resolution.

The process of authorisation is therefore critical to the success of the UK as a financial centre. It needs to be effective and efficient in order to encourage new entrants, maintain its standing, yet discourage the ungodly.

2.5   As will be seen below at **2.10**, the decision making process to assess whether an institution needs authorisation or not has become considerably more complex. One of the drivers for this increased complexity has been the introduction of European regulation in financial markets, first through the Investment Services Directive (ISD), more latterly through its successor, the Markets in Financial Instruments Directive (MiFID), and most recently through the Markets in Financial Instruments Directive II and Markets in Financial Instruments Regulation (MiFID II/MiFIR). The most recent measures are part of a raft of around forty new measures introduced as a rather knee jerk regulatory tsunami response to the financial crisis, which has actually turned out to be the greatest depression in world financial history. The European measures represent a compromise between a wide variety of cultures and approaches to financial markets, and many European states set up financial market regulators for the first time in order to be able to implement the ISD. There has also been a substantial increase in the size of the European Union and the European Economic Area, from the original six to 31, and the creation of pan European financial market regulatory associations to co-ordinate the individual Member State financial market regulators. These pan European financial market regulatory associations have turned into regulators in their own right, and are now known as 'authorities' (European Banking Authority (EBA), European Securities and Markets Authority (ESMA) and the European Insurance and Occupational Pensions Authority (EIOPA)).

For the present, however, authorisation of financial institutions remains in the hands of national Member State financial market regulators, though there are moves afoot to create a Banking Union between certain Member States. The rights in the Treaty of Rome (as amended) to freedom of movement of goods, services, capital and people have further complicated the authorisation environment. Broadly speaking, if a financial institution has been authorised in one Member State, then it is able to establish a branch in a different host Member State, or provide services on a cross border services basis (without a local branch) into a host Member State, without requiring further local authorisation. Such financial institutions need to have separate European Economic Area legal personality to take advantage of the rights, and the rights can be exercised under the Treaty or under the directives. There is separate European legislation in respect of the main pillars of the financial sector, namely banking, investment services, insurance and pensions. See **2.9** below for a more detailed explanation.

2.6   The authorisation environment has also been further complicated by the increasing scope of regulation, and the movement of other parts of the financial sector to be regulated by the single regulator.

The extent of the regulatory net has increased inexorably over the years. It has never contracted:

- At the time of introduction of the Financial Services Act 1986, certain anomalies were discovered, which resulted in the creation of special regulatory regimes from the outset, such as the oil market participant regime. 'Locals', those individuals trading on derivatives exchanges for themselves as principals, were required to be authorised, despite the fact that they could have theoretically relied on the 'principal dealing exclusion' (provided they dealt only with authorised persons, which of course could not be guaranteed since there were other locals involved in trading on exchanges), the regulator stating that it was a regulatory expectation that all those involved in trading on the exchange would be regulated

- In 1998, responsibility for regulating banks moved from the Bank of England to the Financial Services Authority

- In the late 1990s it was concluded that the difficulties at Lloyd's meant that self regulation should be terminated and that the financial market regulator should take over. Advising on participation in a Lloyd's syndicate, managing the underwriting capacity of such a syndicate and arranging Lloyd's insurance contracts became regulated activities and Lloyd's managing agents and members' agents were required to become authorised at the end of November 2001.

- Not long thereafter, the provision of prepaid funeral plans (January 2002), the deposit taking activities of credit unions (July 2002) and mortgage lending and long term care insurance (October 2004) became regulated activities

- general insurance broking became a regulated activity in January 2005

- payment services have become regulated and payment institutions need to be regulated as Small Payment Institutions or Authorised Payment Institutions

- electronic money has become regulated and Electronic Money Institutions need to be regulated as Small Electronic Money Institutions or Authorised Electronic Money Institutions

- consumer credit regulation is the latest to be transferred to the regulator, along with regulation of companies providing pay day loans

- a special regime is currently under consideration for crowdfunding platforms

Key Concepts

2.7   There are a number of key concepts in authorisation:

- If a firm is carrying on investment business in the UK, it needs to be authorised under the Financial Services and Markets Act 2000 (FSMA 2000), s 19, unless an exclusion or exemption applies. Failure to be so authorised is a criminal offence which is punishable by up to two years' imprisonment and/or an unlimited fine. Those contracts entered into when a firm should have been authorised are voidable by the counterparty. In addition, carrying on investment business illegally is unlikely to endear a person to a regulator in respect of any future application for authorisation. There is a separate offence for a person who is not authorised or exempt, to hold himself out as such.

- If a firm is authorised pursuant to European legislation, and has European legal personality (ie is established as a legal entity in one of the 31 Member States of the European Economic Area (EEA), rather than being simply a branch of a legal entity established in a state other than a Member State of the EEA), then that person will be able to 'passport' its services into the other Member States of the EEA, either through local branches, or on a cross border services basis, without requiring further authorisation locally

- The regulator will not authorise a business if it does not appear to be commercially viable, so effort needs to be spent in producing a credible business plan and marketing plan. This should include a vision, mission and culture of the business. See below for further detail

- The business will have to work economically too and a balance sheet, profit and loss account, and cashflow statement in detail for the first 12 months of operation will need to be produced

- It will need to be demonstrated that the key people involved in the business of a financial institution are 'fit and proper' to be involved. This includes shareholders and beneficial owners, as well as key officers and managers. Fitness and propriety in essence means competence (demonstrated by qualifications and experience), integrity (demonstrated by a lack of criminal convictions for offences involving dishonesty), and solvency (demonstrated by a lack of insolvency or bankruptcy)

- Authorisation also entails approval of individuals holding certain key roles within a financial institution (known as 'controlled functions')

- Once authorisation is granted, the business needs to start within 12 months or there is a possibility it will be withdrawn. Changes to the scope of authorisation will take place via a Variation of Permission (VoP), which is usually a quicker process that an application for authorisation ab initio.

- There are separate rules applicable to financial promotion, and these need to be considered independently of the question as to whether authorisation is required. The term 'financial promotion' is very broad and covers all forms of media from printed copy to audio and TV advertising, and presentations. It is defined as an invitation or inducement to engage in investment activity. An unauthorised person may not communicate a financial promotion in the UK, in the course of business, unless either its contents are approved for the purposes of FSMA 2000, s 21 by an authorised person, or it is subject to an exemption under the Financial Services and Markets Act 2000 (Financial Promotion) Order 2005 (FPO)[1].

1 SI 2005/1529.

The UK Financial Market Regulatory Architecture

2.8   The most recent financial crisis, and subsequent great depression, has sparked considerable introspection again and a plethora of proposals for adjustment of regulatory architecture and introduction of vast amounts of new regulation. This time, the previously rejected 'Twin Peaks' model has been instituted in the UK. Regulation is now split into conduct regulation and prudential regulation. The Financial Services Authority has been transformed into the Financial Conduct Authority (FCA), largely to look after regulation of market conduct. The Prudential Regulation Authority (PRA), established within the Bank of England, has been created as a separate new regulator largely to look after prudential regulation. In terms of authorisation, application for deposit taking activity (essentially banks and building societies) and insurance has been moved to the PRA. Authorisation for other financial activities rests with the FCA.

As mentioned above, financial institutions require to be authorised to carry on investment business in the UK. Individuals holding certain positions in financial institutions also need to be approved for those roles. Financial institutions may either be directly authorised or be appointed representatives of a financial institution which is directly authorised. The split between those financial institutions which are directly authorised and those which are authorised representatives, operating under the regulatory umbrella of a directly authorised firm, is roughly 50/50. This is not repeated at the level of approved individuals, however, and of the 130,000 registered individuals, 115,000 are registered to directly authorised firms and 15,000 to appointed representative firms. Of those approved individuals, around 100,000 are customer facing staff. There are proposals to increase the ambit of individual approval to cover less senior staff, which will naturally increase the number of approved individuals.

Grandfathering

2.9   Grandfathering refers to the permission for financial institutions authorised under a current regime to be automatically authorised under a new regime without having to go through the authorisation process of the new regime, whereas financial institutions established after the date of creation of the new regime will need to apply for authorisation under the new regime and go through the new authorisation process. Thus, in the most recent restructuring of the UK's financial market architecture, those who were previously authorised by FSA will be grandfathered into authorisation by the FCA (and/or PRA as appropriate) without having to go through some form of reauthorisation process.

Grandfathering is subject to a firm continuing to conduct the same activities, and not new ones, as well as continuing to meet the threshold conditions. Permission to conduct any new activities will have to be applied for separately. Limitations, requirements, waivers and passports are also carried over into the new regime. Grandfathering also covers individuals as well as firms.

Scope of Authorisation

2.10   To assess the scope of authorisation requires examination of certain key legislation and regulation. The key legislation is the FSMA 2000, as amended. This represents the legislative architecture in strategic terms and is an act of Parliament. Below that is the Financial Services and Markets Act 2000 (Regulated Activities) Order 2001 (RAO)[1], as amended. This is secondary legislation which can be amended much quicker and easier than the primary legislation through a government department, in this case HM Treasury. The views of the regulator are clearly important and there is a lot of guidance on the authorisation process itself. In addition to this general guidance, the 664 page 'Perimeter Guidance' (PERG) describes the investment and services regulated, in greater detail, and is vital to assess.

It was mentioned above how complex the decision making process has become. The following page shows the current decision tree. The regulator has stated that this is high level guidance only, and that legal advice should be taken to ascertain the exact position. Given the complexity of primary and secondary legislation, this is unsurprising, but do bear in mind that the following is not set in stone, and there may be more than one interpretation of it:

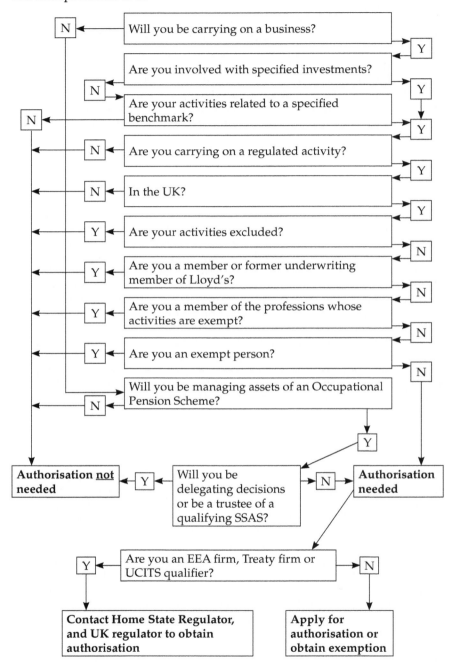

A.   WILL YOU BE CARRYING ON ANY ACTIVITIES BY WAY OF BUSINESS?

2.11   Under FSMA 2000, s 22 for an activity to be considered a regulated activity, it must be conducted by way of business. The Financial Services and Markets Act 2000 (Carrying on Regulated Activities By Way of Business) Order 2001 (Business Order)[1] makes provision for persons to accept deposits or carry on certain kinds of dealing and investment activity, without being regarded as doing so by way of business. Conversely, a person who manages the assets of an occupational pension scheme will normally be regarded as doing so by way of business, unless certain circumstances apply. For most, the only reason to be carrying on the activities in the investments concerned will be to create a business, and profits and losses will arise in the normal commercial manner, so the activities will be carried on by way of business (see PERG 2.3 for further detail).

1 SI 2001/1177.

B.   ARE YOU INVOLVED WITH SPECIFIED INVESTMENTS OF ANY KIND OR ESTABLISHING, ETC, A COLLECTIVE INVESTMENT SCHEME OR STAKEHOLDER PENSION SCHEME?

2.12   Specified investments are defined in Part III of the Financial Services and Markets Act 2000 (Regulated Activities) Order 2001 (RAO)[1] (see **Chapter 1**) and comprise:

- deposits
- electronic money
- rights under a contract of insurance
- shares
- instruments creating or acknowledging indebtedness
- sukuk (shariah compliant debt instruments)
- government and public securities
- instruments giving entitlement to investments
- certificates representing certain securities
- units in a collective investment scheme
- rights under a stakeholder pension scheme
- rights under personal pension scheme
- options
- futures
- contracts for differences
- Lloyd's syndicate capacity and syndicate membership
- rights under funeral plan contracts
- rights under regulated mortgage contracts

- rights under a home reversion plan
- rights under a home purchase plan
- rights to or interests in anything that is a specified investment listed, excluding 'rights under regulated mortgage contracts', 'rights under regulated home reversion plans' and 'rights under regulated home purchase plans'

1 SI 2001/544.

C. ARE YOUR ACTIVITIES RELATED TO A SPECIFIED BENCHMARK?

2.13   See RAO, arts 42, 630.

D. ARE YOU CARRYING ON A REGULATED ACTIVITY?

2.14   Specified activities are defined in RAO, Part II (see **Chapter 1**) and comprise:

- accepting deposits
- issuing e-money
- effecting or carrying out contracts of insurance as principal
- dealing in investments (as principal or agent)
- arranging deals in investments
- arranging home finance activities
- operating a multilateral trading facility
- managing investments
- assisting in the administration and performance of a contract of insurance
- safeguarding and administering investments
- sending dematerialised instructions
- establishing collective investment schemes
- establishing stakeholder pension schemes
- providing basic advice on stakeholder products
- advising on investments
- advising on home finance activities
- Lloyd's market activities
- entering funeral plan contracts
- entering into a home finance activity
- administering a home finance activity
- agreeing to do most of the above activities

See Part III RAO for detail on the investment activities concerned.

E.   ARE YOU CARRYING ON A REGULATED ACTIVITY IN THE UK?

2.15   The UK being the leading financial centre worldwide, one of the main policy considerations is to protect the UK's reputation in this sector. Accordingly, carrying on a regulated activity in the UK has been given a broad interpretation. It is not only carrying on business in the UK which is covered by this term, but also carrying on business from the UK, so it is not possible for a firm to establish a business in the UK, ensure that it only has clients in another country, and argue that UK regulation does not apply. See FSMA 2000, s 418 for further detail.

F.   ARE YOUR ACTIVITIES 'EXCLUDED ACTIVITIES'?

2.16   There is often understandable confusion about whether exclusions or exemptions apply, especially since the end result in both cases is that the operation concerned falls outside the regulatory net. Exclusions are activities which were it not for the exclusion, would fall to be regulated in the normal manner, so they fall within the scope of regulation, only to be taken out of regulation by the exclusion. Exemptions are those which are prescribed not to fall within the scope of regulation in the first place, and are discussed in greater detail below.

Examples of exclusions include:

- the introducer exclusion
- the overseas persons exclusion

The exact scope of the exclusions needs to be examined closely. For example, it is not the case that all introducers fall outside the scope of regulation. What is meant by 'introducer' is defined very narrowly, and only relates to those who merely introduce a potential client to a financial institution in return for an introducer's fee, but no more than that, in other words, a 'bare introducer'. Naturally, if the value of the service provided to a client can be increased, then so can the fee. However, this added value may take the person concerned out of the scope of the exclusion, and into the scope of regulation. It is therefore a question for commercial consideration and cost benefit analysis. Falling within the scope of regulation may increase compliance and regulatory costs, but on the other hand, the knowledge that a person is regulated may increase the confidence of potential clients and lead to increased 'client ownership' and therefore more business.

2.17   Naturally, if a regulatory net has been broadly created then it will encompass many who from a commercial perspective it may not make much sense to bring within the scope of regulation. Another long established exclusion is the overseas persons exclusion. This was created for those established outside the UK but wishing to do business with those in the UK. For the UK to remain a leading financial centre, it must retain its attractiveness to those from other parts of the world, financial sector business being one of the easiest to carry on internationally. Requiring everyone who is established overseas to become regulated in the UK makes no strategic sense and is largely unenforceable anyway. On the other hand, making it possible for anyone to establish offshore and carry on business into the UK without restriction would drive a coach and horses through the concept of investor protection for clients based in the UK. All UK financial institutions would need to do to avoid UK regulation would be to move their establishment offshore. Accordingly, the overseas persons exclusion excludes those established outside the UK to carry on what would otherwise amount to regulated activity, provided such activity is conducted with or through regulated persons. That way, all such business conducted in the UK should at some stage go through a regulated entity and protection of investors should be assured.

See RAO, Part II and, if an investment firm, RAO, art 4 for further details.

G.   DO YOU CONDUCT REGULATED ACTIVITIES ONLY AS A MEMBER OR FORMER UNDERWRITING MEMBER OF LLOYD'S'?

2.18   Lloyd's of London is a special market with a number of considerations which are different to other sectors of financial markets. This specialised area is outside the scope of this chapter, but see FSMA 2000, Part XIX for further details.

H.   ARE YOU A MEMBER OF THE PROFESSIONS WHOSE ACTIVITIES ARE EXEMPT UNDER FSMA 2000, PART XX?

2.19   Exemptions include a professional firm (ie a firm of solicitors, accountants or actuaries) carrying on certain regulated activities that are incidental to its main business. See FSMA 2000, Part XX, the Non-Exempt Activities Order and FSMA 2000, Part XIX for further details.

I.   ARE YOU AN EXEMPT PERSON?

2.20   There are a number of exemptions under FSMA 2000, ss 38 and 39. The RAO also sets out certain exemptions and these are mentioned below. It is not possible to be an authorised person and an exempt person at the same time, so the two are mutually exclusive. Previously it was possible to be authorised in respect of one activity, but exempt through being an authorised representative in respect of another activity. However, this was thought to be a rather confused regulatory scenario, such that the concept of mutual exclusivity has been introduced.

HM Treasury may issue an order exempting certain persons or types of person from the need to obtain authorisation. The Financial Services and Markets Act 2000 (Exemption) Order 2001 (Exemption Order)[1] sets out a number of exemptions, including central banks and international development banks such as the World Bank, European Bank for Reconstruction and Development, where authorisation is considered inappropriate or unnecessary by the UK government, etc. This is not to say that such banks are immune from the risks faced by other banks, but that regulation by one of the Member States which is a part owner of such bank is deemed politically impossible. These international development banks usually police themselves through some form of internal oversight function, and of course the owners are able to question the bank's activities. See the Exemption Order for further detail as to exemptions from the need for authorisation.

1 SI 2001/1201.

2.21 A person who is an appointed representative is also exempt from authorisation. This is a person who is appointed as a representative of an authorised person, in other words, someone who operates under the regulatory umbrella of another who is authorised. The appointment needs to be pursuant to a service contract between the authorised person and the appointed representative under which the appointed representative can carry on certain activities only. These activities are set out in the Financial Services and Markets Act 2000 (Appointed Representatives) Regulations 2001 (the Appointed Representatives Regulations)[1]. They are arranging deals in investments, giving investment advice and arranging for the safeguarding and administration of investments. The service contract must include the provisions set out in the Appointed Representatives Regulations, and the authorised person must take responsibility for the regulated activities of the appointed representative. It works a little like contracting out regulatory responsibilities to the authorised person, so the authorised person needs to ensure that the appointed representative understands the rules to which it is subject and the authorised person will then have to monitor and supervise the appointed representative fully, in order to cut down on its own regulatory risk. Operating as an appointed representative is popular in terms of numbers of firms, as indicated above, though in terms of the numbers of approved individuals operating as appointed representatives, the percentage of appointed representatives is far lower. Appointed representatives are primarily used to give authorised firms greater marketing reach to potential investors.

1 SI 2001/1217.

2.22 FSMA 2000, Part XVIII exempts investment exchanges and clearing houses from the requirement for authorisation, though they do need to be Recognised Investment Exchanges (RIEs) and Recognised Clearing Houses (RCHs) under FSMA 2000, which means that the exemption is somewhat circular as they are nonetheless subject to regulatory oversight.

Lloyd's managing agents and members' agents need to be authorised, though members of the Society of Lloyd's, ie the individual Names, do not themselves need to be authorised in respect of the insurance business they conduct in this capacity.

2.23 Some, such as members of the professions, also carry out what would be regulated activities, but in a way which is incidental to the professional services which they provide. Subject to them meeting certain conditions, they are also allowed to carry on regulated activities without authorisation. The main condition is that they are members of Designated Professional Body (DPB). HM Treasury has set out a list of DPBs in the Financial Services and Markets Act 2000 (Designated Professional Bodies) Order 2001 (the Designated Professional Bodies Order)[1]. Such firms are known as exempt professional firms. They can conduct regulated activities without authorisation provided that such activities are incidental to their professional services, they do not hold themselves out as undertaking mainstream regulated activities, and they do not receive any remuneration from such incidental regulated activities for which they do not account to their clients. If a professional firm wants to carry out regulated activities which are more than incidental to its professional services, it has to apply to the regulator for authorisation in the usual manner. The Financial Services and Markets Act 2000 (Professions) (Non-Exempt Activities) Order 2001 (Non-Exempt Activities Order)[2] ensures that certain activities are always subject to regulation and prescribes that certain regulated activities, such as accepting deposits, effecting insurance contracts or operating a collective investment scheme, can never be undertaken by a professional firm without obtaining authorisation. If a professional firm does become authorised, it has to distinguish between mainstream and non-mainstream regulated activities. Non-mainstream regulated activities are those regulated activities which would have been exempt if they had been the only regulated activities undertaken by the firm. The firm's mainstream regulated activities will fall within the scope of regulation and be governed by the regulator's handbook, but the non-mainstream regulated activities will instead be subject to the supervision of the DPB. Rules and guidance on the distinction between mainstream and non-mainstream regulated activities are in the Professional Firms Sourcebook of the FCA Handbook, which applies both to authorised professional firms and exempt professional firms.

Other exemptions include a local authority or certain kind of housing body carrying on insurance mediation or mortgage activities.

See the Exemption Order and the Appointed Representatives Regulations.

1 SI 2001/1226.
2 SI 2001/1227.

J. WILL YOU BE MANAGING THE ASSETS OF AN OCCUPATIONAL PENSION SCHEME (EG AS A TRUSTEE)?

K. WILL YOU BE DELEGATING DECISIONS OR BE A TRUSTEE OF A QUALIFYING SSAS AS PROVIDED FOR IN THE BUSINESS ORDER?

L. ARE YOU AN EEA FIRM, A TREATY FIRM OR A UCITS QUALIFIER IN RELATION TO THE REGULATED ACTIVITY?

2.24   If a firm is an EEA firm, a Treaty firm or a UCITS qualifier in relation to the regulated activity then it will need to contact its Home State Regulator, and the appropriate UK regulator, to obtain authorisation under FSMA 2000, Schs 3, 4 and 5 (see PERG 5).

If a firm is not an EEA firm, a Treaty firm or a UCITS qualifier in relation to the regulated activity, then it needs to apply for FSMA 2000, Part 4A permission or obtain exemption as a s 39 Appointed Representative, RIE or RCH.

Applying for Authorisation

2.25   Authorisation is not a carte blanche to carry on any regulated activity. Authorisation allows financial institutions to carry on regulated activities, but each activity in each type of instrument and in respect of particular classes of customer have to be applied for. If a firm carries on activities for which it does not have permission then this will amount to a breach of the rules and the firm will become subject to the disciplinary procedures of the regulator. This means that once a firm is authorised it needs to ensure that its business development and compliance processes are hardwired together such that if the firm wishes to carry on a new kind of activity, or in new investments, or with different kinds of client, then the scope of the firm's permission needs to be checked before the new activity, investment or client is carried on, and further permission requested and obtained if necessary. Once granted, then an activity needs to be carried on in accordance with the rules of the regulator. In general, the regulator splits up the regulated activities in the same way as they appear in the RAO, but in certain respects there are differences. For example, there are differences between operating regulated collective investment schemes and unregulated collective investment schemes (the latter recently changing in light of implementation of the Alternative Investment Fund Management Directive (AIFMD)), advising on personal pension transfers is treated separately to advising on other investments, and arranging safe custody facilities is separate to provision of such facilities. Similarly, certain investments are singled out for separate treatment such as spread betting and rolling spot FX. In the application forms there is a matrix of activities to complete. These need to be realistic and tie in with the business plan. They should cover the first 12 months of operations, and the regulator will not be expecting a change of activities within this timescale unless there is sudden change. The permissions will appear on the regulator's website in the register section. This will include basic details of the financial institution concerned, scope of permitted activities and any restrictions, individuals registered to the firm, passport details, and disciplinary history (see, eg, www.fca.org.uk/register). The register has been partitioned, so separate searches will need to be made on payment institutions, for example. The register can be out of date or incorrect, however, which needs to be borne in mind when carrying out due diligence on firms and individuals.

2.26   Firms themselves need to check that information is accurate and up to date, not least because it is this information upon which their regulatory fees are based. Regulatory fees are charged on the basis of various fee blocks which depend upon the nature of the permitted activities being carried out, and the scale of activity. The different fee blocks use different methods of calculation of the scale of a firm's business. There is a minimum fee but no maximum. The minimum level is apparently designed to discourage firms from applying for authorisation on a precautionary basis when in fact there is no regulated activity being carried on. The regulator does put out a consultation paper on its fees for the coming year.

Amendment of the matrix of permitted activities is possible, by submitting a Variation of Permission (VoP). The regulator will expect all aspects of the new activities to have been thought through, including staffing, qualifications, systems needed, IT, impact on the business, capital adequacy, etc. VoPs cover removal or cessation of activities as well as addition of them.

2.27   Greater regulatory flexibility is achieved by enabling the regulator to impose limitations or requirements on firms. For example, it was considered that banks conducting wholesale deposit taking activity alone did not need the same regulatory regime imposed upon them as others conducting retail deposit taking. A new regime was set up for banks in this category, which also made London more attractive to those banks who would otherwise consider the costs of UK branch establishment uneconomic, and at the same time improved competition in this area of the market ('the Grey Paper regime', named after the colour of the document concerned).

The permitted activities may be carried on without restriction, or the regulator may impose limitations on them. Such limitations may include a limitation on the type or number of customers, or on the type of investments which a firm may deal in.

The regulator is also able to impose requirements if it considers these appropriate. These may be requirements to do something, or refrain from doing something. The requirement may apply to some of a firm's activities, or all of them. It may also cover a firm's non-regulated activities. For example, firms are asked during the application process whether they intend to hold client money. Those that do are subject to a number of strict requirements and are required to demonstrate their ability to comply. Those that don't may be required to exclude such activities.

Threshold Conditions

2.28   Firms are required to meet five threshold conditions and be able to demonstrate that they will be able to meet these conditions on a continuing basis after authorisation. These conditions are set out in Schedule 6 to FSMA 2000.

Legal Status

2.29   The general approach is that an applicant can take any form of legal status, ranging from a natural person to a limited company, partnership, limited partnership, limited liability partnership, unincorporated association, etc. However, for certain types of financial institution, the legal status needs to be of a particular form. For example, a deposit taker must be a body corporate, a partnership or limited liability partnership. To carry on insurance activity an applicant must be a body corporate, a registered friendly society or a member of Lloyd's.

Place of registration and head office

2.30   The second threshold condition arises from the collapse of the Bank of Credit and Commerce International (BCCI). It was felt that one of the key issues in BCCI's collapse was that the bank was registered in one jurisdiction but had its head office and principal business in another, making effective regulation difficult. Accordingly, a directive was issued, the 'BCCI Directive' (95/26/EC). Thus the second threshold condition requires those constituted under the laws of a part of the UK to have their registered office and principal place of business in the UK. This should help the regulator to identify where the legal seat of the business is and where its management is conducted from, so as to make supervision more effective.

Close Links

2.31   This is designed to establish the depth and breadth of corporate groups to ensure that effective supervision is possible. Here, shareholdings in related companies over a certain percentage need to be disclosed.

Resources

2.32   The fourth threshold condition is that firms must have sufficient resources to conduct the activities which they wish to carry on. This condition refers not only to financial resources but also to the other resources required to run the activities effectively, so finance, management and staff. These resources must be sufficient not only in terms of quantity but also in terms of quality and availability. Sufficiency depends upon the situation, and one man firms are allowed.

Suitability

2.33   The fifth threshold condition is that firms must be suitable for the activities wished to be carried on, that the firm is fit and proper having regard to all the circumstances. There is detailed guidance as to what is meant by fitness and propriety, but in essence this means management competence, integrity and compliance commitment.

The latter three threshold conditions relate to the regulated activities which a firm wishes to carry on, as the regulator will need to assess whether the firm is ready, willing and organised to comply with specific requirements related to management systems and controls, prudential and anti financial crime controls, for example, as well as the relevant conduct of business regulation. Being adjudged to be fit and proper to carry on one investment activity does not mean that a firm is automatically considered fit and proper to carry on other activities as well, so extension of a firm's permission to cover other activities pursuant to a VoP will entail examination of the fitness and propriety of the firm to carry on those extra activities.

Approved Persons

2.34   It is not only firms which require authorisation, but also the people within them who manage and run the firm. Authorised individuals are known as approved persons. The regulator is allowed to designate certain positions within firms as controlled functions and these are set out in section 10 of the supervision manual (SUP) and below.

Number	Controlled Function
CF 1	Director (executive)
CF 2	Director (non-executive)
CF 3	Chief Executive Officer
CF 4	Partner
CF 5	Director of an unincorporated association
CF 6	Small friendly society
CF 8	Apportionment and oversight
CF 10	Compliance
CF 10a	CASS oversight operation
CF 11	Money Laundering Reporting
CF 12	Actuarial
CF 12a	With profits actuary
CF 12b	Lloyd's actuary
CF 28	System and controls
CF 29	Significant management
CF 30	Customer function
CF 40	Benchmark submission
CF 50	Benchmark administration

Functions are controlled if the person carrying on the function is exerting significant influence on the running of the firm, dealing with customers, or handling customer property. This authorisation of individuals is intended to help stress personal responsibility for compliance. Individuals must seek approval to carry on a controlled function before carrying on that function. Those holding controlled functions are for the most part individuals, but may also be corporate bodies. The general philosophy is that senior management must take responsibility, and most directors and partners will be seen as exercising a significant influence function. In large organisations, the senior management will also be seen as carrying out this role and will therefore require approval.

The Authorisation Process

2.35 Authorisation is seen as a fundamental part of regulation in that this is the stage where the regulator decides who is fit and proper to participate in financial markets. It is one of the key regulatory processes, along with supervision and enforcement. Prevention is seen as better (and cheaper) than the cure and it is much simpler to deny those thought not to be fit and proper entry to financial markets than to catch and deal with miscreants. Naturally, given the numerous scandals which have hit the financial sector, some have questioned whether the application of this theory has seen much benefit in practice, and there are well publicised cases where it seems incredible that the senior individuals concerned have been let near financial markets. Equally, there are times where the regulator acts in an over zealous manner, so there are procedures for redress so as to ensure that individuals are not used as scapegoats, or that cases of simple error can be rectified. In practice, this happens rarely unless a financial institution is prepared to stand up to regulatory injustice.

The authorisation process takes some commitment, financially, commercially and emotionally. It is not difficult, but there is a lot to do. As a general rule of thumb, it takes most around a month of fairly diligent work to put the application together, and a further three months for the application to be considered and approved by FCA. These time periods are longer for more complex applications, such as establishing a bank or an insurance company, for which application is made to PRA. If there is an attempt to establish something more innovative, such as in the area of crowd funding, authorisation can take longer as the regulator becomes comfortable with a new approach and how it ties in with regulatory principles. The regulator will usually raise a number of questions on the application. It is important to recognise that 'the clock stops' during the time period between asking the question and the response being provided.

2.36 The regulator also scores the risk of the firm's proposed business against the probability of an event occurring and the significance of its impact should it occur. The risks vary according to the nature and complexity of the business proposed, the investments, activities and clientele. More importantly, the regulator needs to be assured that a firm is capable of risk identification and management. This assessment is less onerous for firms which wish to carry on lower risk activities. It is possible to approach the regulator with any queries relating to authorisation, but it is unlikely that a pre inspection visit will take place or an interview, unless the application is a complex one, or there is some issue with the personnel or owners.

For smaller firms, the regulator has developed several standard permission profiles for different regulated activities and investment types (eg advisor and arranger of investment activities). Which one is relevant to a proposed business depends on the answers to a number of generic questions about how the business will be structured. At the end of this process the appropriate application pack should be selected. If none of these profiles match a business, then a tailor made application will need to be submitted. There will be a general application form to complete, together with a supplement relevant to the type of proposed business under consideration. This will need to be supported by a fairly detailed and credible business plan. It will need to cover the proposed services and instruments, systems, people, and marketing to target clients. The regulator is looking to see a plan which is commercially viable. There will also be a financial application to complete, which will need to be accompanied by projections in some detail for the first 12 months, covering a monthly profit and loss, balance sheet and cashflow analysis. There are further forms for certain key individuals involved, including the proposed owners. Even if the individual has performed the function at a previous firm, he will still need to submit an application. The forms are accompanied by guidance notes. A compliance monitoring plan needs to be assembled. The regulator does not need to see a copy of any compliance manual, but does need to know that it has been drafted.

2.37   Consideration also needs to be given to the firm's prudential requirements. There are two key elements to this. There is a minimum capital requirement, the level of which depends upon the business to be carried on. There are also ongoing capital requirements which will need to be calculated and which vary over time, such as the position risk requirement. The firm must at all times hold capital sufficient to meet the higher of the minimum initial requirement, or the fluctuating ongoing requirement. The regulator is also able to take into consideration the capital position of any other entities in the same group as the firm. This may entail the regulator liaising with relevant regulators in other jurisdictions, not only as to sufficiency of resources, but systems, and the ability to ensure ongoing monitoring and supervision between the jurisdictions concerned. There is usually some discussion as to how regulation will take place on a daily basis, with a system of limitations, restrictions and waivers likely to form part of the regulatory solution. The capital does not have to be in place at the time of application, but will need to be there before authorisation is granted.

The minimum amount varies according to the activity. In general, the levels are:

Minimum	Type of firm
€50,000	Not authorised to hold client money, deal on own account or underwrite
€125,000	Authorised to hold client money, but not deal on own account or underwrite
€730,000	All other firms

The risk based elements are calculated on the position or market risk, counterparty or settlement risk, and base risk. The regulator will want to see the calculation of the financial resources requirement for a firm. Applicant firms will need to demonstrate a certain level of realism in the projections, and commercially it will be important to demonstrate cashflow at certain levels of income and expenditure, so projections will need to be stress tested.

2.38   The regulator will also look at any connected persons. These may include controllers, group companies, shareholders, outsourced support or anyone else influencing or capable of exerting an influence over the applicant. Again, if this requires liaison with other regulators, then that will be undertaken.

Authorisation used to be granted on a monthly basis by an authorisation committee. Now it occurs on an ad hoc basis. Applicants need to be ready, willing and able to conduct investment business, as well as being adjudged fit and proper and fulfilling the threshold conditions. The regulator used to operate an Authorisation Manual, but this part of the handbook has been moved to the supervision module.

No fees are usually charged for involvement in a grandfathering process, unless changes are desired to be made to activities undertake by the financial institution concerned, etc. There are regulatory fees for an application, however, which vary according to its complexity. Fees for straightforward applications are currently running at £1,500, for more complex ones £5,000 and for complex ones £25,000. Such fees are non-refundable.

Applications need to be considered within six months if complete, and within 12 months if incomplete. However, these limits are maxima, and the regulator will try to get the authorisation through in shorter time if it can. On average, there are around 100 applications a year, and three months for the regulator to consider an application is a standard time, though the time has been lengthening of late.

When authorisation is granted, full details will be posted on the regulator's website.

For a copy of practical guides to the authorisation process, please see www.fmli.co.uk or email info@fmli.co.uk.

Decision making and appeals

2.39   The regulator has published details of its procedures for making decisions on applications for authorisation in the decision making part of the regulator's handbook. There are occasions when a financial institution will not agree with the regulator, and there are also procedures for appeal of those decisions. The regulator also has procedures for the investigation of complaints about its use or failure to use its administrative functions. This gives applicants another route to complain to an independent complaints commissioner about the regulator's handling of the application, whether of the firm or the individuals concerned. In addition, the Financial Services and Markets Tribunal has been established to resolve any disputes about the use of the regulator's legislative powers.

The regulator has always discouraged the making of precautionary applications. It also spends more time than it used to on assessing the firm's business plan, not only for the purpose of not wasting its own time on applications for businesses which are unlikely to be started, but also for the protection of consumers from institutions with a weak model. The regulator will expect a firm to commence its regulated activities shortly after granting authorisation, and if there is no sign of activity within 12 months, then the regulator may withdraw the permission.

Obligations of Authorisation

2.40   Applicants need to demonstrate that they are ready, willing and able to commence business and conduct it in accordance with the relevant rules in the regulator's Handbook. The Handbook is a very lengthy and complex document, covering the many varied elements operating in the financial market in the UK. It grows the more the regulatory net is extended. However, in the case of fairly standard financial institutions, it is possible to design a more bespoke Handbook which covers only those rules with which the particular financial institution will need to comply.

High Level Standards

2.41   This section of the Handbook applies to all regulated financial institutions. It consists of 11 key principles. This arose after the early, detailed rulebooks were criticised for being too formulaic and legalistic. It was felt that a number of financial institutions were complying merely with the letter of the regulation, rather than the spirit behind certain regulations. The regulator thus introduced certain high level principles to act as a guideline as to how a particular regulation should be interpreted. This was then further developed such that a financial institution could be disciplined for a breach of the principles, despite not being in technical breach of any regulation. However, whereas a private individual may take action against a financial institution in relation to breach of a rule of the regulator, this is not so in the case of breach of a principle. A number of financial institutions complained that the pendulum had swung too far in the opposite direction and that now it was much less clear what the regulator's interpretation was going to be of any particular scenario, which made it difficult to carry on business with regulatory certainty.

The principles apply to all of a financial institution's regulated business, and in certain circumstances to its non-regulated business and non-UK business. Although they are fairly obvious, they are generic enough to enable considerable room for interpretation in any given scenario.

No	Principle	Explanation
1	Integrity	A firm must conduct its business with integrity
2	Skill, care and diligence	A firm must conduct its business with due skill, care and diligence
3	Management and control	A firm must take reasonable care to organise and control its affairs responsibly and effectively, with adequate risk management systems
4	Financial prudence	A firm must maintain adequate financial resources
5	Market conduct	A firm must observe proper standards of market conduct
6	Clients' interests	A firm must pay due regard to client interests and treat them fairly
7	Communications with clients	A firm must pay due regard to client information needs, and communicate information to them in a way which is clear, fair and not misleading
8	Conflicts of interest	A firm must manage conflicts of interest fairly, both between itself and its clients and between a client and another client
9	Clients: relationships of trust	A firm must take reasonable care to ensure the suitability of its advice and discretionary decisions for any client entitled to rely upon its judgement

No	Principle	Explanation
10	Clients' assets	A firm must arrange adequate protection for clients' assets, when it is responsible for them
11	Relations with regulators	A firm must deal with the regulator in an open and co-operative way, and must disclose to the regulator appropriately anything relating to the firm of which the regulator would reasonably expect notice

A firm will also need to consider the regulator's stance on senior management responsibilities. A firm must maintain effective systems and controls. It is the Senior Executive Officer, or Chief Executive Officer, who is seen by the regulator as having overall responsibility for compliance with the rules. Where responsibilities are shared out between senior management, the regulator expects this to be achieved in a clear manner and that an individual takes responsibility for the apportionment and oversight.

2.42 There are also separate statements of principle which apply to the approved individuals operating in the business. Here the regulator has attempted to give examples of what it would regard as inappropriate conduct. Breach of these statements of principle could render the individual concerned liable to regulatory action.

No	Statement	Inappropriate Conduct
1	An approved person must act with integrity in carrying out his controlled function	Deliberately misleading (or attempting to mislead) by act or omission; a client, the firm or the regulator, falsifying documents, misleading a client about the risks of an investment, providing false or inaccurate documentation or information. Deliberately misusing a client's assets or confidential information, including front running client orders, churning, misappropriating client assets.
2	An approved person must act with due skill, care and diligence in carrying out his controlled function	Failure to inform a client or the firm of material circumstances where he was aware, or ought to have been aware, of such information and of the fact that he should provide it, for example, failure to disclose dealings covered by the firm's Personal Account Dealing Rules. Failing to provide adequate control over client assets. Failing to explain the risks of an investment to a client.

No	Statement	Inappropriate Conduct
3	An approved person must observe proper standards of market conduct in carrying out his controlled function	The regulator will take the individual's compliance with the Inter-Professional Code (IPC) and the Code of Market Conduct (MAR), into account when deciding whether an individual has observed proper standards of market conduct
4	An approved person must deal with the regulator and with any other regulator in an open and cooperative way and must disclose appropriately any information of which the regulator would reasonably expect notice	Failure to report information which it would be reasonable to assume would be of material significance to the regulator, whether in response to questions or otherwise, promptly in accordance with ACUK internal procedures
5	An approved person performing a significant influence function must take reasonable steps to ensure that the business of the firm for which he is responsible in his controlled function is organised so that it can be controlled effectively	Failure to take reasonable steps to apportion responsibilities for all areas of the business under the Approved Person's control, for example unclear/misleading job descriptions. Failure to act if an individual's performance is unsatisfactory.
6	An approved person performing a significant influence function must exercise due skill, care and diligence in managing the business of the firm for which he is responsible in his controlled function	Permitting transactions without a sufficient understanding of the risks involved. Accepting implausible or unsatisfactory explanations from sub-ordinates without testing the truth of those explanations. Failing to obtain independent expert opinion where appropriate
7	An approved person performing a significant influence function must take reasonable steps to ensure that the business of the firm for which he is responsible in his controlled function complies with the regulatory requirements imposed on that business	Failure to take reasonable steps to monitor compliance with the regulatory requirements of the business

Business Standards

2.43   The business standards block of the Handbook contains a number of sourcebooks relating to the way in which the business of a firm should be conducted on a daily basis:

* prudential sourcebooks which cover capital adequacy requirements

* conduct of business sourcebook which governs the relationship between a firm and its clients

* client assets sourcebook

* market conduct sourcebook which governs the relationship between authorised firms on the markets

* training and competence sourcebook

There used to be a Money Laundering sourcebook, but this was removed, with the main elements of it finding their way into the systems and controls part of the Handbook.

The extent to which these sourcebooks will apply depends largely on the business which a firm conducts and the type of client which it services. Other sections of the Handbook cover issues such as supervision and enforcement, redress, handling customer complaints, and specialist requirements for credit unions, professional firms, and Lloyd's. The regulator also has a role as the listing authority, since this function was taken from the stock exchange, and a section of the Handbook relates to this aspect.

Ongoing Relationship of the Regulator with the Regulated

2.44   The application process is also important for another reason in that it sets the stage for the future of the relationship with the regulator. In the earlier days, firms used to have a pre-authorisation visit from the regulator, but even pre-authorisation meetings are now rare except for where the application is complex or innovative. In the course of the application process, the regulator will examine the application from the perspective of risk, and will allocate the financial institution to one of a number of risk categories. Those in the highest risk category will be assigned a contact team at the regulator and the relationship can be expected to be a fairly constant and regular one. Those in the lowest risk category will not have a personal relationship with any individual at the regulator, but with a generic contact centre. They can expect to be visited by the regulator once every four years, or even longer. This does not mean that there will be no regulatory contact and indeed various returns will need to be completed and submitted, which will be monitored from a distance. Indeed, the risk categories will have no impact on the need to comply with the applicable rules of the regulator.

Applicants can reduce their regulatory risk profile in a number of ways, if they wish, such as by arranging for another regulated financial institution to handle client money, rather than handling it themselves. Demonstrating stronger management controls and undertaking less risky business will result in lowering the risk profile of the financial institution, and therefore the risk category into which it falls. Lower regulatory risk means less time spent on regulatory matters and more on business generation. In essence, this is a question of balance against the business plan and objectives, and there is always risk in every business, so this is just a question of management of that risk against the returns involved.

Special Cases

2.45   There are a number of special cases which need to be mentioned.

Credit Unions

2.46   Credit unions are a small and specific kind of deposit taking and lending institution. They exist to assist those who would otherwise be excluded from the financial system as the banks would not extend account facilities to them for commercial reasons. The regulator has introduced a two tier category of authorisation. Those which will not lend more than £10,000 in excess of a member's shareholding are known as Version 1 credit unions, and are subject to a lighter level of regulation as more appropriate to the volunteers who run such institutions. Those lending larger amounts are subject to a greater degree of regulation and are known as Version 2 credit unions. All credit unions are subject to the fundamental rules of the regulator, however.

Oil Market Regime

2.47   There is a special regime for the oil markets known as the Oil Market Participants regime, with a lighter touch of regulation than most of the rest of the regulatory regime, though as in the case of credit unions, the fundamentals of financial market regulation apply across the board. It was felt that the heavier regulatory touch that as used elsewhere was inappropriate as the normal retail investors found as product users and buyers in much of the rest of the financial services industry do not tend to be involved here.

Payment Institutions

2.48   The UK is a multi-cultural environment and has been for centuries now. There are many groups of nationalities working in the UK who wish to send monies back to their families in the countries with which their heritage is associated. However, the mainstream banks levy charges on cross border transactions to the extent that transfer of small sums, which nevertheless make a considerable difference in the countries to which they are transmitted, is not economic. Accordingly, a number of firms emerged offering services to such groups of nationalities at much more attractive fee rates. Such firms nonetheless need the banks to make the transfers, even if on an omnibus basis. Similarly to credit unions, payment institutions only offer at most a few basic facilities, the main one of which is money transmission. A number of payment institutions have joined together to form the UK Money Transmitters Association. Those offering only the basic services and taking a relatively small amount of business a month are known as Small Payment Institutions (SPIs), and those offering a wider range of services, taking a larger amount of business every month and wanting to be able to conduct their business across the Member States of the European Economic Area pursuant to the Payment Services Directive are known as Authorised Payment Institutions (APIs). Both SPIs and APIs are subject to the basic standard of financial markets regulation, APIs being subject to more stringent standards.

More recently, the mainstream banks have been more selective about those APIs and SPIs to which they will offer services. Many have withdrawn from offering services to payment institutions altogether, often citing the money laundering risk as the key concern. However, given that the AML procedures of the payment institutions are in many cases superior to those of the banks, the payment institutions see their withdrawal as driven by competition reasons. The issue has become somewhat charged politically, both in the US as in the UK, but there is no sign of resolution as yet.

Electronic Money Institutions

2.49   Issuers of electronic money, Electronic Money Institutions (EMIs) are treated in a similar fashion to payment institutions, though the laws and regulations here emanate from implementation of the second Electronic Money Directive by the Electronic Money Regulations. In similar fashion to payment institutions, there are authorised Electronic Money Institutions and small Electronic Money Institutions, the former being larger and able to use a pan European passport. These types of organisation are developing in popularity with the creation and usage of other forms of money, the rise of social media and the ventures into the payment sector by search engines and social media alike.

Crowdfunding

2.50   The protracted financial depression and lack of growth on both sides of the Atlantic made difficulties of funding for SMEs and start ups more acute. Life was also tough for investors as banks are offering extremely unattractive rates of interest. At the same time, the development of the internet and social networks has reduced standard degrees of separation from six to less than three, and considerably increased potential marketing reach. Crowdfunding has developed as a potential escape from both of these key issues.

Meanwhile, the FSA has shown a certain amount of regulatory unease towards crowdfunding. A statement in August 2012 warned potential investors that most Crowd Funding Platforms (CFPs) are unauthorised and that there will be no access to the Financial Ombudsman Service (FOS) or Financial Services Compensation Scheme (FSCS) if needed. FSA's view was that most CFPs should be targeted at sophisticated investors who know how to value a start up business and understand the risks involved, including the risk that investors could lose all of their money. FSA wanted it to be clear that investors in a CFP have little or no protection if the business or project fails and that they will probably lose all their investment if it does. FSA was also concerned that some CFPs may be handling client money without permission or authorisation, and may not have in place adequate protection for investors.

2.51   In assessing whether the CFP will work from a regulatory perspective, the role of a number of participants will need to be assessed, including potential investors, those wishing to raise funds, the CFP platform and its operators, those managing relevant funds and holding client money, those involved in marketing and any others to whom certain functions may be outsourced.

The answer will also depend on the model of CFP under consideration:

- Donation model – funders provide funds either for no return or for a non-financial return
- Lending model – funders provide funds as a loan to be repaid with interest
- Share model – funders provide funds in return for shares in the CFP
- Fund model – funders provide funds in return for a right to a certain share in the revenue or profits generated by the fund

There are changes mooted, with a number of bodies lobbying for the introduction of a different regulatory regime specifically for crowdfunding. Similar moves are afoot in the United States for a regime more appropriate to crowd funding. These potential changes are discussed below.

2.52   Although CFPs are growing in popularity at present, few are authorised. More recently, however, a number of crowd funding platforms have been granted authorisation.

Issues of consumer credit may arise if the lending model is used. Certain specific corporate law issues may arise if the share model is used. Depending on the way in which the CFP is put together and the sizes involved, a prospectus may be needed.

The regulatory future in substantive terms is unclear for crowd funding at present. In the area of collective investment vehicles for example, the general rule is that for funds to be offered to the public the funds themselves have to be authorised, as well as those who promote and manage the funds. Unregulated funds can be offered, but only to specific classes of investor, which generally will not include members of the public, but sophisticated or high net worth individuals who can be taken to understand the risks involved.

A number of market participants are advocating the introduction of a lighter regulatory regime for CFPs. Potential risk to investors could be reduced by other means. These include restricting the amount investors are allowed to invest to a small sum, amounting perhaps to a few hundred pounds each, or to a certain percentage of income, or to limiting the amount which any one investor could invest in a particular fund or project, or to limiting the size of fund which may be allowed. Only funds over a certain size could be required to produce a prospectus. The UK government has established a Business Funding Taskforce which has included crowdfunding in its remit.

The European Dimension

2.53   The UK approach to regulation has to be placed in the context of European regulation. In the earlier days of the European Union, European law consisted mainly of competition law. However, gradually the remit spread to specialist sectors, including the financial sector. The original key EU measures relevant to financial markets were the Investment Services Directive and Capital Adequacy Directive, with copycat legislation applicable to banking and life insurance. However, the amount of EU legislation has mushroomed through the Financial Services Action Plan and at present there are around 40 new legislative measures going through the process in Brussels which will have an impact on the financial sector.

What is Europe?

2.54   These measures apply not only across the EU, but also across the European Economic Area (EEA). The 31 Member States of the EEA are Austria, Belgium, Bulgaria, Croatia, Cyprus, Czech Republic, Denmark, Estonia, Finland, France, Germany, Greece, Hungary, Iceland, Ireland, Italy, Latvia, Liechtenstein, Lithuania, Luxembourg, Malta, Netherlands, Norway, Poland, Portugal, Romania, Slovak Republic, Slovenia, Spain, Sweden and the United Kingdom.

Certain European countries currently lie outside the EEA, such as Switzerland, which nonetheless feel the influence of European law and have similar laws themselves. Some countries have made applications to join the EU some quite some time ago such as Turkey. Other countries either have recently made or are about to make an application to join the EU, such as Serbia, and other Balkan states. Many European micro states lie outside the EU and EEA and are likely to remain so, such as Monaco, Andorra, San Marino and the Holy See. A lot of these states have laws and regulations which are very similar to EU and EEA standards, however.

Passporting

2.55   The key aim was to improve the ability to conduct financial markets business across the EEA. The way of doing this was to introduce a 'passport'. The concept of the passport is that once a financial institution has been authorised for the provision of a service in one EEA Member State, then it should be able to provide such services in another EEA Member State, without that second Member State ('host Member State') requiring further authorisation. 'Passporting is possible in two ways. The first is by establishing a branch (as opposed to a separate legal entity) in the host Member State. The second is to provide services on a cross border basis without having a local branch. The passport is only available to those financial institutions which have separate legal personality in an EEA Member State, so it is not available to the branch of a non-EEA financial institution, for example. Such latter financial institutions may still carry on business in other EEA Member States but will have to be authorised in each of those Member States. The passport only covers investments and investment activities for which the financial institution is authorised by its home Member State regulator. Application for a passport is made to the home Member State regulator. There then follows a period of three months in which to object to the application in the case of a branch, and one month in the case of cross border services without a branch. Originally, the idea was that the home Member State would focus on prudential regulation and the host Member State on conduct of business regulation, such that the latter could impose additional marketing restrictions, for example. Over time, conduct of business regulation has been harmonised so that this element cannot be used as a barrier to market entry.

2.56   The application to passport into another Member State can be made at the same time as the application for authorisation, though cannot be granted until such time as authorisation to trade in the home Member State has been achieved. The regulator will need to be satisfied that the systems and resources exist to do so. Non-UK EEA firms do not therefore need to apply to the UK regulator to establish a branch or provide services into the UK, but to their own regulator. This is in the case of services and instruments covered by the European rules, however, so if a non-UK firm wishes to provide services into the UK in respect of services and instruments which fall outside the scope of the relevant directive, but which are regulated in the UK, then the non-UK firm needs to apply for authorisation in respect of those services and instruments. This does not need to be for a separate firm (unless the services and instruments are run in a separate firm), but can be in addition to its passport where it has one (known as a 'top up permission'). The procedures for a top up permission are akin to those for an application for authorisation however.

There is a route of 'passporting under FSMA 2000, Sch 4 as a 'Treaty firm'. This is where there is no right to passport under a directive, but the firm concerned is authorised in its home Member State to provide such services and instruments. This is not a particularly common route to cross border business however.

Collective investment schemes have been able to passport too, under a separate route, and this has been extended to funds other than UCITS under the Alternative Investment Funds Directive (AIFMD).

Level Playing Field

2.57   Another key aim was to create a level playing field not only as between Member States, but also as between banks and non-banks, particularly in relation to capital adequacy requirements. Although a laudable aim at country level, this has proved extremely difficult between different kinds of financial institution as banking is fundamentally a different business to trading investments.

Investment Services

2.58   The list of investment activities and investments is different from the UK definition, in 'Eurospeak' if you like. This means there is a difference between the two sets of regulation, further complicating matters.

Investment Services and Activities

2.59

- Reception and transmission of orders in relation to financial instruments
- Execution of orders on behalf of clients
- Dealing on own account
- Portfolio management
- Investment advice
- Underwriting or placing financial instruments on a firm commitment basis
- Placing financial instruments without a firm commitment basis
- Operation of multilateral trading facilities

Ancillary Services

2.60

- Safekeeping and administration of financial instruments for clients
- Granting credits or loans to investors
- Advice to undertakings on capital structure, industrial strategy, M & A
- Foreign exchange services related to investment services
- Investment research and financial analysis
- Services related to underwriting
- Investment services and ancillary services related to the underlying of derivatives

Investments

2.61

- Transferable securities
- Money market instruments
- Units in collective investment undertakings
- Options, futures, swaps, forward rate agreements, on financials or commodities
- Credit derivatives
- Contracts for differences

The Future

2.62　　It remains to be seen what will happen in relation to authorisation in the future. To some extent it will depend on whatever the future regulatory architecture may be. If recent developments are followed, then the future may well consist of a pan European regulator of massive proportions, with every financial institution governed according to a set European model which may not suit the specific local needs of industry or the population that well. The scope of regulatory coverage will continue to expand and the vast majority of the financial sector will be regulated under one roof. The decision tree set out above will become ever more complex, but to what end? Innovation will need to be encouraged for the financial sector to grow and service the needs of industry. The goal at the introduction of MiFID was to encourage the growth and rationalisation of financial institutions to become of a size large enough to compete with others on the other side of the Atlantic, but precious few large organisations appear at the top of reviews for customer service, and it is the over-large financial behemoths which very nearly brought the world's financial system down, rather than the smaller ones. Barriers to entry are currently quite high, and it is to be hoped that they will be lowered and competition encouraged. The current tidal wave of financial market regulation from Europe heralds a challenging time for the future. The introduction of MiFID is now widely acknowledged to have stifled European financial markets, rather than enabling them to flourish and Member State economies to grow. Europe currently has the lowest economic growth rates in the world and over regulation is part of the explanation for this. Logically, the constant imposition of tougher and tougher regulation can result in one outcome only, the death of financial markets. We have already seen the scenario where banks are unwilling or unable to lend because of over-burdensome regulation introduced at the wrong time in the regulatory cycle. Regulators need to work out where the tipping point is and not stray over that line. Many have stated that they want to be the 'toughest' regulator, or that 'financial institutions should be afraid of [the regulator]. Why? The goal should be to be the most effective and efficient regulator, rather than having regulatory policy grounded in some form of ill founded machismo. Regulation needs to be collaborative and co-operative, in the needs of the markets which they serve, not combative, stifling or bureaucratic. In terms of authorisation, this means that access to markets should be opened up and innovation encouraged. Three months should be the maximum time for a regulator to be allowed to consider a standard application, with six months the limit for more complex ones.

Chapter 3

The Approved Persons Regime

Peter Bibby

INTRODUCTION

3.1   Individuals (and corporate bodies) who carry out certain roles in authorised firms are required to be individually approved by the FCA and/or PRA (for PRA regulated firms). This is designed to ensure that only those who are fit and proper will be in charge of authorised firms or will be permitted to deal with customers in relation to regulated activities.

The approved persons regime was introduced in the Financial Services and Markets Act 2000 ('FSMA') and was amended by the Financial Services Acts of 2010 and 2012, the latter of which made changes to cater for the division of regulatory responsibility between the FCA and the PRA. The effectiveness of the regime was considered in depth by the Parliamentary Commission on Banking Standards in 2013. The Commission made recommendations designed to strengthen the regime, and amendments to the relevant provisions of FSMA were included in the Banking Reform Act 2013. Those changes have not (at the time of writing) come into force and the purpose of this chapter is to describe the regime based on the law as it stands at 1 February 2014 (which in any event will remain the relevant framework in relation to any conduct that occurs before the Banking Reform Act changes are implemented). A brief description of the changes introduced by the Banking Reform Act appears at the end of the Chapter.

THE STATUTORY AND REGULATORY PROVISIONS

3.2   The relevant statutory provisions are at Part V of FSMA.[1] The relevant parts of the regulators handbooks that set out the rules of the regime are SUP10; FIT; APER.[2] In addition, the DEPP[3] and TC[4] sections of the handbook and the provisions of the Enforcement Guide[5] (EG) are relevant.

1 FSMA 2000, ss 56–71.
2 SUP10 is chapter 10 of the Supervision Manual (SUP10A sets out FCA provisions and SUP10B sets out PRA provisions); FIT is the Fitness and Properness Test for Approved Persons; APER is the Statements of Principle and Code of Practice for Approved Persons.
3 DEPP is the Decision Procedure and Penalties Manual which contains FCA's policies and procedures for disciplining approved persons. FCA has the power to take disciplinary action against any approved person even if that approval was granted by PRA.
4 TC is the Training and Competence module of the handbook. It sets out requirements as to initial and ongoing qualifications and training standards for individuals.
5 EG is the Enforcement Guide which provides a guide to the FCA's use of its enforcement tools.

OVERVIEW OF THE REGIME

3.3   FSMA provides that an authorised person must take reasonable care to ensure that no person performs a controlled function under an arrangement entered into by it (or its contractor) in relation to the carrying on by it of a regulated activity, unless that person is approved by the appropriate regulator.[1] If the authorised person breaches this requirement then it may be disciplined for the breach in the same way as it could be disciplined for any other breach of any other requirement.[2] If a person performs a controlled function without approval and that person should have known that he required approval then he too may be disciplined.[3]

A controlled function is a function specified by either PRA or FCA as one which requires approval. In relation to firms that are solely regulated by the FCA approval for a person to perform a controlled function will always have to be sought from the FCA. In the case of firms that are regulated by both the FCA and the PRA ('PRA firms') approval for a person to perform a controlled function will have to be sought from the regulator that specified the function as a controlled function (referred to as the appropriate regulator[4]). The PRA only has the power to specify functions as controlled functions where they are functions that may enable the person performing the function to exert significant influence over the business of the authorised person so far as relating to a regulated activity (significant influence functions) and of course only in relation to PRA firms. PRA controlled functions are therefore limited to significant influence functions for PRA firms. All other controlled functions are specified by FCA (including certain FCA significant functions that apply to all firms and all customer dealing functions[5]).

FSMA gives the FCA and the PRA power to issue Statements of Principle together with a Code of Practice setting out the conduct expected of approved persons.[6]

Approved persons may be disciplined where they are guilty of misconduct.[7] An approved person is guilty of misconduct where he breaches a Statement of Principle, one of the FCA/PRA rules or where he has been knowingly concerned in a breach of a requirement by the firm on whose behalf he has been approved.

1 FSMA 2000, s 59(1) and (2).
2 The authorised person would be in breach of a relevant requirement and could be disciplined under FSMA, Part XIV.
3 FSMA 2000, s 63A – the penalty will be determined taking into account not only his failure to be approved but also any matter for which he could have been disciplined had he been approved.
4 Where the PRA has specified the controlled function then approval is granted by the PRA with the consent of the FCA.
5 For further details on significant influence functions and customer dealing functions see 'The Functions that can be Specified as Controlled Functions' below.
6 FSMA 2000, ss 64 and 65.
7 FSMA 2000, s 66.

THE IMPORTANCE OF AN ARRANGEMENT

3.4   Approval is only required where a person is performing a controlled function (i.e. a function that has been specified as such by the appropriate regulator) under an arrangement with an authorised person or with a contractor of the authorised person. The arrangement can be a written agreement which clearly sets out the terms and the role and responsibilities of the person and this will be the usual situation. However, the absence of a written agreement will not necessarily mean that an arrangement does not exist and that the person does not require approval. In many firms arrangements may have grown up as a result of custom and practice and those arrangements may involve a person performing a controlled function as a matter of practice. If that is the case then the firm will be in breach of a requirement if it allows that arrangement to persist without the person being approved, and the person himself will be liable to disciplinary action if he carries out his duties under that arrangement if he knew, or should have known, that he should have been approved.

THE FUNCTIONS THAT CAN BE SPECIFIED AS CONTROLLED FUNCTIONS

3.5   FSMA provides that controlled functions can only be specified (and therefore can only require approval) if they fall into one of two categories. The two categories are 'significant influence function'[1] and 'customer dealing function'.[2]

In order to be a significant influence function, the function must be likely to enable the person carrying out the function to exercise a significant influence on the conduct of the authorised person's affairs so far as they relate to the carrying on of regulated activities. In order to be a customer dealing function, the function must involve the person who carries out the function dealing with customers of the firm or with the property of customers of the firm in a manner connected with the carrying on of a regulated activity. If the function does not meet either of these criteria then it cannot be specified as a controlled function by FCA or PRA. Not all functions that meet those criteria will be controlled functions. Controlled functions are only those specified by the FCA or PRA as such.

1 FSMA 2000, s 59(5).
2 FSMA 2000, s 59(6)–(7).

THE ROLE OF THE FCA AND THE PRA

3.6   The FCA and the PRA are given discretion by FSMA to specify functions as controlled functions provided the function meets the relevant criteria.[1] The FCA can specify both significant influence functions and customer facing functions for all firms that it regulates (including those where PRA also regulates). The PRA may only specify significant influence functions for PRA firms. The FCA is under a statutory obligation to try to limit the need for a person to require approval from both the FCA and the PRA to perform a significant influence function where the firm is a PRA firm.[2]

1 Ie it is a significant influence function or a customer dealing function.
2 FSMA 2000, s 59A.

WHERE ARE THE DETAILS OF THE CONTROLLED FUNCTIONS

3.7   The controlled functions that have been specified by FCA are set out in Chapter 10A of the Supervision Manual. The controlled functions that have been specified by the PRA are set out in Chapter 10B of the Supervision Manual.[1]

1 Where a firm is a PRA firm then it will need to consider both Chapter 10A and 10B of the Supervision Manual since it may have persons performing both FCA and PRA significant influence functions and FCA customer dealing functions. Where a firm is only regulated by FCA then it need only consider Chapter 10A of the Supervision Manual.

SIGNIFICANT INFLUENCE FUNCTIONS[1]

3.8   There are four separate categories of Significant Influence Functions: governing functions;[2] required functions;[3] systems and controls functions;[4] and significant management functions.[5]

1 The FCA significant influence functions other than the FCA required functions and, if the firm is a MiFID investment firm, the FCA governing functions do not apply to the activities carried on by a firm whose principal purpose is to carry on activities other than regulated activities and which is: (i) an oil market participant; (ii) a service company; (iii) an energy market participant; (iv) a wholly owned subsidiary of a local authority or social landlord (v) a firm with permission to carry non-investment insurance mediation activity but no other regulated activity. A firm should ensure that it can demonstrate that its principal purpose is to carry on activities other than regulated activities if it wishes to take advantage of this exemption.
2 The PRA will approve a PRA firm's governing functions. The FCA will approve an FCA firm's governing functions.
3 The PRA's required functions are limited to the actuarial functions; the 'with profits' actuary function; and the 'Lloyds' actuary function. Other required functions for a PRA firm will be approved by the FCA.
4 Separate approval for the systems and controls function is only needed from the FCA or the PRA if the person filling the function is not already approved for a governing function (other than 'non-executive director' function). Where a PRA firm requires separate approval for the person filling the systems and controls function then the PRA will approve that person.
5 The significant management function is only specified by the FCA and therefore if a PRA firm has a person filling the significant management function then approval for that person will need to be sought from the FCA.

Governing Functions[1]

3.9   The governing functions that are relevant for a particular firm will depend on the form that the firm takes (ie whether it is a company, partnership or unincorporated organisation) and how its overall management is organised.

There are six separate governing functions that may be relevant for a particular firm: director; non-executive director; chief executive; partner; director of unincorporated association; and small friendly society. The same governing functions are specified by both FCA and PRA and where the firm is a PRA firm then any application in relation to a governing function should be made to the PRA.[2] Where the firm is regulated only by the FCA then the application should be to the FCA.

1 Where a firm carries on insurance mediation activity and is not a sole trader then it must allocate to a director or senior manager performing a governing function the responsibility for the firm's insurance mediation activity. The person so allocated will have the words 'insurance mediation' inserted after the relevant controlled function on the FCA register.
2 Where a PRA firm applies for approval for an individual then the PRA will discuss the matter with FCA. The PRA will consider the application from a prudential perspective and the FCA from a conduct perspective. The PRA approvals will normally be granted with the consent of FCA, although s 59B of FSMA 2000 provides that the FCA may make written arrangements with PRA under which the PRA may give approval without consent of the FCA.

Director (CF1)[1]

3.10   The 'director function' applies where the firm is a body corporate. It is the function of acting in the capacity of a director of the firm. A director is any person who is appointed to direct the affairs of a firm including a member of the firm's governing body whether they are called by the name of director or not and irrespective of whether they are a statutory director. It extends[2] to any person in accordance with whose directions or instructions (not being advice given in a professional capacity such as legal advice from a solicitor) the members of the governing body of a firm are accustomed to act.[3]

The definition of the 'director function' means that the assessment of who needs approval to perform the 'director function' must extend beyond those who are formally appointed as statutory directors of a corporate body, and firms will need to consider whether individuals carrying out a role in a parent or holding company require approval.[4] FCA gives a number of examples[5] of where a person who is not on the governing body of the regulated firm may require approval because he is performing the 'director function'. These include the chairman of an audit committee of a holding company where the audit committee also acts on behalf of the regulated group company. The chairman of the committee will be performing the 'director function' because the function of the chair of the audit committee will enable the person to exert a significant influence over the regulated firm given that the audit committee is operating in place of the regulated firm's own audit committee. The same will apply where a director of a holding company operates under an arrangement where he can exercise significant influence over the regulated firm because of his involvement in decision making for the regulated firm. Again if a senior manager[6] of a holding company operates under an arrangement which gives him the power to set the remuneration or objectives of the executive directors of a regulated firm then given his ability to exert significant influence over their behaviour he will be performing the 'director function' and will require approval as such.

The 'director function' does not include the director of a holding company if the holding company is regulated by an EEA regulator or if the holding company itself has a Part 4A permission. However, where a person is formally appointed as a director of both a regulated holding company and the regulated firm then he will need to be approved for the 'director function' for both.

In each case it is for the firm to determine whether the arrangement under which a person who is not appointed as a statutory director of the regulated firm operates is such that the person requires approval for the 'director function'.

A director does not have to be a natural person but can be a body corporate and where it is a body corporate then it will require approval in the same way as a natural person would.

1 SUP10A.6.7 (FCA); SUP 10B.6.1 (PRA).
2 FSMA 2000, s 417 defines a director.
3 Whilst the 'director function' is a function that only applies to a body corporate, the definition of a 'director' in the glossary to the rulebook is a generic term that applies to all

firms and denotes those individuals who direct the affairs of a firm. In relation to: (a) an unincorporated association; (b) a body corporate; (c) a partnership; or (d) a sole trader, any person appointed to direct its affairs, including a member of its governing body and:

(i) a person occupying in relation to the position of a director (by whatever name called); and

(ii) a person in accordance with whose directions or instructions (not being advice given in a professional capacity) the directors of that body are accustomed to act.

4 The 'director function' includes any officer or employee of a parent undertaking or holding company of a firm whose decisions or actions are regularly taken into account by the governing body of the firm (see SUP 10A.6 and 10B.6).

5 SUP 10A.6.9G (FCA).

6 A 'senior manager' is defined by the glossary so as to mean an individual other than a director who is employed by a firm or by a body corporate within a group of which the firm is a member who has been given responsibility by the governing body or a member of the governing body either alone or jointly with others for management and supervision. Where the individual is employed by the firm he must report directly to: (a) the governing body; (b) a member of the governing body; (c) the chief executive; or (d) the head of a significant business unit. If the person is employed by a body corporate within the group then he must report to a body or person who is the equivalent of (a)–(d) above.

Non-Executive Director (CF2)[1]

3.11   The 'non-executive director' function applies where the firm is a body corporate. It is separate to the 'director function' and applies to those persons who act in the capacity as a non-executive director of the firm. As with the director function this will include those who are non-executive directors of a parent or holding company where their decisions or actions are regularly taken into account by the governing body of the regulated firm. This will not apply where the holding company is regulated by an EEA regulator or where the holding company itself has a Part 4A permission. However, where the person is formally appointed as a non-executive director of both the regulated holding company and the regulated firm then he will need to be approved for the 'non-executive director' function for both.

FCA gives examples of where the non-executive directors of a holding company who are not appointed to the board of the regulated firm will require approval because they are performing the 'non-executive director' function for a regulated firm.[2] These include a non-executive director of a holding company who takes an active role in the running of the regulated firm, for instance where he is a member of a committee such as the audit or remuneration committee of the firm. Likewise where a non-executive director of a holding company has responsibility for setting or scrutinising the strategy of the regulated firm or for scrutinising the performance of the directors of the regulated firm then he is likely to require approval.

1 SUP 10A.6.12 (FCA); SUP 10B.6.3 (PRA).
2 SUP 10A.6.14 (FCA).

Chief Executive Function (CF3)[1]

3.12   The 'chief executive function' is the function of acting as the chief executive of a firm. The chief executive function (unlike the 'director' and 'non-executive director' function) can apply to a firm irrespective of whether the firm is a body corporate or not. A chief executive may or may not be appointed by a firm.[2] If a chief executive or chief executives are appointed then they will require approval to perform that function. The chief executive is the person (or persons who jointly) are responsible for the conduct of the whole of the firms business. A chief executive may be a member of the governing body of the firm and if he is then he will require approval in that capacity as well as in the capacity of chief executive. In a firm with a principal place of business in the UK then the chief executive is the person (or persons) with responsibility for the conduct of the whole of the business under the immediate authority of the directors. Where the principal place of business is outside the UK and the activities in question are carried out by a branch in the UK then the chief executive will be the person with the responsibility for the conduct of regulated activities within the UK. The question of whether the person located in the UK who is responsible for the conduct of the UK business is performing the 'chief executive function' will depend on what powers and responsibilities he has and the extent to which he is supervised from overseas. Where the business is carried out by a branch in the UK then the chief executive of the firm as a whole will not normally be expected to be approved by the FCA or PRA provided the person in the UK has sufficient responsibility for the business in the UK.

The 'chief executive function' is only filled where there is a person (or some group of people) who have responsibility for the conduct of the whole of the business. If the responsibility for the conduct of the whole of the business is divided between a number of people (each with separate responsibilities) then the firm will not have a chief executive. If the responsibility is shared (other than between each member of the governing body[3]) then those by whom it is shared will be filling the 'chief executive function'. The chief executive can be a body corporate and will require approval in the same way as a natural person.

Where the firm does have a chief executive then in normal circumstances he will also be required to fill the apportionment and oversight function for the firm (CF8 required function see below).

1 SUP10A.6.17 (FCA); SUP 10B.6.7 (PRA).
2 There is no requirement to appoint a chief executive because it is not a required function.
3 If the responsibility is shared between each member of the governing body the firm will not have a chief executive since the board will have collective responsibility.

Partner Function (CF4)[1]

3.13   Where the firm is a partnership then the partners make up the governing body of the firm and the partner function is the function of acting in the capacity of a partner of the firm. Where the principal purpose of the firm is to carry on regulated activities then all of the partners will require approval for the partnership function. Where the principal purpose of the partnership is not to carry on regulated activities but the firm is nonetheless authorised then the partner (or partners) with responsibility for regulated activities will require approval. However, in such a case if the responsibility for regulated activities has not been apportioned to a particular partner or partners then each partner will require approval.

There may be a number of different variations in arrangements with a partnership. For example where a professional firm (such as a firm of lawyers or accountants) is authorised and carries on both mainstream and non-mainstream regulated activities then a partner who only has responsibility for non-mainstream regulated activities which are incidental to the professional services that he provides will not require approval for the partner function. A partner with responsibility for mainstream regulated activities (in an authorised professional firm) will require approval for the partner function.

Where a firm is a limited liability partnership then the members of the firm are treated as partners for the purpose of the partnership function. If the firm is registered under the Limited Partnership Act 1907 then the function of a limited partner does not fall within the partner function.

1 SUP 10A 6.23 (FCA); SUP 10B 6.12 (PRA).

Director of Unincorporated Association Function (CF5)[1]

3.14   The 'director of unincorporated association function' applies to those who act as directors of unincorporated associations in the same way as the director function applies to directors of a body corporate.

1 SUP 10A 6.29 (FCA); SUP 10B 6.15 (PRA).

Small Friendly Society (CF6)[1]

3.153   Non directive friendly societies are treated in a similar way to partnerships. Where the principal purpose of the firm is to carry on regulated activities each person with responsibility for directing its affairs requires approval. Where the principal purpose is not to carry out regulated activities then only those to whom responsibility for regulated activities has been apportioned will require approval. If the firm apportions responsibility to a particular individual where the principal purpose of the firm is regulated activities then if the apportionment is reasonable it will only be that individual who will be carrying out the function and will therefore require approval.

Most non directive friendly societies will be credit unions that will be regulated by the PRA and where this is the case then approval will be required from the PRA.

1 SUP 10A 6.31 (FCA); SUP 10B 6.16 (PRA).

REQUIRED FUNCTIONS

3.16   The required functions are, as their name suggests, those functions that the regulator requires a firm to fill. Certain of the functions are required for all firms and certain of the functions are only required where a firm meets a particular set of criteria or carries out a particular type of business.

There are six FCA required functions: apportionment and oversight; compliance oversight; CASS operational oversight; money laundering reporting officer; benchmark submission; benchmark administration. These apply to both FCA and PRA firms to the extent that they are relevant to their business. There are three PRA required functions: actuarial; with-profits actuary; and Lloyds actuary. The PRA required functions are only relevant for PRA firms and then only to those required to appoint actuaries. These are generally insurance firms. The precise requirements in relation to actuaries are set out at SUP 4.

FCA Required Functions

Apportionment and Oversight (CF8)[1]

3.17   SYSC 2.1.3 and SYSC 4.4.5[2] require firms to allocate the responsibility of dealing with the apportionment of responsibilities and the oversight of the establishment and maintenance of systems and controls to one or more individuals. The person or persons to whom that responsibility is allocated will need to be approved as CF8. There are detailed provisions[3] setting out which individual or individuals must be allocated the responsibility of dealing with the apportionment of responsibility and oversight of the establishment and maintenance of systems and controls. Where a firm has a chief executive then he must be allocated the responsibility of dealing with the apportionment of responsibility and oversight of the establishment and maintenance of systems and controls. He can be assisted in this by the directors and senior managers of the firm. Where the firm is a part of a group then the responsibility may be given to a director or senior manager who is responsible for the overall management of the group or for the regulated activities of the group. This is only likely to be appropriate if that director or senior manager is at least equivalent in seniority to the chief executive.

The responsibilities need to be apportioned amongst the firms directors and senior managers and must be done in a way so that: (i) it is clear who has which of the responsibilities; and (ii) the business and affairs of the firm can be adequately monitored and controlled by the directors, senior managers and governing body of the firm.

An incoming EEA or Treaty firm only needs to allocate responsibility for dealing with the apportionment of overseeing the establishment and maintenance of systems and controls. This is because the apportionment of responsibilities is a matter for the home state regulator. The relevant systems and controls for an incoming EEA or Treaty firm are those in relation to the matters that the FCA is entitled to regulate. In general these are the systems and controls in relation to the firms conduct of business from its UK branch.

PRA firms do not need separately to seek approval for a person to perform the FCA apportionment and oversight function provided it is to be performed by a person who is approved to perform a PRA governing function (other than the non-executive director function) and it is made clear at the point of application for PRA approval that the person will be filling the apportionment and oversight function.[4] If a person ceases to perform the PRA governing function for which he is approved then he may continue to perform the 'apportionment and oversight' function for a period of three months without seeking separate approval from the FCA.

1 SUP10A.7.1 (FCA).
2 SYSC is the Senior Management Arrangements, Systems and Controls section of the hand-book. The SYSC part of the handbook describes the systems and controls that firms will be expected to operate.
3 SYSC 2.1.4R and SYSC 4.4.5R comprise tables detailing those persons to whom the re-sponsibility of dealing with the apportionment of responsibilities and the oversight of the establishment and maintenance of systems and controls must be allocated.
4 SUP 10B.7.3 (PRA).

Compliance Oversight (CF10)[1]

3.18   SYSC 3.2.8 and SYSC 6.1.4 require a firm to appoint an individual to have oversight of compliance with the rules in COBS; COLL; and CASS.[2] The person appointed can be either a director[3] or a senior manager.[4] The requirement applies to any firm which carries on designated investment business with or for retail or professional clients. It excludes firms that are merely carrying on non-investment insurance business. A similar require-ment to appoint a person with compliance oversight is imposed by the AIFMD for a full scope UK AIFM. Applications for approval for the com-pliance oversight function are made to the FCA.

1 SUP 10A.7.8.
2 COBS is the Conduct of business Sourcebook; COLL is the Collective Investment Schemes Sourcebook; CASS is the Client Assets Sourcebook. These all relate to a firm's conduct of business.
3 Director for this purpose is the glossary definition and applies to a body corporate, unin-corporated association, a partnership and a sole trader (as opposed to the 'director func-tion' which only applies to a body corporate) and includes 'any person appointed to direct [a firm's] affairs including a person who is a member of its governing body' and '(i) a per-son occupying in relation [to the firm] the position of director (by whatever name called) and (ii) a person in accordance with whole directions or instructions (not being advice given in a professional capacity) the directors of that body [the governing body] are ac-customed to act.' Accordingly a partner in a partnership could fill the role of compliance oversight since he would satisfy the glossary definition of director as being a person who, in relation to partnerships, is a member of the partnership's governing body.
4 Senior manager is a person employed by a firm or by a body corporate within a group of which the firm is a member who is not a director but to whom the governing body has given responsibility either alone or jointly with others for management and supervision and who reports directly to the governing body, a member of the governing body, the chief executive or the head of a significant business unit (or where employed by a group mem-ber he reports directly to a person who is the equivalent).

CASS Operational Oversight (CF10a)[1]

3.19   Firms which are CASS large firms[2] or CASS medium firms[3] are required to appoint an individual to fill the CASS operational oversight function.[4] The person to whom the responsibility must be allocated has to be a director or a senior manager. Firms which hold below the threshold of client money and client assets to be classed as CASS large firms or CASS medium firms do not need to appoint a person to the CASS operational oversight function but do need to allocate responsibility for oversight of the firms compliance with CASS and for reporting to the firms governing body in respect of that oversight to a director or senior manager who is approved to perform a significant influence function.

1 SUP 10A.7.9 (FCA).
2 A CASS large firm is a firm which has held in the previous year or projects it will hold in the next year over £1 billion in client money or over £100 billion in client assets.

3 A CASS medium firm is a firm which has held in the previous year or projects that it will hold in the next year between £1 million and £1 billion in client money or more than £10 million and less than £100 billion in client assets.
4 The CASS operational oversight function is the function set out at CASS 1A.3.1AR which is the function of:
  (1) Oversight of the operational effectiveness of that firm's systems and controls that are designed to achieve compliance with CASS;
  (2) Reporting to the firm's governing body in respect of that oversight; and
  (3) Completing and submitting a CMAR to the FCA in accordance with SUP16.4.

Money Laundering Reporting (CF11)[1]

3.20   The person acting in the capacity of money laundering report-ing officer in a firm requires approval. The money laundering reporting officer is not required to be a director or senior manager of the firm, but is required to have an appropriate level of authority and independence within the firm and to have access to resources and information that is suf-ficient to enable him to carry out his responsibility to oversee compliance with the FCA's rules on systems and controls against money laundering.

1 SUP 10A.7.10 (FCA).

Benchmark Submission Function (CF40)[1]

3.21   Where a firm carries on the regulated activity of submitting infor-mation in relation to a specified benchmark (at the time of writing the only benchmark that had been specified is LIBOR) then the firm must appoint a person to have oversight of its compliance with the requirements in relation to the submission of information. As with the money laundering reporting officer the firm must ensure that the benchmark submitter has an appropriate level of authority and access to resources and information sufficient to enable him to carry out that responsibility.[2]

1 SUP 10A.7.12 (FCA).
2 See MAR 8.2.3R.

Benchmark Administration Function (CF50)[1]

3.22   Where a firm carries on the regulated activity of administering a benchmark then it must allocate to a person the responsibility for oversee-ing the arrangements for compliance with the rules relating to administer-ing that benchmark. As with the money laundering reporting officer and the benchmark submission function the benchmark administrator must ensure that its benchmark administration manager has a level of authority and access to resources and information sufficient to enable him to carry out that responsibility.[2]

1 SUP 10A.7.13.
2 See MAR 8.3.5R.

PRA Required Functions

3.23   A PRA firm will need to consider whether any of the PRA required functions apply to its business, in addition to the relevant FCA required functions. There are three PRA required functions which all relate to actuarial roles. They are relevant for insurance businesses that are PRA firms.

Actuarial Function (CF12)[1]

3.24   This is the function of acting as an actuary appointed by a PRA regulated firm under SUP4.3.1R to fulfil the duties set out at SUP 4.3.13R.

SUP 4.3.1R applies to certain long term insurers.[2] SUP 4.3.1R requires the firm to appoint one or more actuaries to carry out the actuarial function in respect of the firm's long term insurance business. The firm is required to take reasonable steps to ensure[3] that the actuary has the necessary skills and expertise and that he is a fellow of the Institute of Actuaries or the Faculty of Actuaries.

1 SUP 10B.8.1 (PRA).
2 SUP 4.3.1R (PRA) does not apply to registered friendly societies which are non-directive friendly societies; incorporated friendly societies that are flat rate benefits business friendly societies; incoming EEA firms.
3 SUP 4.3.9R.

With-Profits Actuary Function (CF12A)[1]

3.25   This is the function of advising the board of the firm in relation to the with profits funds that the firm operates. The duties of the With Profits Actuary are set out under SUP 4.3.16AR.

1 SUP 10B.8.2.

Lloyds Actuary Function (CF12B)[1]

3.26   This required function applies to the Society of Lloyds. It is the function of acting as a Lloyds actuary to perform the duties set out at SUP 4.6.7R

1 SUP 10B.8.3 (PRA).

REQUIRED FUNCTION SPECIFIED BY BOTH FCA AND PRA

Systems and Controls Function (CF28)[1]

3.27   The Systems and Controls function is a significant influence function that has been specified by both FCA and PRA. The function applies to the individual who has responsibility for reporting to the firms governing body or the audit committee in relation to the firm's financial affairs; the setting and controlling of its risk exposure; and adherence to internal systems and controls procedures and policies. The function will be performed where a firm has a separate risk department and a separate internal audit department.

A firm does not need to seek separate approval for a person to perform the systems and controls function where that person is seeking approval to perform a governing function (other than the 'non-executive director function'). This is because approval for a governing function will include approval for systems and controls function. A person will require separate approval for the systems and controls function if they are not approved for a governing function. Where the function is not performed by a director (as defined by the Glossary[2]) then it should be performed by a senior manager.[3]

For PRA firms, if separate approval is required for a person to perform the function (because it is not being performed by a person seeking approval to perform a governing function) that approval will have to be sought from the PRA. In all other cases if separate approval is required it will have to be sought from the FCA.

1 SUP 10A.8.1 (FCA); SUP 10B.9.1 (PRA).
2 In relation to: (a) an unincorporated association; (b) a body corporate; (c) a partnership; (d) a sole trader, any person appointed to direct its affairs, including a member of its governing body and:
   (i) a person occupying in relation to the position of a director (by whatever name called); and
   (ii) a person in accordance with whose directions or instructions (not being advice given in a professional capacity) the directors of that body are accustomed to act.
3 A senior manager is defined by the glossary so as to mean an individual other than a director who is employed by a firm or by a body corporate within a group of which the firm is a member who has been given responsibility by the governing body or a member of the governing body either alone or jointly with others for management and supervision. Where the individual is employed by the firm he must report directly to: (a) the governing body; (b) a member of the governing body; (c) the chief executive; or (d) the head of a significant business unit. If the person is employed by a body corporate within the group then he must report to a body or person who is the equivalent of (a)–(d) above.

FCA SIGNIFICANT MANAGEMENT FUNCTION (CF29)[1]

3.28 The FCA significant management function is the function of acting as a senior manager[2] with responsibility for a significant business unit that:

1   carries on designated investment business or other activities such as retail banking or corporate lending;[3]

2   effects contracts of insurance;

3   makes material decisions on the commitment of the firm's financial resources and carries out other treasury functions;

4   processes confirmations, payments, settlements, insurance claims, client money and similar matters; and

5   carries on deposit taking for an EEA firm from banking customers and connected activities.

The significant management function is an FCA specified function. Therefore if a person is performing the function they will need to seek approval from the FCA. The function is only relevant for those firms which are so complex and large that individuals who are not otherwise approved for governing functions or required functions or the systems and controls function have responsibility for a significant business unit. FCA anticipates that this will apply to few firms and that most firms will apportion responsibility for significant business units to those who are approved for other governing or required functions or for the systems and controls function. Where responsibility lies with a person who is approved for a governing or required function or the systems and controls function then separate approval is not required to perform the significant management function. However where significant responsibility for a significant business unit has been allocated to a senior manager and that person is not otherwise approved for a significant influence function (excluding the non-executive director function) then separate approval will be required from the FCA.

For the significant management function to apply to a firm it must either:

1   have apportioned a significant responsibility within the description of a significant management function to a senior manager of a significant business unit; or

2   be undertaking proprietary trading; or

3   in the case of an EEA firm undertake the activity of accepting deposits from banking customers and connected activities.

FCA rules[4] set out a number of factors that a firm should consider when deciding whether it is sufficiently complex or large that an individual who is not approved for another function is filling a significant management function. Examples of factors that a firm should take into account include the size of the firm's business in the UK for instance if it has over 100 approved persons or insurance premium in excess of £100 million. Firms should also take into account the number of regulated activities that they carry out or propose to carry out and the management structure and the group structure where they are part of a group.

The activities of a business unit will be relevant when assessing whether a senior manager in charge of the unit requires approval. When assessing whether a business unit is significant the firm should take account of all relevant factors in relation to its current circumstances and its plans for the future.[5]

In each case it will be for the firm to review the activities of the business unit and the responsibility of the person in charge to assess whether that person requires approval. The firm will need to consider the detail of the arrangement entered into with that person and the extent to which that person's responsibility is subject to control or oversight.

Proprietary traders who commit the resources of the firm may be performing a significant management function even if they are not in charge of a business unit. This will depend on their role and the levels of resources that they are authorised to commit. Where they are able to exert a significant influence over the firm then they will require approval. Given that proprietary traders are dealing with the property and assets of the firm and not that of its customers they will not be approved for customer dealing functions.

1 SUP 10A.9.9 (FCA).
2 Where all significant business units are the responsibility of a director then no-one will be performing the 'significant management function'. It is only where responsibility for a significant business unit has been apportioned to a senior manager that the senior manager will need to be approved to perform the FCA significant management function.

3 SUP 10A.9.12 (FRA) gives examples of other activities in addition to designated investment business that will be relevant.
4 SUP 10A.9.4 (FRA).
5 SUP 10A.9.5 (FRA) sets out relevant factors to be considered in relation to the business unit. These include the risk profile of the unit; how much of the firm's capital it uses or commits; how much it contributes to the firm's profit and loss; how many employees and approved persons are in the unit; the number of customers in the unit.

FCA CUSTOMER DEALING FUNCTIONS

3.29   FSMA permits only the FCA to specify functions as customer dealing functions.[1] Therefore all firms (including PRA firms) have to apply to the FCA for approval for those performing customer dealing functions.

1 FSMA 2000, s 59(5)(a).

The Customer Function (CF30)[1]

3.30   The customer function (CF30) is the only customer dealing function which the FCA has specified as a controlled function. However, it applies to a number of different activities and persons carrying out any of those activities will need to be approved for the customer function. The customer function applies to persons who give advice on, deal and arrange deals in and manage investments. It does not apply to banking business nor does it apply to general insurance business. It only applies to activities carried on in the UK from an establishment maintained by the firm or its appointed representative in the UK.

1 SUP 10A.10.

Advising on Investments[1]

3.31   Those individuals who advise on investments other than non-investment insurance contracts (general insurance such as house or motor) and who deal with customers will need to be approved for the customer function. A person performs the function where they give advice and also where they perform related functions such as dealing and arranging. It does not apply where they give basic advice on stakeholder products. Wealth management advisors within a bank will be caught (because they give advice on investments) but counter staff will not be caught. Those advising on investment products will fall within the definition but those advising on protection products will not be covered.

1 SUP 10A.10.7(1).

Corporate Finance Advice[1]

3.32   Those who give advice to clients in connection with corporate finance business alone and perform other functions in connection with corporate finance business are required to be approved under the customer function.

1 SUP 10A.10.7(2).

Pension Transfers and Opt-Outs[1]

3.33   Approval is required for individuals who advise on pension transfers and opt-outs. Such individuals are expected to have a detailed knowledge and understanding of the products and the transactions in question. Firms are required to have any recommendations to carry out a pension transfer or opt-out reviewed by a pension transfer specialist. A pension transfer specialist is a person appointed by a firm who checks the suitability of a pension transfer or opt-out and who has passed prescribed examinations.

1 SUP 10A.10.7(3).

Advice in Relation to Lloyd's[1]

3.34   Approval is required under this category for those who advise on membership of a Lloyd's syndicate.

1 SUP 10A.10.7(4).

Dealing and Arranging[1]

3.35   Those persons who deal (as principal or agent) or arrange deals for or in connection with customers where the dealing is covered by COBS 11[2] require approval under the customer function.

1 SUP 10A.10.7(5).
2 COBS 11 is the Conduct of Business Sourcebook chapter that sets out the rules in relation to dealing and managing.

Investment Manager[1]

3.36   Those persons who manage assets under either a discretionary or non-discretionary investment management agreement require approval under the customer function.

1 SUP 10A.10.7(6).

Bidder's Representative[1]

3.37   This applies in relation to bidding in emissions auctions and covers those who act as bidder's representative under subparagraph 3 of article 6(3) of the auction regulation.[2]

1 SUP 10A.10.7(7).
2 Commission Regulation (EU) No 1031/2010, 12 November 2010.

APPLICATION TO PARENT AND OVERSEAS COMPANIES

Application of Controlled Functions to Parent Company with UK Subsidiary

3.38   Where a parent company (whether overseas or UK) has a UK subsidiary that carries on regulated activities in the UK then the subsidiary itself will be the regulated firm. The approved persons regime will apply to the subsidiary as it would to any other UK incorporated firm. However, in addition to those operating within the UK subsidiary, certain persons based in the parent or holding company may need to be approved. To the extent that individuals within the holding or parent company exercise significant influence over the subsidiary then their role may fall within a governing function.

Management of Overseas Firms Operating through a Branch

3.39   Where an overseas firm is operating through a branch in the UK then the regulated entity will be the firm as a whole and as a result it is likely that a number of those who govern the firm as a whole will have little or no significant influence over the UK regulated activities. In such a case then the FCA and PRA will wish to approve those individuals who actually exert significant influence over the activities of the branch.

The question of who will require approval will depend on the extent of a person's role and authority within the regulated firm under the terms of the arrangement that he has with the firm or with a contractor of the firm.

Where an overseas firm is operating through a branch in the UK then the following controlled functions apply to the firm's operations in the UK:

Director Function (CF1) and Non-Executive Director Function (CF2)

3.40   The 'director function' or 'non-executive director' function where the person performing the function:

(a)   has responsibility for the regulated activities of a UK branch which are likely to enable him to exercise significant influence over that branch; or

(b)   is someone whose decisions or actions are regularly taken into account by the governing body of the branch.

It follows therefore that not all of the governing body of the overseas firm is likely to require approval.

Chief Executive Function (CF3)

3.41   The chief executive function applies to a UK branch of an overseas firm. The chief executive will be the person who has responsibility for the conduct of the regulated activities in the UK. This is unlikely to be the chief executive of the firm as a whole if a chief executive has been appointed for the UK business. The chief executive could be a director of the overseas firm but need not be since the role can be filled by a senior manager.

FCA Required Functions and PRA Required Function

3.42   These will apply to the UK branch as they would apply to a UK incorporated firm.

The Systems and Controls Function

3.43   This will apply to the UK branch in the same way as it would apply to a UK incorporated firm.

The Significant Management Function

3.44   This is an FCA function. It will apply to the UK establishment of an overseas firm if the UK branch is a significant business unit undertaking designated investment business (other than dealing in investments as principal) or processing confirmations, payments, settlements, insurance claims, client money and other similar matters in so far as this relates to designated investment business. The function will only apply where responsibility for the significant business unit has not been allocated to a person who is otherwise approved.

APPLICATION OF SIGNIFICANT INFLUENCE FUNCTIONS TO INCOMING EEA FIRMS OR TO TREATY FIRMS OR TO UCITS QUALIFIERS

3.45   Where a firm is authorised by an overseas regulator and then operates in the UK under a passport or treaty arrangement then the approved person regime will not apply to that firm to the extent that the question of whether a person is a fit and proper person to perform a particular function in relation to the firm is reserved to the firm's home state regulator. This means that members of the governing body of the firm or the branch manager of a UK branch who in accordance with the process for exercising a right to operate in the UK has been notified to the firm's home state regulator will not fall to be approved by the FCA or PRA[1,2].

In relation to the FCA significant influence functions, the FCA money laundering reporting function will apply with respect to the firm's activities carried on from its branch. The FCA significant management function will apply where the significant business unit undertakes designated investment business (other than dealing in investments as Principal) and other ancillary activities or the accepting of deposits from banking customers. If the firm is an EEA pure reinsurer then none of the FCA controlled functions apply in relation to its passported activities carried on from a branch in the UK.

Where a firm has a top up permission (i.e. it exercises the right to carry out regulated activities from a branch in the UK under a passport or treaty arrangement but the passport or treaty arrangement does not cover all of its activities and it has a permission from the UK regulator to carry out the activities not covered by the passport or treaty) then in relation to the activities covered by the top up permission the following apply:

(a)   the FCA or PRA required functions but excluding the FCA functions of apportionment and oversight and compliance oversight;

(b)   the FCA significant management function in so far as it relates to designated investment business (other than dealing in investments as Principal), processing and other matters in relation to designated investment business and accepting deposits from banking customers;

(c)   the customer function.

1 FSMA 2000, Sch 3, Pt II sets out the provisions for the Exercise of Passport rights by EEA firms. These provide for applications to provide services in the UK to be made to a firm's home state regulator which then notifies the UK regulator. Schedule 4 of FSMA sets out the provisions in relation to Treaty Rights. These provide that a firm authorised in an EEA state will qualify for permission to carry out those activities in the UK.

2 Where the firm is passporting PRA regulated activities into the UK then the notification by the overseas regulator is to the PRA. The firm's activities will (as with a UK firm) be regulated by both the PRA and the FCA. Where the firm passporting on is an FCA firm then the notification to the overseas regulator is by the FCA. In each case it will only be FCA controlled functions that will apply to the firm. The controlled functions that will apply will not include the governing functions.

THE CUSTOMER FUNCTION FOR OVERSEAS FIRMS

3.46   The customer function applies to those individuals carrying on business for an overseas firm from an establishment based in the UK in the same way as it applies in the case of a firm incorporated in the UK. Accordingly, to the extent that their activities fall within the description of the customer function they will require approval.

THE CUSTOMER FUNCTION FOR INDIVIDUALS BASED OVERSEAS

3.47   Where a person is based overseas then there are a number of questions to ask in order to establish whether they need to be approved to perform the customer function. The first question is whether the person carries out the customer function in the UK (ie, do they advise, manage or deal etc from an establishment in the UK). If they do not carry out the function in the UK they do not need to be approved. If they are carrying out the function in the UK then the next question will be which aspect of the customer function they are carrying out. If they are advising on pension transfers or advising on Lloyd's syndicates then they will require approval. If on the other hand they are performing the other aspects of the customer function in the UK then they will not need approval if they spend less than 30 days in the UK in a 12-month period and they are appropriately supervised by a person approved for the function. The firm will have to be satisfied that the individual based overseas has three years up-to-date relevant experience obtained outside the UK and the FCA will expect the firm to ensure that the person is accompanied on any visit to a customer.

TEMPORARY APPOINTMENTS

3.48   Firms may sometimes find themselves in the position where due to an absence which is temporary or unforeseen they need to appoint a person to perform a function that is a significant influence function on an interim basis. Where the appointment is to provide cover for an approved person who performs a significant influence function and the appointment is for less than 12 weeks in a consecutive 12-month period then the activities of that temporary appointee are excluded from the description of the significant influence function and they and the firm will be able to proceed without the threat of discipline. Once it becomes apparent that a person is likely to be absent for a period of more than 12 weeks then approval will need to be sought from the appropriate regulator for a replacement.

APPOINTED REPRESENTATIVES

3.49   Appointed representatives are exempt persons[1] for whom a principal has accepted responsibility in writing for their regulated activities. The approved persons regime applies to appointed representatives except for introducer appointed representatives. The FCA governing functions apply to an appointed representative except for a tied agent of an EEA Mifid investment firm. The customer functions will apply to the appointed representative in the same way as they apply to a regulated firm. The investment management function will not apply because an appointed representative will not be carrying on investment management.

1 FSMA 2000, s 39 exempts an appointed representative from the requirement to be authorised in relation to regulated activities. To be an appointed representative a firm must have entered into a contract with an authorised principal under which the principal agrees to be responsible for the representative's business.

THE APPLICATION PROCESS

3.50   Once a firm has determined which of the individuals performing roles in the firm require approval then the next step is for it to make an application for approval on behalf of those individuals. Where the firm is seeking authorisation for the first time then the applications for approval will be made at the same time as the firm's application for authorisation is made. Where a firm is already authorised then the application for approval will need to be made before the person is moved to a role that requires approval.

An application for approval is made by the firm on whose behalf the individual will be undertaking the controlled function. For an appointed representative the application will, be made by the appointed representative's principal since it is the principal that takes responsibility for the regulated activities of the appointed representative.

The application is made on a prescribed form[1] which requires details of the role that the individual will perform and details of his history and prior activities. It is signed by the candidate to confirm that they have fully and properly answered all the questions and is also signed by the firm making the application to confirm that they believe on the basis of reasonable enquiry that the person is fit and proper to perform the role. On receipt of an application for approval the appropriate regulator will make their own enquiries.

1 Form A.

THE REQUIREMENT TO BE FIT AND PROPER

3.51   The application stage for authorisation of firms and approval of individuals is a key stage in the regulatory process. The process is central to the regulators ability to be able to protect the integrity of the markets, deliver a fair deal for customers and further the prudential security of firms. A robust process will enable the regulators to authorise and approve only those who are fit and proper. The matters that the regulator will take into account when determining fitness are set out in the FIT[1] module of the handbook. The regulator will consider the candidate's honesty integrity and reputation (FIT 2.1); competence and capability for the role (FIT 2.2) and their financial soundness (FIT 2.3). The regulator will carry out its own background checks as part of the process and will take into account the answers to the questions on the application form (form A). Form A contains a detailed set of questions for the candidate to answer. It requires details of any past convictions or involvement in companies which have gone into liquidation or which have been the subject of any regulatory or similar investigation.[2] It is imperative that candidates make full and frank disclosure of all relevant matters since the regulator will view a failure to disclose as a serious failing. A failure to disclose is often the ground on which applications for approval are rejected.[3]

Guidance in FIT explains that the regulator will take account of all the facts and circumstances of any issue that has been disclosed when deciding whether or not a person is fit and proper. Accordingly whilst all criminal convictions must be disclosed (even where they are spent), the existence of a criminal conviction will not necessarily disqualify a person from being approved. If the conviction involves dishonesty or financial mismanagement the regulator is more likely to refuse approval than if it involves a non-financial crime. The regulator will also take account of the period of time since the offence was committed and the subsequent conduct of the individual.

For certain roles the regulator will require the individual to have obtained a particular qualification in order to demonstrate competence and capability.[4] As regards financial soundness the regulator will take account of whether the person is the subject of any judgement debt or whether he has entered into any arrangement or compromise with creditors or has been made bankrupt.

The regulator will take into account the role and responsibilities of the approved person when determining the candidate's competence and capability.

When an application for approval is made it is for the applicant to satisfy the regulator that the candidate is fit and proper. The burden of proof therefore operates differently than in a disciplinary case where it is for the regulator to prove his case to the appropriate standard. Applications for approval will be rejected where the regulator is not satisfied about a candidate's fitness and properness. For example if a candidate is the subject of an ongoing regulatory investigation then, despite the fact that there may have been no findings against him, the regulator may be entitled to reject the application on the basis that it cannot at that point be satisfied that the candidate is fit and proper. The mere fact that the candidate may be subject to an investigation will not of itself be sufficient to reject the application. However, the seriousness of the allegations which have prompted the investigation could be.

A finding of regulatory misconduct and the imposition of a disciplinary sanction will not automatically exclude an individual from being approved. Where an individual has been disciplined but the regulator has not imposed a prohibition order then it suggests that the regulator has not found that the person is not fit and proper. However, that would not automatically entitle a candidate to be granted approval since the regulator could decide on a subsequent application that it was not satisfied that the candidate was fit and proper.[5]

1 FIT is the Fit and Proper Test for Approved Persons.
2 The questions in form A mirror the matters set out in the Fit and Proper Test which is in FIT 2.
3 The regulator will view a failure to disclose a relevant matter as evidence that a person may not be relied on to be open and candid with the regulator.
4 The Training and Competence (TC) module of the FCA handbook sets out the qualifications that are required in order to be eligible to perform certain functions.
5 Given the different burden of proof on an application for approval and in a disciplinary case it is possible that the regulator could rely on the same facts to find that it was not satisfied an applicant was fit and proper on a subsequent application as it had relied on to impose a disciplinary sanction notwithstanding the absence of a prohibition.

THE STATEMENTS OF PRINCIPLE AND THE CODE OF PRACTICE FOR APPROVED PERSONS

3.52   Once a firm has determined that a person will perform a role for which approval is required and has made an application for approval then the candidate will need to make sure that he is aware of the additional duties and obligations he may have as a result of becoming an approved person and what the implications of approval may be. The Statements of Principle and Code of Practice for Approved Persons set out the standards of behaviour expected of Approved Persons. They are found in the APER[1] part of the handbook.

There are seven Statements of Principle: Nos 1–4 apply to all Approved Persons[2] and Nos 5–7 apply in addition to those who are approved for significant influence functions. The purpose of the Code of Practice is to help determine whether or not an approved person has complied with a Statement of Principle. It sets out descriptions of behaviour that in the opinion of the FCA does not comply with a Statement of Principle and factors which the regulator considers are relevant when determining whether the approved persons conduct does comply[3].

The Statements of Principle apply to the conduct of an approved person in performing his controlled function and also to the conduct of an approved person carrying on any other function for his firm in relation to the firm's carrying on of regulated activities even if it is not a controlled function.

The Statements of Principle are consistent with the Principles for Business[4] and are as follows:

1 APER in the Statements of Principle and Code of Practice for Approved Persons module of the handbook.
2 FCA and PRA have both issued the same Statements of Principle save that PRA has omitted the Principle in relation to market conduct (Statement of Principle 3). This is because the responsibility for market conduct lies with the FCA. The FCA has the power to issue Statements of Principle with respect to the conduct expected of persons in relation to whom either regulator has given its approval. Accordingly even though PRA has not issued Statement of Principle 3 it will still apply to a PRA approved person. Likewise FCA and PRA have issued the same Code of Practice save that the PRA Code of Practice omits material relevant to Statement of Principle 3.
3 FSMA 2000, s 64. The code does not include any descriptions of conduct which in the opinion of the regulator comply with a Statement of Principle.
4 There are 11 Principles for business which are found in the PRIN module of the Handbook.

Statement of Principle 1

3.53   An approved person must act with integrity in carrying out his accountable functions[1].

1 Accountable functions are an individual's FCA controlled functions and PRA controlled functions and any other functions that the approved person performs in relation to the carrying on of a regulated activity by the authorised person in respect of which he is approved.

Statement of Principle 2

3.54   An approved person must act with due skill, care and diligence in carrying out his accountable functions.

Statement of Principle 3

3.55   An approved person must observe proper standards of market conduct in carrying out his accountable functions.

Statement of Principle 4

3.56   An approved person must deal with the FCA, the PRA and other regulators in an open and cooperative way and must disclose appropriately any information of which the FCA or the PRA would reasonably expect notice.

Statement of Principle 5

3.57   An approved person performing an accountable significant-influence function must take reasonable steps to ensure that the business of the firm for which he is responsible in his accountable function is organised so that it can be controlled effectively.

Statement of Principle 6

3.58   An approved person performing an accountable significant-influence function must exercise due skill, care and diligence in managing the business of the firm for which he is responsible in his accountable function.

Statement of Principle 7

3.59   An approved person performing an accountable significant-influence function must take reasonable steps to ensure that the business of the firm for which he is responsible in his accountable function complies with the relevant requirements and standards of the regulatory system.

THE CODE OF PRACTICE

3.60   The Code of Practice provides examples of behaviour that the regulator considers to be in breach of the Statements of Principle. These examples were drawn from an analysis of regulatory breaches that had occurred prior to the publication of the Statements of Principle and reflect many of the common themes in enforcement cases. The examples are grouped by reference to the individual Statements of Principle. The examples are non-exhaustive and while they may assist in proving a breach of a Statement of Principle (and in helping approved persons to avoid behaviour that the regulator may consider to be in breach) in a particular case they are not a prerequisite of proving a breach. An approved person may be disciplined for a breach of Statement of Principle.

The Code of Practice explains that a person will only be in breach of a Statement of Principle where he is personally culpable. This means that his behaviour was deliberate or it was below that which would be reasonable in all the circumstances[1]. The application of this test was considered by the Tribunal in the FSA's case against John Pottage[2]. Mr Pottage had been chief executive (CF3) and apportionment and oversight (CF8) for UBS AG and UBS Wealth Management UK. The FSA imposed a fine of £100,000 on Mr Pottage finding that he was in breach of Principle 7 by failing to take reasonable steps to identify and remediate serious flaws in the design and operational efficiency of the business for which he was responsible. Mr Pottage referred the FSA's decision to the Tribunal[3]. The Tribunal found that the FSA had not satisfied it that Mr Pottage's actions was 'below that which would be reasonable in all the circumstances (APER 3.1.4G).' The Tribunal found in particular that his failure to act sooner than he did and in the way FSA argued he should have acted 'was not beyond the bounds of reasonableness' and therefore FSA had not proved its case.

The examples of behaviour that the regulator considers are in breach of a Statement of Principle are unsurprising. Under Statement of Principle 1 the examples include, amongst others, deliberately misleading customers; mismarking positions; providing false or inaccurate documentation or information. The examples of behaviour are not exhaustive and therefore even if a particular behaviour does not appear in the Code of Practice the regulator is not prevented from alleging that a breach of the Statement of Principle has occurred. The descriptions of behaviour extend beyond positive action and include examples of a failure to act. For example under Statement of Principle 1 failing to inform a customer that their understanding of a material fact is incorrect is a breach of the Statement of Principle where the approved person was aware that their understanding was incorrect.

Statement of Principle 2 requires approved persons to act with due skill care and diligence and the examples of the behaviour that the regulator considers are in breach of the Statement of Principle listed are similar to those listed under Principle 1, albeit that instead of being deliberate they are negligent. Statement of Principle 3 requires approved persons to observe proper standards of market conduct and therefore the regulator will take account of whether the person has complied with the requirements of the Code of Market Conduct or the relevant market codes and exchange rules. Statement of Principle 4 requires approved persons to deal with the regulators in an open and cooperative manner and to disclose to the regulator anything of which the FCA or PRA would expect notice. In order to avoid approved persons circumventing internal rules and procedures relating to the disclosure of matters to the regulator, the Code of Practice provides that an approved person will satisfy his own obligations under Statement of Principle 4 where he reports a matter to the individuals within the firm who are charged with the responsibility of considering whether matters should be reported to the regulator. In assessing whether an approved person is in breach of Statement of Principle 4 by failing to report matters internally within his firm the regulator will take into account the likely significance of the information to the regulator which it was reasonable for the person to assume; whether the information related to the individual himself or to the firm; and whether any decision not to report the matter to the regulator was taken after reasonable enquiry and analysis of the situation. Where a person is responsible under a firm's procedures for reporting matters to a regulator and receives a notification from an approved person then he will need to take into account the nature of the information provided to him and whether in relation to the approved person concerned it would be a matter that would require disclosure by the firm. Notification requirements in relation to approved persons are in SUP 15[4] and SUP 10[5]. Where the matter disclosed by an approved person relates to the firm itself then those charged with deciding whether to report will need to consider the firms reporting obligations under SUP 15 and the wider duty to report under Principle 11 of the Principles for Business. The lack of a specific requirement to report in SUP15 should not be seen as a safe harbour since the effect of the Principles for Business is to require a more general and holistic approach to be taken to reporting and in particular to require the firm to consider its responsibilities against the aims and objectives of the regulators.

The regulator's expectations of those exercising significant influence functions differs dependant on the nature, scale and complexity of a firms business and the role the person performs. Where a firm's business is more complex and involves higher risk products then the regulator's expectations will be greater than where the business is simpler and smaller.

Statement of Principle 5 deals with the organization of the business for which an approved person is responsible. Under Statement of Principle 5 the approved person is required to take reasonable steps to ensure that the business for which he is responsible is organised so that it can be controlled effectively. The Code of Practice provides that a failure by an approved person to apportion responsibility adequately for all areas of the business for which he is responsible would breach the Statement of Principle. Examples given of such a failure include uncertain reporting lines and confusing job descriptions and authorisation levels. The Code of Practice states that where the strategy of the firm is to enter into high risk transactions then the degree of control and strength of monitoring reasonably required will be greater.

Statement of Principle 6 deals with the management of the business for which an approved person is responsible. Under Statement of Principle 6 the approved person is required to exercise due skill, care and diligence in managing the business of the firm for which he is responsible. An approved person will be in breach of the Statement of Principle if he fails adequately to inform himself about the business. Examples given of such a failure include the approved person permitting transactions without understanding the risks; allowing expansion without assessing the possible consequences; failing adequately to monitor highly profitable transactions; accepting implausible explanations; and failing to obtain independent verification and expert opinion where that would be appropriate. Other examples of behaviour in breach of the Statement of Principle include delegating to an individual or outsourcing in circumstances in the absence of reasonable grounds to believe the delegate had the appropriate capacity competence or capability properly to perform the responsibilities assigned. Statement of Principle 6 expects an approved person to delegate rather than abdicate, and an approved person will be in breach of the Statement of Principle if once he has delegated responsibility he disregards the business or he fails to follow up on an issue or more generally he accepts implausible or unsatisfactory explanations.

Statement of Principle 7 concerns compliance with the requirements of the regulatory systems. Under Statement of Principle 7 an approved person must take reasonable steps to ensure that the business for which he is responsible complies with the requirements of the regulatory system. An approved person will be in breach of the Principle if he fails to take reasonable steps to implement adequate and appropriate systems and controls. The approved person need not do it all himself and can fulfil the responsibility through the actions of a compliance department. An approved person will, however, be in breach of the Statement of Principle if he fails to take adequate steps to monitor the business and if issues are identified fails to act quickly enough and decisively enough to investigate and rectify failures which may have occurred[6]. An approved person will be in breach if following the identification of a problem and recommendations for improvement he fails to act quickly enough to implement improvements.

1 APER 3.1.4G.
2 *John Pottage v FSA* FS 2010/33.
3 The recipient of a decision notice from FCA (previously FSA) has the right to refer the decision to the Upper Tribunal for a full hearing.
4 SUP 15.3.11 requires a firm to notify of any significant breach of a Statement of Principle by an Approved Person. SUP 15.3.17 requires notification of fraudulent activity by an employee. SUP 15.3.1 requires notification of any matter that could have a significant adverse impact on the firm's reputation. This could be relevant where the behaviour of an employee could bring a firm into disrepute.
5 SUP 10 requires a firm to notify the regulator of any issue that would reasonably be material to the assessment of an Approved Person's fitness and properness. Whilst not limited by the matters listed in FIT2 or the information required for Section 5 of Form A it includes all those matters.
6 Assuming his behaviour is below the standard which it is reasonable to expect in all the circumstances.

THE PROCESS FOR CHANGES TO APPROVED PERSONS STATUS

3.61   Once an individual is approved then there are a number of changes that can occur to his status. He may change roles; information about him may change; he may be suspended or dismissed; or he may simply move firms. There are a number of prescribed forms that are to be used where changes are to be made to an approved person's status or details. Where an application to withdraw an application for approval is made then form B is used. Form C is used where notice is being given that a person is ceasing to perform a controlled function. Form D is used for changes to a person's details and form E is used where a person is making an internal change from one controlled function to another.

A firm may only withdraw an application for approval where it has the consent of the candidate and where the candidate is not to be employed by the firm (but by a contractor of the firm for instance by an appointed representative) then with the consent of that person.

Where a person who is approved moves from one firm to be an approved person at another firm then a form A must be used albeit that where the regulator already has the relevant information concerning the candidate a shortened form A may be used. The notes to the form explain when a shortened version can be used.

REQUIREMENTS ON FIRMS TO NOTIFY IN RELATION TO APPROVED PERSONS

3.62   As indicated above in relation to Statement of Principle 4, firms are required to notify matters to the regulator under Principle 11 of the Principles for Business and under the provisions of SUP 15 and SUP 10. In relation to an approved person the firm is required to notify if they have reason to believe that the approved person is in breach of a Statement of Principle and the breach is significant[1]. A firm is also required to report if it suspects that an employee (including an approved person) is guilty of serious misconduct concerning his honesty or integrity where this is connected with the firm's regulated activities[2]. Where a firm becomes aware of a matter which would reasonably be material to the assessment of an approved person's fitness and properness then this must be notified to the regulator on form D[3]. This requirement extends to any of the matters that would normally be declared to the regulator on the application for approval form[4].

1 SUP 15.3.11.
2 SUP 15.3.17.
3 SUP 10A.14.17 (FCA); SUP 10B.12.18 (PRA).
4 See FIT 2.

DISCIPLINE OF APPROVED PERSONS

3.63   Approved persons can be disciplined by the regulator if it appears to the regulator that they are guilty of misconduct and 'the regulator is satisfied that it is appropriate in all the circumstances to take action against him'. Misconduct is defined as being in breach of a Statement of Principle or being knowingly concerned in a contravention of a relevant requirement by the firm on whose behalf the approved person is carrying on a controlled function[1].

A person who requires approval but who does not obtain approval where he ought to know that it is required can also be disciplined for that failure and can be disciplined as if he had been approved[2].

Sanctions include fines, suspensions, limitations and restrictions and statements of misconduct[3].

Where the regulator considers that a person is no longer fit and proper to carry on a controlled function that the person is currently carrying out then the regulator can withdraw the approval[4]. If the regulator takes the view that the person is not fit and proper to carry out a range of controlled functions or to be engaged in connection with an authorised firms regulated activities then the regulator can prohibit an individual[5]. Prohibition is normally reserved for circumstances where the regulator believes that the person does not demonstrate the appropriate levels of honesty and integrity.

1 FSMA 2000, s 66.
2 FSMA 2000, s 63A.
3 FSMA 2000, s 69 requires each regulator to prepare and issue a statement of policy on the imposition of penalties, suspensions or restrictions under s66 of FSMA; the amount of any penalties; and the period for which such penalties or supervisions are to take effect.
4 FSMA 2000, s 63.
5 FSMA 2000, s 56: a prohibition order may relate to a specified regulated activity, any regulated activity falling within a specified description or all regulated activities. The prohibition order can be in relation to a description of authorised or exempt person or in relation to all authorised or exempt persons.

CHANGES TO THE APPROVED PERSONS REGIME

3.64

The Banking Reform Act 2013 set out a number of changes to the approved persons regime including (amongst others) the creation of a senior manager function and the introduction of statements of responsibilities for senior managers. Senior managers of 'relevant authorised persons' (PRA authorised banks and PRA authorised firms that deal as principal in investments) will be guilty of misconduct if a regulatory failure occurs in an area of the business for which they are responsible unless they are able to satisfy the regulator that they took all the steps that it would be reasonable to expect from someone in their position to prevent the breach or its continuation. FSMA sets out a new certification regime for relevant authorised persons in relation to employees who could cause significant harm to the firm or its customers and requires the firm to certify on an annual basis that those individuals remain fit and proper. The FCA is given power to discipline any employee of a relevant authorised person. The Statements of Principle and Code of Practice for approved persons will be replaced by a new set of individual conduct rules. These changes will come into force once the regulators have consulted and have made changes to the rules concerning approved persons.

Chapter 4

Retail Products

Robert Surridge

The following summary broadly follows the FCA Handbook definition of 'retail investment products' although certain sections relate to occupational pension schemes which do not fall within this definition as only personal pension schemes and stakeholder pension schemes fall within this definition. In view of the range of products considered space only allows for a brief summary of the legal structure and other issues and the reader is encouraged to consult more detailed works for a more in-depth understanding where necessary.

LIFE ASSURANCE

Introduction

4.1   The number of life assurance products offered to the public is vast. However, the variety of underlying contracts is actually quite limited and all life assurance products are essentially only variations or combinations of a few basic types. These are set out at paras **4.5-4.11**.

What is life assurance?

4.2   Fundamentally, life assurance involves the payment of money, known as the 'premium' to the life office in return for a payment in the future of a sum of money, on the occurrence of specified events, namely death, expiry of a fixed term ('maturity'), or surrender. The sum paid on death or maturity is known as the 'sum assured' and on surrender a 'surrender value' may be payable. The sum received from the life office is usually in the form of a single lump sum but may occasionally be in the form of regular payments. The premiums paid to the life office may be regular (usually monthly or annually) or a single premium. The various purposes of life assurance are most easily and conveniently considered in conjunction with an examination of the types of life assurance set out at paras **4.5–4.11**.

Is there a technical legal definition of life assurance?

4.3   While in most cases there will be no difficulty in deciding what is or is not a life assurance policy, the case of *Fuji Finance Inc v Aetna Life Assurance Co Ltd*[1] investigated in detail an example of one of the contracts set out below under 'Investment bonds'[2]. On appeal, counsel for Aetna argued that a contract, which whilst described as a life assurance policy offered no more on surrender (after the first five years) than it did on the death of the life assured, and which in many respects closely resembled a pure investment contract, was nevertheless a life assurance policy and as there was no insurable interest[3] it was null and void. Counsel for Fuji argued that it was not a life assurance policy and so was not affected by the Life Assurance Act 1774 (LAA 1774) (which contains the requirements relating to insurable interest). Furthermore the effect of the Insurance Companies Act 1982 (ICA 1982), s 16[4], was not to avoid such contracts but to provide a means for intervention by the Secretary of State for Trade and Industry. The Department of Trade and Industry were also represented at the appeal and, for their part, stated that they recognised such contracts as life assurance policies.

1 [1997] Ch 173, [1997] 1 WLR 482, [1996] 4 All ER 608, (1997) CLC 14; Times, July 15, CA.
2 See para **4.10**.
3 See paras **4.17–4.25**.
4 See now *FCA and PRA Handbooks*, INSPRU 1.5.13R.

4.4   It was unanimously held that the policy in question was a policy of life insurance. The fact that no greater amount was payable on surrender than on death was not sufficient to prevent the contract being recognised as a policy of life insurance. The important point was that the events on which payment would be made were sufficiently life or death related. As it was a life assurance contract the fact that there was no insurable interest rendered the contract 'null and void' and so the appeal was allowed. Therefore there was no need to consider the ICA 1982, s 16 point (whether the policy was unenforceable as a result of the application of this section). However, opinions were expressed. Morritt LJ said it was not unenforceable. Sir Ralph Gibson said it was unenforceable and Hobhouse LJ declined to express a view except to say that legislation was required. This aspect of the decision is therefore disappointing as the uncertainty currently remains. Leave to appeal to the House of Lords was granted but the case was settled beforehand.

Types of life assurance

Whole of life

4.5   Payment of the sum assured occurs on death whenever that occurs. Alternatively, the policy may be surrendered prior to death for the surrender value (if a surrender value has been acquired). Indeed, single premium investment bonds[1] are designed as medium to long-term investment products. In most cases, with regular premium policies, especially in the early years, the surrender value will often be considerably less than the total premiums paid.

1 See paras **4.10–4.11**.

4.6   The purpose of non-investment based whole of life policies is to provide a substantial sum on death whenever that occurs, for example to provide for a spouse and/or family who could otherwise face financial difficulties; or to provide a sum to pay inheritance tax (IHT) in respect of the deceased's estate; or to provide a sum to enable business associates to purchase the deceased's interest in the business; or to enable a company to protect itself against the loss of a key employee ('key man' assurance). Indeed, in any situation where a substantial lump sum is required on death. Such policies are broadly known as 'protection' policies as are 'temporary' (or 'term') policies as referred to below.

Temporary (or term)

4.7   As the name suggests cover only lasts for a limited time. If death occurs during that time then the sum assured will be payable. There are no amounts payable in any other circumstances, eg on surrender, or on death outside the term of the policy. This is generally the cheapest type of life assurance available. Some term assurance policies contain an option to convert into other types of policies. Some may be combined with other benefits such as critical illness benefit.

4.8   Term assurance is suitable where a substantial sum of money may be required as a result of death during a given time period, for example, on the death of the borrower before repayment of the amount of an out-standing loan. Another purpose is to cover death before retirement where the loss of an earner's income prior to retirement (when his pension would otherwise commence) could leave his family in financial difficul-ties. Temporary assurances can also be suitable in connection with gifts, and more specifically, potentially exempt transfers for IHT purposes. IHT can be due in respect of lifetime gifts or transfers if death occurs within seven years. A variant of such a policy would be what is known as a 'decreasing term assurance' where the sum assured gradually decreases over the term.

Endowment assurance

4.9   This type of policy provides cover during the term of the policy but, unlike temporary assurances, also provides a payment at the end of the term and a surrender value after the early period of the policy. Gener-ally this is the most expensive form of life assurance. Endowment policies used to be commonly used in connection with house purchase as a means of repaying the sum borrowed at the end of the term whilst also providing life cover equal to the outstanding amount of the loan during the term. Endowment assurances are also used as pure savings vehicles with the amount of life cover being quite small but the minimum necessary for 'qualification' purposes[1]. Endowment assurances for mortgage repay-ment purposes were the subject of considerable regulatory attention as a result of concern at amounts payable on maturity not being sufficient to repay borrowings. There have been some high profile enforcement actions undertaken by the FSA in connection with endowment mortgage missel-ling.

1 See paras **4.52–4.58**.

Investment bonds

4.10   These are whole of life policies (see para **4.5** above) but because of their purpose, specific consideration is merited. These policies are designed purely for investment purposes with the amount of life cover generally being minimal – often an additional one per cent of the surren-der value. In some cases the amount of life cover is no more than the ongo-ing investment value of the bond. In this respect the case of *Fuji Finance Inc v Aetna Life Assurance Co Ltd*[1] is important. At first instance doubt was cast on the validity of life assurance policies with no life cover in excess of the ongoing investment value.

1 [1997] Ch 173, CA.

4.11   The premium for such policies is invariably a single premium which is invested in one or more of the life office's range of unit-linked investment funds or in its with profits fund. Recent years have seen the proliferation of external fund links through a variety of routes so it is increasingly common to effect a policy with a life office where the underlying fund is managed by an otherwise unconnected fund manager, for example, to a collective investment scheme or, via a reassurance agreement, to a fund managed by another life office. The policy is usually issued as a series of identical policies known as 'segments'. This can have taxation advantages.

Contractual issues

4.12   A life assurance policy is merely one species of contract and the normal contract law rules are applicable. There are, however, certain idiosyncrasies in addition to a range of legislative and common law provisions which are applicable to contracts of life assurance. Life assurance contracts have posed interesting questions in the areas of offer and acceptance. In *Canning v Farquhar*[1] it was made clear that the so-called 'letter of acceptance' from a life office did not necessarily constitute acceptance in terms of contract law. Generally, in modern life assurance contracts the proposer makes an offer by submitting the proposal with the premium which is usually by direct debit instruction for regular premium contracts or a cheque for single premium policies. The life office (if prepared to do so) then accepts and in practice communicates acceptance of this offer by issuing the policy (although it may communicate acceptance separately). However, each case needs to be judged on its own facts and the wording of the proposal/application form is of course crucial. Some offices offer guaranteed acceptance where the proposal/application form will be an acceptance of the life office's offer on the terms set out.

1 (1886) 16 QBD 727.

The proposal form

4.13   Although not technically a requirement a prospective policyholder will generally initiate the application process by completing a proposal form supplied by the life office. If the policy in question offers a significant element of life cover it is usual for a range of questions to be asked to assist in underwriting. These questions will deal with such issues as age, medical history and certain lifestyle questions, and information as to previous applications for life assurance. Gender is no longer relevant following the *Test Achats* case (see below) The proposal form is also likely to contain authority to obtain information from any doctor who has treated the proposer. This area is governed by the Access to Medical Reports Act 1988. If the prospective policyholder consents the life office may have access to a medical report on the individual. The individual in question may request sight of the medical report before it is sent to the life office in which case the life office must inform the doctor of that request. On receiving the application the doctor may release the report to the life office either once the individual has had access to it or after 21 days from making the application in the absence of the individual having contacted the doctor. The individual can request amendments to it if he thinks parts are misleading or untrue. If he wishes to see the report before it is passed to the life office the doctor may delete any part of it which he believes would be likely to cause serious harm to his physical or mental health.

It is no longer permissible to differentiate between male and female applicants in terms of premium levels or benefits under insurance policies following the European Court of Justice case ('Test Achats'[1])

1   *Association Belge des Consommateurs Test Achats and Others* (C-236/09), 1 March, 2011.

4.14   Prior to the enactment of the Consumer Insurance (Disclosure and Representations) Act, 2012, ('CIDA') the consequences of failure to disclose all 'material facts' could have been the avoidance of the policy from the start even if no specific question about the material fact had been asked on the application form. CIDA abolishes the residual duty of disclosure (which has led to clearer but longer application forms as the insurer needs to ask specific questions on all the matters in relation to which it will make its assessment). There is also categorization of non-disclosure or misrepresentation so that there is a proportionate remedy or approach available to the insurer depending on the type of non-disclosure/misrepresentation. If the insured has behaved honestly and reasonably the insurer will have no right to refuse a claim. If the misrepresentation is careless a new concept of proportionality is introduced so that the insurer is placed in the position it would have been in had it known the true facts. So if the insurer would have charged a higher premium the claim would be reduced proportionately to the under-payment of premium. Only if the customer has effectively acted dishonestly (by making a deliberate or reckless misrepresentation) will the insurer be entitled to avoid the policy.

The proposal form or a supporting document should also include a statement that a copy of the completed proposal form and the policy conditions is available on request.

4.15   It is also possible that proof of identity, in accordance with the Money Laundering Regulations 2007[1], may be requested in the proposal form. Permissions for the processing of data and possibly also for future marketing exercises for Data Protection Act 1998 purposes, may also be included.

1   SI 2007/2157.

4.16   For proposals on the life of someone other than the proposer ('life of another' cases) the underwriting questions are normally answered by the life to be assured who, it should be noted, is not a party to the contract. The proposer would generally be required to declare that the answers are correct to the best of his knowledge and belief. The signature of agents, such as attorneys, in respect of medical questions would not normally be satisfactory to life offices as they would not have the personal medical or other knowledge possessed by the applicant. In many circumstances (eg 'off-the-page' advertisements for policies with modest sums assured) simplified proposal forms are used which require few or possibly no medical questions.

Insurable interest

4.17   As the term implies this is a concept limited to insurance contracts. It became a focus of attention in the life assurance industry as a result of the *Fuji Finance Inc v Aetna Life Assurance Co Ltd*[1] case[2]. Unfortunately, the governing legislation in this area is over 200 years old. The LAA 1774 was introduced in order to bring an end to gambling on the lives of public figures. The LAA 1774 provides that no life insurance shall be made unless the person effecting the insurance has an interest in the life to be assured and any life insurance made without such interest shall be 'null and void' and no greater sum shall be recovered than the amount or value of the interest of the assured. Also, the name of the person(s) interested should be inserted in the policy.

1 [1997] Ch 173, CA.
2 See also para **4.10**.

4.18   Insurable interest need only exist at the outset of the policy and the fact that insurable interest ceases before the time of the claim is not relevant[1]. The requirement for insurable interest can also be defeated (in a sense) by assignment of the policy.

1 *Dalby v India and London Life Assurance Co* (1854) 15 CB 365.

4.19   Apart from insurances made by a person on their own life or on the life of a husband or wife, where insurable interest is presumed, the insurable interest must be a pecuniary interest, capable of valuation in money and must be based on an obligation or liability which will, or will be likely to result from the death, or the loss or diminution of any property right which would be recognised at law or equity. A moral obligation or an expectation, for example, the prospect of benefiting under a will, is not sufficient.

4.20   The LAA 1774, s 3 provides that no greater sum shall be recovered from the insurer than the amount or value of the assured's interest. The sum assured at the outset must be supported by an insurable interest of an equivalent amount. Apart from those cases set out above, examples of insurable interest which have been recognised include a creditor on the life of a debtor (to the extent of the debt and accrued interest); employer and employee in each other's lives (where the employer is an individual) to the extent of the value of services to be performed (in the case of an employee's life), or the remuneration for the agreed period of service for fixed term contracts, or notice period in other cases (in the case of an employer's life where the employer is an individual). However, in practice more extensive sums assured are accepted[1]. Other examples are pension scheme trustees on the life of a member (where the member has an enforceable right to death benefits).

1 See para **4.21** with regard to 'key man' policies.

4.21   In other situations the position may not be so clear although in practice the proposal is often accepted. In 'key man' cases a policy is effected by a company or partnership on the life of a director/partner/ manager etc on the basis that the loss of the key man's special services would involve the business in reduced profits and the expense of finding a suitable successor. There must be some doubt in many cases about whether there is technically any insurable interest as there is not necessarily any pecuniary loss, merely an expectation of loss. Nevertheless, this possible objection has not been taken by, for example, Her Majesty's Revenue and Customs who permit the premium payments under a key man policy to be deducted as a business expense for corporation tax purposes.

4.22   In the case of co-directors and co-partners again there is no automatic insurable interest. In some cases the articles of association or partnership deed or other agreement will require the purchase of the deceased's shares or interest and this can form the basis for an insurable interest. Even in cases where there is no certainty that pecuniary loss would result, in practice many life offices seem to be happy to issue such policies.

4.23   Trustees of a trust or settlement do not necessarily have an insurable interest in the lives of beneficiaries. However, there are many possible exceptions in theory or practice to this generally accepted position. In view of the fact that the purpose of the LAA 1774 was to prevent 'a mischievous kind of gaming' then it seems inappropriate that this should prevent trustees effecting policies on the lives of beneficiaries when those persons will be those who are ultimately likely to benefit (and in most cases the policy in question will be an investment orientated one with limited life cover or no life cover in addition to the investment value). In some cases inheritance tax (IHT) will be payable on the death of a beneficiary who has an interest in possession under the trust. As the trustees would be accountable for any tax payable in respect of that interest in possession then they may effect a policy for the probable amount of tax payable. Also, trustees would have an insurable interest in the life of the settlor during the seven years after the gift where this would be a potentially exempt transfer for IHT purposes.

Parents and children do not, as such, have an insurable interest in each others' lives.

4.24   What is the position where insurable interest does not exist? There is a general consensus that the LAA 1774 is in many respects unnecessary today. Furthermore, many observers view it as a hindrance to the modern commercial transaction of life assurance business. It would be extremely unlikely that if the LAA 1774 were repealed life offices would be prepared to issue 'gaming' contracts.

The Law Commission undertook a review of Insurance Contract Law which covered insurable interest. It reported on 2 January, 2008, tentatively proposing liberalisation in this area which to date has not been progressed.

4.25   The LAA 1774 does not prescribe penalties for infringement. Policies which infringe the LAA 1774 are technically 'null and void' although for life offices it would rarely make sound business sense to raise the lack of insurable interest in refusing to make payment out under such a policy.

In many cases life offices are prepared to issue policies where it is clear that no insurable interest exists. In doing so life offices should be aware of the provisions of INSPRU 1.5.13 R of the *FCA Handbook* as contravention of the LAA 1774 (especially on a deliberate and systematic basis) may not constitute insurance business. Also, questions could arise regarding the taxation treatment of such business.

Non-disclosure and misrepresentation

4.26   Unlike other forms of contract the contract of insurance is subject to the principle of 'uberrimae fides' or 'utmost good faith'. The facts on which the risk is to be computed generally lie exclusively in the knowledge of the person proposing. The insurance company must trust the proposer's representations and proceed on the basis that he does not keep back any relevant circumstances in his knowledge or mislead the insurance company. However, this long-held principle has been severely eroded by the Consumer Insurance (Disclosure and Representations) Act, 2013 ('CIDA')

4.27   Prior to CIDA the position was that in order to satisfy the duty of disclosure the proposer must voluntarily disclose, without misrepresentation, all material facts known to him or which the proposer ought to have known if he had made reasonable enquiries[1].

1 *Rozanes v Bowen* (1928) 32 Ll L Rep 98.

4.28   The position now is that the insurance company must now ask the specific questions it requires answers to in order to reach its decision. There is no longer a general duty on an applicant to disclose any other 'material facts'. This has been replaced by a duty to take reasonable care not to make a misrepresentation (section 2(2)). Therefore, the applicant is no longer required to volunteer information but only to respond honestly and with reasonable care to questions asked. Prior to CIDA the proposer could not withhold material information merely because no specific question on the point is asked on the proposal form or in the medical examination, although in practice this had been eroded by statements of practice issued by the Association of British Insurers (ABI).

4.29   The duty to disclose extends beyond the time of proposal up until the time the contract is binding on both parties. There is generally a provision in the proposal/application form that the insurer will not become bound until receipt of the first premium, and the inclusion of a provision that the information supplied is still accurate at the time the policy is issued.

4.30   Section 4 of CIDA retains the concept of inducement. Therefore the policy is not automatically rendered void. In order to avoid a contract in these circumstances the life office must show that it has been induced by the non-disclosure to enter into the contract[1]. It must also show that a reasonable customer would not have made the representation

1 *Pan Atlantic Insurance Co Ltd v Pine Top Insurance Co Ltd* [1995] 1 AC 501, HL; *Narinder Pal Kaur Mundi v Lincoln Assurance Ltd* (2005) Ch D (LTL 1/12/05).

4.31   If the life office avoids the contract then it is set aside from the outset and not merely for the future. Therefore the office would be able to recover any sums paid out (as a mistake of fact). Similarly, any premiums paid would be returnable unless there has been wilful or fraudulent non-disclosure. But if premiums continue to be accepted with full knowledge of the actual facts the life office cannot afterwards repudiate liability on the grounds of non-disclosure[1]. The duty of good faith also requires the insurer to be accurate in its representations.

1 See *Joel v Law Union and Crown Insurance Co* [1908] 2 KB 863.

4.32   Knowledge gained by the life office concerning the policyholder may be imputed to the life office in respect of other policies effected by the proposer, although the precise circumstances are important. Therefore imputed knowledge may not arise unless the information is received by a person authorised and able to appreciate its significance[1].

A breach of the duty of disclosure may in extreme circumstances amount to fraudulent misrepresentation.

1 See *Malhi v Abbey Life Assurance Co Ltd* [1996] LRLR 237, CA.

Policy document

4.33   Although in theory it may not be necessary for a policy document to be issued, in practice some form of policy documentation is almost always issued setting out the main terms and conditions of the contract between the insurance company and the policyholder.

4.34   A life policy is generally issued under hand, as a 'simple' contract, although it may on occasions be issued as a deed and thus be a 'specialty contract'. The policy must be executed in accordance with the constitution or regulations of the life office. The current practice is to provide a standard universal printed set of terms with a schedule containing the terms which are of specific application, such as the policy number, the name of the insured and the life assured, the nature and amount of the benefit, when and to whom payable, the amount(s) of premium and when payable. The conditions and benefits of the policy usually form part of the standard printed terms and would include, for example, provision as to payments of claims, days of grace for payment of premiums, protection against forfeiture, details of how surrenders and conversions may be effected and the options available under the policy, details of charges and, for unit-linked policies, provisions as to the calculation of fund prices. Provisions relating to amendment of policy terms may also be included. The Policies of Assurance Act 1867, s 4 requires the policy to specify the principal place(s) of business at which notices of assignment may be given.

4.35   The growth of unit-linked life assurance business led to the introduction of 'cluster' or 'segmented' policies. Therefore, the proposer will receive a number of policies of equal value for his premium rather than one single policy often within what is termed an overall 'Plan'. Such policies offer more flexibility and opportunities for tax planning.

4.37   Other statements and documents such as marketing literature, quotations and proposal forms do not normally form part of the contract unless they are incorporated in the contract by reference or otherwise.

Statements in marketing literature would not generally form part of the contractual terms of the policy, although if there is a misrepresentation this may afford grounds for rescission of the contract and return of the premiums. An aggrieved policyholder is likely to have more success in pursuing a claim through the Financial Ombudsman Service which also has the advantage for complainants of being free.

Unfair Contract Terms Directive (UCTD)

4.38   The UCTD[1], which came into force in the UK on 1 July 1995 and now takes effect via the Unfair Terms in Consumer Credit Contracts Regulations 1999, SI 1999/2083, provided something novel in insurance contracts-the requirement of fairness. It may also, in time, help remove the public perception of insurance companies being able to rely upon 'small print' to avoid paying legitimate claims, a perception which may in some part be due to the fact that insurers were able to avoid the effects of the Unfair Contract Terms Act 1977 (UCTA 1977), by means of non-statutory adherence to the ABI Statements of Insurance Practice. Unlike UCTA 1977, which applies only to exemption clauses, the UCTD applies to *all* terms of a contract which are subject to the directive. In 2001 the Financial Services Authority was added to the list of 'qualifying bodies' so that it was able to apply for an injunction to prevent the continued use of an unfair contract term (as defined in regulation 5 of the 1999 regulations)[2]. This function is now undertaken by the Financial Conduct Authority.

1 Council Directive 93/13/EEC.
2 Unfair Terms in Consumer Contracts (Amendment) Regulations 2001, SI 2001/1186.

Exclusions

4.39   The UCTD[1], article 4 (2) (and SI 1999/2083, regulation 6(2)(a)) effectively excludes from the requirement of fairness terms which reflect the main subject matter of the contract or the question of adequacy of the price, in so far as those terms are in plain intelligible language. A recital to the directive also excludes terms in insurance contracts which define or circumscribe the risk. However, the Department of Trade and Industry did not adopt this in the regulations as it considered that it was only one example of the main subject matter exemption.

1 Council Directive 93/13/EEC.

Unfair terms

4.40   The UCTD[1] provides that:

> 'A contractual term which has not been individually negotiated shall be regarded as unfair if, contrary to the requirement of good faith, it causes a significant imbalance in the parties' rights and obligations arising under the contract, to the detriment of the consumer.'

From this it is clear that the directive applies to individual terms (not just to contracts in their entirety) which have not been individually negotiated, in contracts between a seller/supplier and a consumer. The regulations define consumer as a 'natural person who in contracts covered by these regulations, is acting for purposes which are outside his trade, profession or business'. A seller/supplier, conversely, is someone acting in the course of their business. Clearly, insurance companies will be dealing in the course of their business but when is a person dealing as a consumer? It is straightforward in most cases but there are potentially difficult situations.

1 Council Directive 93/13/EEC.

4.41   The UCTD[1] specifically provides that a term shall always be regarded as not having been individually negotiated where it has been drafted in advance and the consumer has therefore not been able to influence its substance. This would appear to apply to almost all insurance contracts where virtually all of the terms will be in a standard printed form and any negotiation will be likely to have been in relation to price (price being excluded from the scope of the directive).

1 Council Directive 93/13/EEC.

4.42   It can be seen from the definition above of 'unfair' that it has three limbs:

(1)   contrary to the requirement of *good faith*;

(2)   the individual term causes *a significant imbalance in the party's rights* and obligations arising under the contract;

(3)   to the *detriment of* the consumer.

The requirement of good faith in contracts is not something with which English lawyers, unlike many European lawyers, are familiar. There is, of course, the overriding obligation of 'utmost good faith' (*uberrimae fides*) in insurance contracts but this has historically been used by insurers against policyholders to avoid contracts for 'non disclosure' (see paras **4.26-4.33** above).

4.43   As the definition of 'unfair' hinges on this requirement of good faith the directive provides in an Annex the following guidance:

'In making an assessment of good faith, particular regard shall be had to:

–   the strength of the bargaining position of the parties;

–   whether the consumer had an inducement to agree to the term;

–   whether the goods or services were sold or supplied to the special order of the consumer; and

–   the extent to which the seller or supplier has *dealt fairly and equitably with the other party whose legitimate interests he has to take into account.*' [emphasis added].

4.44   The essential point, in most cases appears to be fairness in relation to a consumer's legitimate interests. Hence, where a consumer takes out a contract to cover a particular loss, then it is presumably not dealing equitably with the consumer's legitimate interests for the insurer to avoid paying at all, or to pay less than the sum insured, whether as an abuse of stronger bargaining position or a technicality. Conversely, it is arguable, where powers expressed in the contract to be exercisable at the discretion of the insurer have to be exercised in a reasonable manner, that the objectivity of the requirement of reasonableness is indicative of the insurer dealing fairly and equitably with the consumer's legitimate interests, particularly where such powers have been disclosed to the consumer before he became bound by the contract.

4.45   The second limb of the definition of unfair terms appears somewhat superfluous, particularly in insurance contracts where the inequality of bargaining power will almost always exist. The requirement of detriment to the consumer is an uncertain concept, as neither the UCTD[1] nor the regulations (SI 1999/2083) define detriment. The requirement of detriment is familiar in issues of contractual consideration or equitable estoppel, in the sense of a financial loss to the innocent party or arranging affairs in an irrevocable way.

1 Council Directive 93/13/EEC.

Relevance to life contracts

4.46   Clauses in life contracts that might be caught are as follows.

(1)   Terms excluding liability – limitation clauses or exemption clauses not related to the nature of the risk (ie not covered by the main subject matter exemption).

(2)   Terms requiring payment of disproportionate amounts for failure to fulfil obligations – early surrender charges and penalties.

(3)   Clauses irrevocably binding the consumer to terms with which he had no real opportunity to become acquainted before the conclusion of the contract. This could apply to all terms of an insurer's standard contract which do not circumscribe the risk. It is arguable where cancellation rights exist and the policyholder receives the policy within that period that the consumer is not then irrevocably bound. In addition the policy terms must be made available to the proposer under the FCA requirements.

(4)   Power of unilateral variation – any power of alteration which is discretionary (subject to some possible exceptions).

(5)   Power to change charges – any terms allowing charges or fees to be increased without allowing the consumer a right to cancel could be caught. However, there is an exemption which permits indexation of charges provided the basis is explicitly described.

(6)   Terms requiring formalities – such as imposing time limits (for example for claims), requirements of notification in a particular form (eg writing) without a valid reason.

The list above is derived from what is known as the 'Grey list' as set out in Schedule 2 to the regulations.

Clear disclosure

4.47   With regard to proposed changes or variations to the contract if there is a valid reason for the change which is expressly set out in the contract then the likelihood of the clause being held to be unfair is considerably reduced. Customers should also be given reasonable notice. If there is a valid reason which is not set out in the contract then if the proposed change is disclosed to the consumer at the earliest opportunity and the consumer has the right to dissolve the contract when they are notified of a change, then the term will generally be fair. This is coupled with and to a certain extent exemplified by the requirement in the UCTD[1] that all written terms be drafted in *plain, intelligible language*. Where there is doubt about the meaning of a term, the interpretation most favourable to the consumer shall prevail. The requirement of plain, intelligible language has an added importance regarding terms dealing with the main subject matter of the contract, as this is a condition of the exemption.

1 Council Directive 93/13/EEC.

4.48   The European aspect of this should also be noted. If a policy-holder is resident in another member state and the law of that country applies then, unless a choice of law is available in that country, the requirement may be that the policy be in the language of that country. It should also be noted that member states are required by the UCTD[1] to ensure that if the consumer has a close connection with the territory of a member state, he does not lose the protection granted by the directive by virtue of a choice of law of a non-member state as the law applicable to the contract. However, there is an inference from this wording that where a choice of law is permitted in a member state, the insurer can insert a choice of law clause of another EU member state (namely the UK) and thereby ensure that 'plain intelligible language' means English, although this could be subject to the Consolidated Life Directive[2] domestic public policy requirements stipulating that the contract, or parts of it, be written in an official language of the host state.

1 Council Directive 93/13/EEC.
2 'Directive Concerning Life Assurance' 2002/83/EC).

Burden of proof

4.49   The burden of proof that a term has been individually negotiated is on the seller/supplier (ie the insurer) and a term shall always be regarded as not individually negotiated where it has been drafted in advance.

Effect

4.50   As the UCTD[1] applies to contracts made after 1 July 1995 insurers should have reviewed their contractual documents to ensure that they comply with the terms of the directive and, in particular, the requirement for plain intelligible language. The emphasis in sales literature should therefore be to produce an understanding of the contract concerned in a manner which is intelligible to the consumer when he/she is deciding whether or not to enter into the contract. The Consumer Rights Bill (2013) is proposing to consolidate the regulations with the Unfair Contract Terms Act, 1977, and to provide greater clarity about which types of contract terms can be assessed for fairness.

1 Council Directive 93/13/EEC.

Early cancellation of policies

4.51 The cancellation rules give investors the opportunity to make considered and well informed investment decisions. The cancellation provisions are set out in Chapter 15 of the Conduct of Business Sourcebook issued under the Financial Services and Markets Act 2000 (FSMA 2000), and generally provide (where applicable) for at least 14 days in which to cancel.

Concept of 'qualification'

4.52 The concept of qualification is important for income tax purposes. The definition of a qualifying policy is complex but, broadly, the policy must be on the policyholder's or his or her spouse's life and it must secure a capital sum on death, earlier disability or on the expiry of at least ten years after the policy is taken out.

4.53 The premiums must be reasonably even and paid at yearly or shorter intervals. There are additional requirements relating to the amount of the sum assured and sometimes also as to the surrender value. Providing these conditions are satisfied the policy proceeds are tax free (although the underlying fund will be subject to tax). However, where a qualifying policy is surrendered less than ten years after it was effected (or, for endowment policies, before the expiry of three quarters of the term if that is less than ten years) any profit is charged to tax at the excess of higher rate tax over basic rate to the extent that the profit falls within the tax payer's higher rate income tax band (but see later with regard to 'top slicing relief'). There will be no tax liability at the higher rate if the proceeds are no greater than the premiums paid, because there has been no profit.

4.54 For non-qualifying policies the proceeds are not wholly tax free. Whilst free of Capital Gains Tax (CGT), if the capital appreciation on realisation is such as to put the individual within the higher rate tax band when added to income in the tax year in which the chargeable event occurs, it is chargeable to income tax at the excess of higher rate tax over basic rate, subject to certain special provisions.

4.55 'Top slicing relief' is available to lessen the impact of the higher rate charge. The gain on the policy is divided by the number of complete policy years the policy has been held and the amount arrived at is treated as the top slice of income to ascertain the tax rate which is then applied to the full gain. The longer the policy has been held the smaller the annual equivalent on which the tax charge is based.

4.56 Switching between the underlying funds to which a life assurance policy benefits are referable, for example from an equity fund to a gilt fund, will not have any taxation effects, although there may be an administration charge for doing this.

4.57 Non-qualifying policies often take the form of single premium investment bonds. It is possible to make withdrawals of not more than five per cent of the initial investment in each policy year without attracting a tax liability at the time, such withdrawals being treated as partial surrenders which are only taken into account in calculating the final profit on the bond when it is encashed[1]. The five per cent is a cumulative figure and amounts unused in any year increase the 'tax-free' withdrawal available in a later year. If more than five per cent is withdrawn tax will be charged on the excess but only if (taking this withdrawal into account) the policyholder's taxable income exceeds the basic rate limit, so that if the excess occurs in a year when the taxpayer is solely a basic rate taxpayer no charge will normally arise. Similarly, if final encashment of the bond can be delayed to a time (perhaps in retirement) when the taxpayer's income, even with the addition of the policy profit, will not attract the higher rate no tax will normally be payable. Where the bond is encashed on death any mortality element of the profit as distinct from the surplus on the underlying investments is not taxable and since the income in the year of death will usually not cover a full tax year, even on the taxable portion there may be little tax liability at the higher rate.

1 Income and Corporation Taxes Act 1988, s 546.

4.58 Encashment of the bond or an earlier chargeable event may affect entitlement to age related allowances even where the taxpayer does not pay tax at the higher rate. A new annual premium limit of £3,600 for qualifying life insurance policies took effect from 6 April 2014.

Trusts and uses of life assurance

4.59 In broad terms life assurance is used either for protection or investment purposes (or a combination of these). The former can generally be facilitated by the use of trusts. The subject of trusts is dealt with in depth in the standard works and in relation specifically to life assurance in the *Law of Life Assurance*[1]. One of the better definitions of a trust is given by the Inland Revenue in its 1991 Consultative Document. This is as follows:

> 'A Trust is a legal obligation which binds a trustee (or trustees) to deal with property or income in a particular way, usually for the benefit of another person or class of persons (the beneficiaries). The person who provided the original funds for the trust (the settlor) may also be a trustee or beneficiary'.

The reason why trusts are so important with regard to 'protection' life policies is easily demonstrated by considering what would happen if, for example, a life policy with a sum assured of £425,000 is effected. If that policy is merely left to be dealt with in accordance with the policyholder's estate then, unless for example a surviving spouse benefits from the proceeds, there will be an Inheritance Tax (IHT) charge of £40,000 in respect of these proceeds alone, ignoring any other assets which may be contained in his estate. Had this policy been written subject to a suitable trust this charge would have been avoided. The fact that policy monies are payable outside of the taxable estate on death can also be used to provide a convenient fund to pay any IHT which does become due on the death of the testator so that assets (for example, the home) do not have to be sold in order to pay the tax.

1 *Houseman's Law of Life Assurance* (14th edn, 2011).

4.60   Apart from taxation mitigation trusts are used as an alternative to wills or intestacy in the devolution of assets. Moreover, unlike wills, trusts can become effective during lifetime as well as on death.

4.61   Effecting policies in trust also has an advantage over wills in that provided there is a surviving trustee then on the death of the life assured the trustees can claim the proceeds immediately from the life office on production of the death certificate. If the policy had not been written in trust (or there are no surviving trustees) the beneficiaries of the estate would have to wait until a grant of probate (where a valid will has been left) or letters of administration (where there is no valid will) have been obtained.

4.62   In appropriate circumstances trusts can also be used for the purpose of creditor protection. In these circumstances it will be necessary to satisfy the provisions of the Insolvency Act 1986. It should be noted that there are particular provisions with regard to life policies effected in trust for spouses and/or children under the Married Women's Property Act 1882, so that even if fraud can be proven with regard to placing the policy in trust, the most that can be claimed back is the amount of premiums paid.

4.63   Trusts are also frequently used in connection with business assurance arrangements. Directors or partners effect policies in trust for their co-directors or co-partners so that on death the surviving directors or partners have a fund from which they can purchase the deceased's interest in the company or firm. There will often be an agreement to buy and sell shares, and it is generally advantageous that this be drafted on an 'option' basis for IHT business relief purposes. The issues and planning in this area can be very complex.

Financial Services Compensation Scheme

4.64   The Policyholders Protection Act ('PPA') 1975 was introduced largely as a response to a number of insurance company failures. The PPA 1975 introduced a compensation scheme to assist policyholders of an insurance company which has been wound up. The scheme was administered by the Policyholders Protection Board.

4.65   FSMA 2000 provided for the new Financial Services Compensation Scheme (FSCS), one of the objects of which was to merge all the existing compensation schemes which existed with regard to retail investments and provide a single point of contact for consumers in the event of a firm being unable to pay claims against it. However, merger did not necessarily mean harmonisation of levels of cover. Indeed, priority was stated to be maintaining the levels of consumer protection offered by the existing schemes and only change arrangements where believed to be clearly justifiable.

The functions under FSMA 2000, Pt XV are undertaken by the Financial Services Compensation Scheme Limited (FSCS Limited), a company limited by guarantee which acts as the scheme manager and was appointed by the FSA for this purpose. It is independent of the regulator (now FCA or Prudential Regulation Authority (PRA)) but accountable to it.

FSMA 2000 sets out the required constitution and essential provisions of the scheme and provides for the FCA or PRA to be able to make rules relating to the scheme and also provides for the scheme manager to be able to impose levies. FSMA 2000, ss 216 and 217 relate to the continuity of long-term policies and the provisions relating to insurers in financial difficulties respectively.

4.66   Chapter 3 of the COMP Rules contains key provisions for life assurance companies. When an authorised insurer which provides long-term insurance cover is declared in default, FSCS Limited must try to arrange to continue cover with another insurer if this is more cost effective than paying compensation. 'Financial difficulties' encompasses provisional liquidation; inability to pay debts under formal insolvency proceedings or an application has been made to court to secure a voluntary creditors arrangement, but the firm is not yet in liquidation or being wound up. Chapter 3 also sets out the qualifying conditions for paying compensation which are explained more fully in following chapters.

Eligibility to claim compensation is set out in the COMP Rules, Chapter 4. Protection offered by the scheme is aimed at ordinary retail consumers. The provisions work on the basis that all persons are eligible to claim and then sets out a table of exclusions. Essentially, all long-term policyholders will continue to be protected (even if they are large companies) unless they are connected with the insurance company in some way.

The claim must also be a 'protected claim' which is defined in the COMP Rules, Chapter 5. One of these can be in respect of a 'protected contract of insurance' (which includes pension contracts etc). The establishment of the relevant person in default must be in the UK, another EEA state, the Channel Islands or the Isle of Man. The commitment (the person covered) must also be habitually resident in one of these territories at the time the policy is entered into.

4.67   The 'relevant person' (such as a life assurance company as an 'authorised firm') must be in default in order for claims to be made against it. Also described in this chapter are the circumstances in which a relevant person is in default. Examples include insolvency or bankruptcy. If compensation is offered the claimant may be required to transfer to FSCS Limited his rights to claim against other parties. The reasoning behind this is to maximise recoveries by FSCS Limited and prevents the affected consumer from taking action against the party/parties in default. Offers may be withdrawn if disputed or not accepted within 90 days. Offers may be re-issued or varied. The COMP Rules, Chapter 9 sets out time limits for payment of compensation. The limits on the amount of compensation payable for long-term insurance contracts remain as they were under the PPA

1975, namely at least 90% of the value of the policy, including future benefits declared before the date of default. Unlike bank and building society deposits and retail investments such as unit trusts there is no maximum payment. Payments in respect of life policies are to be made directly to the claimant or on his instructions. Partial payments or payments on account are also permitted where there may be some uncertainty about paying the full amount. Interest may also be payable on compensation payments at the discretion of FSCS Limited.

Guaranteed products

4.68   In the aftermath of stock market falls in 2001 and 2002 many life offices began to offer 'Guaranteed products'. In most cases this was a type of single premium investment bond although there are also guaranteed unit trusts, open ended investment companies (OEICS) and ISAs. The products in their various forms tended for marketing purposes to be aimed at building society investors and persons who (while still nervous of the stock market) would still like some exposure to equities.

4.69   Guaranteed products generally guaranteed a return based on the value of the FTSE 100 or other stock market index. At the same time, the product offered a minimum cash guarantee or other limitation to the potential downside. As stock market indices do not generally allow for the reinvestment of dividends in their day-to-day price the dividend income is effectively forfeited and generally used to meet the cost of the guarantee, expenses and profit margin of the life office.

4.70   At maturity (usually five years) the investor received an amount either based on the pre-agreed index element of the investment or some fixed, guaranteed, sum. Death benefit is usually stated to be a value no less than the original investment. Surrender values were not, however, usually guaranteed and may well be substantially lower than the original value.

4.71   For the taxation treatment of such products where these are insurance bonds (which are 'non-qualifying' policies) this is described above with regard to 'qualification'[1]. Where the guaranteed product is based on a unit trust vehicle or OEICS any gains on encashment from the unit trust (or OEICS) would be treated as capital gains and are liable to Capital Gains Tax (CGT).

1 See paras **4.52–4.58**.

4.72   In order to provide the guarantee the product generally combined an equity investment and what is known as a 'put option' with an exercise price equal to the guaranteed amount. A put option gives the purchaser the right to sell the underlying asset in question at a predetermined price. This underlying asset can be any of a wide variety of assets, and for the purpose of guaranteed products is likely to be stock indices. The product provider therefore backs his liabilities by buying a combination of suitable assets and tailored 'over the counter' options from an investment bank.

4.73   The FSA took a particular interest in the marketing of these products which are usually highly complex[1]. This culminated in some high profile fines, for example in 2011 the FSA fined Credit Suisse (UK) Limited £5.95 million for systems and controls failings in relation to sales by its private bank of such structured capital at risk products (SCARPs). SCARPs provide an agreed enhanced level of income to customers over a specified period, but also expose them to the potential loss of part or, under certain conditions, all of the initial capital invested.

Credit Suisse UK failed to:

- Have in place adequate systems and controls in relation to assessing customers' attitudes to risk.

- Take reasonable care to adequately evidence that the SCARPs it recommended to customers were suitable, given the assets and investments held by those customers at the time.

- Have in place adequate systems and controls surrounding the recommendation of leverage to customers.

- Have in place adequate systems and controls surrounding the levels of issuer and investment concentration within customers' portfolios.

- Monitor effectively its staff to ensure that they took reasonable care to ensure that the advice given to customers was suitable.

As a result of these failings, Credit Suisse UK's customers were exposed to an unacceptable risk of being sold a SCARP that was unsuitable for them.

1 See for example 'The FSA's regulatory approach to financial promotions' (April, 2002).

INDIVIDUAL SAVINGS ACCOUNTS (ISAS)

4.74   ISAs are designed for investment or savings purposes and have favourable tax treatment. They are not 'stand-alone' in that they will always have an underlying investment such as stocks and shares, OEICS, unit trusts, bank accounts etc. Anyone over the age of 18 and resident in the UK for tax purposes can take out an ISA. Crown employees working overseas and their spouses are deemed to be resident for this purpose. If a plan holder subsequently becomes non-resident, the plan can be maintained and its tax benefits preserved but no further subscriptions can be made in respect of that plan. Many restrictions were significantly relaxed from June 2014 when the New ISA ('NISA') name was introduced

4.75   The tax benefits take the form of total exemption from CGT and income tax on realised capital gains and investment income earned from the underlying investments of the plan. A plan can be terminated at any time and the proceeds withdrawn without loss of the tax benefits. An additional benefit is reduced or zero paperwork as a result of no reporting of income or capital gains.

4.76   There are two types of plan. 'Stocks and shares' or 'cash' (insurance was removed as a separate type of plan as from 6 April 2005 but can still be part of a stocks and shares ISA)[1].

1 ISA (Amendment No 2) Regulations 2004, SI 2004/2996.

4.77   There is no restriction on the investment switches that can be made and no income tax or CGT liability arises as a result. An ISA can be transferred from one account manager to another.

4.78   Prior to 1 July, 2014 the maximum investment into a stocks and shares ISA was £11,520 per tax year and £5,760 into a cash ISA with an overall maximum of £11,520. From 1 July 2014, the maximum overall investment is £15,000 with no additional separate limits for cash or stocks and shares ISAs. An ISA can only ever be an individual investment and so it would not be possible to have a joint ISA. It is not possible to use an ISA as security for a loan.

4.79   Tax relief is not available for investment into the ISA, as it is with pensions. However, the fund is virtually a gross fund in the same way as a pension fund. With ISAs all proceeds are tax free whereas at least part of what emerges from a pension scheme will be taxable. The Individual Savings Account Regulations 1998[1], regs 6–9 (the ISA Regulations 1998) prescribe what ISA subscriptions may be invested in.

1 SI 1998/1870 (as amended).

4.80   Each plan must be managed by an account manager authorised under the FSMA 2000, or approved in some other way as set out in the ISA Regulations 1998[1], reg 14 and approved by HM Revenue and Customs (HMRC). The ISA agreement or terms and conditions will contain various provisions concerning the conduct of the investor's investment, for example, arranging for the investor to receive copies of the reports and accounts of the companies in which he is invested. All records, dealing and other paperwork is the responsibility of the account manager whose function it is to deal with HMRC on behalf of the investor. Also likely to be included in these terms will be provisions relating to charges and to termination of the plan.

1 SI 1998/1870 (as amended).

4.81   The fundamental governing regulations for the operation of ISAs are the ISA Regulations 1998[1], which have been amended on various occasions. Junior ISAs were introduced on 1 November, 2011 for persons under 18 and replaced child trust funds. The limit was raised on 1 July 2014 to £4000. Unlike an adult ISA a child can only hold a total of one cash ISA and one stocks and shares ISA, including for all money from past years, but transfers of these two accounts can be carried out between providers as for adult accounts, except that transfers from one type of ISA to the other are permitted. An additional adult cash ISA can be held between 16 and 18. In the year in which a child becomes 18 the full adult and child ISA limits can both be used.

Each junior ISA has a person with parental responsibility as a single registered contact. From age 16 a child can register to be their own contact and this registration cannot normally be reversed. Except in that case and adoptive parents registering, the previous registered contact will be contacted to obtain their consent to a change of contact.

1 SI 1998/1870 (as amended).

UNIT TRUSTS

Introduction

4.82   As the name suggests the underlying legal basis for this type of investment is the trust. The investors are the beneficiaries and there will be a trustee appointed (which will be a corporate professional trustee) who will look after the trust assets. Unit trusts are, in the eyes of the investor, recognised more particularly by the manager (in whose name the unit trust will be branded and promoted) who will be responsible for the administration of the trust and for the management of the underlying investments. The constitution, management and marketing of unit trusts and the various rights, duties and obligations of the manager, trustee and investors are governed by the applicable trust deed and the various applicable statutes. In 1988 the responsibility for authorisation for new unit trusts passed from the Department of Trade and Industry to the FSA (now FCA). The regime concerning regulation, establishment and running of unit trusts, is contained in FSMA 2000, ss 235–284.

4.83   The definition of 'collective investment scheme' includes unit trusts (FSMA 2000, s 235). Specific reference to 'unit trust schemes' is contained in FSMA 2000, s 244. Unit trusts are therefore a type of collective investment scheme.

Legal nature

4.84   The underlying unit trust deed, as mentioned, is made between the managers, who are the promoters of the scheme and who are responsible for the conduct of the investment and administration, and the trustee (usually a trustee company subsidiary of a bank or building society), which is responsible for ensuring that the managers act in accordance with the trust deed, and which holds the assets of the trust on behalf of the unit holders (possibly via a custodian). The underlying investments are registered in the name of the trustee or custodian which also holds any cash forming part of the fund. The trustee receives all income and other distributions in respect of those assets, such as dividends in respect of shares.

4.85   The trust deed and regulations also set out a formula for valuing a trust to determine the prices at which units must be bought back by the manager from unit holders and this is subject also to regulation [1]. Additional units may be created to meet demand from investors or existing units may be cancelled as a result of the subsequent repurchase of units from investors. A unit trust is therefore 'open ended' and will expand and contract depending on whether there are more buyers or sellers.

1 See the Collective Investment Schemes Sourcebook (COLL).

4.86   The ability of a unit trust to borrow (known as 'gearing') is limited to 10% of the value of the property of the Scheme[1].

1 See COLL 5.5.5 R of the Collective Investment Schemes Sourcebook.

4.87   Subject to the provisions of relevant regulations the trust deed may make provisions as to termination and also specify circumstances in which the approval of unit holders at a general meeting is required. For example, approval is required in order to vary certain provisions of the trust deed, such as to change the investment objectives or to amalgamate with another unit trust.

Authorisation

4.88   The central requirement for authorisation is that a trust deed conforming with the requirements of FSMA 2000, s 243 is executed between a management company and an independent trust corporation to hold the trust's investments and supervise the managers[1]. Both the managers and the trustee must be both authorised and have the relevant permissions under the FSMA 2000.

1 See COLL 2.1 of the Collective Investment Schemes Sourcebook.

4.89   The directors of the management company must be approved by the FCA. The trust deed would provide for a number of issues, for example:

(1)   managers' investment and borrowing powers and limits on investment of the trust assets;

(2)   the manner in which prices and yields are calculated and provisions as to the repurchase of units from investors;

(3)   setting up the register of unit holders, with procedures for issuing certificates and dealing with transfers;

(4)   managers' and trustees' remuneration;

(5)   periodic audits of the trust and the issue of financial statements to unit holders, with reports by the managers, trustees and auditors;

(6)   classes of units.

See COLL 4.2.6 R for the full table of required contents.

4.90   One of the main consequences of authorisation is that it makes it possible for the managers to advertise units for sale to the public and carries with it certain taxation advantages.

Authorisation under the FSMA 2000, s 243 (unit trusts); FSMA 2000, s 262 (Open-ended Investment Companies ('OEICS')

4.91   In order to be marketed to the general public the provisions of FSMA 2000, ss 243 and 262 as appropriate must be complied with. The general rule (as set out in FSMA 2000, s 238) is that authorised persons must not promote collective investment schemes but this is subject to exceptions in the case of authorised unit trust schemes and a scheme constituted by an authorised open-ended investment company (see **4.115–4.118**). Other exceptions relate to 'recognised' schemes which generally means schemes constituted in other EEA states (FSMA 2000, s 264), schemes authorised in designated countries or territories (FSMA 2000, s 270) and individually recognised overseas schemes (FSMA 2000, s 272). Also, if the communication originates outside of the UK the restriction in FSMA 2000, s 238 only applies if the promotion is capable of having effect in the UK.

Unit trust pricing

4.92   Unit trust managers can deal either on a 'forward price' basis, ie at the next price to be calculated, or at prices already calculated and published, ie an 'historical price' basis. However, there are situations where the company would have to change to forward pricing and the general evolution of the rules in this area is in favour of forward pricing.

Purchase of unit trusts

4.93   Individuals, corporate bodies or trustees may all purchase units subject to any limitation which may be imposed on their own investment powers. Unit trusts were specifically mentioned as 'wider range' investments under the Trustee Investments Act 1961. This has now been replaced by the Trustee Act 2000, which introduced a general wide power of investment which would permit investment in unit trusts for all trusts unless there was (unusually) something prohibiting investment in unit trusts in the trust instrument. Life assurance and pension companies also often invest in unit trusts or OEICS via what is often termed a 'fund-link agreement' in order to give their policyholders access to the funds of other fund managers.

4.94   Most unit trusts specify a minimum investment limit with specialist funds tending to have a higher limit. In many cases monthly savings plans are available. As unit trusts are open ended there is no maximum holding though corporate or trustee investors may be restricted by their own investment limitations.

4.95   Non-UK residents may invest in unit trusts subject to the domestic laws and regulations in their countries of residence or domicile. Many UK managers and OEICS will specifically not deal with foreign residents.

Investments of unit trusts

4.96   Unit trusts must invest their portfolios in accordance with the investment and borrowing powers as set out in COLL 5 of the *Collective Investment Schemes Handbook* which specifically deals with investment and borrowing powers. Managers must also take into account the trust deed and prospectus.

4.97   Most unit trusts invest predominately in equity shares although preference shares, gilts and other fixed interest investments are also held for the purpose of generating a yield.

4.98   Traditional authorised unit trusts generally only invested in securities although newer classes of unit trusts are permitted to invest in other financial instruments, or property, and mixed funds invest in several different types, including commodities. These schemes have certain rules and regulations which apply only to those particular schemes. Unit trusts may make use of traded options (in a prescribed manner) for efficient portfolio management purposes. Any call options written and put options bought must be covered by the relevant securities held in the trust.

4.99 Although all unit trusts will have their own particular objectives in terms of stated investment powers in the trust deed itself, all unit trusts share certain general characteristics.

Spread of risk

4.100 An investor can achieve a much wider spread of risk by purchasing a unit trust, which in turn invests in a wide range of securities, than he could himself achieve economically with limited resources. The risks inherent in holding shares in one company or a small number of companies are therefore avoided. The result, in theory, should be a more even progression of income and capital growth. This is reinforced by regulations regarding the maximum investment of a trust's assets in a single company or issue. In practice, unit trusts usually hold between 30 and 100 different securities which is well in excess of the required minimum of 16.

Professional management

4.101 Investment in a unit trust effectively involves a delegation of the day-to-day management of an investor's portfolio to the unit trust managers. Unit trust management companies seek to maximise the investment returns of the trust(s) for which they are responsible. The advantage to the investor is that his investments are under the continuous supervision of professionals whose business it is to keep under review economic, political and corporate developments.

Simplicity and convenience

4.102 The paperwork involved in owning a portfolio of securities is usually avoided. Decisions relating to rights and scrip issues, mergers and takeovers are all taken by the managers. Dividends are received by the trustee and distributions of the trust income are made to unit holders together with reports on the progress of the trust.

Marketability

4.103 As an open-ended investment units can therefore be created or cancelled to meet the requirements of investors. Unit trusts are therefore a generally very liquid investment with none of the restrictions on marketability encountered with some other types of investment.

Types of unit trusts

4.104 There is a wide range of unit trusts which offer a variety of investment objectives designed to suit different categories of investors. The main types are as follows.

(1)   *Balanced* – investment mainly in 'Blue Chip' shares with the aim of achieving steady growth of both income and capital.

(2)   *Income trusts* – aim is to achieve an above average yield to investors seeking a high and growing income. They may purchase convertible shares as a way of achieving their yield objectives.

(3)   *Capital trusts* – these are designed to seek maximum capital growth and the income produced is likely to be low.

(4)   *Fixed interest trusts* – these generally invest in government bonds, corporate bonds and convertible shares. They may be income or capital trusts.

(5)   *Overseas trusts* – investors have the opportunity to invest through these in stock markets in other countries in the world. The complexity involved in overseas investment for the private investor can be avoided by investment via unit trusts. Overseas investment can be rewarding if sterling is weak or economic conditions are more buoyant in overseas regions.

(6)   *Specialist trusts* – these invest in particular sectors of the securities market (eg commodities, smaller companies or new technology companies). They are inherently more risky than more balanced trusts.

(7)   *Accumulation trusts* – certain trusts within all the above categories are structured on the basis that they will accumulate the income rather than distribute it.

(8)   *'Tracker' trusts* – certain trusts are structured to imitate the performance of a stock market index.

Taxation

4.105   Authorised unit trusts attract the relevant CGT treatment described below[1]. For taxation purposes an authorised unit trust is one which, for any accounting period, is a unit trust scheme that has been authorised under, currently, the FSMA 2000, s 243. By virtue of the Income and Corporation Taxes Act (TA) 1988, s 468, for taxation purposes an authorised unit trust is effectively treated as a company with unit holders being treated in the same way as shareholders in a company, with distributions of income treated in the same way as dividends paid to shareholders. A major advantage for unit holders is that within the unit trust itself there is an exemption from taxation on capital gains by virtue of the Taxation of Chargeable Gains Act 1992, s 99. However, the unit holder would be personally liable for any gains made by him on a disposal of units. The taxation provisions relating to unit trusts were, with certain modifications and exceptions, extended to OEICS under the Open-ended Investment Companies (Tax) Regulations 1997, SI 1997/1154.

1 See para 4.107.

4.106   In common with the taxation position of companies, unit trusts are not taxable on UK dividend income (franked investment income) whether this is paid by a company or another unit trust. All other forms of income are taxable as appropriate under the schedular system.

Capital gains of unit-holders

4.107   Capital gains made on units in authorised unit trusts are treated in the same way as gains made on any other type of security, ie the gain, after allowing for indexation, is added to the taxpayers' income for tax purposes. Currently, capital gains up to £11,000 (for 2014 to 2015) are exempt from tax.

Charges in respect of unit trusts

4.108   Some unit trusts are 'dual priced' (essentially there is a 'bid' (buying) and 'offer' (selling) price). On purchase this initial charge is payable to the managers which is incorporated in the unit price. The trust deed must contain a figure for the maximum permissible charge. Initial charges may be up to 5–6 per cent. More managers are moving to a system of no initial charges ('single priced') but with exit charges on encashment in the early years. Following the implementation of the Retail Distribution Review by the FSA, which came into force on 1 January, 2013, it is no longer permissible for managers to pay commission to advisers where a personal recommendation is made. Instead, advisers will be paid an adviser charge agreed with the client in advance.

4.109   Annual management fees based on the value of the trust are deducted by the managers. Such fees may be taken from the unit trust income or from the capital. The maximum permitted level of annual management fees may only be increased if investors are given 90 days' written notice. Fees charged are usually around 1.00 per cent per annum.

4.110   Certain other costs, for example, custody fees for holding overseas investments and collecting foreign dividends, may be paid out of the scheme property.

Offshore funds

4.111   This is a broad term applied to a range of investment mediums whether it is a unit trust, an investment trust company or an investment oriented life assurance policy which is issued by an insurer outside of the UK, often in a so-called 'tax-haven'. The jurisdictions in which such funds are based are usually those which attract little or no local tax, such as the Channel Islands, Isle of Man, Bahamas, Bermuda, Cayman Islands, British Virgin Islands and Luxembourg. The precise taxation effects depend upon a range of factors, such as residence of the unit trust, investment company or life office, where it invests and the existence, or otherwise, of double taxation treaties.

Offshore funds may or may not be recognised under the FSMA 2000, s 264, 270 or 272.

Advertising unit trusts

4.112   The statutory basis permitting the promotion of authorised unit trust schemes is contained in the FSMA 2000, s 238. The provisions relating to Financial Promotion of Collective Investment Schemes is set out in the Conduct of Business Sourcebook, Chapter 4 (COBS 4).

The UCITS Directives

4.113 The Council of the European Community adopted the Undertakings for Collective Investment in Transferable Securities (UCITS) Directive[1] in December 1985 which concerned the co-ordination of laws, regulations and administrative provisions relating to undertakings for collective investment in transferable securities. The intention behind the UCITS Directive was to harmonise laws in this area throughout the European Community (now the European Union) and to facilitate the cross-border marketing of collective investment schemes which comply with its provisions. In order to qualify as a UCITS certain investment and other limitations must be complied with. The influence of the UCITS Directive in the UK can be seen in the FSA rules (now FCA) and subsequent legislation.

1 Council Directive 85/611/EEC.

4.114 Further Directives[1] have subsequently been adopted. UCITS III enlarges the scope of investment assets available to UCITS funds to include money market instruments, derivatives and units of other schemes, and UCITS II makes changes relevant to the management companies. For example, it introduced the requirement for a 'simplified prospectus' (implemented by the FSA under its rules as set out in Policy Statement 05/4 (Implementation of the Simplified Prospectus requirements), which came into force on 1 May 2005. It also introduced a passporting regime to facilitate cross-border investment services throughout the EEA. The UCITS IV Directive came into force on 13 July 2009[2]. This updates the UCITS III Directive by introducing certain further changes, for example, notification procedure; Key Investor Information Document; adapted framework for mergers; master feeder structures; co-operation between member state supervisory authorities and a management company passport.

On 3 July 2012 the European Commission adopted a proposal for a directive amending those parts of UCITS IV which deal with depositary functions, remuneration policies and sanctions for failure to comply with the Directive ('UCITS V'). Shortly thereafter, on 26 July 2012, the European Commission published a consultation paper seeking views on proposals for additional wide-ranging amendments to the UCITS Directive. These changes are referred to as 'UCITS VI'.

1 Directives 2001/108/EC and 2001/107/EC.
2 Directive 2009/65/EC.

OPEN ENDED INVESTMENT COMPANIES (OEICS)

4.115 OEICS were first introduced into the UK in 1997. Whilst there has been a degree of replacement of unit trusts it is probably true to say that this has not been as extensive as was originally anticipated. In terms of spread of risk, professional management, simplicity and convenience, types of investment fund and reasons for investing, OEICS have virtually identical characteristics to unit trusts as set out above.

4.116   Regulations were introduced in order to put in place the regulatory framework for OEICS in the form of the Open Ended Investment Companies (Investment Companies with Variable Capital) Regulations 1996[1].

1 SI 1996/2827. (Although now revoked by the Open-ended Investment Companies Regulations 2001, SI 2001/1228 (which have themselves been partly amended and revoked) which are regulations issued under the FSMA 2000.)

4.117   OEICS are collective investment schemes under the FSMA 2000. Unlike unit trusts, OEICS are corporate bodies and thus have a separate legal existence. OEICS must have an 'Authorised Corporate Director' (ACD) responsible for running it on a day-to-day basis and the ACD will often be the only director of the company. This position has many similarities in practice to that of the unit trust manager. It must also have a depositary responsible for safekeeping of the assets. The depositary must be independent of the OEICS and its directors. Although the legal basis is different, in practice it exercises a similar function to that of the trustee under a unit trust. Both the ACD and the depositary must be authorised under the FSMA 2000. OEICS are able to offer a variety of share classes whereas unit trusts could only offer two types of units. Whilst unit trusts have tended in the past to operate a dual pricing system, OEICS all operate 'single pricing'.

4.118   A further advantage of OEICS is that it is easier to convert or amalgamate them than unit trusts. Unlike unit trusts, OEICS can operate as an umbrella scheme holding various sub-funds each with their own investment goals and held separately from other sub-funds.

The Investment Management Association

4.119   The Association of Unit Trusts and Investment Funds ('AUTIF') was originally established by the industry in 1959 as the Association of Unit Trust Managers (later renamed the Unit Trust Association). In 1993 the name was amended to AUTIF to reflect the interests of its members in PEPs, open-ended investment companies, investment trusts and UCITS funds set up in other EC member states, as well as unit trusts. On 1 February 2002 AUTIF merged with the Fund Managers Association (FMA) to form the Investment Management Association (IMA). The Association acts as a consultative body in agreeing industry standards and as a representative body for dealing with governmental and regulatory bodies. The Boards of the Association of British Insurers (ABI) and the Investment Management Association agreed in principle in April 2014 to merge the investment activities of the ABI, including the Institutional Voting Information Service (IVIS), with the IMA.

PENSIONS

4.120   Apart from those provided by the state, pensions can in general terms be divided into occupational schemes and personal schemes. The former relate to an individual's employment and the latter generally relate to either an individual's self-employment or to situations where no occupational scheme is available, or where the employee chooses not to be a member of his employer's scheme or where an individual wishes to set up a separate or additional pension plan. Within each of the above broad categories there are a range of variations. For example, it is possible to have occupational pension schemes with a few members and group personal pension schemes with hundreds of policyholders. Although all personal pensions are provided by a pension provider (usually an insurance company) the position with regard to occupational schemes can be much more varied. They can be provided fully by an insurance company at one extreme or, at the other, fully self-administered. There can be a range of intermediate schemes where part is insured and part is self-administered (known as 'hybrids').

4.121   The entire framework of private pension provision is underwent substantial changes as a result of the Pensions Act 2004 (which was mainly brought into force throughout 2005 and 2006) and the relevant provisions of the Finance Act 2004 (Pt 4) which introduced a new single tax regime for all types of pension schemes as from 6 April 2006 (referred to as 'A-day').

Introduction

4.122   State pensions only provide a modest income in old age, even though employees' pensions are increased by an earnings-related addition (unless 'contracted out' – see para **4.123** below). This used to be known as the State Earnings Related Pension Scheme (SERPS). From 6 April 2002 the State Second Pension ('S2P') replaced SERPS. In order to encourage individuals and their employers to make pension provision for themselves and reduce the burden of pension provision on the state the government therefore gives generous tax treatment to occupational and personal pension schemes.

4.123   Provided an employer's scheme provided at least equivalent benefits to S2P, employees used to be able to 'contract out' of the earnings-related element of the state scheme, thus paying lower contributions to it in the form of lower national insurance contributions. However, contracting out was abolished as from 6 April 2012 for defined contribution schemes (unless such schemes were contracted out on a salary related basis)

4.124   Many employers, particularly smaller ones, preferred to remain contracted in to the state scheme and provide their own pension scheme in addition. The employee then had the full benefits under the state scheme (and paid full contributions) plus the additional benefits provided by his employer's scheme.

Auto Enrolment

4.125   The pensions landscape has changed further with the introduction of the auto-enrolment reforms. The government set up the Turner Commission in December 2002, following long-standing concerns about the adequacy of pensions saving in the UK. They recommended, amongst other matters, a national pension saving scheme, supported by compulsory employer contributions. As a result primary legislation implementing auto-enrolment was enacted in the Pensions Act 2008 (PA 2008). The main provisions were brought into force on 30 June 2012 by the Pensions Act 2008 (Commencement No 13) Order 2012, SI 2012/1682). Many of the detailed measures relating to the regime are contained in secondary legislation made under the PA 2008. Once subject to the auto-enrolment duties, an employer is required to automatically enrol an eligible jobholder as an active member of an auto-enrolment scheme with effect from the date the jobholder becomes eligible, unless he is already an active member of the employer's qualifying scheme (PA 2008, s 3(2)) The new employer duties are being implemented month by month over a five-and-a-half-year staging period that started on 1 October 2012. Larger employers passed their staging dates first. An employer can choose to bring forward its staging date if it wishes.

An eligible jobholder can opt out of his employer's scheme if he chooses. The employer of an eligible jobholder who is auto-enrolled (and does not opt out) must pay mandatory minimum contributions to a defined contribution (DC) scheme or offer a minimum level of benefits in a defined benefit (DB) scheme. Eligible jobholders who have opted out will be automatically re-enrolled every three years. Workers who are not eligible jobholders may have the right to opt into their employer's qualifying scheme or, in some cases, a different scheme. Once it has passed its staging date, an employer must make regular future assessments of whether its workers are eligible for auto-enrolment or if they need to be told about their right to opt into a scheme.

There are detailed provision-of-information requirements that employers need to comply with.

Annuitisation versus Income Drawdown

4.126   Those in personal pension schemes have been able on retirement to defer using their pension fund to buy an annuity and have some flexibility as to how much income they draw in the meantime. This is termed 'Income Drawdown' or 'Pension Fund Withdrawal' (from A-day known as 'Unsecured Pension' as pension payments are not 'secured' by an annuity contract).

The whole area around how a person takes his pension benefits is being radically altered as a result of the Budget announcements in March 2014. There are a number of interim measures which took effect from 27 March, 2014, for example increasing the amount which can be taken under capped drawdown from 120% to 150% of the levels set out in the tables provided to HM Revenue & Customs by the Government Actuary's Department (GAD). This is ahead of even further liberalisation in 2015 after which, in effect, pensioners can take their benefits in any way they wish.

The trust as the basis of occupational pension schemes

4.127   Except in very limited circumstances the underlying structure of an occupational pension scheme is the trust and, in general, this has worked well as the effect of a trust is to separate the pension scheme assets from the assets of the employer. The pension trustees' duties arise not only from the terms of the trust deed but from the general law relating to trusts and increasingly by statute and especially the Pensions Act 1995, the Trustee Act 2000 and the Pensions Act 2004. In addition, The Pensions Regulator has issued a number of codes of practice.

4.128 The importing of the trust concept into occupational pension schemes has not been universally easy as the law relating to trusts originally evolved in the context of family trusts and not commercial operations. There is a contractual as well as a trust relationship underpinning occupational schemes. Nevertheless, the Goode Committee in 1993 expressed its faith in trust law as the continuing basis for occupational schemes.

Documentation for occupational pension schemes

4.129 In order to provide an idea of the type of documents encountered in the establishment and running of an occupational scheme the following list sets out the most common ones:

- Interim Document;
- Definitive Trust Deed (the core document);
- Deed of Adherence (to enable associated companies to join in);
- Deed of Alteration/Variation;
- Deeds of Appointment/Retirement of Trustees;
- Winding up documentation (Resolution or Deed);
- Transfer Agreement (eg on a takeover);
- Application for Membership;
- Indemnities;
- Employee Announcement;
- Reports, etc under disclosure regulations;
- Investment Management Agreements (where outside investment managers are to be employed).

Membership of occupational pension schemes

4.130 Employees cannot be obliged to be members of their employers' schemes, unless the scheme is non-contributory and provides only death benefits. Employees are able to take out personal pension plans instead (or as well as) or rely on the state pension scheme. In practice this would be very rare as it would normally be in the employee's interest to be a member of the employer's occupational scheme. Pension rights from an existing occupational scheme may be transferred to a personal pension plan if the receiving scheme permits. It is also possible to transfer back from a personal pension plan to an employer's scheme, again if the receiving scheme so permits.

Inland Revenue registration for pension schemes[1]

4.131   As mentioned above (para **4.121**) significant changes were made in this area from 'A-day'. A new single tax regime applied from 6 April 2006 in place of the previous eight pension tax regimes. This regime applies to both occupational and personal pension schemes and is along the lines of the then existing personal pension regime. In general, the tax advantages will only apply to 'registered' schemes (which broadly replaced the concept of 'approved' schemes).

1 Finance Act 2004, ss 149–284.

4.132   Registration of pension schemes (and associated matters) is dealt with under ss 153 to 159 of the Finance Act 2004, and its broad effect is similar to that of 'approval' under the old regime. Virtually all approved schemes automatically became 'registered' schemes on A-day. Registration of new schemes requires an application to the Inland Revenue on a prescribed form and a declaration from the scheme administrator that the scheme will satisfy all the statutory requirements.

What is the purpose in becoming registered?

4.133   The following sets out the taxation advantages of registered schemes:

(1)   the employer's contributions reduce business profits for corporation tax purposes;

(2)   the employer's contributions are not treated as a benefit in kind to the employee (and so the employee is not subject to income tax in respect of those contributions), nor do they count as the employee's earnings for national insurance contributions;

(3)   an employee's own contributions reduce his earnings for tax purposes (but not for national insurance contribution purposes);

(4)   a tax-free lump sum (obtained by commutation of pension benefits) can be paid to the employee on retirement;

(5)   provision can be made for a lump sum to be paid on an employee's death in service, which is usually free of IHT;

(6)   the income and capital gains of the fund are not taxed, although since 2 July 1997 the government has removed the ability of pension funds to reclaim tax credits in respect of dividends arising from UK companies.

Retirement age

4.134   The concept of normal retirement date for tax purposes disappeared under the simplified regime as did the restrictions on drawing occupational scheme benefits and continuing to work for the scheme's sponsoring employer. There is, however, a 'normal minimum pension age' which from 5 April 2010 is 55. Transitional protections for retirement at age 50 (the previous minimum) may be met if a person was a member of a scheme prior to A-Day. There is no maximum age for taking benefits but stricter rules now apply after age 75.

Contributions

4.135   There is a lifetime allowance (LTA) on the amount of pension savings that can benefit from favourable tax treatment and an annual allowance on the value of inflows which will receive tax relief. The LTA replace the limits (known as the 'Earnings Cap') on the earnings on which contributions may be paid.

Lifetime Allowance and the Recovery Charge

4.136   The standard lifetime allowance will be £1.25 million for the tax year 2014/15 which is a reduction from a high of £1.8 million. Pension fund values are assessed against the LTA when benefits are about to come into payment (a benefit crystallisation event). For defined contribution scheme members, it is simply a case of comparing an individual's accumulated pension fund with the LTA. For defined benefit scheme members the position is more complicated because the pension built up must be converted into a value. The new regime does this by using a factor of £20 for every £1 per annum of pension, regardless of age or sex. The 20:1 factor applies provided attaching pension increases do not exceed inflation (or 5%) and dependants' pensions on death do not total more than the member's pension. For people who have already built up pension funds in excess of the LTA certain protections may be available.

Amounts above the LTA will be taxed through a 'recovery charge' of 25% or 55% depending on how benefits are taken.

Annual Allowance

4.137   There is an annual allowance on the value of amounts which will receive tax relief. This is £50,000 for the tax year 2013/14, reducing to £40,000 in 2014/15. Payments in excess of the AA will be subject to tax.

Employees: benefits

4.138   Essentially, the post A-day regime removed the limits on benefits as the benefits are inherently restricted by a combination of the LTA and the AA. However, this is subject to certain exceptions.

Retirement Lump Sums

4.139   The rules permit a lump sum to be taken up to one third of the value coming into payment, subject to this amount not exceeding 25% of the LTA at that time. Transitional protection for pre A-day lump sums exceeding 25% is available.

Death Benefits

4.140   Employers typically provide four times salary lump sum death cover for employees. The restriction for Death in Service of four times earnings was removed and lump sum death benefits are allowed up to the LTA. Any widows' or dependants' pension will be payable in addition to this.

Early Retirement and Continued Employment

4.141   The minimum age for taking benefits is 55 having risen from 50 in 2010. Retirement as a result of incapacity may be permitted at any age.

Members of occupational schemes can retain any right they may have under the scheme to retire between the ages of 50 and 55 provided such rights existed throughout the period from 10 December 2003 to A-day. This right can be lost on transfer to another scheme.

From A-day members are allowed to receive a pension whilst remaining in pensioned employment and, subject to scheme rules, draw part of the pension while deferring the rest.

Unapproved pension schemes

4.142   In addition to registered schemes it is possible to establish unapproved pension schemes either alongside registered schemes, or on their own. Unapproved schemes are known as 'employer-financed retirement benefits schemes' (EFRBS) (previously referred to as Funded Unapproved Retirement Benefit Schemes ('FURBS')). They do not have any tax privileges under the simplified regime. Employer contributions to EFRBSs are, following a period of uncertainty, subject to national insurance contributions which means they have no advantage compared to direct pay. Their general taxation and NIC treatment combined with their administrative complications make them less attractive post A-day.

Unfunded Unapproved Retirement Benefits Schemes suffer from the potential lack of security and the potential large provisions on the balance sheet of the employer.

Contributions to such schemes do not count towards AA or LTA.

Effects of leaving service ('preservation' requirements)

4.143   When an employee leaves employment, then provided he has been in the pension scheme for at least two years, he will be entitled either to have a preserved pension (within the former employer's scheme) which will become payable on retirement, or a transfer payment to a new scheme (if the scheme will accept it) or to an insurance company in order to purchase a 'buy out' policy (still known colloquially as a 's 32 policy' after the FA 1981, s 32 under which such policies were originally issued – see more recently ICTA 1988, s 591(2)(g)) or a personal pension plan. Section 264 of the Pensions Act 2004 introduced a fifth chapter into Pt 4 of the Pension Schemes Act 1993 consisting of new ss 101AA to 101AI. These make provision for members who leave after three months pensionable service to be entitled to a cash transfer or a refund of employee contributions although short service refunds will be abolished under the Pensions Act 2014. However, these are not 'preserved' rights in the pension scheme.

'Surpluses'

4.144 The tax simplification measures in the Finance Act 2004, remove the requirement to dispose of an excessive surplus. However, it remains the case that a payment of surplus to an employer would be subject to tax.

Section 250 of the Pensions Act 2004 substitutes a new s 37 of the Pensions Act 1995, to govern the circumstances under which trustees may make a payment to an employer from an actuarial surplus, and how such a surplus should be determined. The previous rules are repeated in that payments can only be made from an ongoing scheme if the scheme rules permit and that such power must be exercised by the trustees. Subsection (3) of the new s 37 requires certain provisions to be satisfied, eg, a certificate from a prescribed person concerning the assets and liabilities of the scheme and stating the maximum amount of the payment which can be made. The trustees must be satisfied it is in the best interest of the members, no freezing order is in place and scheme members have been notified. In practice, very few schemes are now in surplus partly due to the intervening financial downturn.

Master Trusts

4.145 Master trusts are defined by the Pensions Regulator as occupational trust-based pension schemes established by declaration of trust which are or have been promoted to provide benefits to employers which are not connected and where each employer group is not included in a separate section with its own trustees. A master trust is therefore a multi-employer occupational pension scheme where each employer has its own division within the master arrangement. There is one trust and, therefore, one trustee board. The trustee retains decision making independence for each division on things such as investment funds and service providers under a trust wide governance structure. The decisions over benefit and contribution levels are normally decided on by the employer. With the implementation of the Pensions Act 2012 the requirement for automatic enrolment of employees has commenced. Master trusts are therefore viewed by pension providers as an alternative means of helping meet employers' auto-enrolment obligations and are therefore establishing occupational defined contribution (DC) Master Trusts that can manage the pension investments of many individual companies, and their employees, within a single entity.

Payment of pensions

4.146 Tax on pension payments is taxed as pension income and dealt with under the PAYE scheme, with coding adjustments being made where some or all of the available allowances have been used against other income, such as state pensions.

Personal Pensions

4.147 Persons contributing to a registered personal pension scheme are entitled to tax relief on the contributions they pay. Of course, it is now also possible now for someone to be both a member of an employer's pension scheme and have their own personal pension.

4.148   Pre-1 July 1988 contracts for the self-employed or those not in an occupational pension scheme were known as retirement annuity policies ('RAPs'). Contracts starting on or after 1 July 1988 are called personal pension plans (although they are not limited in the same way regarding who can effect them). All personal pensions operate relief at source for personal contributions although higher rate taxpayers need to claim any additional tax relief through their tax return.

4.149   Personal pension schemes generally allow members to direct where their funds are to be invested, subject to restrictions to ensure that the scheme still meets the conditions necessary for its tax status. A particular variety of personal pension scheme is the Self Invested Personal Pension Scheme (SIPP) which enables the individual to enjoy a range of wider investment powers. A SIPP is generally referred to as a 'wrapper' and were introduced by the Finance Act, 1989, In October 2012, the FSA published the results of a thematic review of SIPPs which concluded that there was potential for significant customer detriment and in November 2012 published proposals to strengthen capital standards for SIPP operators.

4.150   Personal pension contributions can be paid to any 'personal pension provider'. In addition to insurance companies this includes friendly societies, banks, building societies or unit trust managers. In all cases, any annuity is purchased from an insurance company with the fund at retirement and the 'best buy' available at that time can be selected by exercise of the 'open market option'. A plan holder must be given the opportunity to choose the insurance company from which a lifetime annuity is purchased. The Association of British Insurers (ABI) have designed a code imposed on its members which requires full disclosure to plan holders of the options available to them. COBS Rule 19.4 of the FCA Rules also requires certain information to be provided to plan holders.

4.151   The fund into which premiums are paid is free of tax on both income and capital gains, although since 2 July 1997 it is no longer possible to reclaim tax credits on dividends in respect of UK companies.

Deferring personal pension annuity purchase

4.152   For schemes approved or amended after 1 May 1995, a person with a personal pension contract may defer buying an annuity perhaps because rates may be low which has increasingly been the case. A tax-free lump sum can still be taken at retirement and taxable income withdrawals can be taken from the fund during the deferral period up to a maximum of (since 27 March 2014) 150% of the Government Actuary department (GAD) rate. The residual fund remains fully invested, but further contributions may not be made once any benefits (including income withdrawals) have been taken.

4.153   If the pension scheme member dies during the deferral period, a surviving spouse or dependant will be able to take the fund in cash (subject to a tax charge), or buy an annuity immediately, or continue making income withdrawals and buy an annuity later on. If the survivor dies before buying the annuity, the fund may be paid in cash to his or her heirs (net of tax).

4.154 From A-day it became possible to continue with withdrawals beyond age 75 although this is limited. This is known as 'Alternatively Secured Pension' (ASP). As indicated in **4.126** above the announcements in the March 2014 Budget will ultimately lead to the removal of all restrictions over how pension benefits are taken.

Stakeholder pension schemes[1]

4.155 Stakeholder pension schemes have their statutory origins in the Welfare Reform and Pensions Act 1999 and were originally designed for people earning between £9,000 and £18,000 per annum and were intended to be low cost and easy to understand. They were not, however, available to the public until April 2001. Stakeholder schemes may be run either on the basis of a trust (ie similar to an occupational pension scheme) or on a contractual basis with the scheme being run by an FCA authorised 'stakeholder scheme manager'.

1 Welfare Reform and Pensions Act 1999, ss 1–8, and Stakeholder Pension Schemes Regulations 2000, SI 2000/1403 (and subsequent amending regulations).

4.156 Schemes must permit the payment of contributions from a bank or building society account by either cheque, direct debit, standing order or direct credit. Schemes are not obliged to accept payment by cash or credit card. There can be no restriction on the minimum amount of contributions that can be made to the scheme with the exception that schemes are not obliged to accept contributions below £20. (This is the amount actually paid, ie net of income tax relief at the basic rate for a member, gross for an employer.)

Charges

4.157 The annual management charge prior to 6 April 2005 for each member must not exceed one per cent of the fund value. This limit is expressed in the legislation as $\frac{1}{365}$ per cent of the fund value for each day the fund is held under the scheme. From 6 April 2005 the maximum charge was raised to 1.5% of the value of the fund for the first ten years which thereafter reduces to 1%.

4.158 Charges incurred in operating the investments under the scheme (such as dealing charges) can be accounted for in full when determining the value of the fund for the purpose of applying the management charge. Schemes are not allowed to make any additional charges for administering incoming transfer payments, nor for making transfer payments out of the scheme.

4.159 Schemes are allowed to levy charges to cover the administrative expenses incurred in addition to the 1% or 1.5% management charge. Therefore pension providers may recover costs and charges for such things as stamp duty or other charges for buying and selling investments for the fund, or for particular circumstances such as the costs of sharing a pension when a couple divorce.

4.160   Schemes must provide basic information and explanatory material within the maximum annual management charge. Any extra services and any extra charges not provided for by law must be optional. Extra services must be offered under a separate arrangement with clearly defined costs for the services being offered;

Miscellaneous Stakeholder Provisions

4.161   It is possible to make contributions on behalf of other people. In such cases, the contribution is treated as having been made by the recipient for tax purposes and thus, if the recipient is a higher rate taxpayer, additional relief can be claimed in the normal way. The donor makes the contribution net of income tax relief at the basic rate even if he or she is a non-taxpayer.

4.162   Contributions made in this way are gifts for inheritance tax purposes but the donor's annual exemption or the 'normal expenditure out of income' exemption may be available to exempt the gift.

It is also possible for an employer to make contributions in respect of a person who is not an employee – for example a director's wife or child. It seems unlikely that such a contribution would be treated as 'wholly and exclusively for the purposes of the trade' and thus would not be allowed as a deduction when calculating profits liable to corporation tax.

4.163

- Stakeholder schemes must accept transfers in, and there must be no additional charges for this or for transferring to a different stakeholder pension;

- In order to protect the interests of their members, schemes must have either trustees (if trust-based) or stakeholder managers;

- For trust-based schemes, a third of the trustees must be independent;

- Schemes must appoint an auditor or a reporting accountant to check the annual declaration required to be made by the trustees or managers to ensure that the scheme is within the charging regulations;

- Schemes must have a statement of investment principles;

- Schemes must have a default investment option which is subject to lifestyling (which means that during the years leading up to retirement a member's pension is gradually moved into investments that are considered to be less volatile with the aim of providing greater security as they approach retirement).

Personal pensions and bankruptcy

4.164   Unlike with occupational schemes, 'forfeiture clauses' may not be as effective to prevent a trustee in bankruptcy from being able to claim the proceeds of a bankrupt's personal pension (although in effect it is only once the policyholder has reached 55 that the policy is of any value to the trustee in bankruptcy as he can be in no better position than the policyholder himself). This stems from the 'personal' nature of personal pension schemes and the effects of the Insolvency Act 1986. The Pensions Act 1995, s 191 provided for a statutory 'inalienability' clause for occupational schemes whilst omitting personal pension schemes from the ambit of the rule. Concern was expressed at this apparent unequal treatment afforded to personal schemes and eventually the situation was addressed by the Welfare Reform and Pensions Act (WRPA) 1999. Section 11 of the act provides that where an individual with an 'approved pension arrangement' becomes bankrupt on or after 29 May 2000 then this will be excluded from their estate. There are exceptions to this rule. The ability for the Trustee in Bankruptcy (TIB) to apply to court for an Income Payments Order in respect of 'surplus' income is available in respect of pensions in payment before the bankrupt becomes discharged. A TIB can apply to the court to recover 'excessive' contributions paid to the pension scheme, if it is established that the member deliberately intended to deprive creditors of money owed. This could cover contributions paid up to five years prior to bankruptcy, personally, or via a company. A further provision under the WRPA making forfeiture clauses ineffective came into force from 6 April 2002.

4.165   The case of *Re Landau*[1] confirmed that a retirement annuity constituted 'property' in accordance with the definition in the Insolvency Act 1986 and hence was available to the TIB. It is generally thought that the same principles would apply to personal pensions. The cases of *Krasner v Dennison: Lawrence v Lesser*[2] specifically considered personal pensions. It was held that statutory restrictions on assignment do not restrict the rights of the TIB and so policies automatically vest in the TIB. Therefore it is not necessary to obtain an income payments order to make income available to creditors. Many personal pensions have been written subject to 'forfeiture clauses' (also known by other names and many inserted into schemes after their inception) but there has been lengthy debate as to their effectiveness. The case of *Lesser v Lawrence* was the subject of an appeal to the House of Lords but this was not ultimately proceeded with and, although there was a consideration of the validity of forfeiture clauses in this case, it must be borne in mind that the scheme in question did not actually contain a forfeiture clause. In broad terms those arguing against forfeiture clauses argue that such a clause cannot operate to remove rights to benefits which have already vested whilst those arguing for such clauses would say that the rights to pension payments do not arise until each such payment is made. The position for bankruptcy petitions presented before 29 May 2000 and the validity or otherwise of forfeiture clauses is becoming an increasingly rare consideration with the passage of time.

1 [1997] 3 All ER 322.
2 [2000] 3 All ER 234.

4.166   The recent case of *Raithatha v Williamson*[1] has added something of a caveat. The defendant was made bankrupt in 2010. At the time he was entitled to draw his personal pension benefits but had chosen not to. However, before the bankrupt was discharged, the TIB applied for an IPO, claiming three years of pension income and the pension commencement lump sum, despite the fact the bankrupt hadn't crystallised their benefits. The TIB claimed this constituted a 'payment in the nature of income which is from time to time made to him or to which he from time to time becomes entitled', that is, within the meaning of s310(7) Insolvency Act 1986 and therefore constituted income in respect of which the court was entitled to make an IPO. While submitting that pension income did fall within the definition of income for an IPO, the defence argued this didn't extend to include the right to draw on benefits where the bankrupt had chosen not to do so. The court disagreed concluding there could be no logical reason why legislation should distinguish between a bankrupt who had drawn pension benefits and was therefore susceptible to an IPO and one who was entitled to draw benefits but had chosen not to do so. This meant the TIB could apply for an IPO against the bankrupt's pension benefits – both the annuity income and the lump sum.

1 *Raithatha v Williamson* [2012] EWHC 909 (Ch)

Pensions Act 1995 (PA 1995)

4.167   The PA 1995 reflected a recognition that legislative overhaul was necessary in terms of the protection of pension schemes and their members. The provisions of PA 1995 were a response to a variety of issues of concern to the pensions industry. However, the late Robert Maxwell's widely reported activities in relation to the Mirror Group's pension funds was probably one of the main catalysts for the PA 1995.

4.168   The Social Security Select Committee conducted investigations into the ownership and control of pension fund assets which led to its call in its March 1992 report[1], for further investigation into the precise structure of a Pensions Act. The government obliged in June of that year and established the Pension Law Reform Committee to:

> 'review the framework of law and regulation within which occupational pension schemes operate, taking into account the rights and interests of scheme members, pensioners and employers; to consider in particular the status and ownership of occupational pension funds and the accountability and roles of trustees, fund managers, auditors and pension scheme advisers; and to make recommendations.'

The Committee's report (the Goode Report) made over 200 recommendations, the main one being for a Pensions Act to 'lay out a properly structured framework of rights and duties, and a Pensions Regulator. with overall responsibility for the regulation of occupational pension schemes'. These recommendations were adopted by the government in its White Paper (*Security, Equality, Choice: The Future of Pensions*). The intention being that it would provide for greater pensions security by measures designed to achieve 'the greatest practicable security' and that the new legislation would provide a clear framework of statutory obligation on employers, trustees, managers, professionals and members.

1 Second Report, *The Operation of Pension Funds* (HC Paper 61-II (1991–92)).

4.169   In brief terms the PA 1995 provided the following main measures:

(1)   a public regulator of schemes with specific statutory duties and powers for enforcing the terms of the PA 1995. Namely, the Occupational Pensions Regulatory Authority (OPRA) which is itself now being replaced by the Pensions Regulator under the Pensions Act 2004;

(2)   statutory crystallisation of the duties and responsibilities of scheme trustees and provisions to tighten up scheme management;

(3)   duties in relation to investment requirements were made more stringent. The position of the trustee in scheme security and operation is reinforced;

(4)   obligation on professionals involved with schemes to be part of the policing of those schemes – the 'whistle blowing' provisions;

(5)   a quota of trustees to be made up of those nominated by members;

(6)   a compensation scheme;

(7)   men and women to be provided with equal benefits and the equalisation of the state pensions scheme;

(8)   stringent requirements as to payment of surplus to the employer;

(9)   obligations with regard to indexation of pensions after retirement;

(10)   new minimum funding, winding-up and transfer value requirements;

(11)   provisions regarding pensions and divorce (see below for more detail).

The result was a large and complex statute comprising 181 sections and seven Schedules. It also authorised the making of regulations which provide much of the detail to the PA 1995.

Pensions and divorce

4.170   Prior to the PA 1995, there was not much that divorcing spouses or the courts could do about pensions, other than to take them into account when allocating the matrimonial property (known as 'offsetting'). The case of *Brooks v Brooks*[1] brought this issue very much into public focus. The divorce and pensions law reforms in the PA 1995 gave a new range of options.

1 [1996] AC 375.

4.171   In 1993, the Pensions Management Institute (PMI)/Law Society working party reported on this issue. Its conclusions were endorsed in the Goode Report. It recommended that pension splitting should be introduced which involved allowing the court to award part or all of the cash equivalent to a spouse on divorce. The spouse could then leave his or her pension rights with the scheme, or move them to a personal pension. However, many commentators were not keen about pension splitting and the significant problems in practice were set out in a green paper 'Treatment of pension rights on divorce', published by the DSS in July 1996.

4.172 The government agreed to compromise when it was outnumbered during the passage of the PA 1995. In exchange for dropping it, 'earmarking' provisions were agreed. Earmarking is an order given to the pension scheme trustees, which stipulates that at retirement, part or all of any lump sum or pension payable to the member shall be paid instead to the ex-spouse. These provisions appeared as the PA 1995, s 166 inserting new ss 25B and 25C into the Matrimonial Causes Act 1973. They came into force on 1 August 1996, dated back to petitions issued after 1 July 1996. Orders can be made against the pension scheme immediately for lump sum orders and from April 1997 for pension orders.

4.173 Pressure for 'pension splitting' or 'pension sharing' (based largely on the argument that it was preferable because it met the clean-break objectives of modern divorce law) resulted in the introduction of the Welfare Reform and Pensions Act 1999, introducing appropriate new rules. In effect the new rules allowed an immediate transfer of benefits rather than simply earmarking deferred maintenance. This introduced the novel principle that benefits could be taken away from a member. The relevant order is therefore unaffected by the member's death or the claimant's future remarriage. Other notable aspects of the pensions sharing rules are that they are not retrospective; earmarking remains an option (but renamed 'pension attachment orders'); all rights (including AVCs) are included; the claimant does not have to transfer (in which case he or she becomes a member of the scheme); the system operates on the basis of 'debits' against the member's rights and 'credits' for the claimant; pension sharing provisions must be included in new scheme rules[1].

There are two main types of pension sharing post-divorce. An internal share is where the spouse receives a pension share and is granted a pension entitlement in the same pension scheme as the member. The benefits granted to the spouse are independent of those of the member and will usually be payable from the time that he or she reaches the normal retirement age of the scheme in question, (typically age 60 or 65, though other ages may apply in some cases). An external share is where the spouse receives a pension share but is required to invest this in an alternative pension arrangement of their choice. This may be a personal pension, or an occupational scheme which is able to take receipt of the pension credit.

1 See further PSO update No 62, and Finance Act 1999, s 79, Sch 10.

Pensions Act 2004 (PA 2004)

4.174 The main aim of this Act was to introduce increased security for members (mainly of defined benefit schemes), revised administrative and compliance procedures and several proposals of the Department of Work and Pensions report *'Simplicity, Security and Choice: Working and Saving for Retirement'*. The following sections set out some of the main provisions of the Act but are by no means exhaustive.

Pension Protection Fund

4.175 This provides compensation to members of eligible defined benefit/final salary schemes (and in some cases their beneficiaries) if an employer becomes insolvent after 6 April 2005 and the scheme is sufficiently underfunded. It is funded by compulsory levies on the trustees and managers of eligible schemes.

The Pensions Regulator (see below) can issue contribution notices, restoration orders and deliberate failure to act orders. There is also be a 'green light' clearance system in connection with corporate restructuring so that genuine corporate transactions are not caught by provisions designed to disallow reconstructions/mergers which were in fact devices to offload deficiencies.

The Financial Assistance Scheme

4.176 This Scheme was introduced for persons whose schemes went into wind-up between 1 January 1997 and 6 April 2005 and who are not covered by the Pension Protection Fund and who suffered loss when their schemes had wound up.

The Pensions Regulator

4.177 The Pensions Regulator replaced the Occupational Pensions Regulatory Authority (OPRA) and acts on major issues such as member protection from fraud and administrative problems. The regulator is also given powers to counter pensions liberation. In addition to OPRA's powers the new Regulator has a number of additional powers such as a power to issue improvement notices; the ability to freeze a scheme whilst investigations take place; increased powers to suspend, prohibit and remove trustees; imposing 'whistleblowing' obligations; measures to combat pensions 'liberation'; powers to issue contribution notices and financial support directions; and increased information gathering powers.

The Regulator also has educational and information functions and will issue Codes of Practice. An independent Pensions Regulator Tribunal deals with referrals by persons who wish to contest determinations.

Winding Up

4.178 The Act provides for a statutory priority order that will continue to apply when a scheme winds up, whether the employer is solvent or insolvent. Schemes which commenced wind up on or after 11 June 2003 with solvent employers require the statutory debt to be calculated on a full buy-out basis. Where the employer is insolvent these may be ordered to be wound up if in the interests of the members. The Pensions Regulator can impose civil penalties for failure to comply with such an order, and the Pension Protection Fund Board may assume responsibility for the scheme. The Regulator may make a temporary freezing order if there is a risk to members' interests.

Registration of Schemes

4.179 The registration requirements for occupational pension schemes and personal pension schemes are set out in ss 59–65 of the Act. The Regulator is obliged to compile and maintain a register of occupational pension schemes and personal pension schemes which are (or have been) registrable schemes. The Act sets out what constitutes registrable information.

4.180   Trustees or managers of a registrable scheme must notify the Regulator when it is established within the initial notification period (together with the required information). The initial notification period is three months from the establishment of the scheme or, if later, the date on which it becomes a registrable scheme. The Regulator must be notified of any changes to the information provided as soon as practicable.

Trusteeship

4.181   At least one-third of scheme trustees must be nominated and selected by a process involving the active and pensioner scheme members (a recommendation from the Myners' Report and known as 'member nominated trustees'). Trustees must develop sufficient understanding of scheme documentation and pensions and trust law. They must also have an understanding of the principles underpinning investment and funding, and disclose investment principles to members.

Limited Price Indexation (LPI)

4.182   LPI is the minimum annual rate of indexation which must be applied to pensions in payment or deferred pensions, where they relate to service after 5 April 1997.

The LPI cap on defined benefit pension schemes was reduced from 5% to 2.5% but only in respect of pension rights accrued on or after 6 April 2006. LPI was removed completely from defined contribution benefit rights which come into payment on or after 6 April 2005.

Schemes may make increases in pension payments over and above LPI if they wish and the rules allow

THE OFFICE FOR FAIR TRADING (OFT) MARKET STUDY ON WORKPLACE DEFINED CONTRIBUTION PENSIONS

4.183   The OFT published its study on the DC workplace pensions market on 19 September 2013 which identified multiple concerns arising from employees' lack of understanding of pensions and the complexity of pension products, particularly in relation to charging levels. In the opinion of the OFT these points combine to reduce competition in the market on charges and quality.

The OFT has therefore recommended new scheme governance standards to be set by the Department of Work and Pensions (DWP), along with the creation of a value for money framework, under which all costs and charges associated with pension schemes will be disclosed to members. Smaller trust-based schemes should be required to report to the Pensions Regulator after evaluating the extent to which they comply with this framework. The Regulator has agreed to assess which smaller schemes are not delivering value for money, while the DWP has also agreed to consider whether the Regulator needs new enforcement powers to address this issue. Additionally, the ABI has agreed that its members will establish independent governance committees in order to identify value for money issues and raise these at board level.

In view of the actions that seem likely on many of these recommendations, the OFT provisionally decided not to refer the market to the Competition Commission for further investigation.

The Department of Work and Pensions ('DWP') issued its 'Better workplace pensions' command paper in March 2014 which sets out its proposals on defined contribution ('DC') quality standards and charging caps.

The command paper confirms that, from April 2015, the government intends to introduce a set of minimum mandatory DC governance standards for all DC schemes – both trust and contract-based – the focus being on a DC scheme's default investment strategy, costs and charges and administration processes. Perhaps most significantly being a charges cap of 0.75% to apply to management charges for the default funds of all qualifying schemes. From April 2016, it will no longer be possible to deduct commission from members' accounts and active member discounts will be prohibited.

INVESTMENT TRUSTS

4.184   An investment trust is a form of collective investment and, unlike OEICS, are closed-end funds. They are constituted as public limited companies. The name is something of a misnomer as they are not legally 'trusts' but a company. Investors' money is pooled together from the sale of a fixed number of shares which a trust issues when it launches. The board will delegate responsibility to a professional fund manager to invest in the stocks and shares of a range of companies and other permissible assets. The investment trust often has no employees, only a board of directors comprising only non-executive directors. More recently, this has started to change, especially with the emergence of both private equity groups and commercial property trusts both of which sometimes use investment trusts as a holding vehicle.

Shares in investment trusts are traded on stock exchanges, like those of other public companies. The *share price* does not always reflect the underlying value of the share portfolio held by the investment trust. In such cases, the investment trust is referred to as trading at a discount (or premium) to NAV (*net asset value*).

'Traditional' investment trusts normally issue only one type of share (ordinary shares) and have a limited life. Split Capital Investment Trusts have a more complicated structure. Such trusts issue different classes of share to give the investor a choice of shares to match their needs and normally have a limited life determined at launch known as the wind-up date. Typically the life of a Split Capital Trust is five to ten years.

Chapter 5

Customer relations

Andrew Haynes[1]

INTRODUCTION

5.1   The rules relating to the relationships between firms and their customers are to be found principally in the Conduct of Business Sourcebook (COBS). COBS primarily applies in relation to regulated activities, conducted by firms which fall within the definition of designated investment business. COBS therefore has only limited application to deposits. General insurance mediation activities[2] and mortgage activities are subject to their own conduct of business requirements (ICOB for insurance and MCOB for mortgages. These are not covered in detail in this chapter.) The provisions of COBS are at a level of detail which underpin the relevant customer focused Principles for Businesses (see Chapter 1).

1 This chapter is developed from an earlier one written by Peter Bibby
2 This applies to pure protection contract and general insurance contracts and assisting in the administration and performance of a contract of insurance.

5.2   The regulatory framework seeks to provide a level of protection that is appropriate to the type of investor a firm is dealing with. The rules provide a comprehensive system for the classification of investors. This system of investor classification works:

(1)   by defining what is and is not a client;

(2)   by drawing a distinction between different classes of client; and

(3)   by applying specific rules to different classes of client.

5.3   The category into which an investor falls determines which rules apply. Of particular importance is the distinction between retail and professional clients, since COBS compels firms to provide a much greater degree of protection to the former than the latter.

5.4   Where relevant to customer relationships, this chapter examines the appropriate sections of FSMA 2000, FSA 2010 and FSA 2012 as well as COBS together with the Principles for Businesses. In considering the relations between a firm and its customers, this chapter covers COBS:

(1)   general application;

(2)   conduct of business obligations;

(3)   client categorisation;

(4)   communicating with clients;

(5)   distance communications;

(6)   information about the firm;

(7)   insurance mediation;

(8)   client agreements;

(9)   suitability;

(10)   appropriateness (for non-advised services);

(11)   dealing and managing;

(12)   investment research;

(13)   preparing product information;

(14)   providing product information to the client;

(15)   cancellation;

(16)   reporting information to clients;

(17)   claims handling for long term care insurance;

(18)   specialist regimes;

(19)   pensions, supplementary provisions;

(20)   with profits;

(21)   permitted links;

(Sch) transitional provisions and schedules

Territorial application

5.5   COBS 1.1 sets out the territorial application of COBS and in general the whole of COBS will apply to an activity which falls within the definition of designated investment business carried on from an establishment maintained by the firm or its appointed representative in the United Kingdom. In general, where the activity is carried on with or for a client in the UK but not from an establishment maintained by the firm or its appointed representative in the United Kingdom then COBS will apply unless, if the office were to be treated as a separate person (ie separate from any UK establishment with which it may be connected) it would be treated as an overseas person within Article 72 of the Regulated Activities Order (RAO)[1] or the activity would not be regarded as carried on in the UK.

1 SI 2001/544, as amended.

The regulations and customer redress

5.6   As noted above the detailed COBS rules underpin the customer focused Principles for Businesses. There is a distinction between the Principles and the COBS rules which is significant in the event that a 'private investor', which will tend to replicate the definition of 'retail client' in the COBS, can take legal action under FSMA under s 150. In summary such a person can sue an FCA authorised firm or person who has broken the FCA rules and caused loss to the client. The action is brought on a strict liability basis. In practice however many such cases would be actionable for negligence and/or breach of contract. A private investor may bring an action for breach of any of the COBS Rules. The Principles do not give rise to any right of action under s 150 for any investor, including a retail client because by their nature they represent a series of generic commands rather than precise instructions. The Principles can, however, be used by the FCA in taking disciplinary action against an authorised person and, if appropriate, an approved person.

FSMA 2000, s 66 provides that action may be taken by the FCA against an Approved Person if he is guilty of misconduct and the authority is satisfied that it is appropriate in all the circumstances to take action. The action that can be taken covers a financial penalty, a suspension of the FCA license for up to two years[1], the imposition of limitations on the license and making a public statement regarding the misconduct[2]. Suspensions and limitations may be on the whole of part of a license[3]. Misconduct includes knowing concern in a contravention by a relevant authorised person of a requirement under the FSMA or in the case of an authorised person include the Principles for Businesses.

1 Financial Services and Markets Act 2000, s 66(3A).
2 Financial Services and Markets Act 2000, s 66(3).
3 Financial Services and Markets Act 2000, s 66(3B).

The application of COB to different types of business

5.7   COBS 18 sets out the particular provisions of COBS which apply to stock lending activities (COBS 18.4); corporate finance business (COBS 18.3); and energy market activity (COBS 18.2). These are useful reference sources when seeking to determine the particular requirements which do apply to particular types of business.

THE DIFFERENT CATEGORIES OF CLIENT

5.8   The term client includes eligible counterparties and customers are categorised as retail clients and professional clients. (COBS 3.1.2G)

5.9   The term client is defined to include any person with or for whom a firm conducts or intends to conduct designated investment business or any other regulated activity[1]. The majority of COBS however, provides, protections to such clients. There is a separate regime for inter professional business, ie, that carried on between eligible counterparties (see definition at COBS 3.6 and Annex 1). Eligible counterparty business is regulated by COBS 1, 2.4, 4.4.1R, 4.4.2G, 5, 6 (other than 6.1), 7, 9, 11 (other than 11.2, 11.3 and 11.6), 12 (other than 12.3.1R to 12.3.3R), 13, 14 (other than 14.3), 15 and 17 – 21.

Classification of Client

5.10   Under COBS 3.3 a firm is required to take reasonable steps to establish whether a client is a retail client, professional client or an eligible counterparty before it conducts any designated investment business with or for the client. The firm should also inform a client in writing or a retrievable form that the client has the right to request a different categorisation and of any limitations to the level of client protection that would entail.

5.11 A firm must notify a client that is classified as a professional client or eligible counterparty of its right to request a different categorisation whether or not the firm will agree to them[1]. It only needs to notify a client of a right to request a different categorisation including a lower level if it is prepared to consider doing so. It is the responsibility of a professional client or eligible counterparty to ask for a higher level of protection when it deems it is unable to properly assess or manage the risks involved (COBS 3.7.2G).

1 COBS 3.3.

5.12 A firm can either at its own behest, or at the clients, provide a lower level of protection, ie, a professional or retail client can request to be treated as an eligible counterparty and a retail client can request that they be treated as a professional. A written agreement reflecting the arrangement is then necessary (COBS 3.7.3 and 3.7.5)

5.13 If an eligible counterparty requests re-categorisation to obtain more protection but does not specifically request being made a retail client, then they should be re-categorised as a professional client (COBS 3.7.4)

Potential client

5.14 The inclusion of a potential client in the definition of client means that a firm must comply with the rules governing that type of client when marketing investment services, ie before carrying on any investment business. This approach is also consistent with the Regulated Activities Order[1] which includes agreeing to undertake Regulated Activities within its ambit as a Regulated Activity.

1 RAO, art 64 (except agreeing to accept deposits (art 5); effecting and carrying out contracts of insurance (art 10); establishing etc. a collective investment scheme (art 51); establishing etc a stakeholder pension scheme (art 52).

Client of an appointed representative

5.15 A client of an appointed representative of a firm is treated under COBS as a client of the principal firm. This is because the firm accepts responsibility under FSMA 2000, s 39 for specified investment business transacted by the appointed representative. FSMA 2000, s 39 makes clear that anything done or omitted by an appointed representative, as respects business for which the firm has accepted responsibility in writing, is to be treated as having been done or omitted by the firm in determining whether the firm has complied with FSMA 2000 or provisions made under it (that includes in determining whether the firm has complied with COBS). Therefore a firm has a responsibility for ensuring its appointed representatives properly classify their clients before undertaking any designated investment business for the client. It is also therefore very important for a principal taking on appointed representatives carefully considers the business for which the principal will accept responsibility. If the principal chooses to take responsibility for particular types of business then it may be liable to pay compensation in the event that the business is carried on in breach of the rules and a loss is suffered. Whilst the principal is likely to have a claim for indemnity against the appointed representative under the terms of its agreement with the appointed representative that claim may be valueless if the appointed representative is without substance.

Clients for whom agents act

5.16   Under COBS 2.4.3 the presumption is that where a firm is dealing with an agent of a disclosed principal then it will treat the agent and not the disclosed principal as its client except where there is an agreement to the contrary or the agent is neither a firm nor an overseas financial services institution and the main purpose of the arrangement is to avoid duties the firm would owe to the principal for whom the agent is acting. In such cases the principal is also the client.

5.17   In cases where the agent is the client then the firm is likely to be dealing on an eligible counterparty to eligible counterparty basis.

5.18   These provisions do not alter the general agency principles under the normal laws of contract; do not relieve the firm of its obligation to identify its client under the Money Laundering Regulations 2007 and relevant statutes[1]; and do not have relevance when considering the identity of the firm's counterparty for the purpose of the relevant prudential rules. An agent should consider very carefully whether it wants to be treated as a client. If it is and the principal is a retail client then the agent will owe all the duties under COBS in respect of, for example, suitability and understanding of risk to the principal.

1 Terrorism Act 2000 and the Proceeds of Crime Act 2002.

The definition of customer

5.19   The starting point when determining who the client is, is to identify whether the client with whom the firm is dealing is in fact a customer. If the entity does not fall within the definition of customer, then minimal obligations under the rules are owed (see above in relation to inter professional business). If the firm is dealing with a customer, the application of the COBS Rules differs depending on whether that customer is classified as a retail client or professional client.

5.20   A 'customer', as defined by the FCA Glossary, essentially means any person with or for whom an authorised firm conducts designated investment business other than an eligible counterparty. A customer can be a natural person or a body corporate. It may be that a firm conducts designated investment business with a trustee acting on behalf of a trust or a partner acting on behalf of a partnership. Trusts and partnerships are customers only in so far as the individual trustee or partner has authority to bind his fellows. Special arrangements exist with regard to insurance business and there "customer" does not include a policy holder or prospective policy holder who does not make the arrangements preparatory to him concluding the contract of insurance[1].

1 ICOBS 1.

Investors falling outside the definition of customer

5.21   Eligible counterparties are clients but are excluded from the definition of customer. As noted earlier only limited Rules and Guidance apply governing transactions between eligible counterparties. Most important here is the MAR section of the handbook. Eligible counterparties are defined by COBS 3.6.1 as an investment firm, a credit institution, an insurance company, a collective investment scheme authorised under the UCITS Directive or its management company, a pension fund or its management company, any other financial institution (which included regulated institutions in the securities, banking and insurance sectors) authorised under EU legislation or the natural law of an EEA member state; an undertaking exempted from the application of MiFID either under Art 2(1)(k) (certain own account dealers in commodities or commodity derivatives) or 2(1)(l) (locals), a national government or its corresponding office. This includes a public body that deals with public debt, a central bank or a supranational organisation.

Professional clients

5.22   A professional client can either be so by classification and be determined a 'per se' professional client, or by choice, when they are determined to be an 'elective' on. The following are per se professional clients unless they choose otherwise:

– A credit institution;

– An investment firm;

– Any other authorised or regulated financial institution;

– An insurance company;

– A cis or its management company;

– A pension fund or its management company;

– A commodity or commodity derivatives dealer;

– A local; or

– Any other institutional investor

– Whether authorised in an EEA member state or a third country.

– In relation to a MiFID or third party business, a large undertaking which meets two of the following:

  ● A balance sheet total of over € 20 million;

  ● A net turnover of over € 40 million; or

  ● Own funds of over € 2 million.

5.23   A firm will be treated as an elective professional client if it complies with the following. Firstly, the firm must undertake an adequate assessment of the expertise, knowledge and experience of the client that provides them with reasonable assurance that the client can make their own decisions. In addition the client must have made the choice in writing, the firm must give a clear written warning of the protections that will be lost and the client must respond in writing that it is aware of this. Where a MiFID or equivalent third country business is involved two of the following must also apply. The client must have carried out significant transactions at least ten times per quarter over the last four quarters; the financial instrument portfolio must exceed € 500,000 and the client must have worked for at least a year in a position that has given them relevant knowledge.

Trust beneficiaries

5.24 Where investment services are provided to a trust, it is the trustee who must be treated as a customer. The classification of the trust (as a private client or professional client) will depend on its size and the nature of its business. Under the rules, the interests of beneficiaries are protected by requirements that investments must be suitable for the objectives and purposes of the trust which will be found in the trust documentation. The trustee is under a fiduciary duty to act in the interests of the trust.

Eligible counterparty as a private customer

5.25 COBS provides flexibility for firms which only wish to deal with private customers to treat any client as a private customer. This means that, notwithstanding the rules on client classification, a firm could choose to treat those with whom it carries on investment business as private customers. The advantage of this for a firm is that it can apply the same systems and processes to all its customer base. The disadvantage for the client is that it may receive protections, such as suitability and best execution, that it does not want and does not wish to pay for. The remedy for the client is to find a firm which is prepared to deal with it as an eligible counterparty or professional client. To treat one of these two categories as a private customer the firm must notify the client of its intention and explain that notwithstanding such treatment he may not necessarily have rights under the Financial Ombudsman Service or the Financial Services Compensation Scheme because the definition of private customer for eligibility under those schemes does not include all those customers given private customer status voluntarily[1].

The general application rule

5.26 COBS does not apply to a deposit taking institution with regard to taking deposits. Except for COBS 4.6 (past, simulated past and future performance), COBS 4.7.1 R (direct offer financial promotions), COBS 4.10 (systems and controls and approving and communicating financial promotions), COBS 13 (preparing product information) and COBS 14 (providing product information to clients).

Classification of a collective investment scheme

5.27 A collective investment scheme will be classified as a professional firm under COBS 3.5.2 unless re-categorised by arrangement with the firm.

5.28 The client of a trustee of a unit trust will usually be the scheme itself and is therefore likely to be a professional client. If an investment manager or custodian is appointed then he is likely to be carrying on activities with or for the trustee, operator or depositary and therefore it and not the scheme, is likely to be his customer. The trustee should therefore give very careful consideration as to whether it wishes to be treated as a professional client. This is because, while COBS 3.5.2 will ensure that a collective investment scheme itself is normally treated as a professional client. If it is the trustee which is the customer then unless there is a written agreement under COBS 3.7.5 the trustee will be treated as an eligible counterparty. The trustee will then need to deliver the protections of intermediate customer status to the collective investment scheme but will not himself be receiving those protections from his service provider, the manager.

Treating professional clients as eligible counterparties

5.29 Under COBS a firm may treat a professional client as an eligible counterparty if before commencing business with the client it advises the client that it will be classified as an eligible counterparty; has given a written warning of the protections that will be lost under the regulatory system and has provided the necessary notices in the appropriate way to the customer.

Communicating with clients

5.30 COBS 4 explains the position on communicating with customers. The specific rules are consistent with the more general requirements imposed by Principle 7 which provides:

> 'A firm must pay due regard to the information needs of its clients and communicate information to them in a way which is clear, fair and not misleading'.

The provisions of COBS has only limited application to financial promotions, ie, all communications that are marketing communications within the meaning in MiFID. (This is discussed in detail in Chapter 7). Essentially, financial promotions are covered by the Financial Promotions Order 2005, as amended[3]. This requires any such promotion to be issued by a frim regulated by the FCA[4]. There are also requirements imposed by the statutory instrument in terms of content.

1 SI 2005/1529, as amended.
2 Financial Services and Markets Act 2000, s 21.
3 SI 2005/1529, as amended
4 S.21 Financial Services and Markets Act 2000

Communication to be fair and not misleading

5.31 COBS 4.2 provides a basic requirement, which is for communications to be clear, fair and not misleading. The rule is applied in a way which is:

'appropriate and proportionate taking into account the means of communication and the information the communication is meant to convey.' (COBS 4.2.2).

This covers not only the wording of a communication but also the manner in which it is presented. For instance, where the investment contains a degree of risk then disclosure of that risk should be given equal prominence to the reward that may be achieved through good performance. The rule extends to all communications with customers which are not caught by the Financial Promotions regime[1]. The Rule will apply to all client agreements, periodic statements, financial reports, telephone calls etc. In considering what constitutes clear, fair and not misleading the firm should take account of the customer's knowledge of the designated investment business to which the information relates. This means that if the customer is a retail client classed as a professional client by virtue of expertise then a different (and lower) standard will be applied in assessing the communication than if the customer were a private client.

5.32 Specific requirements in the rules (COBS 4.2.4) state that promotions should satisfy the following requirements:

- Is the client's capital will be at risk, this should be made clear;

- If a yield figure is quoted it must give a balanced impression of the short and long term prospects of the investment;

- There must be a clear, fair and not misleading explanation of any charges and sufficient information to make matters clear where the charging structure is complex and the firm will receive more than one element of remuneration;

- If the FCA and PRA are mentioned, it must be made clear which matters are not regulated by them (if any); and

- If it relates to packaged or stakeholder products not produced by the firm, a clear, fair and not misleading impression must be given of the producer or the manager of the underlying investments.

Particular care needs to be taken with regard to "clear, fair and not misleading" when using words such as "guaranteed", "protected" and "secure"[1]

1 COBS 4.2.5

5.33 Any reference to the investors' compensation scheme must be limited to a factual description.

Communicating with retail clients

5.34 Where a communication relating to designated investment business is likely to be received by a retail client then it must contain the name of the firm, be accurate and not emphasise the potential benefits without also giving a fair and prominent indication of any relevant risks. This rule does not apply to a third party prospectus, image advertising or MiFID or equivalent third country business. Nor does it apply to excluded communications or a prospectus where PR 3.3 applies.

5.35 A frim must also consider whether the omission of a fact might result in the communication being insufficient, unfair or misleading[1].

1 COBS 4.5.5

5.36 Comparative information must be provided in a fair and balanced way and where it relates to MiFID or equivalent third country business, the sources of the relevant information must be specified and the key facts and assumptions must be set out[1].

1 COBS 4.5.6

Simulated performance

5.37 Where a simulated past or future performance is indicated then, in essence:

–   The indication must be the most prominent part of the communication;

–   The period covered must be the previous five years, the whole period for which the investment has been offered (or index established) if less than five years and it must show a full twelve month periods;

–   The reference period and source of information must be stated;

–   It must clearly state that past performance is no indicator of the future;

–   If the currency used is not that of an EEA state in which the retail client is resident, the currency must be stated as must the currency fluctuation risk; and

–   If gross figures are used, the impact of commissions, fees and other charges must be shown[1].

There are additional rules[2] where past performance is simulated.

1 COBS 4.6.2
2 At COBS 4.6.6

5.38 Communications referring to future performance must satisfy the following. Namely that it:

–   is based on simulated past performance;

–   is based on reasonable assumptions supported by objective data;

–   Discloses the effect of commissions, fees and other charges if based on gross performance; and

–   Contains a prominent warning that such forecasts are not reliable indicators of the future[1].

1 COBS 4.6.7

Provision of information

5.39 COBS 6 provides the relevant details that need to be provided to retail clients, and in the case of MiFID or equivalent third country business clients, in a durable medium, in a clear and accurate manner in the relevant language. The information is set out clearly in COBS and requires no analysis or explanation. Essentially it covers information about the firm and its services, primarily being information concerning safeguarding of designated investments belonging to clients and client money, costs and associated charges together with timing and medium of disclosure.

Insurance Mediation (COBS 7)

5.40 Prior to a life policy being entered into a firm must, as a minimum, tell the client:

- The firm's name and address;
- That it is registered with the FCA and its number or alternately if registered elsewhere, the register on which it is registered;
- Whether it has more than ten per cent of the voting rights in an insurer;
- How to complain to the Financial Ombudsman;
- Whether the firm gives advice on the basis of a fair assessment of the market;
- If it has any exclusive arrangements with insurers, and if so the client must be told that they can request the names; and
- That the firm is not obliged to conduct its insurance mediation business exclusively with one or more issuer and does not give advice on a fair analysis of the market, and if that is the case the client must be told they can request the names of the insurers that the firm does business with.

5.40 If the client has been told the firm gives advice on a fair analysis of the market, there must be a sufficiently large number of life policies available on the market to facilitate this[1].

1 COBS 7.2.3

5.41 A demands and needs statement should be provided to the client to facilitate determining whether the client has other insurance needs.

TERMS OF AGREEMENT AND CLIENT AGREEMENTS

5.42 COBS requires, with limited exceptions, firms to issue terms of business to a customer before providing investment services. In certain cases firms are required to enter into client agreements with retail clients. There are detailed provisions in COBS concerning the content of such agreements. The type of agreement and the circumstances in which it is required will be determined by the investment services to be provided and whether the firm is dealing with a retail or professional client.

Terms of business

5.43 Terms of business are required to be provided by a firm to a customer with which or for whom it is intending to or does conduct designated investment business unless it falls within an exception (see below). COBS 8.1.3 provides that the client agreement must set out the basis on which the designated investment business is to be conducted. This must in all cases be provided in good time before designated investment business is conducted. COBS 8.1.3 (3) provides that it will be sufficient if the agreement is provided immediately after the client is bound by an agreement provided that the firm could not do so sooner because the client had requested a means of distance communication that made doing so earlier impossible.

5.44   Client agreements may be set out in more than one document provided it is clear that they constitute terms of business and the use of more than one document does not materially diminish the significance of the information provided or the ease with which it can be understood. However, they must be in a durable medium of offered through a website, though in the latter case additional requirements are imposed on the firm.

5.45   It should be remembered that eligible counterparties fall outside the definition of clients covered by these rules and firms are not required by the rules to issue terms of business to them[1]. Nor does this part of the rules apply to firms effecting life assurance contracts as principal.

1 COBS 8.1.1 (1)

5.46   The firm must notify the client in good time if there are any changes to the agreement and do so in a durable medium.

5.47   The firm has to keep a record of client agreements setting out the terms for the longer of: five years, the client relationship or in the case of a pension transfer, pension opt out or FSAVC, indefinitely.

EXCLUSION CLAUSES

Duties and liabilities under the general law

5.48   There are a range of legal limitations on the capacity of a firm to impose restraint clauses. Any FCA registered firm must act in line with this.

Unfair Contract Terms Act 1977 and Unfair Terms in Consumer Contract Regulations 1994

5.49   Customers seeking to avoid unfair terms may also be able to rely on the test of 'reasonableness' under UCTA 1977 and 'good faith' under UTCCR 1994, although their application to investment agreements is limited. UCTA 1977 applies to contracts for investment advice and investment management, but not to contracts of insurance or contracts for the creation or transfer of securities. The UTCCR 1994 apply, inter alia, to customer agreements for 'the sale and purchase of securities and for the provision of advice and other services, such as portfolio management'.

SUITABILITY

5.50   The requirement that firms ensure investments are suitable for customers is a major feature of the system of investor protection introduced in this country. The precise nature of the rules has been amended because of depolarisation and the removal of the requirements either to be an independent intermediary or a tied advisor. The framework is designed to achieve suitability of investments for investors through the interaction of a number of rules and principles. This section considers the regulations that must be observed by firms when selecting investments for their customers.

5.51   The COBS rules on suitability apply to firms which are making personal recommendations about designated investments to a retail client or acting as investment manager for a retail client. The rules also apply to a firm when it manages the assets of an OPS or a stakeholder pension scheme and when it promotes a personal pension scheme by way of a direct offer financial promotion[1] to a group of employees. In the latter case this may well involve a comparison of a group personal pension scheme and a stakeholder pension scheme since they will be required as a firm to satisfy itself on reasonable grounds that the group personal pension scheme is at least as suitable for the majority of the employees as a stakeholder scheme and to record why it thinks the promotion is justified[2]. If there is a personal recommendation for a pension transfer or opt out this must be decided by a pension transfer specialist[3]. Suitability also applies if the firm is not an insurer and it makes a personal recommendation to an intermediate customer or market counterparty to take out a life policy. Suitability in the case of personal recommendations[4] and discretionary transactions is determined by reference to the facts disclosed by the private customer and other facts about him of which the firm is or reasonably should be aware.

1 This is a promotion which: (a) contains: (i) an offer by the firm to enter into an agreement with anyone who responds to the financial promotion; or (ii) an invitation to anyone who responds to the financial promotion to make an offer to the firm to enter into an agreement; and (b) specifies the manner of response or includes a form in which any response is to be made (for example by a tear-off slip). In summary, a controlled agreement is an agreement which constitutes the carrying on of designated investment business.
2 COBS 19.1.2
3 COBS 19.1.1
4 Those are recommendations made to a specific person. In order for it to amount to designated investment business the recommendation must go beyond a general recommendation of a type of investment product and must be specific to a particular product.

5.52   In essence the rule requires a firm to take reasonable steps to ensure that any recommendations or transactions are suitable for the client where the rule applies. The specific transactions to which the Rule applies are set out at COBS 9.2.1 to 9.2.3. The rules do not apply where basic advice is being provided on stakeholder products. Separate rules apply there.

5.53   The COBS rules relating to standards of investment advice are considered below. They are supplemented by FSA 2012, s89 - 91 which have replaced FSMA 2000, s.397; and by Principle 9 'Customers: relationships of trust' which approaches the question of suitability. Specifically it states: "A firm must take reasonable care to ensure the suitability of its advice and discretionary decisions for any customer who is entitled to rely upon its judgment."

FSA 2012, ss 89, 90 and 91

5.54   These sections make it a criminal offence to mislead investors in relation to investment agreements or rights arising from investments.

5.55   Section 89(1) applies to any person who essentially:

(a)   makes a statement, promise or forecast which he knows to be misleading, false or deceptive in a material particular; or

(b)   dishonestly conceals any material facts whether in connection with a statement, promise or forecast made by him or otherwise; or

(c)   recklessly makes (dishonestly or otherwise) a statement, promise or forecast which is misleading, false or deceptive in a material particular.

5.56   Section 89(2) provides that such a person is guilty of an offence if he makes the statement, promise or forecast or conceals the facts for the purpose of inducing, or is reckless as to whether it may induce, another person (whether or not the person to whom the statement, promise or forecast is made) to enter or offer to enter into, or to refrain from entering or offering to enter into, a relevant agreement or to exercise, or refrain from exercising, any rights conferred by a relevant investment.

5.57   Section 90 extends this to criminalise any act or course of conduct which creates a false or misleading impression as to the market in or the price or value of any product. It also covers such behaviour causing someone to refrain from acquiring an investment.

5.58   Section 91 is of less relevance in the context of this chapter. It extends liability for the same type of behaviour as sections 89 and 90 in the context of benchmarks such as LIBOR.

Principle 9, Customer: relationships of trust

5.59   Principle 9 is directly aimed at enshrining the concept of suitability in a high level principle as stated above.

5.60   It should be noted that the principle (like the detailed COBS Rules on suitability – except for the specific provision relating to life products) does not apply to eligible counterparties but only to retail and business clients. Further it only applies to clients entitled to rely upon the firm's judgement. A client will be entitled to rely upon the firm's judgement where the COBS rules impose a suitability requirement and also where there is a suitability obligation in the agreement between the firm and the customer even though the rules may not apply. The obligation will not, of course, apply to execution-only transactions since in such cases the firm is not applying any judgement but is simply following an order.

In general, the position is that the suitability obligation applies where the firm is dealing with a private customer. The obligation on the firm under the principle is one of reasonable care to ensure suitability. This is not an absolute requirement and is an objective test the precise formulation of which will depend on the nature and extent of the business undertaken. Reasonable steps may include training, systems monitoring and oversight implementation by the firm. The rules do not prescribe what will amount to reasonable steps.

Suitability under the COBS Rules

5.61   The rules (COBS 9.2.1 in particular) require that firms must take reasonable steps to ensure that personal recommendations to and discretionary transactions for retail clients are suitable. Under the rules, firms do not need to take reasonable steps to ensure suitability for recommendations made to other clients except where a personal recommendation is made to an intermediate customer or market counterparty to take out a life policy. This explains for instance why firms must be particularly careful when classifying retail clients as professionals due to their expertise. The rules on suitability do not apply to execution-only customers. The suitability rule also applies to a firm which acts as investment manager for a retail client. Here the obligation is an ongoing one in that the firm is required to take reasonable steps to ensure that the retail client's portfolio or account remains suitable. Again, suitability will be tested by reference to the facts disclosed by the retail client himself and other relevant facts about the retail client of which the firm is or reasonably should be aware. Suitability requirements will also apply where with a retail client's consent a firm has pooled funds together with a view to taking common discretionary management decisions. Here the firm must take reasonable steps to ensure a discretionary transaction is suitable for the fund having regard to the investment objectives of the fund.

Suitability in practice

5.62   The suitability of an investment for a particular customer will be determined by the particular facts about and circumstances of that customer. To ensure investment decisions are suitable, a two stage process must be undertaken by a firm. First, information concerning the customer's circumstances and investment objectives must be established. Second, the firm must ensure this information is taken into account when deciding which type of investment is suitable. In short, the investment should be appropriate for the customer.

Information about the customer

5.63   The COBS Rules require firms to obtain information about the customer in order that a suitable investment can be selected as a 'know your customer' requirement is reflected in COBS 9.2.1.

5.64
The Rule applies to any firm that:

(1)   gives a personal recommendation concerning a designated investment to a retail client; or

(2)   acts as an investment manager for a retail client; or

(3)   manages the assets of an OPS or personal pension scheme for a retail client and the firm is not a MiFID or equivalent third country business; or

(4)   restricted rules apply where a firm recommends a life policy to a professional client. In that case the Insurance Mediation Directive's rules apply

5.65   Under COBS 'know your customer' information is not required in respect of an execution only transaction. It should be noted, however, that know your customer information may be required to satisfy the requirements of the Money Laundering Regulations 2007. In relation to a life policy, a demands and needs statement will have to be provided irrespective of the status of the client.

5.66   The requirement in COBS under 9.2.1 states that when making a personal recommendation or managing his investments the firm must determine the client's knowledge and experience, financial situation and objectives. It must also[1] obtain such information from him as is necessary for the firm to understand his investment objectives, that he can carry any related risks and that he has the necessary knowledge and experience to understand the risks. Without this a firm cannot make a personal recommendation[2].

1 See COBS 9.2.2
2 COBS 9.2.6

Personal circumstances and objectives

5.67   The personal circumstances and objectives of the customer should first be established. This is because the firm must have regard to the facts disclosed by that customer before making a recommendation or effecting or arranging a discretionary transaction. The firm should be able to show a correlation between the information gathered and a personal recommendation given or, where relevant, discretionary management decision taken. The guidance makes clear that the aim of gathering the information is so that a clear identification of the client's needs and priorities can be established and that this, combined with details of a customer's attitude to risk, will enable a suitable investment to be recommended.

5.68   In order that information concerning the customer's circumstances and objectives are recorded, firms typically interview the customer. There is, however, no requirement in the rules that a customer be interviewed in person and it is acceptable that adequate information is established by correspondence or telephone.

5.69   In practice, firms usually complete a 'fact-find' to retain details about a customer. A permanent document such as this also serves as evidence of the information obtained. Reliance by firms on standard pro-forma 'fact-finds' for all investment services, however, may not be appropriate since different investments will require the firm to gather different amounts and types of information to ensure suitability.

5.70 The information required from a customer, and to which a firm must have regard, will vary depending on the type of transaction under consideration. For instance, details of a customer's rights under an occupational pension scheme will be highly relevant to the question of whether a pension transfer is suitable for the customer, but is unlikely to be relevant to the question of whether a fund managed with discretion for the customer should increase its exposure to particular securities. In those circumstances, the customer's attitude to risk and his investment objectives in terms of income generation or capital appreciation are far more likely to be relevant.

Information from clients

5.71 Information required from the customer for the purpose of compliance with the rules is not just financial, such as affordability (although this is very important particularly where long-term regular premium investments with high early surrender penalties are concerned), and may for instance require firms to be aware of a customer's health, domestic and employment circumstances. Information concerning the customer's attitude to risk will be required. If an investment represents a long term financial commitment to the customer, more information will be needed to ensure suitability. In particular care will need to be taken to assess whether the customer has access to sufficient short-term funds to warrant his spare cash being tied up in a long term investment where early surrender may lead to significant penalties. Savings endowments are good examples of products where surrender penalties may make it unsuitable unless the customer can be sure that he can afford his funds to be tied up for a lengthy period without obtaining access.

5.72 Where a firm makes a personal recommendation to a client to acquire or sell a regulated c.i.s., an investment trust savings scheme or one held in an ISA then a suitability report must be prepared[1].

1 COBS 9.4.1

5.73 Guidance[1] makes clear that the record of the personal and financial information gathered by the firm can be retained either electronically or on paper. COBS 9.5.2 requires such records to be kept and retained indefinitely in the case of a pension transfer, pension opt-out or FSAVC; five years for a record relating to a life policy or pension contract, including a stakeholder pension scheme and relating to MiFID or third country business, and three years in any other case (ie. for the same period as customer classification).

1 COBS 9.5

5.74 With regard to affordability the guidance suggests that due regard should be given to the customer's current level of income and expenditure and likely future changes in income and expenditure. Particular specific guidance is also included in respect of low premium (less than £50 pa or £1 pw) friendly society life policies. This includes keeping a record of the reasons why this particular transaction is suitable for that individual customer[1].

1 COBS 9.2.9

5.75 The suitability report must, as a minimum, specify the client's demands and needs, explain the conclusion that the recommendation is suitable and show any possible disadvantages[1]. The obligation does not apply if the firm is acting as an investment manager for a retail client and recommends a regulated c.i.s. or if the client is habitually resident outside the EEA. Nor does it apply where small premiums of £1 a week or less payable to a friendly society are involved or if it is just increasing premiums to an existing policy[2].

1 COBS 9.4.7
2 COBS 9.4.3

5.76 It should be noted that information about customers retained by a firm remains confidential under fiduciary duties owed by the firm, the rules and, where relevant, the Data Protection Act 1984.

STANDARDS OF ADVICE FOR PACKAGED PRODUCTS

5.77 The previous rules in respect of advice on packaged products have been amended as a result of depolarisation. The basic position is now that the general rule relating to suitability applies but, in addition, if the recommendation relates to a packaged product then (subject to certain exceptions set out below) it must be the most suitable product from the range of packaged products on which that firm gives advice and if there are no packaged products in the firm's relevant range of products which are suitable then no recommendation must be made.

Suitability for whole of market advisors

5.78 If a firm holds itself out as a whole of market advisor then it must carry out a reasonable analysis of a sufficiently large number of packaged products based on criteria which reflect adequate knowledge of the packaged products generally available from the market or from the sector of the market on which it gives advice. Any recommendation must, in order to meet the general suitability requirement to take reasonable steps, be in accordance with the results of its analysis of packaged products. The recommendation should be for the packaged product, which, on the basis of that analysis, is the most suitable to meet the customers need's. Where a firm holds itself out as giving recommendations on life policies from the whole of market then equivalent requirements will apply. In such cases the suitability requirement applies to personal recommendations made to intermediate customers or market counterparties as well as to private customers.

BASIC ADVICE AND STAKEHOLDER PRODUCTS

5.79 The FCA has been concerned that not every customer wants, or can afford, fully tailored advice on their savings and investment needs and, therefore, a more 'off-the-peg' style of selling that should suit the needs of consumers who are looking for an alternative to full advice has been developed. The FCA believes that the basic advice regime will offer a simple, quicker and lower-cost form of advice to consumers interested in buying these products.

5.80   The Financial Services and Markets Act 2000 (Stakeholder Products) Regulations 2004[1] define the term 'stakeholder product' for the purposes of the Financial Services and Markets Act 2000 (Regulated Activities) Order 2001[2] and sets out the conditions which need to be satisfied in order to classify a product as a stakeholder product. The range of stakeholder products includes a cash deposit account, a medium term investment product and child trust funds. Providing basic advice to a retail customer on a stakeholder product has been a regulated activity. The rules on what firms must do when providing basic advice on stakeholder products are found at COBS 9.6. The rules are designed to enable firms to provide simple, quick and limited advice to persons who may be interested in buying a stakeholder product and assume that firms will provide basic advice to persons who have no practical knowledge of investing in stakeholder products or investments.

1 SI 2004/2738
2 SI 2001/544 as amended

What is basic advice?

5.81   The COBS Rules enable firms to give simple, quick and limited advice to people who are interested in buying stakeholder products. Basic advice is a short, simple form of financial advice which uses pre-scripted questions to identify the customer's financial priorities and decide whether a product from within their range is suitable for that customer. Basic advice establishes only broad financial priorities and takes limited account of the customer's financial circumstances. It also provides for advisors to offer suitable recommendations, not the most suitable recommendation. Sales people providing basic advice are not required to hold formal financial planning qualifications, however they must be competent to administer basic advice.

STAKEHOLDER PRODUCTS

Basic advice

5.82   Firms can follow the rules in COBS 9.6 and just give basic advice where stakeholder products are concerned. **More than one range of stakeholder products can be maintained. A range of such products can include:**

–   More than one deposit based stakeholder product;

–   The stakeholder products of more than one provider;

–   But must not include more than one out of (1) a c.i.s. stakeholder product or linked life stakeholder product, (2) a stakeholder CTF or (3) a stakeholder pension scheme.

5.83 'Basic advice' consists of explaining why the stakeholder products and providers were chosen and providing the client with a list of the stakeholder products and advisers in the range.

5.84 When a firm first has contact with a retail client to give basic advice on a stakeholder product it must give them the following in a durable medium: the basic advice disclosure information which is set out at COBS 9, Annex 1 R unless it has already done so and the information is unlikely to be out of date, or the contact is not face to face and it is impractical to provide the information in a durable medium. It must also give them an explanation of how the advice will be paid for and the fact that any commission will be disclosed.

5.85 Basic advice can be given by firms to retail clients as part of either a services and costs disclosure document or a combined initial disclosure document rather than in isolation. In the latter of the two instances the firm must have reasonable grounds to believe that the services it is going to provide include either a stakeholder product, a non-investment insurance contract an equity release transaction or a home purchase plan. If either are done the firm must comply with COBS 2.2.1R(1)(a) and (d), COBS 9.6.5R and 9 Annex 1. If distance marketing is involved COBS 5 Annex 1 R (1), (2), (4), (5), (19) and (20) and where duties relating to information provided to the firm by an insurance intermediary are concerned, COBS 7.2.1R(1) and (2).

5.86 A firm can satisfy the obligation to provide written disclosure concerning breadth of advice[1] by providing with its basic advice initial disclosure information.

1 COBS 6.2A.5R

5.87 If the firm's first contact with a retail client is not face to face the firm must tell the client that the firm will provide basic advice without a full assessment of the client and that this information will be confirmed in writing. If the initial meeting had been initiated by the firm it must also tell the client the name of the firm and the commercial reason for getting in touch[1]. In any event the basic advice initial disclosure information must be sent in a durable form as soon as reasonably possible after the first contract is concluded, at the latest. If the contract is set up by verbal interaction with the client (deposit based stakeholder products excepted) the information for additional oral disclosure should be provided to the effect that restricted advice is offered[2].

1 COBS 9.6.8
2 COBS 9.6.8 (3) and 6.2A.9R

5.88 If a firm is giving basic advice it must do so on a single range of stakeholder products and do so by putting pre scripted questions to the clients. However, they must not describe a product outside the firm's range or a smoothed linked long term stakeholder product. They cannot describe fund choice or recommend one if a stakeholder product offers a choice of funds. Nor can they recommend the level of contributions to be made to a stakeholder pension or recommend that a client makes ISA contributions that exceed HMRC limits[1].

1 COBS 9.6.9 and 9.6.10

Stakeholder recommendations

5.89   A firm can only recommend a stakeholder product to a retail client if it has taken reasonable steps to assess the client's answers to the scripted questions and any other information they have provided. It must reasonably believe the product recommended is suitable for the client, though there is an exception for deposit based stakeholder products where this requirement is not imposed. The firm must also reasonably believe that the client understands the advice.

5.90   To satisfy these suitability requirements the following is provided by the FCA as guidance[1]. This is set out as an appendix to this chapter.

1 COBS 9 Annex 2 G.

5.91   A firm giving basic advice to a retail client to the effect that they should buy a stakeholder product must make sure that before the contract is concluded, the firm's representative has explained to the client the information needed to make an informed decision about what a stakeholder product is and the most vital parts of the key features document. These are determined to be "aims", "commitments" and "risks". This can be done in an abbreviated form. This is not needed when the client is entering into a deposit based stakeholder product. It must also provide the client with a summary sheet in a durable medium and set out for each of the products it is recommending the amount the client wants to pay in and the reasons for the recommendations made. This must take into account the client's attitude to risk and the information the client has provided. It must also tell the client if they later complain to the Ombudsman, it will be taken into account if they have failed to provide the firm with sufficient information[1].

1 COBS 9.6.14

5.92   Once a contract involving a stakeholder product is concluded for a retail client the firm must let the client have a copy of the completed questions and answers in a durable medium as soon as reasonably possible[1].

1 COBS 9.6.16

5.93   A firm must make sure that none of its representatives are influenced by the way in which they are remunerated to give unsuitable advice on stakeholder products for retail clients. It must also make sure that none of its representatives refer a retail client to another firm in return for a fee or commission.

5.94   Records must be kept of the basic advice given to retail clients along with the summary sheet for each client. The firm must also have an up to date record of its scope of basic advice and also any such advice along with its range of stakeholder products. This extends to any such activity carried out by appointed representatives. Records must be kept for five years.

CUSTOMER UNDERSTANDING OF RISK

5.95   The essential element is that the firm seeks to ensure the customer understands the nature of any risks in an investment. The steps that must be taken by a firm for each transaction will depend on the customer's ability to understand and his experience of the investment. Firms may need to repeat warnings already given to a customer if necessary. Principle 7 requires a firm to pay due regard to the information needs of a client and communicate in a way that is clear, fair and not misleading.

When should risks be notified?

5.96   Notification of the risks should be made before or at the same time as the recommendation of an investment or, in the case of discretionary management services to be provided by a firm, prior to the service being provided. For packaged products sold by any regulated firm the key features document issued by the product provider will address risk factors . The adviser cannot simply rely on key features to ensure understanding of risks and will need to consider separately whether that is adequate to explain the risks.

5.97   The risks which should be communicated to a retail client go beyond a mere explanation of potential loss when purchasing an investment of fluctuating value. Explanations may be required concerning, for example: loss of cancellation rights, surrender values of life policies, possible exchange rate losses and, in certain circumstances, potential tax liabilities.

APPROPRIATENESS (NON-ADVISED SERVICES)

5.98   When carrying on investment business *other* than making personal recommendations or dealing with the course of MiFID or equivalent third country business, a firm must ask the client to provide information regarding their knowledge and experience relevant to the product and service provided[1]. The firm may rely on information already in its possession for this purpose[2]. This is carried out for retail clients to see if they understand the risks involved, but is not necessary for professional clients. Retail clients must be warned if the firm does not think the investment is appropriate in the light of that information. A warning should be given to the client if they do not provide the firm with the necessary information so that the firm cannot determine what is appropriate[3].

1 COBS 10.2.1
2 COBS 10.2.5
3 COBS 10.3.2

5.99   Appropriateness does not need to be determined in execution only arrangements if the client has been told that the suitability check will not be carried out and the firm does not allow a conflict of interest to manifest itself[1]. This rule applies where the relevant investments are either listed shares, money market instruments, bonds, securitised debt, units in a scheme covered by the UCITS Directive and any other non-complex investment, ie, it is not a derivative or a leveraged product and there must be a liquid market in it.

1 COBS 10.4.1

5.100   Records of all this must be kept for five years.

APPROPRIATENESS (ADVISED SERVICES)

5.101   A firm must determine whether a product or service is appropriate for a client and obtain sufficient information from them to do so when providing services in the course of a MiFID or equivalent third country business other than managing investments and making personal recommendations. This rule is therefore relevant when a firm is arranging deals in relation to non-realisable securities, derivatives or warrants for a retail client and where the firm ought to be aware that the client is acting in response to a financial promotion that is a direct offer. This approach also applies where the firm is assessing appropriateness for another MiFID firm so that the second firm can rely on it. In either case the firm must warn the client if it believes the product or service is not appropriate for them. The client should also be warned if they are not providing the firm with sufficient information[1].

1 COBS 10.1.1, 10.1.2, 10.2.1, 10.1.3, 2.4.4 and 10.3.1

5.102   In making this assessment the firm has to take into account whether the client has the knowledge or experience to understand the risks involved. However, if it is a professional client this can be assumed if the firm is acting in the client's area of expertise[1].

1 COBS 10.2.1

5.103   The firm does not need to bother making such an assessment where all the firm is doing is executing or transmitting client instructions in relation to traded shares, money market instruments, bonds securitised debt, units in a UCITS Directive governed scheme and other non-complex instruments. The client does not have to be told that the firm is not required to make the assessment and make sure there is no conflict of interest[1]. With ongoing activity for a client a new assessment is not required each time.

1 COBS 10.4.1

5.104   Relevant records must be kept for five years[1].

1 COBS 10.7

BEST EXECUTION

5.105   A firm has to take reasonable steps to get the best possible result when executing client transactions whenever there is a contractual or agency obligation to do so[1]. It is recognised that because of the different market structures that exist for different types of investment there is no uniform method for achieving this[2]. In achieving this the firm has to factor in whether the person concerned is a retail or professional client, the order they have placed, the investment involved and the execution venue. If a management company is involved its objectives and policies have to be taken into account. Generally speaking, the aim of best execution will be to obtain the best price but there may be cases where other factors are more important[3].

1 For a useful discussion on this see 320.pdf
2 COBS 11.2.1 and 11.2.5
3 COBS 11.2.9

5.106   Retail clients must be given details of the firm's execution policy stating which factors the firm regards as execution criteria, the execution venues that it uses and a clear statement that specific instructions from the client might stop this operating[1]. The client's consent must be obtained if orders are to be executed outside a regulated market or multilateral trading facility unless the firm is engaged in portfolio management for a UCITS scheme. Client orders must be handled promptly and efficiently, though portfolio management services operate outside the rule[2].

1 COBS 11.2.23
2 COBS 11.3.1

RECORD KEEPING

5.107   Proper record keeping is required, as would be expected. In relation to all client orders to deal, the records must cover:

–   The name or designation of the client;

–   The name or designation of someone acting on the client's behalf;

–   Points 2, 3, 4, 6, 16–21 of Table 1 of Annex 1 of the MiFID Regulation, being:

2.   Trading day. The trading day on which the transaction was executed.

3.   Trading time. The time at which the transaction was executed, reported in the local time of the competent authority to which the transaction will be reported, and the basis in which the transaction is reported expressed as Co-ordinated Universal Time (UTC) +/– hours.

4.   Buy/sell indicator. Identifies whether the transaction was a buy or sell from the perspective of the reporting investment firm or, in the case of a report to a client, of the client.

6.   Instrument identification. This shall consist of:

–   a unique code to be decided by the competent authority (if any) to which the report is made identifying the financial instrument which is the subject of the transaction;

–   if the financial instrument in question does not have a unique identification code, the report must include the name of the instrument or, in the case of a derivative contract, the characteristics of the contract.

16.   Unit price. The price per security or derivative contract excluding commission and (where relevant) accrued interest. In the case of a debt instrument, the price may be expressed either in terms of currency or as a percentage.

17.   Price notation. The currency in which the price is expressed. If, in the case of a bond or other form of securitised debt, the price is expressed as a percentage, that percentage shall be included.

18.   Quantity. The number of units of the financial instruments, the nominal value of bonds, or the number of derivative contracts included in the transaction.

19.   Quantity notation. An indication as to whether the quantity is the number of units of financial instruments, the nominal value of bonds or the number of derivative contracts.

20.   Counterparty. Identification of the counterparty to the transaction. That identification shall consist of:

–   where the counterparty is an investment firm, a unique code for that firm, to be determined by the competent authority (if any) to which the report is made;

–   where the counterparty is a regulated market or MTF or an entity acting as its central counterparty, the unique harmonised identification code for that market, MTF or entity acting as central counterparty, as specified in the list published by the competent authority of the home Member State of that entity in accordance with Article 13(2);

–   where the counterparty is not an investment firm, a regulated market, an MTF or an entity acting as central counterparty, it should be identified as 'customer/client' of the investment firm which executed the transaction.

21.   Venue identification. Identification of the venue where the transaction was executed. That identification shall consist in:

–   where the venue is a trading venue: its unique harmonised identification code;

–   otherwise: the code 'OTC'.

–   The nature of the order;

–   The type of order;

–   Any other details;

–   Date and time.

5.107   All transactions must have records kept that show the name or designation of the client, the table set out at 5.106 above, the price and quantity, the nature of the transaction and the individual responsible for execution.

5.108   If the investment firm transmits the execution order to another firm for execution there must be a record of the name of the client concerned, who the order was transmitted to, the terms of the order and the date and exact time of transmission.

5.109   Firms must take reasonable steps to record telephone conversations and relevant telephone conversations provided by the firm and on which the employees carry out their duties. They must be kept for at least six years[1]. There are some allowances for discretionary investment managers. Even here firms would be wise to err on the side of caution and keep such records.

1 COBS 11.8.5 and 11.8.10

PRODUCT DISCLOSURE AND KEY FEATURES

5.110 COBS requires that written details or 'product particulars' of life and non-life packaged products together with cash ISAs and cash deposit child trust funds be issued to private customers when making a purchase. The product provider or stakeholder pension scheme operator is required to produce these documents. The document required is a key features document in the case of a packaged product. In the case of life policies the information must be prepared on the basis of the Consolidated Life Directive information[1]. This section does not go through these requirements in detail. The purpose of this section is to give an overview of the circumstances in which such documents are required and the point in the process at which they are required.

1 COBS 13.1.2

Nature of a key features document

5.111 There are exceptions; for example a firm is not required to prepared documents if another firm has agreed to do so or it is a key features document for a unit in either a UCITS, an EEA UCITS, and key features scheme (if a simplified prospectus is issued) or a stakeholder pension scheme that is not a personal pension. Neither do they have to do so if it is a key features illustration for a unit in a UCITS and EEA UCITS, if it is information from a key features illustration or where it is a packaged product with the return of the initial capital and a specified level of growth. Finally they do not have to do so for reinsurance or pure protection policies. The firm can combine more than one key features scheme, document or simplified prospectus if the schemes are offered through a platform service and the difference between the schemes is described.

Issue of key features document

5.112 In practice, the key features document will be prepared by the packaged product provider, such as the insurance company or unit trust operator and firms arranging such products may rely on this to discharge their duty to prepare key features. This obligation on product providers and stakeholder pension scheme operators to produce key features provides that the key features or information must be provided in a durable medium. Guidance reminds firms that a key features or information document is a financial promotion and that therefore the rules on financial promotions will apply.

5.113 The rules concerning issue of key features documents are designed to ensure that it is sent to retail clients as early as possible in the process of buying the packaged product. COBS requires, in the case of life policies, for the firm to provide the private customer with key features before the private customer completes an application for the policy. Where the policy is sold on the recommendation of an intermediary then the obligation to provide the key features is with the intermediary.

5.114 Key features documents must contain enough information about the nature and complexity of the product, explain how it works, the standards that apply and the benefits and risks. The extent of the information is determined by what the client needs to know to make an informed decision. To this end it must explain complaints handling, compensation available under the financial services compensation scheme whether there are cancellation rights and if so the terms, in the case of CTFs which types are available and for personal pensions schemes the fact that stakeholder ones are available as well.

5.115 Where packaged products are concerned the key features document must include the title: 'key features of the [name of product]'; describe the product in the order of the following headings, and by giving the following information under those headings:

Heading	Information to be given
'Its aims'	A brief description of the product's aims
'Your commitment' or 'Your investment'	What a retail client is committing to or investing in and any consequences of failing to maintain the commitment or investment
'Risks'	The material risks associated with the product, including a description of the factors that may have an adverse effect on performance or are material to the decision to invest
'Questions and Answers'	(in the form of questions and answers) the principle terms of the product, what it will do for a retail client and any other information necessary to enable a retail client to make an informed decision[1].

1 COBS 13.3.2

5.116 Where a packaged product or cash deposit ISA or CTF is sold to a retail client special rules apply. The firm must provide a key features document and illustration, though this is not necessary where the product is a unit in a UCITS scheme, simplified prospectus scheme or an EEA UCITS scheme.

Life Policy Information

5.117 If the firm is selling a life policy it must provide the information required by the Life Consolidation Directive to the client. Namely,

(1)   The firm's name and its legal form;

(2)   The name of the EEA State in which the head office and, where appropriate, agency or branch concluding the contract is situated; and

(3)   The address of the head office and, where appropriate, agency or branch concluding the contract.

Information about the commitment

(4)   Definition of each benefit and each option;

(5)   Term of the contract;

(6)   Means of terminating the contract;

(7)   Means of payment of premiums and duration of payments;

(8)   Means of calculation and distribution of bonuses;

(9)   Indication of surrender and paid-up values and the extent to which they are guaranteed;

(10) Information on the premiums for each benefit, both main benefits and supplementary benefits, where appropriate;

(11) For unit-linked policies, definition of the units to which the benefits are linked;

(12) Indication of the nature of the underlying assets for unit-linked policies;

(13) Arrangements for application of the cooling-off period;

(14) General information on the tax arrangements applicable to the type of policy;

(15) The arrangements for handling complaints concerning contracts by policyholders, lives assured or beneficiaries under contracts including, where appropriate, the existence of a complaints body, without prejudice to the right to take legal proceedings; and

(16) Law applicable to the contract where the parties do not have a free choice or, where the parties are free to choose the law applicable, the law the insurer proposes to choose.

5.118   If a life policy or personal pension scheme is varied for a retail client so that the client can make income withdrawals or take out a short term annuity then sufficient information must be provided so that the client understands the consequences of their decision.

5.119   If a firm sells a unit in a simplified prospectus scheme to a client it must offer the scheme's simplified prospectus and if it is a retail client in the EEA, must also provide them with sufficient information for the client to be able to make an informed decision on whether to hold the units in a wrapper, on the three main types of CTF available and on the type of CTF the firm offers.

5.120   If the firm is selling units in a UCITS or an EEA UCITS scheme it must provide the client with a copy of the scheme's key investor information document and if it is a retail client provide the additional information in COBS 13.3.1.R, ie, standard key features information.

5.121   There are special arrangements available whereby operators of non UCITS retail schemes can get dispensation from the FCA to provide more limited information.

5.122 Authorised fund managers of an ICVC who sell UCITS scheme units directly or through a third party must make sure investors are provided with appropriate key investor information free of charge[1]. If the units are not sold in this way the firm still has an obligation to provide the information on request to product manufacturers and intermediaries selling them or advising on them. The information can be provided either on paper or in a durable form other than this, eg, a satisfactory website, but the firm must be prepared to deliver a paper copy on request free of charge.

1 COBS 14.2.1 A

5.123 A firm is not required to produce documents if they have arranged for another firm to do this subject to some minor exceptions[1].

1 See COBS 14.2.5 to 14.2.10

CANCELLATION RIGHTS

Rights to cancel and withdraw

5.124 COBS provides private retail clients with rights to withdraw before sale together with post sale rights to cancel. Rights to cancel are rights to cancel an investment agreement after the agreement has been signed and after the investor has received a post-sale notice[1] from the firm. A right to withdraw applies to certain investments and prevents the firm from accepting the offer from the customer for at least seven days after the offer is made. Rights to withdraw and to cancel apply to individual customers and to certain products. They are not therefore limited to private customers and will apply to individual intermediate customers.

1 A post-sale notice is a notice advising the investor of his right to cancel.

5.125 The general position is that for up to two weeks after the purchase of certain investments[1], customers are able to cancel the investment. If the right to cancel is exercised, the firm must refund all moneys paid by the customer, subject – in the case of lump sum investments only - to a potential shortfall deduction. Some cancellation rights only apply where advice is given. Certain other policies see this cancellation period extended to thirty calendar days[2].

1 Cash deposit ISAs; regulated collective investment schemes; child trust funds, Enterprise Investment Schemes, accepting deposits and issuing electronic money.
2 These are: life policies, personal or stakeholder pension schemes, pension transfers, a contract to vary such a scheme by making income withdrawals.

5.126 A firm can elect to provide a longer cancellation period and additional cancellation rights.

CHURNING AND SWITCHING

5.127 Remuneration in the investment industry is often commission based and a firm that effects a greater number of transactions is likely to see a commensurate increase in income. 'Churning' or 'switching' is the practice of generating additional income for the firm by recommending, or effecting with discretion, unnecessary transactions for customers. The

COBS Rules are designed to prevent such unjustifiable transactions. The provisions apply where a firm conducts designated investment business with or for a customer (that includes both retail and professional clients).

Churning: personal recommendations

5.128   In short, the rules at COBS 9.3.2 provide that a firm must not make a personal recommendation to a private customer to deal; or to switch within, or between, packaged products, including life policies, unless it has taken reasonable steps to ensure that the switch or deal is in the customer's best interest when viewed in isolation and in the context of earlier transactions.

5.129   The key to assessing whether churning has taken place is whether, in all the circumstances, the dealing would appear to be too frequent. It should be noted that perfectly legitimate switching may take place where tied salesforces become independent and are then in a position where they can advise on a wide range of products. In making recommendations to existing customers to switch to different products, advisers will need to take account of the surrender penalties or charges that may be incurred by the investor.

Churning and switching: discretionary management

5.130   When undertaking decisions with discretion, the COBS Rules prevent firms effecting transactions for private and intermediate customers if the dealing would reasonably be regarded as too frequent in the circumstances. The requirement applies to firms exercising discretion in respect of any dealing; or in relation to a switch within, or between, packaged products for private customers. Firms must have taken reasonable steps to ensure that the deal or switch is in the customer's best interests both when viewed in isolation and taking account of other transactions.

INFORMATION REPORTING

5.131   Clients must be sent adequate reports of the financial services provided by a firm[1] and these must be provided promptly in a durable form. Where a retail client is involved it must include transaction confirmation information no later than the first business day following, and in any event as soon as possible. If it has been received from a third party it must be sent on no later than the next business day[2]. The specific information is set out at COBS 16 Annex 1R. This rule does not apply to management activities if it would merely duplicate information sent by a third party.

1 COBS 16.1.1
2 COBS 16.2.1

5.132   Matters are slightly different where the firm is carrying out orders for a retail client in that there is an alternative method available where the client is provided at least bi-annually with the relevant trade confirmation material[1].

1 COBS 16.2.1(5)

5.133 Where the firm is managing investments an alternative approach exists whereby a bi-annual statement is provided in a durable form. It should be provided quarterly where a retail client requests it. In situations involving straightforward investments that do not involve cash settlement it can be done on a transaction by transaction basis, in which case there must also be an annual periodic statement. If the manager is handling a leveraged portfolio for a retail client the statement must be produced monthly[1]. In addition, if the client money is held than unless this has been covered in the periodic statement an annual one must be sent.

1 COBS 16.3.2

5.134 If client assets are held the details of all designated investments or client money held by the firm, the extent to which it is subject to securities financing transactions and the extent to which any benefit has accrued to the client must be set out in a statement.

5.135 Records must be kept for a minimum of five years from the date of despatch unless it is not MiFID or equivalent third country business in which case it is three years[1].

1 COBS 16.3.11

Appendix

COBS 9 Annex 2 G

SALES PROCESSES FOR STAKEHOLDER PRODUCTS

This Annex gives guidance on the standards and requirements to which a firm may have regard in designing a sales process for stakeholder products and assumes that firms will provide basic advice to retail clients who have no practical knowledge of investing in stakeholder products or investments.

General Standards – all sales

1. A sales process for stakeholder products may allow the representative administering it to depart from scripted questions where this is desirable to enable the retail client to better understand the points that need to be made provided this is compatible with the representative's competence and the degree of support offered by the firm's software and other systems. A software-based system is more likely to provide an adaptable means of providing prompts and support for representatives which may accordingly support a more flexible sales process.

2. Questions, statements and warnings provided should be short, simple and in plain language. Questions should address one issue at a time.

3. The sales process should enable the retail client to exit freely and without pressure at any stage. It should also allow the representative to terminate the process at any stage if it appears unlikely (for affordability, mismatch, risk or other reasons) that there is a suitable product for the retail client.

4. Where necessary the sales process should incorporate procedures to allow uncertainties in the retail client's answers to be addressed before proceeding and should generally reflect caution about proceeding if clarification or further information cannot be obtained during the process (for example if a retail client cannot confirm whether he or she is eligible for membership of an occupational pension scheme).

Preliminary – all sales

5. The retail client should be given the following preliminary information:

   (a) the retail client will only be given basic advice about stakeholder products;

   (b) stakeholder products are intended to provide a relatively simple and low-cost way of investing and saving;

(c)   the range of stakeholder products on which the representative will give advice to that retail client;

(d)   the retail client will be asked a series of questions about his or her needs and circumstances and, at the end of the procedure, he or she may be recommended to acquire a stakeholder product;

(e)   the assessment of whether a stakeholder product is suitable will be made without a detailed assessment of the retail client's needs but will be based only on the information disclosed during the questioning process; and

(f)   the retail client's answers will be noted and, at the end of the process, if a recommendation to acquire a stakeholder product is made, the retail client will be provided with a copy of the completed questionnaire.

6.   Following 5, the retail client should be asked if he or she wishes to proceed and, if not, the sales process should cease.

Affordability – all sales

7.   If it appears that the retail client is unlikely to be able to afford a stakeholder product, the sale should be terminated and the retail client given an explanation together with a copy of the questions and answers completed to that point.

Financial Priorities and Debt – all sales

8.   A retail client should be assessed to ascertain other possible financial priorities -for example, does the retail client need (a) insurance protection; (b) access to liquid cash to meet an emergency; or (c) to reduce existing debts? If appropriate, the retail client should be given an unambiguous warning about the desirability of meeting those priorities before acquiring a stakeholder product.

9.   A stronger warning about the desirability of addressing debt as a priority should be given if it appears that the retail client is significantly indebted, especially if there is a strong indication that the debt commitments may render any new commitment unaffordable in the short-term. For this purpose a firm should consider using a threshold or indicator to decide whether a retail client should be excluded on the basis of affordability. Examples may include where the retail client has (a) annual unsecured debt repayments in excess of 20% of gross annual income or (b) four or more active forms of unsecured debt or (c) has consistently reached his overdraft limit. A firm should review its chosen indicator or threshold regularly to ensure that it reflects prevailing economic conditions and takes account of industry best practice.

10.   A firm should clearly explain what it needs to know about a retail client's debt and consider using a range of alternative words (eg 'loans', 'student loans', 'borrowing' and 'other forms of credit') to ensure all relevant information is obtained. A firm may use a simple reckoner to assess retail client debt, but should be conscious of the

nature of, and not give the impression that it is providing more than, basic advice.

11. If a firm gives a warning about the desirability of meeting other priorities before acquiring a stakeholder product, or about affordability, it should also invite the retail client to consider terminating the sales process.

Saving and investment objectives - all sales (except establishing a stakeholder CTF)

12. A retail client's savings and investment objectives, including the period over which the retail client wishes to save or invest, should be ascertained including whether the retail client:

    (a) may need early access to some or all of the amount saved or invested; or

    (b) wishes to save or invest for retirement; or

    (c) wants to accumulate a specific sum by a specific date.

13. If that information indicates that the retail client's objective is:

    (a) to accumulate a specific sum by a specific date; or

    (b) to save or invest only for the short term; or

    (c) early access may be required to the whole of the sum saved or invested;

    the firm should not normally recommend a CIS stakeholder product, a linked life stakeholder product, a stakeholder pension scheme or topping up of a stakeholder CTF.

Tolerance of risk – all sales

14. If a retail client is not willing to accept any risk of the capital value of an investment being reduced then CIS stakeholder products, linked life stakeholder products and stakeholder CTFs should not usually be recommended. However, a firm may, if appropriate, explain the effect of inflation on long-term savings especially in relation to pensions and invite the retail client to consider his attitude to risk in the light of that explanation.

15. If a retail client is willing to accept the risk of capital reduction in some circumstances but not others then, before any recommendation to acquire a CIS stakeholder product or linked life stakeholder product is made, the retail client should be reminded of the other circumstances in which he or she is unwilling to accept risk to capital.

Stakeholder pensions

16. A stakeholder pension scheme should not be recommended, and the retail client should be advised to seek alternative or further advice, if it appears that the retail client:

    (a) has or will have access to an occupational pension scheme; or

(b) is likely to view income in retirement from state benefits as sufficient; or

(c) already has a pension to which he or she could make further contributions; or

(d) wishes to retire within five years.

17. It may also be appropriate to advise the retail client that other courses of action may be more beneficial than buying a stakeholder pension scheme (for example joining an occupational pension scheme).

18. A firm designing a sales process for use in the workplace may take account of the benefits offered by the employer. If a firm recommends a stakeholder pension scheme on the basis of benefits provided by an employer, then it should explain the basis of the recommendation to the retail client and suggest that the retail client seek advice if he or she has any concerns.

19. A firm should design its processes with a view to addressing the risk that retail clients will fail to appreciate the significance of questions about their pension provision and should accordingly incorporate a range of questions and information designed to foster the retail client's understanding of the issues and to elicit appropriate information.

20. Retail client should be told that a stakeholder pension scheme is lifestyled and what this means.

21. 2 A firm may provide a copy of the table setting out initial monthly pension amounts, found within the "Stakeholder pension decision tree" factsheet, available on www.moneyadviceservice.org.uk in accordance with COBS 13 Annex 2 1.8R, but in doing so should also provide and explain the caveats and assumptions behind the table. A firm should make it clear that the decision on how much to invest is the retail client's responsibility and that he should get further advice if has any concerns.

ISAs

22. A firm should ascertain whether the retail client has already opened a mini or maxi ISA and, if so, whether it would be appropriate for the retail client to open a non-ISA version of the same product.

Chapter 6

Financial Promotion

Owen Watkins

INTRODUCTION

6.1   In keeping with the general philosophy behind the Financial Services and Markets Act 2000 (FSMA 2000), the financial promotion regime seeks to rationalise and modernise, into a single consolidated whole, the existing requirements applying to investment promotions. In this case, however, the consolidation has also resulted in a new vocabulary. No longer does the statute speak of an 'advertisement' or of an 'unsolicited call'; instead, it covers 'an invitation or inducement to engage in investment activity' – that is, a financial promotion[1].

1 FSMA 2000, s 21(1). The words 'financial promotion', though not appearing in the actual text of s 21, are used in the heading and the marginal note.

6.2   Given that one of the main purposes behind the FSMA 2000 was the consolidation of existing requirements in banking, financial services and insurance legislation, it seems at first sight strange that the FSMA 2000 should in s 21 seek to change concepts with which firms and their advisers were well familiar, and instead introduce ones that are new. But throughout the consultation process on the new regime, the Treasury emphasised that its aim was to move to a more 'media neutral' concept. Recent technological developments in communications (in particular, the growth of the Internet) had meant that the existing legislation was becoming increasingly strained to accommodate electronic media within 'advertisements' and 'unsolicited calls'. It was a key Government aim that the financial services system in the United Kingdom should be best placed to reflect, and continue to reflect, the opportunities afforded by electronic commerce[1].

1 See HM Treasury, Financial Promotion – A Consultation Document (March 1999), part 1, paras 1.2–1.3; Financial Promotion – Second Consultation Document: A New Approach for the Information Age (October 1999), part 1, paras 1.2, 3.3; Financial Promotion – Third Consultation Document (October 2000), para 1.7.

THE STATUTORY PROVISION

6.3   The restriction on making a financial promotion (referred to in this chapter as 'the basic prohibition'), and the main circumstances in which the basic prohibition is lifted, are set out in the FSMA 2000, ss 21(1) and (2).

> '(1) A person ("A") must not, in the course of business, communicate an invitation or inducement to engage in investment activity.
>
> (2) But subsection (1) does not apply if—
>
> (a) A is an authorised person; or

(b) the content of the communication is approved for the purposes of this section by an authorised person.'

The FSMA 2000, s 21(5) gives the Treasury the power to create by order further exclusions, by specifying circumstances in which the basic prohibition will not apply. The Treasury has accordingly made an order under this section, the Financial Services and Markets Act 2000 (Financial Promotion) Order 2005[1].

1 SI 2005/1529, as amended, referred to in this chapter as the Financial Promotion Order and discussed further at 6.20 ff. This Order revokes and re-enacts, with certain amendments, the Financial Services and Markets Act 2000 (Financial Promotion) Order 2001, SI 2001/1335, as amended.

6.4   Breach of the FSMA 2000, s 21 is a criminal offence under s 25. This reflects the previous position regarding advertisements issued in breach of statutory requirements, but is tougher (at least compared to the Financial Services Act 1986 (FS Act 1986)) on a person who makes what would previously have been classified as an 'unsolicited call'[1]. A person in breach of the FSMA 2000, s 21 is subject to a maximum sentence of two years' imprisonment and an unlimited fine. The offence is one of strict liability, although it is a defence under s 25(2) to show that the person making the communication believed on reasonable grounds that the communication was prepared or approved for the purposes of s 21 by an authorised person, or that he took all reasonable precautions and exercised all due diligence to avoid committing the offence.

1 Under the FS Act 1986, a person who entered into an agreement with an investor following an unsolicited call in breach of s 56(1) did not commit a criminal offence, though in general he could not enforce the agreement against the investor. By contrast, breach of the unsolicited calls provision in respect of deposits was a criminal offence under the Banking Act 1987, s 34(3).

6.5   Any agreements made as a result of a communication that is in breach of the basic prohibition are generally unenforceable against the person who has entered as a customer into the agreement. In addition, the customer is entitled to recover any money or other property that he has paid or transferred under the agreement, as well as compensation for any loss that he has suffered as a result[1]. Likewise, if as a consequence of an unlawful communication a person exercises any rights conferred by an investment, any obligation to which he is subject as a result is unenforceable against him and he has a similar entitlement to recover money, property and compensation[2]. Only if the court decides that in the circumstances it is just and equitable will the agreement or obligation be enforced or the money or property be allowed to be retained[3].

1 FSMA 2000, s 30(2).
2 FSMA 2000, s 30(3).
3 FSMA 2000, s 30(4).

The key concepts

6.6   The FSMA 2000, s 21(1) introduces four concepts that are key to whether the basic prohibition applies or not. These are as follows.

(1)   A person must be acting in the course of business

6.7   Under the FSMA 2000, s 21(4), the Treasury has the power to specify by order circumstances in which a person is to be regarded as acting, or as not acting, in the course of business. The Treasury indicated back in 1999 that it had no present intention to do so, and that in the absence of such an order the phrase 'in the course of business' is intended to have its ordinary meaning[1]. It will thus be for the courts to decide, in the light of the circumstances concerned, whether or not a person is acting in the course of business. However, the fact that no order has been made since the FSMA came into force indicates that in practice this concept does not cause any material difficulties.

1 Financial Promotion – Second Consultation Document: A New Approach for the Information Age (October 1999), part 1, paras 4.5–4.6.

6.8   The requirement to act in the course of business means that personal communications will not fall within the scope of the FSMA 2000, s 21(1). So correspondence from one close relative to another, conversations between friends, and e-mails posted on a bulletin board or sent to an internet chat room will not be covered, provided that there is no commercial motivation behind the communication.

6.9   The requirement to act in the course of business is not limited to the carrying on of a regulated activity. Firms making communications to their employees, for example, may be affected by the FSMA 2000, s 21(1), even if their business is not a financial services business.

(2)   A person must communicate

6.10   Under the FSMA 2000, s 21(13), 'communicate' includes causing a communication to be made. So the range of potential communicators includes the author of the communication, the person who causes the communication to be made (if a different person) and any third party who passes on the communication. But 'communicate' itself is not defined. The Oxford English Dictionary definition of 'communicate' as 'transmit' suggests that the scope of the word is very wide and would cover any process whereby information is passed from one person to another. However, it seems doubtful whether A could, for the purposes of the FSMA 2000, s 21(1), make a communication to B without intending to do so. Thus if B overhears a conversation between A and C, it would appear that neither A nor C are communicating to B. This result is consistent with the 'directed at' test in the Financial Promotion Order[1] (where the fact that a communication is included in a newspaper or magazine principally accessed in or intended for a market outside the UK is to be taken into account in determining whether the communication is directed at the UK, even if the communication was in fact received by someone in the UK). It also accords with the Treasury's view of the meaning of 'invitation or inducement', discussed below.

1 SI 2005/1529, art 12(4)(e) with art 12(3)(c). See further 6.37.

(3)   The communication must consist of an invitation or inducement

6.11   Neither 'invitation' nor 'inducement' is defined in the FSMA 2000, s 21. The Treasury has indicated that the intention:

'is to catch only promotions containing a degree of incitement and not communications comprising purely factual information where the facts are presented in such a way that they do not amount to an 'invitation or inducement'[1].

This reflects the views given by a Government Minister during the parliamentary debates on the FSMA 2000, s 21[2], though how large a degree of incitement is required is perhaps open to question. On this interpretation, the facts of the case determine whether a communication is caught or not.

1   Financial Promotion – Third Consultation Document (October 2000), para 2.2.
2   See 613 HL Official Report (5th series) (18 May 2000) cols 387–388 (Lord McIntosh of Haringey) and compare 611 HL Official Report (5th Series) (20 March 2000) col 105 and 612 HL Official Report (5th series) (18 April 2000) col 567.

6.12   The difficulty with the Treasury view is that the dictionary definition of 'inducement' suggests that a communication amounts to an inducement if the result is that a person takes a particular course of action as a consequence, regardless of the intention of the person making the communication[1]. It remains to be seen whether the dictionary definition, or the view of a Minister in Parliament, will prevail if the meaning of the expression falls to be determined by a court[2].

1   See Oxford English Dictionary, 'inducement', 2 – 'something attractive by which a person is led on or persuaded to action'. The dictionary definition is also consistent with the decision in *Commission for Racial Equality v Imperial Society of Teachers of Dancing* [1983] ICR 473 at 476, where 'to induce' in the context of the Race Relations Act 1976 was held to mean 'to persuade or to prevail upon or to bring about'.
2   Although courts have been able, since the decision of the House of Lords in *Pepper (Inspector of Taxes) v Hart* [1993] AC 593, to look to statements in Parliament in certain circumstances as a guide to the intention of the legislature, this will apply only where the meaning of the text is ambiguous. A court could well conclude that the meaning of 'invitation or inducement' in the FSMA 2000, s 21(1) was abundantly clear.

6.13   Whatever the meaning of 'invitation or inducement', it is clear that the expression covers a far wider area than the 'advertisements' and 'unsolicited calls' of the previous regimes. In particular, and in marked contrast with the regimes that the FSMA 2000, s 21 replaces, it includes circumstances where the invitation or inducement is made orally (for instance, via a personal visit) and is solicited by the recipient of the communication. The thinking behind this is that solicited oral communications are potentially no less harmful than those that are unsolicited, so it would be anomalous to exclude them[1].

1   HM Treasury, Financial Promotion – A Consultation Document (March 1999), part 1, para 3.2.

(4)   The invitation or inducement must be to engage in investment activity

6.14   'Engaging in investment activity' is defined in the FSMA 2000, s 21(8) as:

> '(a)   entering or offering to enter into an agreement the making or performance of which by either party constitutes a controlled activity; or

(b) exercising any rights conferred by a controlled investment to acquire, dispose of, underwrite or convert a
controlled investment.'

The FSMA 2000, s 21(9) and (10) give the Treasury the power to specify
what constitutes a 'controlled activity' or a 'controlled investment', and
the Treasury has done so in the Financial Promotion Order, Sch 1[1]. In general, controlled activities and controlled investments are the same as regulated activities and specified investments under the Regulated Activities
Order[2], but this is not always the case: for instance, the controlled activity
of providing qualifying credit, which applies to all secured loans where
the lender carries on the regulated activity of entering into or administering regulated mortgage contracts, is far wider than the regulated activity
of entering into a regulated mortgage contract as lender, or administering
regulated mortgage contracts, which applies only to loans secured by a
first legal mortgage on land and which meet other conditions[3].

1 SI 2005/1529.
2 Financial Services and Markets Act 2000 (Regulated Activities) Order 2001, SI 2001/544.
3 Compare the Financial Promotion Order 2005, SI 2005/1529, Sch 1, para 10, with the Regulated Activities Order 2001, SI 2001/544, art 61 as amended by the Financial Services and
   Markets Act 2000 (Regulated Activities) (Amendment) Order 2001, SI 2001/3544.

Authorised persons

6.15 Where a communication that falls within the FSMA 2000, s 21(1) is
made by an authorised person, the basic prohibition does not apply. The
authorised person does not commit a criminal offence and any contract
that results will be enforceable. However, the authorised person will be
subject to the FCA's rules in respect of the communication[1].

1 See 6.73 ff.

6.16 The fact that an authorised person has made a communication
to a third party that falls within the FSMA 2000, s 21(1) does not, in itself,
relieve the third party from the basic prohibition if he is unauthorised and
wishes to communicate the promotion to a wider group of recipients. In
order for this to occur, the authorised person will need to approve the
content of the communication under the FSMA 2000, s 21(2)(b). Should the
third party materially alter the communication after it has been approved,
the original approval will no longer apply and the third party will be committing an offence under the FSMA 2000, s 25, unless he can show that
an exemption in the Financial Promotion Order[1] applies[2]. In the circumstances, the defence provided by the FSMA 2000, s 25(2)(a) (belief on reasonable grounds that the content had been approved by an authorised
person) is unlikely to be available.

1 SI 2005/1529.
2 HM Treasury, Financial Promotion – Third Consultation Document (October 2000), para
   2.18.

Territorial scope

6.17 As far as communications from within the UK are concerned
(sometimes referred to as 'outward promotions'), the basic prohibition

applies without limitation. Some respondents to the Treasury's consultations on financial promotion had argued that the FSMA 2000, s 21 should not apply to communications made to persons in an overseas jurisdiction, if those communications were lawfully made in that jurisdiction; but the Treasury has maintained the position that although this might extend the scope of regulation when compared to the previous regime, the result is justified on the grounds that this 'will help to maintain the highest confidence in the UK as a safe place to do business' (unsurprisingly, the UK Government attaches the utmost importance to safeguarding the UK's reputation as a financial centre)[1]. Certain communications made to overseas recipients are however excluded under the Financial Promotion Order[2].

1 HM Treasury, Financial Promotion – A Consultation Document (March 1999), part 2, para 1.4; cf. Financial Promotion – Second Consultation Document: A New Approach for the Information Age (October 1999), part 2, paras 2.7–2.9; Financial Promotion – Third Consultation Document (October 2000), para 2.6.
2 SI 2005/1529, art 12 and see 6.36–6.41.

6.18   Where the communication originates outside the UK, the FSMA 2000, s 21(3) provides that the basic prohibition applies only if the communication is capable of having an effect in the UK. However, since 'capable of having an effect' covers a wide area – it applies even if in actual fact the communication did not have such an effect – in practice persons making non-oral communications are likely to rely on the Financial Promotion Order, art 12[1] rather than the FSMA 2000, s 21(3) to provide them with an exclusion.

1 SI 2005/1529, art 12.

6.19   The FSMA 2000, s 21(7) gives the Treasury the power to repeal s 21(3). This power should be read together with the power in the FSMA 2000, s 21(6) which allows the basic prohibition to be disapplied to communications of a specified description originating in specified countries or groups of countries outside the UK. The Treasury has indicated that in light of developments in the European Union towards a 'home state' regime for financial services (as illustrated in the 'country of origin' approach to transactions in the e-commerce directive[1]) it wished to retain in the FSMA 2000, s 21 the flexibility to make the financial promotion regime in the UK a pure 'home state' regime when the time is right (that is, when other Member States agree to operate on a 'home state' basis). Whilst in theory the UK could do so unilaterally, this is not in practice acceptable, since it could leave UK consumers vulnerable to unregulated financial promotions communicated from outside the UK. And in any event, since it is unlikely (whatever the ultimate position within the European Union) that all countries will adopt a 'country of origin' approach, it will remain appropriate for s 21 to apply to some communications, at least, made into the UK from abroad[2].

1 Council Directive 2000/31/EC. The 'country of origin' approach has subsequently been adopted in MiFID (Directive 2004/39/EC): for the effect on the FCA's rules see 6.80.
2 See HM Treasury, Financial Promotion – Third Consultation Document (October 2000), paras 2.10–2.13.

THE FINANCIAL PROMOTION ORDER

6.20   The FSMA 2000, s 21(5) gives the Treasury the power to specify circumstances in which the basic prohibition does not apply. The order which has been made under this power, the Financial Promotion Order[1], contains over 70 sets of circumstances which constitute exemptions from the basic prohibition, divided into three categories:

(1)   exemptions applying to all controlled activities (Pt IV);

(2)   exemptions applying to deposits and insurance (Pt V); and

(3)   exemptions applying to certain controlled activities (Pt VI).

1 Financial Services and Markets Act 2000 (Financial Promotion) Order 2005, SI 2005/1529.

6.21   Under the Financial Promotion Order, art 11[1], exemptions may be combined where the circumstances of a particular communication are such that no one exemption will cover it. The original Financial Promotion Order 2001, SI 2001/1335, art 11, placed restrictions on the extent to which combinations of exemptions could be used. This has now been relaxed so as to allow firms to advertise their deposit-taking, investment services and insurance business in a single communication exempt from the basic prohibition in FSMA 2000, s 21(1) where relevant exemptions apply[2].

1 SI 2005/1529.
2 HM Treasury, Financial Services and Markets Act two-year review: changes to secondary legislation (February 2004), volume 1, Proposals for change, para 5.7.

6.22   The Financial Promotion Order[1] states, in respect of each exemption, the type of communication to which it applies. Whether an exemption applies depends on whether a communication is 'real time' or 'non-real time'; and if the former, whether it is solicited or unsolicited. For convenience, the application of the exemptions to the various types of communication is summarised in the tables below[2].

1 SI 2005/1529.
2 See 6.23–6.25.

Exemptions applying to various types of communication

Solicited real time communications

6.23   All the exemptions in the Financial Promotion Order apply, except:

Article 18A	Electronic commerce communications: mere conduits, caching and hosting
Article 20	Communications by journalists
Article 20B	Incoming electronic commerce communications
Article 22	Deposits: non-real time communications
Articles 24–25	Relevant insurance activity: non-real time communications
Article 28A	One off unsolicited real time communications

Articles 31–33	Overseas communicators: non-real time communications and unsolicited real time communications
Article 55A	Non-real time communication by members of professions
Articles 70, 71	Promotions included in listing particulars and material relating to prospectus for public offer of unlisted securities

Unsolicited real time communications

6.24   All the exemptions in the Financial Promotion Order apply, except:

Article 14	Follow up non-real time communications and solicited real time communications
Article 16	Exempt persons (where the exempt person is not an appointed representative)
Article 18A	Electronic commerce communications: mere conduits, caching and hosting
Article 20	Communications by journalists
Article 20B	Incoming electronic commerce communications
Article 22	Deposits: non-real time communications
Articles 24–25	Relevant insurance activity: non-real time communications
Article 28	One-off real time communications and solicited real time communications
Article 30	Overseas persons: solicited real time communications
Article 31	Overseas communicators: non-real time communications to previously overseas customers
Article 34	Governments, central banks etc
Article 35	Industrial and provident societies
Article 36	Nationals of EEA states other than the UK
Article 37	Financial markets
Article 40	Participants in certain recognised collective investment schemes
Articles 41, 42	Bearer instruments: promotions required or permitted by market rules and to existing holders
Article 43	Members and creditors of certain bodies corporate
Article 44	Members and creditors of open-ended investment companies
Article 48	Certified high net worth individuals
Article 51	Associations of high net worth or sophisticated investors

Article 52	Common interest group of a company
Article 55A	Non-real time communications by members of professions
Article 58	Acquisition of interest in premises run by management companies
Article 61	Sale of goods and supply of services
Articles 67–71	Promotions required or permitted by market rules, in connection with admission to certain EEA markets, of securities already admitted to certain markets, included in listing particulars, and material relating to prospectus for public offer of unlisted securities

Non-real time communications

6.25   All the exemptions in the Financial Promotion Order[1] apply, except:

Article 23	Deposits: real time communications
Article 26	Relevant insurance activity: real time communications
Article 28A	One off unsolicited real time communications
Article 28B	Real time communications: introductions
Article 30	Overseas communicators: solicited real time communications
Articles 32–33	Overseas communicators: unsolicited real time communications to previously overseas customers
Article 55	Communications by members of professions

1 SI 2005/1529.

6.26   The relevant definitions are contained in SI 2005/1529, arts 7 and 8. A real time communication is 'any communication made in the course of a personal visit, telephone conversation or other interactive dialogue' (art 7(1)). All other types of communication are non-real time (art 7(2)). Non-real time communications include 'communications made by letter or e-mail or contained in a publication' (art 7(3)). SI 2005/1529, art 7(3) appears designed to clarify the position over whether communications made by the Internet could constitute real time communications under the Financial Promotion Order; and though not expressly covered in art 7(3), it would seem that other types of electronic communication (such as via WAP phones and to Internet chat rooms, or via social media such as Facebook or Twitter) would also constitute 'non-real time communications'. Broadcasts (whether sound or via television) will also be non-real time communications, even when they are live recordings, as they are 'publications' under SI 2005/1529, art 2(1).

6.27   SI 2005/1529, art 7(5) sets out a number of factors which are to be treated as indications that a communication is non-real time. These are:

(1)   the communication is made to or directed at more than one person in identical terms (save for details of the person's identity);

(2)   the system of communication normally constitutes or creates a record of the communication which is available to the recipient to refer to at a later time; and

(3)   the communication is made or directed by way of a system which in the normal course does not enable or require the recipient to respond immediately to it.

6.28   Although it seems clear that not all of these indicators have to be satisfied for a communication to be classified as non-real time, it is not clear whether a communication that satisfied none of these indicators could still be a non-real time communication. Given, however, that they are indicators only rather than factors that determine the issue, it would appear that in theory at least this should be possible.

6.29   One key characteristic of a real time communication (and one which is not present in a non-real time communication) is that there is interaction between the communicator and the recipient. Thus a communication by telephone where direct contact is established is a real time communication; the same communication left on an answering machine would be a non-real time communication (even if it was intended by the caller to be a real time communication).

6.30   Under SI 2005/1529, art 8, a real time communication is solicited when initiated by or made in response to an express request from the recipient of the communication, and unsolicited in any other case. Article 8(3) provides that the following do not amount to an express request:

(1)   a failure by a person to indicate that he does not wish to receive any or any further visits or calls or to engage in any or any further dialogue; and

(2)   an agreement to standard terms that state that such visits, calls or dialogue will take place, unless he has signified clearly that in addition to agreeing to the terms, he is willing for them to take place.

These provisions are clearly designed to prevent arguments that real time communications are 'solicited' because the recipient has failed to tick a box, or has 'agreed' to pages of small print which contain, among the many terms and conditions, authority for calls to be made upon him. In practice, however, 'signified clearly' may amount to little more than a person providing a separate signature (or electronic equivalent, for instance by ticking a box on screen) beside the relevant term.

6.31   SI 2005/1529, art 8(3) also prevents a communication being classified as 'solicited' when the call, visit or dialogue is initiated ostensibly with one purpose in mind, but then moves to a different area. For example, a customer may have agreed to visits being made to discuss investments in units in collective investment schemes. If, however, the caller in the course of the communication turned to discuss the possibility of the customer investing in futures, that part of the communication would be unsolicited.

6.32   SI 2005/1529, art 8(4) allows a real time communication to qualify as a solicited communication if it is made to a person who has not requested it, provided that that person is a close relative[1] of, or expected to engage in any investment activity jointly with, a person who has solicited the communication. This will enable, for example, solicited real time communications to be made to both a husband and wife if only one party has asked for the communication to be made.

1 'Close relative' for the purposes of SI 2005/1529 includes civil partners: see art 2(2) of the Financial Services and Markets Act 2000 (Financial Promotion) (Amendment) Order 2005, SI 2005/3392.

6.33 A number of exemptions contain details of the 'indications' that the communication is required to contain in order to satisfy the exemption. Thus, for instance, non-real time communications for deposits, or relating to relevant insurance activity[1], will be exempt if they are accompanied by certain indications, such as the name of the depositor/insurer, the place of incorporation, and whether the deposit-taker or insurer is regulated or not[2]. SI 2005/1529, art 9 provides that these indications must be presented to the recipient:

(1)   in a way that can be easily understood; and

(2)   in such manner as, depending on the means by which the communication is made or directed, is best calculated to bring the matter in question to the attention of the recipient and to allow him to consider it.

1 That is, relating to a contract of insurance that is not a life policy.
2 SI 2005/1529, arts 22(2) and 24(2).

6.34 SI 2005/1529, art 9 is designed to prevent 'indications' being made in an obscure and unintelligible way. Clearly, if the basis for the exemption is the disclosure of certain pieces of information to the recipient, it would negate the rationale for the exemption if the relevant information could not be readily obtained from the communication. However, the words 'best calculated' impose a very high standard. Taken literally, they require the person relying on the exemption to find the objectively best way of presenting the material, or else commit a criminal offence. As there will be cases where there may be several ways in which the indications could be conveyed, and where none of these appears 'better' than any other, the strictness of the test seems unhelpful. The FCA has however indicated that the expression 'best calculated' should be construed 'in a sensible manner' and that it would regard SI 2005/1529, art 9 as being satisfied if the indication is given enough prominence, taking account of the medium through which it is communicated, to ensure that the recipient will be aware of it and able to consider it before deciding whether to engage in investment activity[1].

1 FCA Handbook, Perimeter Guidance Manual (PERG), 8.11.5G.

6.35 SI 2005/1529, art 10 places an additional restriction on communications concerning 'qualifying contracts of insurance' (that is, life policies). In such cases, an exemption applies only if the contract is entered into with:

(1)   an authorised person;

(2)   an exempt person in relation to effecting or carrying out contracts of the type to which the communication relates;

(3)   a company with a head office, branch or agency in an EEA state other than the UK which is entitled to carry on in that State insurance business of the type to which the communication relates; or

(4)   a company authorised to carry on insurance business of the type to which the communication relates in Guernsey, the Isle of Man, the Commonwealth of Pennsylvania, the State of Iowa, and Jersey.

Exemptions applying to all controlled activities

6.36   As we have seen, the FSMA 2000, s 21(3) exempts from the basic prohibition communications originating outside the UK which are not capable of having an effect in the UK[1]. The exemption created by the Financial Promotion Order, art 12[2] is in keeping with this. In general, it provides that a communication which is made (whether from inside or outside the UK) to a person who receives the communication outside the UK, or which is directed (whether from inside or outside the UK) only at persons outside the UK, is not subject to the basic prohibition. However, if the communication is an unsolicited real time communication, the exemption applies only if the communication is made from outside the UK and for the purpose of a business which is not carried on in the UK. The exemption does not however apply to an outgoing electronic commerce communication[3].

1 See 6.18.
2 SI 2005/1529.
3 For the definition of this expression, see SI 2005/1529, art 6(h).

6.37   SI 2005/1529, art 12 is therefore capable of applying both to communications designed with a particular person in mind (those which are 'made to' that person) and to those which are addressed to persons generally (communications 'directed at' those persons, for example by means of advertisements). The 'directed at' exemption allows communications to be exempt even if they reach persons for whom the communications were not designed.

6.38   SI 2005/1529, art 12(4) lists five conditions which are relevant to whether the communication is 'directed only at' persons outside the UK. Depending on how many of these conditions are met, satisfaction of the conditions either carries evidential weight as to whether the communication satisfies the exemption (in the words of SI 2005/1529, art 12(3)(c), they will be 'taken into account' in determining the issue), or is conclusive evidence that the exemption is satisfied. Even if none of the listed conditions are met, it will still be possible for the communication to be regarded as directed only at persons outside the UK[1], though given the nature of the conditions, that would seem possible only in exceptional circumstances.

1 Financial Promotion Order 2005, SI 2005/1529, art 12(3)(c).

6.39   A communication will be regarded as directed only at persons outside the UK if all of the following conditions are satisfied:

(1)   it is accompanied by an indication that it is directed only at persons outside the UK (but a communication which is directed from a place outside the UK does not need to satisfy this condition);

(2)   it is accompanied by an indication that it must not be acted upon by persons in the UK (again, a communication which is directed from a place outside the UK does not need to satisfy this condition);

(3)   it is not referred to in or directly accessible from any other communication which is made to or directed at persons in the UK by the person directing the communication; and

(4)   there are proper systems and procedures in place to prevent recipients in the UK engaging in the investment activity to which the communication relates with the person directing the communication, a close relative of his or a company in the same group[1]. 'Proper systems and procedures' are not defined, and to some extent will depend on the facts of the individual case. But they are likely to require in all cases some sort of screening process to identify UK recipients (whether by password protecting the material, if communicated via the Internet, or otherwise).

1 Financial Promotion Order 2005, SI 2005/1529, art 12(4)(a)–(d).

6.40   A further condition which has evidential weight requires the communication to be contained in a website, newspaper, journal, magazine or periodical publication principally accessed in or intended for a market outside the UK, or in a radio or television broadcast or teletext service transmitted principally for reception outside the UK[1].

1 Financial Promotion Order 2005, SI 2005/1529, art 12(4)(e).

6.41   This exemption remains available if promotions are also directed at persons in the UK to which the exemptions relating to investment professionals[1] and high net worth companies and other persons[2] apply. If this is so, conditions (1) and (2) above[3] are to be construed accordingly, and condition (3) above will not apply[4]. The exemption also remains available if the promotion is also directed at previously overseas customers and the exemption in SI 2005/1529, art 31 applies[5]. Given that art 11 makes clear that exemptions in the Financial Promotion Order, Pt IV can be freely combined with other exemptions in Pts IV or VI, the express mention of the arts 19 and 49 exemptions in art 12 is odd. Although it might be taken to imply that none of the other exemptions can be combined with art 12, the better view, based on the unqualified wording of art 11, appears to be that this is not the case.

1 Financial Promotion Order 2005, SI 2005/1529, art 19.
2 SI 2005/1529, art 49.
3 See 6.39.
4 SI 2005/1529, art 12(6).
5 SI 2005/1529, art 12(5)(c).

6.42   The Financial Promotion Order, Pt IV[1] also includes exemptions for:

(1)   communications from customers and potential customers (art 13);

(2)   communications made with a view to or for the purposes of introducing the recipient to an authorised person who carries on the controlled activity to which the communication relates, or to an exempt person whose exemption covers the controlled activity to which the communication relates, provided that certain conditions are satisfied (art 15);

(3)   non-real time communications or solicited real time communications made or directed by exempt persons for the purpose of their exempt business, and unsolicited real time communications made by appointed representatives in respect of their exempt business which, if made by their principal, would comply with any relevant financial promotion rules made by the FCA under FSMA 2000, s 137R (art 16);

(4)   'mere conduits', such as postal and telecommunications services, and internet service providers, provided that the principal purpose of the business is transmitting or receiving material provided by others, the content of the communication is wholly devised by another person, and that no control is exercised over the content prior to transmission or receipt (art 18)[2];

(5)   communications made to investment professionals, such as authorised persons, exempt persons whose exemption covers the controlled activity to which the communication relates, governments and local authorities (art 19); and

(6)   incoming electronic commerce communications (with certain exceptions, such as unsolicited communications made by e-mail) (art 20B).

1 SI 2005/1529.
2 'Control' here does not include the power to remove material which is or is alleged to be illegal or defamatory, or where required to do so by law or by a regulator: SI 2005/1529, art 18(3). Even so, the nature of the relationship between newspaper publishers and broadcasters, and the third-party advertisements that they communicate, suggests that they will not be able to take advantage of this exemption. The exemption does not apply to persons who cause the communication to be made or directed, or where the communication is an electronic commerce communication (defined in SI 2005/1529, art 6(f)).

6.43   Four other exemptions in SI 2005/1529, Pt IV are worth treating in more detail.

Under SI 2005/1529, art 14, communications other than unsolicited real time communications are exempt when the communication follows up an earlier communication, provided that the earlier communication was exempt under the Financial Promotion Order because, in compliance with the requirements of another exemption in the Financial Promotion Order, it was accompanied by certain indications or contained certain information, and that the subsequent communication:

(1)   is made by or on behalf of the same person who made the earlier communication;

(2)   is made to a recipient of the earlier communication;

(3)   relates to the same controlled activity and controlled investment[1] as the earlier communication; and

(4)   is made within twelve months of the receipt of the first communication.

1 For controlled activity and controlled investment, see 6.14.

6.44   SI 2005/1529, art 14 will not be available if the earlier communication did not require certain indications to be made or information to be contained. As some exemptions which mention indications or conditions do not as such require the communication to be accompanied by them or to satisfy them (since the exemption is available where none of the listed conditions or indications are satisfied or made), the scope of the exemption is more narrow than first appears[1]. Since art 28, dealing with 'one-off' communications, falls into this category, it would seem that the exemptions for 'one-off' and follow up communications cannot be combined. Of course, it may well be that if the earlier communication satisfied a particular exemption, the later communication would do so also. But if the art 14 exemption cannot be used for the later communication, this will mean (as in the case of someone seeking to take advantage of the exception under art 19) that the person making the communication may need to repeat information made earlier to the same customer. This is hardly helpful to either communicator or recipient, and seems to run contrary to the motivation for the exemption in the first place.

1 The exemption in SI 2005/1529, art 14 will thus not be available where the earlier communication meets the relevant provisions of arts 12 (communications to overseas recipients), or 19 (investment professionals): see arts 12(3)(c) and 19(3). Contrast, for example, communications which are required to satisfy the specified conditions or indication provisions in arts 24 (relevant insurance activity: non-real time communications) and 50 (sophisticated investors) in order to obtain the benefits of those exemptions.

6.45   SI 2005/1529, art 17 provides an exception for 'generic promotions', that is communications which do not identify directly or indirectly a person who provides the controlled investment to which the communication relates, or any person as a person who carries on a controlled activity in relation to that investment. This enables promotions comparing the merits of, say, ISAs with deposits, or those extolling the virtues of unit trusts in general terms, to escape the basic prohibition. It will also be possible for an unauthorised intermediary to advertise himself and the services that he provides, provided that in so doing he does not carry on a controlled activity. So an intermediary who offered to find the most competitive insurance quotation or the best performing unit trust over a particular period would fall within the exemption, as he would not be identifying anyone that provided a controlled investment or carried on a controlled activity in relation to that investment. But if the communication contained examples which, though disguised to the general reader, would nonetheless be capable of being identified (such as the managers of 'ABC unit trust, the value of which has grown by 189% in the two years to last March'), the communication would fall foul of the wide scope of 'directly or indirectly' and would thus be outside the exemption.

6.46   The exemption for non-real time communications by journalists (SI 2005/1529, art 20) has caused the Treasury a good deal of trouble – as shown by the fact that the exemption in the original Financial Promotion Order, SI 2001/1335 covering this point was subject to early and extensive amendment[1]. There is a difficult line to draw between the freedom of the press, and the role that responsible journalism can play in improving consumer awareness of financial products on the one hand, and the need on the other to protect the public from the possibility that journalists' 'buy' and 'sell' recommendations may not be entirely impartial. Partly, perhaps, as a response to the 'City Slickers' scandal in 2000 (where Daily Mirror journalists had tipped shares in which their editor had a financial interest), the Treasury aim was to allow authors of a communication with a material interest in a particular product to write about that product – they may, after all, be very well qualified to do so – and to have the benefit of the exemption, provided that they disclosed any financial interest that they, or a close relative, had at the same time and in the same place[2]. However, the present text of art 20 means that disclosure of a financial interest is not inevitably necessary in order to take advantage of the exemption.

1 See the Financial Services and Markets Act 2000 (Financial Promotion) (Amendment No 2) Order 2001, SI 2001/3800, art 2.
2 HM Treasury, Financial Promotion – Third Consultation Document (October 2000), para 2.37.

6.47   The Financial Promotion Order 2005, art 20[1] can in effect be sub-divided into two separate exemptions for non-real time communications. First, there is an exemption where the communication does not relate to shares or to futures, options and contracts for differences relating to shares, and:

(1)   the content of the communication is devised by a person acting in the capacity of a journalist; and

(2)   the communication is contained in a qualifying publication[2].

'Acting in the capacity of a journalist' is not defined, although as it presumably requires a contractual relationship between author and publication, it should not be difficult to decide in each case whether this condition is satisfied or not. The FCA has indicated that it sees this expression as having a potentially wide meaning, covering anyone who writes for or contributes to a publication, service or broadcast[3]. 'Qualifying publication' is defined by reference to the Regulated Activities Order, art 54(1) and (2)[4]. It covers newspapers, journals, magazines or other periodical publications, regularly updated news or information services, and television and radio programmes, provided that the principal purpose of the publication, service or programme is not to give advice on the merits of buying or selling, nor to lead or enable persons to buy or sell, securities or contractually based investments. The FCA may certify that the principal purpose test is met, and certification is conclusive evidence that it is[5].

1 SI 2005/1529.
2 SI 2005/1529, art 20(1)(a), (b).
3 FCA Handbook, Perimeter Guidance Manual (PERG), 8.12.25G.
4 Financial Services and Markets Act 2000 (Regulated Activities) Order 2001, SI 2001/544.
5 SI 2005/1529, art 20(5)(b).

6.48   A journalist who authors a communication which constitutes a financial promotion, but whose subject matter does not concern shares, options, futures or contracts for differences relating to shares can therefore take advantage of the exemption without disclosing any financial interest that he or his family has in the matter promoted. If such disclosure was required by the publisher, or under codes of practice that cover the publication concerned, the exemption would apply even if the disclosure was not made. It is probably true that the greatest scope for abuse in this area lies in the tipping of shares where the author stands to gain if the tip is followed by others. However, it seems surprising that the Treasury have apparently concluded that there would be no or no substantial risk to consumers from an author tipping other controlled investments (such as units in unit trusts or listed bonds) in which he has a financial interest.

6.49   The second exemption arises where the communication concerns shares (or futures, options or contracts for differences relating to shares), directly identifies a person who issues or provides the shares (or futures, options or contracts for differences relating to shares), and meets the requirements set out in **6.47**, points (1) and (2). In this case, if an author of the communication[1] or a member of his family[2] would be likely to obtain a financial benefit or avoid a financial loss if persons acted in accordance with the financial promotion, the financial promotion may need to be accompanied by an explanation of the nature of that financial interest if the author wishes to take advantage of the exemption[3]. However, this disclosure is not necessarily required. If the author is subject to proper systems and procedures[4] which prevent the publication of communications that require disclosure of financial interests without an explanation of that interest[5], or the publication in which the communication appears falls within the remit of the Press Complaints Commission's Code of Practice, the OFCOM Broadcasting Code, or the Producers' Guidelines issued by the British Broadcasting Corporation[6], there is no obligation to disclose a financial interest in the product promoted. It is worth noting that it is not a condition of the exemption that the communication be in accordance with the Codes or Guidelines; it simply has to fall within their scope. Nor is it a requirement that the Codes or Guidelines require disclosure of a financial interest. The assumption appears to be that in these circumstances it is appropriate for the body concerned to decide whether disclosure is required and, if so, what steps to take if disclosure is not made. Similarly, if the author acts in breach of the relevant systems and procedures with the result that a required disclosure of a financial interest is not made, the communication would still appear to satisfy the condition in SI 2005/1529, art 20(2)(b). (If it were otherwise, art 20(2)(b) would be unnecessary – the position would be covered by art 20(2)(a).)

1 Under SI 2005/1529, art 20(5)(a), 'author' includes the person who is responsible for deciding to include the communication in a publication. This will typically be the editor, but the language is sufficiently wide to include a particularly 'hands on' proprietor, depending on the circumstances of the case.
2 This expression is far narrower than that in the original Financial Promotion Order 2001, SI 2001/1335, art 20: it includes only spouse (or civil partner) and children under 18, whereas the original text, by using 'close relative', covered the author's spouse, children of any age, parents, siblings, and their spouses.
3 SI 2005/1529, art 20(2)(a).
4 'Proper systems and procedures' are not defined (compare SI 2005/1529, art 12(4)(d)), but they are likely to include the keeping of a list of relevant financial interests of authors and members of their families, and an obligation on authors to notify any changes to those interests.
5 SI 2005/1529, art 20(2)(b).
6 SI 2005/1529, art 20(2)(c).

6.50   The Financial Promotion Order 2005, art 20A[1] provides a further exemption for communications by directors or employees of an undertaking, where the communication forms part of a television or radio programme or is displayed on a website (or similar system) comprising regularly updated news and information, and the programme or website satisfies the principal purpose test in the Regulated Activities Order, art 54(1)(a) and (b)[2]. The exemption is available where the communication is a financial promotion relating to shares (or options, futures and contracts for differences relating to those shares) issued by the undertaking or another undertaking in the same group, or relating to any controlled investment[3] issued or provided by an authorised person in the same group, and the communication consists only of spoken words, or is displayed in writing 'only because it forms part of an interactive dialogue to which [the director or employee] is a party and in the course of which [he] is expected to respond immediately to questions put by a recipient of the communication'[4]. This rather obscure provision appears designed to cover question and answer sessions held over the internet, involving the exchange of e-mails or text messages[5]. In addition, the communication must not be part of an organised marketing campaign[6], and must identify the person making the communication as a director or employee (as the case may be) of the undertaking.

1 SI 2005/1529.
2 SI 2001/544. For the principal purpose test, see 6.47.
3 See 6.14.
4 SI 2005/1529, art 20A(1)(b)(ii).
5 Though if that is the case, the use of the expression 'interactive dialogue' is strange, since communications made in the course of an interactive dialogue are real time, and communications made by e-mail or text message are by definition non-real time (see 6.26). SI 2005/1529, art 20A would thus appear in practice to be confined to non-real time communications, despite the fact that the exemption is not expressly so restricted.
6 See 6.54.

6.51 This exemption appears to have been motivated by the possibility that company directors and employees might inadvertently make unapproved financial promotions when responding to questions from radio and television interviewers about their company, or as part of a live website question and answer session. However, it is not clear whether the presence of subtitles on television broadcasts would negate the exemption. The strict wording of SI 2005/1529, art 20A(1)(b)(i) suggests that it would, although logic suggests that this cannot have been the intention. Indeed, the FCA has indicated that as it understands that the Treasury intention was not to prohibit written words in the form of subtitling, it would not expect to take further action if the only reason why a person may have breached FSMA 2000, s 21(1) was the use of subtitling or captioning that introduced nothing new to the promotion[1].

1 FCA Handbook, Perimeter Guidance Manual (PERG), 8.12.36G.

Exemptions applying to deposits and insurance

6.52 The Financial Promotion Order, Pt V[1] contains exemptions that apply to communications that relate to deposits, and to 'relevant insurance activity' – that is, the effecting and carrying out of contracts of insurance which are not life policies[2]. The scope of the exemptions are similar in both types of case: real time communications are unconditionally exempt[3], and non-real time communications are exempt provided that certain information about the insurer or deposit-taker is disclosed (such as name, place of incorporation, and details of applicable complaints and compensation schemes)[4]. Under SI 2005/1529, art 25, non-real time communications concerning contracts of reinsurance, or insurance contracts concerning 'large risks' (defined in art 25(2)) are also excluded.

1 SI 2005/1529.
2 See SI 2005/1529, art 21.
3 SI 2005/1529, arts 23 (deposits) and 26 (relevant insurance activity).
4 SI 2005/1529, arts 22 (deposits) and 24 (relevant insurance activity).

Other exemptions

6.53 The largest part of the Financial Promotion Order[1] is Pt VI, which contains a number of exemptions applying to certain types of controlled activity. In some cases the exemption may depend upon the maker of the communication[2]; in others, on the recipient of the communication[3]; or the subject matter of the communication[4]. The exemptions likely to be of more general interest are discussed below.

1 SI 2005/1529.
2 See eg SI 2005/1529, arts 34 (governments, central banks etc), 35 (industrial and provident societies) and 37 (financial markets).
3 See eg SI 2005/1529, arts 31–33 (overseas communicators: communications to previously overseas customers and knowledgeable customers), 45 (group companies) and 47 (persons in the business of disseminating information).
4 See eg SI 2005/1529, arts 29 (communications required or authorised by enactments), 59 (annual accounts and directors' report) and 70 (promotions included in listing particulars etc.).

Articles 28 and 28A (one-off communications)

6.54 One-off communications fall outside the restrictions on financial promotion in FSMA 2000, s 21(1). 'One-off' is not defined, but SI 2005/1529, art 28(3) sets out three conditions, the satisfaction of all of which means that the communication is to be regarded as 'one-off':

(1) the communication is made to one recipient only, or to one group of recipients in the expectation that they would invest jointly;

(2) the product or service mentioned in the communication has been determined having regard to the particular circumstances of the recipient; and

(3) the communication is not part of an organised marketing campaign (that is, it is not one of a series of similar communications designed to acquire customers for a particular investment or service).

6.55 If one or two of the above conditions are satisfied, that fact is to be taken into account in determining whether the communication is 'one-off' or not. But a communication can still be one-off for the purposes of SI 2005/1529, arts 28 and 28A even if none of the conditions are satisfied[1].

1 SI 2005/1529, art 28(2), (3). For this three-pronged approach elsewhere in the Financial Promotion Order, see arts 12 (communications to overseas recipients), 19 (investment professionals), 49 (high net worth companies, unincorporated associations etc) and 52 (common interest group of a company).

6.56 The original Financial Promotion Order limited the 'one-off' exemption to non-real time communications and solicited real time communications[1]. Article 28A of SI 2005/1529 extends this so that unsolicited real time communications which are 'one-off' are also exempt, provided that:

(1) the communicator believes on reasonable grounds that the recipient understands the risks associated with engaging in the investment activity to which the communication relates; and

(2) at the time the communication is made, the communicator believes on reasonable grounds that the recipient would expect to be contacted by him in relation to that activity.

1 SI 2001/1335, art 28(1).

6.57 The words 'one-off' are in fact rather a misnomer, as the Treasury has indicated that this exemption can be used on more than one occasion in respect of the same recipient provided that the conditions of the exemption are met on each occasion[1].

1 Financial Promotion – Third Consultation Document (October 2000), para 2.21.

Articles 30–33 (overseas communicators)

6.58 The Financial Promotion Order[1] contains four exemptions that are available for 'overseas communicators' – persons who carry on certain controlled activities outside the UK, but not from a permanent place of business maintained by them in the UK.

1 SI 2005/1529.

6.59 Under these exemptions an overseas communicator when acting as such may, without breaching the basic prohibition in FSMA 2000, s 21(1), make:

(1) a solicited real time communication to a person in the UK (but not if the controlled activity carried on by the overseas communicator outside the UK is accepting deposits, effecting or carrying out contracts of insurance, advising on syndicate participation at Lloyd's, providing funeral plan contracts, or activities relating to home reversion plans, home purchase plans or regulated sale and rent back agreements);

(2) a non-real time communication to a customer in the UK with whom he has done business within the previous twelve months and who at that time (or at an earlier time when the same business was done with the customer) was not resident in the UK and did not have a place of business there (a 'previously overseas customer');

(3) an unsolicited real time communication to a previously overseas customer in the UK, provided that the past dealings between the parties would lead the customer reasonably to expect to receive unsolicited real time communications at that time concerning that type of investment activity, and that the overseas communicator has previously disclosed that the protections of the FSMA 2000 do not apply to the communication and may not apply to any investment activity that results, and described what complaints or compensation scheme (if any) would apply to a transaction between them;

(4) an unsolicited real time communication with a customer in the UK whom the overseas communicator believes on reasonable grounds to be sufficiently knowledgeable to understand the risks to which the communication relates, provided that the overseas communicator has previously made the disclosures mentioned in (3) above and the recipient has clearly signalled, after a proper opportunity to consider the information given to him, that he understands the warnings and accepts that he will not benefit from the protections of the FSMA 2000.

Article 36 (nationals of EEA States other than the UK)

6.60 Communications (other than unsolicited real time communications) made by a national of another EEA State from that state, in the course of a controlled activity lawfully carried on by him in that state, are exempt, provided that the communication conforms with the relevant financial promotion rules made by the FCA[1]. Anyone wishing to take advantage of this exemption will need to have a clear understanding of the relevant FCA rules, since a failure to follow the FCA rules to the letter will result in the exemption not applying, and the commitment of a criminal offence. Given that, it seems unlikely that persons will seek to rely on SI 2005/1529, art 36 without the benefit of specialist outside advice.

1 For these rules, see 6.73 ff.

Article 48 (certified high net worth individuals), art 50 and art 50A (sophisticated investors)

6.61   These three exceptions mark a departure from previous regimes. Prior to the coming into force of the FSMA 2000 and the original Financial Promotion Order[1], promotions of investments to private individuals were required to be made or approved by authorised persons. However, various working groups were concerned that this was too restrictive. On the basis that private investment (as opposed to institutional investment) is an extremely important source of finance for companies in the early years; that the costs of obtaining approval for promotions could be prohibitively high, compared to the amounts of money that firms wished to raise; and that the protection of the promotional restrictions might be disproportionate for private individuals of greater sophistication and resource than the average investor, they argued that companies should be allowed to promote investment opportunities directly to more sophisticated private investors, often known as 'business angels'[2]. Given the importance the Government attaches to small and medium-size companies having access to the capital necessary to expand their businesses[3], and the fact that other jurisdictions (in particular Australia and the USA) have a similar exemption, it is no surprise that a decision was taken to liberalise this area[4].

1 SI 2001/1335.
2 See HM Treasury, Financial Promotion – A Consultation Document (March 1999) part 5, para 1.1.
3 See HM Treasury, Financial Promotion – Second Consultation Document: A New Approach for the Information Age (October 1999), part 2, para 2.50.
4 The Treasury subsequently proposed amendments to make capital raising by unlisted companies still less restrictive, and these are reflected in SI 2005/1529. See HM Treasury, Informal Capital Raising and high net worth and sophisticated investors: a consultation document on proposed changes to the Financial Promotion Order (January 2004).

6.62   SI 2005/1529, art 48 applies in cases where the recipient is reasonably believed by the person making the communication to be a 'certified high net worth individual': that is, a person who has signed, no more than twelve months before the date of the communication, a statement of high net worth complying with Pt 1 of Sch 5 to SI 2005/1529[1]. Where such recipients are concerned, communications other than unsolicited real time communications may be made, provided that:

(1)   they relate only to certain investments (broadly speaking, shares and debentures in unlisted companies, options and futures on such investments, and units in collective investment schemes that invest wholly or mainly in such investments);

(2)   the recipient cannot lose more than the amount invested; and

(3)   the communication is accompanied by a warning that the content of
        the promotion has not been approved by an authorised person, and
        that reliance on the promotion may lead to a significant risk of losing
        all the amount invested[2].

1 SI 2005/1529, art 48(1) and (2). The text of the statement may deviate from that contained in
  Pt 1 of Sch 5 and still remain valid, provided that the deviations are non-material and that the
  words shown in bold in the schedule are so shown in the statement: SI 2005/1529, art 48(3).
  Oddly, perhaps, no such leeway exists in relation to the warning set out in art 48(5), which
  suggests that even a non-material change to the text would render the exemption invalid.
2 SI 2005/1529, art 48(5). The warning must, among other things, be in legible form, unless
  this is not reasonably practical because of the nature of the communication (for instance,
  a communication by telephone). In such cases, the warning must be given orally at the
  beginning of the communication and the legible warning must follow within two business days: SI 2005/1529, art 48(4). The legible warning must satisfy various presentational
  requirements designed to emphasise its importance: SI 2005/1529, art 48(6).

6.63   The statement of high net worth acknowledges that the individual signing the statement understands that he can receive promotions
which may not have been approved by an authorised person; that these
promotions may not conform to rules issued by the FCA; that he may
lose significant rights; that he may have no right to complain to the FCA
or the Financial Ombudsman Scheme; and that he may have no right to
claim compensation from the Financial Services Compensation Scheme.
The individual signing the statement confirms that he had, during the
financial year immediately preceding the date of the statement, an annual
income of at least £100,000, and/or throughout the financial year immediately preceding the date of the statement, net assets of at least £250,000.
'Net assets' excludes certain items that could be classed as assets (such as
the individual's primary residence), but also (more dubiously) excludes
any loan secured on the primary residence. The assumption appears to
be that the value of the residence can never be less that the amount of the
loan, which in a declining housing market will not be the case. This leaves
open the surprising possibility that someone whose net asset position, by
any meaningful measure, is close to or less than zero will still be properly
classified as a high net worth individual under SI 2005/1529, art 48.

6.64   Despite the widespread support for the principle behind this
exclusion[1], and the restricted circumstances in which the exclusion applies,
it remains controversial. It equates suitability to receive an unregulated
communication with financial standing, presumably on the basis that high
net worth individuals have enough money to be able to pay for specialist advice if required, and should have been told about the need to take
such advice. The unwritten assumption appears to be that high net worth
individuals will be able to identify when they need to take advice and
will duly seek it. That seems, at best, an optimistic assumption to make.
Indeed, the FCA's recent changes to its rules dealing with the promotion
of unregulated collective investment schemes suggest that they regard
such an assumption as too optimistic[2].

1 See HM Treasury, Financial Promotion – Third Consultation Document (October 2000),
  para 2.41.
2 COBS 4.12.9G(2). See 6.108.

6.65   SI 2005/1529, art 50 provides a similar, though not identical, exclusion for sophisticated investors. All types of communication may be made

to a person who has a current certificate ('current' meaning here signed and dated within the past three years) signed by an authorised person to the effect that he is sufficiently knowledgeable to understand the risks associated with the type of investment that is the subject of the communication. As with the high net worth individual, the sophisticated investor must also have signed within the previous twelve months a statement in prescribed form (though non-material deviations from the wording are permitted), which requires among other things the investments in respect of which the person qualifies as a sophisticated investor to be expressly listed. The communication must be accompanied by certain information. This, again, is similar to the information given to high net worth individuals, except that the risk warning is of the risk of not only losing the entire amount invested, but also of incurring additional liability[1]. (The latter will be true if the investor is certified as sophisticated in respect of derivatives transactions, for example.)

1 SI 2005/1529, art 50(3)(d).

6.66   There is, however, a potential catch with this exemption. The certificate has to be signed by an authorised person. An authorised person is exempt from the basic prohibition, under the FSMA 2000, s 21(2)(a), so could make the promotion to the investor in any event. In doing so he is, in general, subject to the FCA's financial promotion rules under the FSMA 2000, s 137R. However, those rules for the most part do not apply to circumstances covered by the Financial Promotion Order[1]. So there would be an obvious incentive in many cases for an authorised person to certify someone as sophisticated, if by so doing he could promote his products to the sophisticated investor without the need to worry about the FSA's rules.

1 SI 2005/1529.

6.67   However, perhaps mindful of the possibility of abuse, SI 2005/1529, art 50 provides that in order to qualify for the exemption, the communication must not invite the recipient to engage in investment activity with the authorised person who has signed the certificate[1]. So if authorised person A signs a certificate, the effect will be that unauthorised persons will be able to promote the products and services of other authorised persons – but not those of A – to the sophisticated investor. At first sight there would appear to be little incentive for A to sign a certificate, except at a very high fee.

1 SI 2005/1529, art 50(2)(b).

6.68   Because the Treasury felt that SI 2005/1529, art 50 unduly restricted efforts to raise capital for unlisted companies, it subsequently added art 50A, which is similar to the exemption for high net worth individuals in art 48. Under this exemption, an individual may 'self-certify' his sophisticated investor status by signing a statement complying with Pt II of SI 2005/1529, Sch 5. If he does this, then communications may be made to him, provided that the communicator believes him to be a self-certified sophisticated investor on reasonable grounds, that a warning in prescribed form is given to him at the time of the communication, and that any investment promoted to him is limited to those set out in **6.62** (1). The statement that must be signed is also similar to that required for high net worth individuals (see **6.63**), the main difference being that the signatory here confirms that he falls within one or more of four stated classes of person (broadly those with experience in unlisted company investment, or company directors of companies with an annual turnover of at least £1 million).

6.69   All these exemptions are silent on an important issue: how can persons find out whether a recipient has made the self-certification, or possesses the necessary certificate? On the basis of the wording of the FSMA 2000, s 21(1), it would appear that it would not be a breach of the basic prohibition if the initial communication simply sought to ascertain whether the recipient had a current certificate, as such a communication would not be 'an invitation or inducement to engage in investment activity'[1]; this is, indeed, the view taken by the FCA[2]. And even if the answer to the question was in the negative, it seems doubtful whether a further communication urging the recipient to obtain a certificate would inevitably be in breach of the FSMA 2000, s 21(1), as that too would not necessarily have the required promotional purpose.

1 See above, 6.11–6.14.
2 FCA Handbook, Perimeter Guidance Manual (PERG), 8.14.24G.

Article 49 (high net worth companies, unincorporated associations etc)

6.70   Any communications made to or directed at high net worth companies, unincorporated associations or partnerships, or trustees of high value trusts, are exempt from the basic prohibition. Unlike the case of high net worth individuals, there is no requirement for these entities to self-certify their status; but as in that case, even if the communication is made to persons who do not satisfy the criteria, the exemption will still apply, provided that the persons concerned are believed on reasonable grounds to be of high net worth or of high value, (or the communication may reasonably be regarded as directed only at such persons)[1].

1 SI 2005/1529, art 49(1).

6.71   The requirements are:

(1) for bodies corporate, called up share capital of at least £5 million (or of at least £500,000 if it has more than 20 members or is the subsidiary of a parent with more than 20 members);

(2) for unincorporated associations and partnerships, net assets of at least £5 million;

(3) for trustees, the trust must be a 'high value' trust – that is, a trust which has, or had in the previous 12 months, assets (before deducting liabilities) of at least £10 million.

6.72   SI 2005/1529, art 49(4) sets out three conditions which, if satisfied, will conclusively classify the communication as directed at these entities. The communication must indicate the types of person to whom it is directed, and that the controlled investment or controlled activity to which it relates is available only to such persons; it must indicate that other persons should not act upon it; and there must be proper systems and procedures in place to prevent any other person engaging in the investment activity to which the communication relates with the person directing the communication, a close relative of his, or a member of the same group. As we have seen elsewhere, satisfaction of one or two of these conditions is to be taken into account in determining whether the communication is directed at these entities, though a communication can come within art 49 even if it satisfies none of the conditions[1].

1 SI 2005/1529, art 49(3)(b); for the approach elsewhere, see 6.55, n 1.

THE FSA'S FINANCIAL PROMOTION RULES

6.73   The FCA's power to make financial promotion rules is contained in the FSMA 2000, s 137R. Under the FSMA 2000, s 137R, the FSA may make rules applying to authorised persons about the communication by them, or their approval of a communication by others, of invitations or inducements to engage in investment activity or to participate in a collective investment scheme. In particular, the FCA's rules may make provision about the form and content of communications. The FCA's main financial promotion rules are contained in chapter 4 of the Conduct of Business Sourcebook ('COBS'), but there are also financial promotion rules in chapter 3 of the Mortgages: Conduct of business sourcebook (MCOB) and in chapter 2.2 of the Insurance: Conduct of business sourcebook (ICOBS). In addition, the new Consumer Credit sourcebook (CONC), in force from 1 April 2014, contains detailed financial promotion rules in CONC 3. The FCA has also issued detailed guidance on financial promotion and related activities in chapter 8 of its Perimeter Guidance Manual (PERG).

6.74   Originally the FSMA 2000 contained a provision at s 145(3)(a) which prevented rules from being imposed on authorised persons in respect of communications to which an exemption applied under the Financial Promotion Order[1]. This reflected the Treasury's desire that authorised persons should not be at a disadvantage in this area when compared to unauthorised persons[2]. However, as a result of the implementation in the United Kingdom of various European directives3 this is no longer the case. Under the FSMA 2000, s 137R(4), if the FCA considers that any of the specified requirements relating to communications in these directives apply to the communication in question, and that rules are necessary to secure that the communication satisfies those specified requirements, the FCA may make rules that apply to authorised persons even if an exemption under the Financial Promotion Order would apply.

1 SI 2005/1529.
2 The restriction on the rulemaking power in the FSMA 2000, s 145(3)(b), in respect of the promotion of unregulated collective investment schemes, had a similar effect.
3 Directive 2004/39/EC in respect of markets in financial instruments (MiFID) and, in relation to collective investment schemes, Directive 2009/65/EC relating to undertakings for collective investment in transferable securities (UCITS).

6.75   Under the FSMA 2000, s 137S, the FCA has the power to give directions where:

(a)   an authorised person has made, or proposes to make, a communication, or has approved or proposes to approve, another person's communication; and

(b)   the FCA considers that there has been, or is likely to be, a contravention of financial promotion rules in respect of the communication or approval.

In these circumstances, the FCA may require the authorised person to withdraw the communication or approval, to refrain from making or approving the communication, to publish details of the direction, and to do anything else relating to the communication or approval that is specified in the direction. This is a very wide power and one that is consistent with the aim of the FCA to be more proactive than its predecessor, the FSA. The direction is also capable of applying to other communications that are in all material respects the same as, or substantially the same as, the communication which is the subject of the direction.

The direction takes effect immediately, although the authorised person has the ability to make representation to the FCA to amend or revoke the direction, and may refer the matter to the Tribunal if the FCA decides not to revoke the direction[1].

1 FSMA, s 137S(8)(b).

Financial promotion rules in COBS 4

6.76 COBS 4 has the concept of the 'excluded communication', a financial promotion to which none of the COBS 4 rules apply. As with the exemptions in the Financial Promotion Order[1], different exemptions can be combined in respect of the same financial promotion.

The following are excluded communications:

(1) A financial promotion which would be covered by an exemption in the Financial Promotion Order if it were communicated by an unauthorised person, or which originates outside the United Kingdom and is not capable of having an effect in the United Kingdom.

(2) Communications from outside the UK which would be exempt under the Financial Promotion Order[2], arts 30–33 (Overseas communicators) if the office from which the communication was made were a separate unauthorised person.

(3) A financial promotion subject to or exempted from the Takeover Code or to the requirements relating to takeovers or related operations in another EEA State.

(4) Personal quotations or illustration forms (which will be subject to the protections provided elsewhere in COBS, such as the requirement to provide suitable advice).

(5) 'One off' financial promotions that are not unsolicited real time financial promotions (or 'cold calls' in FCA's language). These are already exempt in part under the Financial Promotion Order[3], art 28; the effect of the exemption in the FSA's rules is to extend the Financial Promotion Order exemption to communications relating to deposits and all contracts of insurance.

(6) A communication that is exempted by the Financial Services and Markets Act 2000 (Promotion of Collective Investment Schemes) (Exemptions) Order 2001[4].

1 SI 2005/1529.
2 SI 2005/1529.
3 SI 2005/1529.
4 SI 2001/1060.

6.77   The FCA's financial promotion rules are in one sense simpler than the financial promotion rules originally made by the FSA under the original FSMA 2000, in that they are shorter and less prescriptive. In another sense, however, they are more complicated, as they apply differently depending on whether the communication is in relation to business governed by MiFID or not 1. And as much of the original FSA guidance has disappeared – something the FSA itself removed when amending its financial promotion rules to implement MiFID in 2007 – firms are left to determine what the rules mean with little assistance from the regulator.

1 It is perhaps surprising that the FCA has not taken the opportunity to harmonise the rules across all types of business, though the FCA may have been wary of attracting criticism for 'gold plating' European requirements.

6.78   The FCA's rules apply when a firm communicates with a client in relation to its designated investment business, or communicates or approves a financial promotion (except a financial promotion for qualifying credit, home purchase plans or home reversion plans, or a non-investment insurance contract, where separate financial promotion provisions apply). The FCA's rules also do not apply where a firm communicates or approves a promotion of an unregulated collective investment scheme that would breach the FSMA 2000, s 238(1) if made by an authorised person, but on the somewhat technical ground that such communication or promotion is prohibited.

In addition, the rules do not apply to an authorised professional firm when communicating a financial promotion if the firm's main business is the practice of its profession, the financial promotion is incidental to the promotion or provision by the firm of professional services or of non-mainstream regulated activities, and is not communicated on behalf of another person who could not lawfully make the communication if he were acting in the course of business[1]. The rules on approving a financial promotion continue to apply[2].

1 COBS 18.11.3R. This rule also provides that in respect of promotions of unregulated collective investment schemes, the authorised professional firm may use the exemptions in COB 4 if it wishes.
2 See COBS 18.11.4G.

6.79   Only a limited number of the rules in COBS apply to financial promotions concerning deposits which are structured deposits, cash deposit ISAs or cash deposit child trust funds (CTFs), or to pure protection contracts which are long-term care insurance contracts the most important of which is that the promotion be clear, fair and not misleading[1]. Financial promotions concerning these types of investments are, in particular, exempt from the provisions relating to direct offer financial promotions in COBS4.7, unless the promotion relates to a cash deposit ISA or cash deposit CTF[2].

1 COBS 4.2.1R.
2 See COBS 4.7.1R(4)(d).

6.80   In broad terms, the FCA's rules apply to communications in respect of activities carried on in the United Kingdom, to financial promotions communicated to persons inside the United Kingdom and to cold calls made from the United Kingdom to persons outside the United Kingdom[1]. However, this is modified to comply with various EU directives (in particular, to comply with MiFID)[2]. That means that in some cases the FCA's rules will not apply to communications made to persons in the UK by EEA firms, for instance by a German firm carrying on MiFID business from Germany and communicating financial promotions to investors in the UK.

1 COBS 4.1.8R. For the definition of 'cold calls', see 6.89.
2 COBS 1 Ann 1.

6.81   The fact that the FSA's COBS rules do not apply to a particular promotion will not inevitably mean that the promotion is free from all restrictions. Apart from regulations or guidelines outside the FCA's remit (such as Advertising Standards Authority or OFCOM codes, and regulations of overseas regulators), FCA's Principle 7 of the Principles for Businesses (communications with clients), which requires a firm to pay attention to the information needs of its clients and communicate information to them in a way which is clear, fair and not misleading may also be relevant.

The detailed provisions

6.82 ·   The key FSA rule in relation to financial promotion is the 'fair, clear and not misleading rule' – that is, a requirement that firms ensure that a communication or a financial promotion be fair, clear and not misleading[1]. This rule applies in relation to all communications to clients in relation to designated investment business, other than third party prospectuses, to financial promotions approved by the firm, and to financial promotions communicated by the firm which are not excluded communications, non-retail communications (communications made to or directed at persons who are reasonably believed to be professional clients or eligible counterparties), or third party prospectuses[2]. This last exclusion applies to other rules in COB 4. Other rules in COBS 4 have exclusions for 'image advertising' – communications restricted to one or more of the name of the firm, the firm's logo, a contact point, and the type of regulated activities carried on by the firm or its fees and commissions[3]. Examples of this would be brand advertising at sporting events, such as on advertising hoardings or via artefacts such as umbrellas or pens.

The FCA makes clear that the fair, clear and not misleading rule applies in a way that is appropriate and proportionate taking into account the means of communication and the information the communication is intended to convey[4]. It is therefore surprising that the rule does not apply to communications to eligible counterparties, although this may simply reflect the disapplication contained in MiFID[5].

In certain circumstances, the FCA fleshes out what 'fair, clear and not misleading' involves. So products that place client's capital at risk should make that clear; products that quote a yield figure must give a balanced impression of both the short and long-term prospects for the investment; and references to the FCA and/or PRA as a firm's regulator in the context of unregulated business should make clear that that neither the FCA nor PRA regulates such business[6]. In addition, words such as 'guaranteed' 'protected' or 'secure' should only be used when that term is capable of being a fair, clear and not misleading description of the product and the necessary information has been presented with sufficient clarity and prominence to make the use of the term fair, clear and not misleading[7]. In general (as with all other conduct of business rules) there is a right of action under FSMA section 138D for breach of this rule, though it is a defence that the firm took reasonable steps to ensure compliance. 'Reasonable steps' in this context might include taking professional advice on the content, such as from a lawyer or accountant.

1 COBS 4.2.1R. 'Communication' is added to financial promotion in order to satisfy MiFID article 19(2). In practice, this adds nothing to the pre-MiFID position since firms were already under an obligation under principle 7 of the Principles for Businesses to communicate information to clients (which includes potential clients) in a way that is clear, fair and not misleading.
2 A third party prospectus is a prospectus satisfying the Prospectus Directive (Directive 2003/71/EC) for which someone other than the firm is responsible.
3 See eg COBS 4.3 and COBS 4.5.
4 COBS 4.2.2G.
5 Directive 2004/39/EC, art 24(1).
6 COBS 4.2.4G.
7 COBS 4.2.5G.

6.83   A firm must ensure that a financial promotion addressed to a client is clearly identified as such[1]. This does not mean that the promotion has to have the words 'This is a financial promotion' attached to it (although that would clearly satisfy the requirement), but simply that the promotional nature of the material be apparent. In practice, this requirement is unlikely to cause difficulty.

1 COBS 4.3.1R(1).

6.84   In order to prevent firms marketing their products on the basis of the compensation available in the case of default (and perhaps drawing unfavourable contrasts with the scope and amount of compensation available for competitors covered by the compensation arrangements of other EEA States), COBS 4.4.1R prohibits firms from including more than a factual reference to the ICS compensation arrangements. Where a firm is issuing electronic money to a person, it must also ensure that that person has been told in good time beforehand that the issue of electronic money is not covered by the compensation scheme[1].

1 COBS 4.4.3R.

6.85   COBS 4 contains various provisions which are confined to retail clients, largely derived from MiFID[1]. So a firm that provides information to retail clients must ensure that the information includes the name of the firm, does not emphasise any benefits of the investment without giving a fair and prominent indication of any relevant risks, does not disguise diminish or obscure important items, statements of warnings, and is sufficient for and presented in a way that is likely to be understood by the average member of the group to whom it is directed or by whom it is likely to be received[2]. Although the concept of the 'average member of the group' appears a difficult one, one suspects that any communication that satisfies the 'fair clear and not misleading' rule will be very likely to satisfy the 'average member of the group' requirement in any event.

1 Directive 2004/39/EC.
2 COBS 4.5.2R.

6.86   Comparative information about types of business, types of investments or persons who carry on controlled activities must be meaningful, presented in a fair and balanced way and, where the business is MiFID or equivalent third country business [1], identify the sources of the information and include the key facts and assumptions used to make the comparison [2].

If any information refers to a particular tax treatment, it must prominently state that the tax treatment depends on the individual treatment of the client [3], and the information in the promotion must be consistent with any other information provided to the client [4], unless the financial promotion relates to a pure protection contract that is a long-term care insurance contract[5].

1 'Equivalent third country business' is business carried on from the UK that would fall within the scope of MiFID if the firm were a MiFID investment firm.
2 COBS 4.5.6R.
3 COBS 4.5.7R.
4 COBS 4.5.8R.
5 COBS 4.5.7R (2)(b) and COBS 4.5.8R(2)(b).

6.87 Because of the risk that investors might be induced by the presentation of performance figures to make investments, the rules in COB 4 contain provisions relating to both past and future performance. Past performance information must not be the most prominent feature of the promotion, and at least the previous five years must be covered (or the whole period the investment has been offered, if shorter), in complete 12 month periods[1]. Further, there must be a risk warning that past performance is not a reliable indicator of future results and, where the information is based on gross performance, the effect of commission, fees or other changes must be disclosed [2]. Simulated past performance figures are allowed only if there is an actual past performance of one or more financial indices or investments which are the same as or underlie the investment concerned, and the actual past performance must comply with the past performance rules[3]. Future performance should not be based on simulated past performance and must be based on reasonable assumptions supported by objective data; if that data is unavailable the firm should not provide that information[4]. If the business is not MiFID business or equivalent third country business, the future performance rule applies only to financial promotions relating to a financial instrument, to a financial index that relates exclusively to financial instruments, or to a structured deposit[5].

1 COBS 4.6.2R (1) and (2).
2 COBS 4.6.2R (4) and (6).
3 COBS 4.6.6R.
4 COBS 4.6.7R and 4.6.8G.
5 COBS 4.6.7R(2).

6.88 Direct offer financial promotions – financial promotions that contain an offer to the recipient and specify the form in which a response to the offer may be made (for instance, by attaching an application form) are also perceived as risky, given that the recipients of the promotion are given the means to respond to the promotion in the promotion itself. Accordingly, COBS 4.7.1R sets out contents requirements so that the retail client is able properly to evaluate the risks and the costs. This information will include information about the firm and its services, costs and associated charges, and the risks of the investment concerned. The FCA's guidance at COBS 4.7.4G suggests that in order to enable the client to make an informed assessment of the investment, firms may wish to include in the promotion information referring to the taxation treatment of the investment and its consequences for the average member of the group to whom the promotion is being made, a statement that the client should seek a personal recommendation if he has any doubt as to the suitability of the investment or services being promoted, and a key features illustration if the promotion relates to a life policy or stakeholder or personal pension scheme. A firm can communicate or approve a direct offer financial promotion to a retail client relating to a warrant or derivative, where the firm itself is not obliged to comply with the rules on appropriateness in COBS 10, only if it has adequate evidence that the person arranging or dealing in relation to the warrant or derivatives will comply with those rules or rules equivalent to them in respect of any order he is aware or ought reasonably be aware is in response to the firm's financial promotion[1].

1 COBS 4.7.6R.

6.89   In April 2014 the FCA introduced new rules for direct offer financial promotions relating to a non-readily realisable security (NRRS)[1]. These rules were prompted by the growth in the volume of investment via crowdfunding websites and the concern that retail clients making investments in this way (mainly, if not exclusively, in start-up companies) might not properly appreciate the risks that they were taking. As drafted, however, the rules apply to promotion of NRRSs generally, not just via crowndfunding websites.

1 A NRRS is a security which is not a readily realisable security (such as a listed share or bond), or a packaged product, or a non-mainstream pooled investment. For the definition of a non-mainstream pooled investment see 6.106.

6.90   The general rule is that a firm must not communicate a direct offer financial promotion to a retail client, or approve the content of such a promotion[1]. However, there are two exceptions to this:

(1)   if the retail client recipient is certified as a high net worth investor, sophisticated investor or restricted investor, or self-certified as a sophisticated investor, a direct offer financial promotion may be communicated (or approved), provided that the firm itself, or the person who will arrange or deal in relation to the NRRS, will comply with the FCA's rules in COBS 10 relating to appropriateness[2]; and

(2)   if the retail client will be advised as to the suitability of the investment in accordance with the rules in COBS 9 (the advice may be give by the firm communicating or approving the promotion, or by another FCA authorised firm), or is a corporate finance contact or venture capital contact (who by definition will not reasonably expect to be treated as a client by the firm).

1 COBS 4.7.7R(1).
2 COBS 4.7.7R(2) and (3). 'High net worth investor', 'certified sophisticated investor' and 'self-certified sophisticated investor' are defined by reference to COBS 4.12.6–8: see 6.108. A 'certified restricted investor' is a person who, within a period of 12 months ending on the day the communication is made, has signed a statement in specified terms to the effect that he has not invested more than 10% of his net assets in NRRSs in the previous 12 months and undertakes not to invest more than 10% of his net assets in NRRSs in the next 12 months after the statement is signed. The definition of 'net assets' in this context is similar to that for high net worth individuals in the Financial Promotion Order: see 6.63.

6.91   The COB 4 rules make provisions about 'cold calls' – unsolicited communications in the course of a personal visit, telephone conversation or other interactive dialogue which are not in response to initiatives taken by the client concerned. In general, cold calls can be made only where there is an existing client relationship where the client envisages receiving cold calls, or the cold call relates to a generally marketable packaged product that is not a higher volatility fund of a life policy with a link to such a fund, or the call relates to a controlled activity to be carried on by an authorised or exempt person and the only controlled investments which are or reasonably could be involved are readily realisable securities (other than warrants) and generally marketable non-geared packaged products[1]. Such calls must be made only at an appropriate time of day; the caller must identify himself and his firm, make clear the purpose of the call, terminate the call at any time that the client requests it, and gives the client a contact point when he arranges an appointment[2]. These rules do not however apply to certain types of communication, including those where an exemption in the FPO applies and where the person called is a professional client or eligible counterparty[3].

1   COBS 4.8.2R
2   COBS 4.8.3R.
3   COBS 4.8.1R. In theory this means that such persons could be cold-called at any time; in practice calling at anti-social hours is likely both to be counterproductive and in breach of principle 4 of the FCA Principles for Businesses: could such a call really be in accordance with proper standards of market conduct?

6.92   COBS 4.9 contains provisions that apply to financial promotions with an overseas element (but not in relation to MIFID or equivalent third country business, where an exclusion in the FPO applies, where the promotion is to persons who are not retail clients, or to the extent that it is a prospectus advertisement governed by prospectus rules or relates to a pure protection contract that is a contract of long-term care insurance). If a firm communicates or approves a financial promotion relating to a relevant investment or relevant business of an overseas person, the firm must ensure that the promotion makes clear who has approved or communicated it, that the rules in the FSMA for the protection of retail clients do not apply, and the extent to which the FSCS will be available. If the FSCS will not be available the promotion must say so, though it is open to the communicator to state what other protection or compensation would be available. In addition, the firm must take reasonable steps to satisfy itself that the overseas person will deal with UK retail clients in an honest and reliable way[1]. Where financial promotions for overseas long-term insurers without an establishment in the UK are concerned, the promotion which is communicated or approved must contain the name and location of its registered and (if different) head office and a prominent statement that the FSCS will not be available to policyholders if the company becomes unable to meet its liabilities to them[2]. Where the overseas long-term insurer is authorised to carry on long-term insurance business in Jersey, Guernsey, the Isle of Man, Pennsylvania or Iowa, additional information must be disclosed relating to the trustee and investment manager of any property retained in respect of the promoted contracts[3]. If the long-term insurer is not identified by name, the promotion must contain a statement in prescribed form to the effect that the FSCS and FOS do not apply in the event that the company is unable to meet its liabilities to policyholders[4].

1   COBS 4.9.3R.
2   COBS 4.9.5R.
3   COBS 4.9.6R.
4   COBS 4.9.7R(1).

6.93   Where a firm approves a financial promotion, it is required to confirm that the promotion complies with the financial promotion rules[1]. If subsequently the firm becomes aware that the promotion no longer complies with the rules, it must withdraw its approval and notify any person it knows to be relying on its approval of the withdrawal as soon as reasonably practicable [2].

The FCA's guidance points out that a firm may wish to approve a financial promotion that it communicates itself. This seemingly bizarre act does in fact have a sensible purpose – such approval makes it possible for an unauthorised person (such as a distributor) to communicate the financial promotion without breaching the restriction on promotion in FSMA s 21[3].

A firm may rely on another firm's confirmation of compliance when communicating a financial promotion produced by another person, provided that it takes reasonable care to communicate the promotion only to recipients of the type intended at the time the confirmation was given, and so far as it is reasonably aware the promotion has not ceased to be fair, clear and not misleading in the intervening period and the original firm has not withdrawn the promotion.

Finally, and perhaps most importantly, a firm is prohibited from approving a financial promotion to be made in the course of a personal visit, telephone conversation or interactive dialogue[5]. This means that oral promotions, with their attendant risks, can be made only by authorised firms.

1 COBS 4.10.2R(1). These are the financial promotion rules that would have applied had the communication been other than in relation to MiFID or equivalent third country business (COBS 4.10.2R(3)) – presumably to avoid any argument that certain rules did not apply to the promotion.
2 COBS 4.10.2R(2).
3 COBS 4.10.3G(2).
4 COBS 4.10.10. This rule does not apply in respect of MiFID or equivalent third country business.
5 COBS 4.10.4R.

6.94   Adequate records of financial promotions (other than promotions made in an interactive dialogue) must be kept for a period the length of which depends on the type of promotion: three, five or six years or (in the case of pension transfers and opt-outs, and free-standing additional voluntary contributions (FSAVCs)), indefinitely [1]. This seems unnecessarily complicated and it is surprising that the FCA has not taken the opportunity to simplify matters.

Where the firm communicates or approves promotions relating to non-mainstream pooled investments (broadly, units in unregulated collective investment schemes, securities issued by special purpose vehicles and traded life policy investments) which are likely to be received by retail clients, the person at the firm allocated the compliance oversight function must certify that the promotion complies with the restrictions in FSMA 2000, s 238 and the FCA's rules, as applicable, and the firm must record which exemption was relied on and the reason why it was satisfied that the exemption applied (including making a record of any certificate or warning required by the exemption)[2].

1 COBS 4.11.
2 COBS 4.11.1R(2A).

6.95   Finally, the FCA has rules in relation to marketing communications relating to UCITS schemes and EEA UCITS schemes. The rules derive entirely from the UCITS directive and contain various disclosure requirements depending on the nature of the scheme concerned. The key requirement is perhaps that a marketing communication which comprises an invitation to purchase units in the scheme, and that contains specific information about the scheme, must indicate that a key investor information document is available and not make any statement that contradicts or diminishes the significance of the information contained in that document or the prospectus for the scheme [1].

1 COBS 4.13.2R(1).

Financial promotion rules in MCOB and ICOBS

6.96   The expansion of the regulatory scope of the FSMA to cover mortgage and non-investment insurance products led to the creation of separate regulatory sourcebooks (MCOB and ICOBS), each with its own section dealing with financial promotion.

MCOB 3 and ICOBS 2.2 take a different approach to financial promotion. Whilst MCOB 3 has detailed rules (including extensive guidance on the types of promotion that will satisfy the requirements of the rules [1], ICOBS 2.2 has very few requirements, the basic one being that the firm should take reasonable steps when communicating financial promotions relating to non-investment insurance contracts that it communicates in a way which is clear, fair and not misleading[2]. The difference between the treatment in ICOBS and that in MCOB (and indeed that in COBS) can be accounted for by the fact that the financial promotion rules in ICOBS do not apply in circumstances where the promotion can be made by an unauthorised communicator without approval[3]. Since the effect of the Financial Promotion Order is that real time promotions relating to non-investment insurance contracts can be made by unauthorised communicators[4], and exemptions in the Financial Promotion Order also cover non-real time promotions of non-investment insurance contracts[5], the application of ICOBS 2.2 to promotions made by authorised persons is significantly reduced. As a consequence, few rules are required to deliver appropriate protection for customers.[6]

1 See eg MCOB 3.6.4E – 3.6.6G, and in particular MCOB 3 Ann 1G.
2 ICOBS 2.2.2R. There are similar provisions regarding a firm approving financial promotions in ICOS 2.2.3R.
3 ICOBS 2.2.1R.
4 SI 2005/1529, art 26.
5 SI 2005/1529, arts 24 and 25.
6 Apart from the 'clear, fair and not misleading' rule, the only additional provision in ICOBS 2.2 consists of guidance on the application of that rule to pricing claims (ICOBS 2.2.4G).

FINANCIAL PROMOTION RULES IN CONC

6.97   With the FCA taking over consumer credit regulation from the Office of Fair Trading on 1 April 2014, a new consumer credit sourcebook (CONC) has been added to the FCA Handbook.

CONC 3 contains provisions relating to financial promotion. In many cases, such as in relation to the clear, fair and not misleading rule[1], the FCA has turned what was previously guidance into rules. There is detailed guidance relating to what the clear, fair and not misleading rule requires[2], as well as provisions relating to financial promotions about credit agreements (whether secured on land or not)[3]. There is also a specific risk warning required for high-cost short term credit – an area which the FCA is likely to be keeping under particular scrutiny going forward[4]. Non written promotions outside the firm's premises are also subject to rules designed to ensure that contact is made only at an appropriate time and that the purpose of the call is made clear at the outset[5]. And as with firms subject to COBS, firms subject to CONC must not approve the content of a real time financial promotion[6].

1 CONC 3.3.1R
2 CONC 3.3.5G–3.3.10G
3 CONC 3.5 (unsecured) and CONC 3.6 (secured)
4 CONC 3.4.
5 CONC 3.10.2R.
6 CONC 3.11.2R.

PROMOTION OF COLLECTIVE INVESTMENT SCHEMES

Restrictions on promotion

6.98   Under the FSMA 2000, s 238, authorised persons can communicate an invitation or inducement to participate in a collective investment scheme only if:

(1)   the scheme is authorised or recognised;

(2)   the communication is in accordance with rules made by the FSA which exempt 'promotions otherwise than to the general public' of specified schemes (this phrase appears to include promotions which are in fact made to the general public but which are designed to reduce, as far as possible, the risk of participation in the scheme by persons for whom participation would be unsuitable[1]); or

(3)   the circumstances of the promotion are exempt under a Treasury order.

1 See the FSMA 2000, s 238(10).

6.99   This restriction reflects the fact that unlike other controlled investments, units in collective investment schemes are generally subject to extensive product regulation for the protection of those who purchase them. Accordingly, it is not regarded as appropriate, even for authorised persons, to promote to the general public collective investment schemes which are neither authorised nor recognised.

6.100   There is no need to apply the FSMA 2000, s 238 to unauthorised persons, as units in collective investment schemes are controlled investments[1]. Communications in relation to them are therefore subject to the basic prohibition in the FSMA 2000, s 21.

1 SI 2005/1529, Sch 1, para 19.

6.101   As with the FSMA 2000, s 21, s 238(1) applies to communications originating outside the UK only if they are capable of having an effect in the UK, and the Treasury has the power to move to 'home state' regulation of communications in relation to units in collective investment schemes should other countries do likewise, by exempting communications that originate in specified countries or territories[1].

1 FSMA 2000, s 238(7); compare 6.19.

6.102   The FSMA 2000, s 240 provides that an authorised person cannot approve the content of a promotion under s 21 if the authorised person would himself be prevented from making the communication himself, or causing the communication to be made, under s 238(1). This reinforces the principle, seen in the Treasury order, that an unauthorised person should not be in a better position than an authorised person to communicate invitations or inducements to participate in unauthorised collective investment schemes[1].

1 See HM Treasury, Financial Promotion – Third Consultation Document (October 2000), para 4.6.

The Financial Services and Markets Act 2000 (Promotion of Collective Investment Schemes) (Exemptions) Order 2001 (CIS Exemptions Order)

6.103 The aim of the CIS Exemptions Order[1] is to ensure that so far as possible the same exemptions as would apply to unauthorised persons under the Financial Promotion Order[2] apply also to authorised persons when making communications relating to collective investment schemes. It would clearly be illogical for unauthorised persons, as a result of exemptions applying under the Financial Promotion Order, to have a more liberal regime applying to them[3].

1 SI 2001/1060, as amended.
2 SI 2005/1529.
3 Illogical, but no longer impossible: see 6.74.

6.104 Consequently, there is a large measure of overlap between the exemptions contained in the Financial Promotion Order[1] and in the CIS Exemptions Order[2]. The definitions of real time, non-real time, and solicited and unsolicited real time communications are the same[3]; exemptions can be combined; and there are similar exemptions for one-off and follow-up communications[4], and for communications to overseas recipients, investment professionals, certified high net worth individuals, high net worth companies, sophisticated investors, and self-certified sophisticated investors[5].

1 SI 2005/1529.
2 SI 2001/1060.
3 SI 2001/1060, arts 4–5.
4 SI 2001/1060, arts 15, 15A and 11.
5 SI 2001/1060, arts 8, 14, 21–23A and the Schedule.

6.105 The Treasury also has the power to make regulations under the FSMA 2000, s 239 for exempting single property schemes from the prohibition in s 238(1). A single property scheme is a scheme where the property subject to the scheme consists of a single building or group of adjacent or contiguous buildings managed by the operator as a single enterprise, and where the units of the participants in the scheme are either dealt in on a recognised investment exchange, or where their acquisition is made subject to the units being admitted to dealings on such an exchange. If the Treasury makes such regulations, the FCA may impose duties on the operator, and (if it exists) on the trustee or depositary of the scheme. Given that no such schemes were created in response to regulations made under a virtually identical power in the Financial Services Act 1986, it would seem unlikely that this power will ever be exercised.

The FSA's rules

6.106 The FCA has recently amended its rules dealing with the promotion of unregulated collective investment schemes in response to what it saw as unacceptable selling practices by IFAs and others. The rules now cover not only unregulated collective investment schemes but also investments thought to be substantially similar to unregulated collective investment schemes. The umbrella term for these investments is 'non-mainstream pooled investments'[1].

1 Apart from units in unregulated collective investment schemes, the definition includes certain securities issued by special purpose vehicles and traded life policies.

6.107   The general rule is that a firm cannot communicate or approve a financial promotion relating to a non-mainstream pooled investment where that promotion is likely to be received by a retail client. However, there are a number of exemptions to this listed in the table at COBS 4.12.3R(5), and, as is normal with financial promotion exemptions, they can be combined in relation to the same promotion.

The exemptions allow promotion in the following circumstances:

(1)   to a person who is already participating in or owning a non-mainstream pooled investment ('NMPI') that is being liquidated, wound down or undergoing a rights issue, provided that the NMPI promoted is intended to absorb or take over the assets of the first NMPI, or consists of securities offered as part of a rights issue;

(2)   to certified high net worth investors (persons who meet requirements similar to those required by the exemption in the Financial Promotion Order, art 48), provided that the firm considers the NMPI in question to be likely to be suitable based on a preliminary assessment of the client's profile and objectives;

(3)   to a person who is eligible to participate or invest in an arrangement constituted under the Church Funds Investment Measure 1958, the Charities Act 2011, s 96, the Charities Act (Northern Ireland) 1964, s 25, the Regulation on European Venture Capital Funds or the Regulation on European Social Entrepreneurship Funds, where any NMPI which is such an arrangement may be promoted (though the class of qualifying persons will be strictly limited, for instance to trustees of charities and of certain trust funds, such as the Central Board of Finance of the Church of England and Diocesan Boards of Finance);

(4)   to eligible employees of an employer which is, or is in the same group as, the authorised person (or who has accepted responsibility for the activities of the authorised person in carrying out the designated investment business in question), provided that the communication relates to certain types of employee incentive schemes;

(5)   to Lloyd's names, provided that the NMPI is in the form of a limited partnership established for the sole purpose of underwriting insurance business at Lloyd's;

(6)   to exempt persons (though not to appointed representatives), where any NMPI may be promoted if the promotion relates to a regulated activity in respect of which the person is exempt;

(7)   to non-retail clients (professional clients and eligible counterparties) where any NMPI may be promoted in relation to which the client is so categorised;

(8)   to certified sophisticated investors, where any NMPI may be promoted (the certification process is similar to that in the exemption in the Financial Promotion Order, art 50);

(9)   to self-certified sophisticated investors, where any NMPI the firm considers is likely to be suitable for that client may be promoted, based on a preliminary assessment of the client's profile and objectives (the certification process being similar to that in the exemption in the Financial Promotion Order, art 50A);

(10) where a client specifically requests advice on investing in an NMPI and the client has not received any previous communication from the firm in relation to that NMPI;

(11) where the communication is an excluded communication (see **6.76**); and

(12) where the NMPI is an EEA UCITS scheme which is not a recognised scheme, and which the firm considers is likely to be suitable for the client based on a preliminary assessment of the client's profile and objectives, and the firm provides the same information as it would have provided if the scheme had been a recognised scheme; and

(13) where the NMPI is an investment company registered and operated in the United States under the Investment Company Act 1940 and the promotion is made to a person classified as a 'United States person' under US legislation or who owns a US qualified retirement plan.

1 COBS 4.12.3R(2), which refers to the restriction on promotion of NMPIs in COBS 4.12.3R(1) not applying to units in unregulated collective investment schemes (on the grounds that they are subject to the statutory restriction in FSMA 2000, s 238), might be taken as meaning that the exemptions in COBS 4.12.4R(5) do not extend to the promotion of units in unregulated collective investment schemes (on the grounds that the exemptions in COBS 4.12.4R(5) are exemptions to the restriction in COBS 4.12.3R (see COBS 4.12.4R(1)), and this restriction is stated not to apply to units in unregulated collective investment schemes). But it can scarcely be the case that FCA would have wished to treat units in unregulated collective investment schemes more harshly than other form of NMPI – for instance, preventing their promotion to professional clients and eligible counterparties generally – without making that point explicit in consultation. It therefore seems reasonable to assume that units in unregulated collective investment schemes are capable of falling within the exemptions in COBS 4.12.4R(5).

6.108   The new requirements remove the former 'category 2 person' exemption which enabled promotion to retail clients on the basis that the firm had taken reasonable steps to ensure that the investment was suitable for the client. As this exemption was found to have been widely abused where unregulated collective investment schemes were concerned[1], the new rules which took effect from 1 January 2014 seek to limit promotion of NMPIs to retail clients who are properly categorised as sophisticated or high net worth investors. Indeed, the guidance at COBS 4.12.9G(2) suggests that a firm should not promote NMPIs to clients, even if they are certified high net worth investors, where the firm considers that the clients would not also be sophisticated investors[2]. This is clearly an area which the FCA has under scrutiny, and it will be interesting to see whether the FCA will seek to take action against firms who promote to high net worth investors on the grounds that those investors are not sophisticated enough to understand the risks involved.

1 The rationale for the change is set out in the FSA's consultation paper CP12/19, 'Restrictions on the retail distribution of unregulated collective investment schemes and close substitutes' (August 2012), paras 1.4 ff.
2 Compare similar qualifications in other exemptions where the need for sophistication is stressed: COBS 4.12.11G(2) (self-certified sophisticated investors); and COBS 4.12.13G(2) (qualified investor schemes)

Chapter 7

Market Abuse

Andrew Haynes

INTRODUCTION

7.1   Market Abuse was first introduced as part of the programme of developments that were brought into the financial services regime by the Financial Services and Markets Act 2000 ('FSMA'). Since then market abuse has seen significant change as a result of the Market Abuse Directive which in turn led to changes to the relevant UK legislation[1]. This Directive is a part of the EU's Financial Services Action Plan which has been created to try and develop a pan EU financial market and to enhance market integrity[2]. Problems had arisen with regard to market abuse because member states had different laws. This meant that if a company in one member state were to mount a takeover bid for a company in another, and that second company had subsidiaries in other member states, the takeover would have to be designed not to fall foul of the market abuse regulations in all those states. By having a single EU approach this problem is hopefully avoided.

1 Financial Services and Markets Act 2000 (Market Abuse) Regulations 2005, SI 2005/No 381.
2 Of specific reference to market abuse/insider dealing are Directive 2003/6/EC on insider dealing and market abuse, Directive 2003/124/EC which established criteria for determining when inside information is precise and price sensitive, Directive 2003/125/EC creating standards for presenting investment recommendations and disclosing conflicts of interest, Commission Regulation 2273/2003 providing technical conditions for share buy-backs and price stabilisation, and Directive 2004/72/EC regarding accepted market practices, inside information, insider lists and notification requirements.

7.2   The key element of the Directive is that it applies to all transactions involving financial instruments that have been admitted to trading on at least one prescribed market in the EU regardless of whether that market is regulated. More than one state may be involved in the matter as the regime results in the state in which the market abuse occurs, and that in which the relevant financial instrument is admitted (should it be a different one) both having jurisdiction. In most instances however, both activities will occur in the same state. The regime extends to cover insider dealing, and to reduce the risk of this occurring a requirement was introduced for disclosure by issuers of inside information, on the basis that once this is done the information is in the public domain and insider dealing should cease to be a risk. There is a requirement to create an 'insider list' of people who have access to inside information. In addition there is an obligation to make sure that those producing or disseminating research make sure that it is fairly presented and any conflicts of interest disclosed. There are also two safe harbours which relate to share buy backs and stabilisation. Powers are also provided to the relevant authorities, in the UK the FCA, to provide guidance on 'accepted market practices'. This is assistance in ascertaining whether a particular trade will give false or misleading impression and whether particular information is inside information. There remains some debate about the precise legal status of such guidance but in practice its status will make little difference. The rules are drafted by the FCA and they are also the body who will determine whether to take steps against someone believed to be in breach of the law. The issue is only likely to arise if FCA guidance is cited in the defence of a criminal prosecution or in an Upper Tribunal hearing.

7.3   The essence of the regime however has remained the same since the passing of FSMA which is that certain types of behaviour are deemed to be in breach of the Act. This does not necessarily mean that the behaviour will amount to a criminal offence, though in some cases it undoubtedly will. What it does mean is that the behaviour will give rise to the FCA having the power to take steps against FCA authorised persons and firms together with anyone else who has committed market abuse[1]. This will result in potential fines and in the case of authorised firms also the possibility of loss of licences[2]. If the person agrees to co-operate with the FCA they will often include an agreement to not work in the financial services sector as part of the settlement. The taking of steps against non FCA regulated people is most likely to impact on commodity companies whose involvement in that sector can have an impact on prices. Indeed one of the cases examined below[3] involved a major oil company. This chapter will consider 'market abuse' itself and also insider dealing which comes within the remit of market abuse. Finally, there will be a consideration of the relevant law relating to misleading statements[4].

1 FSMA 2000, s 123.
2 FSMA 2000, s 123.
3 *Shell Petroleum and Trading Co plc and The Royal Dutch Petroleum Co NV*, FSA enforcement action, 24 August 2004.
4 FSA 2012, ss 89–91.

7.4   One issue that arises here is that of the nature of a civil offence. It is not an approach that has been a significant part of English law. Essentially there is a civil burden of proof coupled with a potentially unlimited fine[1]. There were originally suggestions[2] that the courts would regard market abuse as a criminal offence but the view of the majority is that[3] the power to fine is only unlimited because some of those who might potentially be fined are large financial institutions for whom a fine would have to be large to make any impact. Certainly at this point no tribunal or court has adopted the approach of it being a criminal sanction. However, a common misconception is that as it is a civil offence the standard of the burden of proof is that of the balance of probabilities:

> 'A civil court, when considering a charge of fraud, will naturally require a higher degree of probability that that which it would require if considering whether negligence were established. It does not adopt so high a degree as a criminal court, even when it is considering a charge of a criminal nature, but still it does require a degree of probability which is commensurate with the occasion[4].'

> 'The case, like any civil case, may be proved by a preponderance of probability, but the degree of probability depends on the subject-matter. In proportion as the offence is grave, so ought the proof be clear[5].'

1 FSMA 2000, 123(1).
2 Joint Committee on Financial Services and Markets *'Draft Financial Services and Markets Bill: Parts V, VI and XII in relation to the European Convention on Human Rights'*, 27 May 1999, HC 415, p 82.
3 House of Commons research paper, 99/68 pp 61–3.
4 Denning LJ in *Bater v Bater* [1951] 35.
5 Lord Denning in *Blyth v Blyth* [1966] AC 643.

7.5   Therefore, in those cases where the market abuse alleged would also be a criminal offence then the higher the standard of proof that will be required in the Upper Tribunal. In most cases this has not become an issue as those facing market abuse charges have co-operated and accepted disciplinary action. This is perhaps the true measure of success of the new regime. Few if any would be likely to have so co-operated with a criminal prosecution because of the potential consequences.

7.6   For market abuse the key issues relate to FSMA 2000, ss 96, 118 to 131 (as amended) together the FCA Code of Market Conduct (MAR) and some parts of the FCA Conduct of Business Sourcebook. For insider dealing much of the relevant law is still to be found in the Criminal Justice Act 1993, though the FCA Handbook at MAR 1.3 impacts on the treatment of insider dealing as a category of market abuse rather than as a criminal offence. Misuse of information is dealt with in the FSMA and can also be affected by MAR 1.5.

7.7   Inevitably, the recent developments in this area of law raise the issue of how common market abuse and insider dealing are. The FCA themselves have published an analysis[1] which measured the extent to which share prices moved ahead of the regulatory announcements that companies are required to make. The analysis focused on two areas; those relating to takeover bids and announcements about trading performance made by FTSE 350 companies. An assessment was then made of the proportion of these that were preceded by abnormal share price movements. The research did not prove how much market abuse was taking place but it did suggest that 28.9% of takeover announcements and 21.7% of trading announcements were preceded by transactions that were probably based on inside information. Later analyses have produced lower figures but nonetheless reveal the industrial scale on which market abuse and insider trading exist.

1 Dubow B and Monteiro N *'FSA publishes measure of scale of market abuse'* March 2005, FSA.

MARKET ABUSE

The offences

7.8   Market abuse represents a range of behaviour relating to investments that can result in civil sanctions by the FCA against those who have broken the relevant sections of the Financial Services and Markets Act 2000 (FSMA). In most cases the process consists of an FCA Enforcement Action whereby the matter is conceded by the person or firm being dealt with or whereby they do not concede the action but acquiesce in its outcome. If matters are not agreed then the case may be sent to the Tribunal. Originally this was the Financial Services and Markets Tribunal but in April 2010 this was abolished and the cases are now dealt with by the Upper Tribunal. It is also possible that matters end up in a mainstream court either through the FCA taking a matter there or due to an appeal by either the FCA or a party against whom the FCA have taken action. It is in all these stages beyond an FCA Enforcement Action that the issue of the burden of proof arises (see **4.4** above).

7.9   Turning to the offences of market abuse itself, FSMA s 118 makes it an offence where someone engages in certain categories of behaviour in relation to qualifying investments that are traded on a prescribed market. This does not require the person concerned to have intended to commit market abuse[1]. There are a series of definitions of the sub categories that might be actionable on a civil enforcement basis by the FCA. However, the definitions do not exactly marry with the offences that people have been engaging in, some of which appears to span two or more of the defined offences[2]. The FCA's approach in such cases has tended to be to pursue people on the basis of which of the following seems the closest fit. The categories of behaviour which amount to market abuse are: insider dealing, disclosure of inside information, misuse of inside information, manipulating transactions, manipulating devices, disseminating misleading information, distorting the market and encouraging others to do any of these things. These will be briefly considered in turn.

1 MAR 1.2.3 G.
2 The most relevant cases here would appear to be the FCA Enforcement Actions in *Perkins* 29 June 2010, *Alexander* 14 June 2011, *Swift* 13 August 2011 confirmed by the Upper Tax Tribunal in *Visser and Fagbulu*, 28 June 2013 confirmed by Upper Tax Tribunal 27th August 2011, *Goenka* 9 Nov 2011, *Kahn* 24 May 2011 and High Court injunction *Betton* 6 Dec 2010 and *Winterflood* [2010] EWCA Civ 423.

Insider dealing

7.10   It is determined to be insider dealing where '…an insider deals, or attempts to deal, in a qualifying investment on the basis of inside information relating to the investment in question[1]. This differs from the criminal definition in s 52 of the Criminal Justice Act 1993 which does not include *'attempting'* but as at the date of writing[2] no market abuse enforcement has been taken where an unsuccessful attempt to engage in market abuse has been made. Common sense determines that such a case is very unlikely. In turn an *'insider'* is defined[3] as anyone who has inside information as a result of their membership of a company, whether as an administrator or, manager or a supervisory body, as a result of them holding capital issued by a company, as a result of them having access to the information concerned through carrying out their employment or professional duties, as a result of criminal activities or which they obtained by other methods which they know, or could reasonably be expected to know would be inside information. Essentially this is the same as the criminal offence.

1 FSMA 2000, s 118(2) *ibid* and MAR 1.3.2 E.
2 26th February 2013.
3 FSMA 2000, s 118B.

Disclosure of inside information

7.11   This occurs 'where an insider discloses inside information to another person otherwise than in the proper exercise of his employment, profession or duties[1].' In this context 'inside information[2]' is regarded as information of a precise nature relating to qualifying investments which are not commodity derivatives, which is not generally available, relates directly or indirectly to the issuer of a qualifying investment and would if generally available be likely to have a significant effect on the price of the investment concerned or of a related one. Where commodity derivatives are concerned inside information is that which is of a precise nature which is not generally available and relates directly or indirectly to such derivatives, and users of the relevant markets would expect to be provided with it in line with accepted market practice. This may be because such information is routinely made available to users on that market or because it is required by statute, the rules of the market concerned or custom either on the derivatives market or that of the underlying commodity[3]. General availability in either instance extends to information that is obtainable by research or analysis[4]. Again this occupies essentially the same territory as the equivalent criminal offence.

1 FSMA, s 118(3) *ibid* and MAR 1.4.
2 FSMA, s 118C.
3 FSMA, s 118C(7).
4 FSMA, s 118C(8).

7.12   Information can be disclosed without being in breach of the restrictions provided it causes the person making the disclosure to know or suspect that someone else is engaging in market abuse. That information must have come to them in the course of their trade profession, business or employment and it must have been made to the FCA or the appropriate internal officer as soon as reasonably practicable after it was obtained[1].

1 FSMA, s 131A.

7.13   In the case of whether or not behaviour is improper disclosure amounting to market abuse, the FCA view the following as determining factors: whether the behaviour is permitted by the rules of the market concerned or the Takeover Code or whether the disclosure is accompanied by the imposition of confidentiality requirements on the person to whom the disclosure was made. In this instance it must be reasonable to enable the person concerned to perform their proper functions, or is needed by a professional adviser to give advice on a transaction, or is reasonable to facilitate a transaction, or is reasonable and for the purpose of obtaining a commitment or expression of support or finally that it is in fulfilment of a legal obligation[1].

1 MAR 1.4.5 E.

7.14   There is a different definition of 'inside information' in relation to anyone charged with executing orders concerning qualifying or related investments. Here it includes information received from a client in relation to a pending order. The information must be of a precise nature, not be generally available and relate directly or indirectly to an issuer of qualifying investments. If it were generally available it must be likely to have a significant effect on the price of the qualifying investments, or related ones.

7.15   The preceding two categories of market abuse plus 'encouraging others' which is discussed below are also criminal offences under the

Criminal Justice Act 1993 as discussed. Therefore in terms of the standard of the burden of proof in a civil action they should be categorised as civil cases enforcing something that is also a criminal offence.

Misuse of Information

7.16   In any other case where the behaviour concerned is '…based on information which is not generally available to those using the market but which, if available to a regular user of the market, would be, or would be likely to be, regarded by him as relevant when deciding the terms on which transactions in qualifying investments should be effected, and…is likely to be regarded by a regular used of the market as a failure on the part of the person concerned to observe the standard of behaviour reasonably expected of a person in his position in relation to the market. [1]

1 FSMA, s 118(4)(a) and (b) *ibid* and MAR 1.5.

7.17   When determining whether there is misuse of information amounting to market abuse the FCA are influenced by the extent to which the information is reliable, the closeness to its source of the person passing the information on and its reliability. In addition, whether the information differs from that which is generally available or, where it relates to possible future developments which will require a disclosure in the future and the certainty that the development will happen, and there is no other material information generally available. In determining whether a regular user of the market would reasonably expect information to be disclosed or announced the FCA are influenced by whether the information was disclosed in line with legal or regulatory requirements or if the information is routinely the subject of public announcements. Finally, is the behaviour based on information leading to possible future developments where it is reasonable to believe that the information in question will become one of these categories[1]?

1 MAR 1.5.6 E-1.5.7 E.

7.18   The FCA considers the following behaviour in determining whether this type of market abuse has occurred. These are: the experience and knowledge of the people concerned, the structure of the market including reporting notification and transparency requirements, the legal and regulatory requirements that are applicable, the identity and position of the person concerned and the extent and nature of the visibility of the activity. The FCA take into account whether the transaction was carried out pursuant to a pre-existing legal or regulatory obligation, whether it was executed in a way that took into account the need for the market to operate fairly and efficiently and the characteristics of the market in question. This will take into account any relevant law, rules and code of conduct. In addition the position of the person concerned and the standards that can be expected from someone with that level of skill and knowledge will be considered. It would protect the person under suspicion if it transpired that the transaction complied with the rules of the market concerned. Finally, the protection provided where the necessary information was the other side of a Chinese wall from the person under suspicion will apply here as well[1].

1 MAR 1.9.1 E, 1.9.4 E and 1.9.5 E.

7.19 Criminal liability here will depend upon the precise method with which the information concerned is misused. If communications are involved then FSA 2012, s 89 will be applicable along with either s 2 or s 3 of the Fraud Act; if not then FSA 2012, s 90 may be relevant along with Fraud Act, s 4 if the offender's position is being misused or s 6 and s 7 if the activity has involved utilising software.

Manipulating transactions

7.20 Where transactions are carried out other than for legitimate reasons and in line with '*...accepted market practices...*' on the market concerned which '*...give, or are likely to give, a false or misleading impression as to the supply of, or demand for, or as to the price of, one or more qualifying investments, or...secure the price of one or more such investments at an abnormal or artificial level*[1]' market abuse occurs. Key factors in determining whether market abuse by way of giving a false or misleading impression has taken place are the extent to which:

– the orders to trade are given or transactions undertaken represent a significant volume of transactions in the relevant investment, especially when the trading leads to a significant change in price;

– orders to trade given or transactions undertaken by someone with a significant buying or selling position leads to a significant change in the price of the underlying investment, related derivative or underlying investment;

– the transactions led to a change in beneficial ownership;

– orders to trade given or transactions undertaken include position reversals over a short period, a significant proportion of the daily volume of transactions in the relevant investment and might be associated with significant changes in the price;

– orders to trade given or transactions undertaken are concentrated within a short time span leading to a price change which is subsequently reversed;

– orders to trade given change the representation of the best bid or the representation of the order book available to market participants are removed before they are executed; and

– orders to trade are given or transactions are undertaken at or around a specific time when reference prices, settlement prices and valuations are calculated and lead to price changes which have an effect on this type of price and valuation[2].

1 FSMA, s 118(5)(a) and (b) plus MAR 1.6.
2 MAR 1.6.9 E.

7.21 In determining whether behaviour amounts to securing an abnormal or artificial price level the FCA consider three key factors. The extent to which the person has an interest whether direct or indirect, in the price or value of the investment, the extent to which price, rate or option volatility movements and the volatility of these factors for the investment in question, are outside their normal range and whether a person has successively and consistently increased or decreased the bid offer he has made[1].

1 MAR 1.6.10 E.

7.22   Here any criminal liability is likely to be limited to offences covered by the Fraud Act 2006 where the abuse has fraudulent intent. Where not, no communication has taken place as a vehicle for committing the abuse the other potential criminal liability rests on FSA 2012, s 90 in addition to the Fraud Act as the sub-section covers any 'conduct'.

Manipulating devices

7.23   This is defined as carrying out transactions which employ fictitious devices, deception or contrivance[1]. Market abuse by manipulating devices can occur in a number of ways, perhaps the most obvious of which would be to take a position in an investment and then by access to the media voice anonymous opinions about the investment or its issuer and profit from the subsequent price movement. Another would be to enter into a transaction, or series of them to conceal the ownership of an investment by hiding the real owner to get round disclosure requirements. Nominee holdings do not fall foul of this unless done for illicit purposes. One method is known as 'pump and dump' ie, taking a long position and then putting out misleading information to increase its price, following which the investment is sold at an artificially high price. Another is known as 'trash and cash'. This consists of taking a short position in an investment and then putting out negative information to force down the price to make a profit[2].

1 FSMA 2000, s 118(6) and MAR 1.7.1.
2 MAR 1.7.2 E.

7.24   Factors the FCA will take into account in determining whether manipulating devices have been used will include whether, if orders to trade are given or transactions undertaken following the dissemination of false or misleading information by those people or others linked to them and where orders to trade are given or transactions undertaken by people before or after those same people disseminate research which is biased in favour of their investments[1].

1 MAR 1.7.3 E.

7.25   Clearly FSA 2012, s 90 is relevant here in that a criminal prosecution could be brought as the 'devices' referred to here will potentially fit within the requirement that the accused has engaging conduct which is aimed at inducing someone to enter into a contract and which misleads them as to its value.[1] Where fraudulent intent can also be shown then the Fraud Act 2006 comes into play most probably through possessing or making articles to be used in connection with fraud[2]. Either way this sub-category of market abuse should be regarded as both a civil and criminal offence.

1 For a discussion on this general area see Bazley *supra* at pp 246–247.
2 Fraud Act 2006, ss 6–7.

Disseminating misleading information

7.26   This consists of engaging in behaviour which '…gives, or is likely to give, a false or misleading impression as to a qualifying investment, by a person who knew or could reasonably be expected to have known that the information was false or misleading[1].' It consists of behaviour such as knowingly or recklessly spreading false or misleading information about an investment through the media. Alternately it might consist of undertaking a course of business to give a false or misleading impression of an investment. Another example would be where a person puts false or misleading information on the internet or where someone responsible for submitting information to a regulatory information service provides information that is false or misleading. The FCA will consider whether a normal and reasonable person should have known that the information was false or misleading or whether the person concerned actually did know. They will also form an opinion on whether the individuals responsible for disseminating information could only have known that the information was false or misleading if they had access to information the other side of a Chinese wall. If this is the case it is only going to amount to abuse by dissemination if there is evidence the wall may have been breached. This is an area where good compliance can provide protection[2].

1 FSMA, s 118(7) *ibid* and MAR 1.8.1 E.
2 MAR1.8.3 E–1.8.6 E.

7.27   The comments in the previous section regarding criminal liability in the context of manipulative devices are relevant here as well, although there are differences. Disseminating misleading information will normally require communication and therefore FSA 2012, ss 89 and 90 are likely to be at issue. In the context of fraud, engaging in fraud by false representation[1] and by failing to disclose information[2] are the most likely candidates for a criminal prosecution.

1 Fraud Act 2006, s 2.
2 *Ibid*, s 3.

Market distortion

7.28   Where not already covered above such behaviour as is likely '…to give a regular user of the market a false or misleading impression as to the supply of, demand for, or value of, qualifying investments or…would be…regarded be a regular user of the market as behaviour that would distort, or would be likely to distort, the market…and the behaviour is likely to be regarded by a regular user of the market as a failure on the part of the person concerned to observe the standard of behaviour reasonably expected of a person in his position in relation to the market[1].'

1 FSMA, s 118(8)(a) and (b) as modified by the Recognised Auction Platform Rules (SI 2011/2699) and MAR 1.9.1 E.

7.29   The FCA will regard behaviour as amounting to market abuse by way of manipulating transactions where deals are done at the close of a market to mislead people as to the real value, wash trading (where the trade does not reflect a change in beneficial interest or market risk, or where there is but the deal is between parties acting in collusion), painting the tape (entering into transactions that are shown on public display to give the impression of activity) and entering orders into an electronic trading system at prices that are higher than the previous bid or lower than the previous offer and then withdrawing them before they are executed to give a misleading impression of demand or supply. Examples of behaviour that the FCA that will amount to market abuse through manipulating transactions by way of price positioning are:

– transactions by people acting in collusion to secure a dominant position over the demand or supply of a qualifying investment to fix the price or create unfair trading conditions;

– transactions where both buy and sell orders are entered into at the same time with the same price, quantity and party (or different but colluding parties) for non-legitimate reasons. Sometimes this can be acceptable if the trades are in line with those of the trading platform concerned such as cross trades;

– entering small orders into an electronic trading system at higher prices than previous bids or lower ones than previous offers to move the price;

– abusive squeezes, ie, where someone has a significant influence over the supply or demand or delivery mechanisms of a qualifying investment or the underlying product of a derivative contact and also has a position in an investment under which such investments are deliverable and engages in behaviour which distorts the price;

– parties subject to a primary offering colluding in buying further amounts when trading commences to raise the price;

– transactions or orders used to stop the price falling below a certain level; and

– trading on a market or platform to improperly influence the price of the same or a related investment on another prescribed market; and

– conduct by someone acting in collusion that secures a dominant position over the demand for a qualifying investment and creates a price other than for legitimate reasons.[1]

1 MAR 1.6.4 E.

7.30   In this context the issues the FCA will take into account in determining whether the behaviour concerned is legitimate are as follows. Is the person motivated by a desire to induce others to trade or to move the price of a qualifying investment? Do they have another illegitimate reason to trade and was the transaction executed in a particular way with the purpose of creating a false or misleading impression? Factors that are indications that behaviour is legitimate are: is the transaction entered into pursuant to a prior legal or regulatory obligation, is it executed in a way which takes into account the need for the market to operate fairly and efficiently, the extent to which the transaction opens a new position increasing exposure to market risk and if the transaction complied with the rules of the relevant market. It is unlikely that market users when trading in a manner and on a scale most beneficial to them will be distorting the market and therefore be committing market abuse. Trading on prices outside the normal range will not always be an indication of market abuse as this can happen as a normal part of trading[1].

1 MAR 1.6.5 E, 1.6.6 E, 1.6.7 G and 1.6.8 G taken further by MAR 1.6.9 E.

7.31   As far as ascertaining whether abusive squeezes have taken place the FCA will consider the extent to which the person has been willing to limit their control or influence in order to help maintain an orderly market and the price at which they are willing to do so. If the person was willing to lend the investment there is less likelihood of it being an abusive squeeze. The extent to which the person's activity has caused settlement default on a bilateral or multilateral basis will also be a factor. The more widespread the risk of multilateral default the greater the risk that it is an abusive squeeze. The extent to which prices under the delivery mechanisms of the market diverge from the prices for delivery will be factor. There is direct correlation between the divergence and the risk. Finally, the extent to which the spot or immediate market is unusually expensive compared with the forward market will correlate with the risk of an abusive squeeze. It should be borne in mind that squeezes will occur in the markets on a non-abusive basis. Having a significant degree of control of a market through ownership does not necessarily mean an abusive squeeze has occurred[1].

1 MAR 1.6.11 E–1.6.12 E.

7.32   Market abuse through manipulating transactions may occur if a trader buys and sells at the same time, ie, trades with himself to give the impression of trading taking place outside the normal price range to benefit financially from an option. It can also occur where a trader buys a large volume of commodity futures just before close of trading to create a false price. Alternately it could occur where a trader holds a short position in an investment that will show a profit if it falls out of an index in which it is currently quoted and he then places a large order to sell just before the close of trading. The manipulation here will be the attempt to create a false market causing the investment to fall out of the index. A fund manager would be engaging in manipulation if at the end of a quarter he places a large buy order on relatively illiquid shares which are a component of his portfolio to be executed just before market close to create a false price. Another example would be where a trader with a long position in bond futures borrows a large amount of the cheapest ones and then either will not re-lend them or only does so to those he believes will not re-lend to the market. The aim here will be to force those with short positions to have to deliver to satisfy their obligations, resulting in the trader making a profit.[1]

1 MAR 1.6.15 E 1.6.16 E.

7.33   The way in which criminal liability will potentially emerge in this context depends on precisely how the 'misleading impression' is given to a regular user of the market. If it involves a representation then FSA 2012, s 89 are most likely to be at issue, and/or Fraud Act 2006, ss 2 and 3. However, if a position of responsibility is being abused in the process Fraud Act 2006, s 4 becomes an issue in tandem with FSA 2012, ss 89 and 90 according to the precise circumstances. If computer software is used to carry out the activity s 6 or s 7 of the Fraud Act are relevant and again such parts of ss 89 and 90 as are appropriate given the way in which the software is used.

Encouraging others

7.34   There is also a secondary offence[1] of taking or refraining from taking any action which requires or encourages another person to engage in market abuse. Criminal liability here would be dependent on what activity was being encouraged. FSA 2012, s 90 specifically covers 'any course of conduct' which creates a false impression as to the price of investments and so could potentially catch encouragement. The common law offence of conspiracy to defraud[2] might prove more fertile than the relevant sections of the Fraud Act 2006 here in that encouragement would seem to involve an *'agreement'* to commit an offence by the very fact of encouraging it.

1 FSMA, s 123(1)(b) ibid.
2 Now found in s 5(2) Criminal Law Act 1977.

Safe harbours

7.35   There are safe harbours which apply where the behaviour conforms with a rule which makes it clear that such behaviour is not market abuse, the behaviour conforms with the EU Regulation[1] implementing the Directive[2] regarding exemptions for buy-back programmes[3] and stabilisation rules or it is carried out by someone acting on behalf of a public authority in pursuit of monetary authorities or policies with regard to exchange rates or managing public debt or foreign exchange[4]. In addition, FSMA s 123(2) states that a penalty should not be imposed if having considered the response to a warning notice there are reasonable grounds for the FCA to be satisfied that the person concerned had reasonable grounds to believe he had not committed market abuse and had taken all reasonable precautions. In such cases the FCA does have the option of announcing that such behaviour is market abuse without imposing a penalty[5]. This would then make it possible to punish anyone who engaged in that behaviour in the future. It would also be material in determining whether a criminal offence had been committed.

1 EC No 2273/2003.
2 2003/6/EC.
3 MAR 1 Annex 1.
4 FSMA, s 118A(5).
5 FSMA, s 123(3).

Inside information

7.36   This leads us to the question of what exactly 'inside information' is. It is[1] information of a precise nature relating to qualifying investments (see below) which are not commodity derivatives, which is not generally available, relates directly or indirectly to the issuer of a qualifying investment and would if generally available be likely to have a significant effect on the price of the investment concerned or of a related one. Where commodity derivatives are concerned inside information is that which is of a precise nature which is not generally available and relates directly or indirectly to such derivatives, and users of the relevant markets would expect to be provided with it in line with accepted market practice. This may be because such information is routinely made available to users on that market or because it is required by statute, the rules of the market concerned or custom either on the derivatives market or that of the underlying commodity[2]. General availability in either instance extends to information that is obtainable by research or analysis[3].

1 FSMA 2000, s 118C.
2 FSMA 2000, s 118C(7).
3 FSMA 2000, s 118C(8).

7.37 There is a different definition of 'inside information' in relation to anyone charged with executing orders concerning qualifying or related investments. Here it includes information received from a client in relation to a pending order. The information must be of a precise nature, not be generally available and relate directly or indirectly to an issuer of qualifying investments. If it were generally available it must be likely to have a significant effect on the price of the qualifying investments, or related ones.

7.38 The concept of 'precision' crops up in these definitions. This means[1] information which indicates circumstances or an event that exists or is reasonably likely to and is specific enough to enable conclusions to be drawn as to the effect on the price of qualifying investments or related ones. This is likely to be the case only if it is information which a reasonable investor would be likely to use as part of the basis of his investment decisions.

1 FSMA 2000, s 118C(5).

Protected disclosures

7.39 Information can be disclosed without being in breach of any restrictions provided it causes the person making the disclosure to know or suspect that someone else is engaging in market abuse. That information must have come to them in the course of their trade profession, business or employment and it must have been made to the FCA by the appropriate internal officer as soon as reasonably practicable after it was obtained[1].

1 FSMA 2000, s 131A.

7.40 Certain key issues arise from all this: what is an insider, what should be done by firms to highlight who these people are, to which investments does the regime apply and which markets are affected?

Insiders

7.41 Clearly a key focus point is the nature of an 'insider'. This is defined[1] as anyone who has inside information;

- as a result of their membership of a company whether as an administrator or, manager or a supervisory body;
- as a result of them holding capital issued by a company;

- as a result of them having access to the information concerned through carrying out their employment or professional duties;

- as a result of criminal activities; or

- which they obtained by other methods which they know, or could reasonably be expected to know would be inside information.

1 FSMA 2000, s 118B.

Insider lists

7.42 Lists must be kept which, at the least, must state:

- the identity of anyone having access to inside information;

- the reason why any person named is on the list; and

- the date on which the list was created and updated.

7.43 On any occasion when the list is updated, and when necessary this must be done promptly, there must be a statement as to:

- why there is a change when someone is already on the list;

- why anyone has been added; and

- when anyone previously on the list no longer has access to inside information.

7.44 This list must be kept for a minimum of five years. The people responsible for creating these lists must also make sure that anyone who has access to inside information acknowledges the legal and regulatory requirements and that they are aware of the potential consequences should they be breached.

Qualifying investments

7.45 These are defined[1] as:

- transferable securities;

- units in collective investment schemes;

- money market instruments;

- financial futures contracts including equivalent cash settled instruments;

- forward rate agreements;

- interest rate, currency and equity swaps;

- options;

- commodity derivatives;

- any other instrument admitted to trading on a regulated market in a member state or for which a request for admission has been made.

1 See Directive 2003/6/EC, art 1(3).

Prescribed markets

7.46   These are defined by statutory instrument[1] as all markets that are established under the rules of a UK recognised investment exchange and all other regulated markets. For the purposes of all types of market abuse other than insider dealing, relying on information not generally available[2] and behaviour likely to give a misleading impression and to distort a market[3] it also includes OFEX.

1 Prescribed Markets and Qualifying Investments Order 2001, SI 2001/96, as amended by the Financial Services and Markets Act 2000 (Market Abuse) Regulations 2005, SI 2005/381, art 4.
2 FSMA 2000, s 118(4).
3 FSMA 2000, s 118(8).

Transparency standards

7.47   Those engaged in research and the recommendation of investments to the public or distribution channels must disclose their relevant interests. This is mainly aimed at financial analysts and journalists who profit from this activity.

Reporting requirements

7.48   There are reporting requirements for managers and those closely associated with them. The latter category covers spouses, dependant children and other relatives in the household. The reports must be made within five working days to the FCA covering:

- the name of the person concerned;

- the reason why there is a need to notify;

- the name of the relevant issuer;

- a description of the financial instrument;

- the nature of the transaction;

- the date and place of the transaction; and

- the price and volume of the transaction

7.49   If a transaction is suspicious a report must be made to the FCA and if money laundering is possibly a factor also the National Crime Agency and in either event stating:

- a description of the transaction including the type of order concerned;

- the reasons for believing that the transaction might amount to market abuse;

- the means for identifying the person concerned and anyone else involved;

- the capacity in which the person subject to the notification operates; and

- any other relevant information.

Notices

7.50   The FCA is required by s 124 to issue statements when penalties are imposed providing the relevant details and also whether the behaviour concerned had caused an adverse effect on the market. They should also indicate circumstances in which the person concerned should be taken to have had a reasonable belief that their behaviour did not amount to market abuse or that they had taken all reasonable precautions and exercised due diligence to avoid market abuse.

7.51   There are a range of other notices required under FSMA 2000, ss 92, 126,127, 205, 207–209, 387–390 and 393. FSMA 2000, s 92 requires that a notice be given if the FCA is to take steps against someone under s 91 for breach of the listing rules, s 126 requires that a warning notice must be given to someone against whom it proposes to take action setting out any proposed penalty and warning notice. If it is then decided to take action a decision notice must be sent in similar terms. Section 205 enables the FCA to publish a statement where they believe that an authorised person has contravened a requirement under the FSMA 2000, s 207 extends this to situations where the FCA proposes to issue a s 205 notice or to take steps under s 206 (imposition of a financial penalty on an authorised person). It must give the person concerned a warning notice setting out the terms of any statement and the penalty. Once the decision has been made so to act a decision notice must be issued under s 208 again setting out the terms of any statement to be published and any fine. If a s 205 statement is issued a copy should also be sent to anyone else to whom notice was given. Section 387 determines the content of warning notices, s 388 of decision notices, s 389 requires that a notice of discontinuance be issued if they decide not to proceed and s 390 requires a final notice where the action set out in a decision notice has been taken. Finally, s 393 requires that third parties are identified where the FCA think they will be affected prejudicially and that person should then receive a copy of the relevant notice unless they have already received a separate warning notice in relation to the same matter.

7.52   This was the subject of the dispute in *Watts v FSA*[1] a case concerning the Chairman of the Dutch/Shell group. This matter concerned s 393(4) of the FSMA 2000, which provides a right to anyone who is a third party under a 'notice procedure', ie, someone who is prejudicially identified, to be given a copy of relevant notices and a reasonable period in which to make representations to the FSA as it then was. If action is proposed on the basis of market abuse and breach of the Listing Rules (as it was here) any person concerned should be given a warning notice under FSMA 2000, ss126(1) and 92(1). In the absence of a reference to the Tribunal, in this case because matters were proceeding consensually, a final notice has to be issued under s 390(1). Sir Philip Watts had not been explicitly identified in the FSCA notice, but as a result of it he had been subject to considerable adverse media coverage. He therefore believed that he had been implicitly identified and that notifying a company or accusing it of misconduct is a legal fiction[2] as it can only act through individuals. His challenge under s 393(11) was also partly based on his belief that the FSA investigation was incomplete and flawed. The FSA disagreed that Sir Philip Watts was a third party for these purposes and also felt that if it were required to give notice in all cases such as his it would face a 'potentially massive and administratively impractical task'[3]. It was therefore necessary for the Tribunal to consider the meaning and purpose of such notices. Clearly the key element was to ensure fairness. The Tribunal were influenced by the House of Lords debate in which the relevant amendment was introduced:

> 'The new clause on third party rights...rationalises the existing provisions dealing with the rights of third parties identified in warning or decision notices in a way that is prejudicial to them. These provisions were designed to deal with cases where there is some wrong-doing alleged on the part of the third party who is not himself the subject of action by the FSA. For instance, in disciplinary cases under Part XIV, it was felt that action might be taken against a firm for reasons which implied that there has been some failing by one of its directors or employees; or in market abuse cases, where other parties might well be involved in the transactions giving rise to the allegation that market abuse has been engaged in.
>
> The provisions give third parties, who are identified in prejudicial terms in the reasons for a warning or decision notice, the right to receive a copy of the notice, and to make representations or refer the matter to the tribunal in the same way as the person who is the subject of the FSA's proposed action. We took the view that although these rights create an administrative burden for the FSA, they are necessary to give the third party the right to defend himself against any implied blame arising from the reasons given for the action'. *per Lord Bach.*

1 FSA Tribunal, 25 July 2005.
2 see *Lennards Carrying Company Ltd v Asiatic Petroleum Co Ltd* [1915] AC 705 at 713 per Viscount Haldane LC.
3 FSA Tribunal, 25 July 2005 at 42.

7.53   It was held that although it was not always the case that courts would refer to Hansard[1] it was appropriate here because of the novel nature of the issue being contested. It was also pointed out that there were parallels with DTI procedures[2] where it is required that the investigating body acts fairly and provides the opportunity to anyone who has allegations made against them to have a fair opportunity to answer.

1 See *Pepper v Hart* [1993] AC 593; *R v Sec of State for the Environment, ex p Spath Holme Ltd* [2001] 2 AC 349, and *Robinson v Sec of State for Northern Ireland* [2002] NI 390.
2 See *Re Pergamon Press Ltd* [1971] 1 Ch 388.

7.54   Overall the Tribunal rejected Sir Philip Watts claims and held that s 393(4) afforded third party rights to anyone identified in 'the decision' not 'the matter'. The former did not extend to Sir Philip. This is in line with other uses of 'matter' in the FSMA 2000[1]. There was also a precedent on this point of interpretation in *Parker v FSA*[2]. In addition s 393(4) refers to the FSA issuing a decision notice as the same time that it issues '...the decision notice which identifies him'. In addition, s 393(12) refers to the material relating '....to the matter which identifies the third party'. It was also stated that an allegation against a company would not necessarily imply criticism of particular individuals. The whole point of the notices in this context was to give a right of reply to someone who was identified in the FSA notice. It would have been different had Sir Philip been identified by name or job description.

1 FSMA 2000, see ss 92(7), 127(4), 133(4), 205, 208(4), 388(1)(e) and 390(1).
2 See FSA Tribunal, 13 October 2004.

FCA Regulations

7.55   The FCA Principles (see Chapter 1 at 1.1–1.7) will be relevant here. In addition the FCA has published the Code of Market Conduct pursuant to s 119 to provide guidelines as to what behaviour the FCA will regard as market abuse. Section 122 makes clear that if behaviour takes place that does not amount to market abuse under the Code, then it is not market abuse for the purposes of the FSMA. Thus, if the Code were found to be in error it would need to be amended before anyone could have civil proceedings taken against them. However, in serious cases the option of a criminal prosecution for insider dealing, issuing misleading statements or certain other criminal offences would remain.

7.56   As far as the FCA are concerned behaviour will be carried out 'in relation to' investments prior to an admission for trading or the commencement of trading if the act is in relation to them and it continues to have an effect once the application has been made or it has been admitted to trading[1]. Refraining from action might amount to market abuse if the behaviour satisfies s 118(1)(a) and the person concerned has not carried out a legal or regulatory requirement or if they gave rise to the impression that he would correct previous statements where necessary and he has not done so[2]. When determining whether or not someone could reasonably be expected to know that information in their possession was inside information the FCA are guided by whether or not a normal and reasonable person with inside information would or should have known that the person they received it from was an insider and if a normal and reasonable person in the position of the person holding inside information would or should have known that it was inside information[3].

1 MAR 1.2.5 E.
2 MAR 1.2.6 E.
3 MAR 1.2.8 E.

7.57   The FCA will consider the following factors in determining whether information is generally available and therefore not inside information where information is available within the UK:

- whether the information has been disclosed on a prescribed market through a regulatory information service or in any other way in line with the rules of the market concerned;

- whether the information can be obtained from records available to the public;

- whether the information is otherwise generally available or can be derived from such information even if it is only available on the payment of a fee;

- whether the information can be obtained by observation without infringing confidentiality;

- the extent to which such information can be obtained by analysis of information which is generally available even if that analysis requires abnormal skill or expertise[1].

1 MAR 1.2.12 E.

7.58 As mentioned above particular problems arise in relation to commodity derivatives. In particular, what amounts to inside information in this context is in part determined by what information market participants expect to be provided with.

7.59 The FCA also has its own view on what will amount to insider dealing for market abuse purposes. It falls into four main groupings:

- dealing on the basis of inside information that is not trading information;

- front running (ie, trading on a person's own behalf ahead of a client order whilst in possession of inside information to take advantage of the expected price change in the investment concerned);

- when a takeover is taking place, an offeror entering into a transaction in a qualifying investment on the basis of inside information concerning that takeover which involves exposure to a price movement in the target company's shares. This would cover not only dealing in those shares but also derivatives;

- when a takeover is taking place, acting on one's own behalf on the basis of inside information when acting for the offeror[1].

1 MAR 1.3.2 E.

7.60 In determining whether someone's behaviour amounts to acting 'on the basis of' inside information the FCA will have regard to whether the decision to deal was made before the person possessed the relevant inside information, if they dealt to satisfy a regulatory requirement or legal obligation that came into existence before they obtained the inside information and whether the individuals in possession of the inside information had any involvement with the decision to deal or behaved in a way to influence it or had any contact with those who were dealing[1]. In any event if the FCA believes that the person did or did not act in line with a regulatory requirement, this will be a factor in shaping their view as to whether or not the behaviour amounted to market abuse[2].

1 MAR 1.3.3 E.
2 MAR 1.3.11 E.

7.61 One piece of good news for firms with effective compliance systems is that the existence of effective Chinese walls separating those who deal and who influence them from those in possession of the inside information will be regarded by the FCA as an indication that insider dealing cannot have been taking place[1].

1 MAR 1.3.5 E.

7.62 Market makers also have the capacity to engage in legitimate business when dealing and underwriting even if they are in possession of inside information. However, a factor here will be whether the inside information is limited to trading information. If not this will suggest the trading was not legitimate. This does not extend to underwriting[1].

1 MAR 1.3.7 C to 1.3.9 E.

7.63 The FCA's view on whether a person's behaviour represents legitimate business is shaped by four key issues:

- the extent to which the relevant trading is carried out to hedge a risk arising out of their business and the extent to which that risk is neutralised;

- where a transaction is carried out on the basis of inside information concerning a client transaction that has been executed, that information has not yet been required to be published by the exchange concerned or relevant regulations;

- if the trading is connected with a client transaction and has no impact on the price, or that there has been adequate disclosure to the client who has not objected; or

- whether the person's behaviour was reasonable by the proper standards of the market concerned bearing in mind any relevant legal or regulatory requirements and whether the transaction was carried out in a way that reflected the need for the market concerned to operate fairly and efficiently[1].

1 MAR 1.3.10 E.

7.64 What then does not amount to market abuse? Certainly the dutiful carrying out of client orders or the arranging of the same on behalf of someone else will not be market abuse. It will very probably also be safe if the person acting possesses inside information that is not limited to trading information. Factors to consider are: whether the person has complied with the FCA Conduct of Business Sourcebook and Code of Market Conduct (or overseas the equivalent), whether the person agreed with a client to behave in a particular way, whether the person's behaviour appears to have been the effective carrying out of a client order, the extent to which the behaviour was reasonable by the standards of the market or whether the trading was connected with a client and the trading had no impact on the price. Alternately, there was adequate disclosure to the client that the deal would occur and they did not object[1]. Where takeover and merger activity is occurring there is an obvious risk of market abuse in general and insider dealing in particular. However, trading whilst in possession of inside information as part of a public takeover or merger does not of itself amount to market abuse. Likewise, arranging an issue of securities to be offered as consideration in a takeover or merger or making a cash offer[2]. In addition the FCA are influenced by whether transactions are in the target company's shares and are for the sole purpose of carrying out a takeover or merger. If so, it will not be market abuse.

1 MAR 1.3.15 E.
2 MAR 1.3.17 C.

7.65 In the case of whether or not behaviour is improper disclosure amounting to market abuse the FCA view the following as determining factors: whether the behaviour is permitted by the rules of market concerned or the Takeover Code or whether the disclosure is accompanied by the imposition of confidentiality requirements on the person to whom the disclosure was made. In this instance it must be reasonable to enable the person concerned to perform their proper functions, or is needed by a professional adviser to give advice on a transaction, or is reasonable to facilitate a transaction, or is reasonable and for the purpose of obtaining a commitment or expression of support or finally that it is in fulfilment of a legal obligation[1].

1 MAR 1.4.5 E.

7.66   When determining whether there is misuse of information amounting to market abuse the FCA are influenced by the extent to which the information is reliable, the closeness to its source of the person passing the information on and its reliability. In addition, whether the information differs from that which is generally available or, where it relates to possible future developments that will require a disclosure in the future and the certainty that the development will happen. Finally, if there is no other material information generally available. In determining whether a regular user of the market would reasonably expect information to be disclosed or announced the FCA are influenced by whether the information was disclosed in line with legal or regulatory requirements or if the information is routinely the subject of public announcements. Finally, is the behaviour based on information leading to possible future developments where it is reasonable to believe that the information in question will become one of these categories[1]?

1 MAR 1.5.6 E–1.5.7 E.

7.67   The FCA will regard behaviour as amounting to market abuse by way of market distortion where deals are done at the close of a market to mislead people as to the real value, wash trading (where the trade does not reflect a change in beneficial interest or market risk, or where there is but the deal is between parties acting in collusion), painting the tape (entering into transactions that are shown on public display to give the impression of activity) and entering orders into an electronic trading system at prices that are higher than the previous bid or lower than the previous offer and then withdrawing them before they are executed to give a misleading impression of demand or supply. Examples of behaviour that the FCA will regard as amounting to market abuse through manipulating transactions by way of price positioning are:

- transactions by people acting in collusion to secure a dominant position over the demand or supply of a qualifying investment to fix the price or create unfair trading conditions;

- transactions where both buy and sell orders are entered into at the same time with the same price, quantity and party (or different but colluding parties) for non-legitimate reasons. Sometimes this can be acceptable if the trades are in line with those of the trading platform concerned such as cross trades;

- entering small orders into an electronic trading system at higher prices than previous bids or lower ones than previous offers to move the price;

- abusive squeezes (where someone has a significant influence over the supply or demand or delivery mechanisms of a qualifying investment or the underlying product of a derivative contact and also has a position in an investments under which such investments are deliverable and engages in behaviour which distorts the price);

- parties subject to a primary offering colluding in buying further amounts when trading commences to raise the price;

- transactions or orders used to stop the price falling below a certain level; and

- trading on a market or platform to improperly influence the price of the same or a related investment on another prescribed market[1].

1 MAR 1.6.4 E.

7.68   In this context the issues the FCA will take into account in determining whether the behaviour concerned is legitimate are as follows. Is the person motivated by a desire to induce others to trade or to move the price of a qualifying investment? Do they have another illegitimate reason to trade and was the transaction executed in a particular way with the purpose of creating a false or misleading impression? Factors that are indications that behaviour is legitimate are: is the transaction entered into pursuant to a prior legal or regulatory obligation, is it executed in a way which takes into account the need for the market to operate fairly and efficiently, the extent to which the transaction opens a new position increasing exposure to market risk and if the transaction complied with the rules of the relevant market. It is unlikely that market users when trading in a manner and on a scale most beneficial to them will be distorting the market and therefore be committing market abuse. Trading on prices outside the normal range will not always be an indication of market abuse. This can happen as a normal part of trading[1].

1 MAR 1.6.5 E, 1.6.6 E, 1.6.7 G and 1.6.8 G.

7.69   Key factors in determining whether market abuse by way of giving a false or misleading impression has taken place are:

- the extent to which the orders to trade are given or transactions undertaken represent a significant volume of transactions in the relevant investment, especially when the trading leads to a significant change in price;

- the extent to which orders to trade given or transactions undertaken by someone with a significant buying or selling position leads to a significant change in the price of the underlying investment, related derivative or underlying investment;

- whether the transactions lead to a change in beneficial ownership;

- the extent to which orders to trade given or transactions undertaken include position reversals over a short period, a significant proportion of the daily volume of transactions in the relevant investment and might be associated with significant changes in the price;

- the extent to which orders to trade given or transactions undertaken are concentrated within a short time span leading to a price change which is subsequently reversed;

- the extent to which orders to trade given change the representation of the best bid or the representation of the order book available to market participants and are removed before they are executed; and

- the extent to which orders to trade are given or transactions are undertaken at or around a specific time when reference prices, settlement prices and valuations are calculated and lead to price changes which have an effect on this type of price and valuation[1].

1 MAR 1.6.9 E.

7.70   In determining whether behaviour amounts to securing an abnormal or artificial price level the FCA consider three key factors. The extent to which the person has an interest whether direct or indirect, in the price or value of the investment, the extent to which price, rate or option volatility movements and the volatility of these factors for the investment in question, are outside their normal range and whether a person has successively and consistently increased or decreased the bid offer he has made[1].

1 MAR 1.6.10 E.

7.71   As far as ascertaining whether abusive squeezes have taken place the FCA will consider the extent to which the person has been willing to limit their control or influence in order to help maintain an orderly market and the price at which they are willing to do so. If the person was willing to lend the investment there is less likelihood of it being an abusive squeeze. The extent to which the person's activity has caused settlement default on a bilateral or multilateral basis will also be a factor. The more widespread the risk of multilateral default the greater the risk that it is an abusive squeeze. The extent to which prices under the delivery mechanisms of the market diverge from the prices for delivery will be factor. There is a direct correlation between the divergence and the risk. Finally, the extent to which the spot or immediate market is unusually expensive compared with the forward market will correlate with the risk of an abusive squeeze. It should be borne in mind that squeezes will occur in the markets on a non-abusive basis. Having a significant degree of control of a market through ownership does not necessarily mean an abusive squeeze has occurred[1].

1 MAR 1.6.11 E–1.6.12 E and 1.6.16E.

7.72   Market abuse through manipulating transactions may occur if a trader buys and sells at the same time, ie, trades with himself to give the impression of trading taking place outside the normal price range to benefit financially from an option. It can also occur where a trader buys a large volume of commodity futures just before close of trading to create a false price. Alternately it could occur where a trader holds a short position in an investment that will show a profit if it falls out of an index in which it is currently quoted and he then places a large order to sell just before the close of trading. The manipulation here will be the attempt to create a false market causing the investment to fall out of the index. A fund manager would be engaging in manipulation if at the end of a quarter he places a large buy order or relatively illiquid shares which are a component of his portfolio to be executed just before market close to create a false price. Another example would be where a trader with a long position in bond futures borrows a large amount of the cheapest and then either will not re-lend them or only does so to those he believes will not re-lend to the market. The aim here will be to force those with short positions to have to deliver to satisfy their obligations at a higher level, resulting in the trader making a profit[1].

1 MAR 1.6.15 E.

7.73 Market abuse by manipulating devices can occur in a number of ways. Perhaps the most obvious would be to take a position in an investment and then by access to the media voice opinions about the investment or its issuer and profit from the subsequent price movement. Another would be to enter into a transaction, or series of them to conceal the ownership of an investment by hiding the real owner to get round disclosure requirements. (Nominee holdings do not fall foul of this unless done for illicit purposes). One method is known as 'pump and dump' ie, taking a long position and then putting out misleading information to increase its price, following which the investment is sold at an artificially high price. Another is known as 'trash and cash'. This consists of taking a short position in an investment and then putting out negative information to force down the price to make a profit[1].

1 MAR 1.7.2 E.

7.74 Factors the FCA will take into account in determining whether manipulating devices have been used will include whether, if orders to trade are given or transactions undertaken following the dissemination of false or misleading information by those people or others linked to them. Another would be where orders to trade are given or transactions undertaken by people before or after those same people disseminate research which is biased in favour of their investments[1].

1 MAR 1.7.3 E.

7.75 Market abuse by dissemination consists of behaviour such as knowingly or recklessly spreading false or misleading information about an investment through the media. Alternately it might consist of undertaking a course of business to give a false or misleading impression of an investment. Another example would be where a person puts false or misleading information on the internet or where someone responsible for submitting information to a regulatory information service provides information that is false or misleading. The FCA will consider whether a normal and reasonable person should have known that the information was false or misleading or whether the person concerned actually did know. They will also form an opinion on whether the individuals responsible for disseminating information could only have known that the information was false or misleading if they had access to information the other side of a Chinese wall. If this is the case it is only going to amount to abuse by dissemination if there is evidence the wall may have been breached. This is an area where good compliance can provide protection[1].

1 MAR 1.8.3 E–1.8.6 E.

7.76 Market abuse by misleading behaviour or distortion occurs where the movement of physical commodity shares might create a misleading impression as to the supply of or demand for a commodity or futures contract or the price of the same. The FCA will consider the following behaviour in determining whether this type of market abuse has occurred. These are: the experience and knowledge of the people concerned, the structure of the market including reporting notification and transparency requirements, the legal and regulatory requirements that are applicable, the identity and position of the person concerned and the extent and nature of the visibility of the activity. The FCA will take into account whether the transaction was carried out pursuant to a pre-existing legal or regulatory obligation, whether it was executed in a way that took into account the need for the market to operate fairly and efficiently and the characteristics of the market in question. This will take into account any relevant law, rules and code of conduct. In addition the position of the person concerned and the standards that can be expected from someone with that level of skill and knowledge will be considered. It would protect the person under suspicion if it transpired that the transaction complied with the rules of the market concerned. Finally, the protection provided where the necessary information was the other side of a Chinese wall from the person under suspicion will apply here as well[1].

1 MAR 1.9.1 E, 1.9.4E and 1.9.5 E.

FCA REGULATIONS – CONDUCT OF BUSINESS

Investment research – conflicts of interest

7.77   COBS 12 applies to all types of investment research. The FCA recognise the reality that if research is being carried out for a firm's internal use there is little danger of conflicts of interest arising. However, COBS 12.2.13G makes it clear that the FCA think it inappropriate for internal research papers to be used for the firm's own advantage and then to be given to clients where it is reasonable to suppose it might influence their decisions.

7.78   A firm must take all reasonable steps to identify conflicts of interest between itself, its management, employees and others who may be acting for it and a client[1]. All the measures for managing this must *inter alia* be applied to investment analysts as their research and its dissemination may conflict with the interests of those to whom it is sent[2]. Specifically there must be arrangements in place to deal with situations where:

- the analyst or someone connected with them has knowledge of the content and timing of the research which is not publicly available then the analyst cannot engage in personal trading in relation to the research or instruments to which it relates unless acting as a market maker, or on behalf of a client with an unsolicited client order;

- It is possible to act where the head of the firm's legal or compliance function has cleared it;

- Inducements cannot be accepted by analysts from with a material interest in the subject matter of the research;

- Issuers must not be promised favourable coverage of research; and

- Issuers and others cannot be permitted advance viewing of the research if it includes a recommendation or a target price[3].

1 SYSC 10.1.3 R.
2 COBS 12.2.3 R.
3 COBS 12.2.5 R COBS 11.7 is also relevant to personal account dealing.

7.79 Minor hospitality and small gifts are permissible provided they are within the scope of the firm's conflicts of interest policy[1].

1 COBS 12.2.8 G.

7.80 The financial analyst's objectivity should not be compromised by their involvement with activities other than the preparation of research, for example: participating in investment banking activities such as corporate finance or underwriting, pitching for new business or being involved in any other type of issuer marketing[1].

1 COBS 12 2.9 G.

7.81 If a firm disseminates investment research produced by someone else to its own clients it is sufficient if:

- the person who produces the research is not a member of the firm's group;

- the firm has not substantially altered the research recommendations;

- the firm does not present the research as being its own; and

- the firm verifies that the producer of the research is subject to the rules discussed at 7.78–7.80.

7.82 The FCA requires a firm's conflict of interest policy to provide for investment research to be distributed to clients in an appropriate manner. This is taken to making sure it is only distributed through its normal channels and that it is not distributed by someone other than a researcher, unless something in the firm's policy permits it[1]. That policy should include consideration of restrictions on the timing of the release of research, where appropriate[2].

1 COBS 12.2.11 G.
2 COBS 12.2.12 G.

7.83 The FCA believe that it is inappropriate for the person preparing investment research which is intended for internal use for the firm's own advantage to later publish it where the result might reasonably be expected to have a material influence on a client's investment decisions[1].

1 COBS12.2.13 G.

7.84 Non independent research must be clearly labelled as such and that it has not been prepared in accordance with legal requirements designed to promote the independence of investment research and is not subject to any prohibition on dealing[1]. Non independent research is also subject to the financial promotion rules, where applicable[2].

1 COBS 12.3.2 R.
2 COBS 12.3.3 R.

7.85   A firm must identify and manage conflicts of interest when producing non-independent research such as where they know the firm has, or is to publish before clients have had a reasonable opportunity to act on it. There is an exclusion here however to cover the situation where the firm is acting in good faith as a market maker in the ordinary course of business or is executing an unsolicited client order. There must also be consideration of conflicts of interest where non-independent research is intended first for internal use and later for publication to clients[1].

1 COBS12.3.4 R.

Investment research recommendations – required disclosures

7.86   Research information does not have to be subject to information barriers to avoid conflicts of interest[1], but the firm must make sure that research recommendations are fairly presented and disclose its own interests or any conflicts of interest arising[2]. It must also disclose prominently the identity of the person responsible for producing the research including their name and job title, the firm's name and any competent authority[3].

1 COBS 12.4.3 G.
2 COBS 12.4.4 R.
3 COBS 12.4.5 R.

7.87   A firm must make sure that facts in research recommendations can be clearly distinguished from interpretations, estimates, opinions and anything else which is non-factual. Sources must be reliable and if there are any doubts on this score the fact must be made clear. Projections, forecasts and price targets in research recommendations must be clearly labelled as such and material assumptions indicated. Appropriate records must be kept[1].

1 COBS 12.4.6 R.

7.88   A firm must take reasonable care to make sure that in a research recommendation:

- all substantially material sources are indicated including the issuer and whether the research recommendation has been disclosed to that issuer, and if so whether it has been amended following disclosure;

- there is an adequate summarisation of any methodology used to value securities, derivatives or an issuer;

- there is adequate explanation of any buy, sell or hold recommendation including a time frame and a sensitivity analysis;

- reference is made to the frequency with which updates will be made to the recommendation;

- the first release date must be clearly shown as well as the date and time for any security or derivative price mentioned; and

- if the substance of the recommendation is substantially different from one released in the preceding twelve months the change and date of the earlier recommendation must be prominent[1].

Therefore not all research is caught by these rules, it depends on the use that is put to it. There are also exceptions for the media[2].

1 COBS 12.4.7 R.
2 Investment Recommendation (Media) Regulations 2005.

FCA Principle 5

7.89   A breach of the market abuse legislation will also be a breach of FCA Principle 5 which requires firms to observe proper standards of market conduct. However, the converse does not necessarily hold as the Principle is wider than the legislation. In appropriate cases the FCA can take enforcement action for a breach of the Principle.

COBS 4.2.1 R and FCA Principle 7

7.90   FCA Principle 7 requires firms to communicate with clients in a manner that is clear, fair and not misleading as does COBS 4.2.1R. In addition to this, the effect of FSMA, s 150 is that a private client affected by a failure to meet this rule or any other rule will have a right of action for any loss resulting.

1 FSMA 2000, s 397(2), (3).

Safe harbours

7.91   There are safe harbours which apply where:

- the behaviour conforms with a rule which makes it clear that such behaviour is not market abuse;

- the behaviour conforms with the EU Regulation[1] implementing the Directive[2] regarding exemptions for buy-back programmes and stabilisation rules;

- it is carried out by someone acting on behalf of a public authority in pursuit of monetary authorities or policies with regard to exchange rates or managing public debt or foreign exchange[3].

1 EC Regulation 2273/2003.
2 Directive 2003/6/EC.
3 FSMA 2000, s 118A(5).

7.92   In addition FSMA 2000, s 123(2) states that a penalty should not be imposed if having considered the response to a warning notice there are reasonable grounds for the FCA to be satisfied that the person concerned had reasonable grounds to believe he had not committed market abuse and had taken all reasonable precautions. In such cases the FCA does have the option of announcing that such behaviour is market abuse[1]. This would then make it possible to punish anyone who in the future engaged in that behaviour.

1 FSMA 2000, s 123(3).

Jurisdiction

7.93   The jurisdictional elements limit the offence to acts carried out in the United Kingdom, or in relation to investments traded on a prescribed market in the United Kingdom or for which a request for admission has been made and related investments in either case[1].

1 FSMA 2000, s 118A(1)(b)(i)–(iii).

Case law

7.94   There have been a number of relevant cases, most of which have been FSA/FCA enforcement actions, though some have involved the accused taking the matter to the Tribunal. There have also been a small number of cases where criminal prosecutions have been brought. Between them they provide some useful illumination of the law and regulations discussed above. The earlier cases tended to be straightforward insider dealing cases but some of the later ones have been more complex and have strayed into other areas of market abuse. The more interesting ones are considered below.

7.95   *Middlemiss*[1] was the first FCA relevant enforcement action. Like the other cases below (between **7.95** and **7.104**) it turned on the earlier wording of s 118. However, there can be no doubt that the new wording would still catch such cases. It concerned a company secretary who became aware that the company, which was listed on AIM, was going to see a significant reduction in its revenue. He therefore sold 70,000 shares he owned in the company to avoid a loss. Following a trading statement released by the company the share price fell significantly and Mr Middlemiss avoided a loss. He was fined £15,000. *Bracken*[1] concerned a Group Head of Communications who became aware that a negative trading statement was in the offing. He therefore short sold shares in the company and made a profit. He also fined £15,000. In *Davies*[1] the person concerned had helped to prepare the interim results which showed healthy profits. He also knew that exceptional items in the previous year's results would not be recurring. He then purchased shares prior to the results being released and sold them at a profit shortly afterwards. He was given a small fine, its size being influenced by his co-operation.

1 FSA Enforcement action, 10 February 2004.
2 FSA Enforcement action, 7 July 2004.
3 FSA Enforcement action, 28 July 2004.

7.96   In *Shell and Royal Dutch Petroleum*[1] it was held that misleading statements in the annual accounts overstating the size of the oil reserves held by the companies over a number of years amounted to market abuse. This was information which the companies knew, or should have known to be inaccurate. This is an unusual case as it is the only one so far where the matter has not involved an FCA regulated firm or person. They were fined £17 million.

1 FSA Enforcement notice, 24 August 2004.

7.97   *Evolution Beeston Gregory Ltd and Potts*[1]. Here the company, an investment bank, short sold shares through Potts in Room Service Group

257

plc. At one point the volume of shares being short sold exceeded 100% of Room Service's share capital. This was done in the expectation that Room Service would engage in a new share issue which would cover the position, which as it transpired did not occur. The behaviour was determined to be market distortion amounting to market abuse as a result of which 250 investors did not receive their shares in a timely manner. The company was fined £500,000 and Mr Potts £75,000.

1 FSA Enforcement action, 12 November 2004.

7.98   *Hutchings and Smith*[1] concerned a fairly straightforward insider dealing case. Hutchings and Smith were fined £18,000 and £15,000 respectively for illegal trading in the shares of Feel Good (Holdings) plc. Smith provided inside information to Hutchings who traded on the basis of it.

1 FSA Enforcement action, 13 December 2004.

7.99   *Isaacs*[1] concerned the misuse of dishonestly obtained information. Isaacs was an experienced private investor who memorised confidential information he saw lying around on a visit to a friend's house. The nature of the information was firstly in relation to the company's products, the second to better than expected sales figures. This would clearly have been regarded by a regular user of the market as being relevant when deciding on the terms of a transaction. He put this information on an internet bulletin board under a pseudonym to try and raise the price of that company's shares. This was behaviour which a regular user of the market would regard as a failure to observe the standard of behaviour that was appropriate. He was fined £15,000.

1 FSA Enforcement action, 28 February 2005.

7.100   In *Arif Mohammed v FSA*[1] an audit manager was fined £10,000 for market abuse. Mr Mohammed traded in the shares of Delta plc on the basis of information he had acquired that it was going to sell its electrical division. He had acquired this information as the firm was an audit client of his employers PwC, and he had worked on the audit.

1 FSA Tribunal, 7–9 March 2005.

7.101   *Malin*[1] concerned market abuse by misusing relevant information. Malins was fined £25,000. He was co-founder of a company, Cambrian which was listed on the AIM. He was also its sole UK director and finance director. He bought 50,000 ordinary shares ahead of an announcement concerning a placement by the company later that day. Later the same day he chaired a meeting discussing the placement at which he requested the company's broker to release the announcement as soon as possible. He did not sell the shares once the market price had risen as a result of the placement but continued to hold them. He later purchased another 20,000 shares ahead of the announcement of the interim results. He also gave a presentation in the City without having checked that the interim results had been released. Due to unforeseen formatting problems they did not come out until an hour after the normal time. He thus committed the offence.

1 FSA Enforcement action, 20 December 2005.

7.102 *Bonnier and Indigo Capital*[1] concerned the issuance of materially inaccurate statements which created a false or misleading impression amounting to market abuse. Bonnier was managing director of ICL, a New York company providing financial advisory services and capital investment assistance in North and Latin America. The second company involved in the matter was Regus plc, a UK listed firm. Mr Bonnier traded in Regus shares and in contracts for differences in relation to them through Cantors. They in turn took up a position in Regus shares to hedge their position. They retained the voting rights under these shares and the right to transfer them. As a result Mr Bonnier did not have an obligation to report the transaction to Regus. He later contracted with Cantors for the transfer of their voting rights to ICL. Regus' registrar then sent Bonnier a request for clarification of the shareholding. He disclosed the shareholdings but not the contracts for differences. In total he made twelve misleading notifications. It gave the impression that ICL's holding in Regus had risen from 3.51% to 15.12% when in fact it had decreased from 2.3% to 0.07%. Regus' registrar deduced the position and informed Regus. ICL later made an inaccurate statement regarding its beneficial interest in Regus. Bonnier was fined £290,000 and ICL £65,000.

1 FSA Enforcement action, 21 December 2004.

7.103 *Baldwin and WRT Investments Ltd v FSA*[1] concerned Baldwin's investment vehicle, WRT Ltd. It was alleged by the FSA that as a result of a telephone conversation with the chief executive officer of another company he discovered that the company concerned had news likely to increase its profits. This was not news that was publicly available. The Tribunal ruled against the FSA on the ground that the evidence did not support the allegation that Baldwin traded as a result of receiving inside information. The evidence was too vague and Baldwin could provide a reasonable alternative explanation for his trading behaviour.

1 FSA Tribunal, 19–21 December 2005.

7.104 *Davidson and Tatham v FSA (2004)*[1] *and (2006)*[2] Mr Davidson was approached by one of the directors of Cyprotex Ltd to provide a financial guarantee for it, and for a period of time following he became one of its directors. He resigned as a director in November 2001 but remained the majority shareholder. The board then decided to float the company on the AIM to raise capital. A second party, Mr Howe became involved with Mr Davidson on another matter and acting on his advice Mr Davidson opened a spread betting account at City Index. When spread bets are placed with City Index on an individual bases they take a hedging position in the underlying security.

On 12th December 2001 a prospectus was issued stating, *inter alia*, that the placing was not underwritten and that a condition of acceptance for listing was that the full amount of the subscription was to be raised through the placing. Mr Davidson and some of the directors also signed lock in agreements to stop them selling their shares for a period after flotation. By Christmas however it was apparent that there was insufficient investor appetite to raise the full amount of £11 million. A later attempt was made to float and raise £6.5 million but difficulties in finding investors to take up the full offer remained. In due course Davidson took out a spread bet with City Index, which they in turn hedged with a contract for differences with Dresdner Securities, who in turn were underwriting the share issue. The FSA Tribunal overruled the FSA's determination that Mr Davidson had committed market abuse. He had not misled anyone, there were no prospectus requirement that the spread bet or contract for differences be disclosed and were there any reporting requirement it would rest on the broker, not Mr Davidson and the latter had fully disclosed to the broker. Also, because of his share lock in agreement Mr Davidson could not sell his shares in Cyprotex, utilising the back to back spread bet/contract for differences to support the price.

1 FSA Tribunal (2004), 30 July.
2 FSA Tribunal (2006), costs hearing, 7 September.

7.105 *Deutshebank and Maslen (2006)*[1] concerned two financial activities. The first was a book build in the shares of Scania AB and the other the stabilisation of Cytos Biotechnology AG. Scania's shares are traded on the Stockholmbörsen which is not a prescribed market for the purposes of the market abuse regime. Deutshe purchased 63.7 million shares costing £1.1 billion from Volvo AB and sought to dispose of them through an accelerated book build. For the purposes of the latter a marketing range price was established, but during the course of that morning the exchange traded price of the shares fell below that level. Deutsche then instructed two external brokers to start buying the Scania shares and the scale on which they did so represented 90% of the shares in that company being traded, and the share price was brought back within the marketing range. The information provided to Duetschebank's clients with regard to Scania's shares was incomplete and inaccurate in that it did not reveal the crucial information concerning their interference with the price at which Scania's shares were being traded on the exchange. In addition some customers were later told of the situation before the exchange was informed.

1 FSA Enforcement action, 11 April 2006.

7.106 With regard to the Cytos transaction, this was stabilised by a Zurich based trader instructed by Deutshebank on the SWX (Swiss Exchange) pursuant to Deutshebank's having agreed to be the lead manager and underwriter on the issue. As part of the agreement Deutshebank were granted an over allotment option to purchase 100,000 shares at the offer price to cover over allotments made and any short positions incurred in relation to the share offer. It was agreed to set the price of the issue at CHF 40 per share. The company's shares had closed the previous day at CHF 42.40. It was also determined that the offer would be scaled back and that the over allocation of 100,000 shares would be covered by the allotment to Deutshebank. This still ended up with an over allocation of 1,209 shares held by the bank as a naked short position which it had acquired as a result of the trader buying them at CHF 43, 3 Francs above the price at which stabilisation trades should have been made under the terms of the bank's stabilisation rules, which had been communicated to the trader. Later a further 5,000 shares had been purchased by the trader at this higher price.

7.107 Deutschebank were fined £6,363,643 (£3.5 million in relation to Scania, £2,363,643 to cover the losses it avoided on Scania and the balance in relation to Cytos) and Maslen £350,000 for market misconduct and breaches of FSA Principles 2 and 5.

7.108 *Jabre v FSA (2006)*[1] Mr Jabre was a senior trader at GLG Partners, a hedge fund manager. He was provided with inside information by a salesman at Goldman Sachs on a restricted basis, meaning that he could not trade on the basis of that information. Further information was provided on the same basis, relating to an issue of convertible preference shares by Sumitomo Mitsui Fin Group Inc (SMFG). Mr Jabre informed the salesman that he had been borrowing and shorting SMFG stock and asked about the effect of the information provided to him on his exiting trading. The salesman informed him that he was *'free to keep his existing trading pattern'*. The FSA's case is that the salesman later rang him and informed him that he should not engage in further trading in relation to SMFG stock. Mr Jabre then proceeded to short sell $16 million worth of shares in SMFG on the Tokyo Exchange ahead of an announcement of a new issue of convertible preference shares by them. The FSA held that as the shares were also sold on the London Stock Exchanges' SEAQ, they were being sold on a *'prescribed market'* and were therefore within the requirements of FSMA, s 118. He was fined £750,000.

1 FSA Tribunal decisions on Jurisdiction and Market Abuse, both (2006) 10 July.

7.109 *Casoni (2007*[1]*)* concerned a former equities analyst at Citigroup. He was head of a team specialising in the Italian leasing sector. He wrote a research report on Banca Italease, an Italian leasing and factoring bank which his bank published, including a recommendation to buy shares in them at a maximum price considerable higher than the then trading price. He then proceeded to disclose the fact and the details of his pricing model to four of his bank's clients over a two week period and in so doing acted in breach of Citicorp's compliance rules. The pricing model itself was original, applying the embedded valuation methodology normally used to value insurance companies. None of these clients dealt in the shares as a result. The FSA's analysis was that *'…it is improper market conduct for an analyst to selectively disseminate valuations…recommendations, or target prices to clients ahead of publication of that research. It is also improper market conduct for an analyst to forward his working model to clients when there is an impending initiation of coverage. This is particularly so when the client is sophisticated and therefore may be in a position to drive benefit from the model'*. He was fined £52,500, being a £75,000 fine reduced by 30% because he settled the matter straight away and co-operated.

1 FSA Enforcement action, 20 March 2007.

7.110 *Eagle (2010*[1]*)* had agreed to buy 85% of the shares in FEI. His intention was to retain 10% and sell the rest. He also bought SP Bell Ltd, an agency only stockbroker and took control of it. He introduced some clients to this firm knowing that they did not have the funds to trade. He used the broker to sell the FEI shares to its clients. Many of these clients did not know that the shares were being bought and sold on their behalf. Many of the trades were rolled over without being settled so that the clients would not have to pay for them. This breached stock exchange rules and caused an artificial increase in the value of FEI shares and created an artificial view of the demand for its shares. He was fined £2.8 million and banned.

1 FSA Enforcement Action, 20 May 2010.

7.111   These cases need to be put in context. So far[1] of the 61 cases[2] brought on a civil bases 32 have been insider dealing cases except a number of disparate cases: *Shell*[3] (misleading statements regarding the level of reserves and failure to correct this), *Davidson* and *Tatham*[4] (alleged failure to supply appropriate information under s 391(4), (6) and (7) and publishing inappropriate information), *Casoni*[5] (market misconduct in the inappropriate distribution of research), *Perkins*[6], *Alexander*[7], *Swift*[8], *Geddis*[9], and *Visser* and *Fagbulu*[10], *Coscia*[11] and *Currimjee*[12]; *Davis*[13] and *Parikh*[14], *Stevenson*[15] and *Hannan*[16] (manipulative trading) *Da Vinci Invest Ltd* and others[17] and *Goenka*[18]; (market manipulation), *Cameron*[19] and *Goenka* again[20]; (making misleading announcements), *Betton*[21], *Winterflood*[22] and *Kahn*[23] plus also *Chaligné* and *Sejuan*[24]; (ramping shares prices) *Gower*[25], *Osborne*[26] and again in *Hannam*[27] and *Osborne*[28] (disclosing misleading information) and the wrongful release of research in the unusual case of *Casoni*[29]. There were also *Davis* and *Parikh*[30] a case of failing to act with due, skill care and diligence whilst trading for a client and *Wolfson Microelectronics plc*[31] and *Entertainment Rights plc*[32] which were both a failure to release inside information and perhaps belong in a different category. Leaving aside *Davidson* where the case failed, that means that including the last two, 24 out of the 61 market abuse cases brought so far fall in the non-criminal category as far as enforcement has been concerned. What it is debateable is the proportion of illegal activity taking place that falls within these cases.

1 As at 26 August 2014.
2 Calculating by treating joint actions as one case eg, *Davidson* and *Tatham* (2006) are treated as one case.
3 FSA Enforcement action 24 August 2004.
4 Tribunal decision 7 September 2006.
5 FSA Enforcement action, 20 March 2007.
6 FSA Enforcement action 29 June 2010.
7 FSA Enforcement action 14 June 2011.
8 FSA Enforcement action 31 August 2011,upheld by Upper Tax Tribunal 28 Jan 2013.
9 Upper Tribunal 2 September 2011.
10 Upper Tribunal, 15 August 2011.
11 FCA Enforcement action 22 July 2013.
12 FCA Enforcement action 8 August 2013.
13 FCA Enforcement action 8 August 2013.
14 FCA Enforcement action 17 September 2013.
15 FCA Enforcement action 20 July 2014.
16 Upper Tribunal 22 July 2014.
17 High Court injunction by FSA 31 August 2011.
18 FSA Enforcement Action 9 November 2011.
19 FSA Enforcement action 6 July 2010.
20 FSA enforcement action 9 November 2011.
21 FSA Enforcement action 6 December 2010.
22 [2010] EWCA Civ 423.
23 FSA Enforcement action 24 May 2011 plus High Court injunction.
24 Upper Tribunal 28 September 2012.
25 FSA Enforcement Action 13 January 2011.
26 FSA Enforcement Action 26 February 2012.
27 FSA Enforcement notice 27 February 2012, referred to Upper Tribunal.
28 FSA Enforcement Action 16 February 2012.
29 FSA enforcement action 20 March 2007.
30 FCA Enforcement action 8 August 2013.
31 FSA Enforcement action 20 January 2009.
32 FSA Enforcement action 23 January 2009.

7.112   It is now necessary to consider the different types of market abuse in the context of potential criminal liability.

Insider Dealing as a criminal offence

Introduction

7.113   Over the last few years there has been an increasing trend for the FCA to utilise the criminal law against the more serious insider dealers rather than just relying on the civil law approach discussed above. For these purposes the law created by the Criminal Justice Act 1993 (CJA[1]) still applies. This is very similar to the civil offence of insider dealing but the criminal offence is slightly narrower in that it does not extend to related derivative contracts and off market transactions. It is not likely that someone would face both criminal proceedings under the Criminal Justice Act and a Market Abuse action under the Financial Services and Markets Act 2000. It would not fall the wrong side of the double jeopardy rule as the market abuse action would be civil, but the FCA have recognised the unsatisfactory nature of permitting something that is so close to double jeopardy and announced that they would not bring proceedings if a criminal prosecution were taking place. It has to be said that the utilisation of criminal law has been so unsuccessful that it was the primary reason for the development of the civil offence discussed above. There have been very few successful criminal prosecutions since insider dealing became a statutory criminal offence in 1980 and hardly any of these resulted in custodial sentences until the last few years. The previous law, that of conspiracy to defraud still exists but proved even less useful[2].

1 Which put into effect Directive 89/592.
2 See *R v de Berenger* (1814) 105 ER 536, for a rare success.

The nature of the offences in the Criminal Justice Act

7.114   There are three potential offences:

Insider dealing

7.115   This occurs when a party who is able to access information relating to the company concerned deals in securities whilst in possession of such information, which must be unpublished and likely to affect the price of the securities concerned. They need not have accessed the information directly.

Encouraging others to deal

7.116   This offence is committed where someone encourages another to deal in securities whose price is likely to be affected by inside information in their possession. The insider will be committing an offence even if the person being encouraged does not know that the person concerned is an insider or that unpublished price sensitive information is involved. A transaction need not actually take place. It is sufficient that encouragement takes place.

Disclosure

7.117   This consists of someone disclosing inside information outside the proper performance of their duties. It is not necessary for a conviction for there to be evidence that the party disclosing intended it to be acted upon.

In any of these instances a prosecution can only be brought by or with the consent of the Secretary of State for Trade and Industry or the Director of Public Prosecutions unless the FCA decide the bring the action themselves[1].

1 Criminal Justice Act 1993, s 61(1) and Financial Services and Markets Act 2000.

Key elements

7.118   What then is an 'insider'? Section 57 CJA defines this as someone who has inside information from an inside source and knows that this is the case. The person concerned will need to have acquired the information as a result of being an employee, a director or a shareholder of an issuer of securities; though it is not necessary for the crime to relate to shares in that company. Thus, the 'insider' might be a professional adviser or someone doing unrelated work for the firm on a temporary basis, eg, a decorator. However, the access to the information concerned should have arisen as a result of that person's employment, office or protection. There are however two statutory limitations which stop this catching those who as a part of their business or professional activities are rightfully involved in price analysis:

- Section 58 which states that information is not inside information if it can be either readily acquired by those likely to deal in securities or be acquired by those exercising due diligence.

- The possibility of interpreting the description of information being accessed by virtue of the insider's employment to exclude situations where an expert accesses information by virtue of his employment. There is no direct case on the point but either *Grey v Pearson*[1] (golden rule) or *Heydon's Case*[1] (mischief rule) would assist.

1 (1857) 6 HL Cas 61.
2 (1584) 3 Co Rep 74.

7.119   Secondary insiders are also caught as are parties they pass the information on to, subject to this not extending to situations where the act of passing on the information has made it public. There is no requirement for the secondary insider to have taken any active steps to acquire the information. It is sufficient that they know that it was inside information and was obtained from an inside source and then acted on it.

7.120   What then is 'inside information'? It is 'specific information' that must relate either to specific securities or a specific issuer of securities. If made public it would have a 'significant effect' on the price of any securities. This is not defined but the relevant Stock Exchange Guidance Note stated: 'it is not feasible to define any theoretical percentage movement in a share price that will make a piece of information price sensitive'. The Takeover Panel suggested a10% price movement in a day.

7.121   The information concerned need not be precise. The crucial element is that it must not be publicly available information. Section 58 provides guidance by providing a non-exhaustive list. It provides two categories:

(1)   Those where information must be treated as publicly available.

   (a)   Where it is published in accordance with the rules of a regulated market to inform investors and their advisers.

   (b)   Where the information is publicly available as a result of being set out in public records, eg, Companies House.

   (c)   Where the information can already be readily acquired.

   (d)   Where it is derivable from publicly available information.

(2)   Those where information may be treated as publicly available even though:

   (a)   it can only be worked out by experts or analysts.

   (b)   Communication has only been to a section of the public.

   (c)   The information can only be found by observation.

   (d)   The money has to be paid to get the information.

   (e)   The information is published abroad.

Such information must in any case be price sensitive. This means that the price or value of the securities concerned is likely to be significantly affected[1].

1 Criminal Justice Act 1993, s 56.

Securities

7.122   Securities themselves have a definition which is idiosyncratic to the CJA. Schedule 2 lists them as:

Shares

Shares and stock in the value of a company.

Debt securities

Any instrument creating or acknowledging indebtedness which is issued by a company or public sector body, including, in particular, debentures, debenture stock, loan stock, bonds and certificates of deposit.

Warrants

Any right (whether conferred by warrant or otherwise) to subscribe for shares or debt securities.

Depositary receipts

(1)   The rights under any depositary receipt.

(2)   For the purposes of sub-paragraph (1) a 'depositary receipt' means a certificate or other record (whether or not in the form of a document):

    (a)   which is issued by or on behalf of any person who holds any relevant securities of a particular issuer; and

    (b)   which acknowledges that another person is entitled to rights in relation to the relevant securities or relevant securities of the same kind.

(3)   In sub-paragraph (2) 'relevant securities' means shares, debt securities sand warrants.

Options

Any option to acquire or dispose of any security falling within any other paragraph in this Schedule.

Futures

(1)   Rights under a contract for the acquisition or disposal of relevant securities under which delivery is to be made at a future date and at a price agreed when the contract is made.

(2)   In sub-paragraph (1):

    (a)   the references to a future date and to a price agreed when the contract is made include references to a date and a price determined in accordance with terms of the contract; and

    (b)   'relevant securities' means any security falling within any other paragraph of this Schedule.

Contracts for differences

(1)   Rights under a contract which does not provide for the delivery of securities but whose purpose or pretended purpose is to secure a profit or avoid a loss by reference to fluctuations in:

    (a)   a share index or other similar factor connected with relevant securities;

    (b)   the price of particular relevant securities; or

    (c)   the interest rate offered on money placed on deposit.

(2)   In sub-paragraph (1) 'relevant securities' means any security falling within any other paragraph of this Schedule.

The securities concerned must either:

(1)   be listed on an official exchange of a State within the European Economic Area; or

(2)   be admitted to dealing on, or have their price quoted on a regulated market.

The Stock Exchange Guidance Note suggested:

(1) develop a consistent procedure for determining what is price sensitive and for releasing that information to the market;

(2) ensure price sensitive information is kept confidential until the moment of announcement;

(3) consider whether unaudited quarterly statements or announcements updating the market at the end of a financial period are appropriate;

(4) brief employees who meet analysts visiting the company's premises as to the extent and nature of information that can be communicated;

(5) obtain and record the consent of parties attending a meeting at which price sensitive information is to be given to the effect that they will not deal in the company's securities before the information is made public.

Dealing

7.123 Section 55 provides three categories.

(1) Acquiring securities. This may be as principal or agent.

(2) Disposing of securities. This may also be as principal or agent.

(3) Procuring another party to acquire or dispose of the securities. This may be done directly or indirectly.

AG's Reference (No 1 of 1975)[1] held that 'procure' means 'to produce by endeavour'.

In none of these cases need the insider be proven to have benefited from the deal, though in practice this is obviously the normal motive.

1 [1975] QB 773.

Defences

7.124 Once the offence has been shown to have satisfied the elements of their definition (as shown above) the burden of proof shifts to the accused to show that there is a valid defence. The defences fall into two categories, General and Specific.

General defences

(1) Where the accused did not expect to make a profit or avoid a loss[1].

(2) Where the accused reasonably believed that the information concerned was widely distributed enough to avoid prejudicing the interests of anyone else involved in the deal[2].

(3) Where the accused can show that they would have entered into the arrangement in any event[3].

1 Criminal Justice Act 1993, s 53(6).
2 Criminal Justice Act 1993, s 53(1)(b), (2)(b).
3 Criminal Justice Act 1993, s 53(1)(c), (2)(c).

7.125   In the event of the accused being charged with disclosing price sensitive information there are two general defences:

- that the accused did not expect anyone to deal in securities as a result of his disclosure[1]; or

- that the accused did not expect anyone to deal at a profit or avoid a loss as a result of the disclosure[2].

1 Criminal Justice Act 1993, s 53(3)(a).
2 Criminal Justice Act 1993, s 53(3)(b).

Specific defences

7.126

(1)   Market makers and dealers can plead that they were acting in good faith in the course of their business[1]. A market maker is someone who holds themselves out as operating in compliance with the rules of a regulated exchange or under those of a prescribed market or Treasury approved organisation.

(2)   Where it was market information and it was reasonable of the accused to act as they did[2]. Market information is that securities are to be traded, or at least that this is being considered or negotiated, and includes information on a number of securities, their prices and the persons involved.

(3)   If it was market information which the insider acquired as a result of being involved in buying or selling securities[3].

(4)   If the insider can show that they acted in line with the FCA's Price Stabilisation Rules[4].

1 Criminal Justice Act 1993, Sch 1, para 1.
2 Criminal Justice Act 1993, Sch 1, para 2.
3 Criminal Justice Act 1993, Sch 1, para 3.
4 Criminal Justice Act 1993, Sch 1, para 5.

Jurisdiction

7.127   The territorial limit for the crimes concerned is the United Kingdom. Thus the accused must either have been within the United Kingdom when the act concerned was committed, the market concerned must have been situated in the United Kingdom, the crime must have involved an intermediary who was situated in the United Kingdom, or either the disclosure must have been made by the accused when they were situated in the United Kingdom or the recipient of the information or of the encouragement to deal must have been so situated.

Penalties

7.128   On summary conviction, a maximum fine of £5,000 or imprisonment of up to six months, or both[1]. On indictment, an unlimited fine or imprisonment of up to seven years, or both[2]. Directors may be disqualified as the crime is one which shows sufficient connection with corporate management: *R v Goodman*[3].

1 Criminal Justice Act 1993, s 61(1)(a).
2 Criminal Justice Act 1993, s 61(1)(b).
3 [1994] 1 BCLC 349.

7.129 Any profits may also potentially be seized under the Proceeds of Crime Act 2002. This permits[1] the Crown Court to order confiscation where two conditions are satisfied. The first is that the defendant has been convicted by the Crown Court or committed to the Crown Court for sentencing because of the seriousness of the offence and the prosecutor or the Director of the Assets Recovery Agency has asked the court to so proceed and the Court thinks it appropriate. Factors the court will take into account are: whether the defendant had a criminal lifestyle, if so whether he benefited from his criminal conduct and whether he has so benefited even if he does not have a criminal lifestyle. This last caveat could be crucial in enabling the seizure of funds from insider dealing as the person so acting will normally have had a respectable lifestyle in all other respects. If the court decides to proceed they must then decide on the recoverable amount and make a confiscation order to that level. There is a statutory requirement[2] that the court should take into account whether a victim of the conduct intends to start proceedings against the defendant, because if this is the case a confiscation order should not be used if it would render the defendant incapable of compensating the victim. It will be interesting to see whether this would apply if an action were brought by the firm employing the defendant for recovery of money made by insider dealing (see below) as here the firm would not have been a victim.

1 Proceeds of Crime Act 2002, 6.
2 Proceeds of Crime Act 2002, 6(6).

Civil law issues other than the Market Abuse regime

7.130 Contracts under this latter category would appear to be unenforceable under the principle in *Mackender v Feldia*[1]. However, this does not appear to be the case with the main offences of insider dealing which are specifically stated not to be void or unenforceable: Criminal Justice Act 1993, s 62(2).

1 [1967] 2 QB 590.

7.131 Any profit wrongly made by a director will belong to the company of which he is a director[1]. This is a consequence of his owing a fiduciary duty when he is held to have acted as a constructive trustee: *Boardman v Phipps*[2] and *AG for Hong Kong v Reid*[3]. See also *Nanus Asia Co Inc v Standard Chartered Bank*[4] where confidential information obtained in breach of an employee's duty of fidelity gave rise to a constructive trust over profits resulting from its use. If a third party in receipt of information should realise that the information was given to them in breach of a fiduciary duty then the same principle will apply. If the information is given in breach of confidence then an action will lie on that basis. This will extend to employees.

1 *Walsh v Deloitte and Touche* [2001] UKPC 58.
2 [1967] 2 AC 46, HL.
3 [1994] AC 324, PC.
4 [1990] HKLR 396.

7.132 Beyond the position stated at 7.131 directors do not normally have a fiduciary obligation to the company or shareholders, but *Coleman v Myers*[1] suggests that they can acquire one where they are dominant directors in a small company. They must however declare secret profits: *Regal (Hastings) v Gulliver*[2]. However, there does not appear to be a basis for shareholders or other dealers in securities claiming compensation because they traded with the insider dealer at what they may later believe to have been an unfair price. In theory a criminal court could consider a compensation payment under s 130 of the Powers of Criminal Courts Act 2000.

1 [1977] 2 NZLR 225.
2 [1942] 1 All ER 378 HL.

Relevant Codes

7.133 *Rule 2.1 Takeover Code* states that anyone who is in possession of confidential information relating to offers must only make it available when it is necessary. Rule 4.1 goes on to bar dealing in the securities of an offeror or offeree prior to the information relating to the deal becoming publicly available.

7.134 *The Model Code for Securities Transactions by Directors of Listed Companies* requires the directors to notify an appointed party on his board of directors before dealing in any of the company's securities. Clearance should not be given for dealing during a close period[1]. He is debarred from dealing if he is in possession of unpublished price sensitive information. Nor should clearance be given whilst any inside information is available. Nor should the dealing be on the basis of short term interests[2].

1 Para 8.
2 Paras 8 and 20.

Misleading statements and misleading impressions

7.135 This is also an area where a criminal conviction could be the result of improper behaviour rather than just civil proceedings under the FSMA. The specific offence s are in ss 89–91 Financial Services Act 2012[1] and states that it is an offence where someone:

89   Misleading statements

(1)   Subsection (2) applies to a person ('P') who:

   (a)   makes a statement which P knows to be false or misleading in a material respect,

   (b)   makes a statement which is false or misleading in a material respect, being reckless as to whether it is, or

   (c)   dishonestly conceals any material facts whether in connection with a statement made by P or otherwise.

(2)   P commits an offence if P makes the statement or conceals the facts with the intention of inducing, or is reckless as to whether making it or concealing them may induce, another person (whether or not the person to whom the statement is made)—

(a) to enter into or offer to enter into, or to refrain from entering or offering to enter into, a relevant agreement, or

(b) to exercise, or refrain from exercising, any rights conferred by a relevant investment.

(3) In proceedings for an offence under subsection (2) brought against a person to whom that subsection applies as a result of paragraph (a) of subsection (1), it is a defence for the person charged ('D') to show that the statement was made in conformity with—

(a) price stabilising rules,

(b) control of information rules, or

(c) the relevant provisions of Commission Regulation (EC) No 2273/2003 of 22 December 2003 implementing Directive 2003/6/EC of the European Parliament and of the Council as regards exemptions for buy-back programmes and stabilisation of financial instruments.

The purpose of this section is to slightly amend parts of FSMA 2000, s 397. The new section makes it an offence where it is a 'false or misleading statement' whereas the old offence referred to 'promise or forecast'. Also the new offence no longer refers to 'deceptive statements'.

1 ReplacingFSMA 2000, s 397.

7.136 In addition s 90 takes matters further. The wording is:

90 Misleading impressions

(1) A person ('P') who does any act or engages in any course of conduct which creates a false or misleading impression as to the market in or the price or value of any relevant investments commits an offence if—

(a) P intends to create the impression, and

(b) the case falls within subsection (2) or (3) (or both).

(2) The case falls within this subsection if P intends, by creating the impression, to induce another person to acquire, dispose of, subscribe for or underwrite the investments or to refrain from doing so or to exercise or refrain from exercising any rights conferred by the investments.

(3) The case falls within this subsection if—

(a) P knows that the impression is false or misleading or is reckless as to whether it is, and

(b) P intends by creating the impression to produce any of the results in subsection (4) or is aware that creating the impression is likely to produce any of the results in that subsection.

(4) Those results are—

(a) the making of a gain for P or another, or

(b) the causing of loss to another person or the exposing of another person to the risk of loss.

(5) References in subsection (4) to gain or loss are to be read in accordance with subsections (6) to (8).

(6) 'Gain; and 'loss'—

    (a) extend only to gain or loss in money or other property of any kind;

    (b) include such gain or loss whether temporary or permanent.

(7) 'Gain' includes a gain by keeping what one has, as well as a gain by getting what one does not have.

(8) 'Loss' includes a loss by not getting what one might get, as well as a loss by parting with what one has.

(9) In proceedings brought against any person ('D') for an offence under subsection (1) it is a defence for D to show—

    (a) to the extent that the offence results from subsection (2), that D reasonably believed that D's conduct would not create an impression that was false or misleading as to the matters mentioned in subsection (1),

    (b) that D acted or engaged in the conduct—

        (i) for the purpose of stabilising the price of investments, and

        (ii) in conformity with price stabilising rules,

    (c) that D acted or engaged in the conduct in conformity with control of information rules, or

    (d) that D acted or engaged in the conduct in conformity with the relevant provisions of Commission Regulation (EC) No 2273/2003 of 22 December 2003 implementing Directive2003/6/EC of the European Parliament and of the Council as regards exemptions for buy-back programmes and stabilisation of financial instruments.

(10) This section does not apply unless:

    (a) the act is done, or the course of conduct is engaged in, in the United Kingdom, or

    (b) the false or misleading impression is created there.

This now draws a distinction between 'misleading statements' in the preceding section and 'misleading impressions'.

7.137 It is difficult to predict how useful these sections will be. They replace and in large measure replicate the old FSMA, s 397. There was one conviction on the preceding FSMA, s 397 in the twelve years it was in force, *R v Rigby, Bailey and Rowley*[1] which involved the criminal conviction of three men; Rigby for recklessly making a statement to the market which was misleading, false or deceptive in a material particular contrary to s 397(1)(c), Bailey for making a statement, promise or forecast which was misleading, false or deceptive in a material particular contrary to s 397(c) and Rowley on both counts. Rigby and Bailey had stated that both turn-over and profit were in line with expectations. For this to have been true the revenue from three contracts totalling £4.8 million had to be included. These contracts did not exist. Just under a month later an update was issued stating that one of these contracts had not been confirmed and that there was a shortfall of £1.1 million. A cash shortfall was also highlighted. Two weeks later a further statement was issued announcing that their pre-liminary results would not be published that day because of issues arising in the audit. A further shortfall in revenue and profit was forecast on the grounds that the company had failed to satisfy the terms of a licensing agreement worth £2.5 million. This was the second of the three contracts referred to above. The first two accused were sentenced to 3 1/2 years, and 2 years respectively and also disqualified from being a director for 6 and 4 years. The prison sentence was reduced by the Court of Appeal.

1 (2005). Unreported.

7.138   The preceding statutes, the Financial Services Act 1986 had an equivalent section which was in force for thirteen years and, that again only resulted in one prosecution, *R v Hipwell*[1] which reached the Court of Appeal in an unsuccessful attempt to overturn the conviction. The case was brought on the basis of facts which today would potentially lead to a prosecution under FSA 2012, s 89.

A journalist had purchased shares, tipped them in his newspaper column and then sold his own shares at a profit as the price rose. It was held at first instance, and confirmed on appeal that in such a situation the journalist must disclose that they hold the shares they are tipping. Failure to do so amounted to a conspiracy to create a misleading impression as to the price of the shares.

1 [2007] 3 All ER 361.

7.139   An additional element was added in the form of s 91 following the recommendations made in the Wheatley Report on the LIBOR scandal to make sure the law clearly stated that manipulating LIBOR was a criminal offence. The section, which has been widely drafted to cover benchmarks generally, rather than just LIBOR, states the law as follows.

91   Misleading statements etc in relation to benchmarks

7.140

(1)   A person ('A') who makes to another person ('B') a false or mislead-ing statement commits an offence if—

    (a)   A makes the statement in the course of arrangements for the setting of a relevant benchmark;

    (b)   A intends that the statement should be used by B for the pur-pose of the setting of a relevant benchmark; and

    (c)   A knows that the statement is false or misleading or is reckless as to whether it is.

(2)   A person ('C') who does any act or engages in any course of con-duct which creates a false or misleading impression as to the price or

value of any investment or as to the interest rate appropriate to any transaction commits an offence if—

(a) C intends to create the impression;

(b) the impression may affect the setting of a relevant benchmark;

(c) C knows that the impression is false or misleading or is reckless as to whether it is; and

(d) C knows that the impression may affect the setting of a relevant benchmark.

(3) In proceedings for an offence under subsection (1), it is a defence for the person charged ('D') to show that the statement was made in conformity with—

(a) price stabilising rules;

(b) control of information rules; or

(c) the relevant provisions of Commission Regulation(EC) No 2273/2003 of 22 December 2003 implementing Directive 2003/6/EC of the European Parliament and of the Council as regards exemptions for buy-back programmes and stabilisation of financial instruments.

(4) In proceedings brought against any person ('D') for an offence under subsection (2) it is a defence for D to show—

(a) that D acted or engaged in the conduct—

(i) for the purpose of stabilising the price of investments, and

(ii) in conformity with price stabilising rules,

(b) that D acted or engaged in the conduct in conformity with control of information rules, or

(c) that D acted or engaged in the conduct in conformity with the relevant provisions of Commission Regulation(EC) No 2273/2003 of 22 December 2003 implementing Directive 2003/6/EC of the European Parliament and of the Council as regards exemptions for buy-back programmes and stabilisation of financial instruments.

(5) Subsection (1) does not apply unless the statement is made in or from the United Kingdom or to a person in the United Kingdom.

(6) Subsection (2) does not apply unless—

(a) the act is done, or the course of conduct is engaged in, in the United Kingdom, or

(b) the false or misleading impression is created there.

Misleading the Financial Conduct Authority

7.141 There is an additional offence in FSMA 2000, s 398, where someone knowingly or recklessly gives false or misleading information to the FCA in purported compliance with a requirement imposed by the FSMA. It can be punished by a fine.

Chapter 8

Money Laundering

Andrew Haynes

INTRODUCTION

8.1   This is an area that is likely to continue in importance due to the continuing threat of terrorism and the financial transactions utilised to facilitate it. It is not only terrorists who launder money; the illegal drugs industry creates huge reserves of cash from drug sales which need to be laundered; heads of state and senior figures in many third world countries also seem to regard their own countries' finances and overseas aid as a source of personal wealth. Organised crime in general also engages in laundering. The purpose of laundering in each instance is to hide the proceeds of crime and get it to re-emerge in a different place, under apparently different ownership, and with an apparently honest source. Such laundering falls into two main categories: that which starts off as cash and that which is already in the banking system. Drug laundering is an example of the former and corrupt governments the latter. Thus, not all laundering will be of the same nature.

8.2   Money Laundering has been defined as[1]:

'...the process by which criminals attempt to conceal the true origin and ownership of their criminal activities. If undertaken successfully, it also allows them to maintain control over those proceeds and, ultimately, to provide a legitimate cover for their source of income'.

1 Joint Money Laundering Steering Group *Guidance Notes for the Financial Sector*, at 1.03.

8.3   Another, briefer definition[1] is:

'rendering the proceeds of crime unrecognisable as such'.

However, the Joint Money Laundering Steering Committee Guidelines adopt a common mistake which provides false security in many of the larger laundering operations, ie:

'Criminally earned money is invariably transient in nature'.

1 Simon Gleeson 'The Involuntary Launderer' in *Laundering and Tracing* 1995.

8.4   This will often be the case as the criminal concerned will be in need of the funds as soon as possible. However, the vast increases in wealth available to the larger organised crime groups in recent years, and possibly some of the smaller ones, means that it may be possible for them to tie up some of their funds for significant periods of time as part of the laundering process.

8.5   The range of methods that can be utilised to launder money are enormous and anyone needing to have a clear understanding of the subject needs to read widely and keep abreast of changes in laundering patterns. The commonest vehicles for laundering are those where large amounts of cash, liquid investments or assets are handled. In the financial markets, banks and investment business firms are the most heavily utilised. In the commercial field there are businesses dealing in high value goods who can prove attractive as they provide the opportunity for moving money by dealing in expensive items, often across international boundaries. Another development, and one that has become more heavily utilised as banks and other financial businesses have attempted to tighten their anti-money laundering operations is to include a firm of solicitors, accountants or other professionals in what appears to be a bona fide scheme to invest or transact money. This provides the attraction of feeding money through a professional's client account to make the transaction appear legitimate to a later party receiving the money. A particular problem in spotting laundering is that most of those with large amounts of money to launder can construct their operations intelligently enough to avoid it looking suspicious. In almost all instances of large movements of laundered money the criminals will be employing experts to advise and assist them.

8.6 The legislation and guidelines focus primarily on laundering the proceeds of crime. A consequence of this is that they are not of great assistance in picking up terrorist monies. In the UK in particular a dissimilarity arises between the patterns of terrorist money and many of the other laundering schemes. There is also a dissimilarity in the legislation in that it is necessary to report the movement of monies which may be utilised to commit a criminal act by a proscribed organisation rather than just money being moved after a crime. This issue is examined more closely below.

8.7 The imposition of money laundering obligations on financial institutions and certain professionals has created a situation where those parties must ascertain whether a particular transaction is 'suspicious' and, if so, potential reporting issues arise. This chapter will consider what circumstances should arouse suspicion, what reporting issues then arise and what to do in borderline situations.

8.8 The law is mainly found in the Proceeds of Crime Act 2002 which creates laundering offences in ss 327 to 339 and 340(3). This Act has been amended by the Serious Organised Crime and Police Act 2005. In addition there are two other relevant statutes: the Terrorism Act 2000 and the Anti-terrorism, Crime and Security Act 2001, which, together with the Terrorism (United Nations) Order 2001[1] and the Terrorist Asset Freezing etc Act 2010, determine the position with relation to funds that are suspected of being used to further the ends of terrorism.

1 SI 2001/3365.

8.9 The overall structure in the UK is as follows:

- **Proceeds of Crime Act 2002**

  ss 327–338 and 340

- **Terrorism Act 2000 etc**

  ss 12–21

- **Money Laundering Regulations 2007**
  Articulating the 3rd EU Laundering Directive

THE CRIMINAL OFFENCES 1 – LAUNDERING DRUG PROCEEDS AND THE PROFITS OF CRIME

Concealing etc the proceeds of crime

8.10   It is an offence under s 327 to conceal, disguise, convert, transfer or remove criminal property from the jurisdiction. This extends to concealing etc its nature, source, location, disposition, movement, ownership or any rights in relation to it. There are defences in as much that it is not an offence if the person concerned has made a protected disclosure under s 338, usually to the National Crime Agency (NCA), and has been given consent to continue to act. Likewise, if he was going to make such a disclosure but there was 'a reasonable excuse' for not doing so. Finally there is a third defence where the act that has been done consists of carrying out a function he has in relation to enforcing any provision of the Proceeds of Crime Act 2002 or of any other statute relating to criminal conduct or benefiting therefrom. 'Criminal property' is defined by s 340(3) as being someone's benefit from criminal conduct where the alleged offender knows or suspects that it represents such a benefit.

8.11   Under s 327(2C) a deposit taking body that converts or transfers criminal property does not commit an offence provided it does the act concerned in operating an account which it maintains and the value of the criminal property concerned does not exceed the threshold amount. At present the threshold amount has been set at £250. This exception is a very limited one as it only applies to those carrying on deposit taking business.

Arrangements

8.12   It is an offence under s 328 to enter into or become concerned in an arrangement which that person knows, or suspects, facilitates the retention, use or control criminal property. There are three defences which are the same as those in para **8.10** above. The same exception for deposit taking bodies that exists for s 327 also applies here.

It is an offence under s 328 to enter into or become concerned in an arrangement which that person knows, or suspects, facilitates the retention, use or control or criminal property. Since the case of *Bowman v Fels*[1] it has been clear than an 'arrangement' will cover the relationship between solicitors and other professionals, and their clients. This case arose as a result of a property dispute between ex-cohabitees. Shortly before a hearing in the County Court the solicitor for one party submitted a suspicious transaction report concerning the other party. The legal adviser to that party then requested an adjournment because 'appropriate consent' was not anticipated. The Law Society intervened, seeking clarification on the meaning of 'arrangements' under s 328 Proceeds of Crime Act. The Bar Council and the NCIS (forerunners of the NCA) were given permission to intervene.

The case was settled between the original parties but the resulting Court of Appeal decision arose from the court wishing to provide clarification on how the Proceeds of Crime Act impacted on litigation. The key point was that certain activities are excluded from the scope of proceedings related to s 328. What appears to be the case is that where litigation privilege applies, ie, a file where litigation is contemplated or has started then the normal rules do not apply.

> 'The principle which runs through all these cases, and the many other cases which were cited, is that a man must be able to consult his lawyer in confidence, since otherwise he might hold back half the truth.'[2]

It was added by the Court that the phrase 'enters on becomes concerned in an arrangement' under s 328 cannot just treat the ordinary conduct of litigation as outside the scope of s 328, but it also covers the parties agreeing on any step involved in its conduct or from agreeing to resolve any of the issues arising by settlement rather than by litigation to judgment. Otherwise the question would arise at what point a legal professional advising on, negotiating or concluding on his client's behalf a settlement of legal proceedings on the merits could find themselves unable to so act. Once the settlement is reached there is no bar to making a report to the NCA as it is no longer a matter operating in privileged circumstances.

1 (2005) EWCA Civ 226, WL 513404.
2 *R v Derby Magistrates Court ex parte B* [1996] 1 AC 487 per Lord Taylor.

8.13 The decision did not specifically go on to refer to alternative dispute resolution arrangements. However, the general view seems to be that they are caught by the judgment as well and would thus operate outside the reporting requirement in POCA 2002, s 328.

8.14 In this context 'legal advice privilege was just as important as litigation privilege'[1].

Thus in cases where a client is seeking legal advice from a solicitor the matter will be exempt from POCA 2002, s 328 just as a litigation matter would be. The immunity would evaporate if the solicitor had reasonable grounds to suppose that the legal advice were being sought to assist in the carrying out of a criminal offence.

1 *Three Rivers DC v Bank of England* (No 6) [2004] UKHL 48, [2004] 3 WLR 1274, House of Lords.

8.15 The effect of this is that those involved in litigation and related settlements are not involved in 'arrangements' under s 328. Essentially, privilege is not overridden by the statute. The only exception to this would be where there appears to be false litigation taking place so that the party defending could settle out of court to launder money to the plaintiff. Any property however dealt with after the judgment could still be criminal property under s 340(3) (an interpretation section). As a result a suspicious transaction report would have to be made at that stage.

8.16   There are three defences which are the same as those in **1** above. The same exception for deposit taking bodies that exists for s 327 also applies here.

8.17   In the case of *R v Geary*[1], the Court of Appeal held that it is not a breach of s 328 where the assets being handled were lawful. The facts were that a man who was expecting to get divorced asked a friend to hold some of his money to hide it from his wife. At the time no divorce proceedings had been instigated and his wife was not contemplating divorce. The party holding the money was therefore not in possession of funds that were the proceeds of crime. The 'arrangement', ie, that the man's friend would hold and return money could not be separated from the lawfulness of the money itself. The case would undoubtedly have gone the other way if a divorce hearing was taking place as then the money would have been transferred to obstruct the course of justice.

1 30 July 2010.

8.18   There are limits on how far s 328 can be taken. This was illustrated in *Dare v Crown Prosecution Service*[1]. This case involved the proposed sale of a car for £800 to Mr Dare. He was aware that the proposed vendor had a past record of selling stolen cars, but nonetheless test drove the car and then asked for a price reduction and time to raise the finance to buy it. In the end no sale occurred, though Mr Dare's plan had been to buy it and sell it on at a profit. He was originally found guilty of entering into an arrangement under POCA 2002, s 328(1) on the basis that the car was stolen and thus criminal property. Therefore as he knew or at least had grounds to suppose that it was stolen, and he intended to sell it on for profit it was argued that he was facilitating the acquisition of criminal property by whoever bought the car from him. The High Court overturned the conviction on the grounds that found this interpretation of section 328 was too wide. It was pointed out that s 328 says that the arrangement must be one which the defendant knows or suspects 'facilitates' the acquisition of criminal property by another; not 'will facilitate'. Therefore no 'arrangement' had taken place and the conviction was overturned.

1 22 October 2012.

Acquisition use and possession

8.19   It is an offence under s 329 for someone to acquire, use or have possession of criminal property. The three defences to s 327 apply here. There is also a fourth, namely where the person acquiring, using or having possession obtained the property for adequate consideration. This is to protect traders who buy goods and are not therefore under a duty to question the source of the money. It would not extend to a situation where the goods or services were being knowingly provided to assist in the carrying out of a crime, or where there was suspicion. The deposit taking exception applies. It should be noted that the definition of 'property' includes money and therefore this section will cover someone in possession of funds that are being or are to be laundered.

8.20   It was determined in *R v Hogan*[1] that the person charged had purchased some scaffolding from his former employers in cash for about on
sixth of its commercial value without a written receipt. He was charged
under POCA 2002, s 329 and a key issue which arose was whether he
had paid 'adequate consideration'. It was determined by the court that
the adequacy of the consideration was an objective question of fact to be
decided by a jury. The Court added that the issue of whether the consideration was adequate was separate from the defendant's state of mind and
this necessitated a second test. Section 329(2)(c) determined that where the
court had concluded that adequate consideration had been given for the
acquisition of property, no offence would be exist under this Act even if
the offender had known that the property had been stolen. Other criminal
offences might have been committed but they are irrelevant for the purposes of an analysis of the money laundering laws.

1 [2007] EWHC (Admin) 978.

Failure to disclose

8.21   It is an offence under s 330 to fail to make a report where someone
knows or suspects (or has reasonable grounds for so doing) that someone
else is engaged in money laundering where the knowledge or suspicion
came into that person's possession in the course of their business in the
regulated sector. The person on whom this legal obligation rests must
either be able to identify the person concerned or the whereabouts of the
laundered property. The report should be made to the firm's nominated
officer or the person authorised for this purpose by the National Crime
Agency. This disclosure should consist of the person's identity, the whereabouts of the laundered property concerned and any information or other
matter on which this knowledge is based which came to him in the course
of his business. Such a disclosure must be made as soon as reasonably
practicable once the information is in that person's possession.

8.22   There is a defence[1] where the person concerned has a reasonable
excuse for not making the required disclosure or where he is a professional legal adviser and if he knows the relevant information because of
facts coming into his hands in privileged circumstances. There is a further
defence that would apply where the person concerned does not know or
suspect that the other person is engaged in money laundering and had not
been provided with money laundering training by their employer. There
is also the possibility[2] that a professional legal adviser can make a communication to the money laundering reporting officer for the purpose of
obtaining an opinion regarding the situation. Any information made for
such a purpose is not regarded as a disclosure. It is useful where the legal
adviser is less *au fait* than the money laundering reporting officer as to
the relevant legal position. Often such information will have come into
the firm's possession in privileged circumstances where a professional
legal adviser has been provided with it in connection with his giving legal
advice or in connection with legal proceedings. However, this exception
does not apply where the communication has been made with the purpose of furthering a criminal purpose.

1 Proceeds of Crime Act 2002, s 330(6).
2 Proceeds of Crime Act 2002, s 330(9A).

Failure to report

8.23 It is an offence under s 331 where a money laundering reporting officer who receives a report which gives them grounds to know or suspect that laundering is taking place does not then make a report to the NCA. The report that he has received should have stated the identity of the suspected person, the location of the laundered property or why he believes (or it is reasonable to expect him to believe) that the information will assist in identifying the person or location of the laundered property. An offence is not committed if he has a 'reasonable excuse[1]' for not making the required disclosure. Unfortunately this is not a defined term and pending judicial interpretation it would be wise to interpret it very narrowly.

The same offence and defence apply under s 332 to nominated officers outside the 'regulated sector'. This is defined in Sch 9 and covers virtually all financial services business.

1 Proceeds of Crime Act 2002, s 331(6).

Tipping off and prejudicing an investigation

8.24 It is an offence under s 333 where someone knows or suspects that a report to the NCA or other appropriate person along the lines set out above has been made and the person then makes a disclosure which is likely to prejudice an investigation which might follow. It is a defence where the person who has done this did not know or suspect that the disclosure was likely to be prejudicial. There is a second defence where the disclosure is made in carrying out a function that person has relating to the enforcement of the Proceeds of Crime Act 2002, or a similar statute. Finally it is a defence where the person who has tipped off is a professional legal adviser and the disclosure was to a client of the adviser in connection with giving legal advice or to anyone in connection with legal proceedings. This last defence would not apply where the disclosure was made for the purposes of furthering a crime.

8.25 There is a separate offence under s 342 of prejudicing an investigation. It is committed if someone knows or suspects that someone is acting or proposing to act in connection with a confiscation investigation or a money laundering investigation. To commit the offence they must make a disclosure that is likely to prejudice the investigation or falsify, conceal, destroy or otherwise dispose of documents relevant to an investigation, or cause or permit that to happen. There are defences[1] where the person concerned does not know or suspect the disclosure will prejudice an investigation, where disclosure is made in the exercise of a function under the Proceeds of Crime Act 2002 (or any other relevant Act) or he is a professional legal adviser acting under privilege.

1 Proceeds of Crime Act 2002, s 342(3).

Appropriate consent

8.26 An individual within a firm may be provided with appropriate consent by the money laundering reporting officer, the NCA, or where appropriate HM Customs and Excise. In the last two instances appropriate consent will exist: where it has been granted, where seven working days have elapsed without permission being refused and where permission is refused but thirty one days have elapsed since that time with no further communication, or if consent is given[1]. In practice this is not particularly helpful because in many instances a quick decision will be needed. For example, a solicitor who has a client arrive at his office for a completion meeting in a conveyancing transaction wishing to hand over the balance of the purchase price in cash, will need a quick decision. In such instances an emailed report can be sent to the NCA marked 'urgent' and a follow up phone call be made. It will normally be possible to get a decision very quickly and if the money is not leaving the jurisdiction or is being moved to a state with very effective anti- laundering systems there is a high likelihood that consent to proceed will be granted.

The money laundering reporting officer must not give consent to a member of staff unless appropriate consent has been obtained from the NCA or another appropriate person[2].

1 Proceeds of Crime Act 2002, s 335(3)–(6).
2 Proceeds of Crime Act 2002, s 336.

Protected disclosures

8.27   A disclosure which satisfies the conditions that it came into a person's profession in the course of his trade, profession, business or employment, that it caused him to know or suspect that a person is engaged in money laundering, and that it is made to the NCA, HM Customs or a money laundering officer as appropriate does not breach any restriction on the disclosure of information[1]. This covers both common law restrictions and those found in statute, in particular the Data Protection Act 1998.

1 Proceeds of Crime Act 2002, s 337.

Authorised disclosures

8.28   A disclosure should be made before acting. However, no offence is committed if the act is still taking place without it being known that laundering was taking place and the disclosure was made as soon as practicable after the person first knows or suspects that laundering is taking place[1].

1 Proceeds of Crime Act 2002, s 338.

Form and manner of disclosure

8.29   It is an offence unless any report made is not on the prescribed form unless there is a 'reasonable excuse'. Unfortunately, this is not defined[1].

1 Proceeds of Crime Act 2002, s 339(1A), (1B).

Prejudicing an investigation

8.30   Where a person knows or suspects that there is going to be: a confiscation investigation, a civil recovery investigation or a money laundering investigation, they commit an offence if they make a disclosure which is likely to prejudice that investigation or they falsify, conceal, destroy or dispose of relevant documents. A defence exists where they do not know or suspect that the disclosure made is likely to prejudice the investigation, the disclosure is required by a relevant statute, or he is a professional legal adviser giving advice in relation to legal proceedings. This last exception does not apply where the disclosure is made with the intention of furthering a criminal purpose. A second defence exists where the person destroying documents does not know or suspect that they are relevant to an investigation or does not intend to conceal any facts contained in the documents[1].

1 Proceeds of Crime Act 2002, s 342.

Penalties

8.31   Anyone convicted under ss 327 to 329 is liable on summary conviction to up to six months in prison and/or a fine. On indictment this rises to prison for up to fourteen years and/or a fine. A conviction under ss 330 to 332, breach of the law on appropriate consent by a money laundering reporting officer and prejudicing an investigation are all liable for up to six months in prison and/or a fine on summary conviction. On indictment this rises to five years (two years in the case of s 333) and/or a fine[1].

1 Proceeds of Crime Act 2002, ss 334 and 336(6).

THE CRIMINAL OFFENCES 2 – TERRORIST FUNDS

8.32   There is a separate set of laws that applies to terrorist money. Primarily, separate laws are needed as terrorist funds are often not the proceeds of crime but are utilised with a view to committing a criminal offence afterwards. These are determined by the Terrorism Act 2000 which, *inter alia*, creates a series of criminal offences relating to handling terrorist money. They are:

- to receive money or other property with the intention that it be used, or where there is reasonable cause to believe it will be used for the purposes of terrorism[1].

- to become concerned in an arrangement which facilitates the retention or control of terrorist property by or on behalf of another whether this be done by concealment, removal from the jurisdiction, transfer to nominees or in any other way[2].

- To fail to report to the police (in practice the NCA) as soon as is reasonably practicable a suspicion that someone has committed a financial offence in relation to laundering where this information has come into their possession as part of their trade, profession, business or employment. They must also report the information on which their suspicion is based. There is a defence of having a 'reasonable excuse' for not making the disclosure. Information obtained by a professional legal adviser is exempt if it is obtained in privileged circumstances[3].

- To disclose information to another which is likely to prejudice an investigation or interfere with material which is relevant to such an investigation where there are reasonable grounds to suppose that the police are conducting, or proposing to conduct a terrorist investigation[4].

1 Terrorism Act 2000, s 15(2).
2 Terrorism Act 2000, s 18.
3 Terrorism Act 2000, s 19(2).
4 Terrorism Act 2000, s 19(5).

8.33   Terrorist offences by their nature relate to terrorist organisations and the Act provides a list of some who are all parties involved in the conflict in Northern Ireland[1]. Since then a statutory instrument has added a rather more cosmopolitan list of additional organisations whose activities relate to overseas conflicts in the Terrorism Act (Proscribed Organisations) (Amendment) Order 2001[2]. Updated information is added to the Bank of England website warning of persons and organisations whose accounts must be frozen and of whom a report must be made.

The penalties for non-compliance are a fine or up to six months imprisonment on summary conviction and a fine or up to fourteen years on indictment[3].

1 Terrorism Act 2000, s 2.
2 As amended by SI 2007/3299, SI 2011/1781, SI 2011/2833 and SI 2012/2298.
3 Terrorism Act 2000, s 22.

8.34   There is a new disclosure requirement added by the Anti-terrorism, Crime and Security Act 2001 that a firm must disclose to the Treasury any knowledge or suspicion that a customer is in one of the categories of proscribed organisations. The Treasury can also direct anyone to provide them with any information in their possession or control or to produce any document in their possession which the Treasury requires to secure compliance with the statutory instrument.

8.35   As a result of the terrorist attack on the world trade centre there was an urgent re-assessment of legislation relating to terrorism. The result was the Anti-terrorism, Crime and Security Act 2001 and the Terrorism (United Nations Measures) Order 2001[1]. The main issue arising in the context of laundering being the seizing of terrorist funds. The Act allows the forfeiture of funds in civil proceedings in a magistrates' court[2] where the monies concerned are:

• intended for use for terrorist purposes; or

• which consists of the resources of a proscribed organisation; or

• which amounts to property obtained through terrorism.

1 SI 2001/3365.
2 Anti-terrorism, Crime and Security Act 2001, s 1.

8.36   An authorised officer is permitted to seize cash if he has reasonable grounds for believing it to be terrorist cash. This extends to seizing cash, only part of which is believed to be terrorist cash where it is not practicable to seize only the relevant part. Seizure is for an initial period of 48 hours, though this can be extended by up to three months from the date of the order, or in the case of a subsequent order for up to two years. If it is held for more than 48 hours it must be placed in an interest bearing account. The application must be made by HM Revenue and Customs, or in Scotland the Procurator Fiscal.

The Treasury may also make a freezing order if they reasonably believe that:

- action that is of detriment to the UK economy has been, or is to be taken; or

- action which constitutes a threat to the life or property is likely to be taken. The person responsible for that act must be an overseas government or resident.

8.37   The statutory instrument mentioned above widens these powers of seizure. It states that where the Treasury has reasonable grounds for supposing that someone on whose behalf funds are being held is directly or indirectly involved in acts of terrorism, it may require that those funds are not released without Treasury consent. The holder of the funds must then immediately notify their owner of the seizure order. It is also an offence to make funds or related services directly or indirectly available to such people.

8.38   There is a disclosure requirement that a firm must disclose to the Treasury any knowledge or suspicion that a customer is in one of the categories of proscribed organisations. The Treasury can also direct anyone to provide them with any information in their possession or control or to produce any document in their possession which the Treasury requires to secure compliance with the statutory instrument.

8.39   There is an additional statute, the Terrorist Asset Freezing etc Act 2010 which empowers the Treasury to nominate someone a 'designated person[1]'. This should be done publicly notifying them[2], normally in the interests of national security[3] but it can also be done to prevent or detect serious crime[4]. One someone is so nominated it is an offence for banks or other businesses to handle their money[5] or other economic resources if they know or have grounds to suspect that the person concerned is a nominated party. Neither can funds or economic resources be made available to such a person[6] or for their benefit. It is also an offence to knowingly circumvent these laws[7]. Crucially there is a reporting obligation to the Treasury if a party believes someone is a 'designated person' or has committed an offence under Chapter 2 of this Act. The nature and amount of the funds concerned must also be made clear[8]. The Treasury may also request information from a person and/or documents, and it is an offence without reasonable excuse or to knowingly or recklessly provide false information.[9] Obeying this statute does not put anyone in breach of the Data Protection Act 1988 or Part 1 of the Regulatory Powers Act 2000[10].

1 Terrorist Asset Freezing etc Act 2010, s 1.
2 Terrorist Asset Freezing etc Act 2010, s 3(1)(b).
3 Terrorist Asset Freezing etc Act 2010, s 3(3)(b)(ii).
4 Terrorist Asset Freezing etc Act 2010, s 3(3)(b)(iii).
5 Terrorist Asset Freezing etc Act 2010, s 11.
6 Terrorist Asset Freezing etc Act 2010, ss 12–15.
7 Terrorist Asset Freezing etc Act 2010, s 18.
8 Terrorist Asset Freezing etc Act 2010, s 19.
9 Terrorist Asset Freezing etc Act 2010, ss 20–22.
10 Terrorist Asset Freezing etc Act 2010, s 25.

THE MONEY LAUNDERING REGULATIONS 2007

8.40   The Money Laundering Regulations 2007[1] determines the range of those caught by the laundering laws to those carrying on 'relevant business'. This is defined as the following regulated activities:

- accepting deposits;
- effecting and carrying out contracts for long term life assurance;
- dealing in investments;
- arranging deals in investments;
- managing investments;
- safeguarding and administering assets;
- sending dematerialised instructions;
- establishing etc collective investment schemes;
- advising on investments;
- issuing electronic money;
- the activities of the National Savings Bank;
- raising money under the National Loans Act 1986;
- bureaux de change;
- banking activities;
- estate agency work;
- casinos;
- insolvency practitioners;
- tax advisers;
- accountants;
- auditors;
- those providing legal services which involves participating in a financial or real property transaction;
- business services involving the formation, operation or management of companies or trusts; or
- dealing in goods whenever the value exceeds €15,000.

1 SI 2003/3075.

8.41   It does not apply to:

- the issue of withdrawable share capital under the Industrial and Provident Societies Act 1965;
- accepting deposits under that Act;
- issuing withdrawable share capital under the Industrial and Provident Societies Act (Northern Ireland) 1969;
- accepting deposits under that Act;

- activities carried on by the Bank of England;

- an activity in respect of an exemption order, Proceeds of Crime Act 2002, s 38;

- an activity which would have been caught by s 45 of the Financial Services Act 1986 before it was repealed. (This covers a miscellaneous range of activities carried out in judicial and quasi-judicial capacities);

- arranging and advising on regulated mortgage contracts;

- dealing, arranging, managing or advising in relation to an insurance arrangement which is not a qualifying one; or

- the Official Solicitor when acting as trustee in his official capacity.

Requirements of the Regulations

8.42   Part II of the Regulations requires those caught by them to engage in certain activities.

Identification procedures

8.43   The Regulations require that the identity of a new client be checked in any of the following situations:

- where it has been decided that a business relationship should be formed with them;

- when the person dealing with the client has reason to suspect that a one off transaction could be part of a money laundering operation;

- where a one off transaction exceeds €15,000; and

- where there are a series of connected transactions exceeding €15,000 in total value.

8.44   It would be wise for most affected firms to require that all new clients have their identity checked at the outset not just those carrying on a financial or real property transaction. Failure to do so could give rise to the risk of someone using the firm on a non-financial or real property matter and then getting round the identity checking requirement because the staff do not remember to check later. Alternately, a client might initially use the firm on a matter below the financial limit of €15,000 and later use the firm on a larger matter with the same results. Generally speaking the client's identity should be checked at the outset but the regulations do permit some variation in this, where the nature of the contact with the client may make this impossible, eg, where they are in another country. In any event it should always be done at the first reasonably possible time. If the person dealing with the financial institution appears to be acting for someone else, that person's identity must also be checked in the same way.

8.45   The regulations require that identity be checked by an approach that is 'reasonably capable of establishing that the applicant is the person he claims to be'. This means seeing original documents that prove that the person is who he claims to be and also that they live at the address they have provided. This will generally mean seeing more than one document. Ideally one should include a photograph and the person's name and the other should include their name and address. Documents that are useful to prove identity are:

● passport;

● driving licence;

● identity card (if from a country that has them); or

● references.

8.46 To prove that the person is resident where they claim to be it is useful to see:

● utility bills;

● a bank statement;

● check the electoral roll; or

● check the telephone directory.

8.47 Once these checks have been carried out and a photocopy of the document concerned has been placed on file the identity checking requirements have been met. However, it should be borne in mind that any criminal seeking to launder money will have no difficulty at all in satisfying the requirement that they produce such documents. They will either have fake or real documents in the name they are using. This is not a reason for being cavalier about checking identity, but it does mean that possession of 'proof' is not a reason for lower a firm's guard when it comes to suspicious activity by a client.

8.48 It is also possible to run computer checks on a client's identity. There are specialist firms offering such services for a fee and some claim to be able to determine whether someone is a 'politically exposed person' (see below). These systems are useful but it should be borne in mind that organised crime groups and terrorists will create false identities for members and operate them for many years. The longer a false identity has been in existence the more difficult it will be to determine that it is not genuine. In addition, the existence of a name on a computerised checklist will not always provide proof that a person is or is not who they claim. Even where issues are raised by such checks the client may be asked to provide further evidence, eg, birth certificate or a certified copy thereof, but criminals will have no difficulty producing forged documents.

8.49 In the case of corporate clients a company search will have to be done to ascertain the owners and directors of the company. The position regarding corporate groups is not fully clear. The safest approach is to also check a controlling company and any company in the same group with which the client company is intimately connected, eg, if it trades heavily with it. Where a client company is part of a group the group structure should be determined. In a few cases the structure itself may look suspicious. Generally speaking the structure should either articulate the history of the group or reflect the current activities. If a group does appear

unusual it is worth asking the clients as such structures are sometimes created to maximise transfer pricing opportunities and so minimise tax bills with international groups. If such a rationale is provided a letter from the client's accountants should be sought on the point.

8.50   A problem can arise where the client is foreign and as a result the relevant documents are not written in a language that anyone in the firm can read. Here the documents should be translated by a certified notary who offers translation from that language. Their certified translation has the same legal status as the original.

Know your client

8.51   Clearly it will not be possible to spot a suspicious transaction unless the solicitor understands the nature of clients' business activities. Suspicions will normally be aroused by a transaction being incongruous given what is known of the client concerned, or incongruous for businesses of that type. Banks, financial institutions, solicitors, accountants etc are thus required to know their customer.

8.52   The Proceeds of Crime Act 2002 requires that a suspicious transaction report be made as soon as possible once a person acting in the course of their trade, profession or business knows or suspects that someone is engaged in drug money laundering. This is discussed below.

Systems to prevent money laundering

8.53   The Regulations also require that a firm should engage in appropriate staff training, have systems in place to facilitate the spotting and reporting of laundering and also to have a money laundering reporting officer to organise this.

Internal reporting procedures

8.54   It is necessary for firms to have in place systems whereby suspicious transactions are reported to 'the nominated officer', in normal parlance, the money laundering reporting officer. That person has the responsibility of ascertaining whether or not the report made to them really does give rise to suspicion and if so they must make a report to the NCA as soon as is practicable.

8.55   When a disclosure is made the party making the report is immune from being sued for breach of confidentiality by the client concerned[1]. It will also be necessary for the party making the suspicious transaction report to enquire of the NCA whether it is acceptable to continue with the transaction. In practice they will normally give consent for the transaction to continue, as they will wish to observe the transaction and compile evidence as to what may be going on. Without such consent, the party who has become suspicious may well be committing an offence such as aiding and abetting a criminal offence or being an accessory after the fact.

1 Proceeds of Crime Act 2002, s 337.

8.56   Problems have arisen where the grounds for suspicion arise at the moment of completion of an arrangement, eg, where the purchaser suddenly indicates that they wish to pay in cash. In such cases the report should be made to the NCA and highlighted as urgent. A follow up call could also be made. The NCA have indicated that in such cases they will do what they can to expedite a response.

4th EU LAUNDERING DIRECTIVE

8.57   At the time of writing[1] a 4th draft EU Directive on money laundering is in circulation. It is anticipated that all those covered by the regime will have to maintain written laundering risk assessment, policies and procedures and create and operate a process which should test their effectiveness. This should be implemented in a manner which is appropriate for the size of the firm. The concept of politically exposed persons is to be extended to include beneficial owners and those with high level appointments in the UK. Enhanced measures should be maintained for 18 months after the PEP leaves office rather than the current 12. There is the probability that simplified due diligence procedures will be reduced, though this may be left to national parliaments to decide. Other elements include clarification of what records should be kept, minimum sanctions for breach and firms being required to hold accurate and up to date information on beneficial owners.

1   December 2013.

WHAT IS 'SUSPICION'?

8.58   Until relatively recently there was no case law in this country on the nature of suspicion on either the current legislation or its predecessors and sadly, despite the issue of suspicion and the reporting of suspicious transactions having been an issue in this country since 1986 there has been no effort made in any relevant statute or statutory instrument to define it. The nature of 'suspicion' until it was finally given a legal definition in the context of laundering by Longmore LJ in *NatWest v HM Customs with the SOCA an intervening party* where he adopted the suggestion in *R v Da Silva*[1] and applied it to both civil and criminal law:

The person must:

> 'think there is a possibility, which is more than fanciful, that the relevant facts exist. This is subject to the further requirement that the suspicion so formed should be of a settled nature.'

There will no doubt be future legal debate surrounding the meaning of 'fanciful' and 'settled nature'. Nonetheless, matters are considerable clearer than they were before. The definition however is a very wide one. It requires those who are regulated to engage in surveillance and reporting requirements on the basis of any activity by one of their clients wherever the suspicion that they may be acting illegally is 'more than fanciful'. This does have worrying connotations in the context of human rights.

1   (2006) EWCA Crim 1654.

8.59 Issues to consider in determining whether a matter is suspicious include:

- the speed with which cash is being transferred to another form of money and to another place. In particular is money, and in particular cash paid into an account and then paid out at unusual speed?

- whether the routing of the funds involve a country with close contacts to drug production, processing or the laundering of proceeds.

- whether the arrangement one which does not make sense from a business point of view. In particular is it an arrangement that did not appear to be designed to make a profit? This is not always an element however. Many criminal organisations now attempt to utilise the laundering process to make a profit, eg, by utilising funds to buy goods which are then re-sold at a mark-up.

- whether the arrangement involve offshore shell companies, trusts and tax haven banks when the purpose of their involvement does not fit in with normal business practice for the type of transaction taking place, Unfortunately, criminals will have constructed their finances to replicate legitimate business transactions and these in turn can optimise their tax position on an international basis by engaging on off-shore transfer pricing.

- whether the transaction involve cash flows in and out of countries where the banking system is heavily permeated by organised crime, eg, Russia. If it does careful note should be made of the exchange rates at which the currency concerned changes from one currency to another. If these appear to be other than market rates, the transaction should be regarded as particularly suspicious.

Note should be taken of structures that seem to be designed to make it difficult for outsiders to ascertain exactly what is going on. An abnormally complex structure of companies should arouse suspicion. There may be issues relating to the client that raise suspicion. This is only likely to occur with the less professional criminals. The rest will have little difficulty in maintaining a credible appearance. The various professional bodies have all produced detailed guidance notes on this area and the relevant ones should be studied.

Making a suspicious transaction report

8.60 Once a suspicious transaction report has been submitted, the NCA will then inform the person who has made the report whether it is acceptable to continue with the transaction. The NCA normally prefer the transaction to continue to facilitate their observation of the transaction and to provide them with the opportunity to analyse the events concerned. It is necessary to obtain consent to act otherwise the party who made the report will almost certainly be committing a criminal offence such as aiding and abetting or being an accessory after the fact.

1 See Proceeds of Crime Act 2002, s 333 discussed above at **8.24**.

8.61 In cases where there are slight grounds for suspicion but the person concerned does not feel there is sufficient evidence to make a suspicious transaction report, it is a good idea to make a file note of the reasons for concern. It may be that as time goes by a succession of other minor issues may arise and eventually there be sufficient grounds for making a report.

OTHER CASE LAW

8.62   There have been recent cases which have clarified how the relevant law operates. A number of others have been discussed at **8.12**, **8.17** and **8.20** above.

Squirrel Ltd v National Westminster Bank Ltd[1]

8.63   The Chancery Division of the High Court heard this decision which involved a bank account that the bank said it was forced to block because of s 340(3). It regarded the arrangements as reportable under s 328. The bank made a report and then blocked the account but felt it could not explain the reasons to the account holder because of the tipping off provision in s 333.

1 (2005) Times, 25 May.

8.64   The Court held that were the bank to have operated the account once they were suspicious they might be committing an offence under s 328. The meaning of the word 'suspicious' was considered and it was held that in this situation a bank did not have powers of investigation and therefore the suspicion did not need any wider justification to be reasonable.

8.65   The combined effect of ss 328, 335 and 338 was to force a bank that made a suspicious transaction report to report suspicions and then not move the funds or property concerned for either seven working days or if notice of refusal was sent, 31 working days from receipt of that refusal. The customer could not be told. Squirrel Ltd who had brought the case for an explanation as to why their account was frozen could not be informed.

8.66   This followed the two cases of *C v S*[1] and *Bank of Scotland v A Ltd*[2] on the earlier legislation. In the latter case the Court of Appeal provided five key guidelines governing the steps a firm or bank may take in dealing with its clients' money:

- freezing orders would not normally be granted;

- where there is a dispute over whether a payment can be made out of the account or a disclosure be made to a client the firm or bank should discuss the matter with the Serious Fraud Office. If this does not lead to resolution an application should be made for interim declaratory relief;

- the bank should consider whether it is worth contesting actions brought by clients in such cases;

- where such a claim is contested consideration should be given as to whether the judge who hears the proceedings should also be the one from whom guidance is sought; and

- if the firm or bank follows the court's guidelines it should not be at risk of bring in breach of the criminal law.

1 [1999] 2 All ER 343.
2 [2001] EWCA Civ 52.

8.67   In the vast majority of cases this should not be necessary. The firm or bank will be able to make a report to the NCA and then act according to its instructions. If this leads to instructions not to release the funds or a response cannot be obtained from the NCA in time and the client then objects, the firm or bank will be unable to inform them as to why. It will then normally be up to the client to decide on the next step.

Fitzpatrick and others v Metropolitan Police[1]

8.68   Two clients of a firm of solicitors were connected with a debt of £33,000 owed from one to the other. The first client was arrested for drug related offences and the other was known to the firm to be someone with a background of drug related criminal activity. The existence of the debt owed by the arrested party became apparent to the firm at a police interview. The firm then submitted a suspicion transaction report in relation to property dealings by the first client, some of which was property subject to a restraint order.

1 14 February 2012.

8.69   The first client concerned then left the firm and instructed another firm of solicitors and in due course the second client instructed the firm to recover the £33,000 debt. The firm made no enquiry about the source of this money, nor did they seek a variation of the restraint order which covered the property which had been purchased with it. They also then repeatedly tried to contact the first client, but rather than do so through his new solicitors, as would have been normal practice they sought to do so directly and in due course gave him a power of attorney to sign so that his father could sign across the property.

8.70   The police then became suspicious as a result of these activities and obtained a warrant to search the solicitors' offices. They arrested both the solicitor involved and the money laundering reporting officer. The solicitors claimed that they had merely been in the preparatory stages of transaction and that they intended to seek consent from the Serious Organised Crime Agency (the forerunners of the NCA) before they used the power of attorney. The case against the solicitors was dropped, but they then claimed that the behaviour of the police was a breach of their human rights.

8.71   Their action failed in the High Court as the court determined that there was sufficient evidence to give rise to a reasonable suspicion that their behaviour amounted to becoming concerned in an arrangement under s 328. That being the case the behaviour of the police was legal.

R v Saik[1]

8.72   In this case Mr Saik was prosecuted for the offence of conspiracy to launder money. He operated a bureaux de change and had been changing foreign currency suspecting that the money concerned represented the proceeds of crime. The House of Lords held that whilst the offences of money laundering require suspicion on reasonable grounds for a success-ful prosecution, one of conspiracy to launder can only succeed where it is demonstrated that the conspirators knew that the property being dealt with represented the proceeds of crime. Thus proving suspicion is suf-ficient for a conviction of laundering money, but if several acts are pros-ecuted together as conspiracy matters become more complex as there then needs to be evidence of a conspiracy from which inferences as to the state of mind of the accused can be drawn[2].

1 [2006] UKHL 18.
2 Para 63 *supra*.

8.73   The only offences under the Proceeds of Crime Act arise where 'suspicion' is the basis or prosecutions are sections 328 (entering into an arrangement) and 330, 331 and 332 (failure to report). Thus, as a result of this case it is clear that a prosecution for conspiracy to commit one of these offences will not be sustainable where the evidence is limited to the accused having mere suspicion rather than knowledge.

CIVIL LAW ISSUES

Introduction

8.74   It is not only the criminal law and regulatory issues that pose a threat when an institution launders funds, there is also the potential threat of civil proceedings to recover them. For this to occur there must be a real owner of the money acting in pursuit of it. Two problems occur: the concept of real owner is widely defined and the area of law concerned is unclear.

8.75   The position is complicated by the doctrine of constructive trusts. These occur where a court decides to determine after the event that a state of affairs shall be treated as though the parties had set up a trust. Thus, the obligations of a trustee can be imposed on someone who had not thought of themselves as being in that position. This was traditionally done where someone was behaving in an illegal or immoral fashion. It has also been used to create liability by creating a situation where the trustee is then held to have knowingly assisted in breaching the trust or having know-ingly been in receipt of funds from one who has.

8.76   This issue often arises because of the doctrine of tracing. This is an old rule of law that permits someone to pursue money they have lost through the wrongful behaviour of another into the place where it now resides. The common law rule of tracing is of limited use because of old case law that said that once money that had been taken from someone had been mixed by a recipient with their own money in a purse, the true owner could no longer use tracing because it was no longer possible to tell which money was which. However, equitable tracing got round this prob-lem by applying relevant maxims of equity which resulted in the court assuming that anyone in possession the property of another would act to try and repay it. Thus, any money they still had would be treated as the injured party's funds. Likewise if they spent all the money, the first money received back would be held for the benefit of the injured person. The only situation that defeated equitable tracing was where the money had been paid through an overdrawn bank account as there the bank would have been a creditor for the overdraft.

8.77   To obtain equitable tracing it is necessary to prove that the funds were subject to a trust or that there was a fiduciary relationship. Thus those who have lost funds usually wish to try and obtain a court declaration that the money was subject to a constructive trust as it will not normally have been not subject to one in an ordinary sense.

8.78   There is also a jurisdictional problem in that, generally speaking, only those jurisdictions that recognise trusts will allow equitable tracing into their jurisdiction. That said it is normally possible to trace through such a jurisdiction into one that does recognise trusts. As a general rule it is the common law countries (generally, former British colonies) together with some others that recognise the concept of trusts.

Grounds for Constructive Trusteeship

8.79   There are two basic grounds used by the courts:

*   knowing receipt; and
*   knowing assistance.

8.80   The classic exposition of English law on the point was stated by Selborone LC in *Barnes v Addy*[1]:

> 'strangers are not to be made constructive trustees...unless (they) receive and become chargeable with some part of the trust property or unless they assist with knowledge that it is a dishonest and fraudulent design on the part of the trustees.'

1 (1874) 9 Ch App 244, 43 LJ Ch 513, 22 WR 505, 30 LT 4.

8.81   Unfortunately the cases that have followed have left this area of law in an unclear state. Perhaps the crucial case is *Royal Brunei Airlines Sdn Bhd v Tan*[1]. Here the airline had appointed Borneo Leisure Travel as its agent for selling seats and cargo space on the airline. The contract stated that Borneo Leisure was to hold any money received on trust for the airline. However, instead of paying these funds into a trust account for their principal Borneo Leisure paid funds received into their own account. The person controlling Borneo Leisure then allowed the company to use the money for its own purposes. Eventually the firm became insolvent and the airline appeared to have lost its money. It then brought legal proceedings against the managing director and main owner of Borneo Leisure alleging that he had knowingly assisted in breach of trust. He claimed that there was only mismanagement, which did not give rise to personal liability. The Privy Council stated that there were certain key issues:

(1)   the liability of an accessory should apply regardless of whether the trustee and the third party have both displayed dishonesty or whether the trustee was innocent;

(2)   that liability could be imposed regardless of whether the third party had procured the breach or dishonestly assisted in it; and

(3)   that the key issue is the state of mind of the third party not the trustee.

1 [1995] 2 AC 378, [1995] 3 All ER 97, [1995] WLR 64, [1995] BCC 899, [1995] 27 LS Gas R 33, [1995] NLJR 888, PC.

8.82   In other words, where someone interferes with a trust and deprives the beneficiary of some or all of their property, the true owner should be able to get it back.

8.83   The Privy Council also approved some earlier cases which could be of particular concern for financial institutions who have laundered funds. One of these cases was *Fyler v Fyler*[1]. Here a firm of solicitors had put funds from a trust into an investment which was unauthorised. They were held liable even though they had believed that the investment would be of benefit to the beneficiary. The other was *Eaves v Hickson*[2]. Here the trustees made a payment on the basis of a forged document that was presented to them and which according to the judge would have fooled anyone not looking for forgery. The person who had produced the forgery was made liable to repay the money in priority to any claim being made against the trustees. However, had they not got the resources to pay the trustees would then have been liable.

1 (1841) 3 Beav 550, 5 Jur 187.
2 (1861) 30 Beav 136, 7 Jur NS 1297, 132 RR 213, 10 WR 29, 5 LT 598.

8.84   Liability was stated to arise where the person concerned was dishonest rather than unconscionable in their conduct. This consisted of not acting as an honest person would and the test was objective. Interestingly, negligence was held to be insufficient to create liability.

Knowing receipt

8.85   There is a dichotomy between two legal issues in many of the cases. This arises between knowing receipt of funds and liability for breach of fiduciary duty. Knowing receipt occurs when property has been received knowingly in breach of trust. Fiduciary duty is a generic term to cover one of a number of situations that occur where someone is held to have particular obligations to another party because of their relationship with them. There does not need to be a trust (though a trust does give rise to a fiduciary relationship) but similar obligations then occur. Again a party who had laundered funds when a fiduciary relationship arose could find themselves faced with a civil claim. To provide such a right the courts have stretched the doctrine further and further over recent years, although surprisingly a thief is not automatically a fiduciary of the true owner.

8.86   The legal consequences of the two states of affairs are different. In cases of knowing receipt an action in equity can be brought to recover the full amount including any capital growth that has occurred since the recipient received it. On the other hand in cases of knowing assistance the liability is for the total amount lost plus simple interest.

8.87   Many of the issues were considered in *Lipkin Gorman v Karpnale Ltd*[1] where a solicitor became an obsessive gambler. He started gambling with clients' money. The firm's bank noticed that client account cheques were being paid to a casino but did nothing about it. A claim was brought for constructive trust, quasi-contract, negligence and conversion. The House of Lords held that a recipient of stolen money who was unjustly enriched was under an obligation to pay the same amount back to the victim. There is however a degree of protection for the recipient if he can show that his position had changed as a result of the arrangements and that he would lose out by having to pay the money back. This defence is of value to the financial extent of the change of position that has taken place. Unfortunately the only issue that was considered on appeal to the House of Lords was a claim for money had and received. However, the Court of Appeal stated that a bank could not be liable to its customer as a constructive trustee unless it was in breach of its contractual duty of care to that customer.

1 [1992] 4 All ER 409.

8.88   In *Agip (Africa) Ltd v Jackson*[1] a firm of accountants had been acting for a fraudulent client. The accountants received funds from their clients and then passed them on as per instructions received. The true owners eventually appeared and claimed the funds back. As there was no financial sense in pursuing the clients the wronged parties sued the accountants. It was held that they were not liable as they had not received the funds for their own benefit. However, it was stated that were a bank to receive funds to reduce an overdraft it would be receiving the funds for their own benefit.

1 [1992] 4 All ER 385.

8.89   In *Polly Peck International plc v Nadir and others* (*No 2*[1]) a claim for knowing receipt and knowing assistance was brought against Asil Nadir and the Central Bank of Northern Cyprus claiming that a huge amount of money had been wrongly transferred out of the company concerned. The Bank had received the funds for foreign currency contracts and in the course of this had not made enquiries about the source of the funds. The Turkish Cypriot bank concerned had £45 million on deposit with Midland Bank in London. The company's administrator sought an order freezing the bank account. The court held that the key issue was whether or not the bank had been involved in any dishonesty or want of probity in that they had actual or constructive notice that they were receiving misapplied funds. The bank did not need to be shown to have been acting fraudulently. One of the judges felt that it was a case of knowing assistance and that the bank would only be liable if they received the money for their own use and benefit. As they received the money as agents and accounted for it to their principals he did not believe that this requirement had been satisfied. Another of the judges however believed that most of the funds had been received as banker because the bank received the funds in their own right as a result of a currency transfer and therefore the issue was one of knowing receipt. The appropriate measure to apply was therefore whether there was knowledge that trust funds had been misapplied.

1 [1992] 4 All ER 769, [1992] 2 Lloyd's Rep 238, [1992] NLJR 671, CA.

Holding property to the order of another

8.90 Sometimes called 'holding in a ministerial capacity' this arises when one person holds property belonging to someone else and mixes it with their own property. This is beyond 'knowing receipt' as discussed above unless an agent is setting up their own title to the funds. Two issues arise here. The first is the principle that an agent who uses their principle's money in good faith to pay off a debt owed by the principal can raise the defence of 'payment over'. In *Holland v Russell*[1] an agent paid money to another as agent for a ship owner whose ship had sunk. It later transpired that the policy was void for non-disclosure. By then the agent of the ship owner had paid some of the money over to his principal. The court held that the action would lie against the principal not the agent for this sum as the money had been properly paid over.

1 (1861) 1 B & S 424; affd B & S 14, 32 LJQB 297, 2 New Rep 188, 11 WR 757, 8 LT 468.

8.91 However, in *Springfield Acres* (in liquidation) *v Abacus* (Hong Kong) *Ltd*[1] the defence failed. A company had successfully sued Springfield Acres for a large sum. Whilst the claim was waiting to be settled, Springfield's assets were transferred to another company outside the jurisdiction. This money was then advanced to another company via a solicitor's trust account. These funds were then transferred to the defendants who in turn paid them on to other parties. In reality these transactions were for the benefit of one man who was the major shareholder of Springfield and whose family were the beneficiaries of the trusts where the money ended up. The claim succeeded as the defendants were knowingly involved. It should be noted that this is a New Zealand case and only of persuasive value in English law.

1 [1994] NZLR 502.

8.92 In *El Ajou v Dollar Land Holdings plc (No 2)*[1] the plaintiff had been defrauded of money. The money concerned ended up being used as part finance for a building project in England and a claim was then brought against the building company claiming knowing receipt. It was held that a claim could only succeed if enquiry was not made in a situation where an honest and reasonable man would have done so.

1 [1995] 2 All ER 213.

8.93 In *Cowan de Groot Properties Ltd v Eagle Trust plc*[1] a claim was brought following an allegation that the directors of a company had sold some of its property at an undervalue. The purchaser was alleged to have been in knowing receipt. The case is not entirely in line with the others but it does appear to accept the doctrine that a defendant's knowledge will be determined on the basis of what a reasonable person would have learned.

1 [1992] 4 All ER 700, [1991] BCLC 1045.

Suspicious transaction reports and civil liability

8.94 When deciding on how to interpret suspicious behaviour there are problems in the context of civil liability. In theory it can depend on the party concerned failing to carry out a professional level of 'knowing their client' or failing to report suspicious transactions. In practice we seem dangerously close to being in a situation where the courts impose a constructive trust wherever it suits them in order to recover illicit funds. The solution is for firms to be scrupulous in maintaining the requirements of the law and their professional bodies as minimum. Wherever they are in doubt as to whether to make a suspicious transaction report they should do so. From the point of view of both criminal liability and constructive trusteeship they should be safe. However this last issue can then arise in a secondary way.

8.95　A suspicious transaction report may have been made internally in a firm to its money laundering reporting officer, or an appropriate report made to the NCA. Once this is done it could be argued that the firm is knowingly in receipt of illegal funds. Once a report has been made the firm will normally request permission from the body to whom they made that report before they act further. In most cases this will be the course of action which the criminal law enforcement bodies will prefer, so that they have the opportunity to observe the transaction and the client. There is no risk to the firm from the criminal courts in such cases, but neither is there a guarantee that the knowing receipt issue will cease to be a problem. It is possible that such a firm could still be held to be a constructive trustee, a risk exacerbated by the firm potentially ending up in a Catch 22 situation. If they refuse to act on the client's instructions whilst waiting for confirmation from the criminal authorities that they can continue, they may be effectively tipping off the client. If however they act on such instructions there may be fear that they could be held to be a constructive trustee. This now seems to be an over cautious interpretation of the position. One High Court judge, Coleman J stated that it was wholly unrealistic that an institution which had followed the relevant case law would find itself held a constructive trustee[1]. Nonetheless he may have missed a key point. If the firm has operated within the laundering laws but accepted, handled and in due course parted company with money in circumstances where it was in 'knowing receipt' regarding the funds, the very suspicious transaction report that protects the firm under the laundering laws would be the evidence that they were suspicious and therefore were acting in knowing receipt!

1 *Hosni Tayeb v HSBC and Al Farsan International* [2004] EWHC 1529 Comm.

THE WOLFSBERG PRINCIPLES

Why were they created?

8.96　Without pressure from regulators or prompting governments a group of international banks created a set of codes which they have publicly issued and to which they have publicly sworn allegiance. The first step occurred in late 2000 when a number of leading banks[1], acting in co-ordination with Transparency International, agreed to take on board a set of general principles to facilitate improving the standards applied in combating money laundering where private banking relationships are concerned. They also accepted as a formal principle, that the responsibility for this rested with the management of the banks.

1 ABN Amro Bank NV, Santander Central Hispano SA, Bank of Tokyo-Mitsubishi, Barclays, Citigroup, Credit Suisse Group, Deutsche Bank AG, Goldman Sachs, HSBC, J P Morgan Chase, Société Générale and UBS AG. ABN Amro and Credit Suisse have since left.

8.97   The background to these banks acting as they did arose in part because of the influence of the Basel Committee of Banking Supervisors[1] and the Working Group on Bribery at the OECD. This was taken further by a specialised group within the Financial Stability Forum[2]. Transparency International also became involved by enlisting the support of a small number of banks in a programme to prevent the abuse of financial centres by launderers. Concerns were also developing amongst some of the banks that money laundering could damage their reputation[3]. As a result of this two of the banks who were later to make up the Wolfsberg Group exchanged their internal compliance regulations. This led to a larger meeting of banks to take matters a step further.

1 Bank for International Settlements: Basel Committee on Banking Supervision: Prevention of Criminal Use of the Banking System for the Purpose of Money Laundering, Statement of Principles, December 1988.
2 Financial Stability Forum, Working Group on Offshore Financial Centres Report, April 2000.
3 Minority Staff Report for Permanent Subcommittee on Investigations; Hearings on Private Banking and Money Laundering: A Case Study of Opportunities and Vunerabilities.

8.98   The resulting Principles (named after the castle in Switzerland where the working sessions took place) were then publicised in the hope that other financial institutions will follow them. Since then the original Principles were amended in 2002 and a second set of Principles issued to deal with the potential abuse of correspondent banking relationships. Early in 2003 a further set of Principles were issued with the view to suppressing terrorist finances and finally in May 2012 a set of regulations was issued for private banking[1].

1 www.wolfsberg-principles.com.

8.99   One reason for the creation of the Principles was to create a common standard to reduce the uncertainties and complexities resulting from running multi-national banks across disparate laundering regimes. This is facilitated by the fact that the banks concerned make up over 60% of the world market in private banking and around 50% of the market share in each of the key offshore financial centres[1]. A set of common requirements operated across the jurisdictions in which an international bank operates, even though more onerous than that imposed in any of the states in which the banks concerned carry on business, makes the running of the banks much simpler and thus reduces risk management costs. In part the Principles were also driven by the belief that the standards required in the U.S. at the time were insufficient, particularly after the Congress threw out one Presidential attempt to tighten up the law[2].

1 See Peith and Aiolfi, '*The Private Sector becomes Active: The Wolfsberg Process*' in A Practitioner's Guide to International Money Laundering Law and Regulation, Ed Clark and Burrell, City and Financial 2003 at p 273.
2 International Money Laundering and Foreign Anti-Corruption Act 2000, House of Representatives Report 106/2728, Committee on Banking and Financial Services, Chairman, Senator Leach.

8.100   The banks involved had become increasingly concerned that the enormous quantities of money laundering currently taking place could pose a threat to them. This could come about as a result of it becoming public knowledge that a bank has laundered money. If the bank concerned has maintained good standards there is still likely to be damage to reputation, even where the regulator does not believe that disciplinary steps are warranted. In many cases however they will. There are clear signs that the regulators had been becoming both more assertive and proactive in this field[1]. As the Basel Committee pointed out[2]:

> 'Reputational risk poses a major threat to banks, since the nature of their business requires maintaining the confidence of depositors, creditors and the general marketplace. Reputational risk is defined as the potential that adverse publicity regarding a bank's business...will cause a loss of confidence in the integrity of the institution...They need to protect themselves by means of continual vigilance through an effective know your client programme.'

1 (2001) Financial Times, March 24, p 3.
2 'Customer Due Diligence for Banks.' October 2001.

8.101   However, paradoxically the Basel Committee have excluded reputational risk from the prudential regime, the argument being that there is no accurate way of quantifying it. It can be countered however[1] that there is no real evidence of banks suffering measurable financial loss as a result of damage to reputation being caused by a money laundering scandal. UK examples include a number of leading banks being fined for money laundering failings only to see their share price rise! In the longer run though there could be the danger of a systemic consequence where the general damage to the image of banks starts to reflect such crises.

1 See for example Emma Codd 'Reputational Risk' in 'A Practitioner's Guide...' *supra*, see footnote 1 above).

8.102   In the UK the FSA (now FCA) have adopted a similar approach to that seen in the Wolfsberg principles. In Consultation Paper 142 it stated:

> '...a firm must take reasonable care to establish and maintain effective systems and controls for compliance with the applicable requirements and standards under the regulatory system and for countering the risk that the firm might be used to perpetrate financial crime.'

8.103   Rather worryingly in this context was an FSA (now the FCA) investigation into banks[1].Four of the main deficiencies that were found related to this. They were:

- inadequate supervision by senior management of account opening procedures by higher risk customers;

- insufficient checks on the identity of the beneficial owners of companies;

- too much reliance on introductions by existing customers; and

- insufficient understanding of the source of customers' wealth.

Recent disciplinary steps against a number of banks both in the UK and US suggest that until recently matters were worse than this.

1 FSA Press Release, March 2001.

8.104 Another key element in the formation of the Wolfsberg Principles has been the perceived threat of formal regulation on the subject. Traditionally, when faced with this banks have tended to adopt self-imposed codes. This way they provide the government or regulator concerned with enough of what is perceived to be required for imposed regulation to cease being a political imperative. The Code is then drafted in a way that the banks find acceptable. In the United Kingdom the Code of Banking Practice adopted at the time of the Jack Report and the more recent Mortgage Code of Practice are cases in point[1]. It might be added that these only really delayed rather than pre-empted regulation.

1 Though this was superseded by events as a result of lending and administering in relation to mortgages on residential property becoming covered by the FCA regime.

8.105 There is also an element of safety in numbers. If the banks in general agree on an approach that appears to satisfy or exceed what regulators are asking for, it provides evidence that the banks taking part are engaged in good practice. This inevitably creates pressure for others to join in.

THE PRIVATE BANKING PRINCIPLES (May 2012 version)

Client acceptance: general guidelines

1.1 General

8.106 The bank will endeavor to accept only those clients whose source of wealth and funds can be reasonably established to be legitimate. The primary responsibility for this lies with the private banker who sponsors the client for acceptance. Mere fulfilment of internal review procedures does not relieve the private banker of this basic responsibility. Bank policy will specify what such responsibility and sponsorship entail.

One aim of this is to deal with the issue of criminals in government who steal and then launder the assets of their country and hide them as a personal investment fund. In addition there are others, particularly criminals involved in the drug trade, illegal arms dealing and people smuggling; to name the biggest operators. The Principle 1.1 has the weakness of only being aimed at private clients. In most instances those wishing to launder large amounts will have no difficulty in establishing a network of companies throughout the world and then get the payments that enter the western banking system to be made out to companies in that group. In the case of corrupt government officials receiving bribes, the bribe will often be paid into a corporate bank account which appears to have no connection with the official in any event. The person receiving the bribe will nominate the account signatories and thus be able to indirectly access the account.

1.2 Identification and verification of identity

1.2.1 Client identity

8.107 The bank will establish the identity of its clients and beneficial owners prior to establishing business relationship with such persons.

Identity is generally established by obtaining the name, date of birth (in the case of individuals), address and such further information that may be required by the laws of the relevant jurisdictions.

This is perhaps all that can be reasonably be expected of a bank, but the effectiveness of such checks is rather limited due to the relative ease with which false documents and real documents in false names can be obtained. (See **8.45–8.50** above). In addition, how does a bank ascertain that the beneficial owner is who they appear to be? It is a relatively straightforward matter for one person to create a false identity or to hide behind the identity of another. The longer such a false identity has been in existence the more difficult it becomes to determine that it is indeed false. A bank cannot become, nor be expected to become a detective agency. The consequence of this is that Principle 1.2 may give a false sense of security to the bank which has taken this step and to others which deal with it. The recent development of identity checking software only makes a slight difference here. Long term false identities and retrospective falsifying of data can still cause false identities to appear genuine.

1.2.2 Verification of identity

8.108   The bank will take reasonable measures to verify identity when establishing a business relationship as noted below, subject to applicable local requirements.

–   Natural persons: identity will be verified to the bank's satisfaction on the basis of official identity papers or other reliable, independent source documents, data, or information as may be appropriate under the circumstances.

–   Corporations, partnerships, foundations: identity will be verified on the basis of documentary evidence of due organization and existence.

–   Trusts: identity will be verified on the basis of appropriate evidence of formation and existence or similar documentation. The identity of the trustees will be established and verified.

The problem here is the general availability of good forged documents and the relative ease in which it is possible to obtain documents in the wrong name. Apparently safe identity documents such as passports, national identity cards and driving licences are no real guide to identity. To give an idea of the scale of the problem, in the United Kingdom there are also estimated to be around one and a half million more national insurance numbers being used than should be the case.

The corporation checking requirement will tend to reduce the number of off the shelf companies created specifically to launder money. However, it may well also accelerate the market in buying small, relatively dormant companies that are a number of years old and less likely to attract suspicion. There is evidence that this has been happening in the West Indies. Recent changes in ownership and radical changes in the financial behaviour of a company following acquisition should thus attract close investigation. Clearly this is an area where experience and staff training could make a vital difference.

Does the client's corporate group structure make sense in terms of the business transactions being carried on? If not, may it be explicable in terms of the historical development of the corporate group. If neither is the case then the reaction should be one of suspicion and the banker concerned should contact the money laundering reporting officer.

A more difficult problem will apply with investment companies. Namely, whose money is being invested? In the case of well known fund managers and investment companies, 'know your client' provisions will normally suffice. However, in cases of firms who are not already known, 'know your client' is going to involve knowing your client's client; or at least being satisfied as to the intermediary's identity checking requirements.

The requirement regarding trusts is going to cause particular problems. It is never going to be possible to be certain whether the trustees are running the trust themselves or as a front for others. In some cases, for example the blind trusts available in Cyprus, the vehicle itself seems to have been designed to facilitate this very state of affairs.

1.2.3 Beneficial owner

8.109   Beneficial ownership, for AML purposes, must be established for all accounts. Beneficial owners will ordinarily include the individuals; (i) who generally have ultimate control through ownership or other means over the funds in the account; and/or (ii) who are the ultimate source of funds for the account and whose source of wealth should be subject to due diligence. Mere signature authority does not necessarily constitute control for these purposes. The meaning of beneficial ownership for purposes of determining who should be subject to due diligence is dependent on the circumstances and due diligence must be done on all beneficial owners identified in applying the following principles:

- Natural persons: when the account is in the name of an individual, the private banker must establish whether the client is acting on his/her own behalf. If doubt exists, the bank will establish the capacity in which and on whose behalf the accountholder is acting.

- Legal entities: where the client is a private investment company, the private banker will understand the structure of the company sufficiently to determine the provider of funds, the beneficial owner(s) of the assets held by the company and those with the power to give direction to the directors of the company. This principle applies regardless of whether the share capital is in registered or bearer form.

- Trusts: where the client is a trust, the private banker will understand the structure of the trust sufficiently to determine: (i) the provider of funds (eg settlor); (ii) those who have control over the funds (eg trustees); (iii) any persons or entities who have the power to remove the trustees; and (iv) the persons for whose benefit the trust is established.

- Partnerships: where the client is a partnership, the private banker will understand the structure of the partnership sufficiently to determine the provider of funds and the general partners.

- Foundations: where the client is a foundation, the private banker will understand the structure of the foundation sufficiently to determine the provider(s) of funds and how the foundation is managed.

- Unincorporated associations: the above principles apply to unincorporated associations.

In each of the above cases, the private banker will make a reasonable judgment as to the need for further due diligence.

Local law may characterise beneficial owners by reference to specific minimum levels of ownership.

The identity of each beneficial owner will be established and, as appropriate, verified unless the identity is previously verified in accordance with the beneficial owner's role as a client. Identity will be verified to the bank's satisfaction on the basis of official identity papers or other reliable, independent source documents, data, or information as may be appropriate under the circumstances. In the event verification is based on identity papers, copies of such identity papers should be obtained.

'Beneficial ownership,' as that term may be used for other purposes, may have different meanings.

While this is an admirable sentiment it seems difficult to see how this is going to be achieved. Those with large amounts to launder should not find it difficult to hire people to front the transactions they need to engage in, and it will usually be impossible for the bank concerned to determine that this is the case. Many of the points made above will also apply here.

1.2.4 Intermediaries

8.110   The nature of the relationship of the bank with an intermediary depends on the type of intermediary involved: Introducing Intermediary: an introducing intermediary introduces clients to the bank, whereupon the introducing intermediary's clients become clients of the bank. The bank will generally obtain the same type of information with respect to an introduced client that would otherwise be obtained by the bank, absent the involvement of an introducing intermediary. The bank's policies will address the circumstances in, and the extent to, which, the bank may rely on the introducing intermediary in obtaining this information.

Managing Intermediary: a managing intermediary acts as a professional asset manager for another person and either: (i) is authorised to act in connection with an account that such person has with the bank (in which case the considerations noted above with respect to introducing intermediaries would apply); or (ii) is itself the accountholder with the bank, to be treated as the client of the bank.

The private banker will perform due diligence on the introducing or managing intermediary and establish, as appropriate, that the intermediary has relevant due diligence procedures for its clients, or a regulatory obligation to conduct such due diligence, that is satisfactory to the bank.

Where known, respectable intermediaries are involved this will not normally represent much of a problem. However, where the intermediary is not playing by the rules it will be almost impossible to determine the fact at this stage.

1.2.5 Powers of Attorney/Authorised Signers

8.111 The relationship between the holder of a power of attorney or another authorised signer, the accountholder and if different, the beneficial owner of the account, must be understood.

The identity of a holder of general powers over an account (such as the power to act as a signatory for the account) will be established and, as appropriate, verified.

As commented at **8.109** above this is not going to be easy to achieve if the client wishes to deceive the bank.

1.2.6 Practices for Walk in Clients and Electronic Banking Relationships

8.112 A bank will determine whether walk-in clients or relationships initiated through electronic channels require a higher degree of due diligence prior to account opening. The bank will specifically address measures to satisfactorily establish and verify the identity of non-face-to-face customers.

1.3 Due diligence

8.113 In addition to the information contemplated in 1.2, it is essential to collect and record information covering the client profile categories outlined in Appendix I.

Applying a risk based approach, the bank will corroborate the information set forth in Appendix I on the basis of documentary evidence or reliable sources. Unless other measures reasonably suffice to conduct the due diligence on a client (eg favourable and reliable references), a client will be met prior to account opening, at which time, if identity is verified on the basis of official identity documents, such documents will be reviewed.

The problem, as already discussed above, is that such information is not easy to determine. Taking references from other respectable institutions seems a sensible precaution but that institution itself will have had little real opportunity to determine the facts in cases where the client has an illegal source of funds. The source of the funds concerned will be hidden at the other side of a laundering trail where criminal funds are concerned. Meeting the client, or the person purporting to be them will rarely make a difference. In short, this rule proposes an approach that cannot easily achieve its aims.

1.4 Numbered or Alternate Name Accounts

8.114 Numbered or alternate name accounts will only be accepted if the bank has established the identity of the client and the beneficial owner.

These accounts must be open to a level of scrutiny by the bank's appropriate control layers equal to the level of scrutiny applicable to other client accounts. Wire transfers from these accounts must reflect the true name of the accountholder.

This is a sensible precaution but as already seen above the identity checking itself has limited chance of successfully determining the person's real identity where criminal funds are involved.

1.5 Concentration Accounts

8.115 The bank will not permit the use of its internal non-client accounts (sometimes referred to as 'concentration' accounts) to prevent association of the identity of a client with the movement of funds on the client's behalf, ie, the bank will not permit the use of such internal accounts in a manner that would prevent the bank from appropriately monitoring the client's account activity.

1.6 Oversight responsibility

8.116 There will be a requirement that new clients, subject to a risk based approach, be approved by at least one person other than the private banker.

This is a sensible precaution because it will be a great deal more difficult for criminals to either bribe or mislead two successive members of staff than one. That said the comments on the difficulty of determining fake identity discussed above apply here as well.

2   Client Acceptance: Situations requiring Additional Diligence/ Attention; Prohibited Customers

2.1   Prohibited Customers

8.117 The bank will specify categories of customers that it will not accept or maintain.

2.2   General

8.118 In its internal policies, the bank must define categories of persons whose circumstances warrant enhanced due diligence. This will typically be the case where the circumstances are likely to pose a higher than average risk to a bank.

2.3   Indicators

8.119 The circumstances of the following categories of persons are indicators for defining them as requiring Enhanced Due Diligence:

- Persons residing in and/or having funds sourced from countries identified by credible sources as having inadequate AML standards or representing high risk for crime and corruption.

- Persons engaged in types of economic or business activities or sectors known to be susceptible to money laundering.

Persons not deemed to warrant enhanced due diligence may be subjected to greater scrutiny as a result of (i) monitoring of their activities, (ii) external inquiries, (iii) derogatory information (eg negative media reports) or other factors which may expose the bank to reputational risk.

2.4   Senior Management Approval

8.120   The bank's internal policies should indicate whether, for any one or more among these categories, Senior Management must approve entering into new relationships.

Relationships with Politically Exposed Persons may only be entered into with the approval of Senior Management.

The second of these requirements is not as easy as seems to be suggested. If a PEP does not wish to be connected with the funds they will place it through intermediaries or launder the funds first and the bank will never know.

2.5   Cash Handling

8.121   The bank's policies and procedures will address client cash transactions, including specifically the receipt and withdrawal of large amounts of cash.

This is useful but in most cases the laundering of funds will involve depositing cash in circumstances where this will not make banks suspicious, though and this will rarely involve private banks. It will almost never involve withdrawing large amounts of cash.

3   Updating client files

8.122   The private banker is responsible for updating the client file on a defined basis and/or when there are major changes. The private banker's supervisor or an independent control person will review relevant portions of client files on a regular basis to ensure consistency and completeness. The frequency of the reviews depends on the size, complexity and risk posed by the relationship.

With respect to clients classified under any category of persons mentioned in 2, the bank's internal policies will indicate whether Senior Management must be involved in these reviews and what management information must be provided to management and/or other control layers. The policies and/or procedures should also address the frequency of these information flows.

Reviews of PEPs must require Senior Management involvement.

4   Practices when identifying Unusual or Suspicious Activities

4.1   Definition of Unusual or Suspicious Activities

8.123   The bank will have a written policy on the identification of, and follow-up on, unusual or suspicious activities. This policy and/or related procedures will include a definition of what is considered to be suspicious or unusual and give examples thereof.

Unusual or suspicious activities may include:

–   Account transactions or other activities which are not consistent with the due diligence file;

–   Cash transactions over a certain amount; or

–   Pass-through/in and out transactions.

4.2   Identification of Unusual or Suspicious Activities

8.124   Unusual or suspicious activities can be identified through:

–   Monitoring of transactions;

–   Client contacts (meetings, discussions, in-country visits etc);

–   Third party information (eg, newspapers, other media sources, internet); and

–   Private banker's internal knowledge of the client's environment (eg, political situation in his/her country).

4.3   Follow up on Unusual or Suspicious Activities

8.125   The private banker, management and/or the control function will carry out an analysis of the background of any unusual or suspicious activity. If there is no plausible explanation a decision involving the control function will be made to:

–   Increase the business relationship with increased monitoring;

–   Cancel the business relationship; and

–   Report the business relationship to the Authorities.

The report to the Authorities is made by the control function and Senior Management may need to be notified (eg, Senior Compliance Officer, CEO, Chief Auditor, General Counsel). As required by local laws and regulations, the assets may be blocked and transactions may be subject to approval by the control function.

5 Monitoring and Screening

5.1 Monitoring Programme

8.126 The primary responsibility for reviewing account activities lies with the private banker. The private banker will be familiar with significant transactions and increased activity in the account and will be especially aware of unusual or suspicious activities (see **4.1**). In addition, a sufficient monitoring programme must be in place. The bank will decide to what extent fulfilment of this responsibility will need to be supported through the use of automated systems or other means.

5.2 Ongoing Monitoring

8.127 With respect to clients classified under any category of persons mentioned in 2, the bank's internal policies will indicate how the account activities will be subject to monitoring.

5.3 Sanctions Screening

8.128 A sufficient Sanctions Programme must be in place. Prospective clients must be screened on the basis of applicable sanctions and existing clients must be screened as applicable sanctions are updated. Transactions must be screened on the basis of applicable sanctions.

6 No Inappropriate Assistance

8.129 Neither the private banker, nor any other bank employee, will provide clients with any assistance with the knowledge that such assistance will be used to deceive Authorities, including Tax Authorities.

7 Control Responsibilities

8.130 The bank's policies and procedures will include standard controls to be undertaken by the various 'control layers' (private banker, line management, independent operations unit, Compliance, Internal Audit). These controls will cover issues of frequency, degree of control, areas to be controlled, responsibilities and follow-up, compliance testing, etc.

An independent audit function (which may be internal to the bank) will test the programmes contemplated by these controls.

8 Reporting

8.131 There will be regular management reporting established on money laundering issues (eg number of reports to authorities, monitoring tools, changes in applicable laws and regulations, the number and scope of training sessions provided to employees).

9 Education, Training and Information

8.132   The bank will establish a training programme on the identification and prevention of money laundering for employees who have client contact and for Compliance personnel. Regular training (eg annually) will also include how to identify and follow-up on unusual or suspicious activities. In addition, employees will be informed about any major changes in AML laws and regulations.

All new employees will be provided with guidelines on AML procedures.

10 Record Retention Requirements

8.133   The bank will establish record retention requirements for all AML related documents. The documents must be kept for a minimum of five years, or longer, as may be required by local law and regulation.

11 Exceptions and Deviations

8.134   The bank will establish an exception and deviation procedure that requires risk assessment and approval by an independent unit.

12 AML Organisation

8.135   The bank will establish an adequately staffed and independent department responsible for the prevention of money laundering (eg Compliance, independent control unit, Legal).

Appendix I
Due Diligence of New Clients and Principal Beneficial Owners

8.136   Using a risk-based approach, the bank must ensure that it collects and records a sufficient amount of pertinent information when establishing a business relationship and must update the client profile with additional information as the relationship develops. The information should enable an independent reviewer (whether internal or external to the bank) to understand the client and the relationship on the basis of the information recorded. In the event the client is not the beneficial owner, not all of the information contemplated by this Appendix will be obtained with respect to the client; however, in these circumstances, the relevant information will be obtained with respect to the beneficial owner(s).

Source of Wealth

In order to evaluate the source of a client's (or beneficial owner's) wealth, the bank should gather information relevant to the manner in which the wealth was obtained. For example, the information collected by the bank will differ depending on whether the wealth was acquired through ownership of a business, employment or professional practice, inheritance, investments or otherwise.

Net Worth

Source of Initial Funding of Account

The financial institution and jurisdiction from which the assets funding the account will be transmitted (eg, a transfer from the client's account at another financial institution). This is distinct from an explanation of the source of wealth.

Account Information

–   Purpose for Account

–   Expected Account Size

–   Expected Account Activity

Occupation

Nature of Client's (or Beneficial Owner's Business)

Role/Relationship of Powers of Attorney or Authorised Third Parties

Other Pertinent Information (eg, Source of Referral)

8.137   These guidelines are very useful. The one troubling element is the suggestion that one of the options is to cancel the business relationship. This will simply warn the client that they have aroused suspicion. Their reaction will be to take their business elsewhere and do a better job of disguising it. If the bank is suspicious it should instead be reporting the matter to the relevant authority and taking their guidance as to whether to continue to take action. The regulators will normally want the bank to continue acting, thus giving them the opportunity of watching what is taking place. The only potential outstanding issue that could then arise is where the bank suspected it to be a situation where a true owner might later arrive in pursuit of the funds. This is a distinct possibility where large amounts of funds have been pillaged from a state. The bank's fear will be that they may then be made liable to repay the funds even if they have parted company with them. As discussed above at **8.75** to **8.96** the best course of action in such circumstances is to seek a closed sitting at the appropriate civil court, seeking an order that having made a suspicious transaction report the bank can continue to act.

Anti-money-laundering organisation

8.138   The bank will establish an adequately staffed and independent department responsible for the prevention of money laundering (eg Compliance, independent control unit, Legal).

In some respects the emergence of the Principles represents a triumph of risk over rule-based management[1]. Indeed there have been conflicting interpretations as to whether the message being sent by the banks involved is a reaction against further regulation or a move to facilitate it[2]. It can also be seen as an attempt to shape its future form[3]. Whichever is the case the Principles should result in a more precise, practice based, focused and appropriately crafted set of regulations than would emerge from the traditional rule based, regulator led, compliance approach. The problem that this potentially opens up is that it leaves it in the hands of the banks concerned to change the rules when they believe it to be appropriate. It thus becomes an internal matter for banks rather than a policy matter for regulators and therefore depends on those engaged in risk based compliance, laundering and risk management in those banks having sufficient power *vis a vis* sales, new products and marketing to hold the most suitable line. Perhaps it is a positive sign that the creation of the Wolfsberg Principles means that for the banks concerned, at least, such matters should now be more visible. A weakness however[4] is that there is no enforcement procedure should one of the banks fail to maintain the Principles. It will be interesting to see the response of the relevant national supervisor should such a failure occur.

1 Peith and Aiolfi, 'The Private Sector becomes Active: The Wolfsberg Process' in A Practitioner's Guide etc, supra.
2 Examples being the New York Times, editorial, 11 June 2000; American Banker, 11 June 2000; Financial Times, 23 October 2000 and The Banker, 1 October 2001.
3 Peith and Aiolfi.
4 See Peith and Aiolfi, p 274.

8.139   In the words of Dr Peter Eigen[1]:

'We fully expect that other banks will recognise these guidelines and volunteer to accept them … We believe it is essential that internationally active investment firms, brokerage houses, insurance companies, property and asset management firms, fully embrace standards similar to those being announced by the banks.' Eigen has gone on to make the point that the Principles involve facing up to five essential points. The first is that they have been drafted to avoid ambiguity. The second is the voluntary nature of the Principles, it being anticipated that banks will engage more fully with the process if they have volunteered in the first place rather than having been coerced. Thirdly, there is the expectation that there will be a systemic spread of the Principles and that they will become the norm. This overlaps with the fourth, which is that non-bank financial institutions should adopt similar principles as well. The final one is that they are designed to catch the full range of laundering.

1 Chairman, Transparency International, 30 October 2000: http://www.transparency.org.

8.140   Reinout van Lennep, head of ABN Amro private banking, recently went on record as saying[1]:

'These principles reflect decent and adequate standards; we neither expect nor wish to see the standards being raised higher.'

The experience of banks since statutory requirements were first brought in during the mid 1980's, suggests that this may be optimistic. Having opted to create principles to manage an ongoing and intractable problem, the banks have already had to amend and develop them. It would be surprising if it were to stop there. Indeed the banks involved in the process are engaged in ongoing monitoring meetings that may facilitate exactly such a process.

1 http://www.moneyunlimited.co.uk.

8.141   There could also be market pressures for other banks to join in. Winer has suggested[1] that international financial institutions should only be prepared to distribute funds via banks that maintain the highest standards. The Wolfsberg Principles would be one of the factors that could be used to measure this. If this were to happen all major banks would find themselves corralled into adopting the Wolfsberg approach. So far at least this has not happened.

1 Jonathan Winer. Globalization, Terrorist Finance and Global Conflict. Time for a White List? EJLR 2002.

Chapter 9

Clients' Money

Susan Brownlie; updated and amended by Andrew Haynes

SOURCE AND GENERAL PRINCIPLES

9.1   The Financial Services and Markets Act 2000 (FSMA 2000) as amended by the Financial Services Acts of 2010 and 2012 sets the framework for the Financial Conduct Authority's (FCA) detailed client money rules. The FSMA 2000 made provision for the FCA to make rules in relation to the handling of money by authorised persons[1]. Broadly, the legislation provides for the FCA to make provision for money to be held on trust. In addition, the legislation covers the treatment of accounts as a single account (see distribution rules)[2] and for rules relating to interest, both payable to clients and retained by the firm. Importantly, the legislation states that[3]:

'an institution with which an account is kept in pursuance of rules relating to the handling of clients' money does not incur any liability as constructive trustee if money is wrongfully paid from the account, unless the institution permits the payment—

(a)   with knowledge that it is wrongful; or

(b)   having deliberately failed to make enquiries in circumstances in which a reasonable and honest person would have done so[4].

1 FSMA 2000, s 139A.
2 CASS 7A.
3 See the FSMA 2000, s 139(2).
4 In the application of the FSMA 2000, s 139(1) to Scotland, 'the reference to money being held on trust is to be read as a reference to its being held as agent for the person who is entitled to call for it to be paid over to him or to be paid on his direction or to have it otherwise credited to him'. See s 139(3).

9.2   The FCA is required to act in a way which is compatible with its regulatory objectives. These objectives include the providing an appropriate degree of protection for consumers[1]. The FCA has defined its principles which are a general statement of the fundamental obligations of firms under the regulatory system[2]. These principles derive from the FCA's rule-making powers as set out in the FSMA 2000, as amended. The principle which deals with clients' assets is Principle 10. This states that: 'A firm must arrange adequate protection for clients' assets when it is responsible for them'. Breaching a principle makes a firm liable to disciplinary sanctions[3]. Some of the detailed rules and guidance in the FCA Handbook deal with the bearing of the principles upon particular circumstances but the principles are also designed as a general statement of regulatory requirements (for example, in new or unforeseen circumstances).

1 FSMA 2000, s 5.
2 *FCA Handbook*, PRIN 2.1.
3 *FCA Handbook*, PRIN 1.1.7G.

THE FCA HANDBOOK AND THE CONDUCT OF BUSINESS RULES

9.3   The FCA has sought to document all its rules and guidance in a single document known as the FCA Handbook. This Handbook is divided into sections dealing with high level standards, business standards (ie detailed rules), regulatory processes (eg the authorisation process), redress (eg compensation arrangements), and specialist sourcebooks (eg a source-book for collective investment schemes). The principles are located in the high level standards section of the FCA Handbook. The detailed rules and guidance relating to the protection of assets for which a firm is responsible are located within the business standards section of the FCA Handbook. These rules are known as the 'client asset' rules and are located in their own CASS Sourcebook. The CASS rules are divided into eleven sections, dealing with (1) application and general provisions[1], (2) firm classification and operational oversight[2], (3) collateral[3], (4) client money arising from insurance mediation activity[4] (5) custody rules[5] (6) client money rules,[6] (7) client money distribution[7] (8) mandates[8] (9) prime brokerage[9] (10) CASS resolution pack[10] and (11) transitional provisions[11]. In this chapter the term 'firm' is used to mean an authorised person[12]. This is the convention adopted within the FCA Handbook. Within this chapter no distinction has been made between rules, guidance and evidential provisions although the references in the footnotes show whether the requirement takes the form of a Rule (R), of Guidance (G), or Evidential provision (E[13]).

1 CASS 1.
2 CASS 1A.
3 CASS 3.
4 CASS 5.
5 CASS 6.
6 CASS 7.
7 CASS 7A.
8 CASS 8.
9 CASS 9.
10 CASS 10.
11 CASS transchedule.
12 *FCA Handbook*, Glossary.
13 The status of the different types of provisions depends on the terms of the FSMA 2000 as amended, and the particular power exercised to create that provision. An introductory description to the terms is provided in the FCA and PRA Handbook.

Scope of the client asset rules

9.4   The client money rules apply to 'a firm that receives or holds money from, or on behalf of, a client in the course of, or in connection with its designated investment business[1]', or its insurance mediation activity[2] except where otherwise provided by the rules[3]. The disapplication for money arising from designated investment business are as follows:

(1)   an investment company with variable capital;

(2)   an incoming EEA firm other than an insurer with respect to its pass-ported activities;

(3)   a UCITS qualifier;

(4)   authorised professional firms with regard to its non-mainstream regulated activities;

(5)   the Lloyd's Society[4].

1 The definition of 'designated investment business' is provided in the Glossary section of the FCA/PRA Handbook. The activities described in this definition derive from activities specified in the Financial Services and Markets Act 2000 (Regulated Activities) Order 2001, SI 2001/544, as amended.
2 The definition of 'insurance mediation activity is provided in the Glossary section of the FCA/PRA Handbook.
3 CASS 1.2.
4 CASS 1.2.

9.5   Whilst most of the provisions in the conduct of business source-book (COB) will not apply to inter-professional business, the requirements in CASS (Client assets) will apply where a firm provides safekeeping and administration of assets. In particular, the CASS requirements in relation to holding money for clients will apply in connection with inter-professional business.

Customer classification[1]

9.6   In order to properly appreciate the FCA's conduct of business rules in general and in particular, their client money rules, it is necessary to understand the FCA's terminology as used to define the different groups of customers and market participants with which they interact. The key definitions used in the conduct of business rules are as set out below[2]. There are various references below to different customer types being reclassified as different types. The rules provide for some clients to be reclassified where certain conditions apply. Consent and/or notification requirements typically attach to these reclassifications.

1 The full definitions from the *FCA Handbook*, Glossary, should always be used when classifying a client. The text in this section is indicative rather than representing precise definitions.
2 See paras 9.7–9.10.

Client

9.7   For the purposes of most sections of the *FCA Handbook* including the Conduct of Business Sourcebook the term 'client' means 'a person to whom a firm provides, intends to provide, or has provided:

(a)   A service in the course of carrying on a regulated activity; or

(b)   In the case of a MiFiD or equivalent third party business, an ancillary service[1].

Every client will be either a customer or an eligible counterparty[2].

1 COBS 3.2.1.
2 FCA Handbook, Glossary at 'client' (1)(a).

Customer

9.8   Essentially[1,] a customer is a client other than one engaged in insurance, insurance mediation and financial promotions.

1 The exceptions being set out in ICOBS, CASS 5, and MCOB 3.

Eligible counterparty

9.9   Broadly, the definition includes per se eligible counterparties covering:

- Investment firms;

- credit institutions;

- insurance companies;

- a collective investment scheme under the UCITS Directive;

- a pension fund or its management company;

- financial institutions authorised or regulated under EU legislation or the law of an EEA member state;

- an undertaking exempted from MiFiD under either Art 2(1)(k) (own account dealers in commodities or commodity derivatives) or locals under the Directive;

- a national government or its corresponding office, including a public body dealing with a public debt;

- a central bank; or

- a supranational organisation.

9.10   A firm can treat a client as an elective eligible counterparty if it is a per se professional client and in relation to business other than MiFiD or equivalent third country business. It must be either a body corporate with a called up share capital of at least £10 million or which is a local authority or public authority other than a regional government[1].

1 COBS 3.5.2R(3)(b).

Identifying client money

9.11   Not all money arising in a regulated entity will automatically fall within the scope of the rules. A key aspect of ensuring compliance with the FCA's client money rules is the correct identification of money which falls within and outside the rules.

9.12   The following notes set out the key criteria to be considered in determining where the client money rules are applicable. In particular the notes examine the terms 'designated investment business' and 'client' which are key to the definition.

'(2A) (in CASS 6, 7, 7A, and 10 and in so far as it relates to matters covered by CASS 6, CASS 7, COBS, GENPRU or IPRU (INV) 11 subject to the client money rules of any currency'.

Such money must be protected by firms holding it by way of segregation from its own money and suitable organisational arrangements to protect it must be provided[3].

1 (1) is deleted.
2 *FCA Handbook*, Glossary.
3 CASS 7.3.1 and 7.3.2

Segregation of client money

9.13   A firm receiving client money must promptly put it in either:

-    A central bank;

-    A CRD credit institution;

-    A bank authorised in a third country; or

-    A qualifying money market fund[1]. In this last instance the unit in the fund should be held in accordance with CASS 6. A client also has the right to oppose this option[2].

That account must involve the firm taking reasonable steps to make sure the client money is held in accounts that identify it as being separate from the firm's money[3].

1 See art 18(1) MiFID implementing Directive and CASS 7.4.1.
2 CASS 7.4.5.
3 CASS 7.4.11.

9.14   A firm that does not deposit client money with a central bank must exercise due skill, care and diligence in the choice of credit institution, bank or qualifying money market fund that it makes. It must also make a record of the basis on which this decision was made and the date. This must be retained for five years after the firm has stopped using that institution to hold client money[1].

1 CASS7.4.10.

9.15   A firm must limit the funds that it deposits with a group entity so that the funds do not exceed 20% of the balance on all its general and designated client accounts and each of its designated client fund accounts[1].

1 CASS 7.4.9A.

9.16   A firm receiving client money would normally either promptly pay it into a client bank account. 'Promptly' in this context is taken to mean by the end of the next business day after receipt[1]. If the money is received by an automated transfer it should be paid directly into a client bank account, and if it is received in the firm's own account it must be transferred to the client account by the end of the next business day[2]. If however the remittance received is a mixed one the full amount should be paid into the relevant client account by the end of the next business day and any money paid into the client account that does not represent client money must be paid out within the same time frame following clearance of the funds[3]. Alternately, it could pay it out in accordance with a rule that permits the firm to discharge a fiduciary duty of the firm to the client.

1 CASS 7.4.17.
2 CASS 7.4.22 G.
3 CASS 7.4.23 G.

9.17   There is an alternate procedure whereby the firm can pay any money due to the client out of its own account and perform a reconciliation of records and accounts in line with CASS 7.6.2R, SYSC 4.1.1R and SYSC 6.1.1R and adjust the balance accordingly. This should include segregating the money in its client bank accounts until the calculation is re-performed on the next business day.[1] Alternately, the firm can pay the money out in accordance with CASS 7.2.15R. This alternative approach is appropriate where the firm operates in a multi-product, multi-currency environment where the normal approach would be burdensome to operate.[2]

1 CASS 7.4.18.
2 CASS 7.4.16 G.

9.18   If a firm adopts the alternative approach it can pay all the client money into its own bank account. It could also choose to adopt the alternative approach for some parts of its business (see 9.20 for examples) and use the normal type for the rest[1]. Here it must use an historic average for uncleared cheques.

1 CASS 7.4.19.

9.19   A firm adopting the alternate approach mentioned in 9.17 must send a written confirmation to the FCA from the firm's auditor that the firm has systems and controls in place which are adequate to facilitate the alternate approach being carried out effectively[1].

1 CASS 7.4.15.

9.20   A firm which operates the normal approach should make sure that it maintains procedures to make sure that money received by appointed representatives, tied agents, field representatives and other agents is paid into a client account in the same manner as at 9.17 above or is forwarded to the firm (or in the case of a field representative to a specified business address of the firm) to make sure it arrives at the firm's address promptly and in any event by the end of the third business day[1]. To this end the agent or other party must keep the client money segregated[2].

1 CASS 7.4.24 G.
2 CASS 7.4.25 G.

9.21   A firm operating the normal approach which receives client money outside the United Kingdom should either pay it in accordance with the client's instructions or into a client bank account within five business days of being notified of its receipt. Also a firm using the normal approach that is liable to pay money to a client must do so no later than one business day after the money is due and pay it either to the order of the client or into a client bank account[1]. If the client money is in a different currency from that of receipt the firm must make sure that the amount held is adjusted each day so that it represents an amount at least equal to the original currency as translated at the previous day's closing spot exchange rate.

1 CASS 7.4.29 G.

Transfer of client money to third parties (CASS 7.5)

9.22   This arises as an issue in a number of situations where the firm passes client money to a third party without discharging its fiduciary duty to a client; one of the commonest being where the firm passes money to a clearing house as a margin payment. It would also be relevant where the firm passes client money to an intermediate broker for contingent liability investments as a margin payment. Where this happens the firm remains responsible for the client's equity balance at the intermediate broker until the contract has ended and the client's positions at the broker closed. Any excess funds however should be held in a client account, not in client transaction accounts. This does not apply however where the client money is provided by the firm to an authorised central counterparty in connection with a contingent liability investment on a clients' behalf and recorded in a client transaction account (individual or omnibus) at the authorised central counterparty concerned.

Statutory trusts (CASS 7.7)

9.23   A firm receives client money as a trustee (in Scotland as an agent) on the following basis:
–   for the purposes agreed in the client money rules and client money distribution rules;
–   for the clients for whom the money is held according to their interests in it. This does not apply to insurance undertaking clients in respect of client money received in the course of insurance mediation. It is also subject to the bullet points below;
–   after all the claims in the preceding bullet point have been met for clients in the insurance undertaking exception;
–   on the failure of the firm, for the payment of proper costs attributable to distributing client money;
–   then to the firm itself.

If the firm is subject to the client money rules because it has received money as part of its designated investment business other than MiFID business in respect of an investment agreement with or for a client[1], it must hold the client money is accordance with the relevant trust instrument.

1 See CASS 7.1.1 R(4).

Notification and acknowledgement of trust (CASS 7.8)

9.24   When a firm opens a client bank account it must require the bank to confirm to it in writing all money in the account is held by the firm as trustee (or in Scotland as agent) and that the bank cannot combine the account with any other or exercise any right of set off or counterclaim against the money. The title of the account must also make clear the account's status. If the confirmation is not received within twenty business days in the case of United Kingdom accounts, the firm must withdraw the money and deposit it in a client account at another bank[1].

1 CASS 7.8.1 R.

9.25 If the firm undertakes contingent liability investments for clients through an exchange, clearing house, intermediate broker or OTC counterparty, it must before the client transaction account is opened with that party:

– notify them that the firm must keep client money separate from the firm's own money in a client bank account; and

– instruct the person with whom the account is to be opened that any money paid into it in respect of that transaction is paid into the firm's client transaction account; and

– require the person with whom the account is opened to acknowledge in writing that the firm's client transaction account is not to be combined with any other account or subject to a right of set off.

If the other party does not provide the written acknowledgement within twenty business days of the notice the firm must cease using the account with that party and arrange for the repayment of the money[1].

1 CASS 7.8.

Type of business (CASS 1.2, CASS 4.1 and CASS 5.1)

9.26 The client money rules apply to a firm that (*a*) receives or holds money from or on behalf of, a client in the course of, or in connection with, its 'designated investment business' or (*b*) receives or holds money in the course of its 'insurance mediation activity', except where otherwise provided in the rules[1].

1 CASS 4.1.1R and CASS 5.1.1R.

9.27 Although firms undertaking regulated activities must be authorised under the FSMA 2000, they are not precluded from undertaking activities which are not regulated activities. In addition, a regulated firm may carry out regulated activities which fall outside the definition of designated investment business and 'insurance mediation activity'. Any firm involved in activities other than designated investment business and insurance mediation activity is not considered to hold client money subject to the rules in CASS in respect of those activities. Separate rules exist at CASS 7A.

Designated Investment Business

Money which is not client money (CASS 7.1.7CG-7.1.7IG)

9.28 CASS 7.1.7CG to 7.1.7 IG contain rules and guidance which specify a number of situations in which firms can opt out of the client money rules, though the opportunity is not available for insurance mediation activities.

Professional Clients (CASS 7.1.7C and D)

9.29 If a firm (other than a sole trader) receives money from a professional client, or holds it for them, other than in the course of insurance mediation activities, and obtains written acknowledgement of the following from that client the money concerned is not client money, then it is not client money under the rules. The three issues which must be so agreed are:

– the money will not be subject to the protection provided by the client money rules;

– as a result this money will not be segregated from the firm's money and will be used by the firm in the course of its own business; and

– the professional client concerned will only be a general creditor of the firm.

Other exclusions (CASS 7.1.7F and 7.1.8)

9.30   The same approach applies in respect of designated investment business other than investment service or activities, ancillary services, listed activities or insurance mediation activities. In addition the client money rules do not apply to a CRD credit institution in relation to deposits[1], which is to be expected. Such banks must notify clients, before providing any services that the money will be held by them as banker (or in Scotland as agent) and as a result the client money rules will not apply[2]. Approved banks holding money do not do so subject to the client money rules it if is undertaking non MiFID business and the clients are notified in writing that they hold moneys as banker (or in Scotland agent) not as trustee and that the client money rules will not apply[3].

1 See art 13(8) MiFID and art 18(1) MiFID implementing Directive.
2 CASS 7.19 G.
3 CASS 7.1.11A.

9.31   In addition there are exclusions for solicitors who are covered by its own client money rules[1], long term insurers and friendly societies unless it is a MiFID investment firm that receives the money in connection with the MiFID business[2]. Insurance companies are covered instead by the insurance client money chapter[3].

1 CASS 7.1.15.
2 CASS 7.1.15A.
3 CASS 7.1.15B.

Transfer of client funds (CASS 7.1.7H)

9.32   When a firm transfers money it must not enter into an agreement of the type set out at 9.29 above with the other person, or make out that the money is not client money.

Affiliated companies (CASS 7.1.12A)

9.33   Affiliated companies are considered to be so closely related to the firm that their money should be treated as the firm's money and should be held separately from any client money. However, where money from an affiliated company belongs to an underlying client the segregation of this money would be in accordance with the principle of investor protection. Hence, the rules specify that the money from affiliated companies should not be given client money protection unless:

(1)   the firm has been notified by the affiliated company that the money belongs to a client of the affiliated company; or

(2)   the affiliated company is a client dealt with at arm's length; or

(3)   the affiliated company is a manager of an occupational pension scheme or is an overseas company and the money has been given to the firm in order to carry on designated investment business for or on behalf of the clients of the affiliated company and the firm has been notified by the affiliated company that the money is to be treated as client money[1].

Whilst the general principle is that group company money should not be treated as client money, in fact the result of these exemptions, in particular those for money belonging to underlying clients of the affiliated company and for situations where the affiliated company is treated on an 'arm's length' basis, is that, in fact, most group company money is held in protected accounts.

1 CASS 7.1.12A.

Trustee firms

9.34   Trustees receiving money in the course of designated investment business which is not MiFID business are only affected by the client money rules as follows.

Application	CASS 7.1.1R to 7.1.6G and 7.1.8R to 7.1.14R
Trustee firms (other than unit trust trustees)	CASS 7.1.15E R and FR
General principle	CASS 7.1.16G
Requirement	CASS 7.7.2R to 7.7.4G
Depositing client money	CASS 7.4.1R to 7.4.6G
A firm's selection of credit institution, bank or money market fund	CASS7.4.7R to 7.4.13G
Reconciliation of client money balances	CASS 7.6.6G to 7.6.16R

Funds transfer

9.35   Where a client transfers ownership of funds to the firm to cover obligations it ceases to be client money[1]. This does not apply if the money belongs to a retail client whose purpose is to cover that client's obligations under a contract for differences or rolling spot forex contract that is a future and in either case the firm is acting a market maker[2]. The transfer must have been made to that firm or someone arranging on its behalf. This also applies where the firm makes arrangements for securing such a position[3].

1 Recital 27 to MiFID.
2 CASS 7.2.3.
3 CASS 7.2.3A.

Delivery versus payment transactions

9.36 Money paid through a commercial settlement system in respect of a delivery versus payment transaction is not client money if it is intended either that the money will be due to the firm in respect of the client's purchase within one business day of a delivery obligation, or it is in respect of a sale and the money is due to the client within one business day following a delivery obligation[1].

1 CASS 7.2.8.

9.37 In the case of collective investment schemes, money received in respect of a delivery versus payment transaction to settle a transaction relating to units in that scheme, the client money rules do not apply. However, there are caveats. The money should have been received by the authorised fund manager in relation to his obligation to issue units in an authorised unit trust, ACS or ICVC in accordance with COLL (the collective investment scheme sourcebook) unless the price has not been determined by the close of business on the following business day following receipt of the money[1].

1 CASS 7.2.8B

Money payable to the firm

9.38 Money due and payable to a firm for its own account is not client money. This may occur because the firm has acted as principal or agent on a contract and has paid for securities using its own money in advance of receiving payment from the client.

Interest

9.39 Any interest due to a client is categorised as client money. All interest received must be paid onto the client unless the client has been notified in writing of other terms on which it will be paid[1].

1 CASS 7.2.14.

Money ceasing to be client money

9.40 Money stops being client money where:

–   it is paid to a client or their representative; or

–   it is paid to a third party on the client's instructions, except where it is to effect a transaction or

–   it is paid to the client's bank account which is not in the firm's name; or

–   it is due and payable to the firm; or

–   it is paid to the firm as an excess in the client bank account; or

–   it is paid by an authorised central counterparty to a clearing member in relation to a porting arrangement; or

– it is paid by an authorised central counterparty to the client; or

– the firm transfers the money to a clearing member in connection with a regulated clearing arrangement and the clearing member remits payment to another firm or clearing member; or

– it is transferred by the firm to a clearing member in connection with a regulated clearing arrangement and that clearing member remits payment to the firm's indirect clients.[1]

1 CASS 7.2.15.

9.41 Money also ceases to be client money if the firm places it at an authorised central counterparty in connection with a regulated clearing arrangement as part of the default management process of that counterparty due to a default by the firm and the money is then either ported[1] or paid directly to the client by the authorised central counterparty[2]. In addition the money ceases to be client money if it is held by the firm and transferred to a clearing member who facilitates indirect clearing with a regulated clearing arrangement. In this instance the clearing member must remit payment to the other firm or another clearing member in accordance with default management procedures or remit payment to indirect clients in accordance with default management procedures adopted by that clearing member[3].

1 CASS 7.2.15A.
2 CASS 7.2.15B.
3 CASS 7.2.15C.

Unclaimed client money

9.42 Client money can cease to be treated as such and returned where reasonable steps are taken to trace the client, such as:

– having a written agreement with clients permitting the firm to release funds after a period of time;

– there having been no movement on a client's balance for six years (interest etc notwithstanding);

– writing to the client at their last known address telling them that the balance will no longer be treated as client money after 28 days;

– keeping all relevant client bank account records;

– undertaking to make good any valid claim against released balances[1].

1 CASS 7.2.20.

Records, accounts and reconciliations (CASS 7.6)

9.43 A firm must keep accurate records enabling it to distinguish client money from that of other clients and its own money at any time[1]. Such records must be kept for at least five years after they are made.

1 Art 16(1)(a) MiFID implementing Directive and CASS 7.6.1 R.

9.44 Internal reconciliations must be carried out in relation to each account as often as is necessary and in any event as soon as is possible after the date to which the reconciliation relates. The FCA's 'standard method of internal client account reconciliation' sets out what in the FCA's view is the appropriate methodology. There must be records showing the method of internal reconciliation used on client money balances and if it is different from the FCA's standard method there must be an explanation that the method used provides an equivalent degree of protection to the firm's clients and in the event of a primary or secondary pooling event the method used enables the firm to comply with the client money distribution rules. The records must be kept for a minimum of five years. In addition if the FCA standard approach is not being used the FCA must be sent a written confirmation from the firms' auditor stating that the firm has systems and controls in place which are adequate to enable it to use its alternate method effectively[1].

1 CASS 7.6.7 R.

9.45 The FCA believe that a reconciliation is adequate when the firm compares the balances on each client account as recorded by the firm with the balance set out on that account on the statement or other form of confirmation issued by the bank. In addition the balance, currency by currency on each client transaction account as recorded by the firm, with the balance on that account as set out on the statement or other form of confirmation, should be carried out. Approved collateral must be included in the reconciliation. Any discrepancies must be identified.

9.46 If a discrepancy arises as a result of the internal reconciliation the firm must identify the reason and make good any shortfall or withdraw any excess by the close of business that day. If the discrepancy arises between the firm's internal records and those of a third party holding client money the firm must identify the reason and rectify it as soon as possible unless it proves to be purely the result of timing differences between the accounting systems. If the difference cannot be resolved by reconciling the firm's internal records with those of third parties holding client money, and one of the records suggest a shortfall of client money or collateral, the firm must assume that this is the case and pay its own money into the account to make the sum up until the matter is resolved[1].

1 CASS 7.6.15 R.

9.47 A firm must notify the FCA if it cannot comply with any of these requirements. The auditor will also have to make such a report.

Pooling events

9.48 The client money distribution rules apply to a firm when a 'pooling event' occurs. There are two types of 'pooling event' which can trigger the operation of the distribution rules. A primary pooling event occurs in the following situations:

- the failure of the firm;
- on the vesting of assets in a trustee in accordance with an 'assets requirement' imposed under the FSMA 2000, s 55P(1)(b) or (c);

- on the coming into force of a requirement for all client money held by the firm; or

- when the firm is unable to identify and allocate in its records all valid claims arising as a result of a secondary pooling event[1].

1 CASS 7A.

9.49 Where certain pooling events, such as the failure of the firm occur, there should be sufficient client money available for all clients to whom money is owed to be paid in full. This outcome is dependent on the daily client money calculation being properly performed and appropriate transfers being made to client money accounts. It is possible that where there has been a breach of the client money rules there may be insufficient funds available even in the event of a primary pooling event. This could also occur where the primary pooling event has been triggered by a secondary pooling event.

9.50 In relation to the final bullet point in para **9.48** (concerning the firm's records), a pooling event will not occur where the firm is taking steps, in consultation with the FCA, to establish those records and there are reasonable grounds to conclude that the records will be capable of rectification within a reasonable period[1].

1 CASS 7A 2.3.

9.51 A secondary pooling event occurs on the failure of a third party to which client money of the firm has been transferred[1]. When a bank fails and the firm decides not to make good the shortfall in the amount of client money held at that bank, a secondary pooling event will occur[2].

1 CASS 7A 3.1 R.
2 CASS 7A 3.4 G.

9.52 In the event of a secondary pooling event it is likely that there will be insufficient funds available to pay in full all those to whom client money is due. In this event the distribution rules seek to provide a mechanism for determining how the remaining funds are distributed.

Objective and operation of the pooling rules

9.53 The basic principle of the client money rules is that when a pooling event occurs the client money held in different client money accounts of the firm is 'pooled' and money from the pool is then distributed to clients on a 'pro-rata' basis[1]. If 80% of the total pooled funds remain at the time of the pooling event each client will receive 80% of their full entitlement.

1 CASS 7A 2.4 R.

9.54 If a secondary pooling event occurs but the firm 'funds' the shortfall as the third party using its own funds, then the 'pooling' rules set out below will not apply[1]. The FCA explains in the guidance to the distribution rules that when client money is passed to a third party a firm continues to owe a fiduciary duty to the client.[2] The guidance explains that a firm's liability for a shortfall will depend on whether it has complied with its duty of care as trustee (or in Scotland as agent).

1 CASS 7A 3 and 8.129.
2 CASS 7A 3.3 G.

9.55   Assuming initially that there are no 'designated client bank accounts' or 'designated client fund accounts', then the rules require the following approach in the event of a 'pooling event'.

9.56   Where a primary pooling event occurs, client money in each client money account of the firm is treated as pooled and the firm must distribute that money so that each client receives a sum calculated on a 'pro-rata' basis[1].

1 CASS 7A 2.4 R.

9.57   Where a secondary pooling event occurs as a result of a failure of a bank, intermediate broker, settlement agent or OTC counterparty, then every client bank account and client transaction account of the firm must be pooled. Any shortfall must be borne by all clients rateably in accordance with their entitlements. The firm must make and retain a record of each client's share of the shortfall until the client is repaid (say by the firm funding the shortfall). The firm must recalculate the client money entitlements for each client to reflect the reduced entitlement (ie reduced to reflect the shortfall). These lower values are then used in calculating the ongoing daily client money calculation[1].

1 CASS 7A 3.10R (1).

Chapter 10

Financial Rules

Ian Kelly and Rebeka Smith

INTRODUCTION

10.1   The assessment and regulation of the adequacy of firms' financial resources is commonly referred to as 'prudential' regulation. Previously the Financial Services Authority ('FSA') was the sole prudential regulator for all banks, insurers and investment firms in the UK. In 2013, the FSA was separated into two new regulatory authorities: the Prudential Regulation Authority ('PRA') and the Financial Conduct Authority ('FCA').

The PRA is responsible for prudential regulation of banks, insurers and a small number of systemically important investment firms. The FCA is responsible for the prudential regulation of all other financial firms, including most investment firms, asset managers and brokers.

10.2   Financial firms in the UK are subject to various prudential regulations depending on their permissions and activities that they perform. The main focus of this chapter is firms that are subject to the European Union's Capital Requirements Directive[1] (the 'Directive') and the associated Capital Requirements Regulation[2] (the 'Regulation'). As the Directive and Regulation replace the previous three Directives of the same name on capital requirements, this legislative package is commonly referred to as 'CRD IV'.

1 Directive 2013/36/EU.
2 Regulation No 575/2013.

CRD IV

10.3   Following the financial crisis that began in 2007/08 policymakers and regulators recognised the need for an overhaul of the capital adequacy regime that applies to banks, particularly regarding the financial resources that they must hold to be able to survive economic shocks. A new international agreement on bank capital standards, Basel III, was concluded in December 2010. The Basel framework consists of three pillars:

- Pillar 1 sets out prescriptive rules on the amount of capital a firm must hold against specific risks;

- Pillar 2 requires firms to conduct regular internal assessments of their exposure to risk in order to determine if additional capital needs to be held;

- Pillar 3 requires firms to publicly disclose their exposure to risk and details of their capital structure.

Basel III is implemented in the European Union through the CRD IV package which came into effect on 1 January 2014. Previous EU law in this area took the form of Directives (rather than Regulations) which had to be transposed into national legislation. However the Regulation component of CRD IV is highly prescriptive and is directly applicable in EU member states. This approach significantly reduces the scope of national governments and regulators to alter or tailor the regulatory requirements for their own financial sector.

10.4 The Regulation sets out specific standards for the measurement of risk and the levels of capital and liquidity that firms must hold to offset the *relevant* categories of risk. Broadly the Directive sets out standards for supervision and corporate governance, restrictions on remuneration and introduces capital buffers.

CRD IV applies to all banks and building societies that accept deposits, and all investment firms regulated by the PRA. It also applies to FCA regulated investment firms that carry out one or more of the following activities:

(1) trade on their own account;

(2) underwrite issues of securities;

(3) operate multilateral trading facilities;

(4) hold client money or assets; and/or

(5) provide safekeeping and administration of financial instruments.

10.5 Less complex investment firms (that do not carry out one or more of the above activities) remain subject to previous EU rules or alternative national regulations. Investment firms that qualify for exemption from CRD IV remain subject to the FCA's previous rules which implemented CRD III in the UK; BIPRU and GENPRU. These firms are referred to as 'BIPRU' firms. The prudential regulation of BIPRU firms is discussed later in this chapter (paras **10.47–10.54**). The European Commission ('the 'Commission') plans to undertake a review by the end of 2015 to assess the appropriateness of the prudential regime for investment firms contained in the Regulation.

10.6 FCA regulated investment firms that are in scope for CRD IV are subject to the rules and guidance outlined in the Regulation (supplemented by additional technical standards and guidelines contained in supplementary EU Regulations) and the FCA's Prudential Sourcebook for Investment Firms ('IFPRU'). However, only those firms that perform the activities of dealing on own account or underwriting of financial instruments and/or placing of financial instruments on a firm commitment basis are subject to the full CRD IV. These requirements will be examined further throughout this chapter.

DEFINITION OF CAPITAL

10.7 The purpose of regulatory capital is to absorb unexpected losses. Capital can be used to absorb losses on a 'going concern' basis (eg capital resources which can absorb losses in real time during difficult trading conditions, such as share capital and reserves) or in a 'gone concern' scenario (eg capital raised through the issuance of debt instruments, which can be used to cover liabilities in insolvency proceedings).

Therefore, regulatory capital can enable a bank or investment firm to survive trading conditions that might otherwise have caused it to fail.

It also provides added protection to consumers and counterparties by ensuring that they can recover all or part of their investment sums and debts following insolvency of a firm. Holding sufficient capital also decreases the risk of national governments and taxpayers having to support public bailouts of insolvent financial institutions (the 'too big to fail' issue) and usually enhances market confidence in those institutions.

10.8   For firms subject to CRD IV, capital is divided into three categories: Common Equity Tier 1 ('CET1'), Additional Tier 1 ('AT1') and Tier 2. Together these three types of capital make up the total regulatory capital resources of a firm. The Regulation sets out strict conditions that financial instruments must meet in order to be eligible for each category.

Common Equity Tier 1

10.9   CET1 is the highest quality and most liquid capital. It is able to absorb losses on a going concern basis, and therefore it is subordinated to all other capital instruments in insolvency. To qualify as CET1 capital instruments must be perpetual (with the principal only to be repaid upon liquidation) and any distributions must be discretionary and paid from distributable reserves. CET1 is primarily made up of paid up ordinary shares and the share premium amounts associated with those shares. Retained earnings and other reserves can also be included.

Additional Tier 1

10.10   AT1 is the next highest quality capital. It usually takes the form of debt instruments with additional features. In particular CRD IV stipulates that for debt instruments to qualify as AT1 firms must be able to 'convert' the instrument from AT1 into CET1 in an emergency. This conversion can be achieved in one of two ways:

(1)   by converting the instrument from debt into ordinary shares, thereby 'bailing in' the investors; or

(2)   by writing off part of the face value of the instrument, thereby reducing the firm's liabilities and boosting its reserves (ie a 'write-down').

The convertibility features of these instruments means that although they are initially issued as debt instruments, they can function as CET1 capital as and when required. Those same features (eg bail-ins and write downs) also leave investors exposed to the risk of potentially much higher losses than would be the case with a standard debt instrument. This feature makes AT1 instruments a less secure investment for investors, and therefore more expensive for firms to issue and service.

Tier 2

10.11   Tier 2 usually takes the form of subordinated debt-capital instruments. The instrument must have a maturity of at least five years with recognition as regulatory capital reducing ('amortising') over the last five years before maturity. The terms of a Tier 2 instrument must not provide any incentive for the instrument to be redeemed.

Tier 2 is generally regarded as 'gone concern' capital because it can usually only be relied upon to absorb losses in insolvency proceedings (ie ranking below depositors and general creditors).

Deductions from capital

10.12   Certain items on the balance sheet may count as assets for accounting purposes but are deemed to be of insufficient quality to be relied upon for regulatory capital purposes. Intangible assets such as goodwill which are not easily realisable are an example of this circumstance. Other items that may need to be deducted include assets that will only be realised in certain future circumstances (eg a deferred tax asset) or because they represent a sum of money that is being double counted within the financial system as a whole (eg investments in capital instruments issued by other financial institutions). Most regulatory capital deductions are deducted from CET1.

MINIMUM CAPITAL REQUIREMENTS (PILLAR I)

Initial capital

10.13   The Directive stipulates that all banks and similar credit institutions must have a minimum amount of initial capital equivalent to €5 million (or local currency equivalent). National regulators can reduce this initial requirement to €1 million for certain small credit institutions. The PRA has implemented this discretion in the UK so the minimum initial capital for small specialist banks in the UK is now £1 million or €1 million, whichever is higher. The minimum amount of initial capital that an investment firm must hold is discussed later in this chapter (see paras **10.31** and **10.54**).

Risk based capital

10.14   The Regulation sets out the minimum level of capital that banks and other credit institutions must hold on an ongoing basis. These minima are expressed as percentages of the firm's risk exposure[1]. Firms must hold total capital at least equivalent to 8% of their total risk exposure, of which CET1 must be not less than 4.5% of risk exposure and total Tier 1 (CET1 + AT1) not less than 6% of risk exposure[2]. The calculation of the risk exposure amount is explained later in this chapter (see para **10.23–10.32**).

In the case of banks and complex investment firms these minima must be supplemented by capital buffers designed to address the risks inherent in large complex financial institutions. Because these capital requirements are based on the firm's exposure to risk, they are usually called 'risk based' capital requirements.

1 'Risk exposure' is defined differently for different types of financial firms. These definitions are explained in paras **10.23–10.27** (for banks) and para **10.28–10.32** (for investment firms).
2 The 4.5% CET1 requirement and 6% Tier 1 requirement are subject to transitional arrangements and do not fully come into effect until 1 January 2015. During 2014 the equivalent requirements are 4% and 5.5% respectively.

CAPITAL BUFFERS

10.15   In practice the risk-based capital requirements will often need to be further supplemented by additional capital requirements known as capital buffers. CRD IV introduced these capital buffers because regulators decided that the basic Pillar 1 capital requirements had been insufficient during the financial crisis of 2008. Unlike Pillar I the capital buffer requirements must be met entirely with CET1 capital. They will apply to all banks and certain complex investment firms (see para **10.29** below).

Capital Conservation Buffer

10.16   Under CRD IV, all banks (and certain complex investment firms) will be required to hold a Capital Conservation Buffer (CCoB) equivalent to 2.5% of their risk exposure. This buffer supplements the basic 4.5% CET1 capital requirement. It is designed to ensure that firms will have sufficient total capital to weather any unexpected shocks. Firms which are unable to meet this CCoB requirement will face restrictions on the amount of dividend payments and discretionary remuneration payments to employees (eg 'bonuses') that they can make.

Countercyclical Capital Buffer

10.17   The Countercyclical Capital Buffer (CCyB) applies to the same banks and complex investment firms that are subject to the CCB. It is a variable requirement that regulators can set between 0% and 2.5%, in 0.25% increments, of CET1 capital – although this 2.5% limit can be exceeded in certain circumstances). The purpose of the CCyB is to require firms to build up capital reserves during favourable economic conditions, which can then be draw down during periods of financial difficulty.

Each EU Member State must designate a regulatory authority responsible for monitoring the financial sector and setting the CCyB rate accordingly. The Bank of England's Financial Policy Committee (FPC) is the CCyB rate-setting authority for the UK.

The CCoB and the CCyB will be phased in between 2016 and 2019.

Systemic risk buffers

10.18   CRD IV provides for a further set of 'systemic risk buffers' which would apply in addition to banks' minimum capital requirements and the buffers outlined above. As with the other capital buffers, any capital requirement arising from these buffers must be met with CET1 capital.

These systemic risk buffers apply to Globally Systemically Important Institutions (G-SIIs) and Other Systemically Important Institutions (O-SIIs) (ie domestically important). Banks are regarded as systemically important if their failure or insolvency would pose a threat to the wider financial system, domestically or internationally. This could be because they hold a large proportion of a member state's deposits or because the business sector is heavily reliant on them for commercial trading purposes. The Financial Stability Board (FSB) maintains a list of banks that are considered to be G-SIIs. National regulators may determine their own list of O-SIIs. The amount of additional capital that a firm has to hold depends on the level of systemic importance of the bank, as determined by the FSB (for G-GIIs) or the national regulator (for O-SIIs).

10.19 CRD IV also provides for a general Systemic Risk Buffer (SRB), which may be used to address risks not covered by the minimum capital requirements or capital buffers. The SRB is not applied to individual banks, but rather may be applied either to the whole financial sector, or to a particular sub-set – eg mortgage lenders. The FPC is responsible for setting any SRB requirement in the UK.

THE ICAAP (PILLAR II)

10.20 In addition to the Pillar I capital requirements CRD IV requires banks and investment firms to assess their own internal risks and submit this assessment to their regulators for review. This process is called the Internal Capital Adequacy Assessment Process, or ICAAP. As part of the ICAAP a firm should consider its ongoing exposure to the risks inherent in its business, how it plans to mitigate those risks, and the level and quality of capital that will be required to cover those risks. It should also conduct stress testing to take account of potential losses that may arise during periods of economic stress or commercial challenges, and/or or due to unexpected losses.

10.21 Once completed, the firm submits its ICAAP to its regulator for review as part of a process known as the Supervisory Review and Evaluation Process (SREP). Following this review, the regulator may apply additional capital requirements to the firm. These are known as Pillar II capital requirements. They may be in the form of Individual Capital Guidance ('ICG') in which the regulator advises a firm how much capital the regulator considers the firm should hold at all times, and, where relevant, requires the firm to hold a Capital Planning Buffer ('CPB') to be drawn upon in times of stress. Regulatory guidance will normally indicate what type of capital must be used to meet these requirements. From 2015 banks must hold Pillar II capital of at least 56% of CET1. This reflects the structure of a bank's Pillar I capital resources requirement.

LEVERAGE RATIO

10.22 The leverage ratio is a new supervisory measure designed to reduce the risk of excessive leverage building up in the financial system. It is effectively a 're-incarnation' of the previous capital requirement that applied to banks before regulators introduced 'risk-based' capital requirements. Leverage refers to the relative size of an institution's assets and off-balance sheet items compared to that institution's capital. It is a percentage calculated by dividing a firm's Tier 1 capital (CET1 plus AT1) by the exposure value of all of the firm's assets and off-balance sheet items that are not deducted from capital.

In general, the exposure value of an asset is the accounting value of that asset, and should not be offset by any collateral, guarantees of other forms of purchased credit risk mitigation. The exposure value for derivatives contracts is calculated in accordance with the rules relating to credit risk and counterparty credit risk discussed later in this chapter (see para 10.25). For certain off-balance sheet items that are listed in the Regulation (eg undrawn credit facilities, trade finance items) an exposure value is determined according to prescribed rules.

CRD IV does not yet contain a minimum leverage ratio requirement; it simply requires banks and complex investment firms to report their leverage ratio to regulators. However, the Basel Committee on Banking Supervision has proposed the introduction of a minimum leverage requirement of 3%.

RISK EXPOSURE FOR BANKS

10.23   Banks' risk exposure is made up of credit risk, market risk and operational risk. The exposure values for these risks are aggregated to produce a total value for risk exposure and this total value determines the firm's capital requirements.

Credit risk

10.24   Credit risk is the risk that a borrower, counterparty or other debtor to the bank will default on their obligations to the bank. The credit risk of each exposure (ie asset) is usually determined by reference to the perceived creditworthiness of that class of asset or debtor. Banks can assess their credit risk using one of two methods: the Standardised Approach or an Internal Ratings Based (IRB) financial risk model.

The Standardised Approach provides a set of prescriptive 'risk-weights' for different asset classes. Asset classes that are perceived as being safe (eg cash or central bank deposits) receive a low or even '0%' weighting while asset classes that are perceived as being higher risk (eg exposures to corporates or institutions with a poor credit history or unrated foreign governments). These figures are then aggregated to produce a figure for risk-weighted assets. Where a firm's portfolio of assets is perceived to be more risky its risk weighted assets figure will be higher and it will need to hold more capital to meet its 8% minimum requirement.

10.25   Firms may apply to their regulator for permission to use their own in-house IRB model to determine the risk-weights for their exposures as an alternative to using the Standardised Approach. These models are typically only used by large and complex firms. IRB models have attracted criticism in recent years because they allow firms significant discretion to determine their own risk exposure (and therefore capital requirements) and they generally produce lower risk weights than the Standardised Approach.

Counterparty credit risk is the risk that a counterparty to a derivative transaction will fail to deliver on its obligations. A capital requirement must be held against this risk. The precise amount of the capital requirement depends on the type and duration of the derivative contract. Firms may choose from a range of calculation approaches set out in the Regulation to assess their counterparty credit risk, or they may apply to their regulator for permission to use an in-house financial risk model to perform the assessment.

Market risk

10.26   Market risk is the risk that a change in market conditions (eg movement of foreign exchange rates or interest rates) will cause an investment or open position to fall in value. It is relevant for banks and investment firms (ie brokerages) that perform brokerage and trading services – ie brokerage firms will typically be exposed to some form of market risk due to the open positions that they hold during trading and at the end of the trading period. In addition, any firms that have exposures or assets denominated in foreign currencies need to consider the foreign exchange risk elements of market risk. The risk-weighted positions are aggregated to produce a figure for market risk exposure.

Most firms assess their exposure to market risk under the rules on the Standardised Approach to market risk in the Regulation. Alternatively, firms may apply to their regulator for permission to use in-house financial risk models to assess their exposure to market risk in real time.

Operational risk

10.27   Operational risk is the risk that an unforeseen event will lead to financial loss for the firm. This event could occur due to employee negligence, fraud or malpractice, or an IT or related systems failure. By its nature operational risk is difficult to identify and measure. Banks and certain complex investment firms are required to assess their exposure to such risks.

Most firms determine their exposure to operational risk by reference to their average annual income. Others may develop their own hypothetical scenarios (ie operational risk models) and stress tests to determine the potential losses they could incur due to operational risk, and the levels of capital they need to hold against these risks.

RISK EXPOSURE FOR INVESTMENT FIRMS SUBJECT TO CRD IV

10.28   The requirements discussed above relate to banks and building societies. Many of these requirements also apply to investment firms. In the UK, investment firms in scope of CRD IV are divided into three categories depending on their investment activities and permissions: IFPRU full-scope firms, IFPRU limited activity firms and IFPRU limited licence firms.

IFPRU full-scope investment firms

10.29   IFPRU full-scope investment firms are investment firms that deal on their own account or perform underwriting of financial instruments and/or placing of financial instruments. Full-scope investment firms are treated in the same way as banks and building societies.

IFPRU limited activity firms

10.30   IFPRU limited activity firms are investment firms which perform the activities of trading on own account and/or underwriting placing of securities but only insofar as is necessary to fulfil client orders. Put differently, they do not engage in those activities for their own proprietary gain. For limited activity firms, the risk exposure amount (which determines their capital requirements) is the sum of the following:

- credit risk exposure;

- market risk exposure; and

- an amount equal to three month's fixed expenditure (referred to as the 'Fixed Overheads Requirement') multiplied by 12.5.

Limited activity firms are exempt from the 'large exposure' regulations (see paras 10.33 – 10.35) and minimum leverage ratio requirements (see para 10.22). Under FCA rules, these firms are also be exempt from the Capital Conservation Buffer and the Countercyclical Capital Buffer if they meet the definition of a 'Small and Medium Enterprise' (SME) as outlined in the Commission Recommendation on SMEs[1].

1 European Commission Recommendation 2003/361/EC on the definition of micro, small and medium-sized enterprises.

IFPRU limited licence firms

10.31 IFPRU limited licence firms are investment firms which do not perform the activities of trading on own account and/or underwriting placing of securities, and are not permitted to do so. For these firms, their risk exposure amount is the higher of the following three amounts (sometimes referred to as the 'higher of' test):

- the firm's base capital resources requirement, which is the equivalent of €50,000, €125,000 or €730,000 depending on the riskiness of the regulatory activities that the firm is authorised to perform;

  or

- the sum of the firm's credit risk exposure and market risk exposure;

  or

- an amount equal to three month's expenditure on fixed expenditure (the 'Fixed Overheads Requirement') multiplied by 12.5.

IFPRU limited licence firms are considered the lowest risk firms in scope of CRD IV. They are exempt from all of the following: the Capital Conservation Buffer, the Countercyclical Capital Buffer, the large exposure rules and the minimum leverage ratio requirements.

10.32 For IFPRU limited activity and IFPRU limited licence firms the credit risk and market risk exposure amounts are calculated as described in paras **10.24–10.26** above. Firms which do not perform brokerage or trading activities must still consider their exposure to foreign exchange risk when determining their exposure to market risk.

As outlined above firms that are not subject to CRD IV remain subject to alternate own funds regimes and rules, which are discussed in paras **10.47–10.54**.

LARGE EXPOSURE LIMITS

10.33 The Regulation sets out limits on the extent to which firms may be exposed to other businesses or counterparties. These rules are intended to force firms to diversify their exposures to different counterparties and ensure that they do not become unduly dependent on (and thereby vulnerable to) a single counterparty's failure to pay a debt or other receivable.

The limit for each business or counterparty is an amount equal to 25% of a firm's 'eligible capital'.

Eligible capital is the firm's Tier 1 (CET1 plus At1) capital, plus Tier 2 which does not exceed 100% of the value of Tier 1. This 100% Tier 2 limit will be reduced on a phased basis to one third by 2017. Accordingly, from 2017 eligible capital will be Tier 1 plus an amount of Tier 2 that does not exceed one third of the value of Tier 1.

10.34   Where the value of an exposure exceeds an amount equivalent to 10% of the firm's eligible capital it must report this exposure to its regulator. Where a firm breaches the 25% limit due to its trading activities an additional capital requirement will apply to the amount of the exposure that exceeds 25%.

10.35   Certain types of exposure are exempt from the 25% limit, although they must still be reported if they exceed 10%. These exposures include any that would be treated as risk-free under the Standardised Approach to credit risk (such as exposures to EU member states' national governments and the European Central Bank), and certain intra-group exposures that meet specified conditions.

These large exposure limits apply to all banks and certain complex investment firms (ie full-scope investment firms).

CONSOLIDATED SUPERVISION

10.36   The financial resources rules summarised above apply to individual firms and are often referred to as the 'solo' requirements. In addition, banks and investment firms that are part of groups may also have to comply with those rules on a consolidated basis for their group. This consolidated supervision requirement includes rules on capital requirements, the leverage ratio and large exposures. It is designed to ensure that the group as a whole is adequately capitalised and that individual financial firms within the group is not vulnerable to risks that arise in other parts of the group.

In general, the requirements will apply on a consolidated basis if:

- the firm has subsidiaries which are regulated entities;
- the firm's parent is mainly involved in financial business;
- the firm's parent is a company that primarily exists to hold shares in subsidiaries, ie a holding company; or
- the firm's parent is itself a regulated firm.

10.37   The financial resources and capital requirements calculations are similar to the requirements that apply at solo level but are based on the consolidated financial statements of the highest EU parent institution or EU financial holding company in the group. Certain low risk investment firms may be eligible for a waiver from the application of own funds requirements on a consolidated basis under the Regulation. This waiver does not exempt them from performing the consolidated calculations, but it means that they are not in breach of the rules if their group financial resources do not exceed their group financial resources requirement. However, the parent holding company in the group must also demonstrate to the regulator that it is adequately capitalised. It can do this by showing that it has sufficient capital to cover its holdings in financial entities that would otherwise be consolidated with it in addition to being sufficient to cover the total amount of its contingent liabilities in favour of those entities.

LIQUIDITY

10.38   Liquidity risk is the risk that a firm does not have, or cannot obtain, the funds it requires to meet its obligations as they fall due. A firm's ability to manage this risk is essential for the firm to be able to operate as a going concern.

Liquidity risk management is a key component of the Basel III reform agenda, with the introduction of CRD IV setting a new liquidity regime that will be consistent across the EU for the first time. This regime includes the Liquidity Coverage Requirement (LCR) which applies from late 2015 and a Net Stable Funding Requirement (NSFR) which applies from 2018. While CRD IV came into force on 1 January 2014, these requirements are not yet in place and will be further defined and calibrated by the Commission in 2014 (for the LCR) and 2016 (for the NSFR). However since 1 January 2014, banks, PRA-regulated investment firms and a small number of IFPRU full-scope firms are required to report the components of these metrics as part of their CRD IV reporting obligations (see para **10.56**). The LCR and NSFR are discussed in further detail in para **10.44** and **10.45**.

10.39   Until the LCR comes into force the Regulation allows EU member states to maintain (or introduce) national liquidity standards. In the UK the FSA introduced a liquidity regime in response to the financial crisis. The regime imposed more rigorous systems and controls for all firms from 1 December 2009, as well as quantitative measures and increased reporting (effective on a staggered basis from May 2010). This regime applied, to varying degrees, to all UK authorised banks, building societies, BIPRU investment firms, and also to UK subsidiaries and branches of EEA and non-EEA banks.

10.40   Pending the introduction of the LCR in 2015, the PRA considers that its pre-CRD IV liquidity regime is appropriate. After the LCR has been fully implemented it intends to continue to carry out supervision of liquidity risk and take appropriate measures (as provided for by CRD IV). The FCA has also continued to apply the pre-CRD IV regime, but requires a small number of investment firms that are both 'significant' and ILAS BIPRU firms (see para **10.41**) to be subject to the binding liquidity requirements in the Regulation from 2015. A firm is deemed to be 'significant' if it exceeds any of the following thresholds:

- total assets of £530 million;
- total liabilities of £380 million;
- annual fee and commission income of £160 million;
- client money of £425 million; or
- client assets of £7.8 billion[1].

1 See IFPRU 1.2.3R in the FCA Handbook.

10.41   As mentioned above, the current UK regime applies with varying degrees to regulated firms. A firm that is subject to the whole UK liquidity regime is called an 'ILAS BIPRU firm'. This category of firm includes banks, building societies and investment firms that trade on their own account and at all times have total net assets of over £50 million.

However, all firms must abide by the PRA and FCA systems and control requirements, including ensuring that they have adequate liquid resources, and appropriate systems and controls in place to identify, measure, manage and monitor liquidity risk. These requirements include setting a liquidity risk tolerance, identifying liquidity stress scenarios, and developing an effective contingency funding plan to address possible liquidity shortfalls.

The ILAA and Supervisory Liquidity Review Process

10.42   In addition, ILAS BIPRU firms are required to hold an adequate buffer of high quality, unencumbered assets, maintain a prudent funding profile and prepare an Individual Liquidity Adequacy Assessment ('ILAA') at least annually. Similarly to the ICAAP discussed above, the ILAA is a firm's own assessment of the liquidity risk faced by its business and the adequacy of its liquidity resources. As part of the process, a firm must undertake prescribed stress testing and assess its exposure to specific sources of liquidity risk identified by the relevant regulator (eg to markets, currencies and intra-group).

10.43   The ILAA is reviewed by the relevant regulator as part of the Supervisory Liquidity Review Process ('SLRP') and results in the firm receiving Individual Liquidity Guidance ('ILG'). The ILG advises the firm of the amount and quality of liquidity resources that the regulator considers are appropriate based on the firm's liquidity risk profile, and advises the firm what it considers to be a prudent funding profile. The PRA stated in 2013 that the ILG issued under its current liquidity framework will remain the primary measure against which it will monitor firms until the LCR is introduced in 2015.

For firms subject to this requirement that operate a relatively simple business model, the PRA or FCA may grant a waiver that allows them to use a simplified approach to calculating the size and content of their liquid assets buffer.

Liquidity Coverage Requirement (LCR)

10.44   The objective of the LCR is to ensure that institutions hold a stock of high-quality unencumbered liquid assets that they can use to cover any possible deficit between liquidity inflows and outflows over a 30 day stressed period. To meet the LCR an institution must, at all times, hold sufficient liquid assets equal to the 30 day net cash outflow under stress. During periods of actual stress institutions may use their liquid assets to cover their net liquidity outflows.

Under the Regulation this requirement will be phased in from 1 October 2015 (starting at 60% of the LCR) until 1 January 2018 (when 100% of it will apply). It will apply to all banks, PRA-regulated investment firms and a small number of IFPRU full scope firms. The Commission plans to issue further guidelines on how the LCR should be calculated in due course.

Net Stable Funding Requirement (NSFR)

10.45   The NSFR, which has been deferred until 1 January 2016, requires banks, PRA-regulated investment firms and a small number of IFPRU full scope firms to ensure that their long term obligations are adequately met with a diversity of stable funding instruments. The European Banking Authority (EBA) intends to evaluate whether and how it would be appropriate to ensure that institutions use stable sources of funding, on which it will report back to the Commission. The Commission then plans to propose rules to the European Parliament and Council by 31 December 2016.

Liquidity Reporting

10.46   Since mid-2014 all firms in scope of the Regulation's liquidity requirements are required to submit regular reports to their regulators on their liquid assets and projected outflows.

They must also report the items providing and requiring stable funding in order to allow regulators to assess the availability of stable funding. Items to be reported in order for the regulator to assess whether firms have stable funding availability include the amount of the firm's own funds after deductions have been made and certain other sources of funding from the liability side of the balance sheet. Items to be reported for assessment of the need for stable funding include those assets that qualify as liquid under the Regulation, securities and money market instruments, equity securities and non-renewable loans and receivables.

BIPRU FIRMS

10.47   As noted above, the FCA has decided to exempt certain investment firms that do not engage in certain complex or risky investment activities from CRD IV. These 'BIPRU firms', as they are now called, are allowed to continue to follow the prudential rules that implemented the previous Capital Requirements Directive (CRD III) ie the BIPRU and GENPRU sourcebooks in the FCA Handbook.

Capital resources

10.48   Under BIPRU and GENPRU, Core Tier 1 (CT1) capital is the highest quality capital. It consists of paid up ordinary shares, share premium, retained earnings and other reserves (except for revaluation reserves).

10.49   Below CT1 is the next highest quality capital: Other Tier 1 (OT1). OT1 consists of three categories of hybrid capital. Hybrid capital instruments combine both debt and equity characteristics (similar to AT1 under CRD IV) and are designed to absorb losses on a going concern basis. Such instruments must contain a mechanism that enables the firm to convert the instrument to ordinary shares, or to permanently or temporarily write down the principal value of the instrument, in order to recapitalise the firm (or have a process in place to achieve the same or greater effect). Examples of hybrid capital are perpetual non-cumulative preference shares and subordinated debt with a conversion or write-down mechanism.

10.50   The next level of capital, Tier 2, usually takes the form of subordinated debt instruments that are either perpetual or long term in nature. It may also include preference shares and revaluation reserves that do not qualify as OT1 either because they are issued for a fixed period or they place a commitment on the issuing firm to pay regular dividends.

10.51   Unlike under CRD IV, BIPRU firms may also use a limited amount of low quality debt instruments to meet their capital resources requirements. These instruments qualify as Tier 3 (T3) capital. T3 includes short term subordinated debt (original maturity of at least two years or subject to two years notice of repayment) and net interim trading book profits. T3 capital is now unique to BIPRU firms because firms in scope of CRD IV are no longer allowed to use these types of instruments as regulatory capital.

10.52   The different forms of capital are also subject to limits on the amount that can count towards regulatory capital. At least 50% of Tier 1 must be made up of Core Tier 1 with the remainder permitted to be composed of OT1. Tier 2 capital cannot exceed 100% of Tier 1 capital and dated debt-capital instruments within Tier 2 (sometimes called 'Lower Tier 2') cannot exceed 50% of tier 1 capital. Tier 3 capital has limited use because it can only be counted towards meeting a firm's market risk requirement and Fixed Overhead Requirement (see para 10.54).

10.53   BIPRU firms are also required to deduct certain items on the balance sheet from capital where they are deemed to be of insufficient quality to be relied upon for regulatory capital purposes. As is the case for firms in scope of CRD IV, these deductions include intangible assets such as goodwill and sums which represent a double counting of capital within the financial system as a whole (eg investments in capital instruments issued by other financial institutions).

Capital requirements

10.54   BIPRU firms calculate their capital requirements in a similar manner to IFPRU limited licence firms. For BIPRU firms, their capital requirements are the higher of the following three amounts:

- €50,000;

  or

- the credit risk capital requirement and the market risk capital requirement;

  or

- A sum equal to three month's expenditure on fixed overheads (ie the Fixed Overheads Requirement).

These firms are also required to conduct an ICAAP (and submit it to the FCA if requested to do so) and may be required to hold additional capital in the form of an ICG as a result. As part of the ICAAP investment firms must assess additional capital required to meet their Pillar II risks. They must also undertake a detailed wind-down assessment to determine how much capital would be required for the firm to wind-down in an orderly manner. The FCA specifies how BIPRU firms must meet their Pillar II capital requirements in their ICG.

OTHER FIRMS

10.55   Many firms in the investment sector do not perform any MiFID[1] activities outlined above and are regulated by the FCA (and PRA in certain instances) in line with the Interim Prudential Sourcebook for Investment Businesses (IPRU (INV)). This sourcebook sets minimal capital and other risk management standards designed to mitigate the possibility that a firm will be unable to meet its liabilities and commitments to consumers and counterparties. These firms are subject to a lower regulatory burden and usually have lower capital requirements. Such firms include investment management firms, personal investment firms, service companies, collective portfolio management firms and certain consumer credit firms.

1 The Markets in Financial Instruments Directive (Directive 2004/39/EC).

REGULATORY REPORTING – COREP FORMS AND FSA0XX REPORTING FORMS

10.56   Firms that are subject to CRD IV are required to report on their compliance with its requirements using a set of harmonised reporting forms. The same forms must be used by firms in each EU member state. This harmonised reporting is known as 'Common Reporting' or 'COREP' for short.

Common reporting enables regulators to make precise comparisons of levels of capitalisation and exposure to risk among firms across the EU. There are separate forms for each element of the Regulation.

Firms are required to complete the relevant forms for those areas of CRD IV for which they are in scope. For example, an IFPRU limited licence firm is required to complete and submit a smaller range of COREP forms than a large bank which uses in-house financial risk models to determine its exposure to risk.

10.57   Previously, banks and investment firms in scope of CRD III could report using the UK regulators' existing reporting form framework: the FSA0xx forms. Because BIPRU firms remain on CRD III rules they continue to use the old FSA reporting forms.

Some investment firms may have to submit a mix of COREP forms and FSA0xx forms for some investment firms. For example, an IFPRU full-scope firm that is not in scope of the liquidity provisions of the Regulation will be required to submit COREP forms along with the existing FCA liquidity forms (ie FSA0xx forms).

CONCLUSION

10.58   Financial rules are becoming ever more complex for banks and investment firms. The new rules may seem onerous but their aim is ambitious: the prevention of future financial crises. It seems likely that they will continue to develop and reform over the coming years as governments and regulators seek to protect consumers and ensure financial stability. Financial firms must stay on top of this area of rules as it is clear they are here to stay.

Chapter 11:

Enforcement

Christopher Robinson
Partner, Freshfields Bruckhaus Deringer.

INTRODUCTION

11.1   Since the financial crisis of 2008 there has been a significant increase in regulatory enforcement activity against financial services firms in most of the world's financial centres. This has been driven by more aggressive regulatory scrutiny of their behaviour and a greater political and public appetite for enforcement action.

11.2   In the UK this trend is illustrated by the increase in the total fines imposed by the former UK financial services regulator, the Financial Services Authority (FSA), from just over £4 million in 2007–8 to over £400 million in 2012–13.

11.3   Enforcement action will continue to be an important feature of the new UK financial services regulatory regime. The new regime replaces the FSA with three regulatory bodies, which have differing enforcement roles:

(a)   The Financial Policy Committee (FPC): The FPC is a committee of the Bank of England, responsible for macro-prudential regulation. It has no direct enforcement powers against individuals or firms, but acts by giving binding directions to the other two regulators and non-binding recommendations to those bodies, the Bank of England and the Treasury.

(b)   The Prudential Regulatory Authority (PRA): The PRA is subsidiary of the Bank of England responsible for the prudential regulation of all deposit-takers, insurers and a small number of major investment firms. The PRA's objective is to promote the safety and soundness of the firms it regulates.

(c)   The Financial Conduct Authority (FCA): The FCA is the successor entity to the FSA. It is responsible for the conduct of business regulation of all authorised firms and the prudential regulation of authorised firms not regulated by the PRA. The FCA also maintains the FSA's previous role as UK Listing Authority and responsibility for the market abuse regime. The FCA's strategic objective is to ensure that relevant markets work well. This is supported by three operational objectives:

(i)   Securing an appropriate degree of protection for consumers (defined widely to include consumers in wholesale as well as retail markets)[1];

(ii)   Protecting and enhancing the integrity of the UK financial system; and

(iii) Promoting effective competition in the interests of consumers.

1 See FSMA 2000, s 1G.

11.4 The PRA and FCA enjoy extensive (and substantially similar) enforcement powers. Their enforcement processes are also similar, although not identical. However, the extent to which enforcement action is taken is likely to vary significantly between the PRA and FCA.

11.5 The PRA intends to adopt a judgment-led and forward-looking approach to prudential regulation[1]. The PRA has stated that, instead of taking enforcement action, its *'preference is to use its powers to secure ex ante, remedial action, given its approach of intervening early to address emerging risks'*[2] and the Treasury has stated that the PRA's approach *"should mean that enforcement actions are rare'*[3].

1 The PRA's approach to banking supervision April 2013, pages 5–6.
2 The PRA's approach to banking supervision April 2013, paragraph 199.
3 The PRA's approach to insurance supervision, Bank of England, October 2012.

11.6 The FCA's regulatory approach is intended to address emerging problems in the financial services markets before detriment results.[1] This approach is underpinned by new powers enabling the FCA to make rules banning or restricting the sale of a financial product and to force firms to withdraw financial promotions viewed as misleading by the FCA. This might in theory be expected to lead to less enforcement action, on the basis that early intervention should mean that breaches of regulatory requirements are prevented instead of being punished after the event. However, the likelihood is that the FSA's increased use of enforcement action will be continued by the FCA. Indeed, the FCA has indicated it intends to bring more enforcement cases and seek to impose tougher penalties[2]. Furthermore, the FCA has been given competition powers that it can exercise concurrently with the Competition and Markets Authority[3]. These powers include enforcement powers to address restrictive practices engaged in by companies operating in the UK that distort, restrict or prevent competition[4], as well as to carry out market studies and make references to the Competition and Markets Authority[5].

1 See for example The Journey to the FCA, October 2012, Chapter 3.
2 Ibid, Chapter 4.
3 Financial Services (Banking Reform) Act 2013, s 129 and Schedule 8.
4 Powers under Pt I of the Competition Act 1998.
5 Powers under Pt IX of the Enterprise Act 2002.

11.7 The focus of this chapter is on the FCA's enforcement powers and processes, although a number of specific PRA enforcement powers and certain differences between PRA and FCA enforcement processes are briefly addressed at the end of the chapter.

11.8 This chapter addresses:

(a) Enforcement Policy: This section explains the purposes of FCA enforcement action, the prompts for enforcement action and the process by which the FCA decides whether or not to take enforcement action.

(b) Overlapping Powers: This section explains the overlap between the FCA's enforcement powers and the powers of other UK authorities.

(c)   International Aspects of Enforcement: This section explains the manner in which the FCA co-operates with overseas authorities in connection with enforcement action.

(d)   Information Gathering and Investigation: This section explains informal investigations and the FCA's formal investigatory powers, both of which can be used to obtain the evidence required to take enforcement measures.

(e)   Enforcement Measures: This section explains the FCA's powers under the FSMA 2000 to publicly censure and fine firms and individuals, the FCA's powers to vary or cancel firms and individuals' permissions and withdraw approval and the FCA's powers to seek prohibition orders, restitution orders and civil injunctions.

(f)   The Enforcement Process: This section explains the process followed by the FCA when imposing enforcement measures and the role of the Tax and Chancery (Upper Tribunal) Tribunal.

(g)   Enforcement and the Principles: This section briefly addresses the difficulties arising from the increasing use of Principles in enforcement action.

(h)   Enforcement and Redress: This section explains the interaction between enforcement action and the compensation of persons who have suffered loss as a result of the underlying conduct.

(i)   The Market Abuse Regime: This section explains the FCA's enforcement role in the market abuse regime.

(j)   Enforcement by the PRA: This section summarises certain key differences between the PRA and FCA enforcement processes.

ENFORCEMENT POLICY

The Purpose of Enforcement Action

11.9   Enforcement action serves four basic purposes[1]:

(a)   to change the behaviour of the person who is the subject of the enforcement action;

(b)   to deter future non-compliance by others. The FCA has recognised that enforcement action is '*a particularly effective way, through the publication of enforcement outcomes, or raising awareness of regulatory standards*'[2];

(c)   to eliminate any financial gain or benefit resulting from non-compliance with regulatory requirements; and

(d)   to remedy the harm caused by non-compliance.

1 The FCA Enforcement Guide (EG), 2.2(4).
2 EG, 2.1.

The Prompts for Enforcement Action

11.10   There are a number of ways that an issue may reach the attention of the FCA[1]:

(a) The FCA may identify an issue in the course of its own supervisory or thematic work, or be alerted to it by another authority. Information provided to the FCA by and complaints against firms made to the Financial Ombudsman Service (FOS) are a particularly important source of information in connection with retail financial services[2].

(b) The firm or an individual at a firm may notify the FCA of an issue pursuant to their respective obligations to deal with their regulators in an open and cooperative way, and to disclose to the appropriate regulator appropriately anything of which that regulator would reasonably expect notice[3].

(c) The FCA may be informed of the issue by a competitor or customer of the firm.

1 EG 2.17.
2 The FOS provides an informal dispute resolution service pursuant to Part XVI and Schedule 17 of FSMA in respect of complaints made by consumers (defined, in broad summary, as retail customers and small businesses) against financial services firms. The FCA and FOS Memorandum of Understanding of 1 April 2013 provides for regular contact and information sharing between the FCA and the FOS.
3 See Principle 11 of the FCA's Principles for Business and Principle 4 of the FCA's Statements of Principle for Approved Persons.

The Decision Whether to Take Enforcement Action

11.11 Regulatory requirements are infringed so frequently that the FCA cannot investigate and take enforcement action in respect of every potential infringement of which it becomes aware. It must therefore decide which instances of potential infringement to investigate.

11.12 There are two broad levels at which the FCA assesses whether to take action[1]:

(a) First, the strategic level. The FCA will consider the extent to which taking enforcement action will assist it in achieving its statutory objectives. It does not have separate enforcement objectives. Therefore issues which the FCA has identified as a threat to its objectives and which have been the focus of informal communications, thematic work or rule development are issues on which the FCA is most likely to wish to take enforcement action, as a means of reinforcing messages sent by other forms of regulatory action[2].

(b) Second, the individual case level. The FCA will not only take enforcement action in priority strategic areas because *'there will always be particularly serious cases where enforcement action is necessary'*[3].

1 EG, 2.5. Due to the special considerations involved, the FCA adopts a different approach to deciding whether to take enforcement action in respect of cases involving failure by firms to meet the threshold conditions for authorisation or unauthorised business. See further the FCA Enforcement Guide 2.11 to 2.14.
2 The FSA's enforcement action in respect of the selling of payment protection insurance and firms' anti-money laundering systems and controls are examples of enforcement action in areas of general regulatory focus.
3 EG, 2.8.

11.13 The FCA has published enforcement criteria setting out the detailed questions it will ask itself when assessing cases at each of these levels[1]. These include the reaction of the firm to the breach of regulatory requirements, the profit to the firm or consumer detriment resulting from the breach, and whether the breach involves a risk of financial crime.

1 http://www.fca.org.uk/firms/being-regulated/enforcement/how-we-enforce-the-law/referral-criteria.

OVERLAPPING POWERS

11.14   Whilst the FCA and PRA are the primary bodies responsible for enforcement action in respect of financial services and the financial markets, they are by no means the only UK bodies with enforcement powers in this area. Various other bodies have responsibility for regulatory enforcement in particular respects, which potentially overlap with those of the FCA.

11.15   These include other UK regulators such as the recognised clearing houses and investment exchanges, including the London Stock Exchange (which have primary responsibility for enforcing trading on their own markets), the Takeover Panel (which is responsible for enforcing the City Code on Takeovers and Mergers), Lloyd's (which retains various responsibilities for the regulation of the Lloyd's insurance market), and the designated professional bodies (which are responsible for the regulation of financial services activities by their members, under FSMA 2000, Pt XX). In relation to most of these, the FCA has an overall supervisory role under the FSMA 2000. In addition, Pt VI of the FSMA 2000 confers various duties and powers on a body called the competent authority, or UK Listing Authority, which is responsible for the admission of securities to the UK's official list and has various enforcement powers in support of its functions. The FCA has been appointed to that role and the powers of the UK Listing Authority are therefore vested in the FCA.

11.16   Where criminal offences may have been committed, a number of bodies may potentially be involved as well as, or instead of, the FCA, including in particular the Serious Fraud Office (where criminal fraud is involved), the Crown Prosecution Service (where other criminal offences are involved) and the Serious Organised Crime Agency (in relation to money laundering).

INTERNATIONAL ASPECTS OF ENFORCEMENT

11.17   Financial services businesses increasingly operate and trade on a global, rather than national, basis. This means that when a problem arises its effects are likely to be felt in more than one country, prompting intervention from multiple regulatory authorities. For example, the recent investigations into the manipulation of LIBOR have been conducted by regulatory authorities in North America, the UK, continental Europe and Asia.

11.18   In the face of the globalisation of financial services problems, financial services regulators have increased their level of communication and information sharing with one another in respect of enforcement action. The FCA has entered into Memoranda of Understanding with a number of overseas regulators, including (for example) the US Securities and Exchanges Commission, to facilitate consultation and co-operation and to provide a channel for the exchange of information in connection with enforcement action[1].

1 Some recent examples include: the FCA's cooperation with the US authorities in parallel investigations and enforcement action against a high frequency trader (FCA press release 22 July 2013); the FSA sought assistance from Canadian and US regulators in pursuing enforcement action against a Canadian company undertaking manipulative trading affecting securities on the London Stock Exchange (FSA press release 28 January 2013); the FSA obtained assistance from a regulator in Cyprus and prosecuting authorities in Germany in the criminal investigation leading to successful prosecution of an investment banker for insider dealing (FSA press release 13 December 2012).

11.19 Co-operation between the FCA and overseas authorities is particularly important with respect to problems affecting multiple countries within the EU, as the Single Market Directives require national regulatory authorities to provide assistance to one another. For example, the Market Abuse Directive (see para 11.154 below) requires regulators in EU Member States, in the context of the Directive, to co-operate and assist each other whenever necessary, supply information to other regulators, launch investigations on request from other regulators and notify other regulators of market abuse[1]. The national legislation implementing the provisions of the Directive on market abuse is not limited to conduct within a particular Member State, as it applies to behaviour both: (i) within or outside a Member State which relates to markets operating within its territory; and (ii) to behaviour within that State that relates to any other EEA regulated market[2]. So, for instance where trading is conducted from the UK on an exchange of another Member State, the market abuse regimes of both the UK and that State will apply[3].

1 See art 16 of the Market Abuse Directive. Similar obligations and powers also exist in the Markets in Financial Instruments Directive (MiFID) (2004/39/EC).
2 See art 10 of the Directive.
3 The EU is in the process of replacing the Market Abuse Directive with a Market Abuse Regulation and a new Directive on Criminal Sanctions for Market Abuse. The Market Abuse Regulation will extend the scope of the market abuse regime to cover abusive behaviour outside of the EU (see para 11.154 below).

11.20 The FSMA 2000 and the secondary legislation made under it provide the necessary framework for international co-operation, often reflecting the provisions of the Single Market Directives, by allowing the FCA to, for example, exercise investigation powers at the request of an overseas regulator (FSMA 2000, s 169), impose requirements on overseas firms at the request of an overseas regulator (FSMA 2000, s 195), exercise its own-initiative variation powers at the request of an overseas regulator (FSMA 2000, s 55Q) and share information with both UK and overseas regulators in many situations (FSMA 2000, s 349 and see the Financial Services and Markets Act 2000 (Disclosure of Confidential Information) Regulations 2001, SI 2001/2188.

INFORMATION GATHERING AND INVESTIGATION

11.21 When a problem arises, the FCA will first need to obtain sufficient information to understand the problem, before it is in a position to decide what, if any, action is appropriate (although, as will be seen, in some cases, particularly where there is an immediate and serious risk to consumers or the financial markets, it may wish to take urgent action before all of the details are known). The FCA's powers of information gathering and investigation are thus central to its enforcement functions. They are, essentially, fact-finding powers.

11.22 The FSMA 2000 contains a raft of different investigation powers, exercisable by the FCA (some can also be exercised by the Secretary of State, but this power is in practice only residual). The main provisions are to be found in Pt XI of the FSMA 2000, and the FCA's policy on the use of these powers is found in its Enforcement Guide at Chapter 2.

11.23 The statutory provisions are also complemented by the FCA's rules, which impose obligations on the regulated community to comply with what might be termed informal investigations by the FCA.

11.24 Not every rule breach requires an exhaustive investigation. Indeed, as noted above, the FCA aims to focus its resources on those cases which disclose serious breaches that undermine its key objectives rather than on more borderline issues. The nature and extent of the FCA's investigation will in any case depend upon the circumstances, particularly the nature and seriousness of the FCA's concerns and the attitude of the firm concerned. In many cases, particularly where more minor breaches are concerned, the FCA will not need or wish to exercise any of its formal investigation powers in order to obtain the information it requires[1].

1 For a further discussion of FCA policy on the use of its powers, see EG, 3.

11.25 The investigation powers of the FCA can usefully be divided into three groups, namely informal investigations, formal information gathering by the FCA, and formal investigations. They are considered in turn.

Informal FCA investigations

11.26 In practice, the FCA can obtain a great deal of information from the regulated community by simply asking for it, apparently without exercising any of its statutory powers. Authorised firms owe the FCA (and PRA) a duty under Principle 11 of the Principles for Businesses to deal with their regulators in an open and co-operative way. Approved persons owe a similar duty under Statement of Principle 4. Chapter 2.3 of the FCA's Supervision Manual (SUP) provides guidance on the extent of the firm's obligation. This makes clear that there is little that the FCA cannot ask of firms, and that the FCA can, for example, request meetings, access to records and systems, and answers to questions. The firm's obligation extends to taking reasonable steps to ensure that its employees and other members of its group provide similar assistance. In addition, firms are required[1] to permit access to their premises, with or without notice. Similar obligations apply to approved persons[2].

1 SUP 2.3.5. The regulators have said that seeking to access premises without notice will only be appropriate on 'rare occasions' (see SUP 2.3.2). This power was rarely used by the FSA in practice, and there is no indication that the FCA proposes to adopt a different approach.
2 Statements of Principle and Code of Practice for Approved Persons (APER), 4.4.

11.27   Principle 11 was relied upon by the FSA in practice as a means of obtaining information in a wide variety of situations, and it is likely the FCA will continue that approach. However, there are limits to the extent to which Principle 11 (and/or Statement of Principle 4) can generally be used as a means of conducting a detailed investigation. The FCA's 'standard practice' is to use its formal statutory powers when it conducts investigations, although it acknowledges there are a variety of circumstances where departing from that practice will be appropriate[1]. There may be other exceptions in practice. Where it relies on these informal powers instead of its formal investigatory powers, the FCA can obtain information only from within the regulated community. In addition, from the firm's perspective, the basis for and scope of an investigation conducted informally may be unclear, the statutory safeguards outlined below applicable to formal investigations do not apply (although some may in practice be conferred by the FCA and others may in any event be available as a matter of law) and, moreover, it may not always be clear that the provision of information 'voluntarily' by the firm in compliance with its obligations under Principle 11 will override any duties of confidentiality it may owe to third parties.

1 See EG 4.8. The FCA has indicated that it will make clear to those affected whether it is exercising its statutory powers or making an informal request: EG, 4.9.

11.28   Finally, 'mystery shopping' is one of the most significant methods by which the FCA obtains information about firms informally (principally in the retail sector). In 'mystery shopping' exercises, FCA representatives pose as retail customers of a firm in order to obtain information about the 'normal' practices of a firm or firms[1]. The FCA may use information obtained in this way in support of its enforcement functions[2].

1 See SUP, 2.4.
2 See SUP, 2.4.5 G.

Formal information gathering by the FCA

Information gathering under FSMA 2000, s 165

11.29   Short of commencing a formal investigation (which, as will be seen, involves the appointment of an investigator), FSMA 2000, s 165, allows the FCA to obtain from authorised persons and certain others[1] specified information or documents, or documents or information of a specified description. The FCA may specify a reasonable time within which the document or information is to be provided and a place at which it is to be provided. It can also require the documents or information to be verified or authenticated. The requirement is normally imposed by written notice, although this is not always used. However, an officer of the FCA who has written authority to do so may require the person concerned to provide information or documents without delay.

1 Former authorised persons and persons connected with an authorised person (or a former authorised person); recognised investment exchanges and clearing houses or a person connected with an exchange or clearing house; the manager, trustee or depositary of certain recognised overseas collective investment schemes, notwithstanding that such a person is not an authorised person.

11.30   The information or documents must be reasonably required by the regulator in connection with the exercise by it of the functions conferred on the regulator by, or under, the FSMA 2000. This is a wide test, and allows the provision to be used to obtain information not only in relation to a particular enforcement issue which has arisen relating to a firm, but also more generally in relation to the other regulatory functions such as supervision[1]. In practice, the FCA is more likely to seek information from an authorised firm without using this formal power, by virtue of the firm's obligations under Principle 11.

1 For the FCA's policy on the use of this power, see EG, 3.2–3.3.

Reports by skilled persons under FSMA 2000, s 166

11.31 FSMA 2000, s 166 allows the FCA to require an authorised person, and certain types of connected persons, to commission an expert report for submission to it, or to appoint such a skilled person and commission such a report itself[1].

1 SUP, 5 Annex 1, provides a number of examples of circumstances in which the FCA might appoint a skilled person directly, instead of requiring the authorised person concerned to do so.

11.32 The report may be on any matter about which the FCA has required or could require the provision of information under FSMA 2000, s 165. It may therefore relate to any matter reasonably required in connection with the exercise by the FCA of functions conferred on it by or under the FSMA 2000. It must be prepared by a person who appears to the FCA to have the skills necessary to make a report on the matter concerned and, where appointed by the authorised person, must be someone nominated or approved by the FCA.[1] A 'skilled person' thus encompasses not only accountants and actuaries but might also include, for example, lawyers, IT specialists, compliance consultants or those with particular business or technology skills.

1 The FCA may provide a shortlist of candidates from which to choose: SUP, 5.4.6.

11.33 Where the regulator appoints a skilled person directly, the authorised person and firm concerned will be notified, but the skilled person will be expected to report directly to the regulator[1]. The firm will nonetheless be required to meet the cost of the skilled person's work[2].

1 SUP, 5.4.1 G and 5.4.10A G.
2 SUP, 5.3.8 G.

11.34 Where the FCA requires the appointment of a skilled person, it is for the firm to contract with that person and to bear the cost of his or her work. The FCA has imposed various requirements on the terms of the appointment. In particular, there must be a contractual term[1] requiring and permitting the skilled person to co-operate with the regulator and to report to them, broadly, any matters of potential enforcement consequence which he or she comes across in the course of his or her duties, and the firm must waive any duties of confidentiality which might limit the provision of information or opinion by the skilled person to the regulator. The FCA has also indicated that the contract should permit the skilled person to provide the regulator on request with, among other things, copies of any interim or draft reports given to the firm[2]. The contract must also include an unrestricted right for the FCA to enforce these terms directly against the skilled person (under the Contracts (Rights of Third Parties) Act 1999). It is thus envisaged that the person appointed will not only report on the particular matter concerned but also will inform the FCA about any other matters of concern which he or she comes across in the course of his or her work.

1 SUP, 5.5.1 R.
2 SUP, 5.5.2 G.

11.35   The firm in question is expected to take reasonable steps to ensure that a skilled person delivers a report in accordance with the terms of his appointment[1]. Firms are required under the regulators' rules to provide all reasonable assistance to the skilled person, whether that person is appointed by the firm or the regulator directly[2]. Failure to co-operate with the skilled person may be a breach of the regulators' rules and of Principle 11. Moreover, the FSMA 2000 imposes a duty on the firm's normal actuary, auditor or other skilled person, to provide all such assistance as the appointed person may reasonably require[3].

1 SUP, 5.5.12 G.
2 SUP, 5.5.9 R for the rule as well as guidance on what this involves.
3 FSMA 2000, s 166(7) and (8).

11.36   The FCA has provided, in Chapter 5 of the Supervision Manual, guidance on the use of this power. It is clearly a broad power, exercisable in a wide range of circumstances[1] and is used not only in the enforcement context but also for a range of supervisory purposes. In the enforcement context particularly, in deciding whether to exercise this power the FCA considers its objectives and the relative effectiveness of its different powers to achieve those objectives[2]. Thus, for example, it should generally not require the firm to commission an expert report where its objectives are limited to gathering historic information or evidence for determining whether enforcement action may be appropriate, but it may do where it needs to obtain expert analysis or recommendations for remedial action.

1 Some examples can be found in SUP 5 Annex 1 G. The use of this regulatory tool is increasing: the number of reports commissioned increased from 17 in 2005/2006 (FSA Annual Report 2005/2006, appendix 11) to 113 in 2012/2013 (FSA Annual Report 2012/2013, appendix 6).
2 EG, 3.5.

11.37   It is also notable that the fact that the firm must bear the cost of such a report being produced is an exception to the general rule[1] that a firm under investigation does not bear the cost of the investigation. Cost is therefore a relevant consideration in whether the power should be exercised[1].

1 FSMA 2000, Sch 1ZA, paras 19–22.
2 For details of the FCA's policy, see SUP 5.3.8 G. See also SUP 5.3.9 G for the factors which the FCA will take into account when having regard to the cost implications of using this power.

11.38   In addition, a skilled person may be appointed to address record-keeping problems. Under FSMA 2000, s 166A, where the FCA 'considers that an authorised person has contravened a requirement in rules made by that regulator to collect, and keep up to date, information of a description specified in the rules', the FCA may appoint, or require the appointment of, a skilled person to collect and keep up to date that information.

Formal investigations

11.39 The FSMA 2000 allows a formal investigation to be carried out in a range of circumstances. The nature and extent of the investigation depends upon the circumstances and the statutory provision under which the investigation was commenced. Such formal investigations involve the appointment of one or more investigators, who can be (and typically would be) a member of the regulator's staff. It is they who carry out the investigation, subject to directions from the regulator on, among other things, the scope, timing, conduct and reporting of the investigation, and they are obliged to provide a report at the end of the process[1].

1 FSMA 2000, s 170(6).

11.40 The regulator is, generally speaking, required to notify the person under investigation that an investigator has been appointed under a particular statutory provision, and to give the reasons for his appointment. However, there are exceptions. In particular:

(a) the regulator need not do so in relation to an investigation commenced under FSMA 2000, s 168(1) or (4) (see below), if it believes that the notice would be likely to result in the investigation being frustrated;

(b) it need not do so in the case of any investigation commenced under FSMA 2000, s 168(2) (this includes in particular market abuse investigations and perimeter enforcement; see further below);

(c) it also need not do so in the case of investigations into collective investment schemes or open-ended investment companies ('OEICs') (see further below).

11.41 The FCA will not normally publicise the fact that it is undertaking an investigation, nor will the information found in, or conclusions of, the investigation be made public[1]. There are, however, exceptions. The FCA may, in exceptional circumstances, make a public announcement that it is or is not investigating a particular matter, for example where the matter has become the subject of public concern or speculation and it is desirable for the FCA to make the announcement in order to address this. The findings or conclusions of the investigation may become apparent if the FCA takes enforcement action against the person concerned, because, as discussed below, that enforcement action is likely to be publicised. In exceptional circumstances, those findings or conclusions may themselves be made public, for example if the FCA concludes that the concerns that prompted the investigation were unwarranted in a situation where it had made an announcement that it was investigating.

1 For a more detailed discussion, see EG, 6.

11.42 The main investigation powers are outlined in turn below, followed by a discussion of whether firms must comply with requirements imposed by investigators. There are various ancillary provisions supporting the investigation provisions, primarily found in FSMA 2000, ss 175, 176 and 176A, which deals with matters such as the retention of documents by the FCA and the searching of premises under warrant. The FCA's procedures when conducting interviews can be found in EG, 4.17–4.27.

Section 167: general investigations

11.43 The FCA has the power to commence a general investigation into the business or ownership of an authorised person under FSMA 2000, s 167, if it appears to it that there is good reason for doing so. Business includes any part of the person's business even if it does not consist of carrying on regulated activities, and the investigation may extend to other group members of the person under investigation or a partnership of which that person is a member. The provision also applies to former authorised persons.

11.44 There is no guidance in the FSMA 2000 as to what might constitute a 'good reason' for appointing an investigator. The FCA has indicated that it will use this power where it has general concerns about a firm or an appointed representative requiring further investigations to be carried out using its compulsory powers, but the circumstances do not at that stage suggest any specific breach or contravention[1].

1 EG, 3.8.

11.45 The powers of an investigator appointed under s 167 are found in FSMA 2000, s 171. The investigator may require the person who is the subject of the investigation, and certain types of connected persons, to attend before him or her at a specific time and place and answer questions or otherwise to provide such information as the investigator may require. He or she has a limited power in relation to unrelated third parties, namely to require them to produce at a specified time and place any specified documents or documents of a specified description. The investigator may only impose such requirements insofar as he or she reasonably considers the question, provision of information or production of the document to be relevant to the purposes of the investigation. The investigation power is therefore extensive as against the person under investigation, and those connected with that person, but more limited as against unconnected third parties.

Section 168(1) and (4): regulatory or criminal offences

11.46 FSMA 2000, s 168(1) and (4) are the main investigation provisions applicable to investigating specific suspected regulatory breaches and suspected criminal offences under the FSMA 2000. The power to appoint an investigator arises where it appears to the FCA that there are circumstances suggesting certain regulatory breaches or criminal offences[1]. The Secretary of State has concurrent powers, but only in relation to criminal offences, not regulatory breaches.

1 For a full list, see FSMA 2000, s 168(1) and (4).

11.47 These investigations are not confined to the regulated community, although in most instances they relate to authorised firms and those who work for them. The test of 'circumstances suggesting' is a low one; there need not be, for example, reasonable grounds for suspicion that a breach or criminal offence has occurred.

11.48 An investigator appointed under FSMA 2000, s 168(1) or (4) has the same powers as one appointed under s 167, as outlined above, but has additional powers under FSMA 2000, s 172 to obtain information from third parties unconnected with the person under investigation. In particular, the investigator may require a person who is neither the subject of the investigation nor a person connected with the person under investigation to attend before him at a specified time and place and answer questions or otherwise to provide such information as he may require for the purposes of the investigation. Such a requirement can only be imposed if the investigator is satisfied that it is necessary or expedient for the purposes of the investigation.

Section 168(2): serious criminal offences and market abuse

11.49 FSMA 2000, s 168(2) allows the FCA (or the Secretary of State) to appoint an investigator where it appears to the FCA that there are circumstances suggesting that certain serious criminal offences may have been committed or market abuse may have taken place. The criminal offences are unlawful financial promotion (FSMA 2000, ss 21 or 238); the perimeter offences of breach of the general prohibition (FSMA 2000, s 23) and falsely claiming to be authorised or exempt (FSMA 2000, s 24(1)); the market misconduct offences of insider dealing (under Pt V of the Criminal Justice Act 1993); misleading statements or practices (under Pt 7 of the Financial Services Act 2012); and the new offence of manipulating benchmarks[1] that was introduced in the wake of the LIBOR-manipulation investigation (Financial Services Act 2012, s 91).

1 At the time of writing, the only benchmark caught by the market abuse regime is the London Interbank Offered Rate (LIBOR), but other benchmarks may be included by the UK government in the future.

11.50 The powers of an investigator appointed under this provision are probably the most extensive of the investigation powers found in the FSMA 2000. In particular, under FSMA 2000, s 173, if the investigator considers that any person is or may be able to give information which is or may be relevant to the investigation, he may require that person:

(a)   to attend before him at a specified time and place and answer questions;

(b)   otherwise to provide such information as he may require for the purposes of the investigation;

(c)   to produce specified documents or documents of a specified description which appear to the investigator to relate to any matter relevant to the investigation; and/or

(d)   otherwise to give the investigator all assistance in connection with the investigation which the person is reasonably able to give.

11.51 As already indicated, there is no statutory requirement for the appointment of an investigator under FSMA 2000, s 168(2) to be notified to the person under investigation. The rationale is that, in many instances, the regulator will at the outset be investigating not a particular person, but rather a situation, such as a suspicious movement in the price of particular securities. The FCA has, however, given guidance[1] indicating that it will consider notifying the persons under investigation when it becomes clear who those persons are and will normally notify them when it proceeds to exercise its statutory powers to require information from them. It will also give an indication of the nature and subject matter of its investigation to those who are required to provide information to assist with the investigation.

1 The FCA's policy on notification to the person under investigation can be found in EG, 4.2–4.4.

Section 169: assistance to overseas regulators

11.52 The FCA may appoint an investigator to investigate any matter (or may exercise its power under FSMA 2000, s 165; see above) at the request of an overseas regulator, under FSMA 2000, s 169. In some instances, a regulator will be required to investigate in response to the request because of the United Kingdom's obligations under EU law, particularly the Single Market Directives[1]. In other cases, where the exercise of its power is not necessary in order to comply with such an obligation, the FCA has a discretion whether or not to investigate in response to the request and the FSMA 2000 prescribes various factors which it may take into account[2].

1 See, for example, the Consolidated Banking Directive (2000/12/EC), the Life Assurance Directive (2002/83/EC), Directives 73/240/EEC, 88/357/EEC and 92/49/EEC (non-life insurance) and the Markets in Financial Instruments Directive(2004/39/EC) (MiFID). On co-operation with overseas regulators, see also the Market Abuse Directive (2003/6/EC) (see Chapter 7).
2 FSMA 2000, s 169(4). See also EG, 3.14–3.15.

11.53 The power to appoint an investigator in response to a request from an overseas regulator is thus different from the other investigation powers, in that there is no particular test for the appointment of the investigator, such as a suspected breach of a particular rule. The FCA simply has to receive a request from an overseas regulator and then has a discretion whether or not to investigate in response to that request (or, where its EU obligations so dictate, no discretion).

11.54 An investigator appointed under this provision has, under FSMA 2000, s 169(2), the same powers as one appointed under FSMA 2000, s 168(1) (see para 11.48 above). In addition, the regulator has the power to direct that the overseas regulator be permitted to attend and take part in any interviews conducted for the purposes of the investigation. In deciding whether or not to make such a direction, the FCA takes into account various factors[1] and it may not give such a direction unless satisfied that any information obtained by the overseas regulator as a result of the interview will be subject to safeguards equivalent to those in Pt XXIII of the FSMA 2000 (the provisions prohibiting the disclosure of confidential information, subject to the so-called gateways). The FSMA 2000 requires the FCA to publish its policy on the conduct of such interviews. This can be found in the FCA Decision Procedure and Penalties Manual (DEPP), 7.

1 The factors can be found in EG, 4.26. They include, but are not limited to, the complexity of the case, the nature and sensitivity of the information sought and the availability of similar assistance to UK authorities in similar circumstances.

Section 284: collective investment schemes

11.55   Unit trusts and other collective investment schemes raise consumer protection issues and the FSMA 2000 contains separate provision for investigations into them. In particular, the FCA or the Secretary of State may, under FSMA 2000, s 284, appoint an investigator to investigate, broadly, the affairs of a unit trust, a recognised collective investment scheme[1] (so far as relating to activities carried on in the UK), or any other collective investment scheme except an OEIC, or the affairs of the manager, trustee, operator or depositary, as appropriate, of such a scheme. The FCA may commence such an investigation if it appears to it that it is in the interests of the participants or potential participants to investigate or that the matter is of public concern. This is therefore a broad power, the use of which is largely within the FCA's judgement. There is no requirement to notify the person under investigation that such an investigation has been commenced.

1 A recognised collective investment scheme means a UCITS scheme recognised under FSMA 2000, s 264, a scheme constituted in designated territories recognised under FSMA 2000, s 270 and an individually recognised overseas scheme recognised under FSMA 2000, s 272.

11.56   The person appointed has extensive powers of investigation, comparable to those applicable to investigations under FSMA 2000, s 168(2). He or she may require any person whom he or she considers is or may be able to give information which is relevant to the investigation, to produce to him or her any documents in that person's possession or control which appear to the investigator to be relevant to the investigation, to attend before him or her, and otherwise to give all assistance in connection with the investigation which that person is reasonably able to give. The investigator may also, if he or she thinks it necessary for the purposes of the investigation, investigate the affairs of other connected schemes or those involved in the management of such schemes.

11.57   The FCA has a very similar power in relation to OEICs, under the Open Ended Investment Companies Regulations 2001[1], reg 30.

1 SI 2001/1228.

11.58   Since those who are involved in the management of collective investment schemes or OEICs will usually be authorised persons, these powers overlap significantly with the FCA's more general investigation powers discussed above. Indeed, suspected breaches of the FCA rules that apply to collective investment schemes could be investigated under FSMA 2000, s 168(4). Therefore, when considering investigating a matter that relates to a collective investment scheme, the FCA may be able to choose which statutory investigation provision to use. The specific provisions relating to investigations into collective investment schemes are, generally speaking, wider than the general investigation provisions and enable a broader range of information to be obtained.

Section 97: investigations by the UK Listing Authority

11.59   In its capacity as UK Listing Authority under FSMA 2000, Pt VI, the FCA may appoint investigators under FSMA 2000, s 97 to conduct an investigation on its behalf if it appears to it that there are circumstances suggesting, broadly, that there may have been a breach of Pt VI of the FSMA 2000 or of Part 6 rules[1] or provisions made in accordance with the Prospectus Directive or that one of the criminal offences under Pt VI may have been committed.

1 The Part 6 rules came into force on 1 July 2005 as a result of the Market Abuse Directive and the Prospectus Directive coming into force in the UK. They include the Listing Rules as well as the Prospectus Rules and the Disclosure Rules. Note that 'Part 6' in this context is a reference to Pt VI of the FSMA 2000.

11.60   An investigator appointed under this provision has the same powers as one appointed under s 167, as outlined above.

Compliance with requirements imposed by investigators

11.61   As the discussion above highlights, the statutory investigation powers are very broad, they cover most of the types of information that might exist and there are few apparent limits on the information that a person could be asked to provide.

11.62   There are, however, certain limits to the investigator's powers, both under the FSMA 2000 and as a matter of general law. These are briefly outlined, followed by a discussion of how a person might make good an objection to complying with a requirement to provide information, and the consequences of not providing information in response to requirements to do so.

Limitations on the material that can be obtained

11.63   The FSMA 2000 contains two main limitations on the material that persons can be asked to provide. Most importantly, a person cannot be required under the FSMA 2000 to produce, disclose or permit the inspection of an item defined as a 'protected item' under FSMA 2000, s 413. A protected item is, broadly, one that is protected by legal professional privilege (including both 'legal advice privilege' and 'litigation privilege'). However, the FSMA 2000 does not adopt the common law definition of legal privilege, but instead uses its own definition. That definition is static, whereas the classes of legal privilege protected by common law may evolve and, whilst the definition is unclear in some respects, it is not necessarily wholly consistent with the common law. Notably, there is no express statutory protection for without-prejudice communications (which the common law treats in a similar way to privileged material).

11.64   A second limitation is the rather limited protection for banking confidentiality, contained in FSMA 2000, s 175(5). However, this does not apply where the person by whom or to whom the obligation of confidentiality is owed is the person under investigation (or a member of the same group), where the person to whom the duty is owed consents, or where the imposition of the requirement to produce the information or document has been specifically authorised by the regulator. The breadth of these exceptions means that in practice this is unlikely to be of material assistance to firms or a material obstacle to the regulator.

11.65   There is no right to refuse to provide a document or information or to answer a question on the ground of any privilege against self-incrimination. The statutory protection against self-incrimination (FSMA 2000, s 174) is limited to the use which can be made of statements made under compulsion. In particular, it prevents such statements from being used in criminal proceedings (or proceedings for market abuse) against the maker of the statement, with certain exceptions. It does not prevent the regulator from using the statement to obtain further evidence which would be admissible and does not affect the admissibility of any other material, for example, documents.

11.66   Beyond the statutory limitations, the public law duties of the FCA and/or the investigator impose a number of additional limitations. Very broadly, investigators are required to act fairly (see *In re Pergamon Press Ltd*[1]), although all the requirements of natural justice do not apply (see *Herring v Templeman*[2] and *Lloyd's v Moran*[3]), they must not act irrationally (in the *Wednesbury* sense) and, in accordance with the FCA's stated policy outlined above, they should act proportionately and consistently. In addition, they must consider the right to respect for privacy under art 8 of the ECHR when exercising their powers in respect not only of individuals but also of firms[4]. This can be overridden but only for certain reasons and, very broadly, the investigator must consider among other things the extent of the intrusion that is merited in the particular case.

1 [1971] 1 Ch 388.
2 [1973] 3 All ER 569.
3 [1981] 1 Lloyd's Rep 423.
4 It has been held that corporate bodies have rights under art 8: see *Societe Colas Est v France* [2004] EHRR 17 (European Court of Human Rights); see also *R v Broadcasting Standards Commission, ex parte BBC* [2001] QB 885, CA (a company has privacy rights under the Broadcasting Act 1996) and *Cream Holdings Ltd v Banerjee* [2003] Ch 650, CA, per Sedley LJ, at para 80.

Objecting to providing information

11.67   If the person feels there is a genuine reason for not complying with a requirement to produce documents or information, there are several courses of action available. He does not, though, have any right to refer the decision to initiate a particular investigation or to impose a particular requirement on him to, for example, the Tax and Chancery (Upper Tribunal) Tribunal. The first potential course of action would be simply not to comply, to wait for the investigator to take action to enforce his request and then to plead the reason in his defence, primarily (as discussed below) as a 'reasonable excuse' why the court should not treat him as being in contempt. Second, he could bring a judicial review or other legal proceedings to challenge the decision to impose the requirements, or in some cases bring a civil claim for the same purpose. Third, he may be able to complain about the FCA's conduct to the independent Complaints Commissioner under the statutory complaints scheme (although this is unlikely to provide an adequate remedy, particularly on a real-time basis)[1].

1 For details, see the regulators' guidance in 'Complaints against the Regulators', published at http://www.fca.org.uk/your-fca/complaints-scheme.

The consequences of non-compliance

11.68   If a person does not, for some reason, comply with a requirement to provide information imposed under one of the statutory investigation powers, there are a number of possible consequences. The primary consequence (under FSMA 2000, s 177(1) and (2)) is that the investigator may certify to a court that the person has not complied, in which case the court, if satisfied that the person failed without reasonable excuse to comply, may deal with him as though he were in contempt of court. The person could, therefore, be fined or, in more serious cases, even be imprisoned[1] or have his assets sequestrated. The need for the court to consider whether the person failed 'without reasonable excuse' potentially gives the person concerned an opportunity to object to the requirement in appropriate circumstances. Either regulator may also be able to obtain a warrant, under FSMA 2000, s 176, authorising the police to search relevant premises and seize any relevant material.

1 For example, Christopher Westcott was sentenced to 28 days' imprisonment for failing to co-operate with an FSA investigation on multiple occasions. The sentence was suspended on condition that he subsequently co-operated with the FSA: see *FSA v Westcott* [2003] EWHC 2393.

11.69   If the person concerned is an authorised firm, or an approved person, then the failure to comply may also carry regulatory consequences. In particular, it could lead to enforcement action in the same way as any other breach of requirements imposed under the FSMA 2000. It may also demonstrate that an approved person is not a fit and proper person to be carrying on a particular controlled function and therefore lead to the withdrawal of that person's approval. This, and the other regulatory enforcement action that may be available, is considered below.

11.70   In addition, the person may commit a criminal offence if he knowingly or recklessly provides false or misleading information in purported compliance with the requirement (FSMA 2000, s 177(4)). There is also a criminal offence under FSMA 2000, s 177(3) of destroying, falsifying, concealing or disposing of documents which a person knows or suspects may be relevant to an investigation which is being or is likely to be conducted, or causing or permitting this to happen.

ENFORCEMENT MEASURES

11.71   The FCA has, by virtue of the FSMA 2000, a range of enforcement powers, each aimed at addressing different aspects of regulatory issues. Thus, whilst some of the FCA's enforcement powers are disciplinary, others are aimed at, for example preventing further harm or at compensating those who have suffered losses from the firm's actions. Generally speaking, the FCA can exercise these powers individually or in combination. Action can be taken against firms, against employees of firms (primarily but not exclusively approved persons) and in some circumstances against third parties. Armed with the results of its investigation, the FCA needs to consider what enforcement action it is appropriate to take in the light of what it seeks to achieve in the circumstances of the particular case. Thus, from the perspective of the regulated community, it is important to have in mind the range of possible action and not to focus purely on the potential disciplinary consequences of the matter.

11.72   In this section, the main enforcement measures are reviewed (the FSMA 2000 provides for a number of other measures applicable in specific areas which are not reviewed here), followed by an outline of the procedures involved where the FCA proposes to take such measures.

Disciplinary action against firms

11.73   Under the FSMA 2000, Part XIV, the FCA may, if it considers that an authorised person has contravened a 'relevant requirement', impose on that person a fine and/or a public censure[1]. In addition, the FCA may, for such a period as it considers appropriate, suspend any permission the person has to carry on a regulated activity, or impose such limitations or other restrictions in relation to the carrying on of a regulated activity by the person as it considers appropriate[2]. Any one or more of these powers may be exercised by the FCA in relation to the same contravention[3].

1 FSMA 2000, ss 205 and 206.
2 FSMA 2000, s 206A(1).
3 FSMA 2000, s 206A(8).

11.74   The phrase 'contravened a relevant requirement' requires further explanation. It is a wide concept, encompassing:

(a)   requirements imposed directly by the FSMA 2000 (such as the requirement on firms under FSMA 2000, s 59, to take reasonable care to ensure that no person performs a controlled function unless they are approved by the appropriate regulator and, probably, requirements under the FSMA 2000 the breach of which also constitutes a criminal offence);

(b)   requirements imposed indirectly under the FSMA 2000 (for example under the FCA's rules made under powers granted to it under the FSMA 2000, or requirements to provide information imposed by an investigator appointed to conduct a formal investigation);

(c)   requirements imposed by the FCA using its powers under the FSMA 2000 (for example requirements on a firm's Part 4A permission under FSMA 2000, s 55L[1]) or

(d)   requirements imposed by a qualifying EU provision specified, or of a description specified, by the Treasury by order.

1 See for example, FSMA 2000, s 204A.

11.75   The FCA is required to issue a statement of its policy with respect to the imposition of penalties and suspensions or restrictions under FSMA 2000, Pt XIV, the amount of any such penalties, and the period for which any suspensions or restrictions are to have effect[1]. In exercising or deciding whether to exercise its powers to impose a financial penalty or suspend or limit a permission, the FCA must have regard to the policy in force at the time when the relevant contravention occurred. The FCA's policy regarding financial penalties and public censures, which can be found at DEPP 6, outlines various factors which the FCA may take into account in deciding whether to impose a fine or issue a public censure, and to determine the appropriate level of any such financial penalty[2].

1 FSMA 2000, s 210.
2 See DEPP, 6.2.1G and 6.4.1G.

11.76 On 6 March 2010, the FSA's new financial penalties regime came into force. It has been adopted by the FCA. In deciding the level of the financial penalty to be imposed on firms and individuals, the FCA now follows a five-step framework. These five steps are: (1) disgorgement (of the financial benefit derived from the breach); (2) the seriousness of the breach; (3) mitigating and aggravating factors; (4) adjustment for deterrence; and (5) settlement discount[1]. Under Step 2, the FCA will determine a figure that reflects the seriousness of the breach (which will be imposed on top of any financial benefit the firm or individual is required to disgorge under Step 1). This figure will generally be determined based on a percentage of the firm or individual's 'relevant revenue' or 'relevant income'[2]. There are five fixed 'levels', with the higher levels representing the more serious breaches[3]. In deciding which level is most appropriate, the FCA will take into account factors relating to the impact and nature of the breach, as well as factors tending to show whether the breach was deliberate or reckless. The regime lists a number of specific factors likely to be considered 'level 1' through to 'level 5' factors[4].

1 The five steps for penalties imposed on firms are set out in at DEPP, 6.5A, and the five steps for penalties imposed on individuals in non-market abuse cases are set out in DEPP, 6.5B.
2 In the case of non-market abuse matters involving a firm, 'relevant revenue' will be the revenue derived by the firm during the period of the breach from the products or business areas to which the breach relates. Where the breach lasted less than 12 months, or was a one-off event, the relevant revenue will be that derived by the firm in the 12 months preceding the end of the breach. 'Relevant income' for individuals will be the gross amount of all benefits received by the individual from the employment in connection with which the breach occurred. It is the FCA's view (DEPP, 6.5B.2) that an individual receives remuneration commensurate with his responsibilities, and therefore the amount of penalty for failure to discharge his duties properly should be based on his total remuneration (including salary, bonus, pension, share options etc).
3 In the case of firms, the levels are: (a) level 1 – 0%; (b) level 2 – 5%; (c) level 3 – 10%; (d) level 4 – 15%; and (e) level 5 – 20%. In the case of individuals (for non-market abuse cases), the levels are (a) level 1 – 0%; (b) level 2 – 10%; (c) level 3 – 20%; (d) level 4 – 30%; and (e) level 5 – 40%.
4 For example, factors likely to indicate levels 4 or 5 include whether the breach 'caused a significant loss or risk or loss to individual consumers, investors or other market users', 'revealed serious or systemic weaknesses in the firm's procedures or in management systems or internal controls', or 'was committed deliberately and recklessly'. Factors likely to indicate levels 1 to 3 include that 'little, or no, profits were made or losses avoided as a result of the breach', 'there was no or little loss or risk of loss to consumers, investors or other market users', and 'the breach was committed negligently or inadvertently'.

11.77 Following the introduction of the new financial penalties regime, the size of the fines imposed by the regulator has increased significantly. For instance, the FSA recently imposed financial penalties of £160 million on UBS, £87.5m on the Royal Bank of Scotland and £59.5m on Barclays for conduct relating to the LIBOR benchmark rate[1].

1 See *FSA v UBS AG* (FSA Final Notice; FSA Ref No: 186958) (dated 19 December 2012), *FSA v Royal Bank of Scotland plc* (FSA Final Notice; FSA Ref No: 121882) (dated 6 February 2013) and *FSA v Barclays Bank plc* (FSA Final Notice; FSA Ref No: 122702) (dated 27 June 2012).

11.78 The FCA will consider it appropriate to impose a suspension or restriction where it believes that such action will be a more effective deterrent than the imposition of a financial penalty alone. Examples of where suspension or restriction may be appropriate include where the FCA has taken previous disciplinary action against the person, where the FCA has previously taken action in respect of similar breaches and has failed to improve industry standards, where the person has failed to properly carry out agreed remedial measures, and where instances of misconduct appear to be widespread (suggesting a poor compliance culture). The FCA's policy regarding suspensions and restrictions, which can be found at DEPP, 6A, outlines the various factors which the FCA may take into account in deciding whether to impose a suspension or restriction, and, if so, deciding the length of the period of suspension or restriction.

Disciplinary action against approved persons

11.79   Individuals who carry out controlled functions for a firm are amenable to the FCA's enforcement jurisdiction under the FSMA 2000[1].

1 Pursuant to the Financial Services Act 2012, there are two generic functions – the 'customer-dealing function' and the 'significant-influence function' (see FSMA 2000, s 59).

11.80   Disciplinary action can be taken against approved persons under FSMA 2000, s 66 provided that two conditions are fulfilled.

(a)   First, it must appear to the FCA that the person concerned is guilty of misconduct, which means that the person, while an approved person, failed to comply with one of the Statements of Principle for Approved Persons[1] (made under FSMA 2000, s 64), or was knowingly concerned in a contravention by the relevant authorised person of a requirement imposed on that authorised person by or under the FSMA 2000 or by any qualifying EU provision specified, or of a description specified, for the purposes of FSMA 2000, s 66 by the Treasury by order[2]. The approved person must therefore either have breached the regulatory general principles applicable to approved persons or have been involved in some way in the firm's breach[3]. In brief summary, it requires actual knowledge of the facts which made the act complained of a contravention (see *SIB v Scandex Capital Management A/S*[4], *SIB v Pantell (No 2)*[5], *R v Shivpuri*[6], *FSA v Fradley*[7], and *FSA v Asset L I Inc*[8]). This provision also allows a former approved person to be disciplined in relation to his or her conduct while he or she was an approved person.

(b)   The second condition is that the FCA must be satisfied that it is appropriate in all the circumstances to take action against the approved person. This will be the key question in many cases. Whilst primary responsibility for regulatory compliance rests with the firm itself[9] the FCA has indicated that it is committed to pursuing more cases against individuals and holding members of senior management accountable for their actions[10], as it believes action against individuals has the greatest deterrent effect[11]. Broadly, whether it will take action against the individual depends upon whether he is personally culpable for the breach, which it interprets as meaning either that his behaviour was deliberate or that his standard of behaviour was below that which would be reasonable in all the circumstances at the time of the conduct concerned[12].

1 See APER, 2. See also the Code of Practice for Approved Persons, which includes descriptions of conduct which, in the FCA's view, do not comply with the statements of principle: APER, 3 and APER, 4.
2 An approved person is also guilty of misconduct if he has been knowingly concerned in a contravention of a requirement imposed on that authorised person by the Alternative Investment Fund Managers Regulations 2013, see FSMA 2000, s 66 (2)(b).

3 The FSA sought to establish a benchmark for holding senior managers personally to account for failures in managing a regulated entity. However, in the matter of *John Pottage v FSA (FS/2010/0033)*, the Tribunal overturned the FSA's decision to fine Mr Pottage, the chief executive of UBS AG and UBS Wealth Management (UK) Ltd, in respect of flaws in the firm's systems and controls which the FSA claimed that Mr. Pottage, should have systematically overhauled earlier than he did. On the facts, the Tribunal found that Mr. Pottage had identified the flaws and taken steps to rectify them within a reasonable period. Despite the Tribunal's decision in this matter it is anticipated that the FCA will not be deterred in the future from taking personal action against senior managers in respect of their oversight responsibilities.

4 [1998] All ER 514.

5 [1993] All ER 134.

6 [1987] 1 AC 1.

7 [2005] EWCA Civ 1183.

8 [2013] EWHC 178 (Ch).

9 See DEPP, 6.2.4G.

10 See *Journey to the FCA*, October 2012, page 37. For examples of recent high-profile cases brought against individuals, see *FSA v Cummings* (FSA Final Notice; FSA Ref No: PJ01301) (dated 12 September 2012) and *FSA v Thiam* (FSA Final Notice; FSA Ref No: CTT01007) (dated 27 March 2013).

11 See EG, 2.31 and 2.32.

12 See DEPP, 6.2.4G.

11.81   As well as considering the responsibilities of those individuals who were directly involved in any breach, the FCA will often focus on the role of the firm's senior management in cases where a failure on their part to take appropriate action has allowed the breach to occur. The FCA has emphasised that it will continue to investigate and take action against senior managers who fail to recognise and manage the risks that their firm is running[1]. Significant changes to the regime for the regulation of senior bankers will come into effect in 2015 as a result of the Financial Services (Banking Reform) Act 2013. These reforms will mean that a senior banker's exposure to regulatory action will no longer arise only where he or she was "knowingly concerned" in a contravention of regulatory requirements or was in breach of the Statements of Principle for Approved Persons. In future (in very broad summary), if a contravention occurs in an area of a bank's business for which a senior banker is responsible pursuant to a 'Statement of Responsibility', that banker will be liable to disciplinary action unless the banker can show he or she took reasonable steps to avoid the contravention occurring (or continuing).

1 See *The FCA's approach to advancing its objectives*, July 2013.

11.82   Where it is appropriate to take disciplinary action against an approved person for misconduct, the FCA may do one or more of the following: (a) impose a financial penalty on him of such amount as it considers appropriate; (b) for such period as the FCA considers appropriate, suspend or impose limitations or restrictions on the person's approval; and/or (c) publish a statement of the person's misconduct. In practice, successful enforcement action is normally publicised[1]. The FCA's policy regarding financial penalties and public censures is described above.

1 As with firms, the FCA normally publicises its enforcement actions through press releases and announcements on its website (www.fca.org.uk).

11.83   There is a three-year limitation period for taking action for misconduct (FSMA 2000, s 66(4)). This will be extended to six years under reforms due to take effect in 2015 (under the Financial Services (Banking Reform)

Act 2013, s 28). The warning notice (which initiates the regulatory proceedings: see para 11.131 et seq below) must be given to the person concerned before the end of the three-year period beginning with the first day on which the FCA knew of the misconduct (which includes having information from which it could reasonably be inferred) (FSMA 2000, s 66(5)).

11.84 Under FSMA 2000, s 63A, the FCA may impose a financial penalty on a person of such amount as it considers appropriate, if it is satisfied that that person has at any time performed a controlled function without approval and, at that time, the person knew, or could reasonably be expected to have known, that he was performing a controlled function without approval. The factors that the FCA will have regard to when deciding whether to take action against the person under s 63A are set out in DEPP, 6.2.1G and 6.2.9AG.

Variation of permission

11.85 'Variation of the firm's permission on the FCA's own initiative' is the somewhat long-winded terminology for the FCA's power to vary a firm's permission.

11.86 The terminology in the FSMA 2000 arises from the means by which intervention is imposed. Since firms have permission under Part 4A of the FSMA 2000 tailored to their specific circumstances, intervention action is taken by the FCA varying that permission to impose limitations, restrictions or requirements on it, thereby directly affecting the business that the firm is permitted to do. Hence, the firm's permission is varied, not on an application by the firm but on the FCA's own initiative, under FSMA 2000, s 55J.

11.87 The power to vary a firm's permission can be exercised as a matter of urgency (see SUP 7.3.4G). The power may be used with immediate effect where there is a need for immediate action to be taken by the FCA in order to protect consumers or if the firm is not complying with the fundamental regulatory requirements found in the threshold conditions. For that reason the procedure for exercising this power is different from that applicable to many of the other enforcement powers.

11.88 Where the FCA varies a firm's permission, this can include:

(a) adding or removing a regulated activity from the firm's permission; or

(b) varying the description of a regulated activity to which permission relates (for example as to the circumstances in which the regulated activity may or may not be carried on)[1].

1 The FCA must cancel a firm's permission if, as a result of a variation of a Part 4A permission, there are no longer any regulated activities for which the authorised person concerned has permission (see FSMA 2000, s 55J(8)). Cancellation of permission is discussed below.

11.89 In addition to varying a firm's permission, the FCA has a separate 'own-initiative' power to impose such requirements upon a person's Part

4A permission as the FCA considers appropriate, taking effect on or after the giving or variation of the permission. This can include imposing a new requirement, varying a requirement previously imposed by the FCA, or cancelling such a requirement. There are no limitations on the types of requirements that can be imposed on firms. The *FCA Handbook* at SUP 7.3.4G gives examples of requirements which may be imposed.

11.90   The FCA's power to vary permission and/or impose requirements is thus a flexible tool.

11.91   There are three main bases for varying or imposing requirements upon a permission, under FSMA 2000, ss 55J(1) and 55L(2). These are that it appears to the FCA that: (a) the firm is failing or likely to fail to satisfy the threshold conditions[1]; (b) the firm has failed to carry on a regulated activity to which its Part 4A permission relates for a period of at least 12 months (in line with the general policy of preventing firms from holding on a precautionary basis permission to carry on activities which they do not in fact carry on); or (c) that it is desirable to exercise the power in order to advance one or more of the FCA's operational objectives.[2] Similar powers to impose requirements upon a firm's permission exist under the FSMA 2000, s 55O where a person acquires control over a UK authorised person that has a Part 4A permission but there are otherwise no grounds for the FCA to exercise its own-initiative power. In addition, the FCA may exercise either of its 'own-initiative' powers under ss 55J and 55L in support of an overseas regulator (FSMA 2000, s 55Q). The grounds for the exercise of the power are thus widely drawn. The FCA has provided guidance on the circumstances when in practice it will seek to vary or impose requirements upon a firm's permission. This can be found in EG, 8 and SUP, 7.

1 The threshold conditions (found in Sch 6 to the FSMA 2000, as supplemented by the rules made under FSMA, s 137O) are the fundamental requirements underlying the firm's permission and its authorisation under the FSMA 2000.
2 See FSMA 2000, s 1B(3).

11.92   A similar power exists in relation to overseas firms authorised under FSMA 2000, Sch 3 or 4, which do not have a Part 4A permission. This is found in FSMA 2000, Pt XIII and the terminology of 'intervention' is still used in that context. (To the extent that an overseas firm does have a Part 4A permission, for example a top-up permission; this permission can be varied in the normal way.) The power in relation to overseas firms that do not have a Part 4A permission is limited to imposing requirements that the FCA could impose under FSMA 2000, s 55L if the firm's permission was a Part 4A permission. In practice, this still gives the FCA a great deal of flexibility. Given that this power is exercisable in respect of firms which do not have Part 4A permission, the statutory grounds for exercising the power differ from those set out above. The FCA may exercise its power of intervention under FSMA 2000, Pt XIII where it appears that: (a) the firm has contravened, or is likely to contravene, a requirement which is imposed on it by or under the FSMA 2000 (in a case where the FCA is responsible for enforcing compliance in the United Kingdom); (b) the firm has, in purported compliance with any requirement imposed by or under the FSMA 2000, knowingly or recklessly given the FCA information which is false or misleading in a material particular; or (c) it is desirable to exercise the power in order to advance one or more of the FCA's operational objectives.

Cancellation of permission

11.93   The most serious exercise of the own-initiative power to vary a firm's permission under FSMA 2000, s 55J, is the power to cancel that permission. The FCA will consider cancelling the firm's Part 4A permission in two main circumstances: (a) where the FCA has very serious concerns about a firm, or the way its business is or has been conducted; and (b) where the firm's regulated activities have come to an end and it has not applied for cancellation of its Part 4A permission[1]. In practice, cancellation under the circumstances set out in paragraph (a) above is reserved for the most serious cases, where the concerns which the FCA seeks to address by varying the firm's permission are so serious or extensive that the most appropriate course is for it to cancel the permission altogether. In addition, the FCA must cancel a firm's permission if, as a result of a variation of a Part 4A permission, there are no longer any regulated activities for which the authorised person concerned has permission. The FCA's policy on the use of this power can be found in EG, 8.

1 See EG, 8.13.

11.94   The cancellation of a firm's permission cannot be achieved as a matter of urgency, although in practice the same effect can be accomplished swiftly by varying the firm's permission to prevent it from carrying on any of its regulated activities[1].

1 See the discussion in EG, 8.16.

11.95   If the FCA does cancel a firm's permission, and as a result there is no regulated activity for which it has permission, the withdrawal of the firm's authorisation will follow under FSMA 2000, s 33. Once its authorisation has been withdrawn, the firm is outside the regulatory arena for most purposes. Because of this, the FCA recognises that there may be benefit in varying a firm's permission to prevent it from carrying on any further activity but not actually cancelling that permission[1].

1 See EG, 8.17.

Withdrawal of approval

11.96   The equivalent for approved persons of cancelling a firm's permission is to withdraw the approved person's approval under FSMA 2000, s 63. The basis upon which the FCA may do so is simply that the person is not a fit and proper person to perform the function to which the approval relates (this is the corollary of the criterion for the grant of approval under FSMA 2000, s 61).

11.97   The withdrawal of approval is a blunt instrument. The FCA does not have any ability to vary the terms of a person's approval; it can only grant or withdraw it. The effect of withdrawing approval is to prevent the person from performing the particular controlled function for which he was approved, but it does not prevent him from carrying on other controlled functions for the firm, for which approval was not withdrawn, or other functions for which no approval is required.

11.98   The FCA's policy on when, in practice, it will consider withdrawing a person's approval can be found in EG, 9.

Prohibition orders

11.99   The power to make prohibition orders against individuals is more far reaching than the power to withdraw the approval of an approved person. Withdrawal of approval is effective only in relation to those individuals who carry out functions that are required to have FCA approval and, in any event, does not prevent the relevant person from undertaking other functions for the firm for which no approval is required. Further, the consequences for both the firm and the individual of the person carrying out a function for which approval is required following the withdrawal of that approval are solely regulatory. Prohibition orders do not suffer from the same limitations and, in addition, can be used in a more flexible way.

11.100   Under the FSMA 2000, s 56, the FCA may make a prohibition order against an individual if it appears to it that he is not a fit and proper person to perform functions in relation to a regulated activity carried on by an authorised person, a person who is an exempt person in relation to that activity, or a person to whom, as a result of FSMA 2000, Pt 20, the general prohibition in FSMA 2000 s 19 does not apply in relation to that activity (that is, the carrying on of a regulated activity by members of the professions: see FSMA 2000, s 327). Fitness and propriety is, thus, the key concept.

11.101   A prohibition order is an order prohibiting an individual from performing either a specified function, any function falling within a specified description, or any function. The prohibition order may prohibit the person who is subject to it from (a) engaging in a specified regulated activity, any regulated activity falling within a specified description, or all regulated activities and/or (b) acting as: (i) an authorised person; (ii) an exempt person; or (iii) a person to whom, as a result of FSMA 2000, Pt 20, the general prohibition does not apply in relation to a regulated activity.

11.102   A prohibition order can therefore be made against any individual involved with a regulated firm, whether or not an approved person. The extent of the prohibition can be tailored to the particular circumstances: it can range from a prohibition from performing a particular function relating to one regulated firm to a general prohibition against performing any regulated function for any authorised person. The FCA's policy on the use of prohibition orders can be found in EG, 9.

11.103   The enforcement of prohibition orders is treated as a serious matter under the FSMA 2000. It is a criminal offence, under FSMA 2000, s 56(4), for a person to perform or agree to perform a function in breach of a prohibition order, unless he shows that he took all reasonable precautions and exercised all due diligence to avoid committing the offence. The breach could also result in regulatory enforcement action against the firm concerned and/or, depending upon the scope of the prohibition order, against the individual.

Restitution orders

11.104 The FSMA 2000 provides a mechanism for the payment of restitution to the victims of regulatory breaches through the imposition of restitution orders.

11.105 The FCA may impose a restitution order, under FSMA 2000, s 384, but only on an authorised person[1] or a recognised investment exchange. Alternatively, the court has the power to impose a restitution order against any person (whether or not authorised or approved) under FSMA 2000, s 382, on the application of the FCA.

1 But note that the FCA may make a restitution order against any person in a market abuse case, as discussed further below.

11.106 A restitution order may be imposed upon a person who has contravened or been knowingly concerned in the contravention of (a) a requirement imposed by or under FSMA or a qualifying EU provision specified by the Treasury by order[1] or (b) a requirement the breach of which is a criminal offence mentioned in FSMA 2000, s 402(1) (principally, insider dealing under Part V of the Criminal Justice Act 1993, the Money Laundering Regulations 2007, and Schedule 7 to the Counter-Terrorism Act 2008 [terrorist financing or money laundering]). Profits must have accrued to the person as a result of the contravention or one or more persons must have suffered loss or been otherwise adversely affected.

1 Or by the Alternative Investment Fund Managers Regulations 2013.

11.107 The restitution order is an order which requires a person to pay such amount as appears to be just having regard to, as appropriate, the profits or losses or other adverse effects. The body that imposes the restitution order (in other words, either the FCA or the court, depending upon the power used) determines how the money is to be distributed. Assessing the amount that should be paid, and how it should be distributed, can cause serious difficulties in practice, particularly where very large numbers of consumers are involved or where the nature of the problem makes it difficult to assess what losses have been suffered. Determining how profits should be distributed may also cause practical difficulties.

11.108 The restitution order power was not extensively used by the FSA. It will not always be an effective use of the FCA's resources to seek a restitution order on behalf of investors who have suffered losses given the other means to redress (see below). The FCA therefore needs to consider in each case whether the use of its power to make, or apply for, a restitution order is an appropriate regulatory response and whether the costs would be justified by the likely benefits, particularly since it may, if it does do so, become embroiled in a contested process. Factors that may be relevant to this decision include whether profits are quantifiable or losses identifiable, the sophistication, resources and numbers of investors involved, the extent of the losses suffered, the FCA's cost of securing redress, and the availability of other means for obtaining redress. The FCA's policy on making restitution orders can be found in EG 11.

Civil injunctions

11.109 The FSMA 2000 allows the courts to make civil injunctions in support of the FCA's enforcement function, in particular in perimeter enforcement. Injunctions are also available in cases of market abuse, as discussed below.

11.110 Under FSMA 2000, s 380, a court may grant three types of injunction, in each case on an application by the FCA[1]:

(a) restraining breaches, or further breaches, of regulatory contraventions, where the court is satisfied that there is a reasonable likelihood that a person will contravene a 'relevant requirement[2]', or that a person has contravened such a requirement and there is a reasonable likelihood that the contravention will continue or be repeated;

(b) to require a person to take steps to remedy or mitigate the effect of a contravention, where it is satisfied that he or she has contravened a 'relevant requirement' and that there are steps which could be taken for remedying the contravention; or

(c) to restrain a person who it is satisfied has contravened or been knowingly concerned in the contravention of a 'relevant requirement', from disposing of or otherwise dealing with any assets of his or hers which it is satisfied he is reasonably likely to dispose of or deal with.

1 FSMA 2000, s 381 contains similar provisions in relation to market abuse cases, as discussed further below.
2 Pursuant to FSMA 2000, s 380(6), 'relevant requirement' bears the same meaning as under s 384 (as discussed above).

11.111 The first type of injunction, restraining breaches, should not in the normal course be required to be obtained against authorised firms, since they ought to comply without the need for an injunction and, if they do not, they could be restrained by the FCA varying the firm's permission (which it can do as a matter of urgency). In practice, injunctions are most commonly sought in perimeter enforcement cases.

11.112 The second type of injunction, requiring a person to take steps to remedy a contravention, clearly overlaps with restitution orders. It can be used in perimeter enforcement cases, but could also be used to require a firm that has committed a breach to take a step not involving the payment of money, for example to transfer assets or unwind a position in the market. In some circumstances, it may otherwise be difficult for the firm to take the step because of its contractual obligations to other parties.

11.113 The third type of injunction, preventing the disposal of, or dealing with, assets is effectively akin to a freezing order. It overlaps significantly with the court's inherent jurisdiction to make such orders. Such an order will normally be granted only in support of some other proceedings which may lead to an order being made against the firm (for example, a restitution order, or a judgment against the firm in civil proceedings), the purpose being to ensure that the firm's assets are not in the meantime dissipated so as to defeat the enforcement of that order.

11.114 In practice, injunctions are often granted on an interim basis in the first instance, in theory to preserve the position until the matter can be determined at a full trial. In deciding whether or not to grant an interim injunction, the court is involved in a balancing exercise, taking into account, very broadly, the prospects of a final injunction being granted when the matter comes to be determined at a full trial and the consequences of granting or refusing interim relief. In practice, the interim injunction usually accomplishes the objective and the question whether an injunction should finally be granted does not fall to be determined at full trial.

11.115 The grant of an injunction, whether on an interim basis or on a final basis, is within the discretion of the court. It may not, therefore, be sufficient for the FCA to show simply that the statutory grounds for granting an injunction are satisfied.

THE ENFORCEMENT PROCESS

11.116 The FCA's enforcement decision-making process can be found in FSMA 2000, DEPP and in the EG.

11.117 There are two main types of enforcement decision-making procedures, which are addressed in turn. The first, and most common, is the warning/decision procedure. The second is the supervisory notice procedure. Essentially, both sets of procedures give firms the option of undergoing a full tribunal process but in practice encourage early settlement by firms of enforcement action. Slightly different enforcement procedures apply in respect of certain types of regulatory action that need to be taken urgently, because under the standard procedures the enforcement decision is not effective until the end of the process.

11.118 In some cases, the FCA may decide that although a breach has taken place, it is not appropriate to exercise any of its formal powers. In such cases, it may issue a private warning, informing the person concerned that in the FCA's view a breach was committed (but without any determination of this having been made) and letting them know that they came close to formal action being taken. Such warnings are retained on the compliance history of the relevant person and may be relevant when the FCA comes to decide in future cases whether to take enforcement action. The FCA's normal practice is to follow a 'minded-to' procedure before issuing a private warning. This procedure (in summary) entails giving the intended recipient notice of the warning and giving them a opportunity to comment. The decision to issue a private warning will be taken by an FCA head of department or a more senior member of FCA staff. A more detailed discussion of private warnings can be found in EG, 7.10 to 7.19.

The Warning/Decision Procedure

11.119 The warning/decision procedure involves the issuance of a warning notice by the FCA to the person concerned when it proposes that the action should be taken and a decision notice when it decides to take that action. The procedure applies in the circumstances set out in DEPP 2, Annex 1 G. These include, for example, disciplinary measures against firms and individuals (including the imposition of civil penalties for market abuse), the cancellation of a firm's permission, the withdrawal of an approved person's approval, and prohibition orders and restitution orders made by the FCA.

11.120 Under FSMA 2000, s 395 the FCA is required to determine the procedure that it proposes to follow in relation to the giving of warning and decision notices. That procedure must be designed to secure that decisions are taken by a person not directly involved in establishing the evidence on which the decision is based or by two or more persons who include a person not so involved[1]. FSMA 2000 therefore requires a degree of separation between the FCA's investigatory and decision making functions.

1 FSMA 2000, s 395 (2).

11.121 The decision making procedures pursuant to FSMA 2000, s 395 are contained within DEPP. This provides that a body known as the Regulatory Decisions Committee (RDC) has responsibility for most decisions to issue warning and decision notices[1]. The RDC is a committee of the FCA Board, but is separate from the FCA's executive management structure. Only its chairman is an FCA employee and it has its own legal advisers and support staff separate from the staff of the FCA's Enforcement Division[2]. The degree of functional separation resulting is therefore greater than is strictly required by the FSMA 2000. Chapter 3 of DEPP describes the nature and operation of the RDC.

1 Certain decisions can be made under the swifter 'executive procedures' route, which is described in DEPP Chapter 4. This involves the taking of decisions by either a senior FCA staff committee or by an individual FCA staff member.
2 See DEPP, 3.1.

The Steps Leading to the Warning Notice

11.122 The first stage in the formal decision-making process occurs when the FCA enforcement staff responsible for the investigation decide whether to recommend the issuance of a warning notice proposing enforcement action. Prior to this, the FCA's investigation will have been completed. The investigation typically involves scoping discussions following the initial appointment of investigators and the collation of information from document requests and witness interviews pursuant to the statutory investigatory powers discussed above. Following the investigation there is usually an internal legal review of the case by a lawyer who has not been part of the investigation.[1] In many instances the subject of the action is sent a preliminary investigation report (PIR) and given a period (typically 28 days) to respond before the recommendation for action is made to the RDC.

1 EG, 2.36.

The Decision to Issue a Warning Notice

11.123   The recommendation for action put to the RDC is typically supported by an Investigation Report reflecting the action subject's response to the PIR. A panel of the RDC (generally consisting of three members including a Chairman or Deputy Chairman[1]) will then consider whether to issue a Warning Notice. If it decides to do so, the warning notice will be issued to the subject of the investigation. The warning notice must be in writing and give reasons for the proposed action[2].

1 DEPP, 3.3.2G.
2 FSMA 2000, s 387 (1).

Publication of the Warning Notice

11.124   Pursuant to FSMA 2000, s 391 (1) (c), the FCA may publish such information about the matter to which a warning notice[1] relates as it considers appropriate after consulting the persons to whom the notice is given or copied. However it may not do so if this would in the FCA's opinion be unfair, prejudicial to consumers or detrimental to the stability of the UK financial system[2]. The FCA has stated that it will normally be appropriate to publish the details of a warning notice, although, in certain circumstances, it may not be appropriate to publish details of the subject of the notice or to identify an individual.[3] The publication of information about the issuance of a warning notice has the capacity to cause significant reputational damage to a firm or individual, which is unlikely to be wholly undone by subsequent communications. It is therefore important that firms are given a proper opportunity to make representations about the publication of information about warning notices before the s 391(1)(c) power is exercised. This is recognised to a certain extent by DEPP, which provides that the RDC will decide whether to publish information under FSMA 2000, s 391 and that before doing so the RDC will normally allow the subject of the publication at least 14 days to make representations about the terms of the proposed publication[4].

1 FSMA 2000, s 391 (1ZB) lists the statutory provisions in respect of which the warning notice publication power arises, covering the principal powers to suspend, fine and censure firms and individuals.
2 FSMA 2000, s 319 (6).
3 See the FCA's Policy Statement, '*Publishing information about enforcement warning notices*', October 2013 (PS13/9).
4 DEPP, 3.2.14F.

11.125   With the exception of publication of the warning notice, the FCA will generally only publish information about enforcement investigations prior to the decision notice in exceptional circumstances[1].

1 EG, 6.1 discusses these circumstances. FSMA 2000, s 391 prohibits recipients from publishing details of warning notices which have not been published by the FCA.

The Response to the Warning Notice

11.126   The issuance of a warning notice gives the recipient:

(a)   Where (in summary) the action is taken on the FCA's initiative[1], a right under FSMA 2000, s 394 of access to the material relied upon by the RDC in taking the decision that gave rise to the obligation to issue the warning notice and certain types of secondary material which might undermine the regulator's decision. Where the s 394 right applies, the FCA must state that it applies in the warning notice and explain whether any secondary material exists to which the person concerned must be allowed access[2].

(b)   A right under FSMA 2000, s 387 (2) to make representations in respect of the notice to the FCA within a reasonable period, which must be at least 14 days. Recipients of notices are typically permitted to make oral as well as written representations[3].

1   A list of the enforcement actions that trigger the s 394 right is contained within DEPP, 2 Annex 1G.
2   FSMA 2000, s 394 (1) (d) and (e).
3   DEPP, 3.2.15G (2).

11.127   Pursuant to FSMA 2000, s 393, a warning notice must in certain circumstances also be provided to third parties who are identified in the notice in a way which is prejudicial to them. Those third parties have rights to make representations in respect of the notice.

The Decision Notice

11.128   After considering any representations made, the RDC can, if it decides that action should be taken, issue a decision notice. If it decides to take no action then a notice of discontinuance must be issued pursuant to FSMA 2000, s 389.

11.129   The decision notice, like the warning notice, must be made in writing and give reasons for the proposed action[1]. The decision notice may propose the same action as the warning notice, or different action provided that the action proposed is under the same part of the FSMA 2000[2].

1   FSMA 2000, s 388 (1).
2   FSMA 2000, s 388 (2).

11.130   The issuance of a decision notice gives the recipient:

(a)   A further s 394 right of access to material relied upon by the RDC. The decision notice must set out this right where it arises.[1]

(b)   The right to refer the matter to the Tribunal pursuant to the FSMA 2000. The decision notice must set out this right and the procedure for making a reference.[2] This right must generally be exercised within 28 days of the decision notice. If it is exercised, the decision notice generally does not take effect until the Tribunal process, and any appeal, has been completed.

1   FSMA 2000, s 388 (c) and (d).
2   FSMA 2000, s 388 (e).

11.131   FSMA 2000, s 394 also gives third parties identified in decision notices certain rights broadly equivalent to those enjoyed by the subject of the notice.

Publication of the Decision Notice

11.132 Pursuant to FSMA 2000, s 391(4), the FCA must publish such information about the matter to which a decision notice relates as it considers appropriate[1]. However it may not do so if this would in the FCA's opinion be unfair, prejudicial to consumers or detrimental to the stability of the UK financial system[2]. The FCA's normal policy is to publish decision notices if the recipient decides to refer the matter to the Tribunal[3].

1 Subject to limited exceptions in FSMA 2000, s 391(5A).
2 FSMA 2000, s 319(6).
3 EG, 6.8.

The Final Notice

11.133 If the right to refer the matter to the Tribunal is not exercised, the FCA will issue a final notice on taking the action pursuant to FSMA 2000, s 390, setting out the action taken. Final notices are also issued by the FCA upon the completion of the appeal process and the taking of the action directed by the Tribunal or the relevant court. Final notices are published by the FCA on the same statutory basis as decision notices.

The Supervisory Notice Procedure

11.134 A slightly different procedure applies to certain types of enforcement action which the FSMA 2000 allows to be imposed as a matter of urgency. The circumstances in which this procedure applies are set out in DEPP, 2, Annex 2 G. The supervisory notice procedure applies to variations of permission and certain intervention action in relation to incoming firms, and other specific powers, typically involving the FCA giving directions for particular purposes. The procedure involves supervisory notices (typically a first and second supervisory notice) rather than warning and decision notices.

11.135 The procedure is similar to the warning/decision notice procedure. The main differences are:

(a)   the action need not wait to take effect until the entire decision-making process has been completed, but it may, in specific cases where this is necessary, take effect immediately on giving the first supervisory notice or on a date specified in the notice;

(b)   the person does not have any right of access to the FCA's material;

(c)   however, the person does have the right to refer the matter to the Tribunal immediately on issue of the first supervisory notice (whether or not the action is specified to take effect immediately);

(d)   in some cases, principally minor or very urgent ones where RDC members cannot be obtained, the RDC will not be involved, but decisions are instead taken by FCA executive procedures, which means by senior FCA staff members. In the case of urgent decisions, this relates only to the initial decision to issue a first supervisory notice.

Settlement of Enforcement Action with the FCA

11.136   The early settlement of enforcement action is often attractive both to the FCA, because it reduces the resources the regulator must devote to procuring enforcement decisions, and to firms, as it enables them to draw a line under enforcement investigations and preserve their regulatory relationships. The EG states that the FCA *'considers it is in the public interest for matters to settle, and settle early, if possible'*. Settlement is encouraged by the FCA's penalties policy, by which firms are entitled to a discount of between 10% and 30% on fines for agreeing a settlement, with the highest reduction applicable where settlement takes place before the end of the written representations stage of the enforcement process[1].

1 See DEPP, 6.7.

11.137   The FCA's settlement decision procedure is set out in DEPP, Chapter 5 and explained further in EG, 5.

11.138   A person subject to enforcement action can engage in settlement discussions with the FCA at any time during the process, provided the FCA has a sufficient understanding of the issue to make a reasonable assessment of the appropriate outcome[1]. Settlement discussions are 'without prejudice' to either parties' position before the RDC or Tribunal[2]. The settlement discussions themselves take place between the investigating FCA staff and the subject of the investigation.

1 DEPP, 5.13G.
2 DEPP, 5.1.4G. However, the EG makes clear that *'This will not…prevent the FCA from following up, through other means, on any new issues of regulatory concern which come to light during settlement discussions'*.

11.139   Once a settlement is agreed in principle between the investigating FCA staff and relevant person, it must be recorded in writing, typically with a draft of the proposed statutory notice[1]. The settlement will then either be accepted or declined by two members of the FCA's senior management known as the 'settlement decision makers' who have not been directly involved in establishing the evidence on which the decision is based. At least one of the decision makers must be from outside the FCA's Enforcement Division[2]. Where a settlement proposal is declined, the FCA staff and person concerned may be invited to enter into further discussions which the settlement decision makers would be prepared to endorse[3].

1 DEPP, 5.1.6G.
2 DEPP, 5.1.1 (4).
3 DEPP, 5.1.8G (1).

11.140   However, the following of the settlement procedure does not extinguish the rights of third parties in respect of notices pursuant to FSMA 2000, s 393. In practice third party objections to the terms of an agreed notice can impede early settlement.

Other Procedures

11.141   Certain types of enforcement decisions by the FCA, notably the decision to apply to a court for an injunction or restitution order, or to institute a criminal prosecution, do not involve any specific procedure under the FSMA 2000. The safeguards from the firm's perspective are found in the procedures of the civil or criminal court concerned. The FCA has, however, stipulated that the decision to institute court proceedings will normally be taken by the Chairman of the RDC[1]. This gives some protection for firms in a situation where even the institution of such proceedings can cause significant cost and disruption.

1 See for example EG, 11.1A and 12.4A.

The Tribunal

11.142 One of the key safeguards for firms is the ability to refer cases to the Tribunal. For example, it is in the Tribunal that the ECHR fair trial safeguards are fulfilled. The Tribunal is an independent body constituted under FSMA 2000, s 133 and Sch 13, and operated by the Ministry of Justice. It is entirely separate from the regulatory authorities and has no regulatory agenda as such. In respect of disciplinary references, the Tribunal is not an appeal body, but a first instance tribunal able to consider any evidence, and to reach its own decision on what action it is appropriate for the FCA to take in relation to the matter referred to it. In respect of other matters, the Tribunal must either dismiss the reference or remit the matter to the decision-maker with a direction to reconsider and reach a decision in accordance with the findings of the Tribunal[1]. The burden of proof in the Tribunal is on the FCA, not on the person against whom the FCA's enforcement action is being taken.

1 See FSMA 2000, s 133(5) to (7A).

11.143 The Tribunal's procedures are found in the Tribunal Procedure (Upper Tribunal) Rules 2008.[1] They do not prescribe in great detail the procedure to be adopted, leaving it largely to the Tribunal appointed to hear each case to decide on the process appropriate for the determination of that case. Broadly, a Tribunal is appointed to hear each case, drawn from a panel of legally qualified chairmen and a panel of lay members with relevant experience. The person commences the process by issuing a simple notice referring the matter to the Tribunal. It is then for the FCA to take the first step in explaining what the case is about, by issuing a Statement of Case, and the person concerned responds to that in its Reply. At the same time, there is a process of disclosure of relevant documents. Generally, the Tribunal will allow the parties to make submissions, will hear evidence from witnesses and, where appropriate, experts, and it also has powers to summons witnesses and to order the disclosure of documents.

1 As amended by The Tribunal Procedure (Upper Tribunal) (Amendment) Rules 2010 No. 747 (L. 5) and The Tribunal Procedure (Amendment No 2) Rules 2013. Schedule 3 sets out the procedure for financial services cases.

11.144 Proceedings before the Tribunal are normally held in public and judgment pronounced publicly, in accordance with the requirements of the ECHR. This may be an important factor for firms considering whether or not to refer a particular decision to the Tribunal. There is a right of appeal to the Court of Appeal, with permission, but only on points of law, and from there to the Supreme Court.

ENFORCEMENT AND THE PRINCIPLES

11.145   The regulator's increasing reliance on the Principles for Business and Statements of Principle for Approved Persons when taking enforcement action against firms and individuals has been one of the most significant developments in enforcement action since the FSMA 2000 came into effect.

11.146   The use of the Principles in Enforcement Action is addressed in DEPP, 6.2.14 and 15G and in the EG, 2.18 to 2.30. The EG makes clear that *'the FCA will, in appropriate cases, take enforcement action on the basis of the Principles alone'*[1].

1 EG, 2.19.

11.147   The high level of the Principles makes it difficult to state precisely what they require of a firm in a specific factual scenario. This gives rise to two risks, both of which are addressed by the FCA, to a certain extent, in its EG.

11.148   The first risk is that guidance and material such as speeches, case studies and Dear CEO Letters are used to establish what the Principles require, effectively allowing enforcement action to be taken against a firm for failure to comply with informal regulatory communications. The EG recognises that guidance and other material *"is not binding"*.[1] However, it also states that such materials *'are … potentially relevant to an enforcement case and a decision maker may take them into account in considering the matter'*.

1 EG, 2.23.

11.149   The second risk is that the Principles are used as a means of applying regulatory standards at the time of the enforcement action, rather than at the time of the relevant events, in determining whether there has been a breach of regulatory requirements. The EG states that *'to determine whether there has been a failure to comply with a Principle, the standards we will apply are those required by the Principles at the time the conduct took place'*[1].

1 EG, 2.21.

11.150   Enforcement cases brought on the basis of the Principles therefore often raise difficulties for the firms involved. It is common for one or both of the risks outlined above to materialise, notwithstanding the contents of the EG.

ENFORCEMENT AND REDRESS

11.151   As set out at para 11.9 above, undoing the harm caused by non-compliance with regulatory requirements is one of the four purposes of enforcement action.

11.152   The FCA has, as described above, a formal statutory power to impose or seek restitution orders in respect of breaches of regulatory requirements. However, there are a range of alternative means of securing redress, which are more commonly used than the formal restitution power:

(a) First, firms may agree with the FCA (as part of the settlement process described at paras 11.137–11.141 above) to undertake a pro-active redress exercise without the FCA exercising its formal statutory powers at all. Details of the exercise may be set out in the final notice. It may involve, for example, the firm writing to consumers to stimulate complaints, or pro-actively making redress payments to consumers who can be identified as having suffered loss as a result of the relevant breach. The cost of such redress exercises can significantly exceed the size of the fine imposed[1].

(b) Second, the publicity arising from enforcement action may stimulate consumers themselves to complain or bring claims in the courts:

    (i) Certain consumers can complain to the FOS[2], which can award compensation on the basis of what it considers to be *'fair and reasonable'*[3].

    (ii) The FSMA 2000 contains various provisions making firms liable to civil claims for breach of statutory duty as a result of regulatory contraventions. The main provision is FSMA 2000, s 138D. This provides that a contravention by an authorised person of an FCA rule is actionable at the suit of a private person who suffers loss as a result[4]. There are three important restrictions on the s 138D cause of action:

        (A) First, it is open only to a *'private person'*. This is defined pursuant to the Financial Services and Markets Act (Rights of Action) Regulations 2001 as (i) any person who has suffered loss other than in the course of carrying on business of any kind or (ii) any individual not acting in the course of carrying on a regulated activity. A company which enters into financial transactions may not be treated as a private person, even if financial trading is not its principal business in circumstances in which the transactions are part of, or integral, to its business[5]. Governments, local authorities and international organisations will not be treated as private persons in any circumstances under the regulations.

        (B) Second, it does not arise in respect of listing, prospectus, disclosure and transparency rules, rules under the threshold condition code, rules in connection with the provision of information by parent undertakings and financial resources rules[6], or rules of the FCA which provide that section 138D does not apply[7]. The Principles for Businesses are specified as falling outside FSMA 2000, s 138D[8]. Enforcement action taken on the basis of infringements of the Principles for Business therefore may not demonstrate a breach giving rise to potential civil liability.

        (C) Finally, the cause of action is *'subject to the defences and other incidents applying to actions for breach of statutory duty*[9]*'*. Thus, for example, the person making the claim must show that he has suffered loss, that the loss was caused in legal terms by the breach, is not too remote and is of a type that a court will compensate with an award of damages, and, moreover, various defences may be available to the firm.

The same provision is applied to certain specific contraventions relating to collective investment schemes[10]. Similar rights of action arise elsewhere in the FSMA 2000, most notably where a firm fails to take reasonable care to ensure that no person performs a controlled function who is not approved for that function or that a prohibited person does not carry out a function from which he is prohibited (FSMA 2000, s 71); where a firm carries on a regulated activity otherwise than in accordance with its permission (FSMA 2000, s 20(3)); where a passported firm breaches a requirement imposed upon it by the FCA or PRA (FSMA 2000, s 202(2)); and for contravention of the prohibition on dealing in transferable securities or requesting their admission to trading on a regulated market without an approved prospectus (FSMA 2000, s 85(4)).

(c)   Third, the FCA may exercise its powers to promulgate a consumer redress scheme under FSMA 2000, ss 404 to 404E. These sections confer wide-ranging powers on the FCA to make rules requiring firms to pay redress in circumstances where:

(i)   It appears to the FCA that there may have been a widespread or regular failure by relevant firms[11] to comply with requirements applicable to the carrying on by them of any activity;

(ii)   It appears to the FCA that as a result of (i) consumers have suffered loss or damage in respect of which a remedy would be available in legal proceedings; and

(iii)   The FCA considers it desirable to make rules to secure redress[12].

Products or business practices in respect of which enforcement action has been taken are potential candidates for consumer redress schemes, as enforcement investigations and actions may provide the FCA with an evidential basis for promulgating a consumer redress scheme[13]. The FSA's Guidance Note 10 (now published by the FCA) contains detailed guidance on the circumstances in which the FCA will use its consumer redress scheme power.

---

1   For example the FCA issued various final notices in respect of a number of financial institutions that sold PPI. The aggregate amount of the fines levied under these Final Notices was insignificant in comparison to the £8.9bn of refunds and compensation paid in respect to PPI between January 2011 and January 2013 (as calculated by the FCA).
2   See para 11.10 above.
3   FSMA 2000, s 228(2).
4   Pursuant to section 138D (1) rules of the PRA are only actionable if they expressly provide they are actionable. The default position is therefore that they are not actionable.
5   See *Titan Steel Wheels Limited v The Royal Bank of Scotland Plc* [2010] EWHC 211. This case concerned FSMA 2000, s 150, the predecessor to s 138D.
6   FSMA 2000, s 138D (5).
7   FSMA 2000, s 138D (3).
8   See PRIN, 3.4.4R.
9   FSMA 2000, s 138D (2) and (4).
10 See FSMA 2000, s 241 and 257 and the Financial Services and Markets Act 2000 (Open ended Investment Companies) Regulations 2001, SI 2001/1228, reg 25(6).

11 Defined in FSMA 2000, s 404 (2) as authorised persons, payment service providers and electronic money issuers.
12 FSMA 2000, s 404 (1).
13 See FCA Guidance Note 10 (2010), 6.4.

THE MARKET ABUSE REGIME

11.153 The FSMA 2000 contained a new civil offence of market abuse when it came into force in 2001 (see Chapter 4). On 1 July 2005, the legislation implementing the Market Abuse Directive[1] came into force in the United Kingdom and the FSMA 2000 was amended by, essentially, grafting the prohibitions contained in the Directive on to the existing market abuse regime. The result of this is that the UK presently has a wider definition of market abuse than that contained in the Market Abuse Directive. At the time of writing it is anticipated that the Market Abuse Directive will be replaced in June 2014 by the Market Abuse Regulation which will be directly effective across EU Member States two years after the date of its publication in the Official Journal. The scope of the Market Abuse Regulation will be broader than that of the Market Abuse Directive. In particular, in the form currently proposed[2], the market abuse regime would be extended to: (i) financial instruments admitted to trading on multilateral trading facilities ('MTFs') and organised trading facilities ('OTFs' – the new trading venue category to be introduced under the revision of the Markets in Financial Instruments Directive), as well as covering financial instruments admitted to trading on regulated markets[3]; and (ii) instruments traded over-the-counter that have an effect on instruments traded on a regulated market, MTF or OTF[4].

1 2003/6/EC.
2 European Parliament legislative resolution on the proposed regulation of the European Parliament and of the Council on insider dealing and market manipulation (market abuse), 10 September 2013. The Market Abuse Regulation will come into force with a Criminal Sanction for Market Abuse Directive (CSMAD). However, CSMAD will not be required to be implemented in the UK unless the UK opts into it. At the time of writing no final decision has been made by the UK Government.
3 Market Abuse Regulation, art 2(1).
4 Market Abuse Regulation, art 2(1)(c).

11.154 As it currently stands, the UK's civil market abuse regime supplements the criminal regime for insider dealing under Part V of the Criminal Justice Act 1993 and the criminal offences under the Financial Services Act 2012 of making false or misleading statements[1], creating false or misleading impressions[2], or making false or misleading statements with respect to particular benchmarks[3]. The civil market abuse provisions allow the FCA to deal with a wider scope of market misconduct than that which falls within the criminal offences, as well as conduct which is not suitable to be dealt with by the criminal justice system.

1 Financial Services Act 2012, s 89.
2 Financial Services Act 2012, s 90.
3 Financial Services Act 2012, s 91.

11.155 The statutory definition of civil market abuse is found in FSMA 2000, ss 118 and 118A. There is both a primary and a secondary civil offence.

11.156 The definition is complex, but in short the primary market abuse offence is behaviour which:

(a) occurs in relation to qualifying investments[1]; and

(b) falls into one or more of the following categories[2]:

    (i) insider dealing[3];

    (ii) improper disclosure of inside information;

    (iii) misuse of information;

    (iv) manipulating transactions;

    (v) manipulating devices;

    (vi) dissemination of information that gives or is likely to give a false or misleading impression; or

    (vii) misleading behaviour and market distortion.

1 Defined in FSMA 2000, s 118(1).
2 See FSMA 2000, ss 118(2)–(8) and s 118A.
3 This civil concept of market abuse by insider dealing sits alongside, but is different to, the criminal offence of insider dealing under Part V of the Criminal Justice Act 1993.

11.157 The secondary market abuse offence under the FSMA 2000 is of taking, or refraining from taking, action which requires or encourages another to engage in conduct which would be market abuse if the person requiring or encouraging the conduct in question had been engaging in the conduct itself[1].

1 Examples are given in the Code at MAR, 1.2.23.

11.158 The statutory definition of market abuse should be read in conjunction with the Code of Market Conduct which the FCA has issued under the FSMA 2000 to give guidance to those determining whether or not behaviour amounts to market abuse. The Code forms the first chapter of the MAR Sourcebook and specifies behaviour that in the FCA's opinion amounts to market abuse, that which in its opinion does not, and that which is to be taken into account in determining whether or not behaviour amounts to market abuse. To the extent that it describes behaviour as not amounting to market abuse, that behaviour is to be taken as not amounting to market abuse (FSMA 2000, s 122[1]). Otherwise, the Code has the status of evidential guidance. Whilst the Code will therefore be at the centre of any consideration of whether a firm or individual can or cannot follow a certain course of action, it remains subsidiary to the statutory definition of market abuse found in the FSMA 2000.

1 At the time of writing, the Code also specifies behaviour which is (and which is not) accepted market practice in relation to one of more specified markets. However, it is proposed that these accepted market practice provisions are to be removed once the Market Abuse Directive is replaced by the Market Abuse Regulation.

11.159 As the conduct regulator, the FCA has the primary responsibility for enforcement in the area of market misconduct in the UK. It is able to investigate the misconduct and to undertake a range of action aimed at addressing different implications of the same matter. The recognised investment exchanges, the Takeover Panel and/or overseas regulators may, however, also be involved in taking action in respect of market abuse.

11.160 It is widely anticipated that the FCA will seek to build on the approach of its predecessor, the FSA, of aiming to be a 'credible deterrent' to market misconduct. As a result it is likely that the FCA will subject market participants to scrutiny and seek to use the full range of its enforcement options with the aim of making the perceived risks associated with market misconduct outweigh the potential gains.

11.161 It is anticipated that the PRA will only be interested in conduct issues such as market abuse to the extent that there are serious prudential ramifications for a dual-regulated firm that engage its statutory objectives.

11.162 Market abuse can be enforced on a number of different levels.

11.163 The first level of enforcement is criminal prosecution. Market abuse overlaps significantly with the criminal offences of insider dealing (under Part V of the Criminal Justice Act 1993) and misleading statements and practices (Financial Services Act 2012, ss 89 and 90[1]). Insofar as conduct constitutes one of the criminal offences, and is appropriate to be dealt with through the criminal justice system, it may result in a criminal prosecution and the FCA may act as the prosecutor. The FCA's policy on the prosecution of criminal offences and, particularly, market abuse criminal offences, can be found in EG Chapter 12 (and, particularly, EG Chapter 12.8[2]).

1 The offence of misleading statements and practices under the Financial Services Act 2012 was formerly to be found in FSMA 2000, s 397, where it was also a criminal offence. The scope of the misleading practices offence under Financial Services Act 2012, s 90 is now somewhat wider.
2 The FSA secured its first criminal conviction for market abuse in August 2005 when Carl Rigby and Gareth Bailey were found guilty of an offence under the FSMA 2000, s 397(1)(c) (recklessly making a statement, promise or forecast which is misleading, false or deceptive in a material particular). By the time it was replaced by the FCA, the FSA had secured 23 individual convictions in relation to insider dealing with custodial sentences being imposed for all individuals.

11.164 Under the FSMA 2000, the FCA has the power to detain suspects for questioning in relation to market abuse. The FCA entered into a Memorandum of Understanding with the Association of Chief Police Officers[1] that formalise the arrangement for the regulator to request that the police use their powers to arrest individuals or execute search warrants for the FCA in cases of suspected market abuse and insider dealing. This arrangement will continue for the FCA.

1 Memorandum of Understanding dated 22 August 2005.

11.165 The second level of enforcement is that the FCA may impose a civil penalty for market abuse or make a public statement that a person has engaged in market abuse, under FSMA 2000, s 123. Penalties and public statements can be imposed against any person, whether or not within the regulated community, who engages in either primary or secondary civil market abuse. The FCA is required, under FSMA 2000, s 124, to prepare and issue a statement of its policy with respect to the imposition and amount of penalties and in exercising, or deciding to exercise, its power under FSMA 2000, s 123, in any case is required to have regard to the policy in force at the time when the behaviour concerned occurred. The FCA's policy can be found in the EG and DEPP. The FCA will not, generally, both prosecute one of the criminal offences outlined below and impose a civil fine for market abuse, although there is nothing in FSMA 2000 to require this[1].

1 EG, 12.10.

11.166 FSMA 2000, s 123(2) provides that the FCA may not impose a penalty on a person if there are reasonable grounds to be satisfied that the person believed on reasonable grounds that his behaviour did not amount to market abuse or took all reasonable precautions and exercised all due diligence to avoid behaving in a way which amounted to market abuse. DEPP, 6.3.2 sets out factors that the FCA may take into account in deciding whether either condition is met. These include the extent to which the person followed established internal procedures, or sought and followed legal or expert professional advice, or sought and followed advice from relevant market authorities.

11.167 The effect of this provision is that the behaviour still amounts to market abuse (and could, for example, still be prohibited by an injunction), despite no penalty being imposed.

11.168 Proceedings for a financial penalty for market abuse attract additional safeguards under the FSMA 2000 because the government recognised the risk that such proceedings might constitute a criminal charge for ECHR purposes[1]. As a result, in accordance with art 6(2) of the ECHR, legal assistance is available for Tribunal proceedings in relation to market abuse (FSMA 2000, s 134) and, in common with criminal prosecutions, information obtained using compulsory powers is not admissible in proceedings against the person who provided that information or statement (FSMA 2000, s 174).[2]

1 At the time of writing, no challenges under the ECHR have been brought in respect of penalties imposed by the FCA or its predecessor, the FSA.
2 In practice the FCA will usually seek to conduct a voluntary interview with an individual who is the subject of a market abuse regime. In circumstances in which the interview is conducted on a voluntary basis and the individual is not compelled by the FCA, the self-incrimination provisions will be unlikely to be engaged.

11.169 The third level of enforcement is regulatory. Market abuse or other misconduct occurring in relation to an authorised firm may be indicative of broader matters of regulatory concern relating to the firm. For example, it may indicate defects in the firm's systems and controls or issues about the training and competence of employees. It may also indicate that particular individuals are not fit and proper to be involved in regulated activities. As a result, the FCA may wish to take other regulatory enforcement action. Depending upon the situation, this might include disciplinary action (although whether the firm or person had been subjected to a penalty for market abuse would clearly be relevant to whether it was appropriate also to discipline it in relation to the same matter), as well as other action such as varying the firm's permission or withdrawing the approval of an approved person.

11.170 Moreover, if an authorised firm or approved person commits market abuse, that may amount to a breach of the regulatory principles requiring firms and individuals to observe proper standards of market conduct (respectively, Principle 5 of the Principles for Businesses and State-ment of Principle 3 for Approved Persons). The predecessor to the FCA, the FSA, indicated[1] that where the principal mischief is market abuse, or requiring or encouraging market abuse, the FSA will take action under the market abuse regime rather than for a breach of Principle 5. However, a breach of the Principles may be committed even where the conduct does not technically amount to market abuse. In such cases, the FSA may take action to enforce the Principles and any specific rules breached.

1 EG, 2.18.

11.171 Finally, injunctions and restitution orders may also be available in cases of market abuse. Under FSMA 2000, s 381, the FCA can seek an injunction to restrain threatened market abuse, require a person to take steps to remedy it, or to freeze assets. The provisions are similar to the injunction provisions discussed above. The two defences to a fine for market abuse do not apply in the context of injunctions, so that an injunc-tion can be granted notwithstanding the fact that a civil penalty could not be imposed. So far as restitution orders are concerned, the provisions (found in FSMA 2000, ss 383 and 384) are similar to the restitution order provisions already discussed, with the notable difference that the FCA may itself make a restitution order in relation to market abuse against any person, not just an authorised person.

11.172 There is a potential overlap between the role of the Takeover Panel and the FCA's policing of the market abuse regime. The FCA has provided detailed guidance on how it will act where there is such an overlap in DEPP, 6.2.19 to 6.2.27.

ENFORCEMENT BY THE PRA

11.173 As explained at para 11.5 above, the PRA is unlikely to be as active in enforcement investigations and action as the FCA, but it has consider-able enforcement powers. The PRA's powers and decision-making pro-cesses are broadly similar to the FCA's. For example, both regulators have warning/decision notice and supervisory notice procedures, and the PRA enjoys broadly the same FSMA 2000, ss 165, 166, 167, 168, and 169 powers as the FCA (as described above).

11.174 However, there are a number of significant differences:

(a) First, the PRA's enforcement decision-making bodies, the Decision Making Committees (DMCs) differ significantly from the RDC. They are not independent of the rest of the PRA, but are comprised of PRA employees, and may include a person involved in the underlying investigatory process (which is permitted by FSMA 2000, s 395). The composition of a DMC in any enforcement case will depend upon the systemic importance of the firm and issue being considered. The most important decisions are taken by the PRA Board. A panel of Heads of Departments and Managers takes less important deci-sions[1].

(b) Second, the PRA has a very wide ranging power under FSMA 2000, s 165A[2] to obtain documents and information from the persons identified in s 165A (3) (defined to include a person who provides any service to an authorised person) that it considers might be relevant to the stability of one or more aspects of the UK financial system. FSMA 2000, s 165B contains a number of 'safeguards' with respect to this power. It requires the PRA to:

(i) give the person in question a warning and an opportunity to make representations before exercising the power (unless the PRA considers it is necessary to obtain the information and documents without delay).

(ii) publish a statement of its policy with respect to the use of the power approved by the Treasury. The Treasury-approved policy appears in FINMAR 1.

(c) Third, the PRA's penalties policy does not contain a sliding scale of fixed percentages to be applied to a firm's revenues to generate a fine like the FCA's, but instead states *'the PRA will apply an appropriate percentage rate[3]'*.

(d) Finally, the PRA may in practice make use of the FCA's greater investigatory expertise by outsourcing enforcement investigations to the FCA pursuant to FSMA 2000, ss 167 to 169, rather than conducting investigations itself.

1 See the PRA's Approach to Enforcement: Statutory Statements of Policy and Procedure (April 2013), Appendix 1 for further information.
2 FSMA 2000, s 169A contains a similar power which may be exercised by the PRA at the request of an overseas regulator with respect to the stability of the financial system of the country of the overseas regulator.
3 See the PRA's Approach to Enforcement: Statutory Statements of Policy and Procedure, Appendix 2, paragraph 19, April 2013.

11.175 Regulatory problems may arise at dual-regulated firms which are of interest to both the PRA and FCA. The FCA and PRA's Memorandum of Understanding addresses the co-ordination of formal regulatory processes and of enforcement and legal intervention[1] in order to avoid conflicting or incompatible action being taken. It provides for co-ordination varying between consent, consultation and notification for different types of enforcement decisions, and specifically provides that where either regulator decides to carry out an investigation in relation to a dual-regulated firm or individual, the regulators will consider whether the investigation should be jointly co-ordinated.

1 See pages 9 to 11 and Annex 1.

Chapter 12

Professionals and Investment Business

Andrew Haynes

INTRODUCTION

12.1   Under the regime created by the Financial Services and Markets Act 2000 and the Financial Services Act 2012 those carrying on regulated activities need to be regulated by the Financial Conduct Authority (FCA) and the Prudential Regulatory Authority (PRA). However, there are exemptions for professionals carrying on investment business where this is 'incidental'[1] to the professional services being provided to the client. Such professionals are: solicitors (whether in England and Wales, Scotland or Northern Ireland), licensed conveyancers, chartered accountants (whether in England and Wales, Scotland or Ireland), certified accountants, actuaries and chartered surveyors. Were there not to be an exception covering them it would be necessary for most such firms to be regulated by the FCA when carrying out even trivial amounts of financial services work. This was deemed unnecessary as they are all covered by existing regulators and have to maintain appropriate professional standards. In addition the firms providing the types of investments with which such professionals might be engaging with are themselves regulated.

1 FSMA 2000, s 327(4).

12.2   Instances where financial services issues are likely to arise with solicitors are: probate and trusts, conveyancing, corporate finance and takeovers, divorce and some litigation. With licensed conveyancers it is normally going to be limited to advising on and/or providing insurance cover. In the case of accountants it is likely to be limited to insurance and corporate finance work. Where consulting actuaries are concerned the activity can only be conducted for clients that are trustees of pension schemes, employers or insurance companies. Chartered Surveyors were so classified to facilitate their members engaging in insurance mediation activities (see below).

12.3   The nature of 'incidental' indicates that the work concerned is a minor part of the task being carried out and is also necessary to its fulfilment. This also relates to whether or not the investment business had been held out as being a separate task in the first place and how the firm promotes its activities via the media[1]. This also brings into play the financial promotion rules which are dealt with in chapter 3.

1 FSMA 2000, s 327(5).

12.4   The relevant recognised professional bodies are termed 'designated professional bodies' for these purposes under the Act[1]. Those designated are:

- the Association of Chartered Certified Accountants;

- the Council for Licensed Conveyancers;

- the Institute and Faculty of Actuaries

- the Institute of Chartered Accountants in England and Wales;

- the Institute of Chartered Accountants of Scotland;

- the Institute of Chartered Accountants in Ireland;

- the Law Society of England and Wales, though in practice the work is carried out by the Solicitors' Regulation Authority (SRA);

- the Law Society of Northern Ireland;

- the Law Society of Scotland; and

- the Royal Institute of Chartered Surveyors

These bodies are therefore able to supervise the firms who they regulate when carrying on exempt regulated activities in addition to the normal professional activities such firms engage in.[2] If the firm carries on investment work outside the definition of exempt regulated activities applicable to their professional body then they must be regulated by the FCA and PRA.

1 FSMA 2000, s 326.
2 FSMA 2000, s 327(8)

12.5   Some firms that act in non-financial services areas can obtain authorisation to carry on limited financial services work and be supervised by their own professional body whilst doing so. The professional bodies concerned which have been given such accredit status are:

- The CFA Society of the UK;

- The Chartered Institute for Securities and Investment (CISI);

- The Chartered Institute of Bankers in Scotland (CIOBS);

- The Chartered Insurance Institute (CII);

- The Institute of Chartered Accountants in England and Wales (ICAEW);

- The Institute of Financial Planning (IFP);

- The Institute of Financial Services (IFS); and

- The Pensions Management Institute.

The function of such an accredited body is to make sure that those they regulate attain and maintain the new professionalism requirement that must satisfy a Statement of Professional Standing (SPS) which they are responsible for issuing. Anyone they supervise who does not satisfy these standards must be reported to the FCA. In so doing the accredited body must satisfy requirements in four broad areas: to act in the public interest and further development of their profession; carry out effective verification services; have appropriate systems and controls in place and provide evidence to the FCA of their continuing effectiveness; and cooperate with the FCA on an ongoing basis. As the FCA's powers cannot be delegated such organisations effectively act on behalf of, and report back to the FCA.

12.6 There is also a Memorandum of Understanding between the FCA and the SRA[1] providing for an equivalent state of affairs whereby the SRA will report to the FCA on which solicitors are carrying out exempt work under s.327 and those who are authorised professional terms. Reports also have to be made regarding any issues arising regarding such firms.

1 Memorandum of Understanding, Financial Conduct Authority and Solicitors Regulatory Authority, 28 March 2013.

EXEMPT REGULATED ACTIVITIES

12.7 These are determined by FSMA 2000, s 327(1)–(7). In addition, s 327(3) requires that the professional person concerned should not be taking any fee or other financial benefit for the work concerned other than one which is being accounted for to the client. This means that the funds must be held to the order of the client. The firm can offset any commission received on the client's behalf against any fee owed by that client. The rule also requires that the client has given informed consent to this prior to agreement for the professional to keep the commission. The client must have had explained to them that the commission belongs to them and the full amount must have been disclosed.

12.8 As the work concerned must be being carried out in a manner that is incidental to the professional activity concerned. Other identifiable professional work must therefore be carried out to which the investment business work must be adjunct. It follows that it is not possible for a firm to carry out even a one-off regulated activity in isolation that is not incidental.

12.9 The FSMA also gives the power to the Treasury to pass regulations determining the activities that cannot be carried on by those acting under the umbrella of exempt regulated activities. Pursuant to this the Financial Services and Markets Act 2000 (Profession) (Non-Exempt Activities) Order 2001[1] has been passed which excludes:

- accepting deposits;
- effecting and carrying out insurance contracts;
- establishing, running or winding up a collective investment scheme;
- establishing, running or winding up a stakeholder pension scheme;
- acting as a Lloyd's managing agent;
- advising someone to become a member of a named Lloyd's syndicate;
- acting as provider of a funeral plan contract; or
- acting as a lender or administering a regulated mortgage contract, a home reversion plan, a home purchase plan or a sale and rent back mortgage.

The firm must not carry on or hold itself out as carrying on a regulated activity other than these or one in relation to which the firm is an exempt person.

1 SI 2001/1227 as amended by SI 2001/3650, SI 2002/682, SI 2002/1777, SI 2003/1475, SI 2003/1476, SI 2004/2737, SI 2006/1969, SI 2006/2383 and SI 2009/1342.

Exclusions from regulated activity status

12.10 Certain activities are permitted in specific situations even though they appear to be caught by the definition of regulated activities. These are set out in the Regulated Activities Order[1], as amended[2]. These orders specify the types of activity and investments that are permitted, and replaced Sch 2, Pts I and II of the FSMA 2000. In the context of this chapter the key issues are the various exemptions that are useful to professionals. The most notable in this context are set out in the paragraphs below.

1 Issued by H M Treasury pursuant to their powers under sections 22(1), (5), 426 and 428(3) and para 25 of Sch 2 to the FSMA 2000.
2 SI 2001/544 as amended by SI 2001/3544, SI 2002/682, SI 2002/1310, SI 2002/1776, SI 2002/1777, SI 2003/1475, SI 2003/1476, SI 2003/2822, SI 2004/1610, SI 2004/2737, SI 2005/593, SI 2005/1518, SI 2005/2114, SI 2006/196, SI 2006/2383, SI 2006/3384, SI 2009/1342, SI 2012/1906, SI 2013/1881 and the Alternative Investment Fund Managers Regulations 2013/1773.

12.11 Under article 5 deposit taking is a specified activity. However, solicitors regularly accept deposits on behalf of their clients. Article 7 confirms that this operates outside Article 5 and that solicitors are not caught by the regime when accepting deposits. As the purpose of including deposit taking within the financial services regime was to catch those who carry on business as deposit takers or solicitors are holding money as either agent or stakeholder, the exclusion is to be expected.

12.12 Article 14 categorises 'dealing as principal' as a specified activity and states:

> 'Buying, selling, subscribing for or underwriting securities or contractually based investments (other than investments of the kind specified by article 87, or article 89 so far as relevant to this article) as principal is specified kind of activity'.

Article 87 governs funeral plan contracts and article 89 rights or interests in investments.

There are exclusions to 'dealing as principal' in arts 15 to 20.

12.13 Articles 15 and 16 deal with the absence of holding out and dealing with contractually based investments. The former states that a party does not carry on a specified activity unless 'dealing' involves:

- holding themselves out to deal as principal to buy, sell or subscribe for investments at prices they determine themselves on a continuous basis;

- holding themselves out as engaging in the business of buying investments of the kind to which the transaction relates with a view to selling them;

- holding themselves out as underwriters of investments of the kind to which the transaction relates; or

- regularly soliciting members of the public with the purpose of inducing them to deal.

This does not apply to someone dealing as a bare trustee.

12.14 The first two of these are aimed at market makers, investment bankers and fund managers who are trading in their own name but often risking their clients' money in the process. Thus it is an extension of the dealing as agent rule (see **12.17** below).

12.15 Article 16 states that a party is not dealing if the transaction relates to a contractually based investment and is carried out with or through an authorised or exempt person. Nor does it amount to dealing if it is carried out through an office outside the UK maintained by a party to the transaction if the transaction consists of: dealing, dealing as agent, arranging, managing investments, safeguarding and administering assets, sending dematerialised instructions, establishing, operating or winding up a collective investment scheme or stakeholder pension scheme or advising on investments.

12.16 The remaining exceptions in articles 17 to 20 cover respectively accepting bonds and other debt paper, a company issuing or dealing in its own shares, engaging in risk management as principal and acting as trustee[1], sale of goods and services[2], sale of a company[3], employee share schemes[4], overseas persons[5], information society services[6] and UCITS and AIF managers[7].

1 Dealt with in Art 66.
2 Art 68.
3 Art 70.
4 Art 71.
5 Art 72.
6 Art 72A.
7 Art 72AA.

12.17 Article 21 renders dealing as agent a specified activity. However, it is acceptable to do this through an authorised person[1] because the financial services risk in such cases is in the hands of the regulated person to whom the financial services work has been passed. For the exception to apply the transaction must be entered into on advice given to the client by an authorised person or it must be clear that the client in his capacity as an investor is not seeking and has not sought advice from the agent as to the merits of the transaction. Alternately the client may have sought such advice but the agent has declined to provide it and suggested the client receive it from an authorised person. This exclusion does not apply if the transaction relates to a contract of insurance or the agent receives a financial reward from the transaction which is not accounted for to his client[2]. Finally there are exclusions for trustees (art 66), the sale of goods and services (Art 68), group and joint enterprises (Art 69), sale of a body corporate (art 70), employee share schemes (art 71), overseas persons (art 72), information society services (Art 72A) and managers of UCITS and AIFs (Art 72AA[3]).

1 Art 22.
2 Added by SI 2003/1476, art 4(2).
3 Art 20.

12.18   Article 25 renders 'arranging' a specified activity. There are three main exclusions from this. Article 27 excludes situations where a party is simply seeking to provide someone with the means to communicate. Article 28 excludes transactions to which the arranger is a party, whether as principal or agent. However, this does not extend to arrangements relating to a contract for insurance unless the person making the arrangement is the only policy holder or would become one. Article 29 excludes deals entered into through authorised persons as the FCA authorised person will be carrying on the investment activity. Article 33 and 33A exclude the introduction of one party to another provided that the person to whom the introduction is made is either authorised or exempt or is a person who is lawfully carrying on business in the UK and whose business consists of dealing, dealing as agent, arranging, managing, safeguarding and administering, sending dematerialised instructions, establishing operating or winding up a collective investment scheme or stakeholder pension scheme or advising. In any of these instances the introduction must be made with a view to providing independent advice or the exercise of discretion in relation to the investments concerned. Article 34 excludes arrangements made by a company for the purpose of issuing its own shares or debentures. Finally Article 36 adds exclusions for trustees (art 66), professional or non-investment business (art 67), the sale of goods and services (Art 68), group and joint enterprises (Art 69), sale of a body corporate (art 70), employee share schemes (art 71), overseas persons (art 72), information society services (Art 72A), managers of UCITS and AIFs (Art 72AA), activities carried on by a provider of relevant goods and services). (art 72B), providing information about contracts of insurance on an incidental basis (art 72C) and large risk contracts where the risk is situated outside the EEA (art 72D).

12.19   There is a further exclusion from 'arranging' in article 72C[1] covering making arrangements for the sale or purchase of an insurance contract or any right or interest in an investment as defined by article 89. However, the activity must be limited to providing information to a policyholder, be carried on in the course of a profession that does not amount to investment business and is incidental to the profession being carried on. There is a further exclusion relating to large risks contracts of insurance where the risk is not situated in the EEA.

1 Added by art 11.

12.20   Article 36A has added credit broking to the list of investments though there are exclusions for a limited range of activities whilst canvassing off trade premises[1], those for which no fee is paid[2] and transactions to which the broker is a party[3] and certain agreements where a regulated mortgage is entered into are excluded[4] (though they could be caught by Article 61) as are those carried out by a solicitor or barrister in the course of contentious business[5]. Finally there are exclusions for trustees (art 66), the sale of goods and services (Art 68), group and joint enterprises (Art 69), information society services (Art 72A), managers of UCITS and AIFs (Art 72AA) and incidental provisions relating to contracts of insurance (Art 72C).

1 Art 36B.
2 Art 36C.
3 Art 36D.
4 Art 36E.
5 Art 36F.

12.21 'Managing' is categorised as a specified activity by article 37 to which there is a key exclusion. Article 38 excludes someone acting under a power of attorney enabling him to manage the assets concerned. The key issue is that the day to day decisions, ie, whether to buy or sell etc, are carried out by an authorised or exempt person. The exclusions in the final sentence of **12.20** above also apply here.

12.22 Assisting in the administration and performance of a contract of insurance is made an investment activity by Article 39A with exclusions for claims management on behalf of an insurer[1] and those added in the final sentence of **12.20** above[2].

1 Art 39B.
2 Art 39C.

12.23 Debt adjusting is also an investment activity[1] as is debt counselling[2], debt collecting[3] and debt administration[4]. There are exclusions in Articles 39 H to L for activities where the person concerned is connected to the agreement, activities carried out by an energy supplier under a green deal plan, in relation to land and by members of the legal profession in the course of contentious business. The exclusion in Article 72A for information society services applies here.

1 Art 39D.
2 Art 39E.
3 Art 39F.
4 Art 39G.

12.24 'Safeguarding and administering' in relation to securities or contractually based investments is made an investment activity by article 40. However, introducing a person to a qualifying custodian is excluded by article 42. A 'qualifying custodian' is an authorised person permitted to engage in safeguarding and administering or someone who is exempt. The exclusions in the final sentence of **12.20** above also apply here.

12.25 'Advising' is deemed a specified investment activity by article 53 in relation to buying, selling, subscribing for or underwriting an investment which is a security or contractually based investment or exercising a conferred right to do one of those things. It also covers advising in relation to mortgage contracts[1], home reversion plans[2], home purchase plans[3] and sale and rent back agreements[4].

There is an exclusion for advice given in newspapers[5] as part of a news service but not if it is essentially an advert or the giving of advice. Others cover activities in the administration of a mortgage[6] or in the list covered in the final sentence of **12.20** above plus large risk insurance contracts where the risk is outside the EEA[7].

1 Art 53A.
2 Art 53B.
3 Art 53C.

4 Art 53D.
5 Art 54.
6 Art 54A.
7 Art 55.

12.26   Entering into a regulated mortgage contacts is deemed to be a specified activity as is administering one[1]. A regulated mortgage contact is one whereby an individual or trustee borrows money, secured by a first legal mortgage on land in the UK. It must be intended to use at least 40% of the property as a residential dwelling by the individual, a related person or the beneficiary of a trust. In this context 'administering' means notifying the borrower of changes in interest rates or payments due and taking any necessary steps to recover moneys loaned. It does not extend to the work carried on by solicitors when acting on behalf of a bank or building society in a conveyancing matter. It has been extended to home reversion plans[2], home purchase plans[3] and sale and rent back agreements[4]. The exclusion which exists under article 62 covers arranging such administration by an authorised person or administering it themselves.

1 Art 61.
2 Art 63B.
3 Art 63F.
4 Art 63J.

12.27   There are important exclusions covering trustees, nominees and personal representatives in article 66. A bare trustee acting on behalf of someone else can deal as an excluded activity. Arranging is also excluded where carried out by a trustee or personal representative acting in their capacity as such or by a beneficiary under the trust, will or on intestacy. Managing is excluded where carried on by someone acting as trustee or personal representative provided they do not hold themselves out as offering such a service or the assets are held for an occupational pension scheme. A trustee or personal representative can act on an excluded basis from the activity of safeguarding and administering provided they do not hold themselves out as being able to do so. They are also excluded from article 39A[1] (which makes it a specified activity to assist in the administration or performance of a contract of insurance) unless they hold themselves out as so doing.

1 Added by SI 2003/1476, art 7.

12.28   Article 67 provides an important exception in permitting certain activities if carried on in the course of a profession or non-investment business and the financial services activity is merely incidental to the legal work. Also any money received from carrying out the financial services activity must be accounted for to the client. Unfortunately Art 67 is not clearly drafted and the best course of action is to turn to SRA Scope Rule 4 which is far clearer and is intended to have the same meaning. (See **12.32** below).

12.29   The sale and purchase of companies can create a situation where professional advisers acting on behalf of the vendor or purchaser seem to be straying into specified activities. For this reason article 70 provides an exclusion from the activities of dealing, arranging and advising where the transaction is the sale or purchase of a company other than an open ended investment company. The key issue is that the object of the transaction is the acquisition of the day to day control of the company. The evidence of this that is normally expected is one of the following occurs, but even if these are not satisfied it is sufficient if a transfer of control has taken place:

- the shares to be transferred represent 50% or more of the shares in that company[1]; or

- the shares, together with those held by the purchaser will add up to at least 50%[2];

- the shareholding achieved by the buyer does not reach either of these figures but the buyer is still becoming a 'controller' as defined by s 422 FSMA 2000. Essentially this means that the buyer has become someone on whose instructions that company will act and who owns at least 10% of the shares in that company or its holding company[3] In reality it is normally necessary to own 50% the shares to be certain of satisfying this requirement, but sometimes classes of shares have different voting rights and it might thus be possible to have 'significant influence' with less than this amount; and

- in any case the acquisition or disposal is between parties each of whom is any one of the following: a company, a partnership, an individual or a connected group of people, ie, there is a transfer of organised control from A to B.

1 Art 70 (2)(a).
2 Art 70 (2)(b).
3 Art 70(1)(b)(ii) and s.422 FSMA 2000, s 422.

SOLICITORS

12.30   The SRA Financial Services (Scope) Rules 2001 have been issued by the SRA with a view to determining the financial services activities of those firms of solicitors that are not regulated by the FCA. This is the vast majority as only a very small percentage of solicitors' practices have adopted the route of FCA authorisation. The rules also apply to FCA authorised firms where they carry on exempt regulated activities rather than relying on their FCA license. This will often be necessary as the FCA authorisation will only provide the opportunity to act within the precise limits of that license. Firms may often need to engage in the other activities that s 327 of the Act permits, thus bringing in to play the Scope Rules.

12.31   The Rules also set out the conditions and restrictions that apply to such firms. The activities that are prohibited of necessity parallel those set out in the Non-Exempt Activities Order referred to above. However, the SRA have taken matters a little further in that it debars the activities of:[1]

- buying, selling, subscribing for or underwriting investments as principal where the firm holds itself out as engaging in the business of buying such investments with a view to selling them; or holding itself out as engaging in the business of underwriting investments of the kind to which the transaction relates; or regularly soliciting the public to enter into transactions with the firm; or

- buying or selling investments with a view to stabilising or maintaining the market price of those investments.

1 SRA Financial Services (Scope) Rules at 3.

12.32   If a firm carries on exempt regulated activities certain conditions must be met. These are:

- the activity must arise out of or be complementary to the provision of the professional legal services which the firm is providing;

- the provision of the service must be in a manner which is incidental to the carrying on of professional legal business;

- any financial benefit accruing to the firm as a result must be accounted for to the client;

- the firm must neither hold itself out as carrying out, nor carry out a regulated activity unless it is either allowed by the SRA Rules or because the firm is an exempt person; and

- there are no other SRA rules, FCA rules or statutory instruments that debar doing so[1].

There are also a range of seven other restricted areas where activities may be carried out but only subject to restrictions[2].

1 SRA Financial Services (Scope) Rules at 4.
2 SRA Financial Services (Scope) Rules at 5.

(i)   Retail Investment Products (except personal pensions)

12.33   Retail investment products consist of life policies, units or shares in regulated collective investment schemes or investment trust savings schemes (whether or not held in an NISA), a personal pension or stakeholder pension scheme or a structured capital retail product scheme.[1] These cannot be recommended by a firm except in certain situations which are: where the firm is recommending or arranging for a client to be assigned the product[2]-which will normally occur in divorce settlements, or where the firm is doing this as a consequence of the firm managing assets;[3] or arranging a transaction for a client on an execution only basis.[4] The last of these has a specific meaning in that the SRA (Financial Services) (Conduct of Business) Rules require at para 8 that if the firm should arrange a packaged product for a client on an execution only basis, the firm must send written confirmation to the client stating that the client neither sought, nor was given advice by the firm in relation to the transaction. If advice were given within the confines of an exempt regulated activity there needs to be a confirmation that the client then confirmed the transaction should be carried out. Such advice would normally consist of suggesting to the client that they see an independent financial adviser rather than the tied agent they will have often arranged to buy the investment product from. The confirmation should also state that the transaction was carried out on the client's instructions and reflected them.

1 FCA Glossary.
2 SRA Financial Services (Scope) Rule 5.1(a).
3 SRA Financial Services (Scope) Rule 5.1(b).
4 SRA Financial Services (Scope) Rule 5.1(c).

12.34   In divorce cases, a problem that commonly arises is that solicitors leave clients to surrender life policies or endowment mortgages when the matrimonial home is sold. Such clients should be advised to seek independent financial advice, especially where the policy has been running for a number of years. Any advice in relation to whether these should be cancelled amounts to carrying on investment business and so can only be done by someone with an appropriate FCA license. In many instances allowing clients to proceed and cancel endowment policies without suggesting they take advice may amount to negligence. In many instances it will make sense to convert joint policies to single ones. If one is to be terminated there is an active second hand market and arranging to sell these can secure a higher return than cancellation. As a rule of thumb, if the contract is more than ten years old, has a cash in value of over £10,000 and is with a company with a good reputation then it will normally be more profitable to sell rather than cash it in. In the cases of policies that are well advanced the client will often be better off financially by retaining them due to the significant terminal bonuses that can apply.

(ii)   Personal Pension Schemes

12.35   A firm cannot recommend that a client buys or disposes of an interest in a personal pension scheme. If the arrangement does not include a pension transfer or opt out, the firm can make arrangements on a client's behalf, but only where there are reasonable grounds for the firm to assume that the client is not relying on them for advice on the merits or suitability of the arrangement concerned. This has the same meaning as discussed in (i) immediately above. A further issue to arise is that it is sometimes the case that solicitors are asked to advise divorce clients where part of the settlement under consideration includes a pension element. This will require the solicitor to take advice on the value of the pension from a suitable consulting actuary. The allowance in rule 5.1 permitting advising and arranging does not extend to personal pensions and corporate pensions are beyond a solicitors' remit.

(iii)   Securities and contractually based investments (except retail products)

12.36   A firm cannot recommend that a client buys or subscribes to such a security or arrangement where the transaction would be made with a person who carries on the business of buying, selling, subscribing for or underwriting the investment, regardless of whether that person is acting as agent or principal. This rule applies not only to investments currently being traded on an investment exchange or other market but also to client responses to invitations to subscribe for new issues of such investments.

12.37   The exception here[1] is essentially a consumer protection one. A solicitor acting for a client who is an individual with no business experience who is buying a company can only provide legal advice. There are no incidental powers to engage in financial services advice or activities.

1 SRA Scope Rule 5.3(b)(ii).

12.38   In relation to leasehold conveyancing, it is sometimes the case that a management company is set up and the various lessees utilise it to give them access to certain rights or the freehold. As shares are a specified investment any specified activity in relation to them would be covered by the regulatory regime. This would include acting, advising or arranging for a client to hold such shares. However, as such shares would have a nominal value the FCA accept that it falls within the complimentary and incidental exemption to legal services.

12.39   Another possibility is that a divorce settlement agreement in relation to a company may involve the transfer of shares, debentures or warrants or a combination of these. Any activity in relation to these beyond the complimentary and incidental exception would require an authorised person to act.

(iv)   Discretionary management

12.40   A firm cannot carry out discretionary fund management on behalf of a client except in certain very limited circumstances. These arise where the firm is a trustee, donee of a power of attorney, a personal representative or a receiver appointed by the Court of Protection. In any of these instances the day to day decisions concerning the fund management must be taken by an exempt person or an authorised person with appropriate permission. Likewise, any decision regarding entering transactions and buying or subscribing for investments must be undertaken in accordance with an authorised person's advice. Again the authorisation must be with relevant permission. In practice this is not usually an issue as:

- a trustee has certain powers but if a discretionary decision regarding 'investments' as defined by the Regulated Activities Order (see Chapter 1) is to be made a stockbroker or other relevant FCA regulated person would need to advise. Thus if trustees decided to sell all the investments the trust owned they could act. However, if discretion were involved because they were buying investments or making a decision to sell some of them, discretion would be involved and that part of the activity would be beyond their powers.

- the donee of a power of attorney would need to take instructions from the donor or an appropriate FCA regulated person, as appropriate should discretion be required;

- personal representatives will normally find that the discretionary decisions were made by the person who wrote the will, or if it is an intestacy, by the relevant law;

- where the Court of Protection[1] are involved they can make the discretionary decision as an exempt party.

1   They are excluded party under FSMA 2000, s 19..

(v)   Corporate finance

12.41   A firm cannot act a sponsor to a securities issue to be dealt with on the London Stock Exchange or act as a nominated adviser in relation to a securities issue to be admitted for dealing on the Alternative Investment Market or as a corporate finance adviser regarding being admitted for dealing on PLUS.

(vi)   Insurance mediation activities

12.42   A firm must be registered with the FCA before it can carry on insurance mediation work. This is not the same as becoming approved but a simpler process of registration to facilitate carrying on this one activity[1]. A compliance officer must also be appointed and their details provided to the FCA.

1 The register is kept under the same statutory provision, namely FSMA 2000, s 347.

12.43   Insurance mediation work consists of carrying on any of the following activities in relation to insurance contracts or life policies:

- dealing as agent;

- arranging;

- making arrangements with a view to transactions;

- assisting in the administration and performance of a contract;

- advising; or

- agreeing to carry on a regulated activity.

(vii)   Regulated mortgage contracts etc

12.44   A firm cannot recommend a client to become a borrower under a regulated mortgage contract, a regulated home purchase plan or a regulated sale and rent back agreement. In the case of the last two 'borrower' is extended to cover entering into the plan.

1 Financial Services and Markets Act 2000 (Regulated Activities) Order 2001, SI 2001/544, reg 61(3).

12.45   Entering into arrangements as lender or administrator of a residential mortgage are regulated activities. Thus the areas of solicitors' work affected that are permissible will tend to be in relation to giving generic advice in relation to mortgages and acting on behalf of the client and bank/building society in relation to the transaction. Endowment mortgages and other specialised types of investment related mortgages such as pension mortgages and ISA mortgages are caught as the investment element is covered by the definition of 'specified investments' so specific advice cannot be given on them. The solicitor can however act provided it is with the Scope rules. This has been extended[1] to cover regulated home purchase plans and regulated sale and rent back agreements.

1 SRA Scope Rules 5.8–5.10.

12.46   Beyond this the firm would need to be regulated by the FCA and the member of the firm providing the advice or acting be authorised to do so. If such a state of affairs does not exist the firm could arrange for advice to be given to the client by a suitably qualified independent financial adviser.

12.47   A common problem arises where the client has been recommended to a particular firm of solicitors by a bank or building society.

They in turn may have arranged a mortgage which may be an endowment or investment related mortgage. Now that mortgages are specified investments it should be the case that the bank or building society have suggested a mortgage that it is suitable to the needs of that client as this is required of them by the FCA Principles and the FCA Conduct of Business Rules. However, as most banks and building societies are a part of tied groups any associated products they will recommend will be from within their own range. The solicitor may have reasons to suspect that the client may get a better endowment policy or investment arrangement elsewhere. As r 1 of the Solicitors' Code provides an obligation to act in the client's best interests the solicitor may well feel that they must do something. The best approach for solicitors whose firms are not appropriately authorised by the FCA would be to suggest to the client that they take independent financial advice. If the firm cannot provide this the client can be told how they may find an independent financial adviser, one could be recommended or an introduction made.

12.48   Independent advice is not being provided if all the solicitor does is explain what the differences are between a repayment mortgage, an endowment mortgage or any other type. This generic advice does not require authorised status.

Breach of solicitors' rules

12.49   The SRA take into account the guidance they have provided in relation to the rules when determining whether a firm had acted in breach of them. In this respect they mirror the behaviour of the FCA. A breach of the rules could have a number of consequences according to the circumstances. A criminal offence could have been committed under the FSMA 2000 and/or the firm could be deemed to be no longer fit and proper and thus be made subject to an order preventing them from carrying on regulated activities. In less extreme cases the SRA may take disciplinary steps[1].

1 SRA Scope Rules 6.

Agencies

12.50   Some solicitors act as agencies for building societies. This is normally limited in practice to accepting deposits on the building society's behalf and making repayments. To do this the firm will have to be covered by the building society's authorised status. A further issue arises when a client of the building society agency asks for advice in relation to the investments related to the building society's products. If the building society offers independent financial advice the solicitor could arrange for this to be done. However, if they are tied the solicitor should either advise the client to take independent legal advice or provide it himself if appropriately authorised.

12.51   Solicitors sometimes act as intermediaries with insurance companies. They must be careful that they do not carry on any regulated activity in so doing as insurance mediation work is now a regulated investment activity.

Conduct of business

Introduction

12.52   The Solicitors' Financial Services (Conduct of Business) Rules 2001 determine the requirements imposed on those firms that carry on the narrow range of financial services work that can be done by those firms which do not have FCA authorisation. It also applies to those who are regulated by the FCA but the activity being properly carried out is not done within the FCA authorisation but as exempt regulated activities under s 327.

Status disclosure

12.53   Before a firm provides a regulated activity it must provide to the client in writing[1]:

- a statement that they are not authorised by the FCA;

- the name and address of the firm;

- which regulated activities are being carried out and the fact that they are limited in scope;

- that the firm is regulated by the SRA; and

- a statement that complaints and redress can be dealt with through the SRA and the Legal Ombudsman; and

- before the firm carries on an insurance mediation activity a statement must be included in a way that is clear, fair and not misleading, stating:

    'This firm is/we are not authorised by the Financial Conduct Authority. However, we are included on the register maintained by the Financial Conduct Authority so that we can carry on insurance mediation activity, which is broadly the advising on, selling and administration of insurance contracts. This part of our business, including arrangements for complaints or redress if something goes wrong, is regulated by the Law Society. The register can be accessed via the Financial Conduct Authority website at www.fca.gov.uk/register.'

1 SRA Financial Services (Conduct of Business) Rules at rule 3.

Execution of transactions

12.54   Once a transaction has been decided on the firm should act as soon as possible. The firm has a discretion to delay, but only where to do so is in the client's best interests[1]. Firms would be wise to interpret this power in a restrictive way as solicitors only have the power to act within the scope of the instructions provided to them. In addition, where investments are concerned, a solicitor's discretionary power to act is very heavily circumscribed by the law discussed in this chapter and chapter one.

1 SRA Financial Services (Conduct of Business) Rules at rule 4.

Records

12.55 Transaction records must be kept showing the client's name, the terms of the instruction and their date. If the firm has given instructions to another person to effect the transaction the record should show the client's name, the terms, the date and the name of the party instructed by the firm. There is no set form for this[1].

1 SRA Financial Services (Conduct of Business) Rules at rule 5.

12.56 Records of commission received in relation to regulated activities should also be kept. This could be by a file copy of a letter or the bill of costs. It should show the amount and how the firm has accounted to the client for the money[1].

1 SRA Financial Services (Conduct of Business) Rules at rule 6.

12.57 If the regulated activity of safeguarding and keeping the title to investments is carried out the firm must keep records of the same. They should also show a copy of the client's instructions to pass them to any third party, which must be in writing, and a receipt from any person to whom the investments were sent[1].

1 SRA Financial Services (Conduct of Business) Rules at rule 7.

12.58 If the firm should arrange a packaged product for a client on an execution only basis, the firm must send written confirmation to the client stating that the client neither sought, nor was given advice by the firm in relation to the transaction. If advice were given within the confines of an exempt regulated activity there needs to be a confirmation that the client then confirmed that the transaction should be carried out. The confirmation should also state that the transaction was carried out on the client's instructions and reflected them[1].

1 SRA Financial Services (Conduct of Business) Rules at rule 8.

12.59 If the firm is carrying on insurance mediation activities it must comply with Appendix 1 to the SRA Financial Services (Conduct of Business) Rules. The effect of these are set out at below from 12.61 to 12.66.

12.60 Records must be kept for a minimum of six years[1].

1 SRA Financial Services (Conduct of Business) Rules at rule 10.

Insurance mediation activities

12.61 If a firm carries on insurance mediation activities it must satisfy Appendix 1 to the SRA Financial Services (Conduct of Business) Rules 2001 which govern disclosure, suitability, demands and needs statements, exclusion for large risks, notification of establishment and services in other member states[1]. In essence the Appendix sets out requirements relating to disclosure, suitability, a demands and needs statement and excludes large risks insurance. These will be considered in turn.

1 SRA Financial Services (Conduct of Business) Rules at rule 9.

12.62   Where a solicitors' firm carries out insurance mediation work it must take reasonable steps to communicate information[1] to the client in a way which is clear, fair and not misleading. Where the communication relates to an insurance policy other than a life policy the client must be told whether the recommendation followed an analysis of a sufficiently wide range of firms to meet the client's needs. If the firm has not carried out such an analysis it must notify the client whether they are able to do so and tell the client that they can have details of the insurance companies with which the firm does business. Such information must be provided in writing in a durable form.

1 Appendix 1.1.

12.63   The firm must also take reasonable steps to make sure recommendations are suitable to the clients demands and needs[1] by considering the details it has, obtaining details of any existing insurance that the client already has, identify any remaining needs and advise accordingly.

1 Appendix 1.2.

12.64   Where the firm recommends an insurance contract other than a life policy it must also provide the client with a written demands and needs statement that sets out the client's demands and needs, explains the reasons for any recommendation that has been made and comments on the complexity[1]. It must be in writing and in a durable form. If however the contract was entered into on an execution only basis the demands and needs statement need only identify the contract requested by the client and confirm the execution only basis of the contract.

1 Appendix 1.3.

12.65   The requirement for a demands and needs statement which should be provided before the contract is finalised does not apply where the firm renews or amends an existing policy (other than a life policy) and the information provided is still accurate and up to date. The client's attention must be drawn to any matters which have changed before the contract is renewed or amended. Likewise it is not needed[1] if the information is provided orally at the client's request, where immediate cover is needed, where the contract is concluded by telephone or where the firm is introducing the client to an authorised person or an exempt one and is taking no further part in the arrangement itself.

1 Appendix 1.3 (c).

12.66   The insurance mediation arrangements are not available for large risks.[1] This covers insurance for commercial clients on rolling stock, aircraft, ships and goods in transit. This category also covers insurance over credit and suretyship. Finally, where the client is engaged in commercial or industrial activity, land vehicles, fire and natural forces, damage to property and general liability contracts are excluded where the client satisfies two of the following:

(a)   A balance sheet total of €6.2 million;

(b)   A net turnover of €12.8 million; or

(c)   An average number of employees in the course of the year of 250 or more.

1 Appendix 1.4.

ACCOUNTANTS

12.67   The issues here in many ways parallel those affecting solicitors, though there is one key difference. Unlike solicitors, accountants are not automatically authorised by their professional body to carry on exempt regulated activities but must apply for appropriate status. There are a wide range of areas of accountants' work that should not raise financial services issues. These are[1]: auditing, acting as reporting accountants, preparing financial statements, bookkeeping, payroll, tax advice and compliance, insolvency work requiring an insolvency practitioners' license, company secretary work, advising on grant availability, preparing cash flow and profit projections, asset valuation, advising on cancelling insurance contracts, mortgage references, advising on unsecured borrowing, pension administration such as calculating payroll deductions and giving generic advice. In practice the risk is mostly associated with work relating to company shares.

1 See the ICAEW, ICAS and ICAI, Designated Professional Body Handbook, Schedule 3.

12.68   The Designated Professional Body Handbook determines what activities chartered accountants may or may not do in the context of investment business. It is a joint document issued by the Institute of Chartered Accountants in England and Wales, Scotland and Ireland. Even if a firm has a license and is thus able to carry on exempt regulated activities they cannot[1]:

●   accept deposits;

●   issue electronic money,

●   effect contracts of insurance as principal;

●   deal in securities or contractually based investments as principal:

●   establish, operate or wind up a collective investment scheme;

●   act as trustee of a unit trust;

●   act as depository or sole director of an open ended investment company;

●   establish, operate or wind up a stakeholder or personal pension scheme;

●   provide basic advice on stakeholder products;

●   manage the underwriting capacity of a Lloyd's syndicate as a managing agent;

●   act as provider of a funeral plan contract;

●   advise a person to become a member of a particular Lloyd's syndicate;

●   unless included in the Financial Services Register a firm cannot deal in the sale or purchase of rights under a contract of insurance as agent, or arrange such deals. Nor can it assist in the administration or performance of such contracts or give advice relating to a transaction for the sale or purchase of rights under such a contract;

- manage assets belonging to another unless all routine day to day decisions are taken by a permitted third party;

- give advice to an individual unless that person is becoming a controller of a company as a result of that transaction. Nor can he give advice as trustee of an occupational pension scheme; recommend someone buy a security or contractually based investment or in relation to a transaction with someone in the course of dealing in securities or contractually based investments on a public market or in response to an invitation to subscribe;

- Give advice consisting of a recommendation to a member of a personal pension scheme to dispose of rights or interests under the scheme;

- recommend an individual to enter into a specific regulated mortgage contract as borrower; nor as lender or administrator unless in the last two instances they are doing so a trustee or personal representative or under a trust, will or intestacy. The same applies to regulated home reversion plans, regulated home purchase plans and sale and rent back agreements; and

- communicate or approve an investment advertisement[2].

1 SI 2001/1227 as amended.
2 All but the last of these are imposed by SI 2001/1227 as amended except the last one which is the consequence of s 21 FSMA 2000.

Corporate work

12.69 Some work, however, can be carried out. For example, effectively the analysis above relating to solicitors under the heading 'corporate work' applies here as well. The types of work that is permissible without an FCA licence tend to be:

- advising and/or arranging a deal involving the transfer of ownership of a company when the client is either the vendor or purchaser. As above the quantity of shares transferred either in this transaction, or this transaction coupled with others must be a minimum of 50% and the purchaser must be acquiring ownership of the control of the business, or the buyer is becoming a 'controller' of the company as defined by s.422 FSMA 2000.

- Arranging such share transactions will also be acceptable provided it is a necessary part of other professional services, it is not remunerated separately and the activity engaged in is not investment business.

12.70 Corporate finance often involves accountants and article 70 of the Regulated Activities Order[1], as amended, is relevant here. Accountants can legally advise companies on the following except where a minority interest is the result:

- company formation;

- company arrangements and valuations;
- issuing shares;
- cash takeover bids;
- management buyouts using a newco;
- takeovers of one company by another;
- advising on and arranging demergers;
- advising on and arranging a share buy back;
- advising on and arranging a reorganisation of a shareholding for a family member for no valuable consideration;
- advising shareholders as to whether to accept an offer during a take-over;
- arranging the sale of shares in a company being sold to the purchasing company;
- advising on a share issue, a restructuring or the creation of new companies;
- providing administration services on the issue of shares provided that this stops short of bringing vendor and purchaser together;
- advising a company, though not its shareholders, on whether to become public;
- advising those engaged in a management buy out
- arranging the purchase of shares in a management buy out; and
- advising a company to engage in a share buy back[2].

1 SI 2001/544 as amended.
2 ICAEW, ICAS and ICAI Designated Professional Body Handbook, Schedule 5.

12.71   Once authorised by the FCA a firm may do whatever is permitted by the FCA licence. In the case of chartered accountants the category chosen will normally include:

- recommending the purchase of a publicly tradable share; and
- advising a shareholder to take up a rights offer in a publicly quoted company.

Insurance activities

12.72   Since the passing of the Insurance Mediation Directive all aspects of insurance are now regulated activities. There are a few minor exceptions such as travel insurance and extended warranties sold with goods. A designated professional body firm of accountants can advise on and arrange contracts of general insurance.

1 ICAEW, ICAS and ICAI Designated Professional Body Handbook, page 5.

Mortgage business

12.73   In this context 'mortgage' is limited to the same area as that covered by 'regulated mortgage activities' in chapter 1, ie, a first legal mortgage over land taken to secure a loan, which land is to be used for residential accommodation by the borrower or their family or the beneficiary of a trust. The requirement of residential accommodation is satisfied provided at least 40% of it is so used. It must also be in the UK. The loan does not need to have been for the purposes of financing the purchase, though in practice this is usually the case.

12.74   In this area any accountancy firm can:

- discuss the need for a loan or mortgage, the type of mortgage in a generic sense and which lender to approach;

- pass on information or leaflets to clients provided that this stops short of recommending a specific mortgage;

- introducing a client to a mortgage broker;

- providing a cash flow forecast to support a mortgage application;

- providing a reference to support a mortgage application;

- advising a client to redeem a regulated mortgage;

- explaining the terms of a regulated mortgage contract to a client;

- assisting a client in completing a regulated mortgage application;

- acting as intermediary between a client and lender to put a mortgage in place provided that no advice is given.

ACTUARIES

Introduction

12.75   Actuarial consultants normally carry on the business of advising companies on a range of investments, most commonly: pensions, insurance policies, pooled investments, annuities and additional voluntary contributions. The nature of the advice focuses on actuarial assessments of future trends, such as life expectancy, future trends in illnesses and so on. However, the provision of this advice can involve getting caught by the regulatory regime. The most likely regulated activity will be that of advising provided it relates to one of the specified investments regulated by the financial services regime[1].

1 Financial Services (Regulated Activities) Order 2001, SI 2001/544, arts 74-89 as amended.

12.76   To be caught by the financial services regime a firm must be either managed or controlled by actuaries. Such firms can be regulated by the Institute and Faculty of Actuaries in its capacity as a Designated Professional Body and such firms can then carry on exempt regulated activities. If the firm is managed and controlled by actuaries they have the option of applying to be regulated by the FCA and can then carry on such business as their license allows. Such firms can also carry on exempt regulated activities. There is also the option of a firm becoming an 'authorised professional firm'. A license must be obtained to this effect from the Institute and Faculty of Actuaries. If the firm wanted to carry on full investment business and obtain an FCA license they could resolve the problem by setting up a separate limited company to carry on investment business and that firm could apply for an FCA license. An accountancy firm that employed actuaries who were carrying on financial services work would also have to follow the FCA authorisation route.

Professional regulation

12.77   The Institute and Faculty of Actuaries has issued a Handbook for licensed firms. Any regulated firm of Actuaries needs to be aware of the contents of this as well as the FCA Professional Firms Sourcebook. The Handbook explains how a license can be applied for and also sets out the powers of an Actuary under FSMA 2000, Pt XX. Actuarial firms face the same restriction on their powers as set out in the Regulated Activities Order as are discussed in the section of this chapter on solicitors above. They are also subject, where relevant, to the rules on money laundering (**Chapter 8**), financial promotions (**Chapter 6**) and market abuse (**Chapter 7**). The relevant rules on these areas are set out elsewhere in this book. The rules on insurance mediation are governed by the same rules as apply to solicitors and these are explained earlier in this chapter.

12.78   In relation to its regulation by the Institute a firm must:

- comply with the Handbook;

- deal with the Institute in an open and co-operative manner; and

- adopt a contact partner who is responsible for making sure that the firm complies with the Institute's practices and procedures, provides an annual declaration on the form required by the Institute including such undertakings and acknowledgements as the Institute may need, who will supply the Institute with such information as it may require and who will undertake the annual compliance review.

12.79   If the firm is licensed by the FCA to carry on insurance mediation activities, it must provide the Institute with:

- details of the firm's trading name;

- its registered address;

- the names of the individual(s) responsible for managing the firm's insurance mediation business; and

- whether the firm has an overseas branch or is providing cross border services in an EEA member state under the Insurance Mediation Directive or a right deriving from EEA membership

12.80   The firm has an obligation to inform the Institute within ten business days whenever one of the following has happened:

- it is no longer complying with the PII regulations;

- there has been a change in a matter which could affects its eligibility to be licensed;

- any change to its details (name, address, contact partner and whether it has ceased to carry on insurance mediation activities).

12.81   The firm must also pay necessary charges, respond to enquiries made by the Institute, deal with any monitoring or quality review the Institute requires of them, inform them if it cannot meet its obligations under the Handbook, comply with the disciplinary process, the PII regulations, send any necessary notice to the Institute and satisfy the Handbook generally.

Which activities may be carried on?

12.82   Under the Handbook[1] a firm can only carry on investment business that arises out of or is complementary to professional services that are not themselves investment business.

1 At the time of writing the latest edition is that of August 2010

12.83   Due to the nature of some actuarial services it may be that the designated professional business activity took place before the professional work. This is acceptable provided that it was always the intention to provide a connected series of services in this way. Examples where this may occur are, a scheme actuary appointment and consulting in relation to a generic investment. There is also a definition of 'client' that is idiosyncratic to this part of the rules. FSMA 2000, s 328(8) defines clients as:

> '(a)   persons who use, have used, or are or may be contemplating using any of the services provided by a member of a profession in the course of carrying on exempt regulated activities;
>
> (b)   persons who have rights or interests which are derived from, or otherwise attributable to, the use of any such services by other persons; or
>
> (c)   persons who have rights or interests which may be adversely affected by the use of any such services by persons acting on their behalf or in a fiduciary capacity in relation to them.'

This enables firms to consider providing exempt regulated activities at the commencement of a group of related professional services.

12.84   Firms must account to their clients for any pecuniary reward or other advantage that results from carrying on designated professional business[1]. This will normally be commission resulting from advising or a client introduction. Accounting for commission means either giving the money to the client or handling it in line with their instructions. There is no de minimis figure[2]. Nor must they hold themselves out as being able to carry on investment business[3].

1 FSMA 2000, s 327(3),
2 FSMA 2000, s 327(3).
3 In addition there should not be any other reason for not acting, eg as a result of the FCA rules, a statutory instrument or anything else in the Institute of Actuary rules.

Prohibited activities

12.85   There is a list of prohibited activities[1] which it has to be said a member of the Institute of Actuaries would be extremely unlikely to want to carry on. These apply to activities carried on in the UK, with the exception of Insurance Mediation Activities where it extends to passported branches. The banned list of activities are:

- Accepting deposits;

- Issuing electronic money;

- Effecting or carrying out contracts of insurance as principal;

- Market making in securities or qualifying contracts of insurance;

- Buying, selling, subscribing for or underwriting securities or qualifying contracts of insurance as principal where the firm:

  - holds itself out as engaging in the business of buying such investments with a view to selling them;

  - holds itself out as engaging in the business of underwriting investments of the kind to which the transaction relates; or

  - regularly solicits members of the public with the purpose of inducing them, as principals or agents, to enter into transactions involving the buying, selling, subscribing or underwriting of investments and the transaction is entered into as a result of the firm having solicited members of the public in that manner.

- Acquiring or disposing of contractually based investments as principal except with or through an authorised person.

- Establishing, operating or winding up a collective investment scheme;

- Acting as trustee of an authorised unit trust scheme;

- Acting as the depositary or sole director of an open-ended investment company;

- Establishing, operating or, winding up a stakeholder pension scheme;

- Managing the underwriting capacity of a Lloyd's syndicate as a managing agent;

- Advising a person to become a member of a particular Lloyd's syndicate unless such advice is an endorsement of the advice of an authorised third party;

- Entering as provider or administrator into a funeral plan contract; or

- Entering into a regulated mortgage contract as a lender, unless acting in the capacity of a trustee or personal representative and the borrower is a beneficiary under the trust or estate.

The last two bullet points also apply to regulated home reversion plans, regulated home purchase plans and sale and rent back mortgages.

1 These are set out in the Non-Exempt Activities Order 2001, SI 2001/1227, FSMA 2000, s 21 and the Financial Promotions Order 2005, SI 2005/1529, plus additional requirements placed on members by the three Institutes' DPB Handbook, August 2010 at Appendix 2.

12.86 A firm cannot use a license permitting them to carry on exempt professional business to manage or agree to manage in the UK any portfolio which includes or may include securities or contractually based investments. Apart from that the rules relating to exempt regulated activities discussed above in this chapter apply here.

12.87 The entitlement of a passported branch in respect of regulated activities only extends to permitted insurance mediation activities. Firms permitted to carry on exempt regulated activities but intending to carry out other regulated activities, from the branch must establish whether local regulatory approval is required.

Permission Lists

12.88 The Institute, as a Designated Professional Body[1], has adopted the policy that firms it regulates for the purposes of exempt professional activities should only carry out those listed in the Handbook subject to the activity being complementary and incidental to the professional work being carried out.

Insurance Mediation

12.89 In this context 'investments' include insurance policies, which fall into three categories:

- qualifying contracts of insurance eg an endowment policy, personal pension policy or annuity;

- long term care insurance contracts, some types of which may also be qualifying contracts of insurance; and

- all other non-investment insurance contracts eg pure protection contracts (not being long term care insurance contracts) and general insurance contracts.

12.90 Long-term care insurance contracts are subject to the rules relating to packaged products whether or not they are qualifying contracts of insurance.

12.91 Contracts of insurance include reinsurance contracts but the latter are excluded from the definitions of qualifying contract of insurance and longterm care insurance contracts.

12.92 Insurance mediation activities in respect of all kinds of policies of insurance can only be carried out by firms as an exempt professional activity if they have specific permission in their licence from the Institute and who are included in the insurance intermediaries register maintained by the FCA. This register is not the same thing as FCA registration. It is a simpler arrangement whereby all of those wishing to carry on insurance mediation activities seek clearance from the FCA. It is much simpler than a license application. As it takes time for information supplied by the firm to the Institute for the purpose of its initial registration to be forwarded to the FCA and then recorded in the insurance intermediaries register it is the responsibility of such firms to ensure that they do not carry on insurance mediation activities until the name of the firm is so recorded. Where a firm is permitted to carry on insurance mediation activities there are additional requirements in the Institute's handbook referable to such activities.

Regulated Mortgage Contracts

12.93   The Institute's list of things that the Institute permits actuarial firms to do within its category as a designated professional body does not cover any regulated activity in respect of regulated mortgage contracts. Such firms may not carry out any such activities and firms which also have a FCA license can only do so if permitted by the Financial Services Authority and in compliance with the FCA rules.

Authorised Professional Firms

12.94   Authorised Professional Firms ('APF firms') can carry on regulated activities within the same scope as those with the capacity to carry on exempt professional activities, but APF firms can also do those things within its FCA license. However, they cannot carry out regulated activities that are not listed in the Schedules to the Institute's Handbook. Instead, so long as the relevant activity is within the scope of the permission granted them by the FCA, they must comply with the FCA rules when undertaking this mainstream regulated activity.

All firms

12.95   Articles 39B and 72D of the Regulated Activities Order excludes from the definition of insurance mediation activities and regulated activity:-

- in the case of assisting, the activities of:
    - expert appraisal; and
    - loss adjusting or managing claims on behalf of a UK or EEA authorised insurer or an overseas reinsurer.

12.96   Loss adjusting or managing claims for an insured is not excluded.

- in the case of all insurance mediation activities, any activity which relates to a contract of insurance for a large risk which is not situated in an EEA state[1].

1 Art 72D.

12.97   The Regulated Activities Order[1] excludes from the definitions of the regulated activities of:-

- arranging a transaction in a contract of insurance
- managing investments if they are only contracts of insurance; or
- assisting in the administration and performance of contracts of insurance;

activities which consist only of the provision of information to the policyholder or potential policyholder, and which are carried on by a firm in the course of carrying on a profession which does not otherwise consist of the carrying on of regulated activities and may reasonably be regarded as being incidental to that profession. The FCA has provided[2] guidance on the application of this exclusion. Specifically, it is available to firms carrying on exempt regulated activities even though they are carrying on other regulated activities under their DPB licence, though this does not apply if information is given, such as on behalf of the client to the insurer or if advice is given.

1 Art 72C.
2 FSA Authorisation Manual, Appendix 5, paras 5.6.5–5.6.9G.

Financial promotions

12.98   DPB firms engaging in exempt regulated activities must consider the financial promotion regime. The definition of financial promotion in s 21 of the FSMA 2000 is very wide and covers communicating an invitation or inducement for someone to engage in investment activity. The latter term includes entering into an investment management or advisory contract as well as any transaction in investments. It does not, however, include a promotion where the only activity promoted is the provision by the firm of:

- advising or arranging services which relate only to general insurance contracts or pure protection contracts or both; and/or

- assisting in the administration and performance of a contract of insurance.

12.99   Firms should note, however, that the promotion of a particular general insurance contract or pure protection contract, as well as of other investments is subject to the financial promotion regime. 'Communicating' includes all forms of communication such as letters, telephone calls, e-mails, web-sites, broadcasts and presentations at meetings which are pre-prepared rather than spontaneous as well as what might generally be understood as advertisements relating to investments. Communications which amount to a financial promotion can only be made by, or if the contents have been approved by, an authorised person. An actuarial firm which is not FCA authorised but which can carry on exempt regulated activities cannot make such a communication in relation to financial services unless it has been approved by an authorised person or the communication is exempt. The Financial Promotions Order 2005[1] divides all promotions into three categories, unsolicited real time, solicited real time and non real time. Real time covers instant communication such as talking and telephone conversations. Non real time covers everything else. The Order contains a number of exceptions allowing some categories of financial promotion to be made by unauthorised persons. A number of these are particularly relevant to actuaries, for example article 26 which exempts real time promotions of general insurance contracts or pure protection contracts and that in article 24 covering all other promotions of such contracts or policies so long as specified information is provided.

1 Financial Services and Markets Act 2000 (Financial Promotion) Order 2005, SI 2005/1529, as amended.

12.100 The FCA has issued guidance on financial promotion[1] which includes their view of what an invitation or inducement means and discusses the various exemptions to the prohibition on financial promotion.

1 Authorisation Manual, Appendix 1.

Conduct of business requirements

12.101 The Institute imposes certain requirements on firms, some of which apply to all firms and some just to DPB or APF firms. All firms must conduct their business with integrity and due skill, care and diligence. The former has been defined as 'wholeness, soundness, uprightness, honesty'[1]. The latter imposes a rather tougher standard of conduct than may be apparent from the wording. It requires a high standard of professional skill, not merely the avoidance of carelessness. These requirements are taken from FCA Principles 1 and 2.

1 Oxford English Dictionary.

12.102 The rest of this section only applies to firms carrying on exempt regulated activities. Such firms must provide certain key information in writing before providing a regulated activity other than insurance mediation. This must state that the firm is not authorised by the FCA. In the case of insurance mediation a specifically worded paragraph must be included setting out the position regarding insurance mediation certificates. In either case the nature of the regulated activities they can carry on, the fact that for these purposes the firm is regulated by the Institute and Faculty of Actuaries, the nature of the complaints and redress mechanism and the fact that the client will not have access to the compensation scheme must be included in a way that is clear, fair and not misleading. They cannot make representations to clients that suggest that they are regulated by the FCA or that associated protections are available. In this context 'client' has the extended meaning discussed above. Both this and the information in the preceding paragraph can be included in the client care letter.

12.103 The remainder of this section also applies to non mainstream regulated activities carried on in, into or out of the UK or in the case of insurance mediation from a passported branch as well as those carrying on exempt regulated activities. Such firms must make sure that they are in full agreement with their clients as to the services that are being provided. There should be evidence of this. The safest way is for the information to be put in an engagement letter which the client signs a copy of and returns it to the firm. This should be set out clearly and in English unless the client agrees to it being in another language. In the case of individual clients subject to the Financial Services (Distance Marketing) Regulations, the information should be provided over the phone before the contract is entered into. These will not normally apply as actuaries cannot advise individuals on investments but only comment on advice given by an authorised third party.

12.104 In the case of insurance mediation work the following information in writing:

- the firm's name and address;

- that the firm is on the FCA insurance mediation register and whether it is also FCA authorised;

- that the above can be checked at www.fsa.gov.uk/register;

- whether the firm has a direct or indirect holding of over 10% of the voting rights or capital of the insurance firm concerned;

- where an insurance firm or group has a direct or indirect holding of over 10% of the voting rights or capital in the firm;

- whether in relation to the insurance contract concerned the firm has carried out a fair analysis of a reasonable number of contracts. This is not needed if the firm has just passed the client to an independent insurance intermediary;

- how to complain to the firm and after that the Institute; and

- in the case of an APF firm the additional information listed in the FCA's Insurance, Conduct of Business handbook[1].

1 ICOB 4.2.8R (8) and (9).

12.105 Every year the firm must review how effectively it is complying with the Institute's handbook; including such obligations as competence, professional indemnity insurance and continuing eligibility. It is vital to make sure that only exempt regulated activities are being carried on. Client files should also be reviewed. All regulated activities must be carried on by suitably qualified, competent and experienced personnel. Where insurance mediation work is carried on a reasonable proportion of the people in the management structure and involved with the activity concerned must have appropriate knowledge and ability.

12.106 Appropriate records must be kept in writing or on microfilm or electronic form of instructions received from clients and work carried out. They should illustrate why particular conclusions were reached. These should be kept for a minimum of six years except where there are grounds for retaining them longer.

12.107 Complaints must be investigated by one of the firm's principals and if the complaint is justified the firm must do whatever is necessary to rectify the situation.

12.108 Firms must also act in the best interests of clients and manage any conflicts of interest in an appropriate manner. Client money should not be held by DPB firms and APF firms can only do so when permitted by the FCA. Client cheques should be made out to the issuer or insurer. Monies paid by issuers and insurers should conversely be made out to the client concerned.

12.109 Firms in receipt of client property should keep a record of receipt and location. If it is passed to a third party on the client's instructions, those instructions should be in writing and a written acknowledgement received from the party to whom it is sent.

12.110   If the firm advises on a packaged product in the context of exempt regulated activity for a DPB firm or non-mainstream regulated activity for an APF firm, it must be reasonably satisfied that there is not another packaged product that would better suit the client's requirements, objectives and interests. A 'packaged product' in this context is 'a long-term insurance policy including a pension and annuity policy (but excluding a pure protection contract (other than a long term care insurance contract) or a reinsurance treaty), stakeholder pension scheme, long term care insurance contract, a unit trust, OEIC or investment trust savings scheme.'. In the case of a packaged product which is a contract of insurance the recommendation must be suitable to the client's needs. A licensed firm cannot give advice to a client on a non investment insurance contract (defined as 'a contract of insurance which is a general insurance contract or a pure protection contract but which is not a long term care insurance contact') unless it has analysed a sufficiently large number of contacts in the relevant sector to be able to give adequate advice. However, a firm can recommend a non investment contract of insurance that does not meet all the client's needs if there is no completely suitable contract within those analysed and the firm identifies the fact to the client. Advice given to clients must be in writing and in the case of insurance contracts take the form of a demand and needs statement. The advice should be given by someone suitably qualified and experienced.

12.111   If a firm seeks advice from an authorised third party it must supply sufficient information about the client and make sure that the advice is independent. Where information is supplied to the authorised third party within the client's knowledge the firm must get confirmation from the client regarding its accuracy. Risk warnings must be passed on and the client must be made aware of the respective responsibilities of the licensed firm and authorised third party.

12.112   If a firm arranges an investment on behalf of a client, written instructions must first have been provided which specify the transaction to be entered into. It is possible for the firm to act prior to receiving the written instructions provided it is confident that the written version will arrive in due course. A firm could still refuse to act in such a case if it thought fit. If a deal is arranged through an authorised third party the firm must make sure that the client is aware of the respective responsibilities of the firm and the authorised third party. Any information received from that third party must be promptly passed to the client.

12.113   A firm dealing in investments on behalf of a client must have written instructions from the client specifying which transaction should be entered into. A firm should not act on a client's behalf if it considers the transaction would be materially detrimental to the client's interests. If the client has been advised in writing and still wishes to act the firm can do so, but can still decide to decline.

12.114   Where a firm arranges a contract of insurance in the course of carrying on insurance mediation activities for a client it must first provide a written demands and needs statement. This asks the client what his requirements are and tells him what he needs to disclose whilst also asking for details of any existing insurance. The firm should have regard to the facts disclosed by the client, any information it already holds, whether the level of cover is sufficient and the relevance of any exclusions, excesses, limitations or conditions. Any recommendations made by the firm must be set out along with the reasons. This is not needed if the client has been introduced by the firm to an authorised third party who then deals directly with the client.

LICENSED CONVEYANCERS AND CHARTERED SURVEYORS

12.115   These two professional bodies have been recognised by the FCA as designated professional bodies (see **12.4** above). The purpose in these instances is simply to permit those regulated by these two bodies to carry out insurance mediation activities.

12.116   For this purpose licensed conveyancers must be included in their regulator's exempt professional firms regulator and the FCA register as well as satisfy any regulations the Council for Licensed Conveyancers.

12.117   Chartered Surveyors can also be licensed to carry out insurance mediation activities and if doing so must abide by the Royal Institute of Chartered Surveyors Designated Professional Body Rules 2009.

Index